PAPERS RELATING TO POLITICAL ECONOMY

PAPERS RELATING TO POLITICAL ECONOMY

BY

F. Y. EDGEWORTH

VOLUME II

BURT FRANKLIN

New York 25, N. Y.

Published by

BURT FRANKLIN
514 West 113th Street
New York 25, N. Y.

ORIGINALLY PUBLISHED
GREAT BRITAIN 1925

Reprinted with the permission of
the Royal Economic Society

PRINTED IN THE U.S.A.

CONTENTS

Section VI.—MATHEMATICAL ECONOMICS

SECTION IV

INTERNATIONAL TRADE

SECTION IV

INTERNATIONAL TRADE

(R)

THE PURE THEORY OF INTERNATIONAL VALUES

[THIS article was published in the ECONOMIC JOURNAL, 1894, in three divisions. The third of these has now been broken up so as to bring together the portions in which the theory is treated on classical lines. In this restatement emphasis is laid on the less familiar, perhaps less edifying, clauses of the theory; and some similarities and differences between international trade proper and transactions between non-competing groups, including the process of Distribution, are pointed out. There follow criticisms of economists who have treated the subject on classical lines. The supplement or superstructure which Mill, under the influence of Thornton, added to the original sections of his great chapter on International Values is found to be, in accordance with Professor Bastable's verdict, "laborious and confusing." A minute examination of this stupendous supplement forms in the original article an elaborate note which it has not seemed necessary to reproduce in this Collection. Mill is also taken to task for underrating the danger to the home country arising from foreign competition. His doctrine that low wages when common to all branches of industry cannot be one of those causes which enable one country to undersell another is shown to be misleading, unless the terms are interpreted in a now very unusual sense.

Cairnes' stronger statement of a similar doctrine is open to even greater objection.

Criticism is also directed against what is new in Sidgwick's theory of international trade.

There followed in the original article some criticism of Professor Bastable's well-known treatise; based largely on the "parallelism" which he affirms between the incidents and effects of import and export duties. But this is one of the passages which have to be omitted from this Collection for the first of the reasons assigned in the Introduction. The asymmetry which I had ascribed to export and import duties is true only of duties *in kind*, and not even all of those—as I pointed out in a later paper (ECONOMIC JOURNAL, 1897, p. 307). With regard to other points of difference with Professor Bastable, I may say generally what I have said with respect to one of them on a subsequent occasion (*loc. cit.* p. 403) : " The continuance of the controversy appears to be hardly justified by its importance. Suffice it to express the summary judgment that on the one hand Professor Bastable's further explanations are quite satisfactory, and on the other hand that my observations were not uncalled for."

The remainder of the article, as now rearranged, consists of the portions in which mathematical language is employed; portions placed here in virtue of the subject-matter rather than the method, which is of a piece with Section VI. There is first a restatement of the theory already presented in the classical form. Not much is gained by this translation into mathematical language; except so far as variation of the expression may tend to avoid the confusion and prejudice which beset the subject. The use of mathematics has, however, not saved Cournot from the serious errors criticised in the second part of this extract. Of all the writers, classical or mathematical, who are passed in review in the article of 1894, Mangoldt is the one who emerges unscathed from the critical examination. His conception of a commodity common to the home and foreign country goes far towards rendering palpable the evasive conception of units of production in different countries, the products of which are not of equal value on the international market (*cp.* Bastable, *International Trade*, Chapter II, Pigou, *Manchester Guardian* cited ECONOMIC JOURNAL, Vol. XXXIII, p. 134). The rate of exchange between the products of the units of production in the respective countries is the key to the relative values of all the commodities which they exchange in the international market, as well as to the values of the non-exportable commodities in each country. The scheme of ratios presented in connection with Mangoldt's theories (p. 53) is designed to illustrate this conception.]

I. *On Classical Lines.*

International trade meaning in plain English trade between nations, it is not surprising that the term should mean something else in Political Economy. In technical usage international is distinguished from home trade by the existence of barriers which prevent owners of the means of production in one region —or, more generally, sphere of industry—from employing those means in another sphere.[1] Or is it easier to say that home trade is distinguished from international by the tendency to equal remuneration of efforts and sacrifices : to an equality of profits, and an equation of the net advantages in different occupations ?[2] The general conditions which determine equilibrium are the same for both species of trade ; the principal difference is that in the case of the home trade there are one or two more equations.

Such is, I think, the essential attribute of the term international trade as used by theoretical economists ; the properties of geographical and political separation, though usually understood, are not those from which the principal conclusions flow.

The flexibility of this definition escapes from the objection that there is no difference in the present age between international and domestic trade. Let it be granted that capital and perhaps business power are free to flow to all parts of the earth.[3] Yet labour cannot be conceived as flowing so freely. The world is not yet in the condition of the American colonies, where, if Virginia damnified Maryland by a tax, it is said that the inhabitant of Maryland would transfer himself to Virginia.[4] Presumably there may be a considerable difference in the level of advantage in different countries before labour flows from one to another.[5] Suppose, however, that the conditions of international trade proper ceased to exist, there would still remain the quasi-international trade between the parties to Distribution. There would still be a great gulf between employers and employed

---

[1] " The immobility of industrial agents," as Professor Bastable says, in his admirable discussion of the definition in question.—*International Trade*, ch. i.

[2] The plan of putting international before domestic trade—treating it as the rule rather than as an exception—may have historical as well as theoretical justification, if we agree with Professor Bastable that " the first exchanges were international (or rather intertribal)."—*Commerce of Nations*, p. 7.

[3] Business power at least, if not labour, has in several cases been transferred from England to foreign countries, in order to avoid hostile tariffs. See Diplomatic and Consular Reports, Spain 1893, C 6855, 112, p. 18. I have heard of other instances consequent on the McKinley Tariff.

[4] *Quarterly Journal of Economics*, October 1892

[5] *Cp.* Bastable, *International Trade*, p. 10.

across which work is transported in exchange for finished products.

According to this view the fundamental principle of international trade is that general theory which Jevons called the Theory of Exchange, and Professor Marshall describes as " an inquiry into the balancing of the forces of Demand and Supply," [1] which constitutes " the kernel " of most of the chief problems of economics. It is a corollary of the general theory that all the parties to a bargain look to gain by it. Foreign trade would not go on unless it seemed less costly to each of the parties to it to obtain imports in exchange for exports than to produce them at home. This is the generalised statement of the principle of Comparative Cost, with respect to its positive part at least. The negative clause, that the value of articles in the international market is not proportioned to the cost—the " efforts and sacrifice " —incurred by the respective producers, is superfluous, if the definition here proposed is adopted. Why should there be any correspondence between cost and value in the absence of the conditions, proper to domestic trade, on which that equality depends ?

In a complete treatise on international trade it would be proper to dwell at length both on the general principle and the corollary; on the one hand contemplating the tendency towards maximum satisfaction,[2] which constitutes the grandest generalisation of Economics; and on the other hand applying the doctrine of Comparative Cost to explain the peculiarities of existing commerce—why such and such articles are exported from one country and imported to another.[3] But it is proposed to confine this study to those portions of the theory which have at once some bearing on practice, and also a high degree of generality.

I. Of the propositions relating to international trade which are at once general and bear on practice the most important, I think, are those which attribute advantage or detriment—whether for one nation or several—to changes in the supply of, or demand for, articles of trade. Such are the answers to the questions : Would

---

[1] *Principles*, Book V. ch. iii.

[2] The principle is employed by almost all mathematical writers on economics ; among whom Professor Marshall may be distinguished as stating carefully the limitations, under the existing social regime, of the " doctrine of maximum satisfaction " (*Principles of Economics*, Book V. ch. xii. § 7); and Dr. Irving Fisher as appreciating the mysterious analogies between the maximum principles in physics and in human affairs (" Mathematical Investigations in the Theory of Value and Prices." From *Transactions of the Connecticut Academy*, Vol. IX., July 1892).

[3] As Professor Taussig has done in his brilliant article on " Aspects of the Tariff Question," in the *Quarterly Journal of Economics* for 1889, p. 291.

a tax or a bounty, an improvement or deterioration in the means of communication, abundance or scarcity of an exported article, be beneficial to the home country, or to all parties ? The answers to such questions vary with the data, which require to be carefully distinguished.

One distinction—which indeed hardly needs to be pointed out, since it is the similarity, not the difference, which generally escapes notice—is that which has been already indicated between international trade proper, relating to separated regions, and the analogues thereof which may be termed quasi-international trade. Another distinction, which one might have *a priori* supposed to be very obvious, is between the interests of the home country and that of the world at large. Yet, strange to say, a confusion between ideas so different as part and whole pervades many of the arguments in favour of Free Trade; the complaints of List [1] against " the School "—the followers of Adam Smith—on this ground are too well founded.[2] The equivocation might be compared to that which it was reserved for Professor Sidgwick to point out in the term Utilitarianism—referring sometimes to the Greatest Happiness of the individual, and sometimes to that of the whole.

Another important distinction is between *small* and *large* changes; the characteristic of the latter being such an alteration in the scale of production that the law of increasing returns is brought into operation [or the converse alteration]. Thus the " improvement " in the process of manufacture of an exported article considered by Mill in his great chapter (Book III. ch. xviii. § 5) is presumably of the order " small "; the change contemplated by him in an earlier section (§ 2), from a time " when each country produced both commodities to an established trade," may well be—but is not necessarily—large. Another distinction to which it is proper to call attention is between an impediment to trade [or an improvement] in general and that particular

---

[1] *National System.*

[2] The amiable confusion between one's own or one's country's exclusive advantage and that of the world at large may be attributed to Mr. Gladstone, when he asks—in his article on " Free Trade or Protection," in the *North American Review*, Vol. CL.—" why, if Protection is a good thing, it should not be adopted by the United States in their *internal* trade."

Even the most clearheaded of writers, James Mill (*Elements of Political Economy*, ch. iii. § 16, p. 159, ed. 1821) and Professor Bastable (*International Trade*, p. 123, and " Incidence and Effects of Import and Export Duties," in the *Report of the British Association* for 1889, p. 6 of the essay, p. 446 of the *Report*), seem not to distinguish very sharply the ideas of advantage to the world and to a particular nation.

kind of obstruction [or encouragement] which a tax [or bounty] constitutes. The proceeds which may accrue from a tax form an item which is sometimes left out of account in the balance of advantages.[1]

Other principles of classification requiring no comment are the distinction between changes originating in the home country, or abroad; between those affecting primarily exports, or imports; between the case of two countries, and that of several countries; and so forth.

It will be sufficient here to select the most instructive cases requesting the reader to attend carefully to the issue, and to stay condemnation until appeal has been made to the tribunal of mathematical reasoning.

The simplest case is where the question is whether the advantage of the home country is increased by an increase in the supply of foreign articles in the sense that the foreigner is willing to give a greater quantity of those articles in exchange for any of the same quantity of native produce, the increase being supposed to be on a small scale. Upon the general principle that a cheap market is advantageous to the buyer, the home country is benefited; whatever the cause of the increased supply, whether it is due to an improvement in the production of the foreign articles, or a greater desire on the part of the foreigners for the produce of the home country, or *ceteris paribus* an increase in their numbers. Conversely a diminution in the supply of foreign goods is detrimental to the home country.

The technical use of the term increase of supply must here be kept in mind. It is quite possible that the home country might suffer by the foreign customer becoming better supplied with commodities in general. It is well observed by Mr. Medley, an ardent free-trader, that the adoption of free trade by all nations—which of course, according to him, implies the increase of their wealth—might prove detrimental to England.[2] The poverty of the foreigner may quite conceivably be advantageous to the native.

Suppose a new country exchanging with an old one food for highly manufactured products. An increased deficiency in

---

[1] Thus the project of a differential tax on foreign produce (in favour of the colonies) is described by an eminent free-trader as a demand that "England should tax herself to the amount of 10½ millions"; as if England would be a loser to that extent. In the view which I adopt the amount received by the Government is to be set against the amount paid by the people.

[2] *Fair Trade Unmasked.*

necessaries on the part of the old country, or of a large section thereof,[1] always supposing—perhaps an imaginary supposition [2]— that their efficiency is not thereby impaired, rendering them more eager for the supplies derived from the new country, is apt to benefit the new country considered as a whole. However, the particular section of the home country which supplies services analogous to those of the foreigner—considered as an isolated group—may well be prejudiced by the poverty of foreign labour.

This last consideration suggests a fresh topic—international competition; which may, however, be subordinated to the present one (the change in the supply of foreign goods) by observing that when a competitor with the home country deals with the foreigner, the " supply " of foreign goods is diminished. Formal reasoning and common sense concur in regarding such competition as an evil to the home country.[3]

The solution is not so simple when we consider changes originating on the side of the home country. Such changes may be divided into two classes, according as they originate on the side of supply, or demand : exports, or imports. Under the former head the simplest case is where there has occurred an improvement [or the reverse], a diminution [or increase] in the cost of production of an exported article ; the case considered by Mill in the fifth section of his great chapter on International Values. As may be gathered from Mill's reasoning, the improvement may prove detrimental to the exporting country. It is true that Mill obscures the subject by taking as the measure of the gain of trade the alteration in the rate of exchange between exports and imports rather than the truer measure of advantage which the principles of Consumers' and Producers' Rent afford. However, a representative case may be put which brings out the implication latent in Mill's reasoning. It will be recollected that Mill supposes an improvement in the production of linen which Germany exchanges for cloth imported from England; in which

[1] *Ceteris paribus*, of course : not supposing that, when the real remuneration of the foreign labourers is diminished, that of his employer is increased; as Mill and Cairnes do in effect; when, discussing the effect on international values of low wages in a foreign country, they use wages in the peculiar Ricardian sense (*Political Economy*, Book III. ch. xxv. § 4, and *Leading Principles*). These passages will be discussed later on.

[2] Professor Walker in his powerful and impartial article on " Protection and Protectionists " in the *Quarterly Journal of Economics* for April 1890, admits it to be quite possible that in some branches of American industry " the manufacturers pay higher wages for a given quantity of labour than are paid abroad.

[3] See Part II. Mill's paradoxically low estimate of this evil will be considered in Part III.

case he shows it to be a possibility that " Germany will obtain cloth on more unfavourable terms and at a higher exchange value than before " (loc. cit. § 5, par. 6). Now suppose that the same amount of productive forces are expended on linen by the German manufacturer before as after the improvement. If the increase in productivity has been ten per cent., where before there were 100 units of linen produced, there are now 110 units produced. But if the demand for linen be increased " in a less proportion than the cheapness," whereas the German used to receive, say, 100 units of cloth, he will now receive less than 100. For an equal outlay in the way of cost he receives a less return. Whence it follows, if we make the further supposition that linen is not an article of German consumption, that the exporting country is damnified by the improvement; and by parity of reasoning may be benefited by a restriction of its exports. It is clear that the data which have been supposed may be considerably modified without the conclusion being destroyed.

But indeed, without invoking Mill's stupendous chapter, the proposition is sufficiently supported by common sense. It is a commonplace that a bad harvest is good for farmers in the absence of foreign competition. As Ricardo says, " if we lived in one of Mr. Owen's parallelograms and enjoyed all our productions in common, then no one could suffer in consequence of abundance; but as long as society is constituted as it now is, abundance will often be injurious to producers, and scarcity beneficial to them." [1] Let us assume, according to Gregory King's law,[2] that a deficiency in quantity by a tenth may raise the value of the harvest by three-tenths. Now, suppose that the harvest has been an average one; but that, as the grain is sent to market, a tenth leaks out, or is intercepted by robbers (to use a favourite free trade metaphor). The total value will be, as before, raised; so beneficent (to one party) may be the effect of what Cherbuliez calls artificial dearth.[3]

An example of an impediment to export, other than a tax accruing to the exporting country, is a transit duty levied on the exports from one country to another by a third party. It is conceivable that the Native States of India might be benefited by the duty which we levy on opium passing through our territory, if China had no other means of satisfying her demand for opium.

[1] Protection to Agriculture, § 4, sub fin.
[2] See Jevons' Theory, p. 168, 2nd edition.
[3] Dictionnaire d'Économie politique, art. " Disette." Cp. art. " Abondance," by Bastiat.

A similar effect might be produced by an increase in the cost of transporting the exported article from the locality of its production to the port, supposing that there is no corresponding drag on importation.[1]

The effect of a variation in the cost of transport generally will be compounded of different tendencies : since an impediment on exportation and on importation in general affects both countries, so far as each both exports and (in return voyages) imports. Since, out of the *four* tendencies thus compounded, one only (variation in the cost of exportation by natives)—and that one only on certain conditions—would lead to a benefit for the natives from an aggravation of the cost of transport, it may be presumed that in general such an aggravation is very unlikely to be advantageous to the home country.

The case of an improvement in the process of manufacture [2] of an article which is both exported and consumed at home, is also a compound between the certain gain to the native consumer and the possible loss to the home country in the way of foreign trade. It is quite possible that the latter tendency may prevail over the former, just as in the case of farmers [3] who may gain more as producers, than they lose as consumers, by a bad harvest.

An instructive example of the principle under consideration is afforded by the question whether a diminution of the output of the home country's exports consequent upon a limitation of working hours is necessarily injurious to the country. That this question is to be answered in the negative is well argued by Mr. Sidney Webb in his article on " Limitation of the Hours of Labour " in the *Contemporary Review* for December 1889.[4] It is noticeable that the advocate of socialistic measures dwells on propositions relating to the trade between two nations ; he does not bring on the scene a third country competing with the socialistic one. An advocate on the other side would probably represent the whole argument as vitiated by this omission. The judicial position is intermediate between these two. If the demand of the foreign customer for our goods, prior to, or abstracted from, the existence of a competing country, is such as to render a restriction of exports advantageous to the home country, it may still be possible, notwithstanding the existence of competition, to obtain that sort of advantage though in a less

[1] As might well occur in a round-about trade.
[2] Mill, *Political Economy*, ch. xviii. § 5.
[3] Above, p. 10.   [4] See p. 878, Vol. LVI.

degree. As Professor Marshall says with reference to this question, "the influence of foreign trade competition in this connection can be proved to be different from what it at first sight appears." [1]

It should not be conceived, I think, that the conditions favouring the successful restriction of exports are altogether exceptional. Mill, after distinguishing three varieties of conditions, inquires "which is the more probable," and decides in favour of that variety which, as we have already seen, is favourable to the policy of restriction. [2] Accordingly, if each nation could only deal with one other, either of the pair might often play the game of restriction with advantage. But no doubt the existence of competition modifies the foreigner's law of demand for the native articles in such wise [3] as to render that game much less gainful.

It is to be observed that the advantage which has been described results from a drag on exports which need not be a tax. A fortiori of course when the impediment is a tax accruing to the exporting country. The latter proposition is much more generally accepted, I think, than the former. [4] It is often stated with the unnecessary limitation that the home country must have an absolute monopoly of the exporting article. [5] That she should furnish a considerable portion of the total supply might suffice.

Coming next to changes originated on the side of imports (to the home country), let us consider a restriction on importation such as a transit duty imposed by a third power on imports into the home country. Such an impediment on imports, unlike one on exports, is never advantageous to the home country. The duty levied by the Indian Government on opium transported through Bombay from the Native States might conceivably benefit those States, but not the Chinese.

A tax indeed on imports the proceeds of which accrue to the home country may be beneficial to that country : but not with as great probability as a tax on exports. This proposition as it now stands * rests mainly on the concrete circumstance pointed out

---

[1] *Principles*, 2nd edition, p. 745, note.

[2] *Political Economy*, Book III. ch. xviii. § 5, last par.

[3] Cp. below, p. 43.

[4] The latter is explicitly admitted even by McCulloch; the former only incidentally by Mill. [Below, p. 24.]

[5] *E. g.* Rogers, *Six Centuries*, p. 79, " there must be no other source of supply."

* This passage has been rewritten (see above, p. 3).

by Professor Bastable, that in the world as it is a buyers' monopoly in the international market is rarer than a sellers' monopoly. The grounds on which the proposition was originally based have been, as stated in the prefatory note, abandoned.

That a tax on imports may prove a net gain to the home country is admitted by the χαρίεντες, but it is denied by the common free-trader and even by competent economists when expressing themselves carelessly. It may be as well to adduce instances of these contrary judgments; so that my argument in favour of the proposition in question may appear neither paradoxical nor otiose.

In favour of the proposition the following high authorities may be cited :—Mill (*Political Economy*, Book V. ch. iv. § 6) :—

" A tax on imported commodities almost always falls in part upon the foreigners." . . . " Those are in the right who maintain that taxes on imports are partly paid by foreigners."

Senior (*Outlines*, 184) :—

" A part of the taxes received by the Government of one country is often paid by the inhabitants of another."

Seligman (*Incidence of Taxation*, ch. v.) :—

" It will be seen how erroneous is the doctrine of those extremists who maintain that the loss to the consumer is measured by the proceeds of the import duties." . . . " The price of Sumatra tobacco has risen by only a fraction of the tax."

Compare the admissions made by Professor Bastable in his Paper on " Incidence and Effects of Taxation " so often referred to, and Professor Nicholson's reasoning in his masterly paper on " Tariffs and International Commerce." [1]

On the other side Mongredien (*Pleas for Protection Examined*):—

" Import duties on foreign goods fall on the consumers of the importing country and are paid by them."

Sydney Buxton (*A.B.C. of Free Trade*) :—

" Duties on goods are paid for by the people who consume those goods, and not by the people who produce them."

Sir J. Lubbock, at the Congress of the Chambers of Commerce of the Empire, 1892, says, " I maintain the proposition that the duties are paid by the consumer " (*Chamber of Commerce Journal*, July 1892, *Supplement*, p. 28).

The opinion is not confined to Free-Traders. Mr. McKinley (*North American Review*, cl. p. 742) writes :—

" If the duty is put on the non-competing foreign products, the consumer in the United States will pay every dollar of that tax."

---

[1] *Scottish Geographical Magazine*, September 1891.

An instructive statement of the common free trade opinion is found in Mr. Strachey's singularly brilliant report on the effect of the German tariff (Parl. Papers, 1884–5, LXXXI.). Mr. Strachey speaks of—

" The axiom of political economy is that a tax on foreign commodities is borne by the importing country. No one could so much as state [the contrary] without exposing himself to the charge of having no sense of humour."

No one certainly will bring this charge against Mr. Strachey; for his report is probably the wittiest blue-book in existence; one of the wisest too, if we except this particular passage. Mr. Strachey seems to himself to have proved his case when he has demonstrated—by some very interesting statistics—that the price of the taxed article in the importing country exceeds its price in the exporting country by just the amount of the tax, abstracting cost of transport. But *quis dubitavit ?* If, as is or was recently the case, there is a tax of two dollars per ton on hay imported from Canada into the United States, the cost of transport being here insignificant, the price per ton on the American side of the frontier will be two dollars higher than on the Canadian side. The question is whether it is the American price that has gone up, or the Canadian price which has gone down. The latter happens to be the case.[1]*

A similar *ignoratio elenchi* is committed by a still higher authority, Roscher, when he argues that Germany must pay the full amount of the tax which she imposed on wheat imported from America; for that the price in Germany (account being taken of cost of transport) exceeds that in England by exactly the amount of the tax.[2] But how does he know that the imposition of the tax did not cause America to offer her wheat to England

---

[1] As shown in the *Report of the Subcommittee of the Committee of Finance* (Senate U.S.) by Senator Merrill (Rep. 788). Here are some extracts from the evidence : " The duty of five cents per dozen imposed upon eggs by the McKinley tariff is paid by the foreign producer not by the consumer." . . . " They have dropped the valuation on most farm products just about the amount of the duty imposed by the McKinley Bill." . . . " No question they have to take 30 per cent. less for their horses."

Mr. Edward Atkinson in his comments on this Report (*Taxation and Work*, ch. xxv.), after ridiculing the " delusion that one of the effects of a duty imposed in this country upon a given import is to depress the price of that article in the country in which it is produced, and that by such reduction the burden of our tax is put upon that country " (p. 193), admits (p. 194) that " our duties upon the products of Canada have unquestionably had that effect."

* Some of the evidence here cited appears to be not trustworthy, or to refer only to a short period (Shearman, ECONOMIC JOURNAL, Vol. IV. p. 524).

[2] *Finanzwissenschaft*, p. 411, Note 4.

on better terms than before ? It may be the American price which has gone down, not the German price which has gone up.[1]

Probably the highest authority and weightiest argument in favour of the proposition in question are those of McCulloch, who holds [2] that the project [of obliging foreigners to contribute to the revenue of the nation] " is wholly imaginary, and that duties on imports are always paid by the importers, and never by the exporters "; the reason being that the exporters must obtain the rate of profits prevailing in their country, and therefore cannot after the tax lower the price which before the tax only just afforded the ordinary profits.[3]

Let us examine this reason.

First, as pointed out by Professor Bastable,[4] price may be lowered without profits being diminished, if the cost of production varies with the margin. Thus a tax imposed by the United States on certain kinds of agricultural produce imported from Canada [5] might result in the diminution of the quantity, the cost of production, and the price of that produce. This idea of a freely sliding margin is indeed highly theoretical, but so is the objector's idea of equal profits in all occupations.

More important in practice, if less familiar in theory, is the analogous case in which the burden falls—not on rent proper—but on " quasi-rent." Suppose an import tax laid on tin plates. The tax might be paid out of the surplus gains of the more successful foreign manufacturers,[6] while the less successful would be driven out of the field.

No doubt if the tax imposed were a very heavy one, such as is now fashionable, say 50 or 100 per cent., it is not to be expected that the foreign exporters should lower their price to that extent. The price of tin plates then will rise in the home country. Accordingly a net loss corresponding to that rise of price appears to be inflicted on the home country. But it appears so only while we confine our attention to immediate effects. When an engine pushes against a carriage the immediate effect is that the buffer of the carriage is pressed back. When the buffer

[1] Cp. Bastable, Incidence, p. 3.

[2] Principles of Political Economy, Part I. ch. v., sub finem. Cp. Taxation and Funding, Part II. ch. v.

[3] McCulloch's argument is employed by Mongredien (Pleas for Protection) and other extreme Free-traders.

[4] Incidence and Effects, p. 3. Cp. International Trade, p. 45. See also Sidgwick, Political Economy, Book III. ch. v. § 3.

[5] Above, p. 14.

[6] See Bastable, Incidence and Effects [Report of the British Association for 1889], and Sidgwick, Political Economy, Book III. ch. v. § 3.

has been pressed back to a certain point the carriage begins to move, and the buffer of the next carriage, and in fine the whole train. The propagated influence of a tax may be similar, in a case where the demand of the foreigner for the products of the home country—say food and raw materials—is very urgent. The export of tin plates being checked, the foreigners find a difficulty in paying for the imports which they so much require. To restore the equation of international trade they are constrained to offer their exports other than tin plates—exports in general—on terms less favourable to themselves. It is quite conceivable that the gain which the home country derives from this readjustment of trade may exceed the loss which it derives from the rise of the value of tin plates. As Mill says in his splendid and candid section on Protectionism : "A country which prohibits some foreign commodities does, *ceteris paribus*, obtain those which it does not prohibit at a less price than it would otherwise have to pay."

An import tax in the case supposed would resemble the export tax before considered, in tending to check the exports from the home country. For a country so circumstanced it might be disadvantageous to "grow more cotton and cereals," [1] as Mr. Gladstone recommends the Americans.[2] How should the native labour, which but for the check to exports would have been employed in producing them, be now most advantageously employed ? Quite possibly on "tin plates"; thereby rendering the native demand for foreign goods less pressing, and thus more fully satisfying the conditions which must exist in order that the foreigner may be taxed.

These arguments are not affected, or rather become *a fortiori*, by the existence of "invisible" exports or imports of the nature of capital lent, or interest paid. For by the operations which have been described the value of money will have been increased in the foreign country and decreased in the home country.[3] Accordingly the natives as lenders or debtors will now have to give less of their own produce, and as borrowers or creditors will receive more of the foreigner's produce.

It has been shown that under conceivable circumstances

---

[1] *Cp.* F. Bowen, *Principles of Political Economy*, p. 467, *et sqq.*

[2] In his article on "Free Trade and Protection," in the *North American Review.* See Mr. Blaine's criticism of his advice. *Ibid.*

[3] See Ricardo, *Political Economy*, Bk. III. ch. xxi. § 2. Mill, *Political Economy*, penultimate par., *sub finem*, Bk. V. ch. iv. § 6, par. 4, latter part. Bastable, *International Trade*, ch. iii., and p. 118. *Incidence*, p. 3, par. 2.

advantage may result to the home country from a tax on exports or imports. But will it result under given circumstances? A negative answer, I think, may be given in some concrete cases; in many " the only answer is that an answer is impossible "; as Professor J. S. Nicholson demonstrates in his essay on " Tariffs and International Commerce." [1] The affirmative answer is described by him as " part of the casuistry of economics," like the discussions of moral philosophers concerning the occasional justification of mendacity. " Free trade, like honesty, still remains the best policy."

This analogy seems singularly just to one who agrees with Mill as a moralist that " even this rule [truth], sacred as it is, admits of possible exception " . . . that " the exception ought to be recognised, and, if possible, its limits defined "; [2] and with Mill as an economist, that in particular cases " taxes on imports are partly paid by foreigners." [3] " England will gain at the expense of Germany not only the whole amount of the duty but more " [4] by an export tax.[5]

Bounties being " negative taxes," as Cournot says, it may be expected that in cases where a tax is detrimental, a bounty would be beneficial.

But when we consider large changes apt to be attended with a reorganisation of trade, many of the preceding propositions no longer hold good. An increased supply, a greater cheapness of foreign goods, may now, I think, prove disadvantageous. A bounty may prove advantageous upon principles indicated by Professor Marshall,[6] by calling into play the law of increasing returns. Upon similar principles, a tax on imports may foster native industries, it may be advantageous in its ulterior as well as its more immediate effects; in the way of protection, as well as in the way of what may be called in a large sense [7] revenue.

I hope it may be allowable to define my subject so as to exclude a detailed examination of the free-trade controversy. On

[1] In the *Scottish Geographical Magazine* for September 1891.
[2] *Utilitarianism*, ch. i.   [3] Book V. ch. iv. § 6.   [4] *Ibid.*
[5] Of course I agree with Mill and living writers that for one nation to benefit itself at the expense of a greater loss to others is contrary to the highest morality, which takes the greatest happiness of all as its end. " The justice . . . of destroying one of two gains in order to engross a rather larger share of the other does not require discussion " (Mill, Book V. ch. x. § 1). But, in an abstract study upon the motion of projectiles *in vacuo*, I do not think it necessary to enlarge upon the horrors of war.
[6] *Principles of Economics*, Book V. ch. xii.
[7] Including producers' and consumers' rent, as well the receipts of the Treasury.

the general issue I have nothing to add to what I have learnt from the first-rate writers who have treated of the subject, in particular Mill, and Professor Sidgwick,[1] and Professor Marshall.[2] As I read, protection might procure economic advantage in certain cases, if there was a Government wise enough to discriminate those cases, and strong enough to confine itself to them; but this condition is very unlikely to be fulfilled.

So far we have been regarding exclusively the advantage of the home country. When we take in the interest of all parties we are met with the axiom that any interference with exchange diminishes the sum total of advantage resulting to all parties concerned. The axiom, like most of the propositions with which we are concerned, presents two aspects according as we consider small or organic changes. With reference to the former case it may be accepted without qualification, except so far as the level of utility, so to speak, is regarded as different in different countries;[3] the exports of one country as compared with another costing more labour, and the imports affording more satisfaction.

When we consider large changes, developing new industries, it is conceivable, as Professor Sidgwick has argued [4] that an interference with the " natural " course of international trade may be beneficial to all parties.

Much of what has been hitherto said refers primarily to the case of trade between two countries.[5] But the transition to the more general case is easy. As Mill says, " trade among any number of countries must take place on the same essential principles as trade between two countries. . . . Introducing a greater number of agents precisely similar cannot change the law of their action " (*Political Economy*, Book III. ch. xviii. § 3).

The preceding propositions relate especially to international trade proper. But many of them may be transferred to that quasi-international trade of which the principal example is the transaction by which the national produce is divided between the owners of the agents of production. The principal characteristic

---

[1] *Political Economy*, Book III. ch. v.; and *Scope and Method of Economic Science*.

[2] Presidential Address to Section F of the British Association, *Report of British Association*, 1890, and *Journ. Stat. Soc.*, December 1890.

[3] Compare Professor Marshall, *Principles*, Book III. ch. vi. § 2, par. 3.

[4] *Political Economy*, Part III. ch. v. § 1.

[5] The competition of a third country affecting the *demand* of one of the two countries for the goods of the other; above p. 12.

peculiar to international trade proper is, I think, the possibility of a nation benefiting itself by a tax on exports and imports. There may indeed be a tax on the transactions between "nations" in the generalised sense—such as a tax on wages—but the proceeds of the tax would accrue to the community, not to one of the groups.

It is useful, I think, to contemplate the theory of distribution as analogous to that of international trade proper. It is seen, for instance, that the intention which seems to inspire some of the leaders of labour to raise wages by restricting the supply of labour is *prima facie* quite consistent with general principles. But a doubt may occur whether the special conditions are favourable for carrying such a policy to any great length, when the transaction between the entrepreneur and the workman, who supplies an agent of production in return for a share of the produce, is likened to that sort of international trade which England used to have with the Southern States of America, when she imported materials (cotton) and exported the finished article.

Again it is instructive to regard the transaction between landlord and farmer as a sort of international trade. The familiar proposition that "rent does not enter into price," or into cost of production, may thus be seen in a clearer light.

The theories stated in the preceding pages are now to be sustained by, or maintained against, the authority of the principal writers on the subject.

I. (1) *Ricardo.*—Foremost is the founder of the theory,

> Quo nihil majus generatur ipso,
> Nec viget quidquam simile aut secundum.

The incomparable vigour of Ricardo's chapter on foreign trade has not been approached by any of his successors. The main propositions of the theory—the principle of comparative cost (McCulloch's edition, p. 77), the change in the quantities and prices of commodities consequent upon foreign trade (p. 73, *cp.* p. 80 *sub finem*), the difference in the value of money in different countries (p. 79 *et sqq.*), are stated by Ricardo more briefly, and perhaps more clearly, than by J. S. Mill. Mill seems to have the advantage only in one respect; his recognition of the case in which an impediment to trade may be beneficial— or an improvement[1] prejudicial—to one of the countries. It

---

[1] As to the case of improvement, see below, p. 24.

may be observed that the circumstance on which this property depends, the demand in the other country being "increased in a greater proportion than the cheapness," to use Mill's phrase (*Political Economy*, xviii. § 5), did not escape Ricardo (p. 73, par. 2).

The only scruples which the chapter may excite are removed by recollecting Ricardo's peculiar phraseology: the sense in which he employs the terms "value,"[1] and "wages" or "real wages,"[2] and his elliptical use of *either* capital or labour where we might expect *both*. These explanations apply to the following passages :

"We should have no greater value if, by the discovery of new markets, we obtained double the quantity of foreign goods in exchange for a given quantity of ours" (p. 72).

"The country may have 'greater skill' and 'better machinery' used in the manufacture of exportable commodities; yet 'the rate of profits will probably differ but little'; wages, or the real reward of the labourer, may be the same in both" (p. 81).

"If capital freely flowed towards those countries where it could be most profitably employed, there could be no difference in the rate of profit, and no other difference in the real or labour price of commodities than the additional quantity of labour required to convey them to the various markets where they were to be sold" (p. 77).

(2) *J. S. Mill.*—Mill's contributions to the subject are contained in his stupendous chapter on "International Values" (*Political Economy*, Book III. ch. xviii.), the chapters on the "Distribution of the Precious Metals," and the "Competition of different Countries in the same Market" (*ibid.* chs. xxi. xxv.), and the sections treating of *the effects produced on international exchange by duties on exports and imports* (Book V. ch. iv. § 6), and the "Doctrine of Protection to Native Industry" (Book V. ch. x. § 1); and the corresponding passages in the *Unsettled Questions.*

Mill's exposition of the general theory is still unsurpassed. He presents clearly all the leading features : the distinction between international and home trade (Book III. ch. ii., last par.), the former requiring us to "fall back upon an antecedent[3] law,

---

[1] *Cp.* Ricardo, *Political Economy*, ch. xx.　　　　[2] *Ibid.*, p. 82, par. 2.

[3] *Cp.* Book III. ch. xvi. § 1.　The term "anterior" in this passage, of which Jevons complains (*Theory*, p. 215, 2nd ed.), fits well that conception of the distinction which has been adopted in this study (see Part I. par. 1).

that of supply and demand " (*ibid*. ch. xviii. § 1); the sense of " cost " in which " a country gets a commodity cheaper when it obtains a greater quantity of the commodity with the same expenditure of labour and capital " (*ibid*. § 9); the peculiarity that international values are not " in the ratio " (*ibid*. and *cp*. ch. xvi. § 1) of cost in that sense; but that a variation of cost in that sense will be attended with a variation—though not in general an equal variation—in international value (Book III. ch. xviii. § 5). The additions and corrections which Mill's work has received will be noticed in the course of the following more detailed review.

Mill begins by considering the establishment of a trade between two nations. His classical illustration—the exchange of English cloth for German linen—has been much imitated, but little improved. The opening of a trade, which is considered in the first four sections of the great chapter, being a change of the kind which we have designated as simple or continuous,[1] does not differ essentially from the facilitation of (an already established) trade which is considered in the fifth section. The latter case may indeed be regarded as the more general since it comprehends both the case in which the facilitation is beneficial to both countries, the case to which the opening of trade presumably belongs,[2] and also the case in which the facilitation is prejudicial to one party.

Mill is, I think, the first—indeed almost the only—economist who has stated the latter proposition. The statement would have been more complete if he had explicitly affirmed the converse proposition that an impediment to trade may be beneficial to one party.[3]

It would have been well too if Mill in his chapters on International Values, and on the " Competition of Different Countries " (Book III. chs. xviii., xxv.), had treated the cost of production in each country not as constant, but as varying with the quantity produced—as his successors[4] have done. The deficiency however is partly made up in the chapter on " Taxes on Commodities " (Book V.), where, with special reference to international trade, it is pointed out that " duties on the produce of land or of mines

[1] Above, p. 7.

[2] The state of null trade, represented by the " origin " at which the supply-and-demand curves intersect, is in general a position of unstable equilibrium, that is, of minimum advantage; advantage less for both parties than that which is incident to the proximate intersection of the curves, which is in general a position of maximum advantage.

[3] But see below, p. 24.   [4] *E. g.* Mangoldt, Fawcett, Bastable.

might be so high as to diminish materially the demand for the produce, and compel the abandonment of some of the inferior qualities of land or mines. Supposing this to be the effect, the consumers, both in the country itself and in those which dealt with it, would obtain the produce at smaller cost " (§ 6).[1]

It is a more serious complaint that Mill takes as the measure of the advantage which a country derives from trade, the increase in the rate of exchange of its exports against its imports.[2] He thus confounds " final " with integral utility; ignoring the principle of " consumer's rent." [3] However, it may be admitted that his definition is adequate to the purposes for which it is used. Where he says that the whole or none, or more or less, of the advantage will accrue to a certain country, it is generally true, I think, not only in his sense, but in the more correct sense.

The splendid edifice of theory constructed in the first five sections is not improved by the superstructure of later date which forms the latter part of the chapter. This second storey does not carry us much higher. What seems at first sight to be an addition will be found, I think, also in the first part; I mean what Cournot calls the " reflux " of capital and labour; the sort of change which occurs when Germany has obtained cloth from England " with only seven-eighths of the labour and capital which she previously expended in supplying herself with cloth, and may expend the remainder. in increasing her own consumption of linen or any other commodity " (ch. xviii. § 8,

---

[1] Compare Ricardo's theory that " by a continued bounty on the exportation of corn there would be created a tendency to a permanent rise in the price of corn " (McCulloch's edition, p. 188). Compare also the observation made by Mill with respect to taxes considered generally, that a tax, by checking the demand for a commodity, may prevent what we should now call the law of increasing returns from coming into operation (Mill, Book V. ch. iv. § 2, *sub finem*).

[2] Cournot's objection on this score is serious if Mill is held to mean—what he certainly suggests—that England's share of the total gain is in the ratio of (17 *minus* 15) to (20 *minus* 15); 20 and 15 (yards of linen in exchange for 10 of cloth) being the limits fixed by the respective costs of production, and 17 the value actually set up. (See ch. xviii. ante-penultimate section, *et passim*.) But Mill need not, I think, be held to that precise statement; and then Cournot's objection amounts to no more than this : that there is a certain asymmetry and inelegance in expressing the share of the total gain in terms of the commodity purchased by one of the parties (" linen ").

Cournot's objection is partly directed against the expression of the gain of one party as a *percentage*—e. g. the gain of England as 20 per cent., if before the trade she obtained 15 of linen, and after the trade 18 for the same quantity of cloth. Has Mill employed such a percentage in the passage quoted in the next note ?

[3] *Cp.* Book V. ch. x. § 1, par. 5. " The amount of national loss is measured by the excess of the price at which the commodity is produced over that at which it could be imported." *Cp.* Jevons' *Theory*, ch. iv., on the gain by exchange.

first paragraph). But the statement in the original part (§ 5, penultimate paragraph) is nearly as accurate : " In the case supposed the consumers of Germany have had part of their incomes set at liberty by the increased cheapness of linen which they may indeed expend in increasing their consumption of that article, but which they may likewise expend in other articles." (Cf. *ibid.*, last paragraph.)

In short, I agree with Professor Bastable [1] in regarding the superstructure as " laborious and confusing." The last epithet seems particularly deserved by a certain passage leading to what I have called the second storey : where Mill notices the phenomenon of multiple equilibrium, and says : " It is conceivable that the conditions might be equally satisfied by every numerical rate which could be supposed." This statement appears somewhat inconsistent with the conception of an equation which Mill has elsewhere (*Political Economy*, Book III. ch. ii. § 3, and review of Thornton, *Dissertations*, iv.) so well applied to the phenomenon of Supply and Demand. However, suppose that the intersections of the curves are very frequent and close together (as may well be when both are inelastic : below, p. 37, Fig. 4, diagram 4), the case supposed by Mill virtually, if not theoretically, comes into existence. It should be added that Mill has done nothing in his later sections to remove that sort of indeterminateness which does occur in the actual case of plural, though definite, positions of equilibrium—not to speak of that sort of indeterminateness which would occur in the case of that *neutral* equilibrium which he imagines.

The chapter on the " Distribution of the Precious Metals " requires no comment.

In the first section of the chapter on " Competition " (Book III. ch. xxv.), the lenient judgment which Mill expresses appears to imply one at least of the following propositions : (1) The rise of a competitor may diminish the value without diminishing the quantity of a country's exports (*ibid.* last paragraph). (2) A diminution in the quantity of exports does no great harm to producers.

The first proposition, I think, cannot be maintained in the light of the reasoning respecting competition.[2] The second proposition may perhaps be maintained on certain abstract assumptions. But on the concrete supposition that the weaker producers of the exported articles may be driven out of their occupation by a fall in price, and may not be able to find an

---

[1] *International Trade*, p. 29, note.   [2] Below, pp. 24 and 43.

equally good occupation elsewhere, the proposition cannot be maintained.

Mill goes on to argue (*ibid.*, §§ 2 and 4) that low wages when common to all branches of industry cannot be one of those causes which enable one country to undersell another. The argument is sound if low wages are understood in the Ricardian sense of a small proportion of the joint product; which is Mill's meaning. But the argument is not sound, I think, if low wages are understood in the sense of low real remuneration received by the labourer per unit of produce; [1] *ceteris paribus*, and in particular not assuming any elevation in the similarly reckoned remuneration of the capitalist-employing class—a very natural meaning to attach to the term. Mill's employment in this connection of the Ricardian dogma that " general low wages do not cause low prices, nor high wages high prices within the country itself " is questionable (§ 4, par. 2). The Ricardian assumption that the labour-value of money (the efforts and sacrifices required to procure a unit of gold) is constant is not very proper to the case of International Trade.[2] It is quite conceivable, if the inhabitants of a country, or a large section of them, are willing to do as much for less remuneration, reckoned in commodities, that the same efforts and sacrifices will procure less gold in the world's market. Accordingly general prices will fall in that country; and in particular the price of exports; thus the country will be able to undersell others where higher wages (in one, and not the least natural, sense of the term) prevail.

In the section on the effects produced on international exchange by duties on exports and imports (Book V. ch. iv.) Mill employs a principle which was noticed above as omitted in his first chapter : the converse of the proposition that an improvement in the production of exports may be prejudicial to a country. For when he concludes (*loc. cit.*[3] par. 4) that by an export tax in certain cases " England will gain not only the whole amount of the duty but more," is not this " more " attributable to the tax *quâ* impediment ? If the tax were intercepted as a

---

[1] Wages in this sense is, or is proportional to, wages in the sense in which the term is employed by Mill in the classical passage at the end of his chapter on Profits (viz. the real remuneration of the labourer per unit of time, *loc. cit.*, par. 2) *divided by* " efficiency " as defined in that section (viz. the amount of work done per unit of time).

[2] Professor J. S. Nicholson, in his masterly article on " Wages " in the *Encyclopædia Britannica* (Vol. XXIV. p. 309a), hints at this exception to the Ricardian principle.

[3] There is a misprint in the fifth sentence of this paragraph. For " so great " read " a greater."

transit duty, or otherwise,[1] this *plus* would still accrue to the exporting country. (The case considered is that which corresponds to Fig. 4 (2) and (4) in the mathematical sequel.)

In the following section (People's Edition, p. 515*b*) there is a little inaccuracy. It is not true that " a tax on rare and high-priced wines will fall wholly on the growers, or rather on the owners of the vineyards." If the tax is specific the price will be raised by the monopolist.[2]

In the section on Protectionism some of the expressions in the 7th paragraph [3] seem appropriate to the case which I have considered in Part I. : that of a country for whose exports there is an urgent demand in foreign countries benefiting itself by an import tax.[4]

On the famous passage. about " infant industries " I have nothing to add to what has been said by Professor Sidgwick as to the removal of a barrier, so to speak, blocking the initiation of an industry,[5] by Professor Marshall as to the possibility of bringing into play the law of increasing returns [6] through an ingeniously devised system of Protection, and by other eminent economists, in particular Professor Taussig [7] and General Walker.[8]

In conclusion I subscribe to the elevated Utilitarianism which inspires several passages in this section. I trust that Mill has not exaggerated the readiness of the nations to follow an example of commercial disinterestedness—as he has elsewhere certainly exaggerated their readiness to abandon war. " Wars," says the sanguine philanthropist, " are now usually confined, in almost every country, to those distant and outlying possessions at which it comes into contact with savages." [9] Perhaps " collective churlishness " (Book V. ch. x. § 1) in commercial relations will die as hard as war.

(3) *Cairnes.*—Cairnes' principal contribution to the subject is his recognition of the part played by " non-competing groups within a nation." [10] Mill indeed had discerned the existence of

---

[1] Above, p. 10.

[2] Marshall, *Principles*, v. 13, 4. *Cp.* E. J. 1897.

[3] People's Edition, p. 554*b*.

[4] Part I. p. 46, and Part II. p. 435.

[5] *Political Economy*, Book III. ch. v.

[6] Address to Section F, British Association, 1890.

[7] *Tariff History of the United States.*

[8] *Quarterly Journal of Economics*, April 1890.

[9] Book IV. ch. i. § 2.

[10] *Leading Principles*, Part III. ch. ii. § 1, p. 386. The subject is well treated by Professor Bastable in his *Theory of International Trade*, ch. vi.

such groups;[1] but he made less use of them than might have been expected, even with respect to domestic trade.[2]

Cairnes has also restated the fundamental distinction between foreign and domestic trade at great length and with added clearness; but without, I think, substantially adding to or taking from Mill.[3]

On the nicer points of theory Cairnes falls behind his predecessor. He does not seem fully to have apprehended the effect of an improvement in the production of an exported article. In the case of " a great improvement . . . in the manufacture of woollen goods in England " he concludes that " English labourers," so far as they were consumers of foreign goods procured through an exchange for woollens, would " obtain those commodities more cheaply." [4] This conclusion is erroneous if " cheapness " is defined with reference to some fixed standard, such as labour-cost, for it may be shown that the effect of an improvement in the production of an export might be to make the terms on which imports are obtained worse.[5] Cairnes' statements are accurate only on the supposition that alteration in the supply of woollen goods makes no difference in international value. It is only on this interpretation that we can understand his conclusion, " the wages of English labourers measured in woollen goods would rise in proportion as the cost of those goods had fallen " (p. 407). This is true of a *small* country, whose influence on international values may be neglected, but is not true in general.

On the important practical question What is the effect of low wages upon the trade of a country ? Cairnes is even more open to criticism than Mill. Putting the case of wheat imported into Victoria from South Australia or South America, Cairnes argues, " inasmuch as a rise or fall in the rate of wages [in Australia] has no effect on the comparative quantities of labour required for the production of different commodities, it is evident that if the received theory be true this circumstance must be incapable of altering in any way the course of foreign trade " (p. 390 top, *cp.* p. 393, par. 2).

Now, as Cairnes fully perceives that comparative cost does

[1] As pointed out by Professor Marshall in his masterly article on Mill's *Theory of Value, Fortnightly Review*, 1876.

[2] Compare Professor Sidgwick, *Principles of Political Economy*, Book II. ch. ii. § 9. See, however, Mill, Book III. ch. iv. § 4.

[3] Compare Professor Marshall, *loc. cit. sub finem.*

[4] *Leading Principles*, Part III. ch. ii. § 5, pp. 404–7.

[5] Below, p. 36, where it is shown that the effect of the change might be to push back the position of equilibrium along the supposed unaltered demand and supply curve; that is, to make the gain in respect of utility less for the exporting nation.

not " determine," but only " controls " value (*Leading Principles*, p. 423), does not fix " a point about which values move, but a circle within which they move " (*ibid*. p. 424)—an area corresponding to that intercepted between tangents at O to the curves at p. 39 on the abstract supposition of cost of production not varying with quantity—it might have occurred to him that, even though " a fall in the rate of wages has no effect on the comparative quantities of labour required for the production of different commodities," yet, if the Australian workers became disposed to give the same quantity of work in return for less commodities, the point of equilibrium might be displaced to a position such that the Australian goods would become cheaper on the international market. This conclusion does not depend upon the imaginary supposition of fixed costs of production.[1]

A similar criticism applies to Cairnes' solution of the following problem : " Suppose a fall of wages to take place in some leading branch of English manufacture—say Sheffield cutlery— . . . accompanied by a corresponding change over the whole field of English industry . . . what would be the effect of this on the external trade of England ? "

The answers given to the problem which is presented by " supposing the fall in wages not to extend beyond the group of trades in effective competition with the principal industries of Sheffield " (p. 397) seem rather loose from the mathematical point of view. Consider, for instance, the second of the cases distinguished on p. 397, " the demand of foreign countries for Sheffield wares " not increased in proportion to their increased cheapness. The answer that there is no answer—" what the exact character of this readjustment would be it is impossible *a priori* to say "—appears to be inaccurate. The case would seem to be that which is represented by our A B C D E f G H variety (2) and (4). Accordingly the exporting country will be damnified [2] by the alteration in the terms of trade.

---

[1] As apparently assumed by Mill above, p. 21.

[2] It is curious that in his Australian and Sheffield examples Cairnes seems to refer principally to that aspect of the problem which may present least practical interest, namely, what would be the effect of a lowered rate of wages upon the country in which they are lowered, abstracting from competition in foreign trade. However, his answer that there is no effect is to be understood as applying to the two more practical questions, (1) what would be the effect on a country dealing with the one in which the wages are lowered ; *e. g.* is America prejudiced by the prevalence of pauper labour in the countries with which she trades ? (2) what would be the effect of lowered wages in the country in which they are lowered with respect to foreign competition ; *e. g.* does, or might, England by lowering wages obtain an advantage over America in dealing with a third country ?

The only defence which can be made is that by a fall of wages Cairnes means only a diminution in the proportion of the national dividend accruing to the wage-earner; not, as it is natural in this connection to understand the term, the diminution in the absolute amount of commodities which the wage-earner obtains per piece.[1] But, as already argued with reference to Mill, this Ricardian definition, however applicable to the case of an isolated country where the labour-cost of money may be assumed to be constant, is less appropriate to a country affected by international trade, with respect to which the Ricardian proposition, " high wages do not make high prices " (invoked by Cairnes, p. 390), is deceptive. Cairnes' statement thus defined no doubt is true; but it is misleading in the absence of a more explicit enunciation of that definition.

It will be understood, of course, that this criticism of details does not touch Cairnes' main contention against popular fallacies on the subject of low wages. The extreme difficulty of our science is illustrated by the reflection that not only are first appearances and common sense—what Cairnes calls "the commercial view of the subject "—altogether wide of the mark, but even the corrections of the economist require themselves to be corrected. The writer of these criticisms does not flatter himself that they form any exception to this rule.

(4) *Professor Sidgwick.*—The new theory of international values which Professor Sidgwick has propounded in his *Principles of Political Economy*, Book II. chap. iii. appears to be tenable upon an assumption which, with respect to modern trade, is plausible, namely, that the difference in " the aggregate of utilities obtainable by similar sacrifices in different localities " (*ibid.* § 3, par. 1, 2nd ed.), is not much greater than might be accounted for by the cost of transport. If we assume that any greater difference in the level of advantage would be annihilated by a flow of population (*loc. cit.*), Professor Sidgwick rightly considers that " an essential part of the reason why a special theoretic treatment has to be applied to the products of international trade is that a double cost of carriage has here to be taken into account " (*ibid.* § 3, par. 2).

The problem which Professor Sidgwick solves might thus be reached, as I understand. First, abstract cost of transport, and let it " not " be " assumed that labour and capital do not move

[1] To interpret " wages " in this connection as *day-wages* is of course out of the question. This sense belongs to the " commercial view of the subject " dissipated by Cairnes.

freely between the trading countries." This is the case of ordinary domestic trade. Now introduce a barrier which it requires a certain cost of transport to surmount; Professor Sidgwick applies the general theory of international trade to determine how values would be affected in this particular case.

Putting this or some similar construction on Professor Sidgwick's theory, I accept the positive part of it as true, and perhaps pertinent to a great part of modern trade. But I am unable to accept the negative part of the doctrine, namely that Mill's theory is erroneous, " unless we further suppose that after the trade is established, there is no product *common* to the trading countries, a supposition manifestly extravagant " in the case considered (*ibid.* § 2, par. 2).

In directing hostile criticism against Professor Sidgwick I feel like a certain attacking party described by Thucydides who, though they had the Lacedæmonians at a disadvantage in the island of Sphacteria, yet were daunted and overawed by the prestige of their adversaries.[1] But, like the Athenians on that occasion, I have numbers on my side—not only Mill and all his followers with respect to the general issue, but also at the particular point on which Professor Sidgwick takes his stand, the case of a common commodity, the weighty support of Mangoldt.

Professor Sidgwick argues in the light of a well-chosen example that, if there is a common product, the theory breaks down.

" For [taking Mill's case of England exchanging cloth for the wine of Spain] let us suppose that there is at least one other commodity—say corn—which is produced both in England and in Spain. According to Mill's general theory of value, discussed in the preceding chapter, the relative values of cloth and corn in England must be determined by their comparative costs of production; and', again, the relative values of wine and corn in Spain must be determined in the same way. But if we suppose cost of carriage to be eliminated, there is no reason why the value either of wine or cloth should be altered by exportation; hence the values of both wine and cloth relatively to corn, and therefore relatively to each other, must be as much determined by cost of production as the values of home commodities are " (*Principles*, Book II. § 2, 2nd edition, p. 207).

It appears to me that an injudicious line of attack upon this theory has been adopted by those who dispute the

---

[1] " ἀνέβαινον τῇ γνώμῃ δεδουλωμένοι ὡς ἐπὶ Λακεδαιμονίους" (Thucydides, Book IV. ch. iii. 4).

possibility of there being a product common to both countries
—cost of transport having been abstracted—except upon the
supposition that the cost of producing the commodities varies
with the amount produced.   It is quite conceivable that, even on
the abstract hypothesis of constant costs of production and no
cost of transport, there should be a common product.   It is
quite legitimate to suppose with Mangoldt,[1] two countries, I. and
II., dealing in three commodities, A, B, C; whereof A is produced
only in country I., B is produced only in country II., while C is
produced in both countries—exported from II. and imported into
I.   One might even regard this phenomenon as normal, on the
plausible hypothesis that there are an indefinite number of
articles of trade, with every variety of cost of production.[2]
Professor Sidgwick, therefore, is quite justified in regarding the
absence of the phenomenon as " rarely likely to be realised in
fact." [3]   It is quite open to him to select this ground on which to
fight out the issue.

Joining issue with him on the proposition above quoted—
" the values of both wine and cloth relatively to corn, and therefore
relatively to each other, must be as much determined by cost of
production as the values of home commodities are " :—

I submit that the word " determine " might here be used in
one of two senses : either to mean that value varies proportionately to cost; or that value varies with, but not in proportion
to cost.[4]   For example, the first sense is to be understood when
Professor Sidgwick, referring on an earlier page of his book to
domestic trade, speaks of " the Ricardian theory of the determination of value by cost of production " ; [5] the second sense is
to be understood when it is maintained by the present writer the
rate of exchange in the international market is determinate.

The first sense, according to which the proposition under consideration contradicts the received theory of international value,[6]

---

[1] See the description of his views below, p. 52.
[2] Below, p. 53.   [3] *Loc. cit.* 1st edition.
[4] I have endeavoured to distinguish the two meanings in the article on Exchange Value in *Palgrave's Dictionary of Political Economy*.   The distinction is
quite clearly indicated by Mill (*Political Economy*, Book III. ch. xviii. § 9 and
§ 5).   [5] *Principles*, Book II. ch. ii. § 9.
[6] It may be observed that the supposed product common to both countries, far
from evidencing the truth of the proposition under consideration—as the turn of
Professor Sidgwick's sentence might suggest—is properly employed by Mangoldt
as the very type and measure of that difference in the productivity of the two
countries from which follows the truth of the received theory, the falsity of the
proposition in the first sense.   See the example cited below (p. 54), where the
(real) costs of producing C, the common product in the respective countries, are
in the ratio 3 : 4.

might have been expected here.   But it is expressly disowned by Professor Sidgwick when he says, " It does not, of course, follow that the wine and cloth will exchange for each other in proportion to their respective costs." [1]

In the second sense the proposition under consideration does not contradict the received theory.   For it is part of that theory that international values are affected by cost in some way, though not in the same simple way as domestic values.   For example, one of the propositions in the fifth section of Mill's classical chapter is that a change in the cost of production of a commodity will in a certain case be attended with a less than proportionate change in its international value.   The principal object of our investigation is to " determine " the changes in international value which are consequent upon changes in cost of production, including under cost taxation.   In the second sense then the proposition is true; but it does not convict Mill of error.   Yet this is the sense in which Professor Sidgwick seems to employ the proposition.   But I hesitate to attribute an *ignoratio elenchi* to the greatest living master of dialectics.

A more certainly valuable contribution to the subject is made in the chapter on Protection; to which our treatment of the subject is much indebted.[2]   In this chapter the distinction between the good of one country and of all (§ 1);   the proof that a country may by an import tax benefit itself in the way of revenue while it protects native industries (§ 2), and that a large section of a community may be injured by free trade (§ 3), appear especially masterly.

II. *Mathematical Theory.*

The mathematical version of the theory consists either of Geometry or Algebra.

Geometry is directly applicable only to the simplest possible cases.   If more than two commodities are considered, solid geometry must be called in.   The dimensions of space are not adequate to represent the case of more than three variables.

Geometry, therefore, might appear to have no application to reality, since countries importing or exporting only one article exist only in imagination.   But the geometrical representation of this imaginary case is useful as suggesting theorems which may be seen to admit of extension to more concrete cases.

The simplest geometrical representation of international trade

[1] Note to p. 207, second edition, and text of p. 218, first edition.
[2] Above, p. 18.   Below, p. 42.

appears to be a construction first used by Professor Marshall and explained by him in the mathematical appendix to his *Principles*.[1]

In Figure 1, the curve OE, which might be called England's Supply-and-Demand curve, signifies that for a certain quantity Ox of English produce, say " cloth," exported, the quantity Oy of German produce is demanded. The supply of linen and demand for cloth on the part of Germany are similarly expressed by the curve OG.

With respect to these curves it is not, I think, necessary to make the supposition which is usually made with respect to more

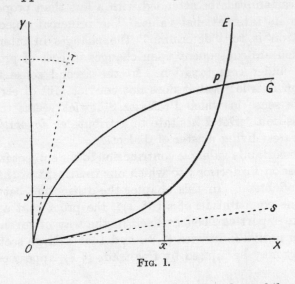

FIG. 1.

familiar demand or supply curves—namely, that while the rate of exchange represented by the curves is varied, the rate of exchange between one of the ordinates and all other articles—the price of all other articles, as it would usually be expressed—remains constant.[2] Rather a movement along a supply-and-demand curve of international trade should be considered as attended with rearrangements of internal trade; as the movement of the hand of a clock corresponds to considerable unseen movements of the machinery. Accordingly, the marginal utility of imports need not be supposed constant[3]; nor the marginal disutility, the cost of production, of exports.[4]

The theory of comparative costs is not very prominent from

---

[1] Note 12, second edition.

[2] *Cp.* Auspitz and Lieben, *Theorie der Preise*, pp. 4, 155, etc.; Cournot, *Principes*, ch. xi. Art. 74; Marshall, *Principles of Economics*, Book III. ch. iii. § 6.

[3] As by Messrs. Auspitz and Lieben when they take money of constant marginal utility as the import.   [4] As by J. S. Mill.

the mathematical point of view.[1] It may be represented geometrically as follows. Let the cost of production at first be supposed constant; then the terms on which England could have obtained linen in the absence of the trade may be represented by a straight line $O\,S$, if tan $S\,O\,X$ = ratio of the cost of production of a unit of linen to that of a unit of cloth. In order that England may obtain linen cheaper with than she could without the trade, the point of equilibrium must be *above* the line $O\,S$. It must be below the line $O\,T$, in order that Germany may be benefited. To generalise this theory there should be substituted for the straight line $O\,S$ (and *mutatis mutandis* for $O\,T$) a curve of constant advantage, or " indifference-curve " (not shown in the figure), representing states for which the advantage to England is no greater than if there had been no trade.[2] That the point of equilibrium falls between the respective indifference-curves is the geometrical version of Comparative Costs. The expression which occurs in some of the best writers, that international value " depends on " comparative cost, is seen from this point of view to be a very loose expression.[3]

In investigating the incidents attending differences in the conditions of supply and demand [4] it is important to distinguish the varieties of data. This purpose may be assisted by the following logical tree, or ramification; where the capital letter corresponds to a positive, the small Roman to a negative attribute.

A, International trade proper; a, quasi-international trade (in particular, distribution).

B, the case of two nations only; b, of several.

C, where we regard the interest of only one, our own, country; c, where we regard the interest of all parties concerned.

D, where we regard present advantage only; d, future also.

E, where we are concerned only with functions of the simple form proper to " short periods " [5] (such as the curves in Fig. 1), and accordingly the changes contemplated are in a sense small; [6] e, where more complicated functions and organic changes [7] are considered.

---

[1] *Cp.* Pareto, " Cambi Forestieri," *Giornale degli Economisti*, 1894, p. 154.

[2] See the present writer's *Mathematical Psychics*, pp. 21–29.

[3] No doubt, as Professor Bastable has pointed out, when there are numerous competing nations, the limits fixed by the principle of Comparative Cost are much narrowed; and accordingly it becomes less incorrect to regard the principle as sufficient to determine international value.

[4] As proposed *ante*, p. 6, par. 3.

[5] Marshall, *Principles of Economics*.

[6] Above, p. 7.

[7] Described below, p. 41.

F, where the change considered originates in a foreign country; f, in the home country.

G, an improvement or impediment other than a bounty or tax; g, a bounty or tax.

H, where the change originates on the side of supply : such as increased facility of producing or exporting native commodities; h, on the side of demand : such as an increased desire for, or facility in admitting foreign commodities.

By ringing the changes on these positive and negative attributes some hundreds of different cases can be distinguished; thus (1) A B C D E F G H, (2) A B C D E F G h, (3) A B C D E F g H, (4) A B C D E F g h; and so on up to 2^8.

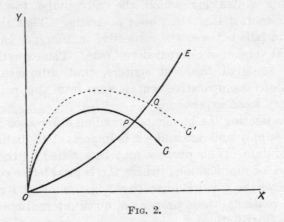

FIG. 2.

But of the compartments thus formed many would be empty, such as those which combine c, regard for the interest of all nations, with F or f, distinguishing natives and foreigners. It is proposed to consider only the more important cases—namely, those which have been summarily treated in the preceding article.

A B C D E F.[1]—This is the case of international trade proper, between two countries, regard being had to the interests of the home country only, and immediate or direct effects only being considered; and a certain simplicity in the law of demand and supply for both countries being assumed, a change is supposed to occur in the terms on which the foreigner is willing to trade.

The increase of the supply of foreign produce (in the sense that more of it is offered at each rate of exchange) is represented in Fig. 2 by the displacement of the foreign curve $O G$

[1] Above, p. 8.

to $O G'$. Whatever the direction [1] of the native or the foreign curve in the neighbourhood of their intersection, it will be found that in every case the new intersection has travelled along the native curve *away* from the origin. Whence the change is beneficial [2] to the native country. Conversely, a diminution in the offer of foreign goods is prejudicial to the home country; as may be seen by taking the dotted curve as the original one.

A B C D E f.—The case of f, a change originating in the home country, is not so simple. [3] The answer varies according as

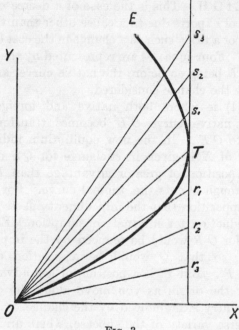

FIG. 3.

the letters, after f, are capital or lower case, designate positive or negative attributes. In each case much turns upon what Mill calls the extensibility of demand. [4] This property may be thus contemplated. Draw a line parallel to the axis Y touching the curve $O E$ in T (Fig. 3). Divide this line into a number of equal small parts: $T r_1$, $r_1 r_2$ below T, and $T s_1$, $s_1 s_2$ above T. Each interval corresponds to an increment in the value of X with respect to Y, that is the number of units of Y given in

---

[1] Consistent with the condition that the equilibrium should be stable.

[2] If this proposition is not self-evident, I may refer for a proof of it to my *Mathematical Psychics*, p. 115.

[3] Above, p. 12.   [4] Book III. ch. xviii. § 1.

exchange for a unit of X. Join r_1, r_2, etc., s_1, s_2, etc. to O; and from the points r_1, r_2, etc., s_1, s_2, etc., let fall perpendiculars—not shown in the figure—on the axis Y. Then it appears that below the point T a decrement in the value of X (relatively to Y) corresponds to a more than proportionate increase in the quantity of Y demanded; and conversely, above the point T. We may describe the curve above T as *inelastic*,[1] below elastic.[*] Each of the cases comprised under A B C D E f are divisible into four subcases, according as the native or foreign curve is elastic or inelastic.

A B C D E f G H.—This is the case of a decrease (or increase) in the supply of exports due to a cause other than the imposition (or remission) of a tax : such as a change in the cost of production, or transport.[2] Four subcases are represented by the four varieties of Fig. 4; $O E$ being as before the native curve, and $O E'$ what it becomes by the change considered.

Subcase (1) is where both native and foreign curves are elastic. The native curve $O E$ becomes transformed by the impediment to $O E'$. In the new equilibrium indicated by the point Q, $R Q$ of X is given in exchange for $Q S$ of Y. But Q cannot be a position of greater advantage than P', where the horizontal through Q cuts the original curve. For, on the most favourable supposition that the impediment affects only exportation, not production for internal consumption,[3] England's offer in exchange for $O R$ would be reduced by the impediment from $O S'$ to $O S$, so that Q would be a position of just equal advantage as P'. But P' is a position of less advantage than P (being nearer the origin as you move along the curve). Thus the native country is prejudiced by the change.

The converse variety of the subcase, where an improvement, not an impediment, has supervened, may be investigated by treating OE' as the original, OE as the displaced curve. Whence it appears that the native country is advantaged by the change.

In subcase (2), where the native curve is elastic, the foreign inelastic, by a parity of reasoning the natives may be benefited by an impediment, and prejudiced by an improvement.[4]

In subcase (3), where the native curve is inelastic, the foreign elastic, the natives are prejudiced by an impediment and benefited by an improvement, as in subcase (1).

[1] *Cp.* Marshall, *Principles of Economics*, Book III. ch. iv.
[*] Compare below, p. 353.
[2] Above, p. 32.
[3] For instance, a transit duty imposed by a third country.
[4] Above, p. 10.

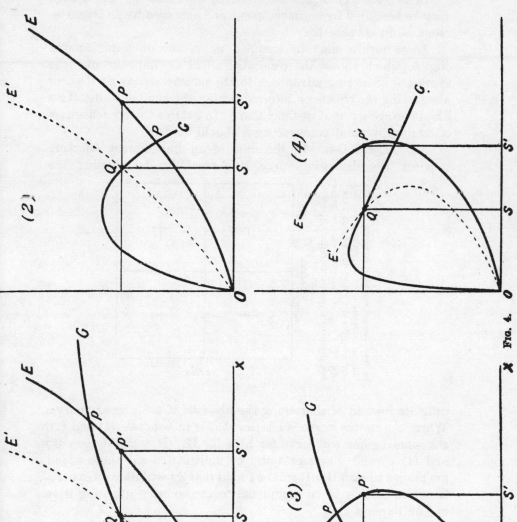

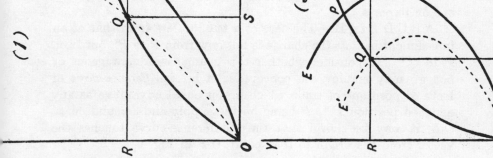

Fig. 4.

In subcase (4), where both curves are inelastic, the natives may be benefited by an impediment and damaged by an improvement, as in subcase (2).

These results may be summed up in the diagram forming Fig. 5, which shows the consequences of an impediment; the symbol + denoting advantage to the natives *ceteris paribus*, or abstracting the effects on internal trade; the symbol — denoting disadvantage without qualification. To exhibit the consequences of an improvement converse signs should be used.

A B C D E F G h.—In the case of an impediment affecting imports, the displaced curve is formed by lengthening the

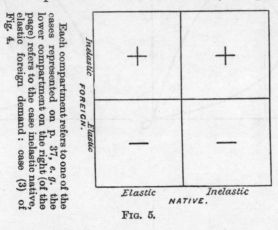

Each compartment refers to one of the cases represented on p. 37, *e. g.* the lower compartment on the right (of the page) refers to the case inelastic native, elastic foreign demand: case (3) of Fig. 4.

FIG. 5.

ordinate instead of shortening the abscissa of the primary curve. Where the native curve is elastic, that is in subcases (1) and (2), the same figures will serve for h as for H. But in subcases (3) and (4) special diagrams must be substituted for those which are proper to case H. It will be found that a restriction on exports is not so certain to be prejudicial to the country imposing it as one on imports.

A B C D E f g H.—The case of a tax [1] differs from that of an impediment in that the change is not now from P to P', but from P to Q.* To consider whether this change is advantageous or not we may employ the conception of an *indifference-curve* or locus of positions of trade which are of equal advantage as any assigned position P.[2] P being on the supply-and-demand curve $O E$, it may be shown that the indifference-curve touches the vector from the origin to that point, $O P$ in Fig. 6.

---

[1] Above, p. 8, first par.

* This statement is true only of certain taxes in kind; as admitted in later writings (ECONOMIC JOURNAL, 1897; S, pp. 71, 72).

[2] *Mathematical Psychics*, p. 21.

Let the native indifference-curve through P cut the foreign demand-curve OG in M. Then, if Q, the new position of equilibrium, on the curve OG (see Fig. 6), is above M, *inside* the indifference-curve, as in Fig. 6, the natives are benefited; if Q is below M the natives are prejudiced. In the subcase illustrated by Fig. 6, viz. subcase (1), it is in general uncertain whether Q is above or below M. The consequence represented by the sign — in the case of an impediment (Fig. 5) becomes now $\pm$.*

The want of symmetry between the effects of restrictions (and of certain unusual taxes in kind) on exports and imports is perhaps the conclusion which can be most peculiarly and exclusively attributed to the mathematical method.

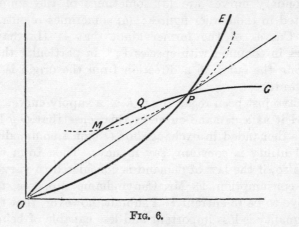

FIG. 6.

A B C e.—So far we have supposed the curves OE and OG to be of the simple form shown in Fig. 1. In considering complicated re-entrant forms like that in Fig. 7, it will be convenient to begin by restoring the usual supposition that the marginal utility of one of the commodities is constant. Thus let us for a moment regard OE as a supply-curve indicating that a certain quantity of cloth OX is supplied in exchange for a certain quantity of a commodity whose marginal utility may be regarded as constant, say money.[1] Then two kinds of supply-curve may be distinguished : (I) representing the amount of cloth which would be offered at each price, no account being taken of the change in the offer due to the alteration in the scale of production for different values of the *primary* supply-curve, as we may call it.

* There are omitted in this context some paragraphs and diagrams which purported in the original to refer to import taxes in general, but are now admitted to be true only of some import taxes *in kind*.

[1] As in Messrs. Auspitz and Lieben's constructions.

It seems to be much the same as Professor Marshall's short period supply-curve. (II) Next let us take account of the change in the offer due to alteration in the scale of production; and so form a series of primaries corresponding to each value of X: Mr. Cunynghame's " successive cost-curves." [1] If now at each point on the abscissa an ordinate is erected, the *locus* of intersection with the corresponding " successive cost "-curve forms a *secondary* supply-curve : Mr. Cunynghame's supply-curve; and, as I understand, Professor Marshall's " long-period " supply-curve.

It is a nice question whether a primary cost-curve can be regarded as re-entrant in the manner represented in Fig. 9. [2] Perhaps we may with sufficient generality consider that it cannot. The secondary curves are (*a*) sometimes of the simpler form represented in the earlier figures; (*b*) sometimes re-entrant as in Fig. 9. Curves of the former kind, that is IIa, have many properties in common with species I; [3] in particular that movement along the curve in a direction from the origin is attended with advantage.

We have just been regarding $O E$ as a supply-curve. Now let us regard it as a demand-curve in this sense that $O y$ linen (see Fig. 1) is demanded in exchange for $O x$ of a commodity whose marginal utility is constant, say money. Then from this point of view also, if the law of demand is considered to vary with the scale of consumption, as Mr. Cunynghame supposes, the curve may prove to be re-entrant. [4] I submit, however, that this cause of abnormality is less important and less capable of being formulated than the influence of the scale of production on cost.

Not that from either point of view an exact determination

[1] ECONOMIC JOURNAL, Vol. II.

[2] As argued by the present writer elsewhere (Address to Section F of the British Association Report, 1889, Note J). Though at a given rate there may be several *maxima* of advantage, there can be only one position of *greatest possible* advantage. Since, then, the motive of the economic man is greatest possible, rather than merely maximum advantage, it should seem that the ordinate of the supply-curve corresponding to each value of tan $P O X$ must be unique; discontinuous for the individual who must be conceived as jumping from one branch to another when a certain value of tan $P O X$ is reached, but continuous for the community since the point of transition will be different for different individuals. On the other hand, there may exist friction obstructing the movement from a small to a large scale of production; and so two branches of the curve exist simultaneously. In this case, as pointed out by the present writer (*Mathematical Psychics*, Appendix 7), the tract between T and T'—points where tangents drawn from the origin touch the curve—is not a genuine demand-and-supply curve, being a locus of *minimum* advantage.

[3] Marshall, *Principles of Economics*, note to p. 484, 2nd edition.

[4] Ascending in Mr. Cunynghame's construction. See ECONOMIC JOURNAL, Vol. II.

of the curve is to be expected; we must be content with general descriptions: such as elastic and inelastic, re-entrant or not. Still less definiteness is attainable when, combining the two views which have just been distinguished, we restore our original view of the demand-and-supply curve $O\,E$: as representing the interchange of two articles of variable marginal utility.

The consequences of the property of re-entrance may be considered under the head (d), which indeed is with difficulty separated from (e); since, in fact, organic changes only occur in long periods.

A B C d.—Many of the propositions, stated under preceding heads, no longer hold when we consider organic changes extending over long periods. Thus it ceases to be universally true that an increase in the supply of foreign commodities is

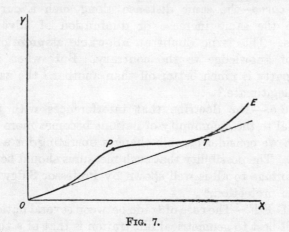

FIG. 7.

beneficial to the native country.[1] For the curve $O\,G$, which had originally, say, cut the curve $O\,E$ a little to the left of P, and not afterwards, being shifted upwards as a whole might strike the native curve in the neighbourhood of T (Fig. 7), corresponding to a lower value of the native produce with respect to the foreign,[2] and a lower value of the native goods may be attended with detriment to the native country.

[1] Above, pp. 8, 34.

[2] The proposition set forth in the books (*e.g.* Mill, *Political Economy*, Book III. ch. xviii.) that the setting up of trade is advantageous to both countries assumes that the curves [or the analogous algebraic functions in the general case] with which we have to deal are of the form I or II (*a*). In that case the position of stable equilibrium may be regarded as a point of maximum of advantage in excess of the *adjacent* minimum formed by the position of null trade, viz. the origin. But, if curves of the form II (*b*) prevail, then a position of stable equilibrium, though a maximum, may be attended with less advantage than the position of null trade.

Again a bounty ceases to be universally disadvantageous. For, in the manner shown by Professor Marshall with respect to a different construction, a bounty may shift the point of equilibrium to a position more advantageous to the community.

A B c D E.—When we consider the interest of both parties, not of one only, the chance of benefit resulting from interferences with trade is diminished. The presumption that any such interference impairs the total utility is well illustrated by Messrs. Auspitz and Lieben, on the tacit assumption that what may be called the hedonic worth of money is the same in both countries. The generalised form of that assumption—appropriate to our system of co-ordinates, which does not represent money—is that if for each party a curve be drawn cutting at right angles the system of indifference-curves—called by the present writer a *preference-curve*—the same distance along such a curve corresponds to the same increase or diminution of advantage on both sides. This is no doubt an allowable assumption, in the absence of knowledge to the contrary. But, when we know that one party is much better off than another,[1] the assumption may be illegitimate.[2]

A B c d e.—The doctrine that interferences with trade are detrimental to the community of nations becomes more questionable when we consider organic changes operating for a considerable time. The possibility that such measures should be attended with advantage to all is well shown by Professor Sidgwick in his chapter on protection.[3]

A b C D E F.—The case of trade between several nations which lends itself best to geometrical illustration is that of a third party competing with the home country, as we may call that one whose advantage is exclusively regarded, for trade with foreigners.

In Fig. 8 let $O G$ be the foreign curve, $O e$ the native, $O \epsilon$ the competing, and $O E$ compounded of the last two, in such wise that if a vector $(O P)$ corresponding to any assigned rate of exchange is drawn through the origin the length $O P$ intercepted by the compound supply-curve $= O \pi + O p$ the corresponding length for the component curves. The detriment inflicted on

---

[1] This is most likely to occur, I think, in the quasi-international trade between the parties to Distribution.

[2] This, if not already evident, may be contemplated by regarding the contract-curve as the locus of points (*Mathematical Psychics*, p. 21 *et seq.*) at which the preference-curves of the two parties coincide with opposite directions. According to the assumption in question, it would be indifferent, from the point of view of the general good, whether all the advantage of trade accrued to one party, or both had a share.

[3] Above, pp. 18, 31.

the home country by the competition may be described as the change in a backward direction along the curve $O\,e$ from the intersection of $O\,e$ with $O\,G$ to p, where the line $O\,P$ cuts $O\,e$.

It is to be observed that competition does not necessarily deprive a country of the advantage which it may derive by a restriction of exports or imports. For suppose that in the absence of competition the conditions were such that the home country could benefit itself by a restriction of exports or imports; then after the rise of competition it may still be possible for the home country to benefit in the way that has been described.[1]

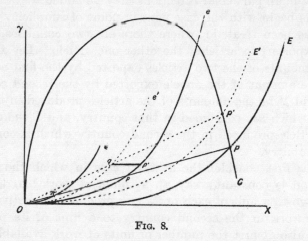

FIG. 8.

The restriction will transform $O\,e$ to $O\,e'$, $O\,E$ to $O\,E'$, P to P', p to q, which is apt to be a position of equal advantage as p', and therefore of greater advantage than p. It may be observed that this species of benefit to the home country may be made possible by competition, not having been so before, if $O\,G$ is inelastic at its intersection with $O\,E$, but not at its intersection with $o\,e$.

a.—The incidents of quasi-international trade—*e. g.* between the parties to Distribution—do not lend themselves to geometry so well as to algebra, on which we now enter.

In entering upon the more complicated part of the subject, it is well to recall Professor Marshall's warning words : " When a great many symbols have to be used, they become very laborious to anyone but the writer himself," and " it seems doubtful whether anyone spends his time well in reading lengthy translations of economic doctrines into mathematics, that have not been

[1] Above, p. 36.

made by himself." [1] It is easier to strike out a new path for oneself than to plant one's steps in the footprints of another.

It is almost sufficient to indicate the general scope of the inquiry—namely, to determine that state of trade for which the sum of the utilities of all parties concerned regarded as functions of the amounts of commodity consumed, less the sum of the disutilities regarded as functions of the amount produced, is a maximum; subject to the conditions that what is bought is sold, what is consumed is produced, the " law of indifference," the existence of non-competing groups, and so forth.[2]

A few more particular directions may be added.

Let us begin with the case next in point of simplicity to that which has been treated : where there are two countries, one of which exports two articles, the other one article. Let x and y be the amounts of the two articles exported by the first country, and z the amount of the article exported by the second country. Let X and Y be the amounts of the articles produced in the first country which are consumed in that country, and Z the amount of the article produced in the second country which is consumed in that country.

Let us first consider the abstract case in which the cost of production is constant; say a_1, a_2 units of work [3] in the first country go to a unit of each of its two products respectively; b_1 units of work in the second country to a unit of its product. Suppose also at first the number of units of work available to be a fixed quantity, say A and B, in the two countries respectively. Then we have

$$(1) \quad \begin{cases} a_1(x + X) + a_2 (y + Y) = A \\ b_1(z + Z) = B. \end{cases}$$

The advantage of the first country which is to be maximised, subject to the first of the above-written conditions, and the corresponding advantage of the second country, may be written—

$$(2) \quad \begin{cases} \Phi (X, Y, z) \\ \Psi (x, y, Z). \end{cases}$$

The position of equilibrium is determined by the values of the variables which make each of the above-written expressions a

---

[1] Preface to *Principles*, 1st edition.

[2] *Cp.* Marshall, *Principles*, 2nd edition, note xii.; and the formulæ given by the present writer in the notes to the Address to Section F of the British Association (1889).

[3] More exactly " effort and sacrifice "; involving at least two dimensions of disutility, labour and waiting.

maximum; subject to the conditions stated by equations (1), and to the further condition—

$$(3)\quad a_1x + a_2y = vb_1z;$$

where v is the rate of exchange between the product of work in the two countries, the number of units of work in the first country, of which the product is equivalent to the product of a unit of work in the second country.*

That Φ and Ψ should each be a maximum, subject to equation (1), may be expressed by proposing each of the following expressions to be maximised—

$$(4)\quad \begin{cases} \Phi\ (X,\ Y,\ z) - \lambda\ [a_1(x + X) \times a_2(y + Y) - A]; \\ \Psi\ (x,\ y,\ Z) - \mu\ [b_1(z + Z) - B]; \end{cases}$$

where λ and μ are indeterminate factors.

The expressions (4) become by equation (3)—

$$(5)\quad \begin{cases} \Phi\ (X_1\ Y_1\ z) - \lambda\ [a_1\ X + a_2Y + vb_1\ z - A]; \\ \Psi\ (x,\ y,\ Z) - \mu\ \left[\dfrac{1}{v}\ (a,\ x + a_2y) + b_1\ Z - B\right]. \end{cases}$$

Differentiating the first of these expressions with respect to X, Y, z respectively, and the second of the expressions with respect to x, y, Z respectively, we have six equations, which with the pair of equations (1) and the equation (3) make nine equations, to determine the nine unknown quantities, x, y, z, X, Y, Z, λ, μ, v.

Eliminating the last six of these variables, we obtained three equations of the form—

$$(6)\quad \begin{cases} \Phi_1\ (x,\ y,\ z) = 0 \\ \Psi_1\ (x,\ y,\ z) = 0 \\ \Psi_2\ (x,\ y,\ z) = 0; \end{cases}$$

which are the analogues of the demand (and supply) curves proper to the case of two commodities; e. g., Φ_1, giving the amount of imports demanded by the first country in exchange for assigned amounts of export, y and z. Ψ_1 and Ψ_2 simultaneously equated to zero determine the amounts of export x and y corresponding to any assigned amount of imports, z. The position of equilibrium may be regarded as the intersection of the three surfaces designated by equation (6).

Conclusions analogous to those which have been obtained for the case of two commodities are easily discerned to be obtainable in the case of three or more variables. Thus, if the second country has an urgent demand for one of the

* Cp. below, p. 53.

commodities, say x, of the first country, it is possible that an export tax on x may be beneficial to the first country; while an export tax on y might not have that effect.[1]

I do not know that any fresh conclusions are presented by the case of many variables. Accordingly it may be left to the reader to elaborate that case.[2] It will be sufficient here to indicate how some of the concrete circumstances which have been abstracted may be restored.

First, the cost of production may be treated as varying with the amount produced by regarding a x (a_2 x, etc.) not as the product of x by a constant, but as a definite function of x.

Again, the amount of work available may be treated as variable, by regarding A (B, etc.) not as a constant, but as a function of disutility, which disutility is to be subtracted from Φ (Ψ, etc.) in order to obtain the expression which is to be maximised.[3]

The cost of transport may be introduced by regarding the littoral of one country as the scene of the market, and treating the cost of importing foreign articles thereto as part of the cost of production.[4]

It is unnecessary to show how the number of commodities and number of countries may be further multiplied. What Mill says of the theory of value in general is particularly applicable to the mathematical version of it: " The further adaptation of the theory . . . may be left with great advantage to the intelligent reader."

It remains only to acknowledge my obligation to Professor Marshall's unpublished chapters on foreign trade. These are the chapters alluded to in the Preface to the *Principles of Economics*

---

[1] *Cp.* above, p. 36.

[2] A statement of the general case is given by Professor Pareto in his able article on " Teoria Matematica dei Cambi Forestieri " in the *Giornale degli Economisti*, 1894, Art. 9 *et seq.*

It may be observed that the formulæ given by Professor Pareto (in the earlier part of his article), after Professor Walras, as proper to the case of industrial competition (domestic trade), are also applicable to that case of trade between " nations (or " non-competing groups ") in which each commodity is produced by only one nation. The formulæ do not express the essential attribute of domestic trade, viz. the tendency to equality in the net advantages of different occupations. Such net advantages, being of the nature of total utility, could not be expressed by formulæ involving only final utility. This is the gist of my criticism of Professor Walras, to which Professor Pareto replies in the article referred to (*loc. cit.* p. 144).

[3] *Cp.* Marshall, *Principles*, Appendix, note xii., 2nd edition.

[4] *Cp.* Pareto, " Cambi Forestieri," *Giornale degli Economisti*, p. 153.

as having been printed for private circulation and sent to many economists. Part of their substance is contained in the first volume of the *Principles ;* part may be looked for in the second volume.* What is written on the subject after a perusal of the privately circulated chapters, and pending the publication of the second volume, can make no claim to originality or permanence—like the light of the planet which precedes the rising of the sun, borrowed from and destined to be effaced by the prime orb.

It remains to test the mathematical theories which have been expressed by critical reference to leading writers on the subject.

(1) *Cournot.* The lesson of caution in dealing with a subject and method so difficult is taught by no example more impressively than by that of Cournot. This superior intelligence, equipped with the most scientific apparatus, seems not only to have slipped at several steps, but even to have taken a wholly wrong direction. He has not only committed errors in formal reasoning, but also has missed general conceptions appropriate to the subject.

Of several paradoxes which occur in that part of the *Principes Mathématiques* which more immediately relates to International Trade,[1] perhaps the first is among the few that are not open to suspicion. This is the proposition that, when a communication is opened between two markets, previously separated by a barrier, the total quantity produced of any commodity which now begins to be exported from one market and imported to the other will not necessarily be increased. For if a flow sets in from market A to market B, the production of the commodity in A must be increased, and its price in that market heightened—the law of decreasing returns prevailing; while in B the price will be lowered, and the quantity produced in that country will be diminished. The increase of the production in A may not compensate the decrease in B; when the demand in A is very inelastic, and the rise in the cost of production with the amount produced very steep, while the contrary properties are true of B (Art. 68).

A similar proposition is true of the total value of the product (Art. 69).

The conditions under which these propositions are true are

* The substance of these papers is now given in Dr. Marshall's *Money, Credit and Commerce* (1923).

[1] *Recherches sur les Principes Mathématiques de la théorie des richesses* (1838), chs. x., xi., xii.

well expressed by Cournot's symbols, in which $\Omega_a(p) =$ the amount offered by the producers in A at the price p, and $F_a(p)$ means the amount demanded by the consumers in A; with similar interpretations of $\Omega_b(p)$, $F_b(p)$. Thus, before the communication,

$$\Omega_a(p_a) = F_a(p_a);$$

p_a being the price of the article in the market A; and, after the communication, if the commodity is exported from A to B, ϵ being the expense of transportation per unit of commodity, and the price in A being changed from p_a to $p_a + \delta$, we have

$$\Omega_a(p_a + \delta) + \Omega_b(p_a + \delta + \epsilon)$$
$$= F_a(p_a + \delta) + F_b(p_a + \delta + \epsilon)$$

(Arts. 67 and 68).[1]

We have now to inquire whether the quantity denoted by either member of this equation is greater than the corresponding quantity before the communication was opened, whether the following inequality holds:

$$F_a(p_a + \delta) + F_b(p_a + \delta + \epsilon)$$
$$> F_a(p_a) + F_b(p_b).$$

Cournot answers this question in the negative by showing that the inequality does not hold in a particular case: namely, when the original prices, p_a p_b, differ from each other, and also from the new price in A, by only a small quantity, in which case also the cost of transport, ϵ, must be small, since otherwise exportation from A to B would not take place on the removal of the barrier. This reasoning, or that which is based on another particular assumption, viz. δ and $p_b - (p_a + \epsilon)$ small (Art. 68, last par.), is quite correct. But the assumption that ϵ should be small leads to an erroneous conclusion in a subsequent problem: to determine the effect of a tax on exports or imports (Art. 70).

If p is the price of the article in the exporting country before the imposition of the tax, u and $p + \delta$ the price after the tax, we have, before the tax, $\Omega_a(p) + \Omega_b(p + \epsilon) = F_a(p) + F_b(p + \epsilon)$.[2]

---

[1] For $p_a + \delta$ being the price of the commodity in A, and accordingly the (net) price which the producers in A obtain (not only for that portion of the product which they sell in A, but also) for that portion of their product which they sell in B at a price heightened by the cost of transport ϵ, the quantity offered by the producers resident in A at the (net) price $p_a + \delta$, together with the quantity offered by the residents in B at the price $p_a + \delta + \epsilon$, is equal to the quantity demanded by the residents in A at the price $p_a + \delta$, together with the quantity demanded by the residents in B at the price $p_a + \delta + \epsilon$.

[2] Compare the last note.

And after the tax u per unit of commodity has been imposed, we have

$$\Omega\ (p + \delta) + \Omega_b(p + \delta + \epsilon + u)$$
$$= F_a(p + \delta) + F_b(p + \delta + \epsilon + u).$$

Cournot now proceeds to draw conclusions from the last equation by expanding and neglecting the powers, not only of δ and u, but also ϵ, above the first power. I submit that Cournot's procedure is inelegant and leads him to an erroneous conclusion. The simpler procedure is first to treat δ and u only as small, δ being the dependent, u the independent variable. Thus,

$$\delta(\Omega'_a(p) + \Omega'_b(p + \epsilon) - F'_a(p) - F'_b(p + \epsilon))$$
$$- - u(\Omega'_b(p \mid \epsilon) \quad F'_b(p + \epsilon)).$$

If now ϵ be small, we may expand both sides of this equation in powers of ϵ, and neglect terms involving powers of ϵ above the first, or rather neglect ϵ altogether. Whether ϵ be small or not, it follows—the law of diminishing returns, as well as that of diminishing utility, prevailing—that δ is negative, and less than u ; or that the price falls in the exporting country and rises in the importing one, contrary to the statement of Cournot (§ 21, par. 1).

I am confirmed in this view by Mr. A. Berry and Mr. C. P. Sanger, who have independently made a similar correction. Mr. Berry writes to me of the corrected reasoning : " This may be confirmed by the fact *a priori* evident that the disturbance of price, δ, must vanish when the tax itself, u, vanishes. This is the case in our equation, not in Cournot's."

It is certainly curious to find a wrong belief as to a matter of fact in business resulting from a slip in mathematical analysis !

Mr. Berry has pointed out to me another slip in Art. 90, pp. 183, 184. There a certain advantage which the author ascribes to domestic as compared with foreign trade does not follow from his own premises.

To this I have to add that those premises are very doubtful. I allude to the theory of " real " as distinguished from " nominal " revenue. To collate here all the passages in all Cournot's versions which bear on this distinction would occupy too much space. It must suffice to submit as the result of such an examination very carefully performed the opinion that, while Cournot's " nominal revenue " is much the same as what would now be called the money measure of national wealth, his " real revenue " signifies, if indeed it is significant, such a measure as that which Mr. Giffen, Mr. Bourne, and others have employed in determining the growth of the quantity of a nation's " capital," or foreign trade. Such a measure is obtained by multiplying the quantities of each commodity at the two compared epochs by its price at one of them, the same price being combined with the two quantities, the one at the initial and the one at the final epoch. Consistently with this view Cournot says that if the price of a commodity rises from p_0 to p_1, corresponding to a diminution of the quantity from D_0 to D_1, whereas the variation of the nominal revenue is $D_0p_0 - D_1p_1$, the loss in real revenue is $(D_0 - D_1)p_0$.

I do not indeed pretend to follow the double route by which Cournot, winding his way through additions and substractions of producers' " and consumers' " gain and loss,[1] reaches this conclusion (*Principes Mathématiques*, ch. xi., and corresponding passages in the *Principes* of 1863 and the *Revue Sommaire*). Nor can I explain why, upon the interpretation of real revenue here suggested, the loss due to a rise of price should be formulated as $(D_0 - D_1)$, multiplied by p_0 rather than p_1; except so far as in the method in question there must be always something arbitrary in the selection of the price to be operated with.

However the conception of " real revenue " may be interpreted, it does not seem appropriate to the problems in hand. According to Cournot the real revenue of a country is diminished by the admission of an additional import through the removal of a restriction on trade. The capital objection to this conclusion is that no account is taken of that sort of advantage coming from cheapness which we should now describe as *Consumer's Rent*. Cournot explicitly makes abstraction of this advantage. He says of it :—

Dans l'évaluation de l'accroissement réel du revenu social, causé par la baisse de prix, on ne tient pas compte de l'avantage qui consiste, pour les nouveaux consommateurs de la denrée, à faire un emploi plus à leur goût d'une portion de leurs revenus ;

---

[1] Professor Seligman seems to follow Cournot without hesitation. He puts the following case (*Shifting and Incidence of Taxation*, p. 153) : " Suppose that the price of the commodity was originally $10, at which price 10,000 pieces were sold. Now a tax of $2 is imposed, all of which is shifted to the consumer. At the new price, however, only 8,000 pieces will be sold." Manipulating the producers' and consumers' loss in Cournot's fashion, Professor Seligman reaches the conclusion that " the diminution in the real revenue = $20,000."

As it seems to me, the essential fact is that there has been a diminution of the national wealth to the extent of 2,000 pieces of the taxed commodity. It is arbitrary whether we multiply this 2,000 by 10, the old price, or 12, the new price, with a view of ascertaining (after the manner of Mr. Giffen) the variation in the total quantity of national wealth, provided that, in dealing with other items of national wealth at the two periods, we employ the corresponding prices— either the old prices or the new. Perhaps the best price to operate with would be a mean of the old and new price, in the case before us $11.

parce que cet avantage n'est pas numériquement appréciable."
(Art 81.)

Of the corresponding loss he says :—

" Il s'agit ici d'un de ces rapports d'ordre, et non pas de
grandeur, que les nombres peuvent bien indiquer, mais non pas
mesurer . . . nos considérations ne portent que sur les choses
mesurables. (Art. 77.)

" Ce dommage n'est pas mesurable et n'affecte pas directe-
ment la richesse nationale, dans l'acception commerciale et
mathématique de ce mot." (Art. 88.)

Real revenue being thus defined, the proposition that it is
diminished by the liberation of trade may be true, but is not
important; as Bertrand urges in an interesting criticism on
mathematical economists.[1]

Another objection to Cournot's proposition raised by Prof.
Bastable is that it uses money as a measure; whereas the value
of money is altered by an alteration in the terms of international
trade. It is tenable, however, that Cournot means to restrict
his theory to small disturbances of trade, the effect of which on
the level of money may be neglected. As far as this objection
goes, his reasoning may be as valid as Professor Marshall's application of Consumer's Rent,[2] or Messrs. Auspitz and Lieben's
reasoning as to the effects of a tax or bounty.[3]

Another objection to Cournot's reasoning is that he does not
take account of the productive factors which, being displaced by
the importation of a commodity which had been produced at home,
are turned to the production of some other commodity. Cournot
himself has stated this objection, and endeavoured to meet it
(Arts. 93 and 86); but I do not feel certain that on this point he
gets the better of Hagen, to whom we now proceed.

(2) *Hagen*.[4]—The mathematical method is not wielded by
Hagen more powerfully in defence of Free Trade than by Cournot
against it. Hagen constructs an " exportation-formula " to
represent the gain (or loss) resulting to the national income
from a new export (p. 11). This gain consists of three parts :
(1) the addition to profits consequent upon the additional production of the exported article; (2) the loss of profits consequent

---

[1] *Journal des Savants*, 1883.

[2] *See* ECONOMIC JOURNAL, Vol. IV., p. 156. Cp. *Giornale degli Economisti*,
September 1894, " Sulla Consumers' Rent."

[3] *Cp.* below, p. 58.

[4] *Die Nothwendigkeit der Handelsfreiheit für das Nationaleinkommen Mathe-
matisch nachgewiesen*, Von Karl Heinrich Hagen, Königsberg, 1844. See article
on Hagen in *Palgrave's Dictionary*.

upon the transference of productive factors from other industries to the production of the exported article; (3) the loss to consumers consequent upon the rise of price. This formula appears open to three serious objections : (*a*) It is assumed that profits in different industries at the same time are a fixed proportion of the expenses of production. This Ricardian assumption may perhaps pass. But not so (*b*) the ultra-Ricardian neglect of all interests but those of the capitalist; no account being taken, as I understand, of the effect of the supposed change upon wages and rent. Lastly (*c*), the effect on the consumers' interest is not rightly formulated. The price being raised from P to $P + p_1$, and the amount consumed being diminished from D to D—d, Hagen puts for the loss of the consumers p (D—d). If he had put $\frac{1}{2} p \times d$, this would have been an intelligible measure of the loss of consumers' rent; being, in fact, the expression which Dupuit—with as much accuracy perhaps as the subject admits of—has put for what is now called consumers' rent.[1]

From this formula Hagen concludes that export trade may or may not be disadvantageous (p. 14). By parity of reasoning he finds that importation must always be advantageous (p. 16). A small bounty may be attended with a slight gain. It may be questioned whether, in view of the unsoundness of the premises, any value attaches to these deductions.

In conclusion, Hagen joins issue with Cournot on two points corresponding to the second and third term of Hagen's exportation-formula (above). On the question whether the productive factors which are displaced by exportation or importation should be taken into account, Hagen seems to have the better of Cournot.[2] In the matter of consumers' rent it is not easy to say which is most in the wrong, Cournot who ignores, or Hagen who falsifies the theory. Indeed, a similar difficulty affects the comparison between the two authors' whole treatment of International Trade.

(3) *Mangoldt*.[3]—This author leads up to the subject of International Trade by some sections on Exchange (§§ 62—74, 1st edition), in which he represents Demand and Supply by curves very similar to those which are now in vogue. In virtue of these constructions Mangoldt, writing without reference to his predecessors, Cournot, Dupuit, and Gossen, may claim to be one

---

[1] See article on Dupuit in *Palgrave's Dictionary*.

[2] Cournot has replied in his *Principes* of 1863, Art. 185. Hagen speaks of reviewing Cournot's work as a whole. Does such a review exist ?

[3] *Grundriss der Volkswirthschaftslehre*, 1st edition, 1863. 2nd edition (posthumous, edited by F. Kleinwächter), 1871.

of the independent discoverers of the mathematical theory of Demand and Supply.

In his Appendix (*Anmerkung*) *On the Equation of International Trade* Mangoldt begins by following Mill's arrangement,[1] dividing the subject according as the demand for a commodity is, or is not, inversely proportional to its price. Under the first head Mangoldt considers first the case of two variables, and deduces conclusions substantially identical with those of Mill, in usefully varied language. Mangoldt then goes on to the case of three or more variables. He discerns the general proposition that—cost of production being supposed constant irrespective of quantity, and abstraction being made of cost of transport—if trade is opened between two countries, the commodities previously produced in both countries will now fall into two groups, each produced altogether in one country; the rate of exchange between the members of each group *inter se* corresponding to the cost of production of each commodity (in the country in which it continues to be produced), and the relation between the two groups being determined by the rate of exchange between the produce of a unit of productive force in one country and that of a similarly defined unit in the other country. This simple truth Mangoldt complicates by positing a commodity as it were intermediate between the two groups, which may serve as a measure whereby to ascertain from which of the countries any particular commodity will be exported.

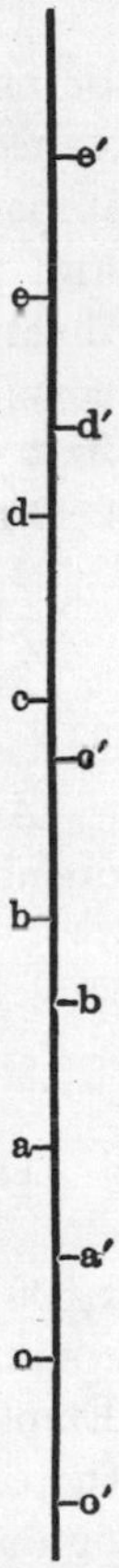

The following construction of our own seems to give the substance of Mangoldt's expositions; it being understood that the substance, as the metaphysicians say, is not a copy of its manifestations. Let us figure the relation between the costs of production of the set of commodities in Country No. I. by a series of points a, b, c, etc., on a right line, any one of which a is obtained by measuring from a fixed origin o, a distance equal to the logarithm of the number of units of productive force which go to the production of a unit of that commodity in Country No. I. Let the natural values of the commodities in Country No. II. be similarly designated by the points a', b', c', etc., measured from o'; o' being taken so that o o' is the logarithm of the number of units of productive force in Country No. II. of which

FIG. 9.

[1] *Political Economy*, Book III. ch. xviii.

the produce is equivalent in the international market to the produce of a unit of productive force in Country No. I. (log. v, or log. $\frac{i}{v}$ in our notation [1]). It appears at once from the figure that, when trade has been established, it is cheaper for Country No. I. to import a′, b′, and c′ than to produce them; and to produce d and e than to export them.

The measure or standard which Mangoldt desiderates would be afforded by the commodity, if the distance between c and c′ vanished. That commodity would be on the line between imports and exports; and it would in general be partly produced and partly imported by one and the same country. Mangoldt illustrates this conception by the following example. Let the costs of production of the three commodities A, B, C, be in the first country 2, 3, 4 respectively, and in the second country 4, 2, 3 respectively, as shown in the annexed scheme.

	A	B	C
I.	2	3	4
II.	4	2	3

And let the amounts demanded by each country before the opening of the trade be as follows:

	A	B	C
I.	1,000	800	600
II.	500	750	600

Then by hypothesis (according to the definition of the first class of cases [2]) Country No. I. lays out a constant cost of $1,000 \times 2 - 2,000$ units of her productive force—in procuring commodity A for her own consumption, 800 on B; and so on. Employing this datum, by a tentative process, Mangoldt reaches the conclusion that A will be produced in No. I. only, B will be produced in No. II. only, C will be produced both in No. I. and No. II. Of A there will be produced in No. I. for her own consumption 1,000, for export $1333\frac{1}{3}$. Of B there will be produced in No. II. 750 for her own consumption, 900 for export. Of C there will be produced in No. I. $533\frac{1}{3}$ for her own consumption, and there will be imported $66\frac{2}{3}$; and in No. II. there will be produced 600 for her own consumption, and there will be exported $66\frac{2}{3}$. The new values are:

$$A : B : C : : 2 : 2\tfrac{2}{3} : 4$$

[1] The v of our formula above, p. 45.
[2] Above, p. 53.

Here C occupies an intermediate position between exports and imports, as may be verified by remarking that, after the trade has been set up, neither country can gain by either exporting or importing C. For it costs 4 units of productive force in No. I. and 3 in No. II.; and the produce of 4 units of No. I. is equivalent on the international market to the produce of 3 units of No. II., as appears from the fact that after the trade has been opened, A and B, each the product of two units in the country in which it continues to be produced, are valued at 2 and $2\frac{2}{3}$ respectively, or in other words exchange at the rate of 8A for 6B.

This theory brings into view an incident which is apt to be masked as long as we confine ourselves to the case of two commodities, the classical " cloth " and " linen "—namely, that it is not in general possible to determine *a priori*, from a mere observation of the costs of production in the respective countries before the opening of the trade, which commodities will be imported and which produced at home. " Comparative cost " cannot be ascertained by simply comparing the costs of different articles in the two countries. Thus if o′ in the figure be pushed up a little, the distances o′ a′, o′ b′, etc., being preserved constant, C will become an export (from Country No. I.) instead of an import. But the position of o′ depends not only on the cost of production in each country, but also on the law of demand in each country for the different commodities.

This incident is illustrated by one of Mangoldt's examples, in which the costs of production of five commodities in the two countries before the trade may be thus represented (p. 218):

	A	B	C	D	E
I.	4	7	6	8	5
II.	5	9	3	7	4

Upon a certain hypothesis as to the amount of each commodity demanded by each country (it being recollected that the real cost laid out on each article by each country is supposed to be constant), it is found that A and B are produced only by No. I., C and E only by No. II., while D—" the measure of the relative productivity of the two countries "—is produced in both. But if the quantities demanded were different, D would be produced only in No. I. (pp. 220–222). From the examples in the textbooks it might have been supposed that D would necessarily have been exported from the second country, and E from the first; since thus the second country could get its E cheaper —namely, at a rate less than $\frac{4}{7}$ D for one of E; and the first country could get its D cheaper—namely, at a rate less than $\frac{5}{8}$ E for one of D. But the truth is that in general no conclusion of the kind can be drawn pending the determination of the relation on the international market between the productive powers of the two countries, the ratio which we have designated as v. It is as the material embodiment of this relation between quantities of labour and sacrifice that Mangoldt's conception of a standard commodity is significant.

But an actual commodity subserving this purpose is not always to be found, as appears from the example which we have just cited, and as Mangoldt himself has pointed out. It may be observed that an actual standard would be forthcoming on one hypothesis—namely, that the volume of trade is split up into an indefinitely large number of items with every variety of cost of production; but in this case the standard commodity, though existent in fact, would probably be insignificant in magnitude.

The results of the abstract problem with which the investigation started are summed up at p. 223 in a set of italicised propositions, which may be read with assent and instruction. The first alone excites some scruple :

" There come first into international trade those commodities of which the costs of production compared with the costs of production of other commodities in the same land differ most widely from each other, then those for which the difference is next greatest."

At first sight there seems to be contained here a statement as to the path or process by which the position of equilibrium is reached; whereas the equations of exchange enable us at best to determine the final position, not the steps by which it is reached. What Jevons called the " Mechanics of Industry " is statical, not dynamical.[1] It appears, however, from the context that the author is aware of this characteristic.[2] The assertion which he makes in the proposition cited relates only to the first step—not to the intermediate path—towards equilibrium; and the affirmation that the first step taken will be the most advantageous one to both parties is tenable.

The simplest case having been discussed, Mangoldt proceeds to restore certain attributes which he began by abstracting.

---

[1] I have had occasion to defend this view against Professor Walras in the *Revue d'Économie Politique* for January 1891. [See below, a, p. 311.]

[2] " Die Art und Weise wie sich der process der Vertauschung der Production vollzeiht ist an sich gleichgültig " (p. 213), [das] " das Endergebniss immer das nämliche bleiben wird " (p. 216, last par.).

First let us no longer suppose the quantity demanded to be in inverse proportion to the labour-cost, but to vary with the rate of exchange between exports and imports, according to some more complicated law. The law which Mangoldt specially affects is such that when the rate of exchange or " price," P, is changed to Pm, m being any factor, the quantity demanded, N, becomes $r \times \dfrac{1}{m} N$; where r is an improper fraction, in cases instanced by the author, $\tfrac{11}{10}$ and $\tfrac{6}{5}$.[1] Employing this conception, Mangoldt enunciates that condition of equilibrium which would now be described as the intersection of two curves.

He then goes on to consider the phenomenon which would now be described as the multiple intersection of demand and supply curves (pp. 228, 229, and cp. § 68). His views on this curious subject are very interesting. He thinks that in general of several possible positions of equilibrium that one tends to be realised which is most favourable to the more *active* of the two nations. But there are stated some probabilities on the other side, which seem not very easy to apprehend (p. 229). It may be observed that Mangoldt, like Mill,[2] supposes neutral equilibrium —the coincidence of the two curves as we may say—to be possible.

So far the cost of production has been assumed to be constant, whatever the amount produced. Mangoldt next supposes (p. 232) the relation between cost and quantity which is now called the law of diminishing returns to prevail, and illustrates the general theory by a particular example, which is rendered more workable by resorting to the simple law of demand at first assumed—namely,,that the quantity demanded is in inverse ratio to the cost.

Finally, the cost of transport is taken into consideration (p. 233). Mangoldt propounds the remarkable theory that upon a certain hypothesis the carrying trade between two countries tends to fall to that one which has the smaller absolute productivity (p. 235). The distinction between the " active " and " passive " nation which we have already met with in connection with

---

[1] As I understand, if (as in Cournot's demand curve) x be the price and y the corresponding quantity demanded, $= f(x)$; we have $f(mx) = \dfrac{r}{m} f(x)$.

In the particular case where the law applies only to small changes of x, put $m = (1 + a)$, a small. Whence $y + a\dfrac{dy}{dx} = y - a r y$.
$$\frac{1}{y}\frac{dy}{dx} = -r. \quad y = Ce^{-rx}.$$

[2] Above, p. 23.

plural equilibrium here recurs (p. 240). Mangoldt illustrates his theories *more suo* by laborious examples. He sums up the section on cost of transport in a series of propositions, among which the following—very freely paraphrased—seem the most remarkable.

(1) The carrying trade between two nations tends to fall into the hands of one, a tendency counteracted by what, with reference to abstract theory, may be described as accidental circumstances.

(2) The carrying trade tends to fall into the hands of that nation the volume and weight of whose exports are greatest.

(3) An improvement in productivity tends to deprive a country of a share in the carrying trade.

(4) Improvements in means of production redound in general, and in the abstract, to the good of the importing people only.

These propositions appear to be, not indeed incorrect—as defined and qualified in the context—yet unimportant. Considering, however, the solidity of the rest of Mangoldt's work, it may well be that one specially interested in the problem of the apportionment of the carrying trade would discern more in this last section than the present writer, after taking a reasonable amount of trouble, has been able to find.

(4) *Auspitz and Lieben.*—In that portion of the *Theorie des Preises* which treats of international trade, the subject is enriched with important propositions and embellished with splendid illustrations. Perhaps the most valuable result due to the authors is the general geometrical proof that a nation may benefit itself in certain cases by an import or export tax. The construction by the aid of which they have discerned this theorem more clearly than their predecessors [1] is much the same as that which has been employed in the earlier pages of our mathematical part : down to the introduction of complicated curves corresponding to organic changes in trade.[2] But there is one important difference between even our simpler constructions and theirs : that theirs are restricted to a small part, ours are applicable to the whole volume of trade. Their abscissa represents a real article, one out of the many items in international trade ; their ordinate represents money, the marginal utility of which is properly considered as not varying with the amount consumed of a single article. Each of our co-ordinates on the contrary represents not so much actual commodities or money, as an ideal article typical of the total volume of trade ; used to suggest conclusions which may be verified by the algebraic analysis proper to the real case of

---

[1] *Theorie des Preises*, fig. 74.   [2] *Ante*, pp. 17, 41.

numerous exports or imports.[1]   Accordingly their supply- or offer- curve is never *inelastic* in our sense of the term ; [2] it continually ascends like the curve O E in the annexed figure; since, if money have a constant utility-value, for a higher price more (or not less) of a product (subject to the law of decreasing returns) will continually be offered. For a converse reason our curve may curl round like the dotted line in the figure. In short, the varieties of curve marked as (3) and (4) in the fourth figure above,[3] do not occur in their scheme. Accordingly they are not conducted to a certain proposition which we have typified by the statement that, if Europe had an urgent demand for the produce of the United States, it might be for the interest of the United States to put an import tax on the produce

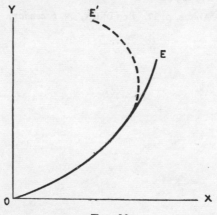

FIG. 10.

of Europe. Now as long as we consider the supply curve for European articles as of the form O E, an import tax thereon cannot come to much, as the authors observe (*Theorie des Preises*, p. 417). The curling round of the curve is required to express the urgency of the European demand for American produce. While we consider the supply curves of particular articles of the form O E, we do not get beyond the effect which we have likened to the buffer of a railway carriage being pushed back ; [4] to contemplate the movement imparted to the whole train, we require a construction such as that which has been employed by us.

Another difference between our and their constructions is that they seem to confine themselves to the simpler species of curve

[1] Above, pp. 31, 44.   [2] *Ante*, p. 35.
[3] Above, p. 37.   [4] *Ante*, p. 14.

which we have called *primary* (above, p. 39). With reference to
the law of supply and demand thus conceived, they rightly
argue that a bounty can never be beneficial to the community
as a whole (*Théorie*, p. 425). They miss Professor Marshall's
conclusion that a bounty attended with what we have called
organic changes, bringing the law of increasing returns into play,
may be beneficial.[1]

I trust that the critical portions of my study on international
value will corroborate the other parts : that the theories enounced
in those parts will be at once confirmed by their general agreement, and not discredited by their occasional discrepancy with
the principal authorities on the subject. I regret that the
negative portion of this result could not be attained without
the use of controversy.

[1] Above, p. 17. See Index, s.v. *Secondary*.

SECTION V
TAXATION

SECTION V

TAXATION

(S)

THE PURE THEORY OF TAXATION

[THIS article, published in the ECONOMIC JOURNAL, 1897, discusses the incidence of taxes, and the criterion of a good tax system, the rule according to which the burden of taxation ought to be distributed among the tax-payers. For the first purpose there is introduced a new classification formed by four dichotomic cross divisions. The leading case defined by the first, or positive, attribute of each division is, contrary to classical tradition, international trade, including dealings among non-competing groups within the same country. The incidence of taxation in this case having been already considered generally (Sect. IV.), there are here discussed only special cases. One such occurs when there is perfect inelasticity on one side of the market, or even on both. Other peculiar cases arise when commodities are *correlated* in respect of Consumption or Production. The genus correlation includes two species, "rivals" or mutual substitutes, when an increase in the possession of one renders the possession of the other less desirable, or an increase in the production of one renders the production of the other more difficult; and "complementary" articles with converse properties. It is shown that (even in a regime of competition) when demand and production are complementary, a tax on one may cause the price of *either* article to fall; with advantage to the consumers as a whole. It might have been added that if the commodities are rivals both in production and consumption, a tax on one may cause the price of *both* to fall. This *curiosum* does not depend on a change in the marginal value of money. The ordinary assumption that the total utility of consumption and cost of production is measured by money of stable value is throughout retained. Corresponding to the last-named paradox is the incident that when both supply and demand are rival, the producers may benefit by the imposition of a tax. *Both* prices may be raised; that of the taxed article to an extent in

63

excess of the tax. A somewhat different paradox—a tax on both commodities (correlated as partial substitutes for each other) benefiting the producers of one of them—is instanced in the text. The instance is furnished by house rent; a topic which is treated at length as illustrating the effects of taxation where mobility of capital and labour acts. The effects of an impost like the Inhabited House Duty vary greatly with the length of the period under consideration.

Monopoly is treated on much the same lines as, but in less technical terms than, in the article of the same date (1797) in the *Giornale* (above, **E.**).

The *curiosa* of the subjects are treated more fully there and in subsequent Papers (see Index, *sub voce* " Paradox "). Attention is called to a peculiar species of semi-monopoly. As mentioned above (**D**), it is one of the concrete cases in which differential prices may prove advantageous to both consumers and producers.

In the latter part of the article there is advocated as the criterion of good taxation, minimum aggregate sacrifice, distinguished from equal sacrifice in the obvious sense of the term, or proportional sacrifice, as the peculiar conception of Professor Seligman and Cohen-Stuart may be called.

The principle of *minimum* sacrifice is now very generally accepted, praised by Cannan, and used by Marshall (see ECONOMIC JOURNAL, 1921, p. 350, and 1917, p. 407). Professor T. N. Carver, who was the first to propound this doctrine, has exhibited its application with convincing clearness in his last work, *National Economy*.]

———

The science of taxation comprises two subjects to which the character of pure theory may be ascribed : the laws of incidence, and the principle of equal sacrifice.

The first subject presents a varietyof distinct cases demarcated by several cross divisions. Of these divisions the following four appear to me the most important for the purposes of theory :—

Either (A) all the transactions [1] under consideration are exposed to competition; or (a) among the parties with whom we are concerned there is at least one monopolist.[2]

———

[1] I suppose in each case parties to an exchange, the play of demand and supply. Taxation in a regime of socialism or of slavery is not considered.

[2] I understand by a monopolist an individual, or a combination, having the sole control of an article of exchange, and dealing with it solely in the interest of the monopolist. I agree with Professor Walras in thinking that much confusion has been caused by extending the term to cases in which a commodity absolutely

Either (B) all the products with which we are concerned obey the law of increasing cost; or (b) some do not.[1]

Either (C) the mobility of capital and labour [2] is not taken account of, or (c) exists and is taken account of.

Either (D) the taxation considered varies with the quantities of articles exchanged (including money, as in the case of a specific or an *ad valorem* tax, or one in kind), and so may be described as a tax on *margin ;* or (d) it does not so vary (as in the case of a tax on profits, or a poll-tax), and so may be described as a tax on *surplus*.[3]

I proceed to consider the more important of the cases formed by the combination of these attributes, giving priority to the first member of each division, the one designated by a capital letter. According to the order adopted, the case first to be considered is that which is defined by taking the first member of each division and which may accordingly be designated as A B C D; indicating that (A) the parties considered consist of two or more groups, the members of each group supplying the same article [4] in competition with each other; (B) each additional increment of every product is obtained by a more than proportional increase of outlay; (C) the groups are " non-competing " in Cairnes'

---

limited, such as land of a certain sort is in the hands of a *plurality* of uncombined possessors (*Éléments d'Économie Politique*, 2nd edition, Art. 408. Cp. *Dictionnaire d'Économie Politique*, Art. " Monopole "). As to the definition of maximum advantage in the case of a *combination*, see the present writer's article on " The Pure Theory of Monopoly " in the *Giornale degli Economisti* for 1897.

[1] I define the laws of increasing and decreasing cost thus. If $\phi(x)$ be the expense—or more generally the equivalent in money of the " real cost "—of producing the quantity x of a certain commodity, the law of increasing cost holds, when $\frac{d_2\phi}{dx^2}$ is *positive ;* the law of decreasing cost, when $\frac{d_2\phi}{dx^2}$ is negative (*cp.* Cournot, *Principes Mathématiques*, Art. 29). Generally if $\phi(x, y, z \ldots)$ is the cost of producing the quantities, $x, y, z \ldots$ of several commodities, the law of decreasing returns does or does not hold, according as the second term of variation of ϕ does or does not fulfil the conditions of a *maximum*. " Decreasing and increasing returns " will be here used as synonyms of increasing and decreasing cost. For fuller explanations and variant definitions, see **C.**

[2] As mobility may exist with respect to some—but not all—of the agents of production (*cp.* article on " International Values " in the ECONOMIC JOURNAL, Vol. IV. p. 35), the more exact distinction might be between (C) a greater and (c) a less degree of mobility.

[3] For certain theoretic purposes it might be better to distinguish the cases in which the tax (D) strikes the variables by the variation of which the parties under consideration seek each his maximum advantage; or (d) strikes the quantity which it is sought to maximise. The distinction between *margin* and *surplus* hovers between this one and the one in the text. (See " Margin," *Palgrave's Dictionary*. *Cp.* below, p. 76.)

[4] Or articles in the case of joint or more generally correlated production (below, p. 72).

sense, " industrial competition " is not supposed to exist; (D) the tax is of the same genus as an export or import tax.

A B C D. The case thus defined is nearly coincident with the case which I have discussed in a former article; that of an export or import tax on an article of international trade; understanding international trade in the generalised sense of ": exchange without mobility." [1] Following Mill, we may begin with the simplest variety where there are only two " nations." The case as conceived by us comprises not only international trade (in the proper sense), say between two islands isolated from the rest of the commercial world, but also a simple abstract market, such as the corn market, of which Professor Marshall has described the " temporary equilibrium " [2] or his ideal nut and apple-market; [3] also the dealings by which the shares of the parties in distribution are determined, the labour market, the loan market, the land market, each considered at first abstractedly by itself, and not yet in its true interdependence with the others.[4]

A tax of the kind now under consideration, affecting such a market, will in general prejudice both parties more or less. If, in the metaphor of a distinguished economist, we represent the undisturbed relation of the parties by the equilibrium of two balls resting against each other in a bowl, it may seem, at first sight, that a wedge inserted between the two balls will raise one of them to the full extent of the thickness of the wedge. But on reflection it is evident that this only occurs in the limiting case when the mass of one ball may be neglected in comparison with that of the other. In the absence of data respecting the relative masses of the balls all we can say is that the distance between them will be equal to the thickness of the interposed lamina. Corresponding to the masses of the two balls are the elasticities of demand and supply for the two parties. The general principle is that the tax inflicts more loss on either party, the less the elasticity of that party's demand or supply; other things, including the other party's elasticity, being the same.[5]

[1] Above, R, p. 5.
[2] *Principles*, Book V. ch. ii., § 1.
[3] *Ibid.*, § 1, *note on Barter* (latter part).
[4] One of the best, and I believe the first statements of the simultaneity, in the mathematical sense, of the several equations pertaining to value and distribution is given by Professor Walras in his *Éléments d'Économie Politique Pure.*
[5] When, as in my Articles on International Value, we make abstraction of money, and consider *price* in the generalised sense of M. Walras, *i. e.* rate-of-exchange, then it is unnecessary to distinguish the elasticity of supply from that of demand. The less the extension of the demand attending a fall of price, the

This proposition has been demonstrated at length in former articles.[1] It must suffice here to add some remarks suggested by an examination of certain extreme cases.

An instance of infinite elasticity of supply is afforded by the labour market upon the Ricardian hypothesis that, in Mill's words, " there is everywhere a minimum rate of wages, that they can never be lower beyond the length of time required for a diminished rate of increase [of population] to make itself felt, and can never long continue higher." [2] Upon this assumption, it is " hypothetically true " that a tax on wages would not permanently rest on the working classes; [3] a conclusion which is justly regarded as the opprobrium of pure theory, if it is applied to justify a tax on wages or on the necessities of the wage-earner. We have, however, Mill's authority for saying that " the assumption contains sufficient truth to render it admissible for the purposes of abstract science." [4]

It should be observed that this perfect elasticity of the supply of labour is predicated only of long periods; for short periods to evoke more work there would presumably be required a higher rate of wages. A similar difference in respect of elasticity between long and short periods is to be noticed in other markets. Thus, according to Professor Seligman, " an equal tax on all capital must fall on the lender, that is the capitalist. There would be no way for him to shift the burden." [5] But he admits that further accumulations might be discouraged. *Pro tanto* then the rate of interest in a long period would be increased.[6] Thus, too, we may

---

less is the extension of supply attending a rise of price. After the point at which demand becomes perfectly inelastic the elasticity may be said to become *negative*. This is the case alluded to in the criticism of Messrs. Auspitz and Lieben (above, **R**, p. 59) as not adapted to a curve which represents the variations of supply with money-price.

[1] The general principle is well stated by Professor Carver in his article on " Shifting of Taxation " in the *Yale Review* for November 1896.

[2] *Political Economy*, Bk. II. ch. xi. § 2.

[3] See Mill's application of the principle, *Political Economy*, Book V. ch. iii. § 4, par. 4.

[4] *Cp.* Adam Smith on taxes upon the wages of labour and the necessaries of life (*Wealth of Nations*, Book V. ch. ii.). McCulloch's remarks on these passages (McCulloch's edition of Adam Smith, Vol. IV. note xxiv.) seem just; his own views (*ibid.* p. 544) human. On this point Professor Seligman, as always where *friction* is the subject, is instructive (*Shifting and Incidence*, p. 174). Among the numbers of other writers who might be referred to, Professor Bastable may be distinguished (*Public Finance*, pp. 358–60, and 436, 2nd edition).

[5] *Shifting and Incidence*, p. 132. Cp. *Wealth of Nations*, Book V. ch. ii : " a tax upon the interest of money could not raise the rate of interest; the quantity of stock or money in the country . . . being supposed to remain the same." But it would not remain the same (*ibid. infra*).

[6] *Cp.* Bastable, *Public Finance*, Book III. ch. v. § 7.

partly account for Mill's statement respecting the " attempt to
tax all purchases and sales " that " neither class [buyers or sellers]
could throw the burden upon the other." [1]   This is true for
instantaneous periods, at least of sellers, so far as they are under
the necessity of selling what they have brought to market. But
can it be affirmed in general of a tax like the Spanish *alcavala*,
that " if levied from the sellers " in the long run it would burden
sellers more than buyers ? [2]

   The difference between the elasticity of supply according as
short or long periods are considered is conspicuous in the case
of houses.

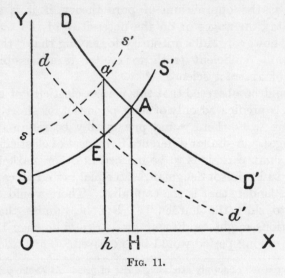

FIG. 11.

   For times so short and in places so limited that the number of
houses offered may be regarded as a fixed quantity,[3] a tax on house
rent, whether imposed on the occupier or owner of the house, is
in general borne altogether by the owner. This conclusion of the
older economists [4] is verified by the newer methods.[5]

   [1] *Political Economy*, Book V. ch. v.
   [2] The effect attributed to a "tax on all commodities " by Mill in an earlier
passage (Book V. ch. iv. § 1, par. 2) would require a long period.
   [3] The case of a commodity of which the quantity cannot be increased may
be regarded as a limiting case of one which can only be increased at an increasing
cost; and so belongs to our class B.
   [4] Mill, *Political Economy*, Book V. ch. iii. § 6, par. 3; Ricardo, *Political
Economy*, ch. xiv., first two pars.
   [5] In the accompanying figure S S' and D D' are taken as, in Professor
Marshall's phrase, " the typical diagram for stable equilibrium for a commodity
that obeys the law of diminishing return " (*Principles of Economics*, p. 425,
ed. 3; *cp.* p. 524).   A is the position of undisturbed equilibrium, O H is then the
supply.   When equilibrium is disturbed by a tax (of the kind now under con-

Some confusion appears to be caused by supposing the law of demand to alter concurrently with the imposition of the tax.[1]

sideration) on the producer, the supply is reduced to O h ; h E is the price received by the producer, E a the tax paid per unit of commodity (Marshall, *loc. cit.*). The figure shows that, if the tax is levied from the consumer, the result is the same. For d d', the demand-curve as displaced by the tax, strikes the original supply-curve in E. This theorem is given by Professor Carver in his article on " Shifting of Taxes " in the *Yale Review* for November 1896 (compare Auspitz and Lieben, *Theorie der Preise*, Art. 82).

Fig. 12 represents the two limiting cases of this theorem. S S′ is the perfectly elastic curve of constant cost, s s' the same displaced by a tax, as in Professor Marshall's Fig. 33; d d' has the same import as in the last paragraph.

In the other limiting case, when the supply is perfectly inelastic, let it equal O κ. Then κ a is the supply-curve. If it is imagined as sloping a little outward, the limiting form not quite reached, the effect of a tax on supply would, as before,

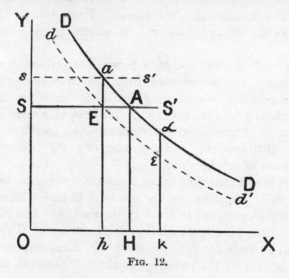

FIG. 12.

be represented by moving (every point of) the curve vertically upwards through a distance corresponding to the extent of the tax. The intersection of this displaced supply-curve—not shown in the figure—would cut the demand-curve in the neighbourhood of a, and accordingly the price paid by the consumer is nearly—in the limit quite—the same as before; the whole tax falls on the other party.

But it is simpler to use the theorem that it comes to the same whether the tax is on supply or on consumption. In the latter case, if d d' is as before the demand-curve displaced by the tax, κ a the price paid by the consumer is unaltered, the whole tax falls on the other party.

Compare Fleeming Jenkin : " If a holder sells unreservedly . . . the whole tax falls on the seller; the supply curve becomes a vertical straight line " (" Incidence of Taxes," p. 114 of *Papers Literary and Scientific*).

Or is it easier to say that, if with Cournot (*Principes Mathématiques*, Art. 51) we represent the equality of *demand* and *supply* before the tax by the equation $F(p) = \Omega(p)$ and after the tax (of u per uni imposed on the supply) by the equation $F(p') = \Omega(p' + u)$; then if Ω is degraded to a constant the equation for p' the disturbed price is the same as the equation for p the original price.

[1] Thus the Report of the London County Council Committee (Lord Farrer,

Is it not competent to the "mechanics of industry" to treat superposed disturbances independently and one at a time? If a person wears high heels, may we not estimate the elevation due to that cause without putting him on a hill? If indeed there is some connection between the artificial elongation and the position of the wearer, it may be proper to note this. Xenophon tells us that the great king alone among the ancient Persians wore his tiara erect. If then the king—as according to Dryden, the conqueror—of the Persians sate " aloft in awful state," the apex of the royal tiara would have been elevated both in itself and on account of the wearer's position. Yet Xenophon's statement is intelligible by itself. So rates on houses when expended in improving the neighbourhood tend to increase the demand for houses.[1] Yet in measuring the burden of the tax to the owner it is allowable in pure theory to abstract its influence on demand.

Another reflex influence of a house-rate on the demand for houses already built—reflected from the quarters where new building is possible—as it presupposes the mobility of capital, must be deferred to a later section. At present we are supposing the offer of built houses to be constant—the *fourth* of the cases so lucidly distinguished and discussed by Mr. Pierson in the second edition of his *Leerboek*.[2]

When it is affirmed that under these circumstances the burden of the tax falls altogether on the owner it is understood that the demand of the occupant is of an ordinary kind—not of that extreme or limiting variety which is perfectly inelastic. The contrary assumption is made by some writers; Mr. Blunden, for instance, who puts houses in the category of those " absolute necessaries

---

chairman) concludes that in prosperous communities house-rate falls on tenants; in declining ones on landlords. Similarly the *Dictionnaire d'Écon. Pol.*, art. " Incidence de l'Impôt." So Lord Farrer in his evidence before the Town Holdings Commission (Q. 1,244) : " The best authorities seem to think that it depends very much on the state of the market." If it is asserted that the incidence of a tax depends on whether the demand is rising in the sense of the demand-curve being raised as a whole, I altogether dissent; if it is meant that the incidence depends on whether the demand becomes more urgent in the sense of the demand-curve becoming steeper, I give only a qualified assent (see p. 71). It is too true that the " best authorities " express themselves carelessly. Pantaleoni forms a brilliant exception when he explains that a rise of rents does not mean shifting of tax (from the owner to the occupier) if the rents would have risen independently of the tax (*Teoria della Traslazione dei Tributi*, p. 226 et seq.).

[1] Mr. Fletcher Moulton, in his evidence before the Town Holdings Commission, has dwelt forcibly on this incident.

[2] Noticed in the Review III. 78.

of life " of which the " prices may rise considerably without appreciably affecting the demand." [1]

No doubt it is so in particular instances, for instance, in the case of the dwelling-houses of the labouring classes in certain localities.[2] But can it be affirmed generally that the demand for dwelling-houses is perfectly inelastic ? " If the tax, indeed, was very high," says Adam Smith, " the greater part of people would endeavour to evade it as much as they could by contenting themselves with smaller houses." And even if the tax be not high, is not a consequence similar in kind, if less in degree, to be apprehended by the owner who offers it for hire ?

In fine, even granted the premiss that the demand for houses is inelastic, the conclusion that the tax falls wholly or chiefly on the occupier does not follow. The supply of houses (already built) being, as here supposed, also inelastic, the price or rent becomes *indeterminate*.[3]

The extreme cases which have been instanced form rather limits than exceptions to the rule that both sides of the market suffer by a tax. An exception is presented by a species of export-tax analysed in a preceding article ; [4] the abstraction of a certain portion of the exports in kind, to be disposed of in a manner not affecting the market under consideration.[5] An instance would be the virtual export-tax which is imposed by the capture of

---

[1] *Local Taxation and Finance*, p. 49. Compare the author's recapitulations of his views in the *Journal of the Statistical Society* for December 1896.

Similarly Professor Seligman : " The landowner is not compelled to part with his land, but the tenant is compelled to occupy some apartments " (*Shifting and Incidence*, p. 111). Elsewhere, indeed (*ibid.* p. 120), he admits that the tax might be " so high as to cause the tenant to content himself with meaner apartments, or rooms in a less desirable locality."

I regard it as the general case, that the tax on the occupier *tends* to diminish his demand for house accommodation. Thus Mr. Bourne, steward of the London estates of the Duke of Bedford, affirmed, " with the greatest confidence," " from the knowledge that I have of everyday work for many years in London," " that the person taking the house is so free in his choice, that he can afford to throw up the houses when he takes into consideration what the rates and taxes are " (Town Holdings Committee, 1887. Q. 11,288–9).

[2] *Cp.* Cliffe Leslie, *Taxation of the Working Classes.*

[3] The intersection of two coincident perpendiculars !

What the actual effect of a tax under such conditions will be would seem to depend on circumstances which from the point of view of pure theory may be called accidents ; among which no doubt the circumstance whether the demand is rising or falling (above, p. 70) may in practice be important.

[4] Above, p. 38.

[5] The condition is stated with much precision by Cournot with respect to the taxation of *monopolies :* " Il peut se faire que le produit de l'impôt en nature soit appliqué à une consommation qui n'aurait pas eu lieu sans l'impôt, et qui n'influe en rien sur la demande que les autres consommateurs font au producteurs " (*Principes Mathématiques*, Art. 42).

smuggled goods; the intercepted goods being destroyed, or so
disposed of as to produce the same effect on the demand
and supply in the two countries as if they were destroyed.
It is not contended that the exception is of any practical
importance.[1]

Another class of exceptions comprises what Mill has called
" peculiar " or " anomalous " cases of value.[2] Such is the case
of " joint production," as defined by Mill, when " the same outlay
would have to be incurred for either of the two [commodities] if
the other were not wanted or used at all." Akin to this case is
that in which the increase of the production of either commodity,
though it does not necessitate, yet facilitates, the increased production of the other.[3] I propose to call products connected by
this relation, which I have elsewhere defined more precisely,[4]
complementary.

If we suppose the degrees of complementariness to be gradually diminished, we shall pass through the zero point of absolute
independence to a relation which may be distinguished as *rival*
production; when the increased production of one commodity
renders the increase of the other more difficult. For instance,
where a limited amount of time, strength, or other resources
may be spent in either of two sorts of otherwise unconnected
production.

The following propositions respecting the taxation of products
correlated in either of the two ways just defined may easily be
proved; it being supposed that the demand for one commodity is
independent of the demand for the other. A tax upon one of two
rival products will raise the price of both. A tax on one of two
complementary products will raise the price of the taxed one, and
lower the price of the untaxed one. In the latter case, it is conceivable that the consumers as a whole might be advantaged by
the tax, if we may set the gain of one class against the loss of
another.

The gain and loss to be balanced would appertain to the
same persons in the corresponding case of correlated demand.
The demand for two products may be called *complementary*
when a rise in the price of one is attended by a fall in the price

---

[1] As this kind of tax is in practice rare, I have to acknowledge that I have,
in a preceding article (ECONOMIC JOURNAL, Vol. IV.) exaggerated the asymmetry
between export and import taxes; and to retract my criticism of Professor
Bastable on that point (*ibid.* p. 624). *Cp.* above, R, pp. 3, 12, 38.

[2] *Political Economy* Book III. ch. xvi. *passim*, and last par.

[3] *Cp.* Marshall, *Principles*, Book V. ch. vi.

[4] *Giornale degli Economisti*, 1897. E, Vol. I.

of the other, *rival* when a rise in the price of one is attended with a rise in the price of the other.[1]

The following propositions respecting the taxation of commodities for which the demand is correlated may be proved. A tax on one of two rival commodities will raise the price of both. A tax on one of two complementary commodities will raise the price of the taxed one, and lower the price of the one which is not taxed. It is conceivable that the latter effect should so exceed the former that, on balance, a gain results to the consumers.

The possibility of a positive gain resulting to one side of the market—one of the two " nations "—from the imposition of a tax[2] is more evident in the case of commodities which are complementary, both as regards production and consumption.* In this compound case it may be shown—but not, I think, very easily, perhaps not without the use of mathematics—that a tax on one commodity may lower the price of either, but not of both.[3]

---

[1] *Ceteris paribus,* and in particular the marginal utility of money being supposed constant. I have used a more essential attribute for the definition of *rival* and *complementary* demand in my paper on " Monopoly " already referred to.

[2] Exclusive of the gain accruing from the tax to the importing country, a gain which must in general be included in order that an import-tax may result in a net gain to the importing country; as maintained by Messrs. Auspitz and Lieben (*Theorie der Preise,* Art. 81), and by the present writer (ECONOMIC JOURNAL, Vol. IV.).

* For a fuller statement see the added note at the end of this Paper:

[3] x and y being the quantities purchased, consider the collective total utility (the *Gesammtnutzlichkeit* of Messrs. Auspitz and Lieben), and also the collective total cost (the *Gesammtkoste* of the same authors), each as a function of x and y. Before the tax, the price of the first commodity = its marginal utility (*i. e.* the differential of the total utility with respect to x) = its marginal cost (*i. e.* the differential of the total cost with respect to x). The price of the second quantity is similarly determined. After the tax—which may be at first supposed small and specific, say u per unit of x, and levied from the producer—if x' and y' be the new quantities then (1) marginal utility of x' = the marginal cost thereof $+ u$; (2) the marginal utility of y' = its marginal cost. Substituting $x + \Delta x, y + \Delta y$ for z' and y', expanding and neglecting higher powers, we obtain two simultaneous linear equations for Δx and Δy. Solving these, we can find the increments of the prices and the decrement of Consumers' Rent, in terms of three kinds of data : (1) the extent of the tax, (2) the rate of decrease of utility and the rate of increase of cost, and (3) the measures of the correlation between the two commodities in demand, and also in supply (the second differential with regard to x and y of the utility-function, and also that of the cost function). These magnitudes must comply with certain conditions; but those conditions are not inconsistent with the statements in the text. But, if only one of these correlations exists, though the price of the taxed commodity cannot fall, yet the Consumers' Rent may rise.

By parity of reasoning it may be shown that though in the case of a single commodity, " if the commodity obey the law of diminishing return . . . the result [of a tax] will be to raise the supply price by something less than the full amount of the tax " (Marshall, *Principles,* Book V. ch. xii. § 4), yet in the case of

Our estimate of the importance of these exceptions to the rule that neither party gains by a restriction of trade depends partly on the question whether the " peculiar cases " are frequent. According to Jevons the cases of joint production, " far from being ' some peculiar cases,' form the general rule, to which it is difficult to point out any clear or important exceptions." [1]

However that may be, the exceptions which have been adduced do not militate against the general rule considered as expressing the most frequent, the typical case. In all the varieties of correlated demand and supply it is still true that most frequently the price of the taxed commodity will be raised, while the price of the correlated commodity will as often be raised as it will be lowered in consequence of the tax. Whence it follows that the cases in which a balance of gain results to one party are a minority.

In these examples we have insensibly passed the frontier, not very important for the present purpose, which separates the case of two " non-competing groups " from that of several. We may now restore to the various markets involved in " Distribution and Exchange," the interdependence which we at first abstracted. We may now suppose a whole system of countries connected by international trade.

The reader may be referred to a former article for a discussion of this general case—the case of several balls in the bowl. It may be well to remark that when in equilibrium one ball presses against another, and that other against a third, it is not in general indifferent between which two balls a wedge shall be inserted. For example, suppose three islands, A, B, C, engaged in this sort of international trade. A imports from B goods, for

---

correlated commodities it is possible that the result of a tax on one may be to raise its price by more than the full amount of the tax; that though in general, the producers' surplus is diminished by a tax, yet in the case of correlated commodities it may be increased. The negative case of this paradox is, that a bounty may prejudice the bountied parties (directly and apart from ulterior effects, and from the cost to their Government).

What has been proved of a small specific tax may be extended (by neglecting higher powers of small quantities) to any small marginal tax (increasing with the increase of the commodity). What has been proved for an indefinitely small tax may be extended to a finite tax by reasoning which Cournot has made familiar. (For further explanations see my article on " The Pure Theory of Monopoly," in the *Giornale degli Economisti*, E, Vol. I.)

[1] *Theory*, p. 217. *Cp.* Preface, p. liii. Jevons is speaking of "joint " products in the narrow sense above attributed to Mill. If Jevons is right in using such strong language (which I am disposed to doubt), then *a fortiori* with reference to the wider category of goods that are *complementary* either in production or consumption.

the manufacture of which B has to import materials from C.[1] An import tax in A (or an export tax in B) on the goods exported from B to A will not come to the same as an import tax in B (or an export tax in C) on the materials imported by B from C. As an extreme case, suppose that the materials imported from our island C are supplied there yearly in constant quantities independently of human effort—*e. g.* seaweed deposited on the shores of C. A tax on the price charged by inhabitants of C for permission to inhabitants of B to remove this seaweed would fall altogether on the inhabitants of C; the price of the goods imported from B into A would not be affected. But a tax on these latter imports would be followed by a rise in the price of those imports, and a fall in the price of the materials imported from C; all three parties will be worse off—in general, and except in the limiting case in which the demand in A for the imports from B is perfectly inelastic; in which case the entire burden of the tax will fall on A, B and C will be unaffected.

A B C d.[2] The possibility which has been shown in the preceding section, that a tax upon products may be in part shifted by the producer, even though he has not the power of changing his occupation, no longer exists when the tax is imposed on profits, or generally *surplus*.[3] The case is not now that of a wedge inserted between two balls in a bowl; it is rather as if the position from which one of the two balls was started to run down to equilibrium was lowered. The height at which it would finally settle would not be altered by this abbreviation of its descent to equilibrium [4] (the bowl being supposed spherical). The

---

[1] Compare Professor Carver's correct decision on the case of a tax that is placed upon an article on its way through the hands of a merchant from the producer to the consumer. (*Yale Review*, Nov. 1896.)

[2] See the explanation of these symbols above, p. 65.

It would have been agreeable to classical tradition to place in this section the theorem, that a tax on rent falls entirely on the landlord. Thus James Mill : "To him [the capitalist cultivator] it is a matter of perfect indifference whether he pays the surplus in the shape of rent, to an individual proprietor, or in that of revenue, to a government collector " (*Elements*, chap. iv. § v. par. 1). So Florez Estrada, Book IV. chap. v.; Professor Seligman, *Shifting and Incidence*, p. 35 and p. 184, and many other authorities.

Yet in spite of the almost universal practice, I venture to think that there is some advantage in the classification here adopted. It may be observed that though under a regime of competition, a tax imposed upon the payment for an article absolutely limited in quantity, such as land, may be viewed as falling either upon margin or surplus, it is otherwise in a regime of monopoly : the tax is there certainly marginal.

[3] Compare Hadley, *Economics*, 512, 3.

[4] Energy representing total utility by a metaphor familiar to the mathematical economist. *Cp.* Irving Fisher's *Mathematical Investigations*, Part II. ch. iii. (*Mechanical Analogies*).

conditions of ecnonomic equilibrium are not affected by a tax on surplus.

This is the first approximation. But it must be remembered that in general it is not possible for the tax-collector to hit a surplus which is altogether "intramarginal." A tax on profits— such as Schedule D of our Income Tax, or such as a payment for a licence to carry on a trade—cannot be levied without some little disturbance of economic margins. This proposition might be illustrated by considering the classical theorem that the remission of rent to all farmers would not lower the price of corn. That is the first approximation. But if the farmers' "margin of saving" was displaced by their increased income, they might be willing to invest more capital in agricultural improvement, and so lower the marginal cost of produce.[1] Contrariwise there might be now required a higher rate of remuneration to evoke the same exertion from the cultivator; his new affluence having displaced the margin at which the decrements of the utility of consumption become equal to the increment of the discommodity of labour.[2] If with Jevons, or still more elegantly with Gossen,[3] we represent that margin by the point along a line at which the ordinates to certain two curves become equal, it will be evident that neither tax on profits, nor poll tax, nor licences, nor any other form of impost under category d will be able to reduce the area representing surplus, without disturbing its boundary.

Some little disturbance of this kind is to be attributed to an income tax, in so far as it strikes the shareholders in a joint stock company. But in so far as it strikes those who are entitled to a fixed payment from the proceeds of a going concern, it affects economic margins only in so far as the reduction of income may cause an alteration in the consumers' scale of demand.[4]

To the present section belong also consumers'—as well as producers'—licences. A tax on licence to consume a thing differs in its effect from a tax upon the thing, when more than one unit of the thing are, or would be in the absence of taxation, consumed

---

[1] *Cp.* Ricardo, *Political Economy*, chap. viii. : " There are no taxes which have not a tendency to lessen the power to accumulate."

[2] Against the probability that taxation will diminish accumulation, there is the possibility that " curtailment of profit may act as a stimulus " (Mill, Book V. chap. iii. § 3). A very bare possibility, according to Bastable (*Public Finance*, Book III. 2nd ed.). For the cognate doctrine that the impoverishment of the labourer will act as a stimulus, see the apt quotations at p. 16 of Professor Seligman's *Shifting and Incidence*.

[3] See Palgrave's *Dictionary*, Art. " Gossen," Fig. 3.

[4] The effect of changes in income upon prices is well analysed by Professor Irving Fisher in his *Mathematical Investigations on Prices*.

during the period within which the licence must be renewed, say a year. If no sportsman wanted more than one gun a year, the effect of a sporting licence in checking demand would be much the same as that of a specific tax on guns. But the licence to drink tea for which, as Adam Smith tells us,[1] people used to pay so much a head in Holland, would act differently from a tax of so much per pound on tea. It would be a tax on surplus. It would knock off all those consumers who do not derive from the consumption of tea a consumers' rent or surplus more than equivalent to the payment of the licence. On the remaining consumers it would act simply as a tax on their income.

A B c.[2] Let us now remove the barriers which have so far been supposed to separate our " non-competing groups." Let us introduce that mobility of the agents of production which is the essential attribute of domestic as distinguished from international trade, which is an important property of long periods as distinguished from short ones. Admitting the classical hypothesis respecting the freedom of capital and labour, we must accept the classical theorems concerning the effects of taxation : that, in the words of Adam Smith—

" A tax . . . upon the profits of stock employed in any particular branch of trade can never fall finally upon the dealers . . . but always upon the consumers, who must be obliged to pay in the price of the goods the tax which the dealer advances " (*Wealth of Nations*, Book V. chap. ii. art. 2).

In the words of Ricardo—

" A tax on the profits of the farmer would raise the price of corn; a tax on the profits of the clothier, the price of cloth " (*Principles*, chap. xv. par. 3).

In the words of J. S. Mill—

" If a tax were laid on the profits of any one branch of productive employment, the tax would be virtually an increase of the cost of production, and the value and price of the article would rise accordingly; by which the tax would be thrown upon the consumers of the commodity, and would not affect profits " (*Principles*, Book V, chap. iii. § 2, par. 1).

I do not know that these expressions can be improved upon. Yet as the attempt to paraphrase our literary classics, which is sometimes made a school exercise, however feeble in itself, brings out more fully the inimitable excellence of the originals, in the

---

[1] *Wealth of Nations*, Book V. ch. ii.
[2] The category thus designated comprises both A B c A and A B c d.

like humble spirit it may be allowable to expand the above cited authoritative dicta.

As I understand the " industrial competition " with which we are now concerned, the conditions of equilibrium are twofold—(1)[1] one common to the " commercial competition," which was supposed to exist in our first two sections, namely, that in any business the outlay in every direction should be pushed up to the " margin of profitableness," [2] and (2) one which forms the differentia of industrial competition, namely, that the " net advantages " in all businesses between which there is mobility should be equal.[3]

Now let a tax on profits disturb the second condition. If equilibrium is restored by the consumers being " obliged to pay in the price of the goods the tax," it follows from condition (1) that the marginal costs of the business taxed must be raised.

This would, I think, be generally allowed in the most familiar case, that of the " margin of cultivation." Consider the following simplified version of an example which Mill has put among " peculiar cases of value." [4] " For simplicity we will confine our supposition to two kinds of agricultural produce; for instance, wheat and oats." There are supposed (by us, not Mill) to exist only " medium soils which, without being specifically adapted to either, are about equally suited to both " products. The relative value of the two grains will of course be determined by the productivity of the marginal dose of outlay on each species of cultivation. Now let a tax be laid on the profits of oat growers. There will be a rush from the cultivation of oats to that of wheat. There will be established a new equilibrium in which, if the demand is constant, the area of wheat-growing is widened, the marginal cost of cultivation diminished; while the converse is true of oats.[5]

I have been supposing the land to be owned by the cultivators. It comes to the same if the land is rented from competing landlords, and a tax is imposed on the rent of oats-growing land. We have then an example of Professor Marshall's theorem that

[1] See *Address to the British Association, Sec. F*, Report for 1889. I have endeavoured to defend this view in an article in the *Revue d'Économie Politique* for January 1891, and in a passage in the ECONOMIC JOURNAL for 1896, Vol. V. p. 173.

[2] *Cp*. Marshall, *Principles of Economics*, p. 433 *et passim*.

[3] Or rather equally attractive, as explained by Professor Marshall in the *Principles of Economics*. I suppose the condition to hold not only for the typical entrepreneur, but also when enterprise delegates the task of superintendence—*e. g.* shareholders in a joint-stock undertaking. *Ceteris paribus*, the chance of profit tends to be the same in one undertaking as another.

[4] *Principles*, Book III. ch. xvi. § 2.

[5] *Cp*. Marshall, *Principles of Economics*, p. 483, note; 3rd edition.

partial rent does enter into the cost of production, taking as a test of such " entrance " the circumstance that a tax on rent will affect price.

The action of mobility is similar when the tax is not on *surplus*, as we began in this section by supposing, but on *margin* —specific, *ad valorem*, or in kind.[1]

I propose to illustrate these principles by considering a tax affecting an industry which presumably obeys the law of decreasing returns,[2] a tax on the rent of urban dwelling-houses.

Let us take as sufficiently general the case put by the Select Committee on Town Holdings in their Final Report :— [3]

" The typical condition of a town holding under this system [the ' leasehold system '] as regards the parties and their respective interests . . . may be described as follows :—

" (A) The occupier of the house holding at a rack-rent, whether on a yearly tenancy or for a longer or shorter term.

" (B) His immediate landlord, the receiver of the rack-rent, who is ordinarily called ' the owner of the house,' and who holds for a term of years, paying during such term to the freeholder a fixed annual sum, generally called the ' ground rent ' . . .

" (C) The freeholder, who receives the ground rent during the term, and on its completion is entitled to the entire property absolutely."

For a first approximation, neglecting the distance in time between the different bargains, we may substitute for the three interests A, B, C, described in the Report the three " nations " A, B, C defined at the end of our first section ; [4] A importing from B, goods for the manufacture of which B has to import materials from C, materials obtained in constant quantities independently of human effort. Only now B is no longer completely insulated, but is connected with a continent of capitalists, whereby the producers in B are kept as it were at a constant level of advantage. With allowance for this difference the solution is as before. A tax on the product houses—whether levied from the occupant or owner—will have the following effects. The occupants will suffer by having to pay a raised price, not in general raised to the full extent of the tax. The capitalist owners will not suffer

[1] Regarding the ascending curve SS' on Fig. 11 as an ordinary short-period supply-curve, we are to consider that it is first raised up, as explained in that context, by a marginal tax, and then further—in general and except when the demand of the consumer is perfectly inelastic—furled in by the migration of entrepreneurs from the industry. In the case of a tax on surplus the curve is not raised up; it is (theoretically) always, not merely generally, furled in.

[2] See Marshall, *Principles of Economics*, *sub voce* " Margin of building."

[3] 1892, No. 214, p. 6. [4] Above, p. 75.

though the price which they receive for their product falls; [1] the net advantage of the industry being kept constant by migration into other industries. The ground landlord will suffer by a diminution of the ground rent. A tax on ground rent, whether levied from the ground landlord or the " owner," falls entirely on the ground landlord.

This is, of course, very pure theory, making abstraction of differences in time, that great source of complications in Economics.[2]

For a second approximation let us distinguish three periods, (1) the average duration of the occupant's lease, (2) the average duration of the owner's lease, (3) longer periods.

(1) It is not questioned that a tax imposed while the occupant's lease is running rests where it strikes during that period.

(2) A first approximation has already been obtained for this case,[3] on the assumption that during this period the offer consists entirely of houses already built. On that supposition the tax falls entirely upon the owner.[4] But we have now to take into account that the offer in general consists partly of houses already built in parts of the town already occupied, say the central area, partly of new houses which may be built on land which has hitherto been agricultural, say for brevity the suburbs.[5] Now if we had an exact measure of the advantage of the central area above the suburban periphery we should have an exact measure of the effect of the tax on house-rent. Suppose, for instance, in the vein of von Thünen, that the net advantage offered by houses of equally costly structure in the respective sites differed only on account of the different fares from each site to a central point. Then since the landlord at the suburbs can only stand out for a certain minimum of rent, that which he might have obtained in the way of agriculture,[6] the occupant in the suburbs has in general

---

[1] The law of decreasing returns being supposed to act.

[2] *Cp.* Marshall, Preface to *Principles of Economics.*

[3] Above, p. 68.

[4] Mr. Cannan clenches the matter thus, "We are not really ' mostly fools.' Who will stand up and confess that he took 76 —— Street at £100 a year, and subject to £20 of rates, when an exactly similar house next door, but in another parish, was to let at £100 a year, and only £12 of rates?" (*History of Local Taxation,* p. 134.)

[5] Our problem is here the same as that which forms Mr. Pierson's *third* case (noticed in the ECONOMIC JOURNAL, Vol. V. p. 436); but our solution is not quite the same as his.

[6] Professor Seligman is alone, as far as I know, in disputing this theorem (*Shifting and Incidence,* p. 106). I cannot agree with him that Mill's reasoning postulates the existence of a no-rent tract. The reasoning is akin to that on p. 78 above, relating to the taxation of rent.

to pay the entire tax, except so far as he reduces his use of house-accommodation; and since the occupants of the central area are better off only in respect of the fares they also have to pay the same price for the same accommodation. The case would be exactly parallel to the familiar case of a tax on agricultural produce. The consumer thereof pays the tax except so far as he reduces his consumption; otherwise the landlords are untouched. This would be the solution, if there were perfect rivalry between central and suburban habitations.

But of course the capacity of houses at the circumference to act as substitutes for houses in the centre is not perfect; there is only a partial rivalry.[1] Since, then, when there is no rivalry, the owners of the central area suffer to the full extent of the tax, and when there is perfect rivalry, they do not suffer at all, it might be inferred that in the intermediate case of partial rivalry the owners would suffer, but not to the full extent of the tax. The inference, however, would not be correct. It is one of the *curiosa* of the theory of *correlated* demand [2] that a tax on house rent might so disturb the balance of demand for urban and suburban accommodation respectively as to cause a positive benefit to the owners.[3] The truth of this proposition is not impaired, because

[1] Compare Fleeming Jenkin: "The rents through the whole town are ruled by those of the new districts. There is a certain selective value between every house in the town, and if the rents of the new houses are dearer, the rents of the old houses are increased in due proportion" ("Incidence of Taxes," p. 117, *Papers, Literary and Scientific.*)   [2] *Cp.* above, p. 73.

[3] Suppose, for simplicity of enunciation, that all the houses in the suburbs are of one kind; and also all the houses in the central area of another kind. Before the tax, let p_1 be the rent of a house, and x the number of houses taken, in the suburbs; and let the corresponding amounts for the central area be p_2 and y. By hypothesis, y is constant. Also, for a first approximation, we may make the classical assumption that p_1, the rent received by the capitalist-builder in the suburbs, does not vary with the tax. Under these conditions, if a tax proportional to the rent, say the ith part thereof (where i is small), is levied from the occupiers in both quarters; for the disturbed equilibrium we have the following equations :—

$$\begin{cases} (1+i)p_1 = p_1 + dx\left(\dfrac{dp_1}{dx}\right) \\ (1+i)(p_2 + dp_2) = p_2 + dx\left(\dfrac{dp_2}{dx}\right) \end{cases}$$

Whence

$$dp_2 = ip_2\left(-1 + \frac{1}{p_2}\left(\frac{dp_2}{dx}\right) \div \frac{1}{p_1}\left(\frac{dp_1}{dx}\right)\right)$$

Whence it appears that the rent received by the urban owner falls to the full extent of the tax when the demands for residence in the respective quarters are quite independent, and does not fall at all when the two articles are perfect substitutes. In the intermediate case the owner's rent falls, or rises, according as $\frac{1}{p_1}\left(\frac{dp_1}{dx}\right) >$, or $< \frac{1}{p_2}\left(\frac{dp_2}{dx}\right)$. The former case is, I think, the more probable; but the

there may be in fact from other causes a centrifugal movement of residents from central quarters. *Pro tanto* the tax may have the effect of diminishing the loss which from other causes is accruing to the owners of residential houses in these quarters.[1]

(3) For long periods the solution above given [2] as a first approximation holds good. We might regard the three interests A, B, C, as three bodies held one above the other by a press or " vice," so that the sum of the depths of three bodies is constant. A wedge being driven in between A and B, the bodies—each obeying its peculiar law of compressibility and resilience—will behave as follows. At first A will be compressed to the full extent of the thickness of the wedge; B and C retaining their full dimensions. After a time A will re-expand, in part at least; B will be compressed to some extent, perhaps nearly to the whole extent of the thickness of the wedge; C will remain firm. But leave the bodies alone for a longer time and B will regain its original amplitude, and the compression due to the insertion of the ·wedge will be divided in uncertain proportions between A and C. It is not to be denied that during the long time required for the working out of these forces, other forces may have come into play. The bodies may have expanded from other causes, the press may have been warped so as to allow room for their expansion. But because the given forces are compounded with others known imperfectly, we are not precluded from calculating the resultant of the given ones.

The proof of the general theory relating to long periods may be verified by an examination of some limiting cases in which the statement of the theory requires modification; the frequent occurrence of which cases may account for the prevalence of opposed theories.

(*a*) In the limiting case when the demand of the consumer,

---

latter is by no means impossible; for all that we know about the relative magnitude of these partial differentials is that $\left(\frac{dp_1}{dx}\right) \times \left(\frac{dp_2}{dy}\right) > \left(\frac{dp_2}{dx}\right)^2$. (*Cp.* **E**, p. 117.)

Probably $\left(\frac{dp_2}{dx}\right)$ is less than either of the two factors of which the product is greater than its square; but not necessarily. *Ceteris paribus*, the event is more likely to occur when the demand for urban houses is very inelastic; for suburban houses very elastic. As to the conditions which the demand-functions must fulfil, see article on " Monopoly " in the *Giornale degli Economisti*, 1897, (**E**).

The proposition is less likely to be true when p_1 is supposed to be lowered (in virtue of the law of diminishing returns). It is strictly proved only for infinitesimal values of i, but may with probability be extended further. (See Index, s.v. *Differential*.

[1] *Cp.* above, p. 70.   [2] Above, p. 80.

the occupier, is perfectly inelastic he will bear the whole tax. This assumption is more readily made, as it is usual, perhaps proper, to make it in problems about agricultural rent. The possibility of this incident has already been admitted with respect to the comparatively short period (2), and may also, though I think less easily, be admitted with regard to period (3).

(β) Suppose that ground-rents are in general very small in comparison with the tax, then of course they can only bear a small part of the tax. May we not explain by this supposition Ricardo's *dictum* ?

" In ordinary cases it may be presumed that the whole tax would be paid both immediately and finally by the occupier." [1]

So J. S. Mill :— [2]

" In the vast majority of houses, the ground rent forms but a small proportion of the annual payment of the house." [3]

This is of course true of houses in the country; [4] not so true now as fifty years ago of urban rates.

(γ) Again, suppose conditions such that only one " dose," so to speak, of building capital can be applied to one parcel of land— say in China or Peru—through the fixity of custom and the mobility of the earth, only a single-storied dwelling of uniform pattern can be placed on each unit of the area available for building. On such a supposition a tax on house-rent would fall in general entirely on ground-rent. [5] For the accommodation of the occupants could not be reduced without some of the sites being left unoccupied. Each landlord threatened with the loss of his entire ground-rent will lower his terms until ground-rent all round has been, if it can be, reduced to the full extent of the tax.

Upon this or some adjacent less extreme hypothesis, we may account for the opinion of some distinguished writers that the tax on house rent in the long run tends to be mostly borne by the ground landlord. Thus, too, we may perhaps explain what otherwise may seem inexplicable—why the successors of Ricardo should attempt to allocate a certain portion of the house rent to the ground rent.

Thus McCulloch :—

" Were the supply of houses easily diminished and increased, a tax on their rents would fall wholly on the occupiers and ground

[1] *Political Economy*, chap. xiv. par. 3.

[2] A different view of the Ricardian dictum appears to be taken by Esquiros de Parieu, *Traité de l'Impôt*, p. 74, and some other eminent writers.

Political Economy, Book V. chap. iii. § 6, par. 5.

[4] Cp. *Wealth of Nations*, Book V ch. ii.

[5] Of course supposing the tax not to exceed the rent.

landlords, and be divided between them in the proportion which the profit of the capital required to build them bears to the rent of the ground on which they stand." [1]

So J. S. Mill :—[2]

" A tax of so much per cent. on the gross rent falls on both these portions [ground rent and building rent]. . . . The incidence, however, of these two portions of the tax must be considered separately.

" As much of it as is a tax on building rent must ultimately fall on the consumer, in other words the occupier." [3]

So Professor Sidgwick distinguishes " the portion of the tax which is paid for the value of the house itself " and the " portion that falls on the ground rent." [4]

Now on our present hypothesis (γ) these statements would be true in a particular case, namely, when the tax was equal to the original ground rent plus the constant building rent.[5] In that case the effects of the tax would be exactly as Mill and McCulloch lay it down. And it was, perhaps, natural to regard this case as typical; at any rate, when the consumer's demand is supposed perfectly inelastic, when our (a) as well as (γ) is present. In that sub-case the true solution, I submit, is that the division of the burden between the occupier and the ground landlord is indeterminate. But the divisions suggested by McCulloch and Mill are plausible.

The consonance of this incident (γ) with authoritative *dicta* moves me to suppose the prevalence of the incident. A house is naturally thought of by Jevons as an instance of an " indivisible " commodity which forms an exception to the general theory of value.[6] And yet, though a house is indivisible, residential accommodation is not. There may be many " mansions " not only in the archaic sense, but in that which is applicable to the modern " flats." " Increments of villa accommodation," in Professor Marshall's phrase, may be added up to the point [7] where

[1] *Taxation and Funding*, Part I. chap. i. § 2.

[2] As against Mill's precise apportionment, Mr. Sidney Webb's contention that " the freeholder . . . has no fixed point of resistance " (*Town Holdings Commission*, 1890, Q. 42–44) is just. His " large jump in value " from agricultural to building land, is not necessary for this conclusion.

[3] *Political Economy*, Book V. chap. iii. § 6.

[4] *Principles of Political Economy*, Book III. chap. viii. § 8.

[5] In the spirit of the classical writers we may here suppose the cost of building constant, even though the supply of buildings should be reduced.

[6] *Theory*, chap. iv.

[7] " The cases in which a man has to live in a house of a size widely different from that which he prefers, because there is none other available," are exceptional (*Principles of Economics*, Book V., p. 592, note, 3rd ed.).

the price just measures both the marginal cost and the marginal utility of an increment. In short, the law of value for house accommodation is (for long periods) essentially the same for house accommodation as for corn. It might be all very well for Adam Smith, who held that "in the price of corn . . . one part pays the rent of the landlord," [1] to say that "the rent of a house may be distinguished into two parts,[2] . . . the building rent and the ground rent." But what have we to do with such apportionment of price, or tax, we who have received the doctrine of Ricardo that "rent does not and cannot enter in the least degree as a component of price"; the doctrine of Professor Marshall that "ground rent does not enter into the expenses of manufacture," on an understanding "exactly parallel to that which has to be supplied in order to make Ricardo's doctrine true, when applied to agriculture ?" [3]

Dwelling-houses, then, belonging to the general category of consumable products, as the highest authorities are agreed,[4] the taxation of such houses obeys the general laws of the taxation of products which have been enunciated above as pertaining to long periods (3) ; [5] abstracting the peculiarities of the "leasehold system" which have been allowed for with reference to short periods (2).

A practical corollary is that a tax on ground rent hurts the ground landlord more, and the occupier less, than *ceteris paribus* a tax on the occupation rent, in the long run ; [6] theoretically even,

[1] *Wealth of Nations*, Book I.   [2] *Ibid.* Book V. chap. i.

[3] See the whole passage relating to the margin of building, in *Principles of Economics*, Book V.

[4] Thus Mr. Goschen in his *Draft Report on Local Taxation ;* "The inhabitant of the house . . . is in reality the consumer of the commodity produced by the builder " (*Local Taxation*, p. 164). So Professor Bastable regards " houses as a particular manufactured commodity " (*Public Finance*, p. 371, 2nd ed.). *Cp.* Mr. Pierson, *Leerboek*, p. 146, 2nd ed.

[5] Above, p. 82. I am confirmed in this view by finding myself able to agree with all that Professor Bastable has said on this subject (*Public Finance*, Book IV. chap. ii. § 5). I concur with his criticism of Professor Seligman that " he seems to give too little weight to the forces that shift taxation on the ground owner."

[6] The reluctance on the part of common-sense and even of trained intelligence to accept the theory here maintained, that there is an essential difference between the effects of a tax on ground rent and a tax on occupation rent, may be accounted for by the tacit assumption that the amount of building is given and constant, irrespectively of the tax. Consider, for instance, the remarkably clear statements of Mr. Clements in his evidence before the Town Holdings Commission (Q. 1,969). The argument which he illustrated by the example of a particular actual house (Q. 1,970) tacitly assumes that the amount of house accommodation demanded by the occupier is constant, whether or not the occupier pays an *ad valorem* tax (see notes).

For other direct contradictions of the theory here advanced see *Town Holdings Committee*, 1887, Q. 3,360; 1888, Q. 2,736, 2,837, 4,446, 9,357 *et passim ;* or put the question to any practical man.

and apart from friction (*a fortiori*, of course, when we restore the concrete circumstance that taxes are very apt to rest where they strike).[1]

In this argument no use has been made of the circumstance that all the leases do not fall in simultaneously. But it will be found that this concrete circumstance does not invalidate the broad conclusion of pure theory, that there is an essential distinction between the effect of a tax on ground rent, and that of a tax on occupation rent. To fix the ideas, we might suppose occupation leases to be on an average for seven years, ground leases for seventy years. Thus every year on an average the leases of a seventh part of the houses in any given urban area would fall in; and in a tenth of these cases the ground leases would also fall in, and the sites would be offered to capitalist-builders; supposing as a first approximation that the duration of the ground lease coincides with the duration of the house. Upon this supposition a tax on ground rent would as before fall entirely on the landlord; a tax on occupation rent would not in general have that effect. The effect of the latter kind of tax would not indeed be exactly the same in the concrete case of rotation and the imaginary case of simultaneous bargains.

But the differences between the abstract and concrete cases will not, I think, repay examination. I am already sensible indeed that the investigation of economic forces which require some seventy years to work themselves out may seem to have been prolonged beyond the limits of applied theory. I submit, however, that the argument is not so abstract, the reasoning is not deduced through so artificial a chain of remote consequences as at least one of the classical theorems of taxation which are still accepted by economists;[2] I mean Senior's doctrine of tithes. In this argument, as interpreted by Mill, the links seem to be as follows : rise in the price of agricultural wages, check to profits, check to accumulation, check to the production of food, check to the growth of population, check to the rise of rent; comparatively to what would have occurred in the absence of the tax. But it is not my design to determine the limits of applied theory, or to uniformly cover with examples the field so demarcated. I aim only, at least in this first article, at a restatement, with slight modifications, of the classical laws of incidence, and a partial exemplification of the restated theory.

[1] Professor Thorold Rogers advocated this view very strongly in his evidence before the Town Holdings Commission.

[2] *E. g.* Bastable, *Public Finance*, and Seligman, *Shifting and Incidence*.

It will be understood that the application of the theory in this section has been adapted to the typical case propounded; modifications of statement would be required by the circumstances that there may be not only one, but several lessees between the ground landlord A, and the occupier C; that the duration of a house may exceed the period of the building lease; that the transfer of accommodation may be effected by sale or " feu," instead of lease; that houses may be used for business, as well as for habitation; that the ground landlord may act as a càpitalist; that rates may differ in different parts of the same town; that house accommodation in different towns forms " rival " commodities; and many other incidents more or less important in practice.

From the point of view of pure theory the following modifications are more interesting. Perhaps the investments which are open as an alternative to an intending builder are not indefinitely extensive in comparison with the house-building industry —at any rate for periods not indefinitely long. The effect of mobility would then be to have connected our island B, not with a vast continent, but only with another island.[1] The joint island might then form a " nation " of capitalists, virtually appertaining to our first section, rather than the present one, obliged to submit in consequence of the house-tax to some permanent reduction in profits.[2]

Again, the building industry may be affected by the law of increasing returns, the operation of which we have next to consider.

A b. The old distinction between increasing and constant (or decreasing) cost presents difficulties to the newer analysis. For if any producer can continually increase his supply at a constant or diminished cost, there appears no general reason why he should not, cutting out his competitors, supply the entire market.[3] The classical conception of constant cost presupposes a limit to the production of each individual. The newer idea of expenditure pushed up to the margin of profitableness, in a regime of competition, implies the law of increased cost.[4] The law of diminishing

[1] Above, p. 79.

[2] This sort of intermediate case between perfect mobility and immobility is treated by Professor Pantaleoni in his highly original *Traslazione dei Tributi.*

[3] *Cp.* Marshall's *Principles of Economics,* 2nd and 3rd editions, Book V. ch. xi. *et passim.*

[4] Thus in the luminous illustration which Professor Marshall has given in note xiv. of the Appendix to his *Principles,* 3rd edition, the total outlay of a master-builder, considered as a function of different classes of labour x_1, x_2, and different kinds of raw materials y_1, y_2, etc., and other kinds of variables, must

costs, as Cournot argues, is only intelligible on the supposition of monopoly.[1]

How then can the law of diminishing cost co-exist with competition ?   How can a larger offer go with a smaller price ?   How can the supply-curves of the kind which Professor Marshall has made familiar be ever conceived as *descending ?*

The better opinion appears to be that such a downward trending *locus* is not to be regarded as a supply-curve in the primary [2] and obvious sense, not as representing the offer which in a given state of industry would be forthcoming at different prices ; but as compounded of, or derived from, a series of such primary curves, which Mr. Cunynghame in his path-breaking essay on the subject [3] has called " successive cost curves."

It has happened to some of us to ascend a mountain slope just up to the point where the desire was just compensated by the difficulty, of further progress.   Such is the position of the economic man on a primary short-period supply-curve sloping upwards.

Suppose that, as a party of mountaineers press up a steep slope, the opposing crest gives way, and they are carried down by a sort of avalanche, and landed on a new inclined plane. Again they urge their toilsome march upwards ; and again, before the crest is reached, they are precipitated on to another ledge below ; and so on till they are brought to a stop on some steep and comparatively firm slope.   Their path in space, though in reality saw-shaped, might appear to one taking a general view to be a curve-line.   Such, perhaps, is the nature of a competitive industry obeying the law of increasing returns : confined for short periods on an ascending supply-curve, extended during long periods down a descending supply-curve.[4]

Suppose that our party, after coming to a stop on a short slope, were to be incited by some fresh stimulus ; they might break through another crest and descend through a distance out of all

be such that the second term of its expansion fulfils all the conditions of a *maximum* (above, p. 65, note 1) ; otherwise the statements made, *e. g. op. cit.*, p. 802, par. 2, would not hold good.

The theoretical difficulties connected with the law of increasing returns are frequently referred to by Professor Marshall in his later editions.

[1] *Principes Mathématiques*, Art. 50, p. 102.

[2] See the reference to the subject in a former article, ECONOMIC JOURNAL, Vol. IV. p. 436.   [3] ECONOMIC JOURNAL, Vol. II. p. 41.

[4] The idea of a curve of many branches was propounded by the present writer in his Address to Section F of the British Association (note J), 1889.   The date explains one serious omission, that of " external economies," pointed out by Professor Marshall in the *Principles of Economics*.   (See a, below, p. 305.)

proportion to the exciting cause. Conversely, the imposition of a new burden might have prevented such progress from occurring. It is thus that, in an industrial regime of the kind considered, a bounty is apt to lower price,[1] a tax to raise it,[2] to a disproportionate extent.[3]

But, if the law of increasing cost is fulfilled in its natural and obvious sense, if the primary or short-period curves are descending, presumably the case belongs to *Monopoly*, the subject to which we next proceed.

Monopoly,[4] the branch of the subject we have now reached, presents a bifurcation peculiar to itself. There is an essential difference between (a_1) the cases in which we are concerned with only one monopolist, and (a_2) those in which two or more monopolists enter. The first subdivision presents ramifications parallel to those which have been traced in the case of competition. The first of these varieties is obtained by combining the just now defined attribute a_1 with the attributes which form the first members of cross divisions enunciated in the first article : namely, B prevalence of the law of decreasing returns, C immobility of capital and labour, D taxation of margin (*e. g.* specific or *ad valorem*, or in kind).

[1] Marshall, *Principles of Economics*, Book V. chap. xii. § 4.

[2] *Ibid.* *Cp.* Mill, *Political Economy*, Book V. chap. iv. § 2, end.

[3] A tax on a rival might of course act as a bounty; *e. g.* duty on foreign imports as a bounty to native producers.

Professor Carver's argument (*Yale Review*, November 1896) that, when an import tax is levied on a commodity which is produced at home under the law of increasing returns, the consumers may possibly bear no part of the tax, is not, I think, as he seems to apprehend, " opposed to the best orthodox teaching "; unless orthodoxy be defined very straitly. The argument is used by some of the highest modern authorities, to whom I have referred in a former article [ECONOMIC JOURNAL, Vol. IV. p. 48, E]. I don't know that they would accept his reply to the objection that the price—after being lowered in consequence of the tax—" might be further lowered by removing the tax." " This might be temporarily," says Professor Carver, " while it is probable that the same forces which kept the price up before the duty was first levied would ultimately bring about the same conditions after it was removed."

[4] The taxation of monopolists and monopolised goods, which is the subject of this article, is not to be confounded with the taxation by monopoly which is practised by several modern governments. The pure theory of the latter form of taxation is simply the pure theory of monopoly in general—a subject which I have attempted to handle in the *Giornale degli Economisti* for 1897 (E). The taxation of monopoly and the taxation by monopoly are connected by a certain analogy, which, as indicated by Messrs. Auspitz and Lieben (*Theorie*, p. 427 and context), exists between monopoly and taxation in general. In ordinary taxation government alters, in taxation by monopoly it makes, prices in its own interest—or rather at its own discretion, as Government need not be perfectly self-interested (*see* Marshall on " Compromise Benefit," *Principles of Economics*, Book V. ch. xiii.).

a_1 B C D. The simplest case under this head is obtained from the case which was first discussed under the heading A B C D, namely a simple market, by supposing one side of the market to be as it were solidified into a monopoly. We have thus the typical case discussed by Cournot : a single monopolist dealing with a body of customers competing with each other, at the same price for all the customers. As demonstrated by Cournot,[1] the effect of a specific tax on the product will be to raise its price to an extent which may be either greater than, equal to, or less than the amount of the tax " selon les circonstances." [2] To which it may be added, I think, that it will probably be less, at least for the case of decreasing returns.[3] In general the addition to the price will be a substantial proportion of the tax.

What is said by many popular writers, and even by some distinguished economists, that a tax (of the kind now under consideration) will not affect the consumer, for that the monopolist has already done his worst, is true only in two special cases. (1) Where it is not in the power of the monopolist to increase or limit his output at will, he will very generally have to bear the whole tax. Cournot has noticed the case of the monopolist who is unable to

[1] *Principes Mathématiques*, chs. v. and vi.

Professor Seligman appears to be under the impression that the only reason advanced by Cournot for the phenomenon that a tax on a monopolised article may raise the price to an extent greater than the amount of the tax was that the price paid by the consumer must include not only the tax but also interest on the sum advanced in order to pay the tax and the profits of middlemen (*Shifting and Incidence*, p. 156). " This theory," says Professor Seligman, " which Cournot invested with elaborate apparatus of mathematical diagrams, is, however, nothing but the accepted doctrine of Adam Smith, Ricardo, and Mill " (*ibid*. p. 157; *cp.* p. 159, par. 1). But it will be evident to any one who studies Cournot's theory of monopoly (*Principes Mathématiques*, p. 78, referred to by Mr. Seligman) that Cournot rests the phenomenon in question, in the case of monopoly, upon a principle other than the accepted doctrine of Adam Smith. Cournot in the passage referred to, has " invested with mathematical apparatus " the law of taxation stated in our text; which is so far from being the accepted doctrine of Adam Smith that it has escaped even Mr. Seligman.

I do not deny that Cournot has also employed the " accepted doctrine "; whether mistakenly, as Professor Seligman holds, will depend on the validity of "the old doctrine of normal or natural profits " (Seligman, p. 158 and *cp.* p. 145), a subject on which I am not called upon in this connection to express an opinion (*cp.* ante, p. 77).

[2] *Principes Mathématiques*, p. 77.

[3] As proved by Cournot (*Principes Mathématiques*, Art. 31) the increase of price due to a small tax u per unit of commodity is of the form $u \times A \div (2A + B + C)$ where A is always negative; B is negative when the law of decreasing returns prevails (and positive in the converse case); of C nothing is known in general, either as to its sign or magnitude, except that the expression $(2A + B + C)$ must be always negative. In such a case, I submit, we are justified in regarding it as probable that A will be (in absolute quantity) less than $2A + B + C$, and therefore the addition to the price less than u—at any rate when B is of the same sign as A, as in the present section.

increase his output.[1] The converse exception may be illustrated by an owner of urban land, if prevented by public opinion from keeping it out of the market. (2) The second exception is where the monopolist is a sole *buyer*, and the supply of the article bought is perfectly inelastic : for instance, a combination of tenants dealing with landlords incapable of combining. But in general the addition to the price will not be zero. I am unable to follow Professor Seligman when he asserts the contrary.

These theorems may be extended from a specific to an *ad valorem* tax. The demonstration is given by Cournot in a passage already referred to (*Principes Mathématiques*, p. 78 *et seq.*). I have endeavoured to give a simplified version of Cournot's reasoning in a note.[2]

---

[1] *Principes Mathématiques*, last paragraph of ch. v. ; first paragraph of Art. 39.

[2] Before the tax, the monopolist will have fixed the price which renders his net profits a *maximum*. He may be supposed to begin tentatively with a very low price, and to go on raising the price as long as the increment of net profit which corresponds to a rise of price continues positive. He will stop just at the point at which that increment ceases to be positive and begins to be negative. That is the required position of *maximum*. A rise of price above that point is attended with a fall in *gross receipts*. For, by hypothesis, the price of rise is attended with a fall in net receipts ; and net receipts equal gross receipts *minus* total cost ; and total cost decreases with the rise of price, since total cost diminishes with the diminution of the quantity supplied, and that quantity diminishes with the rise of price. If, then, gross receipts minus total cost diminishes while the subtrahend total cost diminishes, much more must gross receipts diminish.

After the tax, the quantity which the monopolist seeks to maximise is the net profits in the same sense as before (that is, gross receipts minus total cost) *minus* the amount of the tax, a certain percentage of gross receipts. This quantity will not be a maximum at the point before determined. For if the price be raised above that point, the increment of the quantity to be maximised (net profits *minus* tax) will be 0 minus increment of the amount abstracted by the tax. But the increment of the amount abstracted is negative, since when the price is raised the gross receipts are diminished (as shown in the last paragraph), and therefore the tax which is a fixed percentage of the gross returns is diminished. It will be the interest then of the monopolist to raise the price beyond the old maximum point up to a new limit ; at which the loss in respect of net profits (gross receipts *minus* total cost, which diminishes as the price is raised above the old maximum point) is just compensated by the gain in respect of the diminution of the tax. The new price therefore will be higher than the old.

A scruple may be felt whether, as the price is raised above the old maximum point the loss will overtake the gain, as the reasoning requires. The answer is that the loss (attending the increase of price above the old maximum point) is proportional to the *square* at the increment of the price, while the gain is simply proportional, it being supposed that the tax is small (*cp.* above, p. 74). Whence in general there is a determinate value for the increase of the new price above the old, such that the gain of the monopolist—the net receipts *minus* the tax—should be a maximum.

The mathematical reader will not expect the accuracy of a purist in this popular version ; the general reader will perhaps be disappointed in his expectation of simplicity. I don't know that much has been effected by this cumbrous simplification, except to show the great superiority of the genuine mathematical method.

Cournot's reasoning may be extended to any (small) marginal tax, provided that the aggregate tax increases with the amount supplied.[1]

Throughout all the cases which have so far been considered, there prevails what may be called the general rule, both for competition and monopoly, that both parties suffer more or less from a tax. It remains to point out that in monopoly, as in competition, there are exceptions to this rule. The monopolist, indeed, always suffers, but his customers may be benefited in certain cases.

There is first a peculiar tax in kind noticed by Cournot with respect to monopoly, and described in our former article with respect to competition : " the abstraction of a certain portion of the exports in kind, to be disposed of in a manner not affecting the market under consideration." [2]

The case of several commodities presents a second class of exceptions, even more paradoxical in a regime of monopoly than in that of competition. If a monopolist supply two commodities for which the demand is *correlated*, that is either " rival " or " complementary," then a tax on one commodity may benefit the consumers of both.[3] To fix the ideas, let there be a railway, like our Midland, with two classes of passengers, first class and third class. Let there be imposed a small tax of say 2 or 3 per cent. *ad valorem* on the gross receipts of the first class passenger traffic ; or there being, as in fact, a tax already, let there be

---

[1] As pointed out by Professor Marshall in the passage to which Professor Seligman refers when he says that " most writers, including Marshall (*Principles*, 460) [see p. 462, 1st ed., note, par. 1, p. 538, 3rd ed.] and Pantaleoni (*Traslazione*, 76), overlook this, and confuse a tax on gross receipts with a tax on sales or amount produced."

If the views, here stated summarily, and more explicitly in my article on " The Pure Theory of Monopoly " (*Giornale degli Economisti*, 1897), are correct, there is not the slightest confusion or mistake to be attributed to either of the authors thus disparagingly referred to by Professor Seligman. It is to be regretted that his intellectual sympathy is not always proportioned to his learning.

[2] Above, p. 72. This kind of tax is presupposed in Colonel Barone's theorem respecting a contribution proportional to the quantity; forming the fourth theorem of his " Teoria Matematica dell' Imposta " (*Giornale degli Economisti*, March 1894), p. 207.

[3] In the case of *rival* demand, the theorem makes no postulate about the cost of production. Either the law of increasing or decreasing (marginal) cost may prevail. There may even be no cost, two " mineral springs " controlled by a monopolist (*cp.* Cournot and Marshall) supplying without human effort two waters which may, to some extent, act as substitutes for each other. Or the (total) cost may be constant, not changing with that change in the amounts produced which is consequent on the tax; as it is allowable, though not necessary, to suppose in our example of first and third class accommodation. In the case of *complementary* demand, it must be postulated that production is *correlated* in a certain manner.

superimposed a small additional tax; I say the consequence of the new tax on first-class tickets may be to benefit passengers by lowering the fares of both kinds, both the third class and also the first class.

A mathematical demonstration of this theorem has been offered elsewhere.[1] The reader who has seen how difficult it is to state in ordinary language the proof of the simple proposition that a tax on a monopolised article tends to raise its price (above p. 91, note), will not expect here a full statement of the more complicated argument relating to two commodities. He may be put on the track of the investigation by the following hints.

Let x and y be respectively the first and third class fares (per mile or other unit) before the tax. After the tax let us suppose the directorate of the railway to alter the fares one at a time; and first the first-class fares.[2] By the theory above stated, the first-class fares will be raised in consequence of the tax (the third class being for the time fixed), say to x_1. There will result a diversion from first-class traffic, a rise in the demand for third-class accommodation. There might be expected then a rise of third-class fares in sympathy with the rise in the price of the rival accommodation; for when the demand for an article is raised it is probable[3] that its price will rise, ceteris paribus. But other things are not the same here. For, while the purchasers are now disposed to give more for third-class accommodation, the sellers are more ready to offer third-class accommodation now that it has an advantage over the first-class in not being taxed. Thus the change in the third-class fare will be the resultant of two tendencies, one making for a rise, the other for a fall. There is nothing to show that the latter tendency may not preponderate. Accordingly, the new y, say y_1, may be less than the old one. This low third-class fare will tend—by the sort of sympathy between the prices of substitutes which has just been noticed—to drag down the first-class fare, when we come to the third step, which consists in determining the first-class fare, x_2, which is most profitable to the monopolist, the third-class fare being fixed at y_1.

[1] See *Giornale degli Economisti*, 1887, Vol. I. p. 131 (E). In that article I give an explicit example of a possible curve, or rather numerical law, of demand for first and third class accommodation, such that if a tax of 2 or 3 per cent. is put on first-class tickets, it will be the interest of the management to lower *both* fares.

[2] Of course I do not suppose so delicate an adjustment—such a frictionless movement towards the position of maximum profit—to be realised in the concrete management of an English railway. But I think that it may be of scientific interest to establish the theoretic possibility of the paradox enounced in the text.

[3] Though in a regime of monopoly, not necessary. See Index, s.v. *Paradox*.

It is probable then that x_2 will be less than x_1. And there is nothing to show that it may not possibly be less even than x. There is nothing to show that the series of subsequent steps will not converge to a system of two fares each of which is lower than the original one.[1]

The preceding theorem illustrates a general characteristic of monopoly, that the laws of incidence relating to that regime resemble, but are less exact than, those relating to a regime of competition.[2] To take another example from the case of

[1] An acute friend has objected : If it is advantageous to the monopolist to lower prices after the imposition of the tax, why is it not before ? I reply : Because the conditions of maximum profit are altered by the tax. Let x be the price of first-class accommodation, and y that of third-class accommodation, before the tax; and let the corresponding quantities demanded be D_1 and D_2. After the tax, let x' and y' be the prices, D'_1 and D'_2 the corresponding quantities. Then the profit of the monopolist is D_1x+D_2y before the tax, after the tax $\frac{19}{20}D'_1x'+D'_2y'$; if, to fix the ideas, we suppose the tax to be 5 per cent. $ad\ valorem$ (on the proceeds of first-class tickets), and for simplicity we abstract expenses of production (supposed constant). There is no inconsistency in supposing that it is neither the interest of the monopolist to change the fares from x and y to x' and y' before the tax, nor from x' and y' to x and y after the tax; x being greater than x', and y than y'. It is necessary only that D_1x+D_2y should be greater than $D'_1x'+D'_2y'$, and also $\frac{19}{20}D'_1x'+D'_2y'$ greater than $\frac{19}{20}D_1x+D_2y$; or that we should have at the same time (D'_2y-D_2y) less than $(D_1x-D'_1x')$, and (D'_2y-D_2y) greater than $\frac{19}{20}(D_1x-D'_1x')$. It is not surprising that of two quantities which are known not to be widely different (the tax being small), one should be greater than nineteen-twentieths, and less than the whole, of the other, provided that the quantities are $positive$. Now it is probable that $D_1x-D'_1x'$ is positive, if x is greater than x_1', as D_1 is probably greater than D_1' (the monopolist reducing his offer of the taxed commodity). Nor is it improbable that $D'_2y'-D_2y$ should be positive; nor inconsistent with the supposition that y' is less than y.

The objector may still insist : If Dx is greater than $D'x'$, why not raise x' to x, leaving y' what it is ? To which I reply that the proceeds of the first-class traffic will no longer be Dx in that case, but $x \times$ first-class accommodation demanded at the prices x (first-class) and y' (third class), say $x \times \Delta$. Now Δ may fall off so rapidly, as the first-class fare is raised from x' to x, owing to the counter attractions of the third class (at the price y') that the monopolist will lose more by the decrease in the demand for first class than he gains by that increased demand for the third class which he at the same time causes.

[2] This greater latitude is explained by the circumstance that in monopoly, unlike competition, the producer [or, $mutatis\ mutandis$, the monopolist buyer] must take account of the change in demand price caused by variation in the amount of product which he may offer ($cp.$ Marshall, $Principle\ of\ Economics$, Part II. p. 802, 3rd ed.). If β be that amount and p the price ($ibid.$), the marginal cost is equated in competition to $p\Delta\beta$, but in monopoly $p\Delta\beta + \beta\Delta p$. Accordingly, in determining the variation in the position of equilibrium due to a (small) tax ($cp.$ Cournot, $Principes\ Mathématiques$, ch. vi.), whereas in competition the highest order of differential (of p with respect to β, taking β as the independent variable) which we need take account of, is of the form $\dfrac{dp}{d\beta}$, in monopoly we have also to take account of differentials of the form $\dfrac{d_2p}{d\beta^2}$. The sign of the former is given by the law of diminishing utility. But the sign of the latter is not usually a $datum$.

correlation. We have seen that when production only is correlated, " it being supposed that the demand for one commodity is independent of the demand for the other," in a regime of competition (1) a tax upon two rival products will raise the price of the taxed one, and lower the price of the untaxed one; (2) a tax on one of two complementary products will raise the price of both.[1]

Now let the correlated production be in the hands of a monopolist, the demands as before being uncorrelated. Then (1), as before, a tax upon one of two rival products will raise the price of the taxed one; but it will not, as before, necessarily—it will only probably—lower the price of the untaxed one. Also (2) as before, a tax on one of two complementary products will certainly raise the price of the taxed one, but will only probably raise the price of the untaxed one.

For example in a regime of monopoly it is probable, though not so certain as in a regime of competition, that a tax on malt would tend to lower the price of wheat in a country dependent on a limited area for its supply of both products; assuming that the production was not (otherwise) correlated. Contrariwise if the products are *complementary* in respect of the rotation of crops, as the Malt Tax Committee of 1862 suppose. " The effect of the malt tax," they say, " is to interfere with the due rotation of crops," [2] and therefore presumably to cause wheat to be grown in more unfavourable conditions, at a higher price.

Some peculiar cases of rival production are constituted by the property that in monopoly identical objects may be sold at different prices : for instance seats for men or women at a theatre. If instead of the theatre tax which is now levied in Italy there were imposed a tax on men's tickets only, the ladies would be likely to gain not only in exemption from the tax, but also in having less to pay for their tickets. That is supposing the demand for one kind of ticket to be independent of the demand for the other kind. *A fortiori* if, as it is natural to suppose, the demands are *complementary.*[3] For it is probable in monopoly, as it is normally true in competition, that " a tax on one of two complementary commodities [*i. e.* " for which the demand is correlated "] will

---

[1] Above, p. 73, par. 2, where, by a misprint, or *lapsus plumæ*, the predicates of two propositions were transposed in the original version.

[2] Parly. Papers, 1868, 420. Cp. *Evidence*, 1867 : Q. 2616, 2952, 3023, 3305.

[3] The young man who treats his lady friends to tickets, and the paterfamilias who provides for mixed parties, would be disposed *ceteris paribus* to give more for men's tickets if ladies' tickets were lowered, or more for ladies' tickets if men's tickets were lowered.

raise the price of the taxed one, and lower the price of the one which is not taxed." [1]

Following an order similar to that of the corresponding section on competition, we shall now leave correlation out of sight, and go on to consider the general case in which a monopolist deals with two or more competitive groups. For example, we might imagine one of our islands A, B, C,[2] to be now held by a monopolist. As before, we shall find that it is not indifferent whether a certain tax is levied on transactions between A and B, or on transactions between B and C. If, as before, we suppose the materials supplied by C to be constant in quantity and independent of human effort, we have now three cases, according as A (the consumers), B (the manufacturers), C (the landlords) form a monopoly. In the first case a tax on the product will prejudice both parties, not only in general as in competition, but always—correlation of supply or demand not being now supposed. For the circumstance which forms an exception in competition, the inelasticity of the consumer's [3] demand, cannot occur in monopoly.[4] In the second case a tax on the goods produced by the monopolist B will not prejudice C; for the monopolist will have already done his worst.[5] In the third case a tax on the product will, on the general supposition that the demand of the consumers is not perfectly inelastic, prejudice the landlord in general in monopoly as in competition; but not in monopoly always. For, though in consequence of the tax the demand on the part of the (competitive) producers in B for the (monopolised) article supplied by C falls, yet it does not follow that the price of C will fall. For it is one of the irregularities of monopoly as compared with competition that a rise [or fall] in the demand for a monopolised article is not necessarily, but only probably, attended with a rise [or fall] in its price.[6]

---

[1] Above, p. 73.   [2] Above, p. 75.   [3] Above, loc. cit.

[4] This may be elegantly exhibited by the curves which Messrs. Auspitz and Lieben have employed to illustrate the case in which the monopolist is a sole buyer.   [5] See E, Vol. I., p. 113.

[6] Suppose that the demand for the monopolised commodity increases in the sense that the average consumer " will buy more of it than he would before at the same price, and that he will buy as much of it as before at a higher price " (Principles of Economics, Book III. chap. iii. § 4, 3rd ed.). Then the demand-curve will e shifted outwards, as in Professor Marshall's figures 26, 27, 28. The Monopoly revenue curve (ibid.) will accordingly be modified. The new q_3 will be on a constant revenue curve (ibid.), which is further " out," or away from the axis than the corresponding old curve. But there is nothing to prove that the new Lq_1 is greater than the old one; the displacement of the demand curve may be such that—whatever the shape of the " supply-curve "—the new Lq_1 is less than the old one.

This survey of marginal taxes of monopolised articles may conclude with the reflection that the consequence of such taxes appear to be in general more unpredictable in monopoly than in competition.

a_1 B C d. That taxation upon the profits of a monopolist cannot be shifted is universally acknowledged. It may be observed that this is true not only as stated in the books of a capitation tax consisting of a lump sum, and an *ad valorem* tax directly proportionate to profits, but also of a *progressive* tax on profits (the proportional contribution increasing with the amount).[1] Of course the alteration of the monopolist's revenue may produce, as in the case of competition,[2] an indirect result on the margins of work and saving.

a_1 B c. To attribute mobility to monopoly may appear a contradiction in terms. The designation may, however, be appropriate to a certain mixed case intermediate between monopoly and competition when there is present mobility of labour and capital, but not the other characteristic of perfect competition, unique price determined by higgling of the market.

Crossing Mont Blanc from Italy into France, at a little mountain inn which is perched high above Chamonix I had some refreshment in the charge for which one item was a franc for a slice of bread. I don't suppose that this franc had any exact correspondence with the marginal efforts and sacrifices requisite to produce bread and carry it up to that height. It might have been so if several of the Chamonix bakers had erected each a shop or booth on the rock and competed with each other. Supposing this to be impracticable under the circumstances, it might still be open to any citizens of Chamonix to start a rival *auberge*, if it appeared that the proprietor of the existing one was making more than ordinary profits (account being taken of all the hardships incident to the business). In such a case we have " industrial " without " commercial " competition. The case is perhaps

---

The rationale of this uncertainty, as well as others which have been noticed, is to be found in the same " dominant fact in the theory of Monopoly " (above, p. 94, note). In competition we are concerned only with the rise in the amount demanded at each price, the *variation* of Cournot's function $F(p)$, say $\delta F(p)$. If this is positive, the price must rise, the law of decreasing returns prevailing. In monopoly we have also to look to the sign of $\dfrac{d}{dp} \delta F(p)$, which is not usually given.

[1] See article in *Giornale degli Economisti* (E.)

[2] Above, p. 76. The effect of such a tax on the margin of production is exhibited by Colonel Barone in the second theorem of " Teoria Matematica dell' Imposta " (*Giornale degli Economisti*), 1894.

common where there is a large establishment and a comparatively small number of customers.

As Professor Walras has well observed, these conditions are realised much more often than is supposed—

" tel fabricant de chocolat, qui vend son chocolat 3 francs la livre quand il le débite sous le nom modeste de ' chocolat superfin' enveloppé simplement de papier glacé le vendra 4 francs la livre à la condition de le parfumer à la vanille et de le débiter sous le nom de ' chocolat des princes,' enveloppé de papier doré. Il en est de même des différentes places d'un théâtre, dont les différents prix ne sont nullement proportionels au frais de production de ces places." [1]

In such cases the incidence of taxation will partly obey the law of monopoly and partly that of competition. For marginal taxes not large enough to overcome the friction which resists mobility, it should seem that the law is rather that of monopoly than of commercial competition, our a B C D rather than our A B C D. One difference would be that, where the demand of the consumer is very urgent, the tax would fall on the producer to a greater extent than is to be expected in a regime of perfect competition.[2] In general the consequences of the tax become more unpredictable in virtue of the property under consideration ; a difference which is perhaps aggravated by the circumstance that the case is apt to be one of joint production.

a_1 b. The law of " increasing returns " does not constitute such an important subdivision of monopoly as of competition. There is no difficulty in the case of monopoly in understanding how production should stop short in the full career of the law of increasing returns, the diminution of the cost being more than counterbalanced by the falling off of demand.[3] The principal difference between the case of increasing and decreasing cost, is, I

---

[1] *Économie Politique Pure*, p. 416; *cp.* Schönberg's *Handbuch ;* article by F. Neumann, especially ii. 3 ; Acworth, *Railways and Traders*, ch. iv. So Hermann (*Untersuchungen*, ch. vi. p. 419, ed. 1870) of a shopkeeper who uses smuggled wares along with wares which have paid duty : " Stellen sich die preise höher als die schmuggelpreise tiefer als die preise der verzollten waare." It is not easy to see how this can be, unless the shopkeeper enjoys some of the properties of a monopolist. Professor Marshall points out that the " dominant fact in the theory of monopolies " (*cp.* above, p. 94) " is dominant also in the case of any producer who has a limited trade connection which he cannot quickly enlarge."

[2] Above, p. 90, note 3.

[3] Regarding the action of increasing returns as essentially different in the case of monopoly and competition, I cannot quite accept Professor Seligman's statement with respect to a (specific) tax on a monopolised article. " Of course the same qualifications are to be introduced as before [in a regime of competition] according as the monopoly industry obeys the law of the constant diminishing or increasing returns " (*Shifting and Incidence*, p. 161). Not " of course," surely.

think, that the price is apt to be raised—will be raised *ceteris paribus*—to a greater extent in the case of decreasing than in that of increasing cost.[1]

a_2. The remaining branch is the shortest, yet not perhaps the least fruitful with regard to general economic theory, which rather than finance is here cultivated. Where two or more monopolists take part in a system of bargains there are no laws of incidence, for there are none of value. It has long been recognised that the bargain between two monopolists [2] is indeterminate; it is now submitted that a system of bargains in which two or more monopolists deal, not directly with each other, but with one or more competitive groups, is also indeterminate. Suppose, for instance, a miller dealing with two monopolists, one the owner of the ground, the other of the water-power—as in an example put by Professor Marshall,[3] the only writer, so far as I know, who has given a hint of this theory. Let there be a number of such millers in competition with each other; and let the ground rent and the water rent be subject to revision from time to time, *e. g.* every year. The monopolists might go on for ever shifting the rents, making moves against each other like two chess-players when on each side there survives only the king with one or two inferior pieces.

The theorem may have some bearing on a system which is regarded by some as the ideal of the economic future, that each industry should be consolidated into a " Trust " or combination. Such a system would be characterised by instability, by fluctuations of prices such as now occur in railway wars, but more prolonged; for in so far as the combatants, like the two landlords in the example given, are not direct competitors, the combat seems less likely to be terminated by either the ruin of one party or the amalgamation of the two. That consummation may be more apt to occur when the two monopolists supply, not complementary articles, like land and water-power, but rival commodities. But even in this case the proposition that value is between

[1] I am compelled to differ from Professor Graziani (*Istituzioni delle Finanze*, p. 338) on this point. As already pointed out (above, p. 90) the imposition of a tax u per unit of commodity is in general of the form $u \times A \div (2A + B + C)$; where A is always negative, B is negative or positive according as the law of decreasing or increasing returns prevails; nothing is known of the sign of C—it represents the element of chance in the theory of monopoly (Index, *A priori probabilities*). Accordingly, *ceteris paribus*, A and C being constant, the increase of price is *greater* when the law of increasing returns prevails.

[2] Sidgwick, *Political Economy*, Book II., ch. x., § 3; Jevons, *State in Relation to Labour*, p. 154; Böhm-Bawerk, *Positive Theory of Capital*, Book IV. ch. ii.; cp. *Mathematical Psychics*, pp. 21 *et seq.*, by the present writer.

[3] *Principles of Economics*, Book V. ch. x.

certain limits—over a certain range of price—indeterminate may
well be of considerable theoretical importance.[1]

For further discussion of this and other subjects touched upon
here, I once more refer to the contemporary article on the Pure
Theory of Monopoly in the *Giornale degli Economisti*.

The character of pure theory, deduction from received first
principles, attaches not only to the incidence of taxes, which has
been considered in the preceding paragraphs, but also—in a minor
degree, doubtless—to the distribution of the fiscal burden among
the taxpayers, which is to be considered in what follows.
There is at least one aspect of this subject which may present
sufficient length of reasoning and strength of premises to deserve
the title " pure." The view thus distinguished is that according
to which the sacrifice felt by the taxpayer is a dominant factor
in the apportionment of the fiscal burden, the hedonistic, or in
a special sense utilitarian, principle of taxation, as it may be
called. Some other principle may be held—for instance, that
of " ability," or " faculty," in a more objective sense,[2] but can
hardly be held to belong to the domain of pure theory.

[1] The case of wayleaves on mines to which Professor Marshall directs attention
(*loc. cit.*) may illustrate the general principle, or rather absence of principle. It
appears from evidence given before the Commission on Mining Royalties that it
is not always possible to make the negotiation for royalty and wayleave concurrent
(Q. 590). The lessee who, having sunk much capital on a mine, wants to take
up an adjoining mine " deals with a halter round his neck " (Q. 561); he has been
" got into a cleft stick " (Q. 673; *cp.* Q. 5690). There is also much evidence
that " the royalty is reduced by the rate of wayleave paid " (Q. 13,151). " A
lower royalty is taken than would be if not subject to wayleave " (Q. 1933; *cp.*
Q. 13,218, 11,306, 13,151, 13,749, etc.). Let us imagine these transactions to be
effected successively, as thus : The first step is to take a lease of a coal-field for
a certain period. The second step is to take a wayleave or some other subsidiary
privilege. The terms exacted for this privilege being onerous, the third step
would be on a revision of the first lease to lower the rent for the coal-field. The
fourth step, it may be supposed, would be on a revision of the other lease to still
further raise the wayleave. But this result is not certain, or not certain to
continue as the series of steps is prolonged. It may become the interest of the
owner of the subsidiary privilege to lower his terms in order to encourage the
industry, wayleave being a charge of so much per ton. The principal landlord
may retort by raising his terms; and the see-saw may go on *ad infinitum*. The
lessee would not necessarily be worse off than if he had to deal (for both coal-
field and subsidiary privileges) with a single monopolist—except so far as the
instability of value is harassing to industry.

Of course I do not suppose such a prolonged series of steps as I have described
to occur in the concrete. But I think it is a legitimate fiction in order to bring out
the contrast that, whereas in a regime of competition a series thus continued
theoretically tends to a definite position of equilibrium (as illustrated *e. g.* by
Professor Walras in his *Économie Politique Pure*), in a regime of monopoly there
does not exist, even theoretically, a determinate position of equilibrium.

[2] These terms are often applied to the principle of subjective sacrifice. *Cp.*
Cohen-Stuart, *Bijdrage tot de Theorie der Progressieve inkomstenbelastung*, ch. i

The purest, as being the most deductive form of utilitarianism is that from which Bentham reasoned down to equality.[1] There are those who regard this form as also purest, in that its first principle is the most apt to be universally accepted. That principle proposes as the end of action, or criterion of conduct, the greatest sum-total of happiness; the intensification of pleasure, its prolongation and distribution among increased numbers being approved only when they conduce to that end. The conception has been formulated mathematically by the present writer.[2] In extending the summation of pleasure, according to the formula, over all time and all sentience, it is to be considered that, just as egoism is never so perfect but that distance in time renders pleasure less attractive, so utilitarianism is never so perfect but that persons whose interests are widely separate will not each " count for one " to the other.[3]

This remark may seem particularly appropriate to the adoption of utilitarianism as the rule of political action. The average citizen cannot be expected to care much for the interests of the foreigner, perhaps not very much for the interests of fellow-citizens outside his own class, nor at all for a remote posterity.

The proof of utilitarianism as the principle of political action has been variously conceived. The same speculative height is reached by different paths.[4] There is an approach on the economic side which it may be allowable to point out here. Let it be granted that there is a certain analogy between political and industrial co-operation or concerted action—an analogy admitted by many high authorities with respect to the fiscal action of the State.[5] We must not regard as an essential feature of the

---

The connection between the two meanings is very happily explained by Professor Seligman, *Progressive Taxation*, p. 191. Bentham inveighs with characteristic vehemence against the ambiguity of the term " faculties " in the French Revolutionary Declaration of Rights (*Works*, Vol. II. p. 518).

[1] " Propositions of Pathology upon which the Advantage of Equality is Founded," *Principles of the Civil Code*, Part I. ch. vi. (*Works*, Vol. I. p. 304); *Constitutional Code*, Book I. ch. iii. sec. v. (*Works*, Vol. IX. pp. 14–18) *et passim*. J. S. Mill's doctrine of equality is not so clear (*Utilitarianism*, p. 93). Fitzjames Stephen complains of its obscurity with some reason (*Liberty, Equality, and Fraternity*, ch. v.).

[2] *Mathematical Psychics*, p. 57 *et seq.* On the pleonastic words " of the greatest number " commonly suffixed to " greatest-happiness," see *ibid.* p. 117, and *cp.* some good remarks by Professor Montague at p. 34, of his preface to Bentham's *Fragment of Government*.

[3] *Ibid.*, Appendix IV., " On Imperfect Egoism."

[4] There are some valuable reflections on Bentham's proof, or want of proof, in Professor Sidgwick's article on Bentham in the *Fortnightly Review* for 1877, Vol. XXI. p. 647.

[5] *E. g.* the well-conceived analogy between the State in its fiscal capacity and a

analogy the circumstance that in economic bargains there generally prevails a rate of exchange corresponding to final utility. That circumstance is brought about by competition, which does not exist in the case of the political contract. It is therefore improper, with Lord Auckland, to call income-tax " a fair price for protection," [1] to ask with Thiers, " What is society if not a stock company in which every one has more or fewer shares ? " [2] This is the fundamental fallacy of the " *quid pro quo* principle " or " benefit theory," which is justly rejected by J. S. Mill,[3] Professor Seligman, and other high authorities. The " economic " theory of taxation propounded by Professor Sax, his " conception of tax as a value-phenomenon," [4] appears open to a similar objection. The truer analogy is with those economic bargains which are not governed by competition; for instance, an agreement between an employer or an association of employers and a trade union, or, as in the case of a " boundary " dispute, two trade unions. Is there any general principle governing such agreements ?

The present writer has suggested, as the principle apt to be adopted by two [or, *mutatis mutandis*, a few] self-interested parties contracting in the absence of competition, the greatest-happiness principle, slightly modified : that arrangement to be made which conduces to the greatest sum-total welfare of both parties, subject to the condition that neither should lose by the contract.[5] Of course each party would rather have his own way completely. But the action of self-interest being suspended by mutual opposition, the more delicate force of amity which even in economic men is not entirely wanting,[6] may become felt. Moreover, each party may reflect that, in the long run of various cases, the maximum sum-total utility corresponds to the maximum individual utility. He cannot expect in the long run to obtain the larger share of the total welfare. But of all principles of distribution which would afford him now a greater, now a smaller

co-operative institution in Professor De Viti's *Carattere Teoricetico dell' Economia Finanzieria*, p. 103, *et seq.* *Cp.* Professor Graziani, *Istituzioni*, lib. 3, cap. 4, and authorities there cited.

[1] Quoted by Professor Seligman, *Progressive Taxation*, p. 96, in which context many similar references will be found.   [2] *Ibid.*

[3] *Political Economy*, Book V. ch. ii. § 2, par. 2.

[4] " Die Progressivsteuer," p. 87 *et seq.*, in the Austrian *Zeitschrift für Volkswirtschaft*, Vol. I. Part I.   Cp. *Grundlegung, passim.*

[5] *Mathematical Psychics*, p. 53.

[6] Much evidence was given before the Labour Commission as to the beneficial effects of " closer acquaintanceship between the parties." (Group A, Q. 607. *Cp.* Q. 2,019, 15,072–3, etc.).

proportion of the sum-total utility obtainable on each occasion, the principle that the collective utility should be on each occasion a maximum is most likely to afford the greatest utility in the long run to him individually.[1] Thus the recommendation of utilitarianism to self-interested parties would not be—as Bentham's teaching has been said to be—like making ropes out of sand.[2] *A fortiori*, the higher the degree of public spirit which is ascribed to the parties.

On these or other grounds assuming the greatest-happiness principle to be the test of governmental action, at least with respect to taxation, let us proceed to apply the principle. The primary problem is to determine the distribution of those taxes which are applied to common purposes, the benefits whereof cannot be allocated to particular classes of citizens. The condition that the total net utility procured by taxation should be a maximum then reduces to the condition that the total disutility should be a minimum.[3] From the condition that the total disutility should be a minimum, it follows in general that the marginal disutility incurred by each taxpayer should be the same. But if the inequality of fortunes is considerable with respect to the specified amount of taxation, there may not be taxation enough to go round, so to speak. The solution of the problem is that the higher incomes should be cut down to a certain level. At the same time the fact that the general marginal condition is not perfectly satisfied, suggests the solution of a wider, a *secondary* problem, namely, to determine the distribution of taxation, not being limited to that amount of which the benefit is indiscriminate. The solution of this problem in the abstract is that the richer should be taxed for the benefit of the poorer up to the point at which complete equality of fortunes is attained

[1] Thus it would appear reasonable that a foreman who is insolent to the workpeople, and not particularly serviceable to the employer, should be dismissed, if thereby the employer's profits are not sensibly diminished, while the workpeople gain considerably in freedom from annoyance; or, again, that workmen should consent, on terms not extravagant, to do a little extra work on an emergency, if thereby the employer is saved from considerable loss. But to illustrate fully the applicability of the principle would be out of place in this article.

[2] *Cp.* Professor Sidgwick in *Fortnightly Review, loc. cit.*

[3] The authority of Bentham may be cited in favour of this theory of taxation :—

" It is therefore necessary that those who create wealth by their labour should give up a portion of it to supply the wants of the guardians of the State. . . .

" All government is only a tissue of sacrifices. The best government is that in which the value of those sacrifices is reduced to the smallest amount (*Principles f the Civil Code*, Part I. ch. xiii., *Works*, Vol. I. p. 13, ed. 1859).

" To take care that this pain of constraint and privation be reduced to the lowest term " (*View of a Complete Code of Laws*, ch. xxix., *Works*, Vol. III. p. 204).

The *acme* of socialism is thus for a moment sighted; but it is immediately clouded over by doubts and reservations.

In this misty and precipitous region let us take Professor Sidgwick as our chief guide. He best has contemplated the crowning height of the utilitarian first principle, from which the steps of a sublime deduction lead to the high tableland of equality; [1] but he also discerns the enormous interposing chasms which deter practical wisdom from moving directly towards that ideal.

" In the first place it is conceivable that a greater equality in the distribution of produce would lead ultimately to a reduction in the total amount to be distributed in consequence of a general preference of leisure to the results of labour on the part of the classes whose shares of produce had increased." [2]

There is also the danger—

" That the increase through equalisation of the incomes of the poorer classes will cause the population to increase at a more rapid rate than at present; so that ultimately the increment of an average worker's share will be partly spent in supporting a larger number of children, and partly reduced through the decrease in the efficiency of the more crowded labour." [3]

It is remarkable that Mill should have apprehended the dangers of deficient production and excessive population less than the danger to liberty. The weighty sentence into which he condenses the substance of his teaching on liberty deserves to be repeated.

" It is yet to be ascertained whether the Communistic scheme would be consistent with that multiform development of human nature, those manifold unlikenesses, that diversity of tastes and talents, and variety of intellectual points of view which not only form a great part of the interest of human life, but in bringing intellects into stimulating collision and by presenting to each innumerable notions that he would not have conceived of himself, are the mainspring of mental and moral progression." [4]

Liberty is not the only one of the higher goods which is threatened by a dull equality : there is also the " function of maintaining and developing knowledge and culture," the performance of which function, as pointed out by Professor Sidgwick, has hitherto been largely due to " rich and leisured persons." [5]

[1] *Principles of Political Economy*, Book III. ch. vii. § 1.
[2] *Loc. cit.* § 2.
[3] *Ibid.*
[4] *Political Economy*, Book II. § 3.
[5] *Ibid.*

The transition is easy to another reservation, which is in some sense more intrinsic than the preceding. The Benthamic argument that equality of means tends to maximum of happiness, presupposes a certain equality of natures : but if the capacity for happiness [1] of different classes is different, the argument leads not to equal, but to unequal, distribution. The testimony of Professor Sidgwick that Bentham would probably have recognised this reservation [2] carries a double weight of authority. The possibility corroborated by so high evidence is calculated to temper the more drastic applications of utilitarianism.

The preceding reservations relate to the pursuit of socialistic equality by any methods; the following relate more particularly to the pursuit of that end by means of taxation. A progressive tax rising to such a rate that it would not be the interest of the taxpayer to increase his fortune by saving or enterprise above a certain amount,[3] while improving the distribution, would check the augmentation of the community's wealth. There is, however, to be set off the probable increase of saving among the poorer classes.[4] Especially the investment of capital in persons by way of education might be increased.[5] There would be an increase of production also so far as the proceeds of socialistic taxation are applied to render the poorer classes more efficient.[6] But against this increase in the efficiency of the poor might

---

[1] This terminology has been employed by the present writer (op. cit., p. 57; cp. pp. 64, 125) to designate differences both in the amount of means which different individuals may require in order to attain the threshold or zero-point of happiness, and in the amounts of utility which they may derive from the same additions of means above that point. Compare Professor Carver's weighty observations (American Acad. of Polit. Sci. 1895, p. 82) upon difference in wants—a term which may also refer to differences in the amount of means needed for efficiency.

[2] Professor Sidgwick says : " I do not however think that Bentham intended to deny (1) that one person may be more capable of happiness than another, or (2) that, if so, the former's happiness is more important than the latter's, as an element of general happiness." (Elements of Politics, p. 583, note 2. Cp. note 3 for a fuller statement of Professor Sidgwick's own view.)

[3] The condition which a progressive tax must fulfil in order not to have this effect, is clearly expressed by Professor Ulisse Gobbi in a recent tract to which the chaste use of mathematics lends a peculiar charm. (Sul carattere razionale dell' imposta progressiva, § 3.)

[4] Cp. Bastable, Public Finance, 2nd edition, p. 295, and, with special reference to the problem of distribution with which Trade Unionism is concerned, Professor Marshall's Economics of Industry (1879), p. 202.

[5] Cp. Marshall, Principles of Economics, sub voce, Discount of future pleasure; also Sidgwick's Principles of Political Economy, Book III. ch. ii.

[6] The exemption of a minimum is to be defended not only after Bentham (Constitutional Code, ch. xv., Works, Vol. I. p. 319) on the ground of least sacrifice, but also on the ground of greatest efficiency.

have to be set some decrease in the efficiency of the not very rich.[1]

Again, there is the general presumption against governmental action, the special danger that taxation extended beyond its proper objects will be abused. The warning comes with less weight from those who are ready to employ taxation for a collateral purpose of which they themselves approve—the correction of intemperance.

In fine, the increase of taxation is limited by evasion.

These extensive, though briefly indicated, reservations reduce the *prima facie* revolutionary dictates of pure utilitarianism to the limits of common sense. The position thus defined is much the same as Mill's.[2] " That the State should use the instrument of taxation as a means of mitigating the inequality of wealth " is not to be demanded when a " tax on industry and economy," a check to the growth of wealth, is thereby imposed.[3] But the utilitarian will be as " desirous as any one that means should be taken to diminish those inequalities " : such means as the limitation of inheritances and the taxation of unearned increments, so far as these means are free from the dangers above enumerated. A similar reconcilement between equality and security [4] is taught in an article replete with utilitarian wisdom on *The Ethical Basis of Distribution*, by Professor T. N. Carver.

" The minimum amount of repression [or check to the growth of wealth] is secured by imposing an equal sacrifice on all members of the community, but the minimum amount of sacrifice is secured by collecting the whole tax from those few incomes which have the lowest final utility. No rational writer advocates the latter plan exclusively, but many rational writers do advocate the former plan. Yet it is not beyond dispute that the former plan ought to be followed exclusively." [5]

This passage, read with the context, almost exactly expresses the thesis here maintained; except that the last sentence is asserted rather too diffidently, and the first clause much too confidently. *Minimum sacrifice*, the direct emanation of pure

---

[1] For an instance see below, p. 120.

[2] For some differences from Mill see below, p. 115.

[3] Mill, *Political Economy*, Book V. ch. ii. § 3.

[4] The reconcilement is taught by Bentham with respect to legislation in general. See the forcible chapter on " Security and equality—their opposition," with the context (*Principles of Civil Code*, Part I. ch. xi. *et passim*); *e.g.* " It is not equality itself but only a tendency towards equality, after all the others [security, subsistence, and abundance] are provided for, that is the proper object of endeavour " (*Works*, Book III. p. 294).

[5] *Annals of the American Academy*, 1895, p. 97.

utilitarianism, is the sovereign principle of taxation; it requires no doubt to be limited in practice; but query whether the requisite limitation is to be obtained from *equal sacrifice*, or any of the cognate subsidiary forms of the hedonic principle which are presently to be considered ?

Before leaving the principle of minimum sacrifice, let it be observed that, under the limitations which have been described, this principle may also be applied to justify differential taxation on the ground of differences in other respects besides size of income : for instance, difference in the permanence of the income,[1] differences in civil state,[2] number of children,[3] age,[4] and other attributes.[5]

Besides the principle of minimum sacrifice, which has been considered, there are other species of the hedonic theory of taxation. The most familiar are the principles of equal and of proportional sacrifice : that each taxpayer should sacrifice an equal amount of utility, or an equal proportion of the total utility which he derives from material resources. The former species is the commonest in England; the latter flourishes in Holland.[6] The two species might be included in a genus termed " like sacrifice."

It will be convenient to consider first the practical consequences, next the theoretical proof of these two principles.

In order to deduce conclusions from either premiss, there is required another premiss relating to the law of diminishing utility. There are some reasons for assuming—it is at least the simplest hypothesis—that utility diminishes in inverse ratio to

---

[1] It is hardly necessary to refer to Mill's magisterial discussion of this matter.

[2] An instance of taxation varying according as the taxpayer is married or not is referred to below on p. 133, note 2.

[3] All would not agree with Mill that having a large family, so far as concerns the public interest, is a thing rather to be discouraged than promoted.

[4] See the curious remarks of McCulloch on this subject (*Edinburgh Review*, 1833, vol. 57, p. 156).

[5] Dr. Robert Meyer has given a list of attributes (*Principien der gerechten Besteuerung*, p. 53). Of course it must be remembered that, as Mr. Cohen-Stuart points out, by attempting to make corrections without sufficient data we run the risk of making our result worse.

[6] The honour of clearly distinguishing these principles appears to belong to Mr. Cohen-Stuart (*Bijdrage tot de Theorie der Progressieve Inkomstenbelastung*, ch. i. § 4). He does not seem to deserve Professor Seligman's disrespectful criticisms : " Much ado about nothing " (*Political Science Quarterly*, Vol. VII. p. 337); " Cohen-Stuart takes a long time explaining this, but as we know it is nothing new, being precisely what Mill expressed in other words " (*Progressive Taxation*, p. 184; *cp.* as to Mill's formula, p. 136). It may well be doubted whether Mill entertained the notion of proportional sacrifice, or distinguished it from that of equal sacrifice. It is certain that the ideas have been confounded by other writers.

means, after the law of Bernoulli.[1] Upon this assumption the principle of equal sacrifice gives proportional taxation;[2] the principle of proportional sacrifice gives progressive taxation.[3]

But there seem to be better reasons for assuming that the utility diminishes with the increase of income at a faster rate. There is the testimony of high authorities, Montesquieu,[4] Paley,[5] J. B. Say[6] and many others cited in the learned pages of Professor Seligman. True, Mill regards the doctrine as " too disputable altogether " with regard to the higher incomes. But neither Mill nor any other considerable authority has held that the diminution is *less* than in the inverse ratio of the income. Mill's estimate being the lowest, we may take as the most probable estimate one intermediate between his and others, and assume that the utility diminishes at a rate exceeding the increase of income, if not for the highest incomes, at any rate for incomes considerably above the usually exempted minimum.

This presumption is confirmed by the observation that the property in question, the diminution of utility out of proportion to the inverse income, almost certainly holds for large differences as distinguished from differential variations; as Dr. Robert Meyer has well argued.[7] But, if such is the character of the utility-curve as to finite differences, it is probably also its character as to differential variations.[8] The observed circumstances would not be consistent with the prevalence of Bernoulli's law throughout. It must be assumed that for a considerable tract of the curve—supposed not violently discontinuous—the property in question prevails.

[1] The grounds of this provisional assumption are well stated by Professor Sax, *Die Progressivsteuer* (p. 78).

[2] As reasoned by Fauveau (*Considérations mathématiques sur l'Impôt*). It is important to observe that the proposition applies not only to taxes, which may be treated as infinitesimal, but also to integral imposts (*cp.* Cohen-Stuart, *Bijdrage*, Appendix I. p. 190).

[3] As reasoned by Cohen-Stuart, *op. cit.*

[4] *Esprit des Lois*, liv., xiii., ch. vii.

[5] *Elements of Political Knowledge*, forming Book VI. of *Moral and Political Philosophy*.

[6] *Cours*, Part VIII. ch. iv.; *Traité*, liv. iii., ch. ix. : " Si l'on voulait asseoir l'impôt de chaque famille de manière qu'il fût d'autant plus léger qu'il portât sur un revenu plus nécessaire, il faudrait qu'il diminuât non pas simplement proportionellement, mais progressivement."

[7] *Die principien der gerechten Besteuerung*, p. 333. Professor Sax's criticisms of this passage seem unnecessarily severe (*Progressivsteuer*, pp. 52–3). Professor Sax's own reflections (*ibid.*) confirm the assumption here made as to the character of the utility-curve, up to a certain point at least of the curve.

[8] The converse of this statement is proved by Cohen-Stuart in his first Appendix.

Some doubt may remain as to the extremity of the curve which corresponds to very high incomes. It has been supposed by several high and independent authorities, that ultimately the law of Bernoulli holds good. · Some of the reasons assigned are to be found in the passages cited below from eminent authors.[1] It is here submitted that the character ascribed to the extremity of the utility-curve is not sufficiently evidenced. First, as to capitalisation, regarding it as an application of income to future gratifications (whether personal or vicarious), one does not see why it should not approach satiety with a rapidity greater than that which is assigned by the Bernoullian law. It may be suspected, too, that an improper inference is drawn from the circumstance that as the income is increased by equal increments the differences between the successive increments of utility become less. But it is not with these differences that we are concerned, but with the *ratio* between successive increments of utility. And there is nothing to show that this ratio does not increase more rapidly than according to the Bernoullian law. The pleasure derived from a certain income may well increase with the income somewhat as, according to the theory of errors of observation, the probability that an error will occur within a certain distance increases with the distance.[2] Ultimately the

[1] Professor Sax, *Die Progressivsteuer*, loc. cit., p. 101 : " Durch diese Einbeziehung künftiger Bedürfnisse erfährt der Bedürfnissstand eine Erweiterung welche die grössten Dimensionen annehmen kann, sich dann aber eben auch auf Bedürfnisse von minimalen Stärkegraden erstrekt. Dieser Umstand in Verbindung mit der einleuchtenden Folgerung dass, da der Bedürfnisgrad nicht auf Null sinken kann, von einem gewissen Punkte niedriger Bedürfnissintensität an die Differenzen der durchschmittlichen Intensität auf einander folgender Bedürfnisgruppen rasch abnehmen müssen und somit das Verhältnis der umgekehrten Proportionalität der Einkommen annehmen, bedingt schliesslich die Aufhebung der Progression des Wertstandes, was folgerichtig die Progression der Steuer zum Stillstande bringt."

Professor F. J. Neumann, *Progressive Einkommen Steuer*, p. 146 : " Da in den höchsten Beträgen ein *sehr grosses* Einkommen . . . regelmässig etwas gleich entbehrlichen Genüssen oder aber der Capitalisirung dient."

Professor Treub, in a passage quoted at length by Mr. Cohen-Stuart (*op. cit.* p. 148), speaks of " het punt waarop de nuttigheidsgrad van het inkomen constant bligft."

Professor Graziani, *Giornale degli Economisti*, 1891, p. 164 : " E escluso il concetto d' un saggio [d' imposta] continuamente crescente, pochè s' è dimostrata l'impossibilita d' un continuo accrescimento nella differenza di valutazione fra ciascuna frazione successiva di richezza." Cp. *ibid.* p. 167. Professor Graziani here takes proportional sacrifice as the desideratum (*ibid.* p. 160).

[2] The marginal utility of money—the measure of the increment of welfare which corresponds to an increment of income—might quite well have some such form as the probability-curve, viz.

$$y\left(= \frac{du}{dx} \right) = A e^{-(x-a)^2}$$

additions become imperceptible, but not the less do they obey the law that a disproportionately large increment of the independent variable is required to produce the same increment of the dependent one. In fine the view here combated has no doubt derived some adventitious aid from the supposed practical necessity of adopting a proportional income-tax for very high incomes; which could only be justified by the principle of equal sacrifice upon the assumption of the Bernoullian law.

It is to be admitted, however, that the property in question has been accepted by Mr. Cohen-Stuart, who cannot be suspected of mathematical confusion, and who has expressly distinguished the theoretical and practical points of view.[1]

Here are his reasons :—

" For the millionaire—or rather . . . the *milliardaire*—the possession of his income signifies no more than a cipher, the increase of which has no longer any influence on his consumption. To see the cipher increased by 4 per cent. for instance, if it is a pleasure to a man with 10 millions [francs per annum] or one with 100 or 500 millions, would be, I should say, about the same pleasure to each. . . . As soon as all personal wants are pretty well satisfied, and, *a fortiori*, after the income has passed this limit, its increase proportionately, that is by an equal percentage, must, as it seems to me, tend to afford an equal pleasure. That the addition of the same *amount* should be as strongly desired, should produce equal pleasure, however great the income, seems to me absurd; that the same *proportion* of the income should have this effect strikes me as rational." [2]

The mathematical reader who is not convinced by Mr. Cohen-Stuart on this point will hardly defer to others.

Upon the assumption that the diminution of marginal utility with income is (throughout) in excess of Bernoulli's law, the principle of equal sacrifice and that of proportional sacrifice both give progressive taxation, the latter in a higher degree than the former.[3] Either principle, but more probably the

---

where x, the independent variable, is the amount of income, y, the dependent variable, is the marginal utility of income (the differential of u, the total utility of income); a is the minimum of existence, and A another constant. In order that the sacrifices (first supposed small) made by two individuals having incomes x_1 and x_2 should be equal, the respective contributions should be, not as $x_1 : x_2$, but as $e^{+(x_1-a)^2} : e^{+(x_2-a)^2}$. And this disproportion of contribution to income would not only be maintained, but increased, as the income is indefinitely increased. *A fortiori*, if proportional, not equal, sacrifice is aimed at. *A fortiori*, too, if the sacrifices are not small.

[1] *Op. cit.* p. 134.   [2] *Op. cit.* p. 155.
[3] *I.e.* higher for any assigned form of the utility-curve, and amount of taxation.

.latter, may (upon the assumption above made) lead to a subtrac
tion of income so great as to leave the possessor little interest
in increasing his income beyond a certain limit. The two
varieties of like sacrifice may in this respect resemble the principle
of minimum sacrifice in requiring to be limited by a regard for
other disutilities beside the constraint and privation occasioned
to the taxpayer.[1]

[1] The relation between the different modes of the sacrifice theory might thus be
exhibited diagrammatically. Let Y measured along the axis OY represent size of
income; and construct the curve II' such that the co-ordinate to any assigned Y
represents the number of incomes smaller than Y. Thus the strip of area $Y\Delta X$

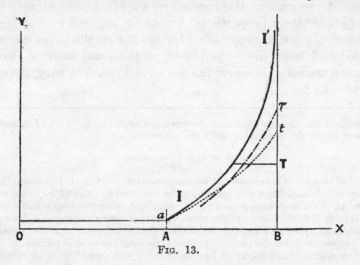

FIG. 13.

represents the portion of the national income which consists of incomes of the
size Y. The curve II' is probably shaped as in the figure; in conformity to
Professor Pareto's beautiful theory of income-curves (" Cours d'Économie politique pure : Courbe des révenus." *Cp.* ECONOMIC JOURNAL, Vol. VI. p. 666) II'
may be regarded as asymptotic to—or at least terminating on—a perpendicular
through B, where OB is the total number of incomes; Aa may be taken as a
minimum exempted from taxation.

Then to apply the principle of minimum sacrifice, find a point, T, on the
ordinate through B, such that the area intercepted by that ordinate, the horizontal
through T and the curve II' should represent a portion of the national income
equal to the required amount of taxation. To apply the principle of proportional
taxation, find t on the same ordinate such that the required amount of taxation
may be equal to the amount represented by the area intercepted between that
ordinate, the curve II', and a curve at which the ordinate η at every point fulfils
the condition

$$(y - \eta) \times \frac{du}{dy} \div u = \text{constant};$$

where u is the total amount of utility derived (on an average) from the income y.
This curve is represented by the continuously dotted curve line in the figure (upon
a certain supposition as to the minimum of exemption, *cp.* Cohen-Stuart, *op. cit.*,
on the " Bestaans-minimum "). To apply the principle of equal sacrifice, find τ,
on the same ordinate, such that the required amount of taxation may be

The method of applying the limitation might well be, for all the forms of the sacrifice theory, the use of such a scale of progression as would be given by the principle of proportional taxation *upon the supposition* that the extreme tract of the utility-curve was such as it has been conceived by Mr. Cohen-Stuart and others. Practical reasons, not deductions from any form of the first principle, would thus lead to a " degressive progression " culminating in a simply proportionate tax of the higher incomes, such as in fact seems to be coming into vogue.[1] Then those who hold the principle of proportional sacrifice might avail themselves of the curious theorem given by Mr. Cohen-Stuart, that an approximately proportional tax being imposed on the higher incomes, the law of progression for the tax on the lower incomes, as deduced from the principle of proportional sacrifice, would be much the same, however the law of utility might vary, between wide limits.[2]

---

represented by the area contained between the ordinate, the curve II', and the curve of which the ordinate η fulfils the condition

$$(y - \eta) \times \frac{du}{dy} = \text{const.}$$

A part of this curve is represented by the discontinuously dotted (broken) line in the figure. If completed this curve may be expected to meet II' asymptotically below A. But, doubtless, regard to efficiency and other practical considerations may lead to the deformation of the curve, so as to join on at an earlier point to II'.

It will be apparent from this illustration that equal sacrifice is less socialistic than proportional sacrifice, and proportional sacrifice less so than minimum. But in what degree either mode of like sacrifice is less socialistic than minimum sacrifice, we have no data, it is submitted, for determining. It is quite possible that the curve through τ, and, *a fortiori*, the curve through t, should prescribe a taxation of the higher incomes, which in the interests of production it would be fatal to carry out. Like sacrifice can no more, or not much more, than minimum sacrifice be trusted to act without checks. What, then, is the ground for preferring like sacrifice ?

[1] Thus Dr. Westerdijk, in his very able article on the progressive income-tax in the Dutch communes in *De Economist* for March 1897, holds that " all reasonable supporters of progression " are at one in approving of Mr. Treub's principle which in practice is the same as Mr. Cohen-Stuart's, though not grounded on the same reasons. The formula which is given by Professor Ulisse Gobbi in his *Carattere razionale dell Imposta Progressiva* (1897) deserves consideration not only on account of its elegance, but also because it is based on an assumption which is frankly arbitrary, not identified with the sacrifice theory. The assumption is that there ought to be an inverse relation between the portion of tax incident on each successive increment of income and the importance of the wants provided for by that increment. Whence for extremely large incomes, as the difference in the importance of the wants provided by successive increments of income becomes indefinitely small, the difference between the portion of tax charged to each increment of income should become indefinitely small; or the tax should become more and more nearly proportional.

[2] Professor Sax's criticism of this arrangement as illogical is not justified by the logic of mathematical science. " From unproved premisses can never follow a

The distinction between like sacrifice and minimum sacrifice is not more serious when the principles are applied to differences in other respects besides amount of income (*cp.* above, p. 556). For example, whether is it easier to say that incomes which are not equally permanent should not be taxed equally, because the sacrifices would not be equal to each other, as Mill has it,[1] or because their total would not be a minimum, as here proposed? So the doctrine of minimum sacrifice, as well as that of proportional sacrifice, may use the proposition affirmed by Mr. Cohen-Stuart, that for the purposes of taxation the married differ from the unmarried chiefly in having a higher minimum of exemption.[2]

To have deduced the precepts will aid us in estimating the authority of *like sacrifice.* This may best be effected, from the utilitarian point of view adopted in this article, by determining the relation of the principle under consideration to the supreme principle. That relation is one of complete autonomy, if like sacrifice is prescribed by intuitive justice. But the utilitarian will not accept this *imperium in imperio.* He will object to like *sacrifice* thus supported, what several acute dialecticians [3] have objected to proportional sacrifice, that its propriety is not self-evident.

A position more neutral with regard to utilitarianism is taken by Mr. Cohen-Stuart when he maintains that proportional sacrifice, leaving the relation between all the parties in respect of welfare unchanged, is *the* principle for the Manchester man.[4]

---

conclusion that is to be regarded as proved; from mere assumptions, never a real fact." And much to the same effect in the context (*Progressivsteuer, loc. cit.* p. 82). Now the character of certainty in the conclusion with uncertainty in the premisses is one which frequently is presented in that branch of mathematical science which, as being applied to human affairs, is nearest akin to pure economics, namely, the calculus of probabilities. In ascertaining the probability that a given effect has resulted from a certain cause, it is generally necessary to deal with certain quantities termed *a priori* or antecedent probabilities, about which nothing is known, except that they are not very small [or very great, or very unequal]. Thus Mill, of such an argument : " it would be impossible to estimate that probability with anything like mathematical precision," yet " a practical decision can generally be come to without much hesitation." *A priori* probabilities of this character are involved in the received treatment of physical observations.

[1] *Political Economy*, Book V. ch. ii. § 4, note.

[2] *Bijdrage*, pp. 140–145. The judicious author here repeats the warning that we may overshoot the mark by attempting too great accuracy. Compare the exemptions in favour of the married in the scheme proposed by the Grand Council of Berne (but rejected by the referendum), *Report on Graduated Taxation in Switzerland.* C. 6856 .—15 (1892).

[3] *E. g.* Graziani, *Istituzioni*, p. 301; Sax, *Progressivsteuer*, p. 62.

[4] *Bijdrage*, ch. v. This proposition can hardly be said to have the character of an axiom. What Walker and Professor Seligman call the " leave-them-as-you-

Somewhat similar appears to be the position of Professor Sidgwick, except that he has explicitly recognised the supremacy of
the greatest-happiness principle, and admits the possibility of its
being employed to promote equality by taxation.   But he regards
this direct interposition of the supreme principle as liable to a
dangerous excess.   The principle of equal sacrifice is therefore
deputed to act, a deputy not liable, like the principal, to be
betrayed into imprudent concessions.   This paraphrase is based
on the following passages and their context :—

" The obviously equitable principle—assuming that the
existing distribution of wealth is accepted as just, or not unjust—
is that equal sacrifices should be imposed on all; and this [is]
also obviously the most economic [1] adjustment of the burden
except so far as it is thought desirable to make taxation a means
of redressing the inequalities of income that would exist apart
from governmental interference."

" The introduction, however, of this latter principle to any
marked extent involves the danger " [described in the preceding
chapter].   " And the danger is much greater here . . . because
if the principle is applied at all, any limit to its application seems
quite arbitrary."

The position of Mr. Cohen-Stuart with respect to proportional sacrifice and that of Professor Sidgwick with respect
to equal sacrifice are tenable, so long as we hold with Mr.
Cohen-Stuart that the utility-curve is ultimately of the Bernoullian form.   But if, as above contended, this premiss is not
tenable, then a rapidly progressive taxation following from the
principle of proportional sacrifice, the Manchester man could
hardly be expected to acquiesce in that principle.   Nor could the
principle of equal sacrifice be safely deputed to act on behalf of
the supreme principle.   Of the deputy as well as of the sovereign,
we might then say : " if the principle is applied at all, any limit
to its application seems quite arbitrary."   At any rate, the
only certain limit to the application of equal sacrifice—viz. that
more than the necessary minimum of taxation should not be

find-them theory " is, in the opinion of many, best carried out by a simply proportional income-tax.   Thus, McCulloch, in the *Edinburgh Review* (Vol. LVII. p.
162), protests against a graduated income-tax, on the ground that " no tax is a just
tax unless it leaves individuals in the same relative condition in which it found
them."   So Courcelle-Seneuil speaks of the proportional income tax as " qui
altererait le moins l'état de distribution résultant de la liberté " (*Traité théorique
et pratique*, ii., p. 218).

[1] " Economic " is, of course, used here in the same sense as in the preceding
chapter; that is, nearly equivalent to utilitarian in our first sense.   (See Book III.
ch. vii. § 1, par. 1)

raised and more should not be required from the higher incomes than would bring down all above a certain level to that level [1]— is greatly in excess of practical limitations. Is it not simpler to dismiss the deputed principle of equal sacrifice, and to adopt as the true norm of taxation minimum sacrifice tempered by a regard for the growth of wealth and other advantages above enumerated ?

The capacity of like sacrifice to act independently is even less upon another view of its authority. What if, as compared with the utilitarian code, it is not a sort of by-law, as just now in effect supposed, but simply a clause, a badly-transcribed clause, of the code itself ? What if *equal sacrifice* is but a corrupt reading for *equi-marginal sacrifice*, the condition of minimum disutility ? [2] Thus Mill, in that classical passage which has influenced the most influential of his successors,[3] in the same breath proclaims the principles of equal and of least sacrifice :—

" Whatever sacrifices it [a government] requires from them [persons or classes] should be made to bear as nearly as possible with the same pressure upon all, which, it must be observed, is the mode by which least sacrifice is occasioned on the whole." [4]

It is remarkable that in support of one of the principal reforms with respect to taxation which he advocated, Mill should have employed the genuine utilitarian reasoning in favour of equality rather than the questionable principle of equal sacrifice.[5] Thus when he first introduces the proposal to limit inheritances :—

" It must be apparent to every one that the difference to the happiness of the possessor between a moderate independence and five times as much is insignificant when weighed against the enjoyment that might be given, and the permanent benefit diffused by some other disposal of the four-fifths " (*Political Economy*, Book II. ch. ii. § 4).

And in a later chapter on inheritance, he refers to " the

[1] As appears from the position of the curve through *t* in note to p. 111.

[2] Above, p. 103.

[3] Both Mr. N. G. Pierson (*Staathuishoudkunde* 1886, p. 310) and Sir Robert Giffen (Evidence before the Financial Relations Commission Q. 7777) profess to follow Mill.

[4] Mill, Book V. ch. ii. § 2, par 1. The divergence between the principle of equal sacrifice presented by Mill and that of minimum sacrifice is indicated by the present writer (*op. cit.* p. 118). Professor Carver calls attention to the fact that Mill affirmed the two divergent principles in the same passage (*Amer. Acad. for Pol. Sci.*, 1895, p. 95).

[5] Bentham is always clearer than Mill in the deduction of equality from greatest-happiness, because he virtually employs the differential calculus : adding and subtracting " particles of wealth," as in *Pannomial Fragments* (*Works*, Vol. III. p. 231).

deeper consideration that the diffusion of wealth, not its con-
centration, is desirable " (Book V. ch. ix. § 2).

So McCulloch can see no halting-place, such as the principle
of equal sacrifice is supposed to supply, between a proportional
income-tax and that levelling of the higher incomes which, as
above shown, is the inference from the principle of minimum
sacrifice.[1]

So Dr. Robert Meyer describes as " the commonest argument "
in favour of progressive taxation one which rests upon an
interpretation of equal sacrifice which makes it virtually identical
with equi-marginal sacrifice.[2]

So some of the high authorities who have advocated progressive taxation on the ground of equal sacrifice may be credited
with an " unconsciously implicit " [3] utilitarianism of the pure
type. Mr. Cohen-Stuart indeed has argued that several of these
high authorities hold the principle of proportional sacrifice. For
whereas they have deduced progressive taxation from the principle of equal sacrifice, *simpliciter* and without any *datum* as to
the law according to which utility diminishes, this fallacious
reasoning is explicable, he thinks, on the former supposition, but
on the latter inexplicable. But what if there was in the confused
minds of these distinguished publicists not *equal* sacrifice nor
yet *proportional* sacrifice, but *equi-marginal* sacrifice (leading
to *minimum* sacrifice) ? It is true that this premiss is less consonant to their statements than the other. But then their
conclusion really does follow from this premiss. Obliged as we
are to make a compromise between obscure premisses and fallacious reasoning, may not the line of least confusion, so to
speak, be—not the assumption that the premiss was somewhat
obscure and the reasoning somewhat erroneous, but—that the
premiss was quite confused and the reasoning quite exact ?

Altogether, whatever view we take of the relation of the
principle of like sacrifice to pure utilitarianism, the sphere of
its action independently of that supreme principle appears to
be insignificant.

The proposal here made to substitute *minimum* for *equal* in

---

[1] *Edinburgh Review*, Vol. LVII. p. 164 (1833).

[2] " Das gewönhlichste Argument dass die proportionale Steuer bei grösseren
Einkomen deswegen ein geringeres Opfer verursache, als bei kleineren, weil sie nur
entbehrlicheren Bedürfnissen die Befriedigungsmittel entzieht beweist zu viel "
[*i. e.* it leads to the conclusion above deduced from the principle of least sacrifice,
that the higher incomes should be cut down to a lower level.] *Op. cit.* p. 331.

[3] The happy term applied by Professor Sidgwick to the utilitarianism which is
latent in current ethical opinion.

the " sacrifice " theory of taxation will not modify considerably
the practical directions afforded by that theory. Rather the
obligation to follow those directions is made clearer. As of old,
before the invention of the compass, the star-steered sailor would
not sensibly have altered his course if he could have discovered,
by the use of a telescope, that what he had regarded as a luminous
point was really a double star, composed of bodies separated from
each other many million miles ; so in the present state of financial
science, affairs being at such an enormous distance from principles,
the discovery that the sacrifice theory comprises several distinct
ends is not calculated to result in a serious alteration of the
line of conduct indicated. Rather the use of our speculative
instruments in separating the species of this theory of taxation
conduces to keeping in view the generic principle, in spite of
distance and obscurity. The use of *minimum*, instead of *equal*,[1]
sacrifice enables us to pierce the sort of metaphysical mist which
has been raised by the question : *Why* should the principle
be adopted ?[2] The question is not embarrassing to those
who regard minimum sacrifice as a deduction from the greatest-
happiness principle—" the only possible, the only conceivable
principle which can guide legislation on a great scale."[3] Again,
there is a want of clearness in the reasoning from the principle
of equal sacrifice, because in order to obtain any conclusion some
assumption must be made as to the rate at which the increase of
utility tends to diminish with the increase of means ;[4] while " to
ascertain the exact relations between something psychical and
something material is impossible."[5] But the reasoning from
the principle of minimum sacrifice assumes no exact relation
between utility and means ; it assumes only what is universally
admitted, that utility does not increase proportionately to
means, the Jevonian " law of diminishing utility." Again,
some confusion is caused by the conflict between the two forms
of equal sacrifice ; equal in a proper sense and proportional.
But the pure utilitarian has no difficulty in accepting both
principles as equally inexact but equally useful approximations
to the true principle ; or rather that of proportional sacrifice
as more exact, being more in accordance with minimum sacrifice,

---

[1] In the following paragraphs dealing with practice it has seemed best as most
agreeable to usage, to occasionally employ the term " equal " generally, covering
proportional as well as *equal* in the proper sense (see above, p. 107).

[2] Asked, *e. g.*, by Professor Graziani with reference to the Dutch form of the
doctrine, *Istituzioni*, p. 301.

[3] Sir Henry Maine, *Political Institutions*, last page.

[4] Above, p. 107.   [5] Seligman, *Progressive Taxation*, p. 136.

equal sacrifice as more useful, in this country at least, as being more familiar.

To take as a concrete example the problem presented by the financial relations between England and Ireland, the general result of the preceding considerations would be to strengthen that argument in favour of the Irish claim which is grounded by some high authorities on the principle of equal sacrifice, and to weaken those objections to the argument which are grounded by other high authorities on the indefiniteness of the principle. This correction would be the less important in so far as the consideration of sacrifice has to be combined with other considerations not admitting of precision.

There are several considerations special to the concrete problem which can only be adverted to here—put in the form of questions to which the answers are not given. (1) What disbursements from the Exchequer are applied to common purposes, the benefits of which cannot be allocated to particular regions, any more than to particular individuals? Does "the expenditure . . . . for the general objects for which a government is carried on, namely, for the administration of justice, the maintenance of order, the maintenance of the poor "[1] and so forth, belong to this class? (2) Whether, if much of the taxation complained of is raised by duties on stimulants, the privation thereby occasioned to the consumers should be left entirely out of account, and no part of it should be reckoned in that total of sacrifice which it is sought to minimise, because some part of the taxed commodities is consumed intemperately? (3) Whether it is any mitigation of such sacrifice that the consumer of the taxed articles was free to abstain therefrom; or whether it is not only demonstrated by the classical political economy [2] that taxes on commodities are not less burdensome, but also demonstrable by the modern mathematical method [3] that they are

[1] Sir Robert Giffen, in evidence before the Royal Commission on the Financial Relations between England and Ireland (Q. 11,024).

[2] See Mill, Book V. ch. vi. § 1. *Cp.* Bastable, ECONOMIC JOURNAL, Vol. VI.; note to p. 202.

[3] If a given amount—which may at first be supposed finite and small—is raised by taxing a few commodities (not specially selected in the interest of the consumer as suggested by Professor Marshall, *Principles*, Book V. ch. xii. § 7), there will in general occur under the head of those commodities a loss of "consumers' rent" which does not occur when the amount is directly subtracted from income, the consumer being free to reduce his expenditure on all commodities without disturbance of prices. The proposition may easily be extended to larger amounts of taxation.

Abstraction is here made of certain secondary advantages attending indirect taxation : that it is apt to escape attention, and that it is taken at a time and in a

more burdensome, than direct taxation? (4) Whether, if a special rate of taxation is claimed by the inhabitants of a peculiarly circumstanced part of a united kingdom, such as Ireland, on the ground of a special predilection for certain now heavily taxed commodities, or on any other *prima facie* reasonable ground, such a claim is not to be entertained, because it would not be practicable to allow a special rate to the inhabitants of some other part of the United Kingdom, such as Wiltshire; or whether, as Mill says, with reference to his proposal to allow a specially low rate of taxation for a class whose sacrifice is specially great, " the difficulty of doing perfect justice is no reason against doing as much as we can? " [1] (5) Whether, if Ireland is overtaxed only because she is poor, it may not be a problem of practical interest to determine by how much her taxation is in excess of what it would be if a just distribution of taxation as between rich and poor prevailed throughout the United Kingdom? (6) Whether and how much the Irish claim is strengthened by the treaty of the union providing for " particular exemptions or abatements "? or (7) on account of the alleged " economic drain from Ireland "? or (8) on old scores, in particular the generally admitted overtaxation in the middle part of the century, and the much-disputed transactions in the first part of the century?

To attempt to evaluate these items in the account between the two countries would be out of place in a discussion of pure theory. It will merely be assumed here, for the purpose of illustration, that the items referred to are not so preponderant as to make the consideration of " sacrifice " of no account. Upon this assumption the first approximation to the solution of the problem is obtained by minimising the total sacrifice, subject to the condition that production is not much diminished. The condition, as above explained,[2] operates at two points. There is danger of diminishing by differential taxation the accumulations of the very rich, the efficiency of the not very rich.

The latter consideration has been urged with great force by Professor Sidgwick and Professor Bastable in the Memoranda submitted by them to the Financial Relations Commission.[3] It

---

manner very convenient. The former advantage, as Mill observes (*loc. cit.*), is dwindling; the latter may find a set-off in the practice of stopping income-tax at the source.

[1] *Political Economy*, Book V. ch. ii. § 4. *Cp.* " It is no objection to this principle [equal sacrifice] that we cannot apply it consistently to all cases."

[2] Above, p. 105.

[3] Vol. II., 182 col. *b.*, and 184 col. *b.*

must be remembered, however, that the consideration figures on
both sides of the account. If the efficiency of the richer country
may be somewhat diminished by increase of taxation, the efficiency
of the poorer country may be considerably increased by relief
from taxation. The gain on balance is especially evident in
the case where the aggravation of taxes is experienced by those
whose income exceeds the necessaries for efficiency, and the relief
from taxation is experienced by those whose income falls short
of the necessaries for efficiency; necessaries being here defined,
as proposed by Professor Marshall, in such wise that the income
of any class is said to be below the necessary level when an
increase in their income conduces to an increase by a greater
amount in their efficiency.[1]

It is not quite clear how far this consideration of efficiency
forms part of the ground on which the exemption of a minimum
income from taxation is ordinarily claimed. It is, at any rate, a
consideration only subordinate to a consideration for the " suffer-
ings of privation " which, as Bentham says, are caused by taxes
levied upon persons who may not have wherewith to pay.

The balance of minimum sacrifice against maximum production being necessarily rough, it is no great objection to any part
of the calculation that it is devoid of numerical precision. Yet
that is the sort of objection which has been brought against Sir
Robert Giffen's estimate of the " taxable surplus " for Ireland and
Great Britain respectively. On this subject Professor Bastable
writes :—

" The fairest rough test—and no test can be looked on as more
than an approximation—of taxable capacity is to be found in a
comparison of total income rather than in any refined and doubtful calculation as to what is left after necessary expenses have
been defrayed." [2]

" The difficulties inherent in any attempt to refine on or
manipulate the total income in order to get a measure of ability,
seems to indicate the convenience of keeping to the plain rule of
taxation according to income." [3]

" The decisive objection to such theories is the difficulty of
their practical application. To estimate income is a task, perhaps,
too difficult for the statistician; but to discover the amount of
' free ' income is quite hopeless, and the employment of conjec-

---

[1] *Principles of Economics*, Book II. ch. iii. § 3. The level of *necessaries* in the
technical sense, is in general different from the " necessaries of life," " the
requisites of life and health " (Mill) usually referred to in this connection.

[2] Appendix to *Evidence of Financial Relations Commission*, Vol. II. p. 185.

[3] ECONOMIC JOURNAL, Vol. VI. p. 200.

tural amounts as guides in so definite a matter as taxation is a dangerous course which might lead to the most paradoxical results. A slight alteration of figures would supply the premisses for an altogether different conclusion." [1]

" In 1886 Sir R. Giffen estimated the taxable surpluses of Great Britain and Ireland respectively at 800 millions and 15 millions; in 1895 he estimated them at 900 millions and 22 millions. From which it at once follows that Ireland's taxable capacity had risen from being less than 1 : 53 to more than 1 : 41. . . . Mr. Lough gets 1,092 millions to 15 millions or $72\frac{4}{5}$: 1 as the ratio." [2]

This argument seems to exaggerate the determinateness of the problem. Taxation is " not so definite a matter." The claim to a special rate of taxation, as Mill says of the claim on behalf of temporary incomes, " does not rest on grounds of arithmetic, but of human wants and feelings." As involving an estimate of immaterial quantities the distribution of burdens in the way of taxation might be compared to the distribution of prizes by way of examination It is not so definite a matter measuring intellectual ability by numerical marks. " The difficulties inherent in any refined attempt to get a measure of ability " might seem to indicate the convenience of keeping to some " plain rule " of examination, e. g. that the marks of a candidate should be proportioned to the *length* of his answers. But this plain rule being plainly unfair is not preferable to more refined estimates which though affected with " personal equations," and all kinds of fortuitous aberrations, still aim at least at ideal fairness. It is quite possible that marks so different as 53 and 41 assigned to the same candidate by different assistant examiners might assist the head examiner in placing the candidate. So the very divergent estimates of damages made by separate jurymen are compounded into a result by which substantial justice is secured. The estimates of taxable surplus must be similarly treated as liable to a considerable " error " or uncertainty. It is in this spirit that the distinguished propounder of the estimates in question has understood his figures.

" When we come to deal with the matter equitably, that is a thing which ought to be allowed for." [3]

" But then of course these are very rough computations indeed,

---

[1] ECONOMIC JOURNAL, pp. 199, 200.   [2] *Ibid.* p. 200, notes.
[3] Evidence of Sir Robert Giffen before the Commission on Financial Relations between England and Ireland (Q. 7777).

and are only meant to be illustrative of what the effect of applying this principle would be." [1]

" Some rough mode of calculation of that kind is all you can do." [2]

" I do not suggest and never suggested such a rule [that the taxable incomes of Ireland and Great Britain are in the proportion 22 : 900] could be applied in a strict arithmetical way." [3]

In short, the general principle for adjusting taxation between two regions—or any classes, whether defined geographically or not —between which it is thought fit to establish distinctions of taxation, is not a simple rule of three applied to incomes, but rather a method such as that which was adopted in Switzerland in 1851, for regulating the contributions of the cantons to the " Federal Expenditure."

" To make oneself familiar with all the different circumstances which have to be taken into consideration in order to form a judgment on the economic situation of a canton; then, using a free judgment, and without taking too rigorous a basis, to tax each canton according to a certain tact." [4]

The alternative plan of " proportioning the normal contributions of different income classes to the *total* incomes of the respective classes, while carrying out Mill's principle of not trenching on the subsistence minimum, by excluding taxes on the necessaries of life as well as direct taxes of the poor," [5] derives, it is here submitted, an undue support from Mill's use of *equal*, instead of *minimum*, sacrifice. Even on the principle of equal sacrifice proportional taxation of income (above the exempted minimum) is an extreme measure. [6] The golden mean is not to be attained by creeping cautiously close to the limiting extreme— *nimium premendo litus iniquum*. The guiding star of Utilitarianism shines in a direction away from that hard coastline, and gilds the bolder course with the light of pure theory.

[Let $F(x, y)$ be the money measure of the satisfaction attending the acquisition of the quantities of the commodity x and y. Let

[1] Evidence of Sir Robert Giffen before the Commission on Financial Relations between England and Ireland (Q. 7778).

[2] *Ibid.* Q. 7780.

[3] *Ibid.* Q. 7787.

[4] Quoted by the Royal Commission on the Financial Relations between England and Ireland, Vol. II., Appendix XVI.

[5] Professor Sidgwick in Appendix I. to Vol. II. of Evidence before the Commission on Financial Relations (C. 7720), p. 183. Compare the very similar language of Professor Bastable on p. 185.

[6] As argued above, p. 114, par. 4.

$f(x, y)$ be the cost of producing those quantities. What the consumers seek to maximise is then

$$(1) \quad F(x, y) - p_1 x - p_2 y;$$

where p_1, p_2, are the prices of the respective commodities. What the producers seek to maximise is

$$(2) \quad x p_1 + y p_2 - f(x, y).$$

Whence
$$(3) \quad \left(\frac{dF}{dx}\right) = p_1 = \left(\frac{df}{dx}\right);$$

$$(4) \quad \left(\frac{dF}{dy}\right) = p_2 = \left(\frac{df}{dy}\right);$$

together with certain conditions which must be fulfilled by the second differential coefficients of the functions in order that (1) and (2) may be each a maximum. We must have $\left(\frac{d^2F}{dx^2}\right)$ and $\left(\frac{d^2F}{dy^2}\right)$ each negative; say $- A$ and $- B$, where A and B are always positive. Also $\left(\frac{d^2f}{dx^2}\right)$, $\left(\frac{d^2f}{dy^2}\right)$ must each be positive, say $+ a$ and $+ b$, where a and b are always positive. Let $\left(\frac{d^2F}{dxdy}\right) = \mp C$, where C is always positive; the upper sign being used when the demand is rival, the lower when it is complementary. Likewise let $\frac{d^2f}{dxdy} = \pm c$, c always positive; the upper sign being used where the supply is rival, the lower when it is complementary. Then the two remaining conditions which must be satisfied by (1) and (2) may be written,

$$(5) \quad AB > C^2; \quad (6) \quad ab > c^2.$$

Now let a tax of τ per unit be imposed on one of the commodities, say x. Thereby there is added to the cost of producing x the amount of the tax, viz. τx; and accordingly to the value of $\left(\frac{df}{dx}\right)$ for any x there is added τ. Equation (3) with this addition and equation (4) will now be true of the new values of x and y consequent on the impost, say $x' + \Delta x$, $y' + \Delta y$, where x', y' are the original quantities. Substituting these values and expanding (3) and (4) thus modified in ascending powers of Δx and Δy, recollecting that those equations are satisfied by x' and y', we obtain

$$(7) \quad \Delta x \times - A + \Delta y \times \mp C = \Delta p_1 = \Delta x \times a + \Delta y \times \pm c + \tau;$$

$$(8) \quad \Delta x \times \mp C + \Delta y \times - B = \Delta p_2 = \Delta x \times \pm c + \Delta y \times b;$$

whence $\quad (9) \quad \Delta x \times - (A + a) + \Delta y \times \mp (C + c) = \tau;$

$$(10) \quad \Delta x \times \mp (C + c) + \Delta y \times - (B + b) = 0.$$

Solving these simultaneous equations for Δx and Δy we obtain

$$\Delta x = \tau \times - (B + b)/D^2; \quad \Delta y = \pm (C + c)\tau/D^2;$$

where D^2 is the determinant $(A + a)(B + b) - (C + c)^2$; which is known to be positive, whether *a priori* as the condition that the total advantage of both producers and consumers *in globo* should be a maximum (*cp.* Marshall, *Principles of Economics*, mathematical note xiv); or as a deduction from the aforesaid conditions of maximum pertaining to each party separately, in equations (5) and (6). Substituting these values in the expressions for Δp_1 and Δp_2 given by (7) and (8) we obtain

$$(11) \quad \frac{D^2}{\tau}\Delta p_1 = - A \times - (B + b) \mp C \times \pm (C + c);$$

$$(12) \quad \frac{D^2}{\tau}\Delta p_2 = \mp C \times - (B + b) - B \times \pm (C + c).$$

Let us begin with the case in which it is proper to take the upper signs before C and c; that is the case of rival demand and rival production. In this case it appears from (11) and (12) that both prices will fall if

$$(13) \quad A(B + b) < C(C + c);$$
$$(14) \quad C(B + b) < B(C + c); \quad Cb < Bc.$$

These conditions are far from exacting. They are satisfied by values of the constants of which two are quite arbitrary, except for the conditions that they must be positive, and the remainder are very slightly restricted. Take *any* (positive) values of a and b and any value of $c < \sqrt{ab}$ (> 0); and *any* (positive) proper fractions r, s, t. Let $C = r\sqrt{AB}$; and for the inequations (13) and (14) write the equations

$$(15) \quad A(B + b) = sr^2AB + sr\sqrt{AB} \times c;$$
$$(16) \quad r\sqrt{AB}b = sr^2t \times Bc.$$

From (15) we have

$$AB(1 - sr^2) + Ab = src\sqrt{AB}$$
$$B(1 - sr^2) + b = src\sqrt{B/A}$$
$$(17) \quad \sqrt{B/A} = (B(1 - sr^2) + b)/src.$$

From (16) we have

$$(18) \quad rb = sr^2tc\sqrt{B/A}; \quad \sqrt{B/A} = b/srct.$$

Substituting this value of $\sqrt{B/A}$ in (17) and reducing we obtain for B $b(1/t - 1)/(1 - sr^2)$. Whence from (17) or (18) $A = \dfrac{s^2r^2c^2t^2}{b} \dfrac{(1/t - 1)}{1 - sr^2}$.

$C = r\sqrt{AB} = r^2sct\left(\dfrac{1}{t} - 1\right)/(1 - sr^2)$. The reader may verify the fulfilment of inequations (13) and (14) by assigning values almost at random to the symbols in (15) and (16). Thus let $a = 1$, $b = 1$, $c(< \sqrt{ab}) = \frac{1}{2}$; $r = s = t = \frac{1}{2}$. Then $A = \frac{1}{2^2 4}$, $B = \frac{8}{7}$, $C = \frac{1}{2^8}$, $A(B + b) = \frac{1}{2^2 4}\left(\frac{15}{7}\right) < \frac{1}{2^8} \times \frac{15}{2^8} = C(C + c)$. $Cb = \frac{1}{2^8} < \frac{4}{7} = Bc$.

Whence $(D^2 = 1 \cdot 865$ nearly) $\Delta p_1 = - \cdot 005\tau$, $\Delta p_2 = - \cdot 287\tau$; both prices fall in consequence of the tax.

So far of rival production and rival consumption.   When both correlations belong to the other species, "complementary," the tax of one article may, as stated in the text, cause the rise of *either* of the articles but not of both.   This case differs from the preceding in that the lower signs in (7) and (8) and the sequel are to be used (C and c still treated as positive).   Then, if it be possible, let there coexist the inequations

$$(19) - A \times - (B + b) < - C \times - (C + c),$$

i. e.
$$A(B + b) < C(C + c);$$

$$(20) + C \times - (B + b) - B \times - (C + c) < 0,$$

i. e.
$$B(C + c) < C(B + b).$$
$$Bc < bC; \quad c < bC/B.$$

Since $AB > C^2$ we infer from the inequation (19) $Ab < cC$. Substituting in this inequation the superior limit for c derived from the inequation (20) we obtain

$$Ab < bC^2/B; \quad AB < C^2;$$

which is absurd, being contrary to (5).

By putting now c, now $C = 0$ we may verify other statements in the text.]

(T)

ANSWERS TO QUESTIONS PUT BY THE LOCAL TAXATION COMMISSION

[THE doctrine of minimum sacrifice is restated in less technical language in answers to a question put by the Royal Commission on Local Taxation. Answers are also given with respect to the incidence of various taxes about which the Commission inquired. The answers were published in the Reprint of the Commission [C. 9528, 1899]. A copy of the Question is here affixed.]

ROYAL COMMISSION ON LOCAL TAXATION

QUESTIONS

1. Is the classification of Imperial Taxation indicated in the accompanying Table a correct classification; if not, what alterations can you suggest? (*See* Table marked A, and memorandum marked B, by Sir Alfred Milner explaining the basis of the Table.)
2. Assuming the classification, is it complete, and are the several items correctly distributed?
3. In particular should such an item as the net revenue of the Post Office be treated as a tax, and if so, under which of the heads specified in the Table?
4. In considering the equity of any tax or system of taxation what tests should be applied?
5. Can you offer any suggestions which would assist the Commission in determining the question of the real incidence of taxation as distinguished from its primary or apparent incidence?
6. Could you, for example, state your view as to the real incidence of—
   - (*a*) The inhabited house duty;
   - (*b*) Rates levied on houses and trade premises;
   - (*c*) Rates levied on agricultural land;
   - (*d*) Taxes on the transfer of property;
   - (*e*) Taxes on trade profits;
   - (*f*) Death duties?

7. Is it possible to frame any criterion whereby the purposes for which taxation should be raised locally can be distinguished from those for which taxation should be raised by the central Government?

8. Should the two kinds of purposes and the expenditure on them be kept distinct or should the expenditure for local purposes be partly borne by the central Government?

9. Should local rates be divided between owners and occupiers of real property, and if so, in what proportions?

10. Should ground values be separately rated for local purposes, and if so, on what principles?

11. Under what conditions and in what manner would the rent which could be obtained by an owner of land on rateable hereditaments be affected, if at all, by—
    (a) The increase of an old rate;
    (b) The imposition of a new rate;
    (c) The reduction or abolition of a rate?

12. Under what conditions and in what manner would the rent which could be obtained by an owner of land or rateable hereditaments be affected, if at all, if an occupier by whom a rate had hitherto been paid were empowered to deduct the whole or a portion thereof from the rent in the same manner as he is now entitled to do in the case of income tax? (Schedule A.)

13. What is the effect, if any, upon rent of rating property—
    (a) On different scales of duty according to the value of the property;
    (b) On different scales of duty according to the character of the property or the purposes for which it is used?

14. Can you make suggestions to the Commission as to any methods of raising revenue for local purposes, otherwise than by means of rates?

15. Does any point not included under any of the foregoing questions occur to you on which having regard to the terms of reference to the Commission you wish to express an opinion?

PROFESSOR EDGEWORTH'S ANSWERS TO THE QUESTIONS SUBMITTED TO HIM BY THE ROYAL COMMISSION ON LOCAL TAXATION

1. A classification may be incorrect in two ways. It may violate the rules of formal or those of material logic. For instance, suppose taxes divided into indirect, and those which are on

commodities; or taxpayers divided into those who are at least six foot high, and those who are under six foot. The first classification is incorrect because the classes formed are not mutually exclusive : the second classification is incorrect because it subserves no purpose of art or science.

The proposed classification, properly interpreted, is not incorrect in either sense. If the terms " incidental to . . . property " and " in respect of commodities " are defined so as not to overlap, then the classification may subserve the purpose of enabling the various items of the national Budget to be held together in thought.

The classification might be considered incorrect, if it was designed to indicate the incidence of taxation. For, certainly, it does not fulfil that purpose, as appears from the cross-questioning to which the author of the classification was subjected by Sir Robert Giffen.[1] But the classification was not designed to fulfil this purpose, as appears from the answers given on the occasion referred to.[2]

I cannot suggest, I do not recommend, any alteration of the proposed classification. The object of such an emendation would be, apparently, to render the classification a better exponent of the real incidence. But it may be doubted whether a classification which fulfils the first purpose—to afford a comprehensive view of the receipts of the Exchequer—admits of being amended so as to fulfil the second purpose—to indicate the real incidence of taxation. It must be recognised that the points of primary percussion and final incidence are not coincident. There is the sort of difference which exists between an ordinary map divided into provinces and counties, and a map of which the divisions are designed to exhibit the variety of geological formations. There is, doubtless, a certain correspondence between the two charts; and it is not only in Greek that mountains are associated with boundaries. But query if it would be worth while to alter familiar demarcations—subtracting a district from one county, and adding it to another—in order to construct a sort of mongrel map, which should subserve at once the purposes of ordinary geography and scientific geology.

2. The questions may be understood to mean : (1) Do the items enumerated in the proposed Table together make up the total taxation raised by Parliament ? (2) Is each item placed in the compartment to which it properly belongs ?

---

[1] Agricultural Commission, Q. 63, 235, and context.
[2] *Ibid.*, Q. 63, 253; 63, 266.

(1) To the first question there can be only one answer. The only qualification to the obvious affirmative is the caution that the amount raised by taxation is not an accurate measure of the real burden. As Mill says of a tax on newspapers, it is " objectionable, not so much where it does fall, as where it does not." The principle has been generalised by Professor Marshall in his theory of " consumers' rent." For example, if the duties on some consumable articles were raised, the burden of taxation would certainly be increased, but the ordinary pecuniary measure of that burden might quite possibly be reduced.

(2) The arrangement of the items appears to me correct enough. I should add that it might have been widely different, without appearing to me incorrect. For the term " incidental to " signifying simply " with respect to "—and divorced, as I contend that it should be, from its association with *incidence*— is so vague and elastic that the compartments which it defines may be made to include more or less, at pleasure. Thus several of the items under Head 4, *e.g.*, bills of exchange and promissory notes, might as well have been, where Sir Alfred Milner was at first disposed to place them,[1] in the category of taxes not incidental to property, as where they are now. Distinctions which turn upon such differences seem hardly worth contending for.

(3) What is the best definition of a tax is an interminable inquiry. There is a whole literature on the subject on the Continent. It may be true, as a French writer has observed, that all this dialectic never brought an additional franc into the Treasury. Yet the discussion exercises speculative faculties which are demanded by some problems in taxation. It will not be expected, however, that this academic exercise should be performed here.

For the present purpose we may accept Professor Bastable's definition of a tax, and understand with him that " when ordinary profit is exceeded, the monopoly possessed by the [public] office is employed for taxation." [2] Or, in Professor Sidgwick's words, " Government avoids interfering with distribution "— whether in the way of tax or bounty—" if it sells the commodity at the price at which it would be sold if provided by private industry." [3] But " we can only conjecture roughly " what that price would have been.[4] We do not know to what extent

---

[1] Memorandum B., p. 4.
[2] *Public Finance*, Book II. ch. I. § 4.
[3] *Political Economy*, Book III. ch. viii. par. 4.
[4] Note to first edition, *loc. cit.*

the service would be monopolised in the absence of Governmental interference. The calculation is further complicated by the possibility that, whether in a regime of perfect competition, or more or less imperfect monopoly, there might be different prices, varying with the cost of service in different localities. It has further to be considered that the burden imposed on the public by the Government monopoly of the post is not to be measured simply by the rise in price which it may occasion. Professor Marshall, in a letter to *The Times*, of April 6, 1891, estimated the loss to the public in the way of " consumers' rent," consequent on the prohibition of private enterprise in postal services, as amounting to some four and a half million pounds sterling annually. It seems to follow that the " net revenue of the Post Office " is a very inaccurate measure of the fiscal burden imposed by the Government monopoly.

4. The equity of any particular tax must be judged by reference to the system of which it forms part. That the same tax may or may not be inequitable, according as the payer is or is not otherwise burdened, is an acknowledged principle.[1] We may go on then to consider the equity of a system of taxation. The following is a summary of views expressed fully in the ECONOMIC JOURNAL for December 1897.[2]

In considering the equity of any political system, the test which should be applied is the greatest happiness principle.[3] From this principle it follows that *ceteris paribus* the sum of privation or sacrifice caused by taxation should be a *minimum*. Therefore, if a certain amount of taxation has to be raised (for purposes of which the benefit cannot be allocated to particular persons), the *primâ facie* best distribution is that the whole amount should be paid by the wealthiest citizens. The incomes above a certain level should all be reduced to that level; the incomes below that level should be untaxed, the level being determined by the amount which it is required to raise.[4]

This levelling principle requires to be corrected by several prudential considerations.[5] There is the danger of driving the rich, or at least their riches, from the country, and checking accumulation; there is the danger of awakening the predatory instinct of the poor, and precipitating revolution. When tempered by ordinary prudence, the suggested rules of equity deduced

---

[1] See Fawcett, *Manual of Political Economy*, Book IV. ch i. Bastable *Public Finance*, 2nd edition, p. 300 and p. 555, note 1. Seligman, *Progressive Taxation* (on the principle of *compensation*).

[2] " Pure Theory of Taxation," above S, p. 100 *et seq.*

[3] *Loc. cit.* p. 101.   [4] *Loc. cit.* p. 103.   [5] *Loc. cit.* pp. 104–5.

from the principle of *least* sacrifice are not, in practice, very different from the received rules which are deduced from the principle of *equal* sacrifice. But there is an important theoretical difference between the two first principles.

I maintain that the principle of equal sacrifice derives its acceptance from its similarity in conception and dictates to the principle of least sacrifice : that the former has no authority independent of the latter. J. S. Mill, the leading authority on the subject, confuses the two principles. In the same breath he enounces the principle of equal sacrifice and identifies it with that of least sacrifice. " Whatever sacrifices it [Government] requires of them [persons or classes] should be made to bear as nearly as possible with the same pressure upon all, which, it must be observed, is the mode by which least sacrifice is occasioned on the whole." [1] The association in Mill's thought between *equal* sacrifice and equality—an inference from *least* sacrifice—is apparent in his method of advocating the limitation of inheritances,[2] and in the juxtaposition noted by Professor Sidgwick,[3] between the first clause above quoted and the dictum in the same section that "the true idea of distributive justice consists . . . in redressing the inequalities . . . of nature."

Many distinguished foreign authorities also seem to hover between the two principles, having " equal sacrifice " on their lips, but using arguments which are germane to " least sacrifice."

The principle of equal sacrifice has sometimes been clearly distinguished from that of utilitarianism pure and simple, and preferred to it as being free from the dangers which, as above admitted, attend the working of the latter principle. But in order to deduce any rule of distribution from the principle of equal sacrifice, there is needed some assumption as to the degree of slowness with which utility tends to increase with the increase of means. Upon a very probable assumption as to that slowness, the principle of equal sacrifice would lead to a progressive taxation almost as drastic as that which has been above described. This is admitted by Professor Sidgwick when he says, " If equalisation of burden were the sole consideration, the equity of a graduated rate of taxation, rapidly increasing as incomes rise, could hardly be denied." [4]

It should seem therefore that, as a working principle, equal sacrifice has no great advantage over least sacrifice.

[1] *Political Economy*, Book V. ch. ii. § 2.
[2] Above, **S**, p. 115.
  Political Economy, Book III. ch. viii. par. 7, 1st edition.
[4] *Politics*, p. 182. Cp. *Political Economy*, Book III. ch. viii. par. 7, sub.

For further defence and qualification of the views propounded the reader is referred to the article already cited. The main result of that investigation is somewhat to weaken the prepossession in favour of taxation proportional to incomes (above a certain minimum), and somewhat to strengthen the arguments in favour of progressive taxation. It may be added that there does not seem to be much weight in the common objection to progressive taxation : that if the proportion payable continually increases, it must ultimately reach 100 per cent., or at least a ratio such that the taxpayer would have no interest in increasing his income. For, first, the point at which these consummations would be attained may well be far above the highest existing incomes, as happens in the case of some progressive systems in Switzerland. And secondly, the dictates of the least sacrifice principle might be approximately satisfied by a law of progression which ultimately, for high incomes, converged to a simply proportional rate of taxation.* If the ultimate ratio was very high, the initial ratio might be very low.

5. I have elsewhere [1] suggested four distinctions which may be of assistance in determining the real incidence of taxation.

There is first the distinction between a regime of monopoly and one of competition. The laws of incidence are not the same for these two cases. Thus it is rightly argued that rates in respect of railways and canals fall upon the shareholders who own the property, while rates in respect of mines and quarries fall upon the consumers of the products; [2] it being understood that monopoly prevails in the former case, competition in the latter. A less familiar inference is that, even if a canal or quarry is monopolised, a rate would not fall entirely upon the monopolist, but partly on the consumer; supposing, as is usual, I believe, that the rate is proportioned to the output.[3]

The second distinction is between products which obey the law of " diminishing returns " and those which do not. This distinction is relevant to the weight rather than the point of incidence. The burden of a tax on products obeying the law of " increasing returns " is apt to be greater. It may be observed that the articles with which the Commission is specially concerned,

---

* Even this degree of proportionality is not necessary as shown below.
[1] Above, S, p. 65.
[2] See Memorandum by Sir Edward Hamilton, p. 55.
[3] See Marshall, *Principles of Economics*, p. 462, and above, S, p. 91.

lands and houses,[1] seem mostly to belong to the category of diminishing returns.

The third distinction is between cases where there exists mobility between different industries and cases where this mobility does not exist. One important case of immobility is that of capital fixed during a " short period "[2] as distinguished from " the long run." Thus there is an essential difference between the incidence of a new house rate, according as it affects the owner of a house already built, or as it enters into the calculation of an intending builder.

The fourth distinction is between a tax which varies with the amount of article (including money) produced or dealt in, and one which is irrespective of that amount. A specific and an *ad valorem* tax belong to the former category; to the latter, a poll tax and a payment for a licence. Consider, for example, different modes which might be imagined of taxing the production of barley—I say barley, not corn, to avoid the complication attending the taxation of labourers' necessaries.[3] Mobility between the farming and other industries being supposed, a tax proportioned to the amount of output falls upon the consumer; since before, as after, the impost the " final " increment of product must just repay the producer.[4] By a parity of reasoning a tax under the form of a licence to grow barley will presumably fall on the landlord; supposing that he has no mobility and must either let his land for the cultivation of barley or not at all. It must be supposed also that he can bear it, that his rent *minus* the licence is a positive quantity. Theoretically it would seem that, in general and when the demand for the commodity is not perfectly inelastic, the consumer would, in the long run, only be affected when the licence exceeds the rent. Nor even then is the operation of the licence quite so simple as it is sometimes taken for granted in the books.[5] More practical

[1] As to lands, see Mill's *Political Economy* passim; as to houses, Marshall's *Principles of Economics*, sub voce " Margin of building."

[2] Professor Marshall's useful phrase.

[3] In this hypothetical analogy the effect of foreign trade on price may be left out of sight as an incident not relevant to the building industry.

[4] In the case of agricultural produce, as Mill points out (Book V. ch. iv. § 3, par. 1), if the tax diminishes consumption, " it to that extent contributes to throw back agriculture upon more fertile lands or less costly processes and to lower the value and price of corn; which therefore ultimately settles at a price increased not by the whole amount of the tax, but by only a part of its amount." There is, theoretically, an analogous diminution of the expenses, with the rise of the " margin," of building (the law of diminishing returns prevailing); but it may be doubted whether this effect is considerable.

[5] See above, p. 78.

exemplifications of these theories will be given in subsequent answers.

6. In the answers which follow relating to imposts on houses, I shall suppose, when the contrary is not expressed, that the so-called " London leasehold system " [1] prevails. Statements made with special reference to that system can easily be adapted to other circumstances.

(a) To determine the incidence of the inhabited house duty is a problem so complicated that it is expedient to break it up by first considering an ideally simplified case, then introducing one by one the concrete complications.

(1) First let us suppose the inhabitants of a town to deal with the owners of houses already built, abstracting the competitive influence exercised by new houses and other towns. For periods and circumstances which permit this supposition a tax such as the Inhabited House Duty will, theoretically, fall entirely on the owners on the expiry of each occupant's lease (that is, on an average, in less than three and a half years after the imposition of the tax, supposing that the term of the occupation-lease is sometimes seven years and sometimes three). For, the supply of houses being perfectly inelastic, the owners have no choice but to throw these their wares upon the market without a reserve price ; they must accept that price which just carries off the supply. Since the imposition of the duty does not increase the demand of the occupants, the payment per house which they can be got to make will not be increased. The payment now made by the occupant, consisting of rent *plus* tax, will be the same as the payment made before by him, consisting of rent alone. The payment received by the owner will be less than before by the full extent of the tax.[2]

(2) Now, let us take into account the circumstance that houses are not eternal. First, let us suppose the town, or other circumscribed region, to be renewed without being enlarged, new houses from time to time being built on old sites, but not on new sites. If the average duration of a house is 50 or 100, or generally n years, then an nth part of the total number of houses in the town will be yearly produced, and offered for occupation by building entrepreneurs. These entrepreneurs, being free to apply their capital otherwise than in building, will require as

---

[1] There is a good description of the system in the final report (1892) of the Select Committee on Town Holdings, p. vi.

[2] The matter is put more technically in my study on the Pure Theory of Taxation (above, 8).

good profits in that industry as in any other not subject to a special tax. Whence it follows, by familiar reasoning, that the duty, being an *ad valorem* tax on the price paid for a consumable article, falls entirely on the consumer—the occupant. The occupants of new houses then pay the entire duty. But it is not theoretically possible that, in the same market, similar articles should be obtained for different prices : old houses for the same rent as before the imposition of the tax, new houses for that rent *plus* the tax. If, as a first approximation, we ignore the difference in the demand for new and for old houses, the pressure exercised by the builders of new houses will, in the course of less than seven years, result in imposing the tax [1] on the occupants of the old as well as the new houses.

(3) A similar conclusion is obtained when we take into account the circumstance that where the population is increasing new houses will be required in new sites as well as old ones; still assuming that new and old houses are exactly similar articles. But, of course, this is a very inexact assumption. New and old houses are not interchangeable like sovereigns of different dates; urban and suburban residences are not identical articles, but more or less perfect *substitutes* for each other.

(4) Account being taken of this relation between new and old houses, we shall find that the effect exercised by the new buildings upon the house-market is similar in kind, but not in general equal in quantity, to that which was described under heading (2). In the limiting case, when the rivalry between the new and old houses is null, the whole tax falls on the owner, as in case (1). In general it may be supposed that the case lies between (1) and (2); that the occupier of an old house pays a part, but not the whole, of the tax. But this natural supposition is not quite correct. The extra payment imposed on the occupants of old houses in consequence of the tax is not limited to the extent of the tax. Zero is, indeed, an inferior limit, but there is no definite superior limit. The imposition of the tax may so disturb the delicate balance of demand for the rival articles, central and suburban—or, more generally, old and new—houses, that in the new equilibrium the occupants of old houses pay a rent increased by more than the tax, the owners of old houses positively gain by the tax.[2] This *curiosum*

---

[1] The whole tax, if we admit what may be called the classical assumption that the expenses of building are not sensibly altered by the diminution of demand for houses which may be caused by the rise of the price paid by the consumer—the occupier. (See the penultimate note to Q. 5.)

[2] Above, S, p. 81.

in the theory of value seems only to be of importance as it tends
to confirm the conclusion that the occupier will bear a considerable
portion of the tax.[1]

(5) There is next to be introduced the competition between
different towns. Residences in different places constituting rival
commodities, we may see, by an extension of the analysis above
employed, that a uniform tax may so disturb the balance of
complex demand as to cause a certain rush of inhabitants to one
town from another. The owners of houses already built may
gain more rent by the increase of demand consequent on such
disturbance than they lose through that more immediate action
of the tax which was indicated under the preceding head. Conversely, they may lose rent through the competitive action
referred to under the present head. As regards the distribution
of the burden between owner and occupier, the competition
between towns does not tend, on the whole, to alter the proportions.

(6) Lastly, account is to be taken of "friction." With
respect to the distribution of the burden between owner and
occupier, friction acts in two opposite ways. It obstructs that
transference of the tax from the occupier to the owner which was
indicated under head (1), and that transference from the owner
to the occupier which was indicated under heads (2), (3), and (4).

In the first case, the process by which the burden tends to
be shifted from the occupiers to the owners is as follows :—If,
before the imposition of the rate, each occupier had as much
house accommodation as he wanted at the old price (the rent of
occupation), thereafter he will have more house accommodation

---

[1] The eminent Mr. N. G. Pierson, of Holland, in his noteworthy discussion
of this subject (in the second edition of his *Leerbock der Staathuishoudkunde,
eerste deel,* p. 166 *et seq.*) has come to a different conclusion, namely, that the
occupier of a house with a high ground rent, as in a central region, will, at most,
pay only as much tax as what is paid by the occupier of an exactly similar house
with [little or] no ground rent, as in a suburban periphery. Mr. Pierson deduces
this conclusion from the assumption that the difference between the rents of the
two houses may be expected to be the same after and before the imposition of
the tax (or, at least, not greater after than before). This assumption would be
appropriate if two similar houses dissimilarly situated ["*twee huizen van ongelijke
ligging en alleen daarom in huurwaarde verschillend,*" loc. cit. p. 178; "*twee
gelijksoortige perceelen,*" p. 171] could be regarded as two units of the same commodity, analogous to two quarters of barley grown on a highly rented site and
at the margin of cultivation respectively. But I submit that the two houses
ought rather to be regarded as *different quantities of commodity,* analogous to the
quantities of barley produced by the outlay of the same capital at the margin
and on a highly rented site. There is no " anomaly " (*loc. cit.* p. 179) in the
supposition that the difference between the prices paid for those two quantities
of produce should be increased by a tax. It is the received theory, as stated,
e.g., by Mill (Book V. ch. iv. § 3, pars. 2, 3, 4).

than he demands at the new price (the rent *plus* the rate). Accordingly, he will seek to disembarrass himself of this superfluous housing by moving, or threatening to move, to less extensive premises. But this action is much clogged by friction. The gain in utility (or " consumers' rent ") which is effected by taking just as much as he wants at the new price may well be overbalanced by the expense and trouble of moving.

Case (2), at first sight, does not seem to admit of as much friction. As the owner of a new house will not pay the rate, the occupier must undertake to pay it; but he will not do so while equally good old houses are obtainable at the same rent and less rates. As Mr. Cannan says : " Who will stand up and confess that he took 76 —— Street at £100 a year, and subject to £20 of rates, when an exactly similar house next door . . . was to let at £100 a year, and only £12 of rates ? " [1] However, in the case before us, it may well be that the paucity of new houses is a circumstance favourable to friction. That nth [2] part of the town or region which is yearly renewed may not be sufficient, so to speak, to leaven the whole region with the effect of the tax. It is, perhaps, significant of the preponderance of friction—the impotence of what may be called the normal forces—in this case, that Mr. Pierson, in his discussion of a rate on houses in a circumscribed region, such as *The City* in London,[3] considered as unaffected by the competition of extra-urban houses, has taken no account of the competitive influence exercised by *new houses within the region*. The action of friction in favour of the occupier in case (2) may be enhanced by the characteristic of case (4), the imperfect capacity of new houses to act as substitute for old ones.

Case (3) is affected less by the circumstance of paucity, and more by the circumstance of imperfect substitution.

The principal forces, normal and frictional, which are at work have now been analysed. But I have not sufficiently accurate knowledge of the facts to determine in concrete cases the resultant of all the forces. Doubtless, in virtue of friction, it may be expected that more or less of the tax will stick where it hits. But whether this expectation is greater when the tax is imposed on the occupier than when it is imposed on the owner, I am unable to say.

So far as to the incidence of the inhabited house duty on occupiers and owners. There is still to be considered its incidence on the ground landlord. This action is, of course, very slow, making itself felt immediately with respect only to the small

---

[1] *History of Local Taxation*, p. 135.   [2] Above, p. 134.   [3] *Loc. cit.* p. 178

proportion of sites for which new leases are being created at any time, with respect to the average of sites not until after many years—perhaps 40 or 50.[1]

Theoretically, a house being regarded as a sort of product grown upon the land,[2] a house tax paid by the occupier tends to diminish the ground rent through the diminution of the demand on the part of building entrepreneurs for sites. The limiting case is when the demand for houses is quite inelastic. Then the same amount of house accommodation is demanded before as after the imposition of the tax. The occupier pays the same rent as before *plus* the duty; the builder obtains the same profits; the ground landlord the same rent. In general, the imposition of the tax causes a diminution of demand for house accommodation; intending builders divert their enterprise to other investments; the ground landlord suffers through slackened demand for sites. But what the Exchequer loses through the diminished use of houses is not, in general, equal to what the ground landlords lose through the diminution of demand for sites.[3] Nor would the equality be of any fiscal significance, since what is lost by the ground landlords is not gained by the Exchequer. Indeed, the question has been raised whether an effect of this sort—detrimental to a certain class, without any corresponding benefit to the Exchequer—can properly be described as the *incidence* of a tax.[4]

(*b*)—(1) The principal difference, with respect to incidence, between the inhabited house duty and house rates is that the former is uniform, the latter may vary [5] from place to place. So far as such variation does not occur, the preceding analysis holds good of house rates. Where one locality is more heavily rated than another, the excess of rates may or may not correspond to extra advantages offered to occupants. For instance, a municipality may give more service in the way of lighting and cleansing than others in return for an equivalently heavy rate, or it may give

[1] Supposing the average term of a building lease to be 80 or 100 years.

[2] See answer to Question 5, last paragraph. Compare Mr. Goschen (*Local Taxation*, p. 164) :—" The inhabitant of the house is, in reality, the consumer of the commodity produced by the builder."

[3] Compare the formulæ given by the present writer in section 1 of the article on the Pure Theory of Monopoly (**E**).

[4] A dictum carrying the combined weight of Ricardo's and Adam Smith's authority can be quoted on the affirmative side of this verbal question. " The payment of this tax, then, would ultimately fall on the occupier and ground landlord, but ' in what proportion this final payment would be divided between them,' says Adam Smith, ' is not, perhaps, very easy to ascertain.' "—Ricardo, *Political Economy*, ch. xiv. (Taxes on Houses).

[5] Dudley Baxter has pointed out this difference very clearly.—*Taxation of the United Kingdom*, p. 65.

the same service, *e.g.*, in the way of drainage, at a heavier rate corresponding to disadvantages of situation.[1]

To begin with the second case, the differential rates will tend to divert demand from the locality, with the following results to occupiers and superior interests. The occupiers who are not driven away suffer the aggravation of rates; the occupiers who are driven away suffer a loss of *utility* (or " consumer's rent "). The owners during the remainder of their terms, and the ground landlords ultimately, suffer a loss of rent consequent on the slackened demand for houses in the locality.

These results are counteracted when the extra rates correspond to extra benefit. If that benefit is immediate, none of the parties need suffer. Demand is not slackened; rents do not fall. If the benefit is a future result of present outlay, both occupiers and owners will suffer temporarily in the ways above described. It is not true of differential rates that the occupier bears all the cost of improvements by which the owner is ultimately benefited.

(2) As pointed out by numerous authorities,[2] a rate on trade premises falls partly on the customer, partly on the trader, partly on the owner, in proportions difficult to determine : *ceteris paribus*, more upon the customer the greater his preference for dealing in the particular locality; on the trader the greater the loss incurred by him in moving to another place (or business); on the owner the longer his term. The only remark not quite familiar which occurs to me is that the owner of old premises is not quite so defenceless as might be supposed, since he benefits by the competitive action which is propagated from new premises in the manner indicated under head (*a*) 2.

(*c*) According to Ricardo, " a tax on rent " [in the proper sense of the *t*erm] . . . " would fall wholly on landlords." But " a tax on rent, as rent is constituted " [*i.e.*, true rent *plus* " quasi-rent," as we might now say] . . . would be a tax on the profits of the landlord." " The capital expended on these buildings, etc. [' the buildings and the improvements which are made by the landlord's stock '], must afford the usual profit of stock; but it would cease to afford this profit on the land last cultivated, if the expenses of these buildings, etc., did not fall on the tenant, and if they did, the tenant would then cease to make his usual profits of stock, unless he could charge them on the consumer."

[1] Compare Mr. Cannan's valuable analysis of the causes of inequality in local rates.—ECONOMIC JOURNAL, Vol. V. p. 31.

[2] *E.g.*, Professor Sidgwick, *Political Economy*, 2nd edition, p. 575, note; Professor Bastable, *Public Finance*, 2nd edition, p. 421; Mr. Blunden, *Local Taxation*, p. 55.

This general theory must be applied with caution to the present circumstances. It may be doubted whether English landlords expect their outlay on their estates to afford " the usual profit of stock "; the supply of such expenditure follows a special law, not that of the general investment-market. Moreover, with respect to produce for which there is a world market, such as wheat, the effect of agricultural rating in one country upon the price must be insensible. From the first incident it is deducible, I think, that the landlord will bear some part of the tax on the quasi-rent; from the second incident, that he will bear the greater part. On the other hand, as Mr. Blunden has ingeniously observed,[1] the farmer will not be able to shift on to the landlord any burden which is common to other industries, in particular that part of the rate which falls on his dwelling-house, say 5 per cent. of the total agricultural rate. Altogether, theory leads to the conclusion that the greater part of an agricultural rate falls on the landlord.

These theoretical tendencies are masked by friction, the action of which seems to vary with the conditions of supply and demand. Under the conditions which prevailed when Mr. Goschen wrote his classical report on local taxation, it may have been true that a farmer could not insist on his landlord's reducing the rent in consequence of the imposition of a rate. Dudley Baxter may have been right when he wrote : " On all the evidence that I can collect, I have little doubt that, although in theory the rates are paid by the landlord, yet in practice and on the average of tenancies, a portion of the rates does fall upon the tenant." [2] This portion was estimated by him as one-fourth. But under the present conditions, the " pull of the market " being against the landlord, " friction " seems to favour the tenant. I know of a case in which a set of agricultural tenants, threatened with a school board rate, declined to trouble themselves about the matter, averring their confidence that the whole rate would virtually have to be borne by the landlord. I know of many cases in which the tithe rent-charge was transferred from the tenant to the landlord, according to the Act of 1891, without any concomitant increase of the rent. Friction, as well as theory, seems now to make against the landlord.

(d) Taxes on the transfer of property fall indifferently on both parties, now on the buyer more, now on the seller.[3] Adam

---

[1] *Local Taxation*, p. 41.

[2] *Taxation of the United Kingdom*, p. 62.

[3] *Cp.* Professor Bastable, *Public Finance*, p. 547, and the present writer, above, S, p. 68.

Smith's *dictum* that " taxes upon the sale of land fall altogether upon the seller," for that " the seller is almost always under the necessity of selling," cannot be predicted generally of the sale of land including hereditaments.[1] But it is true wherever the proprietor has no use for the property except to sell it. One important application of this theorem is that a tax on the sale of urban sites, like a tax on ground rent, falls altogether on the ground landlord.

(*e*) As to the incidence of a tax on trade profits, I have only one remark to add to the received theories on the subject. The difficulties which I have elsewhere raised [2] as to the mode in which a tax on the profits of a particular trade is compensated by a rise in price seem to strengthen the probability of the tax acting as a preventive to improvements of production which would otherwise have been adopted.[3]

(*f*) Adam Smith's *dictum* that taxes on inheritance " fall finally as well as immediately on the persons to whom the property is transferred " is substantially incontrovertible. But there is much to be said for the view [4] that in propriety of speech such taxes fall immediately on the persons *from* whom the property is transferred. It is they who have the power of evading the tax (by donation to the living); it is they who bear the burden of that evasion when they forgo the luxury of bequest. Nor is Adam Smith's " finally " to be interpreted so strictly, but that this tax, like all taxes, will have diffused effects upon accumulation and production.[5]

7 and 8. *Primâ facie* some purposes may be distinguished as purposes for which taxation should be raised locally, namely, those of which the benefit accrues to the inhabitants of the locality exclusively; for instance, amenities which conduce to pleasure rather than efficiency. Conversely the taxation should be raised by the central Government for certain other purposes, such as national defence. But there is a large intermediate class where the benefit cannot be altogether allocated either to the part or the whole, *e.g.*, local police and education.

The criterion thus afforded by the proportion in which the

[1] *Cp.* Mill, *Political Economy*, Book V., ch. v. par. 1, note.

[2] Above, §, p. 78.

[3] This preventive action is indicated by J. S. Mill, *Political Economy*, Book V. ch. iv. par. 2, *sub finem*.

[4] As suggested by Sir Robert Giffen in Q. 63,281 of the Royal Commission on Agricultural Depression.

[5] See Professor Bastable, *Public Finance*, Book IV. ch. ix. par. 9; and compare the present writer, ECONOMIC JOURNAL, Vol. VII. p. 57, par. 2.

benefit is divided between the locality and the nation does not suffice to determine the proportions in which the expenditure should be borne. Where indeed the benefit accrues wholly to the locality, perhaps the expenditure should be wholly borne by the locality. But the converse does not hold, for it seems to be requisite for the sake of economical administration that some expenditure which is chiefly in the interest of the general public— for instance, the maintenance of the poor—should be largely borne by particular localities. *A fortiori*, the criterion is not available where the proportions in which the benefit is divided cannot be ascertained.

As Mr. Cannan says, " the expenditure does not fall into two clearly defined classes, and even if it did, the most consummate statesmanship would find it difficult always to reconcile the extension of the area of chargeability with economy in administration." [1] I am prepared to think that here, as in some other subjects, no principle is available except the general one which justifies the method of comparing, and in some sort averaging, the unanalysable judgments given by competent authorities conversant with the circumstances of each case.

9. It is convenient to answer this question after Question 10, and along with Question 12.

10. Ground rents should be specially rated, when newly created, in localities where an " unearned increment " has accrued to landlords. A contribution may thus be obtained from a source which would not otherwise be tapped.

This conclusion is at variance with reasoning which many experts have put before the Town Lands Committees.[2] It has been argued that as a rate on the occupier's rent ultimately burdens the ground-landlord, so a rate on the ground rent ultimately burdens the occupier. This reasoning seems to be incorrect in that it ignores what may be called the *marginal* character of economic transactions. If to each site there corresponded a building of a certain invariable cost, then it might be true that, if the rate is added to the occupier's payment, an equal amount must be subtracted from the ground-landlord's receipts; and, if the rate is subtracted from the ground-landlord's receipts, an equal amount must be added to the occupier's payment—the builder's profits being constant. But, theoretically, in general the cost of

---

[1] *History of Local Rates*, last page.

[2] See Evidence, 1887, Qs. 3,360 and 11,285; 1888, Qs. 2736, 2837, 3188, 4442, 9355; 1891, Q. 1969 *et seq.* (particularly lucid); see also Mr. Sargant's evidence before the Town Holdings Committee and his *Urban Rating*, pp. 45–52.

the building on each site is not to be considered as fixed beforehand. The builder will push his expenditure up to the point at which his last or " marginal " increment of outlay is likely to be only just compensated by the increase in the rent which he is to receive from the occupier. Accordingly, where there is a virtually *ad valorem* rate, the addition to the rate due to the last increment of value added to the house must be paid entirely by the occupier. Therefore, if we may treat house accommodation as a commodity sold in a market,[1] the rate, not only on the marginal increment but on the whole value of the building, will be paid by the occupier.

It may be objected that if the rate on the ground rent is applied to relieve the occupier, then the demand for houses being thereby increased, occupier's rents and ultimately ground rents will go up; the last state will be no better than the first.

This objection would have weight if it were proposed to apply the rate on each site to relieve the occupiers of that site. This proposal will be considered below as a case of division between the occupier and superior interests (see answer to question 12). But here we are entitled to assume that the proposed ground rate is applied to the relief of occupiers generally, or, what comes to the same, to the execution of improvements for which otherwise additional rates would have been imposed on the occupiers. No doubt the improvements tend to increase demand for residences, and this increased demand will tend to increase the occupiers' rents. But this tendency would equally have operated if the improvements had been executed at the occupier's expense, and the occupiers are gainers, by having them executed at the expense of the ground-landlords. No doubt the increased demand for residences will tend to increase ground rent; but the occupiers will gain by having these fresh accretions of ground rent in part applied to further improvements.[2] It would be a strange com-

---

[1] Compare Marshall, *Principles of Economics*, third edition, Appendix, Note XIV.

[2] The theory, as here stated, is not touched by the examples which Mr. Sargant has adduced in his *Urban Rating* (p. 47 *et seq.*) to prove that rates fall upon ground rent. His arguments are, perhaps, not aimed at, at any rate they do not hit, the position here taken up; that a special rate on the ground rent falls altogether on the ground landlord.

A case which has been confidently appealed to (by the writer of the *Digest of Evidence*, given before the Town Holdings Select Committee, Vol. II. p. 200), adduced by Colonel Sackville West, agent for Lord Penrhyn, in his evidence before the Town Holdings Commission (1888, Q. 11,560 *et seq.*). Of two parishes in the neighbourhood of the Penrhyn quarries, the rates of cottages were paid in Llandegai parish by the lessor, Lord Penrhyn; in Llandechid parish by the lessees, his workmen; and the ground rent per house in Llandegai was greater than the ground rent in Llandechid by almost exactly the amount of the rate per house,

plaint against a newly discovered source that, after it had been tapped, it was apt to be replenished.

While thus holding that the proposal to rate ground rents is theoretically sound, I hesitate in such a matter to follow pure theory very far without the support of specific experience. Possibly a rate of so much per cent. on ground rents generally—or on any other scale that could practically be employed—would prove *differential* in the sense which has just been explained.[1] Perhaps the market for house accommodation is not so perfect as the theory requires. Probably there are serious technical difficulties in the way of applying the theory. It may be difficult to distinguish true ground rent, which is the object of the proposed rating, from returns which the landlord may receive for the execution of improvements preliminary to building—for instance, drainage or road-making. It may be difficult to prevent the ground landlord from evading the proposed rate—for instance, by accepting a fine from the building lessee in lieu of a portion of the ground rent. It may be difficult to define the region in which ground rents, having received an " unearned increment," are a fit object of special taxation. Moreover, the immediate relief to be obtained from this new source of contribution is small; since ground rents form only a fraction of occupation rents, and new ground rents are created infrequently in the situations where the higher ground rents mostly occur, that is, on sites which have already been built on. However, the source is likely to become more considerable with the growth of population.

It will be remarked that the special rating of ground values is here based solely on the presumption that an unearned increment has accrued to the landlord. The proposal is not applied to " improvements " in the ground rent due to the landlord's outlay. It is not applied to ground rents already created. As pointed out by numerous expert witnesses before the Town Holdings Committee, such ground rents are fixed charges, which have not experienced any unearned increment.[2] They have been largely

---

viz. 9s. This case is somewhat peculiar, in that the ground landlord appears to have been virtually a monopolist. Hovever, the general principle that taxes on rent are borne by the landlord does not entirely fail on that account. If the authorities had seen fit to impose a special rate on the ground rent in these parishes, the landlord would probably have had to pay it all in Llandechid. (Theoretically, indeed, he could shift a part of it by restricting the amount of land offered.) In Llandegai, he would certainly have the resource of putting the ground rent on the same footing as that in Llandechid. But where the interests are divided by competition there could be nothing analogous to this latter adjustment.

[1] *Cp.* Answer 12.

[2] I should be prepared to modify this statement upon obtaining evidence that

bought by insurance companies and other prudent investors as specially safe securities; and they would seem to be very unsuitable objects for special taxation.

11. The laws which have been enunciated in Answer 6, for the imposition of a new rate, apply equally to the increase of an old rate. The laws for the reduction or abolition of a rate are given as the negative case of the former. The chief difference —beyond the change of *sign*—between the positive and negative case is due to friction. There is some reason for believing that friction resists an increase less than a reduction of rates. For one of the chief processes by which a change of rate is propagated is the competition between new and old houses, described in sections (2) and (3) of heading (*u*) in Answer (6). In the case of a new rate being imposed, intending occupiers of new houses bid against actual occupiers of old houses whose leases are expiring. In case of a rate being reduced, actual occupiers of old houses whose leases are expiring bid against intending occupiers of new. The competition is naturally keener in the former case. A slight difference of rate may decide an intending owner to apply for an old rather than a new house. But a considerable difference of rate may be required to determine an actual occupier to incur the trouble and expense of a move.

12. Division of rates between owner and occupier, whether by deduction or otherwise, profits little theoretically. If there is a perfect market in any commodity—it may be house accommodation, or it may be tea—the imposition of an ordinary tax (or rate), disturbing the balance of demand and supply, results in a rise of the price paid by the consumer. But it makes no difference to the result, theoretically, whether the tax collector takes his share of the price from the hands of the buyer or those of the seller.

The exceptions to this general proposition are principally due to friction. But there are some exceptions valid even in theory. A tax by way of licence to produce is, under certain circumstances, borne entirely by the producer, as pointed out in the answer to Question 4. If, then, a tax of this sort is commuted in part for an ordinary tax on the consumer, the producer will, theoretically, gain by the division. A consumer's licence presents a similar incident. " In Holland," says Adam Smith, " people pay so

---

the capital value of such fixed charges is generally and materially raised by an increase in the value of the houses on which the ground rent is charged. I am assuming (1) that, as Mr. Sargant says (*Urban Rating*, p. 101), " if it [the charge] is well secured, the addition can be but trifling," and (2) that it generally is well secured.

much a head for a licence to drink tea." If the licence was so
much, irrespective of the quantity of tea drunk, and not large
enough to deter many from becoming tea-drinkers, then, the
" final utility " of tea not being sensibly affected, the tax would
be borne altogether by the consumers. Accordingly, they would
be permanently gainers by the division of the impost with the
producers.

I don't know that this theory has much bearing on house-
rates in this country. Abroad, perhaps, some exemplifications
could be found   In Austria the " house-class " tax is proportioned
to the number of habitable dwelling-rooms irrespectively of the
style of architecture.   " The wealthy owner pays no higher rate
of taxation on a marble edifice . . . than the owner of a common
brick tenement with the same number of rooms." [1]   If this tax
was not large enough to cause a material reduction of the number
of rooms inhabited, the burden would stick where it hit; a
division of the tax between owners and occupiers would be
effectual.

The following theory is more germane to the purpose in hand.
If the occupier of a new house be entitled to deduct a portion of
his rent from the ground rent, then, for reasons above assigned,[2]
the ground landlord will be unable to shift this charge.   Thus
the occupier of a new house will experience a real relief which
will be propagated, by the influence of competition, to old houses
in the neighbourhood.   The rents of those old houses will be
reduced, the rates remaining the same; so that, even without
division, the burden would, *pro tanto*, be shifted to the owners.
Division, thus fortified, would be even theoretically effectual.

The buttress thus afforded to the project of division is itself
liable to give way.   It is threatened by the competition with
houses on cheaper sites.   The ground rents in such situations
will not be large enough to afford substantial relief to the occupiers.
Intending occupiers of such houses will therefore, according to
the theory stated in Answer 6 (*a*) (3), press in and compete against
the occupiers who are obtaining substantial relief by the deduction
of ground rents.   The advantage promised by reduction to the
occupiers of houses with expensive sites will thus be shifted back
to the owners and, ultimately, the ground landlords.   Things will
come round again, after much wasted trouble, to the *status in
quo ante*.[3]

---

[1] O'Meara, *Municipal Taxation*.
[2] See Answer 10.
[3] *Cp*. Answer 10, p. 143.

However, it is a tenable supposition that residences in neighbourhoods where the ground rent of new houses is high and those in which it is low are very imperfect substitutes for each other; that, even in the absence of friction, competition between them is feeble. Accordingly, the relief of occupiers by a certain percentage, say, 30 per cent. of the ground rent, though it would amount to different percentages of the occupiers' rent in different localities, say 12 per cent. in central and 6 per cent. in peripheral neighbourhoods, yet would fail to disturb the balance of demand for houses in those respective situations. On this supposition the division of rates between owner and occupier, buttressed by deduction from the ground rent in new houses with newly created ground rents, might stand. As conducive to the working of this arrangement the deduction of a moderate proportion only, say a third, of the occupier's rent may be recommended. Presumably this proportion should be deducted from the owner in the case of old houses, in the case of new houses with newly created ground rents from the ground landlord up to a certain proportion of the ground rent, say a third, and the remainder from the owner.

It will be remarked that in this reasoning, as throughout the answers, it is presumed that in the case of a new house the owner does not pay the rate, since he expects the ordinary profits on his investment—a circumstance which removes the case from the analogy of the income tax (referred to in Question 12), since the income tax, not being special to investment in building, cannot be shifted by the building owner.

Apart from the special arrangement which is here propounded as even theoretically defensible, I think it probable that in virtue of *friction*, if an occupier by whom a rate had hitherto been paid (Question 12) were empowered to deduct part of the rent from the owner, part of the burden would be thrown on the owner.

Altogether I am disposed to recommend that " local rates should be divided between owners and occupiers " (Question 9) as a means to that end; which appears to me desirable so far as owners are, or are about to be, in the enjoyment of unearned increment.[1] But, before pressing this recommendation, I should require to be satisfied that the principle of taxing unearned increment would be fairly applied. Perhaps some sort of court to make allowance for hard cases would be required. It should be observed that exemptions granted to individual owners would be ineffectual, since no individual could stand out for better terms than would be current in the neighbourhood. Exemptions could

[1] *Cp.* above, p. 142.

only be granted in favour of (the owners in) regions or zones practically isolated from external competition. As an additional precaution it might be recommended that the rule should not come into force until after the expiry of the occupier's lease; or at least not within some three years after the enactment. With these precautions the division could do little harm; it might do some good, and seem to do more. What seems may be as important as what is for the political purpose of appeasing discontent and getting municipal improvements adopted.[1]

Friction is most likely to be effective when the effect required of it is not very great. Friction may resist the force of gravity on a slope of 30 degrees, but fail to do so on a slope of 60 degrees. On the score of friction, therefore, as well with reference to the special deduction from ground-rent above proposed, it may be recommended that the deduction should not be very large; say, a third of the occupiers' rent. This proposal may square with the fact that it is difficult to give the owners a voice equal to that of the occupiers in the imposition of rates.

13. (a) The effect of a *progressive* rate would be to lighten the contribution of the poorer householders and thereby probably to make the distribution of fiscal burdens more equitable; possibly, to make the working classes more efficient. This desirable result is apt to be reduced by friction in the numerous cases [2] in which the rates are paid by the owners. *A fortiori* if, as testified by some,[3] the owners of small tenements act as monopolists. For in this case the relief of the occupiers will be, even theoretically, not indeed null, but probably less than in the case of perfect competition.[4] And practice may lag even further behind theory.

(b) An obvious tendency of rating property differently, according to its character and purpose, is to divert demand to the more favoured conditions. But in the more important existing cases of such difference, *e.g.*, between agricultural and urban rates, between rates on inhabited houses and those on trade premises, I do not suppose that this effect is considerable.

14 and 15. As to methods of raising revenue for local pur-

---

[1] Mr. Costelloe, among other witnesses before the Town Holdings Committee, insisted much on the impossibility of getting improvements adopted—the " deadlock " of the present system. *Cp.* Final Report, 1892, p. xxi : " In our opinion the change would do much to remove the sense of injustice which, whether rightly or wrongly, is no doubt at present very widely entertained."

[2] According to Mr. Sargant, three-fourths of all the cases.—*Town Holdings Committee*, Q. 4364.

[3] *Cp.* Mr. Costelloe's evidence before the *Town Holdings Committee*, 1890, Q. 4529.

[4] See Index, s.v. *Monopoly*

poses otherwise than by rates, I suggest that accurate information should be collected as to the expedients resorted to in foreign municipalities. At the same time, attention might be given to the teachings of experience abroad concerning the incidence of local taxation.

I express the opinion that, if such information is worth obtaining, it is worth printing legibly.

(U)

URBAN RATES

[IN this paper, published under the title of " Incidence of Urban Rates " in the ECONOMIC JOURNAL for 1900, the answers of several leading economists to questions put by the Royal Commission on Local Taxation are discussed with special reference to three leading questions. Firstly, the utilitarian criterion is restated with special reference to Local Taxation. Secondly, the incidence of a tax or rate levied on the occupation and rent of house premises is once more brought up for discussion. There is developed the attack begun in a former paper (S) upon the classical doctrine that the proportion of the impost falling on the occupier can be assigned from the proportion of the ground rent to the total rent of the premises. Lastly, various proposals for raising a revenue from ground rent or site-value are considered. Mill's proposal, confined to unearned increment, is entirely approved. It is shown that had this plan been adopted for London, in the 'sixties of last century, there would in 1900, without any shock having been given to the rights and expediencies of property, be flowing into the local treasury an additional revenue of some two millions annually. Other schemes, not adapted like Mill's to secure equity in distribution, and to avoid discouragement to production, are examined and condemned. The condemnation might have been less sweeping, if I had had before me at the time of writing (1900) the views expressed by Professor Pigou in his *Policy of Land Taxation*, 1909, set forth in the context of the following passage : " Let us eliminate for a moment the consideration of equitable distribution and focus attention upon the varying degree in which different taxes inflict indirect injury on the community in general." That a tax on rent other than what is unearned increment has some advantage on productional grounds was perhaps not sufficiently taken into account in the arguments employed in this paper. But arguments should always be interpreted by what they are intended to refute ; and it will be found that the schemes against which the polemic here reprinted was directed were not characterised by any regard for productional advantages, but were based on erroneous estimates of the income accruing from land as distinct from labour, confusion between rent proper and rent "as it is constituted," in Ricardo's phrase, that is, quasi-rent, metaphysical conceptions as to the peculiarities of property in land, culminating in the dictum of the single-taxer which puts a landowner on a par with a slave-owner, in fine, the influence of Mill's doctrine distorted and misapplied by socialistic rapacity and superstition.]

Incidence here denotes all those effects [1] of taxation with which the economist is concerned. The title thus interpreted covers part of the ground which the Royal Commission on Local Taxation has recently illuminated by the publication of "Memoranda" relating to the "Classification and Incidence" of taxes.[2] The Commission have accomplished a remarkable feat; they have improved on the British Blue Book. The oral examination of witnesses which characterises our Parliamentary inquiries is admirably adapted for eliciting authentic facts and expert opinion. But for the purpose of exhibiting trains of economic theory questions urged without concert are less serviceable—the Platonic dialogue itself would hardly be continuous enough for this purpose. It was therefore a brilliant idea to substitute paper work for *vivâ voce* examination. The reader who compares and combines the different answers given to the same questions may hope to obtain a more accurate and complete statement than if he had followed any one authority. He may not only obtain a corrected result, but may also test its correctness, if he employ this unique opportunity of observing how far propositions in political economy present the essential characteristic of science, consensus. With this *double* object in view it is now proposed to reconsider some of the matters about which the Commission inquired. A *third* purpose may at the same time

---

[1] Compare Mr. Cannan (at p. 166 of the *Memoranda* referred to in the next note) : " I have no doubt that it is better to eschew the use of the term ' incidence ' of taxation. . . . It is far better to consider the *effects* of taxation." Thus the effect of a tax on bicycles, according to Mr. Cannan's usage, reaches "not only to those who use bicycles, and benefit because other people use them, but also to those who would have used bicycles, or would have benefited by other people using them, if the obstruction of the tax had not intervened." According to the present writer's usage, the effect would also reach to the landlords of Coventry, so far as their rent might be reduced by the check to the production of bicycles.

[2] *Memoranda chiefly relating to the Classification and Incidence of Imperial and Local Taxes,* issued by the Royal Commission on Local Taxation, 1899 [C. 9528]; hereinafter referred to as " *Mem.*"

be subserved : to criticise some popular proposals in more detail
than the original questions suggested. The reconsideration
retains the form of answers to an examination paper. The
questions cover less ground than the original ones; the answers
are correspondingly narrowed, and are further abridged by the
writer's contenting himself with a bare reference to much of what
he has said in answer to the Commission.

QUESTIONS.

I. According to what first principles should the burden of
taxation be distributed ?

II. What are the effects of (1) an imperial tax, (2) a local rate,
levied upon the occupiers of houses in proportion to rent or
letting value ?

III. Distinguish and discuss schemes which have been proposed for rating owners of urban lands and buildings.

ANSWERS.

I. *First Principles of Taxation.*—An individual cannot hope to
reveal new axioms of conduct. He can at most fructify principles
already implanted in the mind of his contemporaries; much as
one member of a committee may frame a resolution expressing
the sense of the majority. In this spirit is submitted as a canon
now generally acceptable, that in distributing the burden of
taxation regard should be had to the " wants and feelings," in
Mill's phrase,[1] of the taxpayer. It is not merely that " every
tax ought to be levied at the time or in the manner in which it is
most likely to be convenient to the contributor to pay it "; consideration of the sacrifice incurred by the taxpayer dictates not
only Adam Smith's third and second canon, but also the modern
equivalent of his first. " It was not the amount of taxation,"
writes Sir Alfred Milner of Egypt under Ismail, " which did the
mischief, it was above all the irregular, cruel and arbitrary
manner in which the taxes were collected." In civilised countries
there is no hesitation about condemning an injurious manner
of levying taxes, the question is how the amount should be
apportioned as between the different classes of contributors.
It would be judged intolerable in the present age that the poor
should bear the greater part of taxation, as under the *ancien
régime,* or even a part proportioned to their income, as seemed

[1] Book V. ch. ii. § 4.

reasonable to McCulloch [1] and Cornewall Lewis.[2] The rationale
of the distribution which now finds favour appears to be no other
than those laws of sentience or " pathological propositions," upon
which, according to Bentham, " the good of equality is founded," [3]
by a constructive reasoning which is approved by Professor
Sidgwick.[4] Alike with respect to property and taxation, the
fundamental " law of diminishing utility " would carry us very
far in the direction of socialism, if this principle of utilitarian
distribution were not cut into by another utilitarian principle,
founded on the danger of restricting production.

" In considering the economic effects of taxes, we have to
allow weight to *productional*, as well as *distributional*, consequences,
and sometimes to allow more weight to the former." [5]

" Even in the interests of equity canons based on mere considerations of equity are often of but secondary importance
in practice." [6]

This principle also has what may be called its formal side,
relating to the immediate consequences of taxation, expressed in
Adam Smith's *fourth* canon, and in that which a modern authority
has called the " first and most important of the principles that
should guide the practical financier "—that " taxation should
be productive." [7] It may be, in the present state of civilis-
ation, that this preliminary " productional " condition cannot
be satisfied without prejudice to " distributional " requirements,
and the utilitarian must sadly acquiesce in an otherwise undesirable inequality of taxation as " inequitable and inevitable." [8]
But beyond the condition that taxes should be productive to the
Treasury, there are wider productional advantages to be taken
into account :

" Speaking generally, those systems of finance have caused
the least injustice and hardship which have most favoured the
development of the energies and inventiveness of the people,
which have hindered them the least in the selection of those routes
for the satisfaction of their wants." . . .[9]

---

[1] *Edinburgh Review*, Vol. LVII. p. 162.

[2] Report of the Select Committee on Parochial Assessments [1850. No. 622].
Evidence of Sir G. C. Lewis (Q. 2379). " My own opinion is unfavourable to a
graduated income tax, as I wish to see all persons contribute equally from their
means." [3] *Principles of the Civil Code*, Part I., ch. vi.

[4] *Political Economy*, Book III., ch. vii. § 1. *Politics*, ch. i. p. 9.

[5] Sidgwick, *Mem.*, p. 109. [6] Marshall, *Mem.*, p. 114.

[7] Bastable, *Public Finance*, III. 7, § 5.

[8] Mackay, *Mem.*, p. 220.

[9] Marshall, *Mem.*, p. 114 (immediately following the passage last quoted from
the same expert).

To this head—production, including economy and efficiency —may be referred the following provision (if it does not rather belong to the class of political considerations [1] omitted in this article).

" So long as a person retains the right of voting on the levying and expenditure of taxes, it is not safe that he should wholly escape onerous taxes." [2]

The infraction of utilitarian distribution thus threatened is avoided thus :

" It may be safe and reasonable to return to him or his children the equivalent of his payments in such benefits as will increase physical and mental health and vigour, and will not tend towards political conscription." [3]

When these benefits are set off against that burden, ought the net sacrifice to be the same for every taxpayer ? Or is the criterion not the equal sacrifice of each, but the least sacrifice of all ? The authority of Mill is invoked for the first doctrine ; the authority of Bentham may be invoked for the second. The two varieties of first principle have been balanced elsewhere ; [4] the following additional consideration is now thrown into the scale. It being admitted that the *desideratum* is some compromise between the benefits and burdens of taxation, if with Professor Sidgwick we leave out of consideration the *political* [5] conditions of a good tax (upon which the amount and kind of taxation depend largely), those conditions which the economist is principally concerned to realise may thus *primâ facie* be envisaged : to obtain the nearest possible approximation to equality of sacrifice, with the least possible check to the production of wealth. But this provisional description is not an accurate definition. For in order to obtain a maximum in respect of two quantities, there seems to be postulated a *third* quantity dependent on them, the maximum of which constitutes the *quæsitum*. This *tertium quid* can be nothing else but utility, advantage in general considered as varying both with the totality of production and the equality of distribution. This dialectic is exactly parallel to that by which it is concluded that the first principle of utilitarianism is, *not* " the greatest happiness of the greatest number," but

---

[1] *Cp.* note 5.

[2] Marshall, *Mem.*, p. 114.

[3] *Ibid.*

[4] *Mem.*, pp. 127–8, and references there given.

[5] *Political Economy*, III., ch. viii. § 6. " There are very important political reasons for preferring some laws to others, and for seeking to realise certain ends in taxation generally which lie beyond the scope of a strictly economic discussion."

the greatest quantum of happiness.[1] The more familiar statement has indeed some advantages. That it is more familiar
is no small advantage; another is that it emphasises an essential
condition of greatest happiness, that the means of happiness
should not be monopolised by a few. The popular, as compared
with the exact, formula has only one disadvantage : that it is
nonsense. To find the maximum of one quantity, A, " of " or in
relation to the maximum of another quantity, B, is a statement
of a problem in the calculus of variations which no amount of
authority can render other than inaccurate [2]—not the authority
of Mill, not even that of Bentham. Maine must be understood
as speaking of the substance, not the form, of the Greatest
Happiness principle, when he concludes that

" The only possible, the only conceivable principle which can
guide legislation on a great scale, is the greatest happiness of the
greatest number." [3]

It is a refinement of esoteric philosophy to object that this
only conceivable cannot be conceived; for the purpose of the
author's political argument the popular form is the most forcible.
May we not interpret with a similar freedom the experts who
have professed the principle of equal sacrifice ? Their object has
been evidently to apply the principle to the practical questions of
progressive taxation or exemption of minimum, not to define
with theological precision what Lord Farrer calls " the mysteries
of equal sacrifice." Consider, for instance, Mr. Courtney's [4]
weighty judgment :

" With respect to all services which are recognised as common
and indivisible the apportionment of their cost must follow the
principles of taxation in general. As to this the answer which
has most recommended itself to me is that taxation for common
purposes should be levied from each member of a community
according to the law of equal sacrifice, meaning thereby that each
individual should be mulcted of such a sum as would, having
relation to his means, involve the same sacrifice to the common
want. The suggestion which has often been made of allowing
to each member of the community an irreducible minimum
necessary for the maintenance of existence, before considering
the taxation of the overplus, is founded on an obscure appreciation of this doctrine of sacrifice, since the sacrifice becomes

[1] See Sidgwick, *Methods of Ethics*, Book IV. ch. i. § 2.
[2] *Cp.* below, **X**, p. 241.
[3] *Early forms of Government*, p. 400.
[4] Other experts who have explicitly professed the principle of equal sacrifice
are Giffen, p. 25; Sidgwick, p. 101; Gonner, p. 145; Blunden, p. 188.

infinitely greater when this minimum is trenched upon. Corre-
lative, however, to a reservation of the minimum is the suggestion
that with the extension of the overplus the proportion of the tax
may be increased, since the sacrifice diminishes as this extension
increases. The principle of graduation of taxation thus appears
to be dictated by considerations of pure justice, but it must be
admitted that it is extremely difficult to apply a rule of graduation.
It must be regulated by such conceptions as we may have of the
tenacity of attachment of the normal man to growing possessions,
and of the corresponding sacrifice involved in a tax on this tenacity.
All we can hope for is some rude measure of apportionment
approved by common morality."

The wisdom of these counsels would not be impaired if for
the " same sacrifice " to each taxpayer we substitute the *least
aggregate sacrifice*. What though the principle of least sacrifice
might prescribe a *less than equal* sacrifice on the part of the poor
man, yet, in view of the resistance of the " normal man " and
other practical considerations, the prescription is only a counsel
of perfection not practically distinct in its direction from the
nearer, though still very distant, goal of equal sacrifice. May we
not regard equal sacrifice as conducive to, and, in the phrase of
Mr. Courtney, " founded on an obscure appreciation of," the prior
principle ?

A fortiori, this interpretation is applicable to those who, with
Professor Bastable and Mr. Price, avoiding the mysteries of equal
sacrifice, rest in the happy ambiguity of " taxation according to
ability." Professor Bastable, indeed, when prescribing

" the canon of taxing according to ability, which may most
conveniently be regarded as measured by amount of income," [1]
is presumably to be read in connection with the parallel passage
in his *Public Finance :* [2]

" An equal charge will impose equal sacrifice on persons
of equal ' faculty,' and where abilities are unequal, a corresponding inequality in the amount of taxation will realise the aim of
equality of sacrifice."

But whether it is easier to say " ability " or " equal sacrifice,"
may not the practical arrangements suggested be just as well
regarded as realising the aim of least sacrifice ?

Still less do those who, with Professor Marshall, appeal to the
" obligations of duty," or " the public conscience " [3] discriminate

---

[1] *Mem.*, p. 140.   [2] Book III. ch. iii. § 3.
[3] *Mem.*, p. 113. Compare Mr. Caillie (*Mem.*, p. 244), quoting Montesquieu :
" The public revenues are not to be measured by what the people are able, but

against least sacrifice; upon any system of morals and politics. On the Utilitarian system the public conscience is informed by the Greatest Happiness principle. It is no clause of that principle that happiness, positive or negative, should be equally distributed.[1]

Nor does the equality of sacrifice derive any support from the equality of treatment asserted by some of the experts :

" No inequality of treatment shall be meted out as between individuals possessing similar amounts of wealth " (Cannan, p. 165).

" Equity demands, as a matter of course, that there shall be no exemptions of, or omissions to tax, particular classes or individuals " (Blunden, p. 189).

The equal treatment of different persons in identical cases is a condition underlying every reasoned theory of social conduct : formulated by Clarke as " a rule of righteousness," and sublimated by Professor Sidgwick into an axiom of Utilitarianism.[2] Now Utilitarianism, as stated above on the highest authority, aims at least, rather than equal, sacrifice.

Of course, it is not pretended that the Utilitarian maximum problem has been made easy by being made more intelligible. The difficulty of the *unit*,[3] which some regard as insuperable, still remains. " We cannot hope for more than a very rough approximation." [4] " No near approach to equity in taxation is attainable." [5] " But although the pursuit can never be wholly, or even very largely, successful, the quest is not therefore to be abandoned." [6] Faint as the light is of our guiding principle, it is infinitely preferable to the moral darkness which succeeds

---

by what they ought to give " (Liv. XIII., ch. i.). It is in this spirit that Montesquieu says later : " Dans l'impôt de la personne la proportion injuste seroit celle qui suivrait exactement la proportion des biens " (Liv. XIII., ch. vii).

[1] *Cp.* Sidgwick, *Politics*, ch. xxx. § 2. " If it is meant that equality in the distribution of happiness is in itself to be aimed at, the maxim is certainly different from the general utilitarian principle which I have taken as fundamental. . . ." " To aim at equality in distribution of happiness may obviously be incompatible with aiming at the greatest happiness on the whole."

[2] " That the good of any one individual is of no more importance as a part of universal good than the good of any other." *Methods of Ethics*, Book III. ch. xiii. § 4.

[3] Attention may be called to Dr. A. Voigt's reflections on the measurement of economic advantage by *ordinal* numbers, degrees of utility being distinguished as *first, second*, etc., in the order of magnitude, but not as multiples of a unit. (*Jahrb. f. d. Gesammt. Staats*, 1893, No. 4; noticed in the ECONOMIC JOURNAL, Vol. IV p. 202.)

[4] Sidgwick, *Mem.*, p. 101.

[5] Marshall, *Mem.*, p. 114.

[6] Blunden, *Mem.*, p. 189.

when regard for the feelings of the poor who bear the burden of taxation is extinguished. By what other test than sympathy with sacrifice is judgment to be formed upon what Mill calls [1] "the disproportionate weight" with which the customs and excise duties " press on the poorer classes " ? Without that test could we even condemn the iniquities of the *ancien régime* ? The more objective criterion of "productional" interests might indeed forbid such taxation of necessaries as would prejudice efficiency. But would regard for production be an adequate inducement to exempt a minimum from income tax, or to spare the comforts of the masses ? It is only the more intelligent " shepherds of the people " who, in order the more frequently to shear, will take care never to flay, their flocks.

The taxation thus far considered has been *onerous*, which may be defined as

" taxation to defray expenditure of which the benefit (if any) which accrues to the individual taxpayer is so vague and indirect that the principle of proportioning payment to benefit is inapplicable." [2]

When the benefits of Government can be allocated to individual recipients, the rule is that they should be paid for by the recipients.[3] This is desirable both on productional and distributional grounds; both to prevent the wasteful use of the service, and to secure an equitable distribution of net sacrifice as between those who use and those who do not use the service. But this general rule, as we have seen,[4] has an exception, when a benefit is intended as a compensation for an inevitable burden, and is not likely to be used wastefully. Generally when Government does make a charge for the use of a public service like the Post Office, the price which the consumer has to pay is not the measure of the benefit which he obtains, as in a regime of open competition.[5] Nor, if a service is supplied gratis to private individuals, as the use of a road maintained for military reasons at the national expense, or the free education of children,[6] is the cost to Government a measure of the benefit special to the individuals using the service. The question what services Government should undertake, what things people should be left to do for themselves, is not considered here.

---

[1] *Political Economy*, Book V., ch. vi. § 3.

[2] Sidgwick, *Mem.*, p. 110.

[3] *Cp.* Sidgwick, *Politics*, ch. xi. § 4; *Mem.*, p. 101; Courtney, *Mem.*, p. 85, last par.   [4] Above, p. 154.

[5] Experts in reply to the third question set by the Commission.

[6] Courtney, *Mem.*, p. 85.

These propositions, applied in the first instance to individual taxpayers, may be extended to the financial relations between the sovereign state and corporate units, such as municipalities and the component parts of a kingdom or empire. The large relief from the burden of taxation which *primâ facie* on distributional grounds should be afforded to the less prosperous subordinate communities, is restricted by the productional principle, that those who have a share in calling the tune should have a share in paying the piper.[1] However, the hurt thus done to distribution may be alleviated by imperial subventions. In the result there should be fulfilled the condition that the members of poorer corporations or other sections of the nation should suffer a sense of burden or sacrifice equal with, or at any rate not greater than, the onus felt by the richer classes. But the condition can only very approximately be realised, indeed only very imperfectly defined. For example, some exemption from taxation is reasonably claimed for Ireland, on account of her comparative poverty; but to draw up this claim with the precision of a commercial account shows a misconception of the whole theory. " The claim does not rest on grounds of arithmetic, but of human wants and feelings," as Mill says with reference to the " general principles of taxation." The short method of determining the contribution of the wealthier part of a United Kingdom by means of its available surplus is the more inadmissible in that it ignores the *productional* consideration of part of the " surplus " as necessary for efficiency.[2] But while remembering that the directions of our chief guide are not perfectly precise, let us not forget that they are the best we have; far better than the false simplicity of financial relations, which minds uninformed by Utilitarian philosophy are prone to accept. The specious maxim that the same commodity should be taxed identically in different regions may be instanced as one in which official routine would be apt to acquiesce, if uncontrolled by a regard for the feelings of the people who pay the taxes.

The condition that Governmental aid should not encourage waste is to be construed strictly in dealing with corporations. So insidious is the tendency of " doles " to pauperise. What grant could appear less demoralising than one for the maintenance of pauper lunatics ? Yet, as Mr. Mackay brings evidence to prove,[3] the financial advantage to be gained by a locality if it can get

[1] *Cp.* Farrer, *Mem.*, p. 69.

[2] As pointed out by Professor Sidgwick in the *Memorandum* which he contributed to the " Financial Relations " Commission. *Cp.* above, **S**, p. 119.

[3] *Mem.*, p. 232.

some of its paupers classed as lunatics has led to unexpected abuse. It is pointed out by Mr. Cannan[1] that imperial subventions designed to alleviate the inequalities of natural advantages in different localities would tend to an uneconomic distribution of capital and population—though, on purely distributional grounds, as tending to equalise net burdens, such grants might be advocated. In estimating the benefit derived by a section of the nation from a public service special to that section it would not in general be proper to take the cost to the Government as the measure. Thus the benefit to the Irish people of the Constabulary maintained by imperial expenditure for partly imperial ends, is not to be measured by the whole, but only by a part—Sir Edward Hamilton has suggested half[2]—of that expenditure.

What services should be supplied by the central Government to the subordinate community is a question not considered here. But the case in which a municipality supplies its own wants has an aspect which concerns us. The burden of the contributions required for that purpose is to be distributed among the members of the subordinate community according to the principles which we have been investigating with respect to sovereign communities. Part of the local taxation will be *onerous* in this sense, that the benefit sought by the subordinate community as a whole cannot be allocated to the individual ratepayers. Onerous in a *secondary* sense let us say, in contradistinction to the use of the term with reference to *national* purposes. Is the bulk of ordinary local taxation to be regarded as onerous in this secondary sense? There is much to be said for this usage. As Professor Seligman puts it :

" Even in local finance, where a general tax is levied to defray all the local expenditures, it cannot be maintained that the benefits arising from the action of the local judiciary, of the police, of the fire service, of the Board of Health, or of the other departments of local government, are separately measurable for each individual. . . ."

" Although the particular area which is benefited is put into a separate class, the benefits to the individual of the class are general, not special, exclusive or individual benefits " . . . " as

---

[1] *Mem.*, p. 170.

[2] Evidence before the Financial Relations Commission (c. 7720, II., p. 116). " In order to be absolutely fair towards Ireland, I will consider that half the charge the Irish Constabulary and Dublin Police is an imperial charge, just as if it were a military charge."

to every one within the class, the tax is payable, whether the particular individual receives much or little benefit." [1]

Certainly it would be infelicitous to characterise local taxation as " beneficial " on the mere ground that the expenditure of the municipality is directed to its own as distinguished from the national purposes. The analogy of a corporation supplying its own wants is not with an individual paying beneficial taxation to the central Government, but with an individual who procures commodities for himself. On the other hand, it is to be considered that the expenditure on the usual objects of local taxation is apt to redound to the pecuniary advantage of the contributories more directly than the expenditure of onerous national taxation. The cleansing of streets and sewers has the result that the occupiers of residences in the improved neighbourhood enjoy a commodity of higher market value; but the removal of a stain from the national flag is not an asset to the average citizen even approximately proportionate to his share of taxation. The tendency of a national onerous tax to " make the more roving classes live abroad," acutely noticed by Mr. Sargant,[2] is indeed a phenomenon similar in kind with that competition between localities which renders non-remunerative local taxation distributed according to " ability " or " sacrifice " difficult.[3] But the difference in degree [4] seems to justify the usage of the experts.[5] Though in general theoretically the burden of taxation, in the case where the benefit sought by the community as a whole cannot be allocated among the individual members, ought to be distributed according to the same law of " sacrifice " or " ability " in a subordinate as in a sovereign community, yet in fact in our municipalities there does not occur much onerous taxation of this sort. What is called onerous local taxation is usually that which does not redound to the advantage of the ratepayers as a body directly or otherwise than as they are members of the nation, for instance, as much of the poor rates as does not conduce to the special benefit of the municipality.[6] Of onerous local taxation in this *primary* sense, it is evidently true that

---

[1] *Essays in Finance*, pp. 345-6.   [2] *Mem.*, p. 212.

[3] *Cp.* Cannan, *History of Local Taxation*, p. 132 *et seq.*

[4] *Ibid.* p. 133. " On the whole, it may be said that the [existing] system is more in accordance with . . . the principle . . . of taxation according to benefit than with . . . that of taxation according to ability."

[5] *Cp.* Sidgwick, *Mem.*, p. 111, par. 4; Marshall, p. 113 (on " remunerative " taxes); Bastable, 140, par. 2; Rice, p. 183, par. 2; *et passim*. According to Wagner (*Die Communalsteuerfrage*, p. 31), the principle of benefit has a greater scope in communal taxation, though still only the *second* leading-principle.

[6] Sidgwick, *Mem.*, p. 107.

" onerous taxes, Imperial and Local, must be treated as a whole." [1]
It may be worth observing that this proposition contains a
truth even in the secondary sense in which " onerous " relates
to the purposes special to the municipality, but not assignable to its individual members. For although on productional
grounds only members of the subsidiary community should
contribute to advantages that are enjoyed only by that community,[2] yet the utilitarian distribution of a (substantial) burden
of taxation that is onerous in the secondary sense among members
of the subsidiary community will theoretically affect their
relative prosperity, and thereby affect the distribution of taxation that is onerous in the primary sense. So true in every
sense it is that

" the system of taxation, with regard to which all questions
of equity must be considered, comprises both imperial and local
taxes." [3]

Altogether the distinctions between national [4] and local,
between onerous and beneficial taxation, are not so fundamental
as to be the ground of essentially different regulations. All the
received canons and categories appear subordinate to the golden
rule, that the detriment attending an assigned amount of taxation should be a minimum, and the grand distinction between
modes of detriment, diminution of the total production and
aggravation of unequal distribution.

II. *Imposts on Occupiers*.—The effects of a tax or rate vary
with a variety of cases, of which the definition in each context is
commended to, without being intruded on, the attention of the
critical reader. One essential difference is between new and old
houses, those built and occupied before or after the imposition of
the tax or rate. Let us begin with the first head, and under it
first consider *dwelling*-houses. As to tenure, let us take as
typical the English leasehold system; observing that, for our
purpose, it does not much matter whether the lease is for 99,
or for 999 years, or, as in the case of " feu duties," for ever.[5]
Nor does it matter whether, in addition to the three principal
parties—the ground landlord, the building owner, and the occupier—there is intercalated a fourth or fifth party, such as the holder
of an " improved leasehold ground rent," or other sub-lessee.

---

[1] Marshall, p. 113.   [2] Sidgwick, *Mem.*, p. 99, last and penult. par.
[3] Gonner, *Mem.*, p. 159.
[4] " nicht principiell ganz verschieden," Wagner says of these (*Communalsteuerfrage*, IV.).
[5] The varieties of tenure prevalent in this country are clearly explained by
Mr. Sargant in the first chapter of his *Urban Rating*.

An *ad valorem* tax on the gross rent which the occupier pays will obey the general law which governs taxes of consumable commodities. The economist has not to construct a special law of taxation for the taxing of houses, any more than the physicist has to construct a special law of gravitation for the tumbling of houses. It is deducible by received general reasoning that the three parties in the proposed typical case will be affected as follows. The occupier will suffer not only by paying more for the house accommodation which he continues to use, but also by forgoing part of what he would have used but for the impost.[1] "Residences in different places constituting rival commodities . . . a uniform tax may so disturb the balance of complex demand as to cause a certain rush of inhabitants from one town to another." [2] A similar disturbance of the marginal utility and the quantity demanded of different styles of house accommodation would result [3] (even from the uniform national house tax here contemplated, and, *a fortiori*, from the actual inhabited house duty). The capitalist building owner will not (in the long run) be damnified at all, or only inasmuch as, if house-building is a sensible portion of the total industry, general profits would be depressed.[4] The ground landlord will be damnified by the relaxed demand for sites. The reduction of ground rents will be greater, *ceteris paribus*, the greater the elasticity of the occupier's demand for house accommodation.[5]

[1] *Mem.*, p. 127, par. 1. Compare Mr. Cannan in the passage referred to above, at p. 172.

[2] *Mem.*, p. 130. It is possible that the *minimum* disturbance of this sort would result from a tax *not uniform*.

[3] It is conceivable that the demand for houses of a certain kind might be *increased* by the tax. *Cp.* Marshall, *Principles of Economics*, Book III. ch. iii. § 6, note :—" It is even conceivable, though not probable, that a simultaneous and proportionate fall in the price of all teas may diminish the demand for some particular kind of it." Adam Smith supposes that a tax " payable by the inhabitant " would diminish the competition for houses " of all other rents except the lower rent for which it would for some time increase the competition " (*Wealth of Nations*, Book V. ch. ii.). His reasoning is perfectly correct on a probable supposition that the demand for housing is tolerably elastic for the higher styles and rigid for the indispensable minimum of accommodation—conditions which it is not easy to state exactly without the use of symbols, such as those employed in the treatment of *correlated demand* by the present writer, above S, p. 72; referring to E.

[4] *Cp.* ECONOMIC JOURNAL, Vol. VII. p. 68, where the observation is traced to Professor Pantaleoni's original *Traslazione dei Tributi*.

[5] The evidence of this proposition is of a sort which frequently occurs in mathematical economics. The proposition is true, not universally, but probably, its quality depending on the form of a function which is unknown, but may be presumed in the long run of cases to be favourable to the proposition. Thus, in the case before us, it is conceivable, but improbable, that the less expensive buildings,

These propositions are sufficiently evidenced by the general reasoning of the older economists, supplemented by the modern doctrine of *margins*. If specific experience is demanded, it may be found in the evidence of Sir Sidney Waterlow before the Local Taxation Commission of 1870. The effects which a tax exerts upon the margins of production and consumption are clearly indicated in the following passages :—

" Supposing there were no local rates at all, the profits would have been so large that we should have been tempted immediately to increase supply." (Q. 3411). . . .

" You cannot increase the quantity of land, but you may increase the quantity of building on a given piece of land, and if you put seven storey houses instead of two, of course you get an increased quantity of the article, and then the law of supply and demand comes in and affects the rent." (Q. 3440.)

" There is . . . a limit in height both as affecting the cost of construction and the question of convenience to the tenants." . . . " It is only in districts where there is a great demand for houses that you are able to build the flats one above the other, and the landlord is able at the same time to get a high ground rent." (Q. 3516–7.)

The solution of the problem here offered is confirmed by its agreement with the conclusions of the experts, as evidenced by the following extracts read in connection with their contexts.

Farrer, p. 67 :—" Abolish the house duty and the Duke of Bedford's income would probably be increased."

p. 68 :—" The error of supposing that rates are wholly paid by the occupier of houses in towns, and are not shifted at all on to the reversioner."

Courtney, p. 86 :—" Where there is no special advantage of site or position . . . the abolition of a house duty would be a relief to the occupier only, and the imposition of a house duty would be a burden on the occupier. Even if the duty had the effect of compelling the occupier to live in a house less commodious than he would otherwise obtain, the burden would still

---

which would be resorted to in consequence of the tax, would be of a construction which required a larger area than the many-storeyed mansions which it was profitable before the tax to erect. The proof of the theorem that improvements in agriculture tend to reduction of rent appears to be of the kind here contemplated. (*Cp.* as to this theorem, Marshall, *Principles of Economics*, Book VI. ch. ix. final note.) Other instances occur in the mathematical theory of taxation in a regime of monopoly. (See Index, s.v. *A priori Probability*.)

rest upon him, not by making him pay more, but by giving him less for his money."

Sir Robert Giffen, p. 96 :—" The inhabited house duty is a consumption tax."

Sidgwick, p. 103 :—" When the tax has become *old*, it may be assumed that no part of it is borne by builders as such. . . . The rent paid for a house must be sufficient, speaking broadly, to allow the builder of new houses as much profit as he would have had if the tax had not been imposed . . . the tax must be assumed permanently to reduce in some degree the demand for houses. . . ."

p. 105 :—" The prevalent belief, that the extra burden of the high rates of London and other towns really falls in the main on the occupiers of houses as such, would seem not to be well-founded." . . .

Marshall, p. 117 :—" The inhabited house duty being onerous tends to check building."

Bastable, p. 141 :—" So far as demand for building is reduced by it [the inhabited house duty], the ground landlord is affected."

Conner, p. 153 :—" It is levied on a consumable commodity, namely, a house, and thus will fall, in the first instance, on the immediate consumer. The consumer cannot shift it on to the owner, as in that case the profits of a particular trade would be specially taxed."

Cannan, p. 168 :—" Let us suppose that there has hitherto been no house tax, and that a universal tax of 5*s*. in the £ for unproductive purposes is placed on all dwelling-houses, and levied on the occupiers. Let us suppose also that the occupiers are on quarterly tenancies, all of which expire between the passing of the Act and its coming into force. The immediate effect must be a fall in house rent. All occupiers must restrict either their expenditure or their savings in some direction, and enough of them will try to reduce their expenditure on rent plus house-tax to make a great diminution in the demand for house room. As the number of houses has not yet been altered by the tax, the supply remains the same, and consequently the price must be reduced. But this reduction of rent, of course, reduces the capital value of houses; the capital value being reduced, some professional builders retire from the business and others become bankrupt, and the supply of houses is consequently reduced. Building stops, or proceeds at a slower rate, until building profits are restored to the ordinary level by a rise of house rent and the capital value of houses. The occupiers then have to pay more for the same accommodation, or to be content with worse accommodation for the same money.

"A tax on a particular form of property does damage to the owners of property in general as well as the consumers of the commodity connected with the particular class of property" . . . [a fact] "of trifling importance in the case of a tax on a small class of property."

Sargant, p. 212 :—"Among tendencies of the inhabited house duty . . . which tend to throw by anticipation small part of the constant rates . . . on to the owners of the sites, are (1) the tendency of the tax to make occupiers inhabit smaller houses or tenements." [1]

Mackay, p. 226 :—"There is only one market for capital and enterprise, and if the business of house-building is to go on, it must give the normal rate of profit to those engaged in it. The producer may evade the loss involved in the increased cost of production . . . by limiting supply till increased demand raises the price."

The experts who are not quoted as gathering with the doctrine here propounded are not to be understood as scattering against it. There seems to be only one irreconcilable dissentient, Mr. Gomme,[2] and even he is not very decided. Why then is a larger show of concord not exhibited? The answer to this question may be interesting to other students of synoptic economics.

In the first place writers of answers to the paper set by the Royal Commission very properly remembered that they were not undergoing an ordinary examination; and did not seek to cover the ground evenly, after the manner of a candidate who knows that his examiner is prohibited by an official rule from assigning more than a certain maximum to each answer. Mr. Cannan, for instance, whose answer as to the effect of a house tax on the occupier and building owner is in striking accord with ours, does not go on with us to mention the effect of ground rent on the decline of investment in building, having occasion to invoke that obvious corollary in a subsequent passage in connection with an original theory of his own. Again, Mr. Mackay, resuming the whole theory of incidence from an independent standpoint, gives a general support to our propositions which it is not possible to exhibit by a quotation within our limits.

Other writers have glanced away from our inquiry in an opposite direction, by keeping quite close to the question set by

---

[1] Mr. Sargant's head (2) is referred to on p. 161, above.
[2] *Mem.*, p. 241, last par.

the Commissioners. Their answer relates to the concrète incidents of the British Inhabited House Duty, not to the general question here proposed. It is thus that we may interpret Professor Bastable, when he writes :—

" Broadly speaking, this tax falls finally, as well as immediately, on the occupier. So far as demand for building is reduced by it, the ground landlord is affected, but this influence must be trifling." (*Mem.*, p. 141.)

The inhabited house tax being small, if the demand for house accommodation is of an ordinary kind, not approaching perfect elasticity, which there is no reason to believe, the influence of the tax on the demand for ground must be " trifling." The immediate context about the incidence of rates—said to be more complex owing (*inter alia*) to " their greater amount "— bears out this interpretation. A similar explanation is probably to be given of certain other round statements as to the incidence of the tax on the occupier, *e.g.*—

" Speaking generally, I think the inhabited house duty is borne by the occupier . . . the proposition remains generally true, as far as houses occupied for domestic purposes are concerned that inhabited house duty is paid by the occupier." (Courtney, p. 86.)

It would seem from the context that Mr. Courtney's dictum rests upon a particular matter of fact concerning which the general theory here propounded makes no assumption, namely that the case " where there is no special advantage of site or position " (*loc. cit.*) may be regarded as the general one, rather than the case " where site or position forms an important part in the value of the house." The assumption seems to have been made by some of the older economists,[1] and was probably truer in their time than now. However this may be, to assign a particular value to one of the coefficients in a general formula is not to invalidate the truth of that formula.

This last remark is to be borne in mind in considering Mr. Blunden's attitude of dissent. He finds that—

" the real incidence of this tax [the inhabited house duty] is normally and generally upon the occupier " (*Mem.*, p. 189), by assigning a particular value to a co-efficient which we have left undetermined, the elasticity of demand for house accommodation. He in effect puts *zero* for the value of this coefficient.

" The surrender of some portion of their customary house

[1] *Cp.* J. S. Mill, *Political Economy*, Book V. ch. iii. § 6, par. 5.

accommodation is for many reasons repugnant to the feelings of the great majority of householders, and would only be resorted to under the strongest pressure, and in a small proportion of cases " (*Mem.*, p. 190).

The question here raised is important in its bearing not only on an imperial house duty, but also on local house rates, so far as they are both onerous and uniform, or not tending to divert demand from one locality to another. It appears to the present writer impossible to reconcile Mr. Blunden's statement with general presumptions as expressed by Adam Smith in a well-known passage,[1] or with specific statements made by competent witnesses; for instance, some of those implied in passages above cited from Sir Sidney Waterlow's evidence above quoted, or the following : [2]

" [If we had raised rent] ' those who had three rooms would have gone into two rooms ' . . . ' they are obliged [in such a case] to take . . . a cheaper tenement which is inferior in quality or accommodation.' " [Evidence of Sir Sidney Waterlow, *loc. cit.* Qs. 3433 and 3437.]

" When the distress came on, mechanics, formerly in receipt of good wages, and living in two or three rooms, packed themselves into one." [Evidence of Dudley Baxter before Select Committee on Local Taxation, 1870, No. 353, Q. 5799.]

Nor is Professor Seligman, to whom Mr. Blunden appeals, convincing when he maintains :

" House accommodation is in part an absolute necessity, in part, an expensive luxury. . . ."

" Many people prefer to maintain their supposed station in life at any cost. In such cases, a law on house accommodation tends, as in the case of all taxes on luxuries, to make them forgo other things which they deem less desirable." [3]

---

[1] *Wealth of Nations,* Book V. ch. ii. " He will therefore content himself with a worse house." . . . " The final payment of this tax would fall partly upon the inhabitant of the house, who, in order to pay his share, would be obliged to give up a part of his revenue." *Cp.* above, p. 71, and p. 84, note 7.

[2] It should be mentioned that Mr. Blunden appeals to specific personal experience on the other side. In a letter which he allows the present writer to refer to, Mr. Blunden says : " It is due to my daily observation of the facts (and not to any preconceived theory) that I hold the opinion that there is in actual life a much greater rigidity in the demand than has very usually been assumed. . . . I have for many years past, and in many localities, been engaged more or less in examining returns of rents paid, many of which are accompanied by statements of the income of the rent payers. . . . As a result of my experience, I have become convinced that the effects of high or rising rates in lowering the standard of house accommodation is ordinarily inappreciable."

[3] Seligman, *Shifting and Incidence,* 2nd ed., p. 153.

Upon general presumptions, should we not rather expect that intermediate between the class to whom the amount of house accommodation which they now enjoy is an absolute necessity and the class to whom it is an indispensable luxury, there would be a large class to whom house accommodation would be an article of the kind which has been called a mass-luxury, very apt to be consumed in greater quantities as the price decreases? [1] On the whole, no adequate reason seems to have been shown for dissenting from Professor Marshall's judgment :

" Where the condition of society is healthy, and there is no check to general prosperity, there seems to be an elastic demand for house-room on account of both the real conveniences and the social distinction which it affords." [2]

Mr. Price's position, so far as it is really different from that which is here taken, is to be explained by the last-mentioned circumstance, a different estimate of one of the quantities involved; but the difference is, for the most part, only apparent. Mr. Price says :

" The primary incidence of the inhabited house duty falls on the occupier, and it is probable that to a very large degree the real incidence of the tax corresponds with its primary and apparent incidence." [3]

But there is nothing in the reason which he assigns in the immediate context with which the present writer cannot wholly agree :

" Some, at least, of the reasons, which may be adduced in support of the theory that the burden of local rates is shifted from the occupier, do not apply to the case of the inhabited house duty. The occupier is unable to remove, or diminish, the burden, to any practical extent, by changing his abode. He cannot move to another district where the duty is lower, for it is an imperial tax, levied on uniform principles throughout the country." [4]

It should seem that the writer has here in view the operation of the house duty on occupiers already accommodated with houses; a case which, in our division of the subject, does not yet come up for consideration, upon which, under another head, a complete agreement with Mr. Price will be expressed. It is true that Mr. Price adds :

[1] Compare the examples of different degrees of elasticity in the demand of the same article by different classes of society, given by Professor Marshall, *Principles of Economics*, Book III., ch. iv. §§ 2, 3, 4, ed. 4, p. 178 *et seq.*

[2] *Principles of Economics*, Book III, ch. iv. p. 182.

[3] *Mem.*, p. 180.   [4] *Ibid.*

" His [the occupier's] house accommodation is, within narrow limits of increase or decrease of requirements, a fixed item in his standard of comfort." [1]

" Expenditure on house accommodation is within limits elastic." [2]

Here there seems to be made a particular assumption as to the form of the " demand-curve " for house accommodation : whereas, in the view of the present writer, there is legitimately only a general presumption that the demand is of an ordinary character, neither very elastic nor yet perfectly inelastic.

One more reason for not more largely producing the evidence of the experts is their occasional use of a certain terminology respecting the division of burden between occupier and landlord, which, however justified by authority, the present writer ventures to regard as infelicitous. The following is, perhaps, the most explicit, but by no means the only instance of the usage referred to :

" So much of the house duty as was proportionate to this [the ground] rent and, so to speak, attached to it, would be ultimately borne by the person entitled to receive this rent." (Courtney, p. 86.)

In this and similar passages there seems to be implied the doctrine which McCulloch has expressed with particular clearness :

" Were the supply of houses easily diminished and increased, a tax on their rent would fall wholly on occupiers and ground landlords, and be divided between them in the proportion which the profit of the capital required to build them bears to the ground on which they stand." [3]

It being universally admitted that, in McCulloch's words, " there are few chapters in Dr. Smith's great work more unsatisfactory than his chapter on rent," it will not appear particularly impious to dispute a formula which involves Adam Smith's obsolete conception of rent forming part of price. The formula

---

[1] *Mem.*, p. 180.

[2] *Ibid.*, p. 181, par. 5.

[3] *Taxation and Funding*, Part I. ch. i. § 2; criticised, along with J. S. Mill's parallel statement, by the present writer, above, S, p. 83 *et seq*. It is not quite clear whether McCulloch and the other eminent writers who have adopted this proposition mean the proportion between the profit and the ground-rent as they would have been if the impost had not existed, or as they are after the impost. The question is of the less importance, since for an indefinitely small tax which the appropriate mathematical analysis takes as the typical case the two statements *might have been* equally true, and since in fact they are equally false.

seems to have been repeated by the successors of Adam Smith,[1] much as Adam Smith employed a few expressions savouring of the physiocratic errors which he had himself refuted. To remove the misconception it is sufficient to consider cases in the neighbourhood of the limit at which the demand of the occupier is perfectly rigid. In such cases, whatever the proportion of the ground rent to the gross rent paid by the occupier, the detriment to the ground landlord is nothing or next to nothing, as may be verified by substituting *barley* for *house accommodation*,[2] and employing the received theory of agricultural rent. Whoever heard, outside the pages of Adam Smith, of that part of a tax on barley which falls on rent? In general, the detriment to the ground landlord depends on the *marginal* conditions of production and consumption, and is independent of the *total* magnitudes of the ground rent and the gross rent (and the proportions between them), just as, to adopt an illustration of economic equilibrium which Professor Marshall has made familiar, the position at which two balls moving in a (vertical section of a) circular basin come to rest, is independent of the *distance* through which either body may have slid on its way to equilibrium.[3]

Probably many who have repeated the dictum of McCulloch have meant no more than the truism that, when the ground rent —or rather the excess thereof above the minimum fixed by agricultural rent—is (absolutely) small, then an impost on gross rent cannot reduce the ground rent by (an absolutely) great amount. The experts have acquiesced in the dictum of the

---

[1] Dudley Baxter accepts as the received doctrine a very explicit statement of the theorem in his examination before the Select Committee on Local Taxation, 1870 (Qs. 5811–5819). "That is theoretically the rationale of it," he holds, while pointing out that there are "very great variations in practice," pertaining to what we should now call short periods. Those varieties will find a fitting place in the sequel; here we are only concerned to deny that "theoretically the rationale of it" is as Baxter and his authorities suppose, *e.g.*, in the test case which was put to him (*ibid.*) :—" If the ground rent were very high, with a very small cottage built upon it, the cottage would bear very little of the rates, and the ground rent would bear a greater proportion?" Those who have the courage of abstract theory must reply that the size of the building—provided it is not an irreducible minimum, provided that the margin of building is left free—the amount of the surplusage forming ground rent, and the proportion between those two quantities, are not material circumstances with respect to the incidence of taxation. The elasticity of the demand for housing being kept constant—for instance, at or near zero—the amounts of the ground rent and the building rent (gross rent *minus* ground rent) might be interchanged without any variation of the loss resulting from the tax, both to the occupier and the ground landlord.

[2] *Mem.*, p. 129, par. 3, p. 131, last par., and references given on both pages.

[3] *Cp.* above, S, pp. 74 and 75.

classical economists, very much as they have acquiesced in the Classification emanating from high quarters which was submitted to their judgment. It is a good classification, the majority answer, with almost uniform civility, but not good for the purpose of determining the incidence of taxation. So the classical division of a tax on gross house rent into two portions, " as much of it as is a tax on building rent," and " the portion which is a tax on ground rent," [1] is logically correct, and, like the kindred statement that " rent *does* enter into the cost of production," [2] may be appropriate for certain purposes, in particular to indicate the parties who are sufferers by the tax; [3] but it is not adapted to the present purpose to ascertain the extent to which ground rent tends in the long run to be reduced by a tax upon the gross rent of new houses. There is no objection to speaking of the " portion which is a tax on ground rent," if we are careful to remember that this portion and its proportion to the tax on gross rent has no relation whatever to the amount by which the ground rent tends to be reduced in consequence of the impost.

But the vulgar are apt to take words literally, and the expressions of economists have encouraged the popular exaggerations in the opposite directions of plutocratic and of socialistic error, on the side now of the land-agent now of the agitator. On the one hand the apportionment of the gross rent between occupier and ground landlord, predeterminately and irrespectively of the elasticity of demand and the amount of the tax, is of a piece with and suggests what may be called the fallacy of concrete instances, which is committed when some representative of the landed interest adduces a particular actual house, and argues

---

[1] Mill, *Political Economy*, Book V, ch. iii. § 6.

[2] *Cp.* Marshall, *Principles of Economics*, Book V. ch. viii. 31.

[3] One who disputes a received proposition may be reasonably required to point out how it came to be accepted. This condition is complied with by observing that the theorem in question would be exactly true upon two very natural suppositions : (*a*) That the demand for housing is perfectly inelastic, and (*b*) that a tax proportioned to the ground rent should be levied, directly or by way of deduction, on the ground landlord (or the building owner, who deals with the ground landlord), while a tax proportioned to the difference between gross rent and ground rent was levied on the occupier. Upon these suppositions the ground landlord would bear the whole tax on the ground rent, and he would not suffer any further loss resulting from a diminished demand for sites. Now the assumption (*a*), as we have seen (above, p. 168), is not without evidence; and the confusion (*b*) is plausible and agreeable to popular parlance, more than other propositions which, from the point of view of economic theory, are on the same level of inaccuracy : for example, that it is all the same whether a bicycle tax is levied on the bicyclist who buys and uses the article, or on the landlord of a site which is required for the production of the article.

that, if the rates had been greater by so much, the ground rent must have been less by just that much; since the occupier would not have given more, nor the building owner have taken less than each has done.[1] Whence it is inferred that the ground landlord has already borne his fair share of burden.[2] Now, when it is urged with respect to an actual house that a specified tax levied on the occupier would reduce the ground rent at its creation by so much, it is forgotten that the house would not be what it is if the specified tax had existed at the time of the building. For the amount of building on a site is not a fixed quantity, but is determined by the " margin of building," which varies with an *ad valorem* tax on the price or gross rent of the premises.[3] There has been committed the fallacy which the mathematical economist discerns to be the treatment of a dependent like an independent variable; and even the man in the street recognises when it assumes the gross form of attempting to eat your cake and have it. You cannot eat into the profits of the capitalist by an impost

[1] See the instance referred to above, p. 85, note 6. To the same class may be referred the argument of Mr. Hunt in his evidence before the Local Taxation Commission of 1870, when he adduced the concrete instance of the "plot of land in Parliament Street now vacant, near the Whitehall Club," and proceeded in thought to build and let a house upon estimates based on the existing state of demand.

A similar case is discussed at Q. 13,550 *et seq.* of the evidence given before the present Royal Commission on Local Taxation (C. 9150). The builder having spent £1000 on each of a set of houses, "will want £60 per annum himself from each house." The gross rent paid by the occupier is £100, the rates are £20, and the ground rent is £20. It is argued that "if no rates had existed in the district the landlord would have got £40 a year for his land instead of £20"; . . . "the tenant having calculated that he would pay £20 a year in the rates and only giving £80 to his landlord, it does not make any difference to the tenant whether he pays £80 to the landlord or £20 to the local authority, or whether he pays £100 to the landlord and none to the local authority." According to our view, "if no [onerous] rates had existed in the district," the scale on which the capitalist would have found it profitable to build would not have been what it now is; the builder would have spent £1000 + $16 \cdot 6x$ on each house, and would have wanted (on the same hypothesis as to the net return of the speculative builder, Q. 13,554) £60 + x per annum for himself; the occupier would have given £80 + y for the increased amount of accommodation; the ground landlord would have received £20 + $y - x$; where nothing is known of x and y except that they are positive, and that y is *probably* greater than x (above, p. 163, note 3). There is not the slightest presumption that the loss to the ground landlord in consequence of the imposition of the rates is £20. The loss is $y - x$, unknown quantity *minus* unknown quantity. The same symbols may be usefully employed to expose the dogma of McCulloch, which is classed with that of these witnesses by a parity of misconception, not an identity of misstatement.

[2] It is true that the advocates have often in view the competition between different localities; but, as will be seen when we come to *rates*, the demand for house accommodation in that case is not so different from the simpler case here under consideration, but that the argument in the text is applicable.

[3] Above, p. 185.

which reduces the marginal demand of the occupier, and at the same time have everything as it was before the impost, to be used as an argument against the taxation of ground rents. On the other hand, the advocates of taxing ground rents have also been wildered by the inappropriate conception of demarcating a part of the tax levied on the occupier as " the portion which is a tax on ground-rent." [1] The usual vices of socialist speculation, the confounding of short periods with long periods, of quasi-rents with true rents, are aggravated by this misconception. Under its influence the proposition that a tax on ground value does not hurt the occupier is applied beyond its legitimate limits—not true in the long run, as will be argued in the sequel, of a rate to be levied from year to year, during the currency of the ground lease, in proportion to an ever-growing ground value, upon owners who will have contributed efforts and sacrifices to the production of a house.

The reasons which have been given in the last few paragraphs for not producing a larger array of confirmatory citations from the answers of the experts are applicable with slight change to the discussion of *rates*, which follows next.

The circumstances which for our purpose differentiate a local rate from an imperial tax are mainly two : (1) that a rate is beneficial in such wise as not to reduce the demand for the rated houses at all, or to the same extent as a purely onerous tax of the same magnitude; (2) that rates differ in different districts between which occupiers have a choice. Suppose for a moment that the first attribute is absent, and that all rates are purely onerous, and as a further simplification, suppose at first that there are only two districts, A and B, between which occupiers have a choice. And, the onerous imposts in both equalling, or rather equilibrating each other initially, let a new rate be imposed on houses in A. At first sight it might appear that ground rents in A would be diminished exactly to the extent of the new burden. But this would occur only in the case of a *fixed* burden on the production or enjoyment of premises in A : *e.g.*, a " Church rate," not of the ordinary kind, but of the nature of a fixed charge levied on the owner, or a payment by each occupier for an indispensable right (or rather " servitude ") of way. But the rate which we are considering varies *ad valorem* with the value of the house. Accordingly, as above shown,[2] building will be discouraged in A, and if A were an isolated region, there would be

---

[1] J. S. Mill, *loc. cit.*   [2] Above, p. 173.

simply a reduction of demand in A attended with a diminution of ground rent. But A being in rivalry with B, there will also be a *fall* [1] of demand in A owing to the diversion of occupiers to B, while from the same cause there will be a *rise* [2] of demand in B, with a corresponding readjustment of invested capital. In the result ground rents will have decreased in A, and will have increased in B. It is conceivable that the increase in B should be greater than the decrease in A. But it is not probable. [3] The presumption is that on balance ground rent will be reduced by an onerous impost which checks production.

The conditions on which the extent of this effect depends may be investigated by introducing several circumstances each by itself *ceteris paribus*. Thus (1) let the absolute magnitude of the rate in A be increased, then each of the terms which make up the total diminution of ground rent, viz. (decrease in A *minus* increase in B) being correspondingly increased, it may be presumed [4] that in general the total diminution will be greater. Again, (2) let the elasticity of demand for housing in general in either district be increased, then by parity of reasoning with that employed in the simple case, the decrease in A of ground rent becomes greater, and for a like reason the increase in B becomes greater. Therefore by a parity of presumption the total diminution becomes, in general, greater. Next, (3) instead of two unequal rates in A and B let an average equal rate be imposed on both. Ground rent as a whole might be affected, but there seems no general reason why it should be increased rather than diminished.

Generalising, we may say that, if a system of onerous rates be imposed on a set of districts more or less in competition with each other, the consequent reduction of ground rent will be greater the heavier the average imposts are, and the more elastic the general demand for housing. The imposition of a uniform rate forming a mean of the percentages or shillings in the pound

[1] " Reduction " is here distinguished from " fall " in accordance with Professor Sidgwick's proposal (*Political Economy*, Book II. ch. ii. § 2) that the former term should mean the change in the amount demanded—say x—of a certain commodity consequent on the change in the price of that commodity, the latter term the change in the amount demanded consequent on a change in the law or curve of demand—dx as distinguished from δx in the symbols proper to the Calculus of Variations. In the case of correlated demand with which we are now dealing, the contrast is between $dp_1\left(\dfrac{dx}{dp_1}\right)$ and $dp_2\left(\dfrac{dx}{dp_2}\right)$ where p_1 and p_2 are the prices of x and the correlated article respectively.

[2] See preceding note.

[3] See Index, s.v. *A priori Probabilities*.

[4] *Ibid.*

that originally prevailed, would in all probability not materially affect the sum total of ground rent, supposing that there was originally no correlation between high rents and high rates.[1]

This is a conception very different from the representation made on behalf of the landed interest, that the imposition of a rate in a district causes a reduction of ground rent which may be measured by the amount of the rate, or at least its excess above a certain level common to all districts. It seems to be imagined that the natural advantages of a district and their economic equivalent (rent + rates) form a constant quantity, like the height of the district above the sea. But we ought not to conceive the relative values of different sites as thus " in fluctuation fixed "; the demand-surface with which we have to deal may rather be likened to a sort of an air cushion of which some parts are originally more elevated than others; but when you press down some others go up, and accordingly the total depression caused by certain pressures at different points is not to be expressed by any simple formula.

Thus the reduction of ground rents is much less than appears at first sight even if we could suppose that all the rates were onerous. But it is time to restore the fact that all rates are not onerous; the better opinion is that " those rates which are truly onerous are less in amount and vary less from place to place than is commonly supposed." [2] But in so far as imposts are beneficial the demand of the occupier is increased to the full extent of the impost,[3] and accordingly there is no relaxation in the demand for sites. The supposition that all rates fall ultimately on ground rents becomes twice removed from the truth.

These propositions are in general accordance with the testimony of the " experts." The essential differences between a local rate and an imperial tax are noticed by almost all. The tendency of onerous rates to be shifted on to owners is attested by a great number—with less qualification perhaps than might be recommended.

Sidgwick, p. 104 :—" In this case [that of *old rates*, nearly but not quite corresponding to our category of *new houses*] it

---

[1] *Cp.* Marshall, *Mem.* (Memoranda published by Royal Commission on Local Taxation, C. 9528), p. 119.

[2] Marshall, *Mem.*, p. 118.

[3] It may be worth observing that, though the demand is said to be unaltered by a beneficial impost, this can rarely be true of the demand-*curve*; and, accordingly, although the effect on the superior interests of a beneficial impost is, *ceteris paribus*, *nil*, it does not follow that the effect of a beneficial impost, *plus* an onerous one, is the same as that of an onerous one alone—except in the sense that it may be either greater or less for all we know.

seems clear that the whole burden of the differential rate, so far as it is onerous, must fall on the owner of the ground value, provided that in spite of this burden the land remains still more valuable for the purpose of house building than for any other purpose. . . . ."

Marshall, p. 120 :—" He [the occupier] transfers most of them [rates other than ' rates, the current expenditure of which gives full value to the occupier '] rather quickly to his immediate landlord."

Bastable, p. 141 :—" Where different amounts of rates are levied in different parts of the same district, the [onerous][1] extra rates are shifted back to the house owner, and in the case of new building tend to lower ground rent." . . . " In specially favoured situations, where building sites command a high, or what is usually called a monopoly, value, the ultimate incidence of rates is clearly on the ground owner."

Cannan, p. 170 :—" The consequence, then, so far as distribution is concerned, of rates being for unproductive purposes higher in one place than another, is to cause less creatable immovable property to exist in the high rated and more in the low rated places than would be the case if the rates were equal in all places."

" Everything which tends to discourage the investment of capital in immovable property in a district tends to diminish the demand for ' unimproved land ' or space in that district, and this diminution in the value of space of course mitigates the effect of the discouragement to investment."

Price, p. 181 :—" Some amount of movement, at least, is possible from more to less highly rated districts, and thus the burden of the rates may be partly shifted from the shoulders of the occupiers."

Sargant, p. 213 :—" ' Differential rates,' so far as onerous, and so far as existing or anticipated at the date of the development of land for houses or trade premises, are, in respect of both site and structure, thrown by anticipation on the owner or successive owners of the land at the time when it comes to be developed, and operate by way of diminution of the price or rent obtained by him or them." [2]

The answer to Question II.[3] contained in the preceding paragraphs relates primarily to the case of leasehold tenure,

---

[1] This attribute is implied by the exclusion of " rates, so far as their outlay is reproductive, in addition to the value of houses in the district."—(*Ibid.*)

[2] As to the extent of the reduction Mr. Sargant's authority cannot be claimed.

[3] *Ante*, p. 152.

which may be taken as typical of Great Britain. But the statements may be transferred with little alteration to the case of freehold tenure which prevails in many, perhaps most, parts of England.[1] The *price* which building capitalists are willing to give for freehold will be affected by a tax on occupation rent in the same sense as the ground rent on the former supposition. The demand of the occupier will be affected as before. The consequence to the ground landlord and the occupier would not be materially different in a regime where the occupiers are freeholders who buy land on which to build their own houses.

When we pass from dwelling-houses to houses used for purposes of production, including sale, the scene of consumption is transferred from the house itself to the commodities which are produced in or by the house. The relations between the consumer at one end, the ground landlord at the other end, and the intermediate producers are not materially different. As before, beneficial rates are " paid by no one " in the phrase of Mill adapted by Professor Bastable.[2] " The advantages resulting from a proper expenditure of rates may either recompense the traders, or so attract consumers as to allow of higher prices being maintained." [3]

A uniform *ad valorem* onerous impost on the rent of all premises employed for production would result in a change of the final utilities of buildings, not only as between different places, as in the case of dwelling-houses,[4] but also as between different industries. Those commodities for which the demand is particularly inelastic would tend to be raised in value. Thus, if the demand for bread varies with the price less than the demand for bonnets, the bakers may employ nearly as extensive premises before as after the imposition of the tax which will be almost entirely shifted to the consumer; while the milliners meet the burden by some diminution in the size of their establishments as well as some rise in price. The value of food as compared with finery would be raised *pro tanto*, if abstraction might be made of the law of increasing returns. There is also now a disturbance of the margins of production which in the case of dwelling-houses seemed not sufficiently important to deserve notice. There will be a pressure on " those trades which happen to require large buildings in proportion to their net returns." [5]

---

[1] This estimate appears to be justified by the particulars concerning the distribution of building tenures given in the Report of the Select Committee on Town Holdings, 1889, No. 251, pp. 6–9.   [2] *Mem.*, p. 141.

[3] *Ibid.*   [4] Above, p. 163.   [5] Marshall, *Mem.*, p. 113.

Another effect of more importance in the case of business premises than dwelling-houses is that on the renewal of the occupier's lease the owner is more able to take advantage of the special utility above the market-value which the premises may have for that particular occupier,[1] not a mere *pretium affectionis* in the case of the shopkeeper, but a consequence of the " good-will " created by his own exertions.[2]

An onerous rate on both dwelling-houses and business premises would disturb the marginal utility, and accordingly the quantity produced and the value of the two kinds of building, theoretically, even if the impost on both kinds were of the same magnitude, and *a fortiori* when, as in the case of the Inhabited House Duty, it is different.

As between different places the displacement caused by difference in onerous rates will vary *ceteris paribus* with the capacity of one place to act as a substitute for another in the supply of the consumers' wants. As in the case of dwelling-houses the incidence of an onerous extra rate in a particular locality depends on the elasticity of demand for accommodation in that particular locality. As Sir Edward Hamilton says,[3] "A large part of the rates payable in respect of Bond Street and Oxford Street may be contributed by all of us, in the shape of an enhancement of the price which we pay for our commodities " [so far as the rates are onerous and differential], if " all of us "— or the better halves of us—insist on shopping in those fashionable resorts, notwithstanding the imposition of an extra charge. But if the attempt of shopkeepers in Bond Street and Oxford Street to stick on additional prices would divert a great part of their custom to humbler localities, then, as Professor Bastable says, " the [extra] rates would fall [ultimately] on the ground landlord." [4]

Compare as to these propositions, the following testimony of the experts; the reasons why more of it is not forthcoming being recollected." [5]

Courtney, p. 86 :—" As regards rates on trade premises, these must ordinarily form part of trade expenditure, and be ultimately borne by the customers availing themselves of the services, or consuming the commodities of the trade supplies."

[1] Let us hope that, as witnessed before the Select Committee on Town Holdings, 1889 (Report, p. 11), such cases of exaction are rare.

[2] *Cp.* Marshall, *Mem.*, p. 120, par. 3-4.

[3] *Mem.*, p. 39.

[4] *Ibid.*, p. 142.

[5] *Ante*, p. 166.

Sidgwick, p. 105 :—" The burden of any special taxation of traders not balanced by a corresponding taxation of other classes tends, when the taxation is old, to be partially diffused through the community, through the effect of this industrial disadvantage in diminishing the abundance and cheapness of traders' services."

Bastable, p. 141 :—" Rates on business premises are further complicated by the possible effect they may have on prices to consumers. An equal tax on all business premises in a country would be a tax on profits, since it could not be evaded by change ; but a rate on such premises in a particular locality would appear to be shifted either forward to the consumers in higher prices, or backward to the ground owners in lower ground rents."

Cannan, p. 168 [with reference to a tax on bicycles taken as representative of the imposts inquired about] :—" its effect reaches not only to those who use bicycles and benefit [e.g., by having their errands done cheaper] because other people use them, but also to those who would have used bicycles or would have benefited by other people using them if the obstruction of the tax had not intervened."

Blunden, p. 191 :—" The real incidence of the rates on shops and other business premises would appear to be mainly upon the customers of the goods made or sold therein."

Mackay, p. 228 :—" The question then is, Can an occupier for trading purposes throw forward a part of the burden on his customers ? As in the cases already considered [residences], this appears to me to depend on whether the demand is sufficiently elastic not to be deterred by the increased price which the highly-rated tradesmen will undoubtedly be inclined to ask. To take an instance, the reason that a Bond Street shopkeeper probably charges more than a tradesman in an unfashionable neighbourhood is not because his rent and taxes are high, but because a demand of a very special character, the demand of the fashionable world, concentrates itself on the articles to be sold in Bond Street shops. There is a point, however, at which customers will be deterred and driven to meaner streets ; they are free, so to speak, to buy abroad."

The parallels which have now been exhibited between the typical cases of dwelling houses under leasehold and the other varieties of urban premises and tenure are similarly close, and will not need to be drawn again at length, in the case of *old* [1] houses which is next to be discussed.

Houses built and occupied before the imposition of the tax or

---

[1] See the division at p. 162, *ante.*

rate fall into two categories according as there is or is not competition between old and new houses. The experts seem properly to take the former as the general case. Perhaps they hardly allow enough weight to the circumstance that so far as new houses are often not identical commodities, but substitutes for the old ones, the extent to which an impost will be shifted from the former on to the latter class cannot be predicted accurately. This agency, it should be observed, is distinct from *friction*. It is not the trouble and expense of a move that prevents an intending occupier of a new house on whom the capitalist builder threatens to shift an onerous impost from dealing with the more yielding owners of old houses who must take what they can get, it is that old houses have not exactly the same attractions as new ones.

Friction properly so called no doubt plays a dominant part in the case now under consideration. The occupier, as Mr. Price says with special reference to the existing Inhabited House Duty,

" will probably need a more powerful motive than the payment of a slightly diminished Inhabited House Duty before he takes the unpleasant, and, it may be, difficult, step of changing his abode or manner of life ; and regarding the mass of occupiers as a whole, it is improbable that the payment of duty at an increased rate on houses of higher value induces an appreciably large number to move into tenements exempt from duty altogether, or into those taxed at a lower rate." [1]

The comparative strength of friction in case of business premises and residences is ably discussed by Mr. Price. The difficulties of prediction on a matter of this sort are illustrated by the incident that on the question whether friction is more operative in the case of a reduction or of an increase of (onerous) rates, opposite reasons apparently both valid are adduced by Mr. Price and by the present writer. On the one hand—

" it seems more probable that the *reduction* or *abolition* of a rate would be likely to produce less effect on the rent than the *increase* of an old or the *imposition* of a new rate. The removal of a burden would not, in all probability, so powerfully stimulate the efforts of the other party to obtain a share of the relief, as its imposition would urge the party on whom it primarily fell, to shift a portion to other shoulders."—*Mem.*, p. 186.

On the other hand—

" there is some reason for believing that friction resists an increase less than a reduction of rates. For one of the chief

[1] *Mem.*, p. 180.

processes by which a change of rate is propagated is the competition between new and old houses, described in sections (2) and (3) of heading (*a*) in Answer (6) [*Mem.*, p. 130]. In the case of a new rate being imposed, intending occupiers of new houses bid against actual occupiers of old houses whose leases are expiring.[1] In case of a rate being reduced, actual occupiers of old houses whose leases are expiring bid against intending occupiers of new. The competition is naturally keener in the former case. A slight difference of rate may decide an intending owner to apply for an old rather than a new house. But a considerable difference of rate may be required to determine an actual occupier to incur the trouble and expense of a move."— *Mem.*, p. 135.

Mr. Price's judicious remarks on friction cover also the case in which there is no building of new houses in the neighbourhood in competition with the old houses. In this case theoretically the whole of a tax and of a rate so far as it is onerous is (on the expiry of the occupier's lease) borne by the rack-rent owner,[2] so long as his lease runs, and is ultimately shifted on to the ground landlord. Compare the evidence of the experts :

Sidgwick, p. 103 :—" A *new* tax on inhabited houses proportioned to their annual value tends to cause men to be content with less house accommodation ; and so far as this cause operates, a part of the burden of the tax must fall on the owners of houses. . . ."

" In localities where the demand for houses is so slack that it is not worth while to build, the burden of the tax will remain partly on the owners of houses so far as the demand for them is strictly local."

Marshall, p. 121 :—" Where the population is receding, and building has ceased, onerous rates tend to press on owners."

Bastable, p. 141 :—" Where a locality is stationary, the increase of rates falls on the house-owners, who would otherwise get more rent."

Practically, as several of the experts have pointed out, the transference of the onus from the occupiers is impeded by friction. What is the amount of this force of friction as compared with the simpler motives which the more abstract theory assumes is a question of considerable practical interest which will recur in the

---

[1] It being borne in mind that all the detriment attending the aggravation, and all the advantage attending the reduction, of the rate would redound to the *owner* of old houses in the absence of competition with new houses.

[2] See *Mem.*, p. 129, last par.

sequel. A right conception of the relations between owners and occupiers of old houses is essential to the consideration of proposals for the relief of the occupier which forms the subject of the next answer.

III. *Rates on Owners.*[1]—The schemes which have been proposed for rating owners of urban lands and buildings in this country fall under two heads, (I) the division of rates between occupier and owner, and (II) the imposition of a special rate on site values.

I. The proposed division of the occupier's burden may be either (A) only with his immediate landlord, the rack-rent holder, or (B) with a series of " superiors." [2]

A. The short and simple division is governed by the principle that theoretically in general, apart from " friction," and except for the short period during which the occupiers' leases run, it makes no difference whether the tax-collector takes his share of the price paid for the commodity house-accommodation from the hands of the buyer or those of the seller.[3] Not many occupiers are so incautious as Sir John Thwaite, who stated in evidence that " he had taken a house worth £280 without knowing that there was a land-tax of 2s. 10½d. in the £." [4] Compare the experts :

Courtney, p. 89 :—" At the commencement or revision of a tenancy, rents would be settled in view of the power of deduction supposed to be granted, so that the real burden of rates and the real benefit of rents would remain as before."

Giffen, p. 97 :—" The real incidence is not affected by the question as to who pays in the first instance."

Sidgwick, p. 108 :—" If the land or house is let from year to year, I do not see how the occupier can gain by the power of deduction, except on the assumption that by a strange want of foresight he does not adequately take the rate into account in bargaining about the rent, unless the rate varies materially from year to year."

Bastable, p. 143 :—" With short tenancies and where competition is effective, the question of division is a minor one."

Gonner, p. 158 :—" In abstract theory, and granted the assumptions enumerated in the previous answer, no difference

[1] In answer to the question : " Distinguish and discuss schemes which have been proposed for rating owners of urban lands and buildings."

[2] It is convenient to use this term in a sense wider than the legal definition.

[3] See the present writer's answer to Question 12 in *Mem.*

[4] Select Committee on Local Taxation, 1870, Q. 4038.

would occur through the change of method suggested in the present question." (Q. 12.)

Cannan, p. 171 :—" If occupiers were allowed to deduct either rates, or the cost of getting their hair cut, or any other expense from their rents, then their rents would be that much higher."

Sargant, p. 215 :—" The ultimate incidence of rates is the same whether the occupier pays or the owner."

Gomme, p. 242 :—" Assuming that no other element of value affected the matter, it may be shortly stated that if taxation were deducted from rent, rent would increase by the amount of taxation deducted."

These propositions remain true in the limiting case where the share of the rate levied from the occupier is zero—the case of the " compound householder." [1]

If the experts regard division of rates as a matter of little importance, why do so many of them recommend it ?   " To some extent for the sake of justice, but more to prevent discontent," in the words of Professor Sidgwick.[2]   To some extent the proposed " deduction " by the occupier would be operative in virtue of a certain friction which is described by several of the experts, especially by Mr. Price.[3]   What little advantage may accrue to the occupier from this effect of friction it may seem just to allow him for a reason of which a particularly definite statement is that given by Mr. Cannan :

" So much of the rates as is raised to pay off capital expenditure ought, strictly speaking, to be paid by the owners, since it is payment for a remote benefit (that of being free from the payment of interest on the loan raised for the capital expenditure).   In the case of new occupiers, the payment will be allowed for, just like any other disadvantage, but some injustice is done to old occupiers unable to revise their bargains with their landlords if new and unforeseen payments for capital expenditure are saddled upon them. . . . The occupier receives the benefit of the things provided by the capital expenditure till the conclusion of his term of tenancy, and should therefore pay the interest on the capital.   But it is no advantage to him that the capital should be sunk or written off." (*Mem.*, p. 171.)

---

[1] Even if the landlord is to be regarded as a monopolist, as alleged by some (*e.g.*, Select Committee on Town Holdings, 1890, Q. 4529), it still remains true in abstract theory that it is indifferent on which party the rate is levied.

[2] *Mem.*, p. 107.

[3] *Mem.*, pp. 180, 181, 185.   See also Farrer, p. 79 *et seq.*; Courtney, p. 89; Sidgwick, pp. 107, 108; Bastable, p. 143; Gonner, p. 157.   *Cp.* Report of Select Committee on Town Holdings, 1892, § xiii.

As the only direct method of correcting this hardship it might be suggested that the owner should recoup the tenant at the end of his term of tenancy for that portion of a new rate imposed during the tenancy which goes to paying off a loan for the capital expenditure.[1] But if this remedy is impracticable, then on grounds which the strictest disciple of the Manchester School can accept, it may be wished that the occupier should obtain what little advantage may accrue to him from division of rates. On less definite grounds, those who do not accept the result of Demand and Supply as the criterion of ideal justice may acquiesce in the occupier's obtaining a better bargain than the play of the market assigns to him, by way of a share in the advantage accruing to his landlord from that increase of value which appears to be the general rule (though not without some exceptions) in our growing towns.

There is room for greater difference of opinion about the other motive for introducing a division : in order that the owner should " *appear* to pay " [2] what he does not. It does not redound to the discredit of our science that there should be discrepancy between experts on a question which belongs not to the theory of economics but to the art of politics—what are the legitimate uses of humbug ? It is quite consistent with the uniformity of science that one writer should " never have been able to see the merit of " an arrangement which " keeps up the illusion that the incidence of the tax is upon those who pay the money to the Government; " [3] to another it should seem advantageous " to some extent for the sake of justice but more to prevent discontent," to divide certain rates " between owner and occupier in the manner suggested by Mr. Goschen in 1870 " (that is half and half); [4] while a third, not only on grounds of justice, " so far as owners are or are about to be in the enjoyment of unearned increment," but also " for the political purpose of appeasing

[1] Mr. Sargant has estimated that a rate of 2*d*. in the pound would be sufficient to form a sinking fund for paying off a capital loan (Select Committee on Town Holdings, 1892, Q. 4436). Quoted with approbation by the Committee in their final report (1892). *Cp.* Royal Commission on Local Taxation, 1900 [Cd. 201], Appendix xi, § 11.

[2] Lord Farrer, *Mem.*, pp. 80, 81; and to the same effect in his evidence before the Select Committee on Town Holdings (1890, No. 341). Apropos of this plea of expediency it may be well to recall that even the virtue of the younger Mill relaxed so far as to countenance some illusion as to the incidence of direct compared with indirect taxes, considering that " while any such infirmity of the popular mind subsists . . . while men's minds are so little guided by reason," an addition to " the public dislike of taxation " might present useful reforms, and lead to a repudiation of the national obligations. (*Pol. Econ.*, Bk. V. ch. vi. § 7.)

[3] Sir Robert Giffen, *Mem.*, p. 97.   [4] Sidgwick, *Mem.*, p. 107.

discontent," should be " disposed to recommend " the deduction by the occupier of some proportion of his rent; a particular proportion, " say a third of the occupier's rent," being suggested on the ground that " friction is most likely to be effective when the effect required of it is not very great." [1]

So far it has been supposed that occupiers' leases, as usual in this country, are short. Otherwise it would not be true that division between occupier and owner is a small matter. It is not true of a twenty-one years' lease, such as not uncommonly occurs in the case of high-class residences, open to the tenant only but not to the landlord, to terminate at the end of seven or fourteen years. *A fortiori* it is not true of division between an occupier who is a " feuar " and his " superior." Of all such cases it is particularly true that, as Mr. Sargant says, " if any division of rates between owner and occupier is to be applied to existing contracts . . . there will necessarily be much hardship and loss inflicted on a prudent class of investors." [2] The owner's interest in improvements remaining unexhausted at the end of the period would not compensate his having to pay for so long a period a considerable fraction of rates whereof the benefit accrues to the occupier alone during that period. Accordingly in such cases the objections on the ground of distribution, and even of production, which are directed in a later section against certain schemes for rating site values are to some extent applicable to the method of division considered in this paragraph. Under the existing conditions of tenure, are these objections obviated by the proposal [3] that, beginning three years after enactment, there should be division between owner and occupier of rates in excess of the average for those three years ?

B. The long division between the occupier and a series of superiors is described by Mr. Costelloe in his evidence before the present Royal Commission on Local Taxation under the designation of " rent duty." " This rent duty calls for an even poundage contribution from every receiver of rent right back to the owner of the freehold." [4] In the words of a witness before the Local Taxation Commission of 1870,[5] " You should travel down, catching every interest, until you come to the ground landlord, each

---

[1] *Mem.*, p. 137. Mr. Price has recommended the same proportion on grounds of justice, arguing that " it may theoretically be more equitable than an equal distribution " (*Mem.*, p. 185).

[2] *Ibid.*, p. 215.

[3] Made (in effect) by the Local Taxation Committee of 1870 (*Report*, Resn. 9).

[4] *Minutes of Evidence*, Vol. II. C. 9150. Q. 19,904 and context. Was the scheme first propounded by Lord Hobhouse [*Contemp. Review*, 1888] ?

[5] Sir John Thwaites, Q. 4038.

party paying in proportion to the [his] property or interest in the building." So the very clever writer of the articles on " Financial Reform " in the *Speaker :* " Division of rates would be a complete reform if you define owner properly " [so as to include superior interests].[1] It will be convenient to defer the discussion of this scheme in order to consider it along with others which differ from it in definition more than in effect.[2]

II. Among schemes for rating site value a wide distinction is to be drawn between (1) those which do, and (2) those which do not respect vested interests.[3] J. S. Mill's scheme is the typical example of the former class. It would be superfluous to recapitulate his provisions for intercepting the " future unearned increment " of land value; but it may be well to recall his scrupulous concern for present possessions.

" I see no objection to declaring that the future increment of rent should be liable to special taxation, in doing which all injustice to the landlord would be obviated, since that includes the present value of all future expectations." (*Political Economy,* Book V. ch. ii. § 5.)

" The Society [The Land Tenure Reform Association] do not propose to disturb the landowners in their past acquisitions . . . whatever value the land may have acquired at the time when the principle they [the Society] contend for shall obtain the consent of Parliament, they do not propose to interfere with."

---

[1] *Speaker,* Nov. 11, Dec. 16, 1899.

[2] See below, p. 210.

[3] A cross division is formed by an impost on (*a*) ground-rent only, (*b*) all superior interests (the symbols corresponding to a certain parallelism with the division into A and B). But the subdivisions 1 *b* and 2 *a* can hardly be described as " schemes which have been proposed." The nearest approach to the realisation of the former, known to the writer, is the scheme proposed by the Select Committee of 1892 (No. 214, p. xix), which (properly belonging to the head 1 B) is discussed below at p. 210. The nearest approach to 2 *a* appears to be a scheme, suggested by Mr. Harrison, and discussed by the Select Committee on Town Holdings (Report, 1892, p. xvi), for taxing reversions by means of an impost levied on ground rents payable at present under a lease. This scheme is open not only to the objections stated below under the head II .2 *a*, p. 198, but also, in so far as ground rents consist partly of quasi-rents, to the objections stated under the head II 2 *b*, p. 203. Conceivably indeed the scheme might be defined so as to come under head II 1, the type characterised by the absence of competition. The condition that existing acquisitions should not be disturbed would seem to require that the prospective reduction of the landlord's income during the remainder of the term and after the reversion should not diminish the capital value of his interest to such an extent as to render it no longer possible for him to purchase with that capital the perpetuity of an income at least as great as that which but for the impost he would have enjoyed during the remainder of the term and (with some addition) after the reversion. Such an object would be difficult to hit, even if it were aimed at; which there is no reason to suppose.

(*Papers on Land Tenure ; Dissertations and Discussions*, Vol. IV.
p. 244.)

" These owners should be allowed at any future period to
alter their minds, and give up their lands for the price first
offered." (*Ibid.*, p. 245, *cp.* p. 264.)

" Those whose land might afterwards fall in value would be
able to claim the former price from the State, although they
could no longer obtain so much from individuals." (*Ibid.*, p. 295,
cp. p. 286 *et passim*.)

This scrupulosity contrasts strongly with the plans which are
now in vogue. The leading idea appears to be to impose on
every one deriving an income from land built upon or vacant, a
special rate proportionate to that amount of his net income which
may be attributed to the value of the site. The method of
determining this net income may be thus typified. Let Z be the
rack-rent-owner receiving net rent (clear of expenses for repairs)
z from the occupier. Z pays to his immediate superior Y the
annual income y; Y receives y, and pays x to his superior X, and
so on up to the freeholder, who receives without paying. Accordingly the net income obtained from the premises by Z is $z - y$,
that of Y is $y - x$, and so on. Now, if the object were to exact
from each party a certain quota, say 25 per cent., of his net
income, that object would be realised by exacting $\cdot25\ z$ from Z,
and empowering him to deduct $\cdot25\ y$ from the rent which he pays
to Y; Y being empowered to deduct $\cdot25\ x$ from his payment to X,
and so on. But this would be only " rent duty," a second best
plan according to Mr. Costelloe, in comparison with the special
rate on site value.[1] To pass to this scheme we have only to
substitute for the series of annual payments, z, y, x, etc., that
portion of each payment which is said to consist of ground-value,
say ζ, η, ξ, etc., respectively. Then, if as before, 25 per cent. is
the quota, the occupier deducts $\cdot25\ \xi$ from his payment to Z; Z
deducts $\cdot25\ \eta$ from Y; Y deducts $\cdot25\ \xi$ from X, and so on.

It only remains to determine the amounts ζ, η, ξ. It seems
to be generally agreed that ζ is obtained by estimating the present
value of the land as a cleared site. From this datum η, ξ, etc., are
computed, but there are diversities in the method of computation.
A great variety of practice is covered by the happy ambiguity of
the leading principle as announced in authoritative documents,
such as the Report of the Local Government and Taxation
Committee of the London County Council : " That all persons
deriving a revenue, or use equivalent to revenue from the value

[1] Above, p. 186.

of a site, be liable to such charge," the " direct charge upon owners of site values " to be termed " owners' tax." [1] The *Bill for the taxation for local purposes of ground values in Burghs in Scotland* [2] which embodies the aspirations of the Glasgow Councillors, is not more explicit. Two methods of computing η, ξ, etc., stand out prominently, the first associated with the name of Mr. Fletcher Moulton, Q.C., the second emanating from the London County Council. A general idea of these methods may be obtained from the following metaphorical instance. Suppose that a gold watch has passed from one party to another by repeated sales; and that it is desired to lay a " gold-value " impost not only on the last holder, but also on the whole series of parties who once held the article whether completed or in any stage of its production (these parties being supposed to receive the equivalent of what they parted with in the form of periodical payments). The data for determining the respective contributions of the parties are : (1) the present market value of the watch, say z; (2) the values for which each of the preceding owners parted with their interest in the watch, say y, x, etc.; (3) the estimated present value of the gold case clear of the steel works, say ζ. Then the amount of gold value in the hands of the present owner is ζ, and the amount of gold value held by the first owner, the party who sold the raw material to the goldsmith for the manufacture of the watch, is the whole amount of the value which he received. To determine the amounts of gold value attributable to the intermediate parties *two* methods are suggested. *First*, suppose that the present gold value of the watch ζ subsisted in the past as far back as it can be supposed, that is as long as ζ is not greater than the known total value of the watch. Thus, if the penultimate holder on parting with the watch obtained a value y greater than, or equal to, ζ, there shall be attributed to him gold value of the amount ζ; but if y is less than ζ, then the whole of y is regarded as gold value. The contribution of the antepenultimate holder is determined from that of the penultimate one by the same rule. *Secondly*, suppose that the present value of the steel works subsisted in the past so far back as it is possible to suppose. Then for the gold value at a past epoch we are to put the given value of the watch at that epoch *minus* the present value of the works. Now the present

---

[1] Recommendations of the London County Council submitted to the Royal Commission on Local Taxation, 1898; forming an addendum to Mr. Costelloe's Memorandum in the second volume of *Minutes of Evidence* issued by the Commission. [C. 9150.]

[2] Discussed by Professor Smart in his *Taxation of Land Values*.

value of the works is given as the difference—called " balance "—between the given market value of the watch and the given valuation of the gold case. Accordingly we have for the " gold value " of the watch at the past epoch the then value of the watch *minus* the said " Balance "; always provided that the gold value thus determined is not less than the value of the watch at a stage before the works were put in; for that value, at least, must be considered to subsist in the hands of all the subsequent owners. For example, in the case above typified the " balance " is $z - \zeta$, and accordingly the amount of " gold value " in the hands of the penultimate owner Y, is $y - (z - \zeta)$; provided that this difference is not less than a certain minimum, viz. the value which was received by a former holder for the watch case before the works were put in, say g. This amount of value, at least, must be charged to Y; and accordingly his share of gold-value is *either* the above written *or* g,—whichever is larger. Special arrangements are made for the awkward possibility that, the works being unsuited to the case, the value of the cleared case would be greater than the value of the watch as it is.

But let the advocates of these schemes speak for themselves without parables. Mr. Moulton, in his able pamphlet, *The Taxation of Ground Values* (1889), thus exemplifies a method recommended by him which may be identified with our first :—

" Suppose in the case given in the last paragraph ['if the rate on ground-values be five shillings in the pound, and an occupier pays a rent of £1000 per annum for a building standing upon land whose ground-value is £500 per annum '] the landlord is not himself the freeholder, but holds the land from him at a ground rent of £100 a year. It will be evident that the intermediate landlord is himself the owner for the time being of four-fifths of the annual ground value, and the freeholder is only the owner of the remaining one-fifth. Now the principle of these proposals is, that the rate should follow the ground-value or any part of it, each person paying the rate upon the part of the ground-value which passes into his pocket. In the instance given, the occupier will deduct from the rent which he pays to the intermediate landlord £125, *i.e.*, five shillings in the pound upon the whole ground-value of £500. The intermediate landlord will in a similar way deduct five shillings in the pound upon the rent that he pays to the freeholder, *i.e.*, five shillings in the pound upon £400. This is just, and in accordance with the principles we have enumerated, because he receives and returns that portion of the annual value. In this way, each person who is in receipt of any portion of the annual ground-value will contribute a fair share of it towards the burdens of the community." [1]

The second method of determining the site value attributed to the different parties is illustrated in the " Forms of Demand Note " [2] published by the County Council [9550—9738] referred to in the Report of the Local Government and Taxation Committee on the rating of land values, 1893, No. 127 [9641—9737], in which the method is set forth. The " forms of demand " are accompanied with an explanation by Mr. Harper. Here is one of the examples :

Rateable value A	.	.	.	.	.	£360
Site value B	.	.	.	.	.	200
Balance C	.	.	.	.	.	£160

Interest.	Rent.			Site value rate.		
	Received.		Paid.	Gross amount paid or allowed.	Amount deducted from rent.	Net payment.
	£ s. d.		£ s. d.	£ s. d.	£ s. d.	£ s. d.
A, lessee for 21 years from 1864	543 0 0		255 0 0	10 0 0	4 15 0	5 5 0
B, building lessee for 99 years from 1920	255 0 0		45 0 0	4 15 0	2 5 0	2 10 0
C, freeholder	45 0 0		nil	2 5 0	nil	2 5 0

Mr. Harper thus interprets :—

" B first proceeds to ascertain how much his sub-lessee A is justified in deducting. As the site value is only £200, the rent of £255 clearly falls under rule 2.[3] He must therefore deduct Balance C (£160) from the rent, leaving £95 as the sum upon which A is entitled to deduct, and at one shilling in the pound this gives £4 15s. as the amount to be deducted. B then turns to his own deduction. His rent, £45, is obviously a ground rent,

[1] Loc. cit., p. 12. Compare the very clear account of his scheme given by Mr. Moulton in his evidence before the Select Committee on Town Holdings, 1891 (No. 325). Q. 47—9 et passim, e.g., Q. 866 et seq.; also, Royal Commission on Local Taxation, 1900 [Cd. 201]. Q. 22870. See also below, p. 200, note 2.

[2] Reprinted by the Royal Commission on Local Taxation, 1900 [Cd. 201], Appendix VII.

[3] Rule 1 is : " If the rent you pay is a ground rent, or in respect of land only, deduct $xd.$ in the £ upon the amount of such rent." Rule 2 : " If the rent you pay includes buildings or other property besides land, subtract the balance C from the amount of such rent, and deduct $xd.$ in the £ upon the remainder."

and he can therefore, under Rule I., deduct one shilling in the pound upon it, viz. £2 5s., leaving as the net charge upon himself £2 10s., which is exactly one shilling in the pound on the net annual site value which he personally enjoys." [1]

There are other formulæ for apportioning " site-value," in particular one which was embodied in Mr. Dalziel's Bill,[2] referred to in the Report of the Local Government and Taxation Committee above cited. But the matter is perplexed by an alleged misprint in the Bill, and the comparatively simple types which have been adduced are sufficient for our purpose.

Having then distinguished the principal schemes [3] which have been proposed for rating ground value, let us go on to discuss their advisability, employing the criteria which have been obtained in an earlier section ;[4] that an impost should as little as possible conduce to either restraint of production or inequality in distribution.

(a) The *productional* test is remarkably well satisfied by Mill's scheme; of such an impost it is particularly true that, in Professor Marshall's words,[5]

" a tax upon this rent [rent in the ' strict sense,' as distinguished from that part of the value of land ' which can be traced to the work and outlay of its individual holders '] does not alter the action of the owner; for he takes none in order to earn this rent : it does not ' enter into the cost of production ' of the commodities raised on the land. A tax on it does not alter that cost; does not restrict the supply of commodities; does not raise their value; is not shifted forwards; and, of course, cannot be shifted backward."

As Ricardo says, " a tax on rent " [in the strict sense] . . . " would fall wholly on landlords." [6]   But as he goes on to say, " a tax on rent, as rent is constituted . . . would be a tax on the profits of the landlord." Ricardo is speaking with special reference to agricultural rent. But even the landlord of urban sites is in the concrete not perfectly inert. The " master's eye " produces some of its proverbial effect. If he has not supplied sewers and roads, at least he has supervised the arrangement of streets and type of houses so as to render the neighbour-

---

[1] Roy. Comm., 1900 [Cd. 201], p. 160.

[2] *Land Values (Taxation by Local Authorities)*, 56 Vict., Bill 11.

[3] The scheme mentioned in note 3 to p. 187 seems hardly to deserve this designation.

[4] Above, pp. 152–162.

[5] *Mem.*, p. 116.

[6] *Principles*, ch. x. par. 1.

hood attractive.[1] That the labour of supervision may fall upon an agent does not affect the *productional* aspect of this consideration. On some large urban estates the landlord is content to take a smaller rent if he may impose present conditions as to buildings which are to fall in to the family some eighty years hence. What is this but the sacrifice of a present advantage for a greater future one ? A substantial tax altering the margin of this kind of saving would virtually check accumulation. Moreover the Ricardian statement postulates that the landlord has no other use for his land but to let it. But, in fact, he has the alternative of selling or mortgaging it. As several witnesses explained to the Select Committee on Town Holdings, if feu duties were taxed, proprietors would no longer feu. " It would not work," said one, " it would end in our putting it as a first mortgage." [2] It is not very easy to block these alternative courses by a tax exactly equivalent to a tax on ground rents. In so far as the tax on ground rents might be evaded by legal devices, an added burden would have to be borne nominally by the lessee, the building owner, and ultimately by the occupier.[3] However, with all these reservations it is not to be denied that a considerable part of the productional advantages claimed for the rent in the " strict sense " does appertain to an impost on the ground rent of our large towns, especially on future augmentations of ground rents, as contemplated by Mill.

The *distributional* test, too, is evidently satisfied by an impost on future unearned increase. If we admit the premiss we can hardly reject the inference in what Mill says about the landlords :—

" They grow richer, as it were, in their sleep, without working, risking, or economising. What claim have they on the general principles of social justice to this accession of riches ? " [4]
As Professor Marshall says :—

"The expenditure of such private societies as the Metropolitan Public Gardens Association, and much of the rates raised on building values for public improvements, is really a free gift of wealth to owners who are already fortunate." [5]

[1] *Cp.* Select Committee on Town Holdings, 1891. Qs. 6531, 2138, 5484, etc., and Royal Commission on Local Taxation, 1900 [Cd. 201], Appendices *passim*, in particular Matthews, p. 146.

[2] *Loc. cit.*, 1891, Qs. 6889, 5252; and *cp.* Qs. 5403, 6300 *et seq.*

[3] That a tax on *one kind of rent* may affect price is an admitted proposition (*cp.* Mill, *Pol. Econ.*, Bk. V. ch. iii. § 6, par. 4). It follows from that relation of rent to " one kind of produce " which Prof. Marshall has explained (*Principles of Economics*, Bk. V. ch. viii. § 3).

[4] *Political Economy*, Vol. II. p. 5.   [5] *Mem.*, p. 125.

O

It is true that all owners of ground rents in this country are not already fortunate; however, the future unearned increments even of small fortunes seem a very proper object of taxation. The question now arises, Will they not be sufficiently taxed by our income tax and death duties? It may be replied that the future increase of true rent is in so much higher a degree " unearned " than ordinary acquisitions as to be placed in a distinctly different category for the purpose of taxation. The somewhat fine distinction is thus drawn by Mill :—

" The rights of private individuals to something which they did not make, or help to make, but which came to them by bequest or inheritance from people who also did not make it or help to make it, are a totally different thing from the right of every one to the product of his own labours and sacrifices, or to the product of the labours and sacrifices of those who freely gave it to him." [1]

There are good judges who do not admit that the distinction is workable.[2] However, suppose it granted that the future increased increment when distinctly recognisable should be subject to an extra impost, why is that impost to be a *rate* rather than a tax? Mill does not seem to have ruled on this point. That the proceeds of an impost on ground-rent should be applied to municipal purposes, inasmuch as that rent has been created and maintained by the rates—or, to speak more generally, by the action of the citizens—sounds reasonable, yet is not so cogent as it sounds. The principle that labour has a right to what it produces is hardly relevant here, since the increase of ground rent was not the *motive* for the sake of which cities were formed and improved. It is a by-product, like acorns on oaks which were planted solely for the sake of timber. Does justice demand that we should plant the acorn in the place where it has grown, if the parent forest is already too dense? If crowding into cities is an evil, might it not be argued that, just as temperance reformers propose to apply the proceeds of some public-houses to the extinction of others, so the unearned increment of urban rent might be applied to check the tendency to aggregation, or at least not to aggravate it by rendering cities more attractive. While some attention may be claimed for this dialectic, still it cannot fairly be denied that such an impost as a " fresh-air rate " [3] based on future unearned increase of ground-rent would be just and reasonable.

---

[1] *Dissertations and Discussions*, p. 279.

[2] *E.g.*, Mr. Price, *Economic Science and Practice*, pp. 4—8.

[3] *Cp.* Marshall, *Mem.*, p. 125.

But after Mill's scheme has passed successfully the scientific tests, it still is open to a practical objection, that it is nobody's interest to start it. It might be compared in this respect to the honest species of bimetallism which that just man, Mr. Leonard Courtney, has propounded; to avoid all suspicion of seeking a temporary advantage by the inflation of prices, the value of silver in relation to gold is to be fixed at a ratio *less* than the market value.[1] Such a scheme may embody an eternal verity, but it offers no immediate advantage to the political agitator. There is no money in it ! To show this in the case of a scheme like Mill's, it suffices *a priori* to observe that if the present market value of land is to be guaranteed, or at least not to be attacked, advantage can result from the tax only in so far as Government is more far-seeing, is gifted with greater " longanimity " or " effective desire of accumulation " than the individual capitalist.

To take a concrete instance : say, using the best statistics that are available, that the yearly unearned increment of site-value in London is £300,000.[2] Now all this yearly increase of value is not received in the way of increased ground rent. For ground rents are not created freshly every year, but in London say only once in eighty or more years.[3] Thus the amount of ground rent to be touched in the first year in which the enactment comes into force [4] would be at most only some £300,000 ÷ 80 ; supposing that the houses of London remained constant in number like a stationary population. But as, in fact, London has been growing rapidly, the average number of premises leased by ground landlords eighty years ago must be much less than an eightieth part of the present city. Perhaps not more than 300,000 ÷ 150, some £2,000, can be intercepted on

---

[1] *Nineteenth Century*, April, 1893.

[2] This figure is given by Mr. Sidney Webb in his examination before the Select Committee on Town Holdings, 1891. Compare Tract 30 of the Fabian Society. Mr. Gomme (in the Memorandum contributed to the Royal Commission on Local Taxation, Vol. I., Part II. [C. 8765]), has given some figures which lead to a similar result. House-property in London rose in rateable value, presumably owing to increase of site value, in round numbers by £3,200,000 in the decade 1871—2 to 1881—2, but in the period of fifteen years from 1881—2 to 1896—7 only £2,900,000. It is possible that these increases are in part only apparently due to the increased stringency of the valuation. However, the figures are borne out—at least their magnitude is shown to be not improbable—by the estimates which have been made by foreign statisticians with respect to other capitals. A good *résumé* of these statistics is given in Dr. Einaudi's excellent article in *La Riforma Sociale*, 1900, N.S., Nos. 8, 9.

[3] For various estimates of the average length of the term in London, see index to Reports of Select Committee on Town Holdings for 1886—9 (1889, 251). Mr. Ryde considered the usual term ninety-nine years.

[4] See below, p. 196, note 3.

the occasion of newly created ground rents in the first year; the rest of the annually accruing increment of £300,000 being caught by middlemen whom Mill, if consistent, would presumably not touch.[1] Nor would he touch in the second year, nor for many years, those ground rents which had been docked of unearned increment in the first year.[2] Thus the amount of annual income flowing from the new source into the municipal treasury would be considerably less than £4000 in the first year. In the second that income would continue to be enjoyed, and there would fall to be added the increase since the initial epoch less than another eightieth part of the metropolis, less than $2 \times 4,000$. Similarly in the third year less than $3 \times 4,000$; and so on. In ten years the additional annual income might perhaps amount to some £200,000,[3] not 2 per cent. of the municipality's present annual expenditure. It is to be noted also that this ten years dates not from the present time, the year of enactment, but a year so distant in the future that the prospect of an increment to value in that future year does not seriously affect the present market-price of land [4]—perhaps ten years, and surely not less than five years from the time of enactment.

But because this prospect is not very attractive to the socialist agitator that is no reason why an ideally wise government should not consult for a future generation. Let county councils only persevere in the regulation of newly created ground rents, and ultimately a considerable part of the municipal expenditure will be defrayed out of site values; there will be realised the aspiration of those who " wish the burden of the rates to be transferred from man's action in improving and developing the land to his privileges in holding for private use a part of Nature's free gifts." [5]

[1] " I grant that in many cases the increased value [of works of art] does not reach the artist himself, but is an addition, and sometimes an unlooked for addition, to the gains of a middleman. . . ." *Loc. cit.*, p. 297. Yet Mill does not propose to tax away this unlooked for addition.

[2] Mill would have allowed " a long lease " of " situations advantageous for building or for industrial purposes." *Ibid.*, Vol. IV. p. 249.

[3] In general, we ought to take account of the increment which the yearly addendum, supposed initially about £300,000, is likely to receive if it continues an approximately constant percentage of a continually increased volume of site-value. Initially this volume might be about £15,000,000, Mr. Gomme's estimate for 1897 (*loc. cit.*, Table XII.). So that the yearly increase of the volume would be less than 2 per cent. It will be seen that these estimates are very liberal. Accordingly we have for a superior limit to the total income accruing in n years $(1 + 2 + \cdots + n)(1 + 0.02)^n \times £4000$, in ten years, for instance, about £260,000.

[4] " Taxation would not commence until there had been time for an increase of value to accrue." Mill, *loc. cit.*, p. 245. *Cp.* passages quoted above, p. 187.

[5] Marshall, *Mem.*, p. 124.

Yet laudable and secure as such an object so pursued may seem, its very distance in futurity may give pause. " Spem longam reseca " is the lesson read by Mill's example. Here was the first economist and one of the first intellects of his age, prepared to base a complicated construction, weighted with heavy liabilities, upon the foundation that " the land of the world—the raw material of the globe—in all prosperous countries constantly increases in value." [1] Doubtless there is a certain universality in this proposition. But the course of land value seems to

" crook and turn upon itself in many a backward streaming curve."

At any rate here and now the proposition has proved not true of agricultural rents; and the adoption of Mill's scheme would have resulted in a failure disastrous to this country, as Rogers has impressively pointed out.[2] Is it so certain that the value of central urban sites will go on increasing at the present rate ? Professor Flux's investigation of " internal migration," published in the ECONOMIC JOURNAL, 1900,[3] showing unsuspected movements of population inspires diffidence in prediction. Would it be wise to incur any great liabilities or even working expenses, on the strength of the probable progress of value in a distant future ? However, when the example of Mill is used to point a moral it must be remembered that his disastrous failure would largely have been due to his scrupulous provisions in defence of property already acquired—a weakness which cannot be attributed to the more recent schemes which are next to be discussed.[4]

[1] *Dissertations and Discussions*, Vol. IV. p. 284. Cf. *Pol. Econ.*, Book V. ch. ii. § 3.

[2] *Interpretation of Economic History.*

[3] Vol. X. p. 142.

[4] Here should be placed, if it could be placed, among " schemes which have been proposed " the variety which is formed by applying to the British institution of " rates " the German principle of taxing " Conjuncturgewinn " (as to which see Wagner, *Finanzwissenschaft*, Vol. II. § 232 *et seq.*, and references there given). Some idea of such application may be obtained from Herr Pabst's proposals, referred to in the ECONOMIC JOURNAL, Vol. X. p. 133, with respect to German house-property. The complexity of English tenures would render it particularly difficult to apply the principle to interests other than ground rents. The practical difficulty of touching " Conjuncturgewinn " in general is pointed out with authority by two eminent German economists who admit the abstract justice of Wagner's principle, Prof. Cohn, *System der Finanzwissenschaft* (translated by Veblen), § 342, and Prof. Robert Meyer, *Principien der gerechten Besteuerung*, p. 366. The latter well observes, " There is no universal publicly ascertainable [*ausserlich erkennbares*] test of unearned increment [*conjuncturgewinn*], only on the basis of the most intimate knowledge of the particular circumstances and capacities of each business could the influence of *conjunctur* with certainty be determined." It is an important suggestion that the evil is less than appears; *conjunctur* lose their specific character, " durch die Capitalisirung im Kaufpreis

(2) Contemporary schemes [1] present two aspects which it is important to distinguish : the rating (a) [2] only of " rent proper," rent in the " strict sense," " that part of the (annual) value of land which arises from its position, its extension and so forth," and (b) of rent including quasi-rent, " that part of the (annual) value of land which can be traced to the work and outlay of its industrial holders," of which it is true that " if it had been expected to be less than it actually is, the motive to work and to save the product of work would have been less." [3]

(a) What has been said above about the " productional " aspect of Mill's scheme is true of imposts not only on future increments but also on rent proper generally, with a certain reservation to be mentioned later.[4] We may pass on, therefore, to the " distributional " aspect of the proposed schemes so far

---

. . . bei der fortschreitender mobilisirung der Grundbesitz." In other words, if we might suppose that house property changed hands frequently, say on an average every ten years, for money earned by effort and sacrifice, the prospect of an increase in value in the near future entering into each price, there would not be much play for the taxation of unearned increment as conceived by Mill.

[1] It is not proposed to discuss here the incidental advantage claimed for a special rate on sites in that it lends itself to the rating of vacant spaces. The expediency of this measure depends on questions which the writer has not set himself to answer : (1) What proportion of the vacant land is held by monopolists (account being taken of the competition between different localities) ? (2) To what extent is vacant land in cities to be regarded as a product of effort and outlay (e. g. of companies or private landowners who prepare land by sewering). (Select Committee on Town Holdings, 1891, Q. 239–240)—seeing that in general articles which are not thus produced are not withheld from the market in a regime of competition (the " supply-curve " being a vertical line, above, p. 68), and articles which are thus produced have their supply price raised, not only in a regime of competition, but also in one of monopoly (ibid., p. 227) ? (3) Whether the impost would induce competitive owners of vacant land to sell it to monopolists ? (4) Whether consistency would require that vacant houses should be rated ? (5) Whether the impost would lead to the diminution of gardens and other healthy open spaces ? (6) Whether evasion would be largely practised by the erection of make-believe buildings, cheap and cheaply rated ? (7) What is the amount of vacant land in our towns, and whether the evil of a certain proportion thereof being withheld from the market, and the gain of the additional rate, are so great as to be worth much effort, and the sacrifice of simplicity in our tax system by introducing an impost on capital ? in fine, (8) Whether, if the evil calls for a remedy, the proper remedy is not that the municipalities should buy the vacant land at a fairly valued price ? Most of these points are raised in the Report of the Select Committee on Town Holdings, 1892 (No. 214), p. xxxiv, with evidence there referred to, and (by Lord Salisbury and Mr. Goschen) in the Report of the Royal Commission on the Housing of the Working Cl sses [C. 4402], p. 61, and p. 66, and in the evidence taken by Royal Commission on Local Taxation.

[2] It should be observed that there is a certain correlation between this division a and that suggested above (p. 187, note 3), but not an identity.

[3] Marshall, Mem., p. 115; Principles of Economics, Book V. ch. ix. § 42 et passim.   [4] Below, p. 207.

as they fall on true rents. So far as they will fall on future augmentations of rents proper, the distributional aspect of Mill's schemes and the contemporary ones are much the same; the favourable judgment which has been passed on that may be transferred to these. There are certain differences, however Mill would have guarded against mulcting those who should have suffered a decrement of ground value. Again, Mill's system would presumably have secured that no part of what was taken from the landlord by taxation should be restored to him in the form of an increased rent. But it is not so easy to prevent this consequence in the case of a rate of which the proceeds are laid out in the locality. It has been argued indeed that a ground rent cannot be made to contribute to the local expenditure, since what the landlord loses by the impost he gains through the greater demand for sites. This is true in the long run, and with respect to future contracts, provided that the expenditure of the rate is such as to increase the demand in the requisite degree. This would be the case if the proceeds of the rate were simply deducted from the occupier's rent, other things being unchanged; or were laid out on improvements which add to the premises an attractiveness equivalent to the expenditure. There is some guarantee that this equivalent will exist when the occupiers, through their representatives, are spending their own money. But [1] money extracted from the ground landlords might be expended on objects which, though useful, have not for the many a high degree of *final* utility, such as the higher education or sanitation. Even the lower gratifications may be afforded out of the landlords' pocket beyond the limit for which consumers would be willing to pay at the cost price. It is perfectly conceivable, therefore, that a considerable slice of the ground rent in a locality should be applied to the edification and amusement of the inhabitants, without resulting in such a rush of applicants for residence in that locality as would fully recoup the ground landlord.

The schemes proposed, then, would act as a means towards an end which has been admitted to be desirable, the taxation of future unearned increments. But would the means be the best available; or rather like the method of roasting pork by burning the kitchen? This question arises as we go on to consider that

---

[1] The distinction here taken is the *rationale* of the difference between the answers which the present writer has given to the *ninth* and the *twelfth* of the questions set by the Royal Commission on Local Taxation (*Mem.*, p. 136, referring to *Mem.*, p. 134).

part of the plan [1] which relates to interests already created, to
all manner of fixed incomes secured on rent, ground rents, feus,[2]
or the interest of the lady mentioned by Lord Farrer who derived
a terminable annuity from " leasehold ground rents near King's
Cross bought for her by a thrifty, thoughtful husband." [3]   On
what principle is it equitable or agreeable to utilitarian distribution [4] to dock by a special rate these fixed charges ?   One
answer is that ground rents [5] being created or maintained by
the outlay of the rates ought to contribute to the rates.   But
this argument seems to prove too much.   There are so many
things which go to create and maintain the funds out of which
people pay their debts, that it may seem arbitrary to fix on a
particular kind of debt and a particular condition for the existence of the means to pay it.   The argument, as Mr. Sargant
has objected, is equally applicable to prove that the owners of
railway debentures should be compelled to contribute to the
working expenses of railway.   And, as Mr. Gerald Balfour has
objected,[6] " We might as well argue that it was to the water
companies alone that the increase in value in towns was to be
attributed."   It is proposed on high legal authority to exempt
mortgagees from the action of the principle in question; but to
the lay mind it is difficult to explain why it should be less
equitable—though it may be less feasible—to make mortgagees
contribute to the rates, forasmuch as the rates maintain the
value of the premises on which the mortgages are charged.[7]

    [1] Mr. Fletcher Moulton is honourably distinguished by his wish to deal with
existing contracts " fairly and equitably " (Sel. Comm. " Town Holdings," 1891,
(No. 325), Q. 593.   Cp. Qs. 98, 1786), and evidence before the Royal Commission,
1900.   But the working of his scheme as typified in the example given below
(p. 209) may justify its being placed in the present category (2, defined above,
p. 187).
    [2] Many of these payments, many more than appears at first sight, as
pointed out above, are of the nature of quasi-rent.   It would be often hopeless
to attempt to ascertain how much of a so-called ground rent is " the result of
natural value, and how much is due to the expenditure which he [the land owner]
has incurred " (Sargant, Urban Rating, ch. i.).   In this sub-section (II., 2 a, 1)
these payments are considered so far forth as they are of the nature of " rent
proper "—the case which may seem most favourable to the proposed impost; but
all that is said here against the equity of the impost is to be understood as a
fortiori applicable to these payments, so far forth as they contain a considerable
element of quasi-rent.
    [3] Sel. Comm. " Town Holdings," 1890 (No. 341).   Q. 3990.
    [4] Above, p. 157.
    [5] This allegation has been considered above (p. 194) as an argument for the
application to municipal purposes of an impost supposed to be already accepted as
reasonable, here as proving the reasonableness of a new rate.
    [6] In the debate in the House of Commons, March 8, 1895.
    [7] " Town Holdings," 1891, Qs. 1474, 1795, 892, etc.   Harrison, ibid., 1890,
3715.   Cp. Evidence before the Royal Commission on Local Taxation [Cd. 201],
Q. 22,874 et seq.

It is urged more definitely that the owner of a fixed income charged on land and buildings may fairly be called on to pay for that addition to the capitalised value of his income which results from the security added by the increase in the value of the premises. But there is a good deal of evidence that the capital value of such an interest is not usually much increased by an addition to the value of the premises on which it is charged.

" In any *bona fide* ground rent, the margin was sufficient before, and enough is as good as a feast." (Evidence before Select Committee on Town Holdings, 1891 (325), Q. 1082.)

" No ordinary fluctuation of value would affect the security of the superior." (*Ibid.*, Q. 2240.)

" The feu duty is already so well secured that ' not much difference results from increased value of property.' " (*Ibid.*, Q. 5887.)

The Select Committee on Town Holdings reasonably regards " the benefit to improved ground lease-holding as too remote and indirect." [1] At any rate the projected impost sins against Adam Smith's fourth canon, since the proposal to reduce annuities which are sought out on account of their fixity and security is calculated to diminish considerably their selling value :—

" The capital value of the ground rents would be diminished by much more than the capitalised amounts of the rates charged on it." (Evidence before the Select Committee on Town Holdings, 1891, No. 325, Q. 155.)

" The element of uncertainty introduced by taxation of 2*s.* in the pound would cause loss of *another* tenth." (*Ibid.*, Q. 5881.)

The reason most operative with the general public is doubtless the belief that the owners of ground are affluent landowners, very fit subjects for extra taxation. As Mr. Gillies, a member of the Edinburgh Town Council, said frankly before the Select Committee on Town Holdings,

" I think there is no use in making any great cry about the hardship to others who are in better circumstances." (*Loc. cit.*, Q. 5140.)

But there is evidence that a good number of " small people " in this country are interested in this species of property :—

" The more thrifty people are, the more they prefer ground-rents as an investment." (Evidence before Select Committee on Town Holdings, 1887, Q. 1917, *cp.* Q. 1254.)

Ground rents to the amount of nearly £1,000,000 were, in 1884–85, sold in " small parcels." (*Ibid.*, 1922.)

[1] Report, 1892 [No. 214]. For further proof of this proposition see Mr. Sargant's *Urban Rating* appendix, from which an illustration is cited below.

The Prudential Assurance, essentially an office " for the lower middle class," holds ground rents to the extent of £1,300,000. They form an investment for " a very large number of the industrial classes," for " people of all classes," who invest in " ground rents as provision for their families." (*Ibid.*, Q. 3491.)

The King Edward School derives an income from ground rents of £27,000 a year. (*Ibid.*, 1888, Q. 1399.)

The Harper Charity School has an income of about £20,000 a year from London property. (*Ibid.*, 1887, Q. 11447.)

The Church of Scotland has £40,000 a year from feu duties. (*Ibid.*, 1891, Q. 2378.)

If the amount of taxation now levied on owners of houses in Scotland were transferred to feu duties, there would be a reduction of £7 10s. on an average income of £120 enjoyed by the ministers of 365 churches accommodating half a million people, " chiefly among the poorer part of the population." (*Ibid.*, Q. 6364.)

A certain charitable institution would be deprived of the means of relieving " fifty-four poor girls." (*Ibid.*, Q. 6198.)

There are " hundreds of thousands of the industrial and middle classes who have small savings invested in ground rents through benefit and insurance societies," *e.g.*, a messenger to a firm in the City, a barmaid, a spinster with a legacy of £300, a solicitor's clerk. (*Ibid.*, Q. 987.)

Of course there are rich landlords, but why should they be singled out to bear a greater burden than other equally rich persons ? If a " professional man with several unmarried daughters "[1] has invested his savings in ground-rents, why are they to be deprived of a quarter of their income, while the fortune of another family, invested in mortgages or in railways, is intact ? Is it reasonable that as in a case put by Mr. W. H. Warner in the important memorandum which he has contributed to the Royal Commission on Local Taxation,[2] the same fortune of £20,000 should, owing to the unexpected impost of 6s. in the pound on ground rents, yield £210 per annum less, being invested in ground rents, than if it had been invested in railway debenture stock with an originally equal prospect of $3\frac{1}{2}$ per cent. Is it not a first principle of fiscal equity, and indeed of all morality,[3] that no distinction should be made where there is no significant difference ?

" No inequality of treatment shall be meted out as between individuals possessing similar amounts of wealth."

---

[1] Sargant, *Urban Rating*, p. 96.
[2] *Minutes of Evidence*, Vol. II. [C. 8765], Appendix 4.   [3] *Ante*, p. 157.

" The proposal [of land nationalisers] is, by the ordinary person, very rightly considered unjust, because it deducts unequal amounts from A who has £10,000 worth of land, and from B who has, say, £10,000 worth of ships." (Cannan, *Mem.*, p. 165.)

Why should that " pain of loss " and " fear of loss " which Bentham has so forcibly described in his " Analysis of the Evils Resulting from Attacks upon Property " be distributed unequally among owners of equal properties ? [1]

(b) These considerations become *a fortiori* when we regard the proposed rate as an impost on *quasi-rent*. To the " pain of loss " and " fear of loss," which were considered under the head of rent proper, there is now added in the terms of Bentham " the destruction of property." [2] " The most prudent will begin to contract their enterprises, and by degrees to abandon an uncertain career." [3] As Professor Nicholson has said with reference to still more violent tamperings with property in land than those now under consideration : " The argument against confiscation does not rest merely on instinctive morality." [4] We can see the utilitarian reason for not disappointing the legitimate expectations of Peter in order to confer an unexpected gain on Paul. That method of redistribution is calculated to diminish the total to be distributed. Accordingly, all that has been said in the preceding paragraphs concerning the " distributional " character of the special rate in relation to rent proper is to be read with added emphasis into the following paragraphs in which the " productional " character of the rate in relation to quasi-rent is discussed.

On the borderland between the categories (a) and (b) there is a certain effect which, essential to quasi-rent, incidentally attends rent proper. It has been well said that " when land or other free gifts of nature have once become private property, their rent proper does not act as a direct motive to make and save the means of production ; though, of course, a violent appropriation of it might destroy the security on which all such motives depend." [5] It may be difficult to arrange that the appropriation of rent proper should not be so far violent as to cause some shock to security. Anatomists tell us that portions of the white matter in the brain may be removed without any sensible effect on the animal that is being operated on. But the operation is admitted to be a delicate one, and there is always danger of disturbing some nerve-centre

[1] *Principles of the Civil Code*, Part I. ch. x. Works, ed. Bowring, Vol. I. p. 310.　　[2] Bentham, *loc. cit.*　　[3] *Ibid.*
[4] *Conference on Industrial Remuneration* (1895), p. 462.
[5] Marshall, *Principles of Economics*, Book V. ch. ix. § 4, p. 472, 2nd edition.

of exquisite sensibility. So though rent proper be a sort of " intra-marginal " surplus which may be scooped out without sensible effect upon the economic organism, there is still a danger of disturbing the " grey matter " of the industrial brain. And even where no lesion is inflicted, the mere apprehension thereof may cause the victim of the operation to start back. And such apprehension is to be expected where the victim is the enterprising capitalist and the operator is the socialist politician. Economic anatomy is not minutely studied by those who are absorbed in the practical pursuits of making or of taking money ; and the nice distinction between " proper " and " quasi- " rent is not so familiar to either of the parties as to form a limit to the fears of the one and the rapacity of the other.

Thus even that part of the impost which falls only on rent proper exercises some effect in deterring capital from investment in house-building and the subsidiary industry of sewering, road-making, etc. Much more is this effect produced by the impost so far as it falls on quasi-rent : for instance on that part of an improved ground rent which forms the remuneration of outlay and effort.[1] The essence of the transaction is not affected by the use of deduction from superiors as practised in the collection of the income tax.

" In the case of a new house, the owner does not pay the rate, since he expects the ordinary profits—a circumstance which removes the case from the analogy of the income tax . . . since the income tax, not being special to investment in building, cannot be shifted by the building owner." [2]

In the words of Professor Sidgwick :—

" Income tax laid equally on incomes from different sources . . . has no tendency to be transferred . . . a tax on farmers' [or any other ' particular class ' of] profits would tend to be transferred through industrial competition to other classes of the community." [3]

The example of the income tax, to which the innovators are always pointing triumphantly, proves nothing.

" I have never seen," said Mr. Costelloe, " an answer to the proposition that if this could be done with the income tax, something analogous could be done where Parliament chooses to levy

---

[1] In this connection, as well as with reference to head *a*, may be mentioned the allegation that " the trouble in calculating and apportioning the rates . . . would depreciate the value of property " (" Town Holdings," 1891, Q. 1122). " The fractions are something frightful " (*ibid.*, 6069).

[2] *Mem.*, p. 136.   [3] *Ibid.*, p. 103.

a rate which is intended to be a direct charge coming out of rent receivable by owners." [1]

He might have seen an answer in every treatise on political economy. Thus J. S. Mill [2] :—

" If a tax were laid on the profits of any one branch of productive employment, the tax would be virtually an increase of the cost of production, and the price would rise accordingly; by which the tax would be thrown on the consumer of the commodity."

Ricardo, as usual, puts the case of *hats* :—

" A partial tax on profits will raise the price of the commodity on which it falls; a tax, for example, on the profits of the hatter would raise the price of hats; for if his profits were taxed, and not those of any other trade, his profit, unless he raised the price of his hats, would be below the general rate of profits, and he would quit his employment for another." (*Political Economy,* ch. xv. § 2.)

A " partial " impost on the profits of those engaged in the production of houses will raise the price of house accommodation. This principle is equally applicable to those who prepare the land and those who build the house. It may be thought that building will not be discouraged as the impost is placed on the site. And doubtless this circumstance would make some difference if the impost had been levied on the discounted value which the intending builder was willing to give for the site; it would make all the difference, if that payment were of the nature of rent proper. Suppose a builder is willing to pay a rent of £45 per annum for a site as in the example above cited, [3] if the impost were simply proportional to that rent, the builder would be only so far embarrassed, as land property, sewered and ready for building, would no longer be supplied on the same terms as before; and if we could suppose that no preliminary outlay on the land was requisite, then the case would come under Ricardo's principle. " A tax on rent " would " fall wholly on landlords."

But the proposed impost is not simply proportioned to, nor depending in any direct relation on, the payment which the intending builder offers for a site. It is not, in the example referred to, $\frac{1}{20}$ 45, but $\frac{1}{20}$ $(45+\eta-\xi)$ where $(\eta-\xi)$, say σ, is often an unpredictable quantity. If speculative builders were making ordinary profits before the impost could they continue

---

[1] § 5, Appendix XI., to Vol. II. of *Minutes of Evidence, Royal Commission on Local Taxation.*

[2] *Pol. Econ.*, Vol. III. § 3.   [3] p. 191.

to do so after it without the price of houses being raised ? If a watchmaker [1] were liable to an impost of so much in the pound on a certain—or, rather, an uncertain—amount of " gold value," σ, depending on the valuation of the gold cases at periods subsequent to the manufacture, would not a rise in the price of gold watches be the consequence ?

On general principles then we should expect that

" builders will in future throw on occupiers, in the shape of rent, the estimated amount of this prospective rating just as surely as would be the case with present rates." (Sargant, *Urban Rating*, p. 162.)

And there are special reasons for expecting that the partial tax on profits which we are considering will operate with particular effectiveness to " raise the price of the commodity," houses. (*a*) The amount of prospective rating against which the builder has to secure is likely to be estimated at a higher figure if he regards the impost as the outcome of a prejudice against property in land—as if landowners were entitled to no more consideration than slave owners !—a prejudice which, if yielded to, is likely to result in an additional impost on the remuneration for his house.[2] He may suspect, too, that the datum on which the impost is from time to time to be computed, the value of the cleared site, will be over-valued to his detriment. (β) That datum is at best somewhat vague, with a wide margin of uncertainty.[3] And as the methods of computing from that datum the net rateable quantity of site value, here called σ, agree neither with each other nor with any principle intelligible to the business man, he may regard the result as impossible to reckon on and quite aleatory. Now, as Professor Marshall has pointed out : although

" a risky trade in which there is an element of romance often becomes so overcrowded that the average earnings in it are lower than if there were no risks to be run . . . in the large majority of cases, the influence of risk is in the opposite direction ; a railway stock that is certain to pay 4 per cent. will sell for a higher price than one which is equally likely to pay 1 or 7 per cent. or any intermediate amount."

And (γ) there is no reason to except the building industry from

---

[1] *Cp.* above, p. 189.

[2] *Cp.* Smart, *Taxation of Land Values*, p. 89.

[3] The liability of such a valuation to a considerable " probable error " is suggested by much of the evidence on the subject before the Select Committee on Town Holdings and the Royal Commission on Local Taxation (*cp.* Lord Farrer, *Mem.*, p. 82), and does not seem to be disproved by the evidence to the effect that the valuation is possible.

the large majority of cases. Not " an element of romance," but a special degree of caution is to be attributed to investors of capital in this industry. The supply of capital would be greatly reduced by the proposed imposts.

" They would prevent secured interests in houses from being arranged so as to yield a fixed income, and so would drive cheap or trust capital out of house property and raise rents." (Sargant, *Mem.*, p. 216.)

For these reasons [1] it may be expected that to levy a required amount on the holders of " site-value " as proposed, rather than on the occupiers as at present, would not only not benefit, but would even injure, the occupiers.

But a reason pointing in the opposite direction may be alleged. While it is admitted that, as Ricardo says, " a tax on the profits of the farmer would raise the price of corn," it may be urged that the proper analogue is not corn, but the fruit of the aloe, or whatever produce is not fully reaped till two or three generations after it is sown, at a distance in time beyond the limits of effective prevision. In the case of a harvest so remote, the rapacity of a Government which should seize upon the standing crop might produce less than the usual discouragement to industry. The building owners may continue to perform their usual functions, while that portion of their surplus gains which does not act as a motive to effort and sacrifice is abstracted by a judiciously imposed site-rate; as the bees who used to sulk when robbed in the old-fashioned way now cheerfully go on filling that upper-storey of the hive which modern contrivances continually deplete without impairing the instincts of labour and accumulation.

There appears to be a portion of truth in this representation. There is a limit of time beyond which, if provisions are extended, the contract becomes " blind " as the phrase is. As Dudley Baxter replied in a somewhat different connection when asked,

" You do not think that all these risks were in the owner's mind when he made this contract ? " " I do not think they were," he said.[2]

There may be a prospect, in Professor Sidgwick's words,

" at once sufficiently definite to be made a ground of legislative

---

[1] So far as prediction is possible in a matter so contingent, it may be expected that the *first* of the schemes above described, p. 189, would be more effective in raising the price of house accommodation, the amount of the impost (for an assigned number of shillings in the £) being probably both greater in amount, and subject to a greater probable error.

[2] Select Committee on Local Taxation, 1870. Q. 5870, *et ante.*

action, and yet not definite enough to be taken into account in private bargaining." [1]

What Mr. Courtney says with respect to the occupier and the consumer, may be true also to some extent of the producers :

" Existing rates may be and are taken into account when tenancies are created, but no one can speculate with practical effect on the possibility of a subsequent increase or diminution of them." (*Mem.*, p. 90.)

So far as this non-Ricardian result takes place, the effect of the proposed site-taxes will no longer be either null, or the reverse of that which is intended. Another effect will be produced, yet one that is not desired or desirable. The occupier will not be relieved; but the rack-rent owner will be enriched. The first incident attends the occupier's power to deduct from his immediate landlord; the second incident attends the power of that landlord to deduct from his " superior." The first power of deduction, as shown above, profits little in general. In the long run the pecuniary position of the occupier with respect to his immediate landlord is determined by the conditions of supply and demand, and not the mode in which a rate may be collected. Is the impost beneficial, as generally in the case of rates ? Then the occupier pays for benefits.[2] Is the impost more or less onerous ? Then in the case of new houses, or old houses which are in competitive touch with new houses,[3] the burden is shifted on from the producer to the consumer, that is, the occupier. In the case of stagnant neighbourhoods, and more generally old houses which are not in perfect competitive touch with new ones, the owner already bears all or part of the onerous rates,[4] and—friction being abstracted—will bear the same proportion after the power of deduction has been conferred. The occupier then, having a short lease from his immediate landlord, is not much benefited by deduction. But the landlord having a long lease from his superior is materially benefited.

Mr. Sargant has forcibly illustrated this incident with reference to the first of the schemes now under consideration.[5] He puts the following case, admitted to be fair and typical by the author of that scheme :—

[1] *Mem.*, p. 107.

[2] Some modification of this statement is required in exceptional cases as above (p. 186) mentioned.

[3] *Mem.*, p. 130.

[4] Above, p. 182.

[5] Sargant, *Urban Rating*, Appendix; referring to the first of the schemes described above, p. 189.

" A, a landowner, has leased a site for its full value, £100 per annum, to B, a builder, who has erected thereon a house worth £600 a year (*i.e.*, £500 in addition to the original ground value of £100), and has secured his profit by letting the house to C, in consideration of a premium for the whole term at £500 per annum. The land is then supposed to increase in value to £500 per annum, and therefore the house and land to £1,000 per annum, the whole increase of £400 per annum thus going into the pocket of C."

Thus the site-value is £500,[1] and accordingly C is entitled to deduct from B the whole of the site-rate, say, at 5*s.* in the pound, £125; while B is entitled to deduct £25 from A. Then the consequence of raising a given amount of onerous taxation, say £125, by the proposed method, rather than as at present from the occupier, will be as follows. Whereas at present the £125 will be paid either by the occupier or the rack-rent owner C, or partly by one and partly by the other, the proportions of these payments, apart from friction, will be exactly the same in the proposed as in the present arrangement.[2] The main effect of the proposed change will be to transfer to the pocket of A, who is enjoying an unearned increment of £400, £100 from B,[3] who built the house, and £25 from A, the landowner, who may have made an outlay in roads and sewers [4] and cannot possibly have obtained so large an unearned increment as C.

The proposition that the occupiers are not benefited by the proposed series of deduction is of course only true in the long run, apart from " friction," and except for the short periods required for occupiers' leases to run out. Or not even with that exception in the case of householders who do not pay rates directly, perhaps some *three-fourths* of the total number.[5] Among these the numerous class of lodgers may for the present reasoning be reckoned. But it is objected: Would not the fall of rents

---

[1] Here £500 is the amount denominated ζ in the explanation given above (p. 189), and the case is that in which the penultimate holder obtained a value *equal to* ζ.

[2] Above, p. 487.

[3] The contention that the impost on B is justified by the increase in the capital value of his interest cannot be sustained if Mr. Edward Tewson, the well-known estate agent, to whom the case was submitted by Mr. Sargant, is right in estimating this hypothetical ground-rent as " *before* the rise in ground-value at from 18 to 20 years' purchase, and *after* the rise at from 18 to 21 years' purchase." *Cp.* above, p. 504.

[4] *Cp.* above, p. 183.

[5] Select Committee on Town Holdings, 1891, Q. 953. The argument is not affected by the *monopoly* which the landlord in such cases may enjoy; above, p. 184, note 1.

payable by the landlord benefit persons in the position of his lodgers ? [1] The answer is that, if that fall was due to a fall in the cost of producing a house, or any cause that could be reckoned on by speculative purchasers of house property, then the play of competition would transfer some of that advantage to the consumer. But we have seen that *this* kind of causation does not tend to lower, but rather to enhance, the price of houses under the proposed system. The fall supposed is a mere windfall for the landlords : and that kind of gain is not transferred to the tenants for the reason explained in the text-books, when it is taught that rent of agricultural land does not affect the price of wheat.[2] Thus, even supposing that houses are not to be classed with " hats," even granting that there is some exception to the Ricardian rule that a tax on producers is shifted to consumers, at best the result would be to have transferred windfalls from one to another class of producers.

This then is the outcome of the schemes now popular, to injure one investor for the benefit of another investor. For this is every interest vexed and harassed. Peter is robbed to pay, not Paul, but Paul's landlord. We are told nothing about the owner of the " hired house " in which " Paul dwelt two whole years." [3] He may have been a heathen capitalist. At any rate the modern representative of that party does not appear entitled to especial consideration. Of all the links in the chain of production this last may seem the least deserving to be gilded with unexpected gain stripped from the others. The rack-rent owner is at least as likely as any of his superiors to be enjoying unearned increment. The gains of the builder are at least largely earned; the gains of a rack-rent owner who has purchased a house built by others may be mostly speculative. Above all the rack-rent owner is the only party who can be the recipient of *future* unearned increment, a circumstance which it may be hoped has not become indifferent to the countrymen of Mill.

The reasoning applied to the schemes for rating sites which have just been discussed is applicable with little change to the scheme for dividing rates, defined but not discussed in an earlier page,[4] of which the essence is to lay an impost on each party proportionate to the net income which he derives from the premises. This scheme presents two aspects according as (1) it does, or

---

[1] Cp. *Contemporary Review*, March, 1890, p. 418.
[2] *E.g.*, Mill, *Pol. Econ.*, Bk. III. ch. v. § 2.
[3] Acts xxviii.
[4] 1 B, referred to on p. 187.

(2) does not respect vested interests. To the former (1) class belongs the recommendation of the Select Committee on Town Holdings, 1892— [1]

" that under all future contracts half of the rates should be borne by owners in proportion to the several rents they receive . . . and that the liability to deduction should attach not only to the receivers of the rack-rent, but to the owners of all superior interests."

The objections above stated under the head 2 a [2] do not apply to this case, but the objections stated under the head II. 2 b [3] apply almost equally to this case. It may be thought that, as no distinction is made between income issuing from buildings and from land, this system will discourage building more than the so-called rate upon site-value. But it is very possible that a fixed impost proportional to net profits will discourage industry less than the abstraction of an unpredictable quantity which is called indeed a rate on site value, but might as well be called a rate on an unknown quantity, σ.

" The result would be to make every rent received in respect of every interest in houses a variable one, and so to drive cheap or trust capital out of houses as an investment, and to necessarily raise rents." (Sargant, *Mem.*, p. 215.)

" If, where there are several interests in houses, a proportion of the rates in the £ is to be deducted on each payment between successive interests, the effect will be to rate mere annuitants or rent charges, and to relieve to this extent the real owners " [that is, the parties in this article denominated the rack-rent owners]. (*Ibid.*)

When (2) present as well as future rents and quasi-rents are struck, the check to production is aggravated by the shock to equity. Almost all that has been said as to the productional and distributional imperfections of the site-rate may be transferred to this case. Here, too, appearances are apt to deceive the very elect. The brilliant writer who has been referred to as advocating this scheme is confident that " if you define the term owner so as to cover those persons whom you want to rate, and then proceed to send to each of these ' owners ' a demand note, the relief so given to the occupier will be a real relief." A patient analysis discloses the contrary view. The relief so given to the occupier will not be a real relief, for his rent is likely to be raised at least as much as his rates are lowered, probably more owing to the discouragement of producers. Nor will you render con-

[1] 1892, No. 214.   [2] Above, p. 198.   [3] Above, p. 203.

tributory all " those persons whom you want to rate," for the
rack-rent owner will not only not be amerced, but will even gain,
by your substituting the proposed system for the present one.[1]

It will be understood that the statements in the preceding
paragraphs relate primarily to the typical case of the English
leasehold system; [2] with which, for much of the reasoning, the
system of Scotch feus, Manchester chief rents, and so forth, may
be identified. It has been all along supposed that the owner and
the occupier are different persons, as commonly in our towns.[3]
When this is not the case the schemes in question can no longer
be regarded as inept as well as inequitable. The object being to
relieve, as the phrase is, the ratepaying occupier, this object would
be realised as far as the present occupier-owners are concerned,
even though the whole class of occupiers, including the species
that are owners, might, in the future, be damnified by the check
now given to production. As to the equity of the scheme, if, as
seems to be a frequent case in our large towns, the property
increases without much trouble on the part of the owner and
beyond what he reckoned on when acquiring the property, what
is the claim of the owner-occupier to relief ? Unforeseen rates, it
is said, are imposed. But they are mostly " beneficial." [4] Where
they are really onerous, may not this onus be set against that
increase in value ? Where not, in neighbourhoods that are declining, no doubt a hardship, or at least a misfortune, is made out.
But is the remedy sought equitable ? Is it reasonable that the
superiors, who would not have shared a gain, should have to share
a loss with the owner ? And once more it is to be recalled that
more often than appears there is a *productional*,[5] as well as a distributional, reason against confiscating the interests of superiors.

Upon the whole the schemes which are now in vogue for
rating all kinds of " owners " appear to effect nothing which
could not better be effected by a scheme like Mill's, perhaps
coupled with a division of rates between occupier and " rack-rent
owner " as recommended by many of the experts whom the
present Royal Commission has consulted. If a scheme embody-
ing Mill's principle had been adopted a generation ago with
respect to urban sites, an annual income of some two or three
million sterling [6] would probably now have been flowing into the

[1] Above, p. 208.

[2] Above, p. 162

[3] Reports of the Select Committee on Town Holdings, 1889, No. 251, pp. 9, 10;
and Report, 1892, No. 214, p. xvi.

[4] Above, p. 158.   [5] Above, pp. 193, 200, note 3.

[6] On the basis of the figures given above, p. 195.

municipal treasury from ground rents in London; while the division of rates between the occupier and his immediate landlord, not too suddenly introduced,[1] might possibly have conferred some advantages of minor importance on the occupiers. Nothing better would have been accomplished by the more pretentious schemes which are now in vogue. The apparent gain to the occupier from the diminution of rates would have been compensated by a rise of rent. It would probably have been more than compensated : the check to production would have resulted in a higher price, as measured by rent *plus* rates, being paid by the occupier for house-accommodation. Nothing more would have been effected—nothing but confusion and bitterness, the temporary gains of rapacity, and the useless transference of windfalls from one investor to another.[2]

These conclusions have been reached without bias. The writer holds no brief for urban landlords. He has impartially pronounced against them upon several counts. He has disputed the favourite argument that they have been already rated in that their rents are by so much less than they would have been if the rates had not existed.[3] He would go so far as to allow that, even if it were true that the landlords had paid the rates out of unearned increase in the past, it might nevertheless be reasonable to rate unearned increase in the future. He has met the *recherché* objection that a special rate on ground rent would be nugatory, since the landlord would be compensated by the increased demand on the part of occupiers.[4] He has fully accepted Mill's doctrine on the taxation of " future unearned increment " of rent. He has admitted that the industry of which house-accommodation is the product presents something peculiar and exceptional in the long incorporation of land with labour, in virtue of which an impost on the profits of the producers might have less than its usual effect on the interests of the consumers. He regards it as conceivable that a greater than Mill might succeed in demarcating some portion of the gains of middlemen in this industry as *par excellence* " unearned," [5] so different in kind from the ordinary

---

[1] *Cp.* above, p. 185.   [2] See p. 208.
[3] *Ante*, p. 173.   [4] Above, p. 199.

[5] See note to p. 198, above. A tentative in this direction—the only direction, as it appears to the present writer, in which there is any hope of advancing beyond Mill's position—is made by Mr. Henry, the City Assessor of Glasgow, when he proposes (Minutes of Evidence, Royal Commission on Local Taxation, Vol. III. [C. 9319] Appendix XXV., p. 25, etc. *Cp.* Mr. R. McKenna, M.P., *ibid.*, Vol. IV. Appendix XIX.) that owners of land and buildings should be specially taxed " on all increase of rent of annual value beyond that at the passing of the Act, but providing always that where an increase of rental is obtained from money

blends of work and luck as to become the object of a specially
heavy impost without detriment to the quantity of production
or the equality of distribution.[1] But this problem which Mill
did not attempt has not been solved by his successors. In
a matter so complex and momentous it may reasonably be
demanded that action should not be taken until a scheme is
forthcoming which shall stand the test of abstract general reasoning as well as Mill's scheme. And even then there still should
give us pause the possibility that, though the principles are
sound, some error in a datum, such as Mill committed,[2] might
result in a disastrous failure.

---

spent on improvements, etc., on the property an annual deduction of $7\frac{1}{2}$ per cent.
[on the " money spent," presumably; but for how many years ? for ever, into
whatever hands the premises may pass ?] from such increase of rental be allowed
before imposing such tax." This impost on future unearned increment would
not much offend against the distributional canon of taxation if not too
suddenly introduced. It would offend against the productional canon, so far
as the regulations necessary to the working of the scheme might deter the
investment of capital, and the restriction of profit might discourage the application
of effort and sacrifice, which in many inobtrusive ways are apt to act produc-
tively (above, p. 193); so far also as the working of the system proved costly in
comparison with the yield (as to the amount of which in the case of London,
see above, p. 195), a great part of the " unearned increment " becoming earned
by assessors, accountants, inspectors and lawyers, who would be required in order
to ascertain the increase of rental " obtained from money spent on improvements."

[1] *Ante*, p. 152 *et seq.*; regard to " quantity of production " including the
condition that the tax should be worth the cost of collection (*ibid.*, p. 154).

[2] Above, p. 197.

(V)

FURTHER CONSIDERATIONS ON URBAN RATES

[In V (" Recent Schemes for Rating Urban Land Values,"
ECONOMIC JOURNAL, 1906), there is considered a milder scheme
for tapping site-values, based on the Minority Report of the Local
Taxation Commission and embodied in Parliamentary Bills
which were introduced in 1902 and subsequent years. While
the superiority of this scheme to those condemned in the former
paper is duly admitted, preference is still expressed for Mill's
recommendations.]

Schemes for imposing a special rate on urban site-values were
discussed by the present writer in an article which was published
in the December number of the ECONOMIC JOURNAL for the year
1900, before the appearance of the final report made by the Royal
Commission on Local Taxation. With the aid of criteria established in that article it is proposed now to advert to the Majority
Report of the Commission so far as it relates to the " rating of
land values,"[1] to the " Separate Report on urban rating and site-
values " by a Minority, published in the same Blue-book,[2] and
to the Bills deriving from that separate report which have been
laid before Parliament.[3]

As shown in the article mentioned, the incidence of a rate on
urban site values involves the composition of two laws relating
respectively to the taxation of rent proper and that of " quasi-
rent." The first law alone is operative in those cases to which
J. S. Mill's doctrine of the unearned increment is applicable.
It may be well to reproduce the doctrine in his own words :—
" Suppose that there is a kind of income which constantly tends
to increase without any exertion or sacrifice on the part of the
owners ; those owners constituting a class in the community whom
the natural course of things progressively enriches consistently

---

[1] The subject of the ninth chapter in the Majority Report.
[2] Cd. 638, 1901.
[3] In 1902 and the three following years ; debated respectively on February 19,
1902, March 27, 1903, March 11, 1904, April 14, 1905. There is a good summary
of the Bills in an Appendix to Mr. Wilson Fox's *Rating of Land Values.*

with complete passiveness on their own part . . ." such increase of wealth would be a " fit subject of peculiar taxation." [1]

The opponents of a special impost on site values seldom do justice to Mill's doctrine. The Majority of the Local Taxation Commission argue : " Inasmuch as the value of the land is included in the valuation of the rateable hereditament as a whole, ground rents . . . are already taxed." [2] But the contention is that a special, a " peculiar," impost should be laid on certain ground rents. The Majority pronounce against that contention when they say " nor does land differ so essentially from other property as regards the alteration of its value from time to time as to justify its being rated exceptionally." [3] It is here submitted that a different estimate as to the growth of urban site-value is countenanced by such statistics as are available; in particular, the figures for the growth in recent years of ground-values in Vienna and Berlin, given in the writings of the *Verein für Socialpolitik*, Vol. XCIV. 1901, and other French, Italian, English, and American statistics, well marshalled by Professor Einaudi in his masterly article in the *Riforma Sociale* for August, 1900.[4] To these may be added some striking instances adduced [5] by advocates of Land Values Rating Bills in Parliament. The case seems to be similar to the case for the differential taxation of funded as distinguished from temporary and precarious incomes ; a discrimination which was advocated by Mill, and which has been accepted into the financial systems of many countries, including our own,[*] so far as the Death Duties are defended on this principle.[6] It is not a decisive objectionag ainst such discrimination, that in the words of the Minority Report,[8] with reference to the taxation of the unearned increment of rent from urban land, " a consistent application of the principle would be impracticable," that urban land is " not unique in this respect." As Mill says, with reference to the differential taxation of incomes, " It is no objection to this principle that we cannot apply it consistently in all cases. . . . The difficulty of doing perfect justice is no reason against doing as much as we can."

[1] *Political Economy*, Book V. ch. iv. § 5, and Contents.
[2] *Loc. cit.*, pp. 39–40.
[3] *Ibid.*, p. 45.
[4] Referred to in the ECONOMIC JOURNAL, 1900, p. 609.
[5] *E.g.*, by Dr. Macnamara. Hansard, Vol. 120, p. 473. March 27, 1903.
[*] Written before the change introduced by the Budget of 1907.
[6] *Cp.* Bastable, *Public Finance*, Book IV. ch. ix. § 3. " We are thus led to regard the Death Duties as a capitalised income-tax levied only on accumulated wealth, and sparing those comparatively temporary parts of income that result from personal exertion "   [8] *Loc. cit.*. p. 166.

Justice cannot be defined with objective precision. The equitable distribution of fiscal burdens is based by many on the principle of Retribution rather than of Equal (or Least) Sacrifice They will have it that a special impost on unearned increment from urban land is just, because the possessor has obtained this advantage through the outlay of his fellow-citizens. It may, indeed, be pertinently asked whether landlords are the only class who have indirectly benefited by the improvements which others have made in their own interest; whether the outlay of civic authorities and fellow-citizens is the only cause which has contributed to the growth of rent.[1]   But it is not to be expected that any definition of justice will be free from dialectical objections.   We must count as gathering with us those who do not scatter against us.   They are to be regarded as following Mill, who in their proposals to tax increment of rent, at least emphasise the circumstance that it is " unearned."   Of this type is the remarkable doctrine which Professor Adolph Wagner expressed in a recent address.   Supposing a piece of land to have changed hands for 100,000 marks, and in a year or two to be again sold for 150,000 marks, a capital expenditure of 10,000 marks in the way of improvement having been in the meantime made, Professor Wagner thus goes on :—" There remains of the 150,000 marks 40,000 : that is the unearned increment [konjuncturgewinn]. This 40,000 marks has the owner produced by his own efficiency and labour? No!   Has he paid for them?   No! . . . This 40,000 marks then is to be drawn on for purposes of taxation [gilt es zur Besteuerung heranzuziehen]. You cannot put the rate high enough in my opinion.   I would leave something to the owner who has gained under such circumstances, say, 10 per cent., or as such a measure could not yet be carried through, say 50 per cent., or so far as I am concerned, 30 per cent." [2]

It will be observed that Professor Wagner does not propose to deal in this drastic manner with the original 100,000 marks. It is only a disciple of Henry George that would treat a land-owner like a slaveowner,[3] whose unhallowed property may be confiscated without compensation. It is not proposed to argue here against this principle; argument about first principles is unavailing. There is postulated a general agreement with the

[1] Compare Prof. Einaudi's dialectic in the *Riforma Sociale* for September, 1900.

[2] *Kommunale Steuerfragen* (1904), referred to by R. C. Brooks in the *Political Science Quarterly* for December, 1905.

[3] The parallel is expressly drawn in the Eighth Report of the Illinois Labour Bureau.

doctrine of unearned increment—as taught by Mill, not as caricatured by George.

The application of Mill's doctrine would be simple but that the law on which it is based is cut into by another law of incidence. It is not only true that, in the words of Ricardo, a " tax on rent [proper] would fall wholly on landlords," but also that " a partial tax on profits will raise the price of the commodity on which it falls." Now a site-value tax under the prevalent system of urban tenures is apt to fall to some extent on the profits of the business-men who supply house-accommodation. The prospect of a rise in the value of house property encourages the supply of house-accommodation; the prospect of an additional impost, however named, to be levied in the future on those who in the present are making efforts and sacrifices in the way of production tends to discourage that supply.

It may be objected that the prospect is too remote to affect present action; and it has been admitted that the producer of a house will not be so much affected by the prospect of taxation extending over a series of future years as the producer of a hat—Ricardo's favourite instance—is affected by an ordinary tax.[1] Full allowance being made for this difference, a considerable effect in the way of increased burden to the consumer must still be attributed to the prospect of diminished profits for the producer. The distance in time to which the outlook of the building entrepreneur extends is well illustrated by a form of lease which seems to be not unknown in Chicago, in which the future increase in the value of the property is the subject of stipulation. Here is a specimen : [2] the lease of a certain plot of ground for ninety-eight years and eleven months from June, 1894. The lessee is to construct a first-class building thereon by May 1st, 1895. He is to pay up to April 30th 1895, $5,000, and afterwards annual rents as follows :—

		$
For nine years	..	12,000
For next ten years	.	15,000
For next ten years	..	17,000
For next ten years	..	20,000
For remaining fifty-nine years	..	25,000

The prospect of future increment is evidently not indifferent to the lessee. *Primâ facie*, if the Government exacted from that

---

[1] *Cp.* above, p. 207.

[2] Taken from the aforesaid report of the Illinois Labour Bureau.

entrepreneur, under the title of site-value, a sum in excess of that surplus which he can afford to hand to the ground landlord, the supply of house-accommodation would be restricted.

No ! it may be objected, all that will happen is that the rent of the ground landlord will be *pro tanto* diminished. Fine issues are here raised. Let us approach the question by first considering a rate of the ordinary kind *ad valorem* on the rent payable by the occupier. This impost, if levied on the building owner, would not be thrown by him altogether on the ground landlord, as some high authorities have conceived, but in part at least, and very possibly altogether, on the occupier.[1] Now when we substitute for this kind of impost that reduction of profits which may be apprehended from a site-value tax levied on the building owners, is the case materially different ? The answer of pure theory is, yes. There is in the abstract all the difference between a tax on a margin and a tax on a surplus.[2] But the theory is seldom applicable in all its purity to concrete circumstances. There is not usually a practical difference of first importance between a specific tax and a tax by way of licence. To be sure, there is usually absent a condition which is apt to be present in the case now under consideration—namely, the existence of land for which there is no other use at all comparable in profitableness with the production of that commodity on the producer of which it is proposed to levy an impost. But this condition is not always present in the case under consideration. Suppose the Chicago builder above instanced to foresee that in the first three periods in which he had been ready to give the ground landlord 12,000, 15,000 and 17,000 dollars per annum respectively, he would in consequence of the new impost be exposed to an exaction of 50 per cent. more in each of those periods; will not his enterprise be damped ? He cannot withhold from the ground landlord more than he was prepared to offer him; the prospect of a charge on profits which cannot thus be recouped tends to check building enterprise. Moreover, it is doubtful how far a rate on site value of the kind proposed is to be regarded as a tax on surplus. Suppose that transactions by which the building owner raises money on the security of the premises are hampered by the prospect that the interest payable in return for those advances will be in the future pursued with a so-called site-value tax, even into the hands of the creditor. Lenders would insist on more onerous terms, and the extension of the entrepreneur's operations would

[1] Above, S, p. 80 *et seq ;* Index, s.v. *House Tax.*
[2] See above, S, p. 75.

be checked; the effect of the impost would then be of that *marginal* kind which, as we have seen, restricts the application of building capital, and imposes a burden on the consumer of house-accommodation.

Altogether, the case may be compared, in respect of the uncertainty of its incidence, to a customs duty. The incidence of such a duty is not the same as that of a duty on home-made articles. Theory admits that a part of the tax may fall on the foreigner. But only reckless and ignorant politicians act upon the supposition that all the tax is always borne by the foreigner.

The neglect of the burden repercussively imposed on the occupier is the capital error of the schemes criticised in the former paper; schemes justly described in the Separate Report [1] as " crude and violent," neither " equitable nor workable." The writers of the report honourably abstain from the violent interference with contracts, discerning its tendency to check enterprise. " The proposed violation of contracts would greatly aggravate existing evils by destroying confidence and discouraging building enterprise." [2]

With regard to the incidence of the proposed imposts, unaccompanied by violence, the writers of the Minority Report perceive clearly enough that foreseen rates of the ordinary kind are apt to be in part thrown on the occupier, even though levied from the building owner.[3] But they and the promoters of Bills founded on their report have not equally realised that a foreseen impost levied from the owner does not lose the property of transference to the occupier, because it is called a rate on site-value.

The neglect of this incident exposes to some doubt the Minority's fine reasoning as to the local distribution of the new impost; the consequence thus described by the promoter of a Bill on the lines of the Separate Report :—" The inner ring of the town will move out the outer rings, and the outer rings will push out the population still further outwards." [4]

So far as the proposed rate on site-value acts like a tax on rent proper, doubtless, *ceteris paribus*, the taxation by which the enterprise of the builder is checked will be reduced; and since there is most building at the periphery, building there will be most encouraged.

But whereas the new rate is, after a short interval, to fall upon the building owner [5]—that is, the entrepreneur, or a party from

---

[1] *Loc. cit.*, pp. 162, 166.　　　[2] *Loc. cit.*, p. 164.
[3] *Loc. cit.*, p. 156.　　　[4] Hansard, Vol. 103, p. 483.
[5] Separate Report, p. 171; and the Bills founded on the Report.

whom he obtains payment—it is to be expected that the proposed rate will act partly as a tax on profits. To that extent building enterprise will be checked. The check may be expected to be greater at the periphery than the centre; not only absolutely or *in toto*, because there is more building at the periphery, but also per cent. of the outlay, for a reason above indicated, that the foreseen decrement of profits are less capable of being deducted from ground-rents where ground-rents are low, as at the periphery, than where they are large enough to recoup anticipated loss of profits, as at the centre.

Without insisting on this paradoxical consequence, may we not invoke the general presumption against seeking to compass by taxation ulterior objects other than revenue? Disturbance to industry is in general a much more certain consequence than any beneficial result that is proposed. Thus the promoter of a Land Value Rating Bill, after admitting that in his scheme within " the inner ring of the city " " the tax would increase on each property," goes on :—" But even there there would be no hardship on property owners. For they would only have to build better premises and use their land better, and they would not as now be subjected to a higher tax on their enterprise." [1] If it is meant to suggest here, as in other passages, that the new impost would supply a new motive to the owner to use his land better, the deduction appears to be very questionable. If it did not before pay him to replace an old building, it will not pay him any better to do so, because, under the new system, whether he does so or not, he will be placed under the necessity of paying a site-value rate. This and other points of theory here touched upon are elaborately demonstrated by Professor Luigi Einaudi in his *Studi sugli effetti dell' Imposte*,[2] the most exhaustive and sagacious treatise on the whole subject known to the present writer.

Similar criticisms may be directed against the proposed land value rates in their relation to vacant land. The promoter of such a measure argues,[3] " the landlords will come tumbling over one another in their eagerness to sell, and down will come the value of the land to the price at which it ought to be sold—that is, a little above its agricultural value." In this and like passages there seems to be involved a disputable opinion as to the functions of the speculator in land : too low an estimate of his usefulness, too high an estimate of his power to prejudice the

---

[1] Preface to Zimmermann's *Taxation of Land Values* (1905).
[2] Reviewed in the ECONOMIC JOURNAL, Vol. XIII. p. 237; below, Vol. III.
[3] Preface to Zimmermann's *Taxation of Land Values*.

consumer. As in other industries—if not quite so much as in other industries [1]—the speculator is useful in finding a market for the article. As Mr. Edward Bond, in a debate on one of the Bills now under consideration, urged, " they had to rely principally, if not entirely, on the efforts of speculative builders and commercial men, who went into the business with a view to getting a fair return for their money." [2] The discouragement of this necessary middleman would, he thought, not conduce to the result aimed at, " namely, to bring more land into the market," but to the opposite result. As in other industries, the speculator is not so responsible as he appears to be for high prices. Their fundamental cause—the urgent demand for an article of which the quantity in existence is limited—is not created by speculators. We may therefore apply to the above-cited proposals what is said in the Report (Lord Hobhouse's) of the Local Government and Taxation Committee of the County Council,[3] with respect to certain earlier proposals of similar design. " We doubt first whether it is possible to force the market, as they suggest, by the indirect agency of rates upon landowners. It is the interest of landowners to bring their land into profitable occupation as quickly as they can. We doubt secondly whether, if the land market could be artificially forced by a system of rating, it would be found of advantage to landowners."

In what precedes it has been taken for granted that urban land is not monopolised in the sense of being under the control of a single person (individual or corporate). How far this assumption is illegitimate the writer has no means of forming a judgment based on accurate information. He is not much affected by declamations so loose as not to distinguish between monopoly in the sense pertinent to the reasoning, and monopoly in the sense of limited total supply. There is some trustworthy evidence—that of the careful Professor Voigt in a masterly study on the Housing Question in Berlin [4]—that there at least the complaint against monopoly is not justified. It is to be remembered, too, that the power of large landlords in small towns is checked by the competition which exists with other towns.[5]

---

[1] Can it be maintained that pure speculation in land unaccompanied with any other productive activity—to " buy to hold and sell at a profit," as the advertisements put it—is attended with all the advantages ascribed by economists (J. S. Mill, for instance, *Political Economy*, Book IV. ch. ii. § 4) to speculation (without monopoly) in a commodity like wheat ?   [2] Hansard, Vol. 103, p. 522.

[3] *Minute of the Proceedings of the London County Council for* 1891.

[4] *Schriften des Verein für Socialpolitik.*   Band XCIV. (1901), p. 233.

[5] *Cp.* above, p. 175.

In fine, the interest of monopolists is not always contrary to that of their customers. It is supposed to be, much more often than it is proved to be, in the case of Railways.[1] In the case of land the frequent allegations that a large rise of price has been obtained by holding up land does not prove that the best use of the land has not been made. If it was the pecuniary interest of the owner to prefer the large deferred rent to the small one, which might have been obtained sooner, it was presumably the pecuniary interest of the municipality also to wait. There is no reason to think that they ought to " discount the future " at a less provident rate than the capitalist. The delay which is for the fiscal interest of the municipality may be, indeed, but there appears no presumption that it will be, opposed to the interests of the inhabitants. Forcing the market, " forestalling the blighted harvest " of urban land might have led to undesirable jerry-building and other admitted evils.[2]

The antithesis between the interests of the inhabitants and the monopolist owner is most likely to exist when his interest is other than pecuniary, such as affection for amenities. The interposition of the civic authority is doubtless justified in such cases. But surely a tax is a very clumsy method of applying the required control.

To this reasoning may be opposed the experience of foreign and colonial land taxes. And doubtless if the contention were that the adoption of the proposed site rates would be followed by immediate dissolution, that experience would be decisive. But, whereas, it is contended only that these rates will act like a protectionist duty, indirectly burdening the citizens whom it purports to benefit, against this contention the short experience of very recent legislation in other countries is not available. Perhaps no experience, however prolonged, would be adequate; as in the argument for Free Trade, we must depend largely upon general reasoning.[3]

The suggested analogy with Protection will perhaps be accepted by the advocates of site taxation. Admitting that part of the new burden will fall on the occupiers, they may still take

---

[1] See some instances in Mr. Dudley Evans' articles on "British Railways and Goods Traffic " in the ECONOMIC JOURNAL for 1905.

[2] The authors of the Separate Report, p. 175, and some of their followers (c_p the able article in the *Independent Review* for 1905) are on their guard against these evils. But still the question recurs whether a tax is the best method of securing just the requisite amount and kind of building.

[3] As J. S. Mill (*Logic*, Book VI.) and Sir Robert Giffen (Essay on *Import and Export Statistics*, Sect. VI.) have *inter alios* pointed out.

up the position that this is a very good way of raising additional rates. The more knowing among the town councillors who advocate the current schemes may employ the common doctrine of unearned increment, or the more refined reasoning of the Separate Report, *ad captandam plebem*, as crafty statesmen have been suspected of recommending a modicum of Protection, not being the dupes of their own argument, but because the people could thus be more easily induced to submit to additional taxation. It is as if in a wine-growing country a new tax, really incident on the wine-bibing public, was recommended, partly as extracted from the ill-gotten gains accruing to the lords of the vineyards, partly as inducing the wine-dealers to place their goods on the market sooner instead of waiting for an enhanced price.

If nothing more is meant than a change in the point of percussion of a tax on the householder, like the change in the taxation of the beer-drinking public when a beer-tax or a licence has been added to or substituted for a malt-tax, then *cadit quœstio*. It may be admitted that a site-value tax unaccompanied by interference with contracts, if not more costly to collect and not more harassing to industry than an ordinary rate, would be no worse than an ordinary rate.[1] Indeed, it would be better for a reason like that which is *pro tanto* available in favour of a customs duty in preference to a duty on a home-made article—namely, that a part of the former *may* fall upon the foreigner. So a part of the site tax may fall where it can be borne with least sacrifice.

But it is evidently not on such grounds, not as an ordinary tax, that the authors of the Separate Report and their followers in Parliament defend their schemes, but *bonâ fide* upon the grounds that have been above examined. Some more or less conscious corroboration is also derived by the Parliamentary advocates from the considerations on which Mill's doctrine of unearned increment rest. It is thus that we interpret the emphasis on striking instances of increased value accruing by mere lapse of time. It may therefore be proper to inquire whether the new schemes are defensible as being in accordance with Mill's recommendations.

So far, indeed, as the current schemes involve Mill's principle of taxing unearned increments they are defended by the present

---

[1] The conditions presupposed are not very likely to be fulfilled if the plan is adopted under the misconceptions which make it appear, not an ordinarily oppressive, but an extraordinarily equitable tax. (See above, U, p. 151 *et seq.*)

writer. But the defence on this ground is not so strong as might *primâ facie* appear. The schemes do indeed include taxation of unearned increment as well as other kinds of taxation. But in fiscal science the greater does not always comprehend the less. Compare the working of Mill's principle with the modern form of site-value tax. In the case of premises in the centre of a town when a new lease is created—or the land is otherwise disposed of by the ground-landlord Mill's plan is—with due regard to the interest initially existing—to dock the future receipts of landlords by a substantial percentage, such a percentage as Professor Wagner, in the passage above-quoted, has proposed to take from unearned increment.[1] If this plan had been adopted in Mill's time some two millions sterling might now be flowing into the municipal treasury.[2] But nothing like this could be obtained from the same ground-rents according to the methods now in vogue. Dealing with wheat and tares—earned and unearned increments—promiscuously, as above argued, they could not, under the name of site-tax, impose so drastic an impost, or rather an appropriation. It would be particularly impossible to do so in the case where the value of the cleared site is much greater than that of the site *plus* an existing tenement. Some advocates of new schemes may claim indeed that their schemes will put a stop to that anomaly. But it has been argued above,[3] that this claim is not admissible. If, as appears to be the general design of these schemes, a site-value rate is to be imposed on the land before it changes hands, to follow it into new hands without breach of continuity, and to be fixed at a constant percentage for a whole country, or at least district, then an operation on anything like the scale contemplated by Mill with respect to newly created ground-rent would be impracticable.

Like remarks apply to the proposed taxation of vacant land. Mill's plan would be to wait till the egg is laid, and then if you like, scoop out all the yolk. The plan of taxing the value of the goose derived from the prospect of future eggs cannot well be so drastic. It will be observed that this objection is distinct from and additional to the more familiar objection already in effect urged, that tampering with the process of capitalistic incubation will diminish the number of eggs available for consumption.

If there is no other general principle but Mill's conducting

---

[1] Above, p. 217.
[2] As argued in the former paper, above, p. 195.
[3] Above, pp. 220–1.

to a " peculiar " taxation of site-value, the only question is how far is it in practice safe to follow that principle. May we apply to English tenures the regulations which are now proposed in Berlin. " An increment tax shall be levied whenever the present purchase price or the market value [gemeine wert] of the real estate exceeds by more than 10 per cent. the price paid at the former change of hands," to which price are to be added expenses for improvements and repairs.[1]

Or are such inquisitory methods to be deprecated because, in the words of the Majority Report on Local Taxation, they " would bring into existence new inequalities of liability," and, we may add, check supply by harassing enterprise " unless measures were taken to differentiate not only between district and district, but between property and property—an obligation which in our opinion could not be satisfied by any possible modification of the existing rating machinery." [2]

On this important question the present writer has nothing to add to the considerations summarised in a former article.[3] Possibly, as in the case of agricultural land in Great Britain, the application of Mill's principle may seem, under existing conditions, impracticable. Possibly, as in the case of agricultural land in Ireland, after much boggled legislation, long banishment of political economy to Saturn, the treatment ultimately adopted will embody the ideas of Mill.[4]

[1] " Berlin's Tax Problem," by Robt. C. Brooks, *Political Science Quarterly*, Dec. 1905.
[2] *Loc. cit.*, p. 44.
[3] Above, **U**, p. 213.
[4] See *England and Ireland*, by J. S. Mill, 1868.

(W)

[THE substance of an Address given to the Students' Union at the London School of Economics, January, 1906, is here reproduced. It is admitted that in the more moderate form which the project had by that time assumed it might pass as not an inordinately bad tax.]

The rating of Urban Land Values is a suitable subject to bring before students of Economics because it exercises that faculty of abstract reasoning which is characteristic of Political Economy as distinguished from Political Science in general. The reasoning which the subject requires is particularly difficult, because there is involved the composition of two general laws.

There is, first, the law that, in Ricardo's words, " a tax on rent would affect rent only; it would fall wholly on landlords." If this law only were in operation, there might be a simple case for the application of Mill's principle that the unearned increment of land value should be subject to a special impost; a principle to which a general adherence on the part of students may be presumed.

But, cutting into this simple law, there is another law that, in the words of the same Ricardo, " a partial tax on profits will raise the price of the commodity on which it falls; a tax, for example, on the profits of the hatter would raise the price of hats." Suppose that hats were usually trimmed with a particular kind of old lace, of which the quantity in existence was strictly limited. Suppose that hat dealers were usually paid on the " hire system," by way of instalments of which the payment extended over considerable intervals of time. And let there be imposed a tax on lace-value to be deducted from the payments to the hatter; the amount deducted being proportioned to the value, at the time of each payment, of the lace on the hat in respect of which the instalment is paid. Would not this be in effect a tax on the profits of the hatter, tending to " raise the price of the commodity " hats ? Would not a rate on site-value, to be similarly from time to time deducted from the remuneration of parties who had been concerned in the production of a house, tend to raise the

227

price of house-accommodation paid by the occupier ? It may be objected that the hat dealer, in view of the impost, would recoup himself, not by requiring more from the consumer of hats, but by offering less to the possessors of lace. It might be so under some circumstances; it would not be so in other cases. One case in which the consumer is particularly likely to suffer is where the foreseen amount of the impost exceeds the whole rent. In general perhaps we can know about the incidence of such a tax only as much as we know in general about the incidence of a customs-duty. There is a presumption that some part of the burden will fall on the consumer; there is a possibility that the greater part may fall on a party about whom the consumer is not concerned. Many a politician who advocates the imposition of a special tax on site values, well discerns the absurdity of acting on the supposition that a duty on imports falls altogether on the foreigner. He beholds the beam in his Protectionist brother's eye, but considers not that there may be at least a mote in his own eye.

The neglect of the ulterior consequences which have been indicated form a weighty objection to several of the earlier schemes for rating urban site values—schemes which have been well characterised, in the Separate Report made by a minority of the Local Taxation Commission, as " crude and violent," neither " equitable nor workable." These schemes are crude and unworkable, because they lead to the abandonment of an industrial system which has grown up presumably in the interest of the consumer as well as producer. Capital will not in future be so readily forthcoming for the construction of houses when it is foreseen that the remuneration thereof will be reduced by the " deductions " which form an essential part of these schemes.

The authors of the Separate Report are honourably free from the violence and inequity—if the word may be allowed—which they justly attribute to some of their predecessors. They do not propose, by rescinding extant contracts, to inflict an unexpected and peculiar burden on a class of persons not demarcated by excess of wealth, or any other mark of ability to bear taxation. A particularly respectful consideration is due to proposals which are unbiased by the vulgar predatory impulse.

It is not easy to present a general idea of these proposals, as they vary considerably in details. The following description purports to be only typical; not true, perhaps, as to every particular of any one of the measures which have been fathered upon the Separate Report.

The type is characterised by two features, of which the more conspicuous consists of a plan to encourage building by a well-adjusted rate on site-value. The improvement is partly to be effected in the centre of towns by encouraging building on vacant spots, and by inducing owners of houses unsuited to their sites to substitute more suitable buildings. But it is especially at the outskirts of towns that beneficial effects are expected. As explained by the proposer of the Bill for Land Values Assessment, which was brought into Parliament in 1903, " the chief object of this law was to relieve buildings in the outskirts of a town." Beside this refined plan, forming the main purpose of the new measure, there seems to be a more ordinary motive, disavowed, indeed, by the minority (as well as the majority) of the Commission on Local Taxation; yet perhaps half consciously held by the promoters of measures based on the Separate Report, and actuating many of the supporters of those measures. There is the desire to tap the reservoirs of unearned value, not exactly on the principle of Mill, but rather on the ground that the owners of such value have obtained a pecuniary gain through the efforts and sacrifices of their fellow-citizens. These desirable objects are ensured by means of a tax of so much in the pound on the " site-value " of each plot, supposed to be measurable with sufficient accuracy for the purpose of taxation. This special rate on site-value is to be borne by the occupier so long as his lease runs, and thereafter by the landlord who leased the premises to the occupier. If that lessor is himself a lessee, the rate will be borne by him only so long as his lease runs; and thereafter by another lessor; and so on, until all the leases relating to the plot of land have run out, when the site-value rate will fall upon the ground-landlord. If the ground-landlord create a new lease, presumably he will continue to bear—thrown back upon him by way of " deduction "—the rate upon site-value such as it was at the time of creating the lease; but subsequent additions to the amount payable will be borne by the lessee, up to the time when he, too, may become a lessor; after which he will continue to bear as much of the rate on site-values as he bore before giving a lease, while his lessee will bear the subsequent additions, and so on.

Details may differ, but it results in general that the parties who undertake outlay and risk in the production of houses will have their remuneration diminished by the new impost. They will tend to recoup themselves by throwing the burden partly on their landlords, and partly on their lessees.

So far as the rate acts like a tax on pure, or proper, rent, the main reasoning of the Minority Report and its followers may be accepted. Other things being the same, a less portion of the rates would be raised at the outskirts of a town, where site-values are low, and building there would be encouraged.

So far as the rate acts like a tax on " rent, as it is constituted," in Ricardo's phrase—on the element of profit in concrete rent—building would be discouraged, particularly at the outskirts, for a reason above submitted, because ground rents are there particularly small.

This reasoning is no doubt somewhat abstract, but so is the reasoning to which it is opposed. The counter-argument may serve at least to recall the canon that taxation should be only for the sake of revenue. So little can be known in general about the consequences of a tax, except that it will probably hamper the producer and burden the consumer. Whether we consider the action of the proposed rate at the centre of towns, or at the circumference, hesitation seems justified.

As to the centre, is it so certain that the owner of a site which has not been put to the best use will have a new motive to set his house in order? Let A be the net advantages, in the owner's view, obtained in the present state of the premises; let B be the prospective advantages derivable from rebuilding his house, account being had of risk, trouble, loss in the way of interest, and other items on the debtor side of the balance. If before the imposition of the special rate the present exceeded the prospective advantages, if A is greater than B, this relation will not be destroyed by the imposition of the rate of so many shillings, say r, on the site value, say S. We have now $A - \dfrac{r}{20} S$ greater than

$B - \dfrac{r}{20} S$. To be sure, if r is so large that $A - \dfrac{r}{20} S$ becomes less than nothing, the owner would have a motive to get rid of the premises by sale—presumably to someone who saw his way to making a better use of the site. But such dispossession of unenterprising owners is surely rather too drastic an operation to be contemplated by those who disclaim violence.

Again, as to the circumference, it has already been argued that the expectant stimulus to building might not be effective. There remain to be considered the good effects attributed to the repression of speculation in land. These good effects are to be measured by the bad effects of speculation. Now speculation in land is not so efficacious, nor are its effects so deleterious, as may be

supposed. It is not so efficacious because it is not the only, nor
the principal, cause of high prices paid for urban land. The demand
on the part of consumers, not the operations of speculating middlemen, is the bottom-cause of high prices. Nor are the effects
which may truly be ascribed to speculation in land so bad as they
are described. That speculators subserve a useful purpose in
putting a commodity on the market is an economic truism. The
outcry against speculation in land recalls the prejudices of our
ancestors against " forestallers " and " regraters " and the
monsters described as " badgers."

It is true, indeed, that if a single owner control the whole
supply of a commodity for which the community is hungering,
such a monopolist may raise the price to the great detriment of
the consumer. But first it must be proved that monopoly in the
sense of control by a single will prevails respecting urban or
suburban land. Next it has to be observed how far the monopolist
is exercising his power to the detriment of his customers. In
fine it should be considered whether the probable evils of untem-
pered monopoly—and it may be added the possible evils of
unrestricted competition—are to be corrected by so clumsy an
instrument as a tax, rather than by intelligent governmental
control.

There remains the more generally attractive object which
" unearned increment " constitutes. So far as recent proposals
embody the principle of Mill they must be approved by one who
approves of that principle. Yet he may consistently disapprove
of the way in which the principle is carried out. Roast pork is a
good dish, but burning the kitchen is a bad way of cooking that
dish. Besides the obvious inconveniences of that culinary method,
it is open to two minor objections. The viand is apt to be done
either too little, or too much ; to be only singed, or to be burnt to
cinders.

The first of the objections metaphorically indicated may be
illustrated by comparing Mill's plan with more recent proposals,
in the case of central premises. According to Mill's plan, when—
all old leases having fallen in—the ground landlord creates a new
lease, a very substantial percentage, in the case of distant reversions at least, would accrue to the community. But so drastic
an appropriation of unearned increment may seem to be inadmissible according to the schemes which are now in vogue. If
the rate on site-value were so very heavy, it would be impossible
to preserve that beautiful continuity with which the new rate
on site-value is to be passed back from lessee to lessor on the

termination of each lease. It would not be seriously proposed
that the holder of an expiring lease, with perhaps an old house
unsuited to the site, should be subjected to such a rate as the
incoming reversioner might bear with cheerfulness, or at least
without detriment to future occupiers.

In the case instanced the unearned increment was not fully
taxed; the pork was not completely roasted. It is done to cinders
in the following instance. Suppose that the measures directed
against speculation in land produced the expected slump in land
values. There would be lost large accretions of value, much of
which, according to Mill's plan, might be appropriated by the
community.

Against the reasoning here employed experience may be
arrayed; the experience of Queensland and some other of our
colonies, and some towns in Germany. But experience must
be transplanted with caution from its original surroundings. It
seems that a " sparrow-rate " is leviable in South Australia;
directed against a pest which is not very formidable here. It is
probable that the rate " on the unimproved value of land " in
certain colonies complies with Mill's principle of taxing unearned
increments more nearly than would be possible with our complicated system of tenures. The party who suffers by the imposition
of the rate on site-values may be less frequently in a simple system
a mere capitalist, who counts upon the ordinary profits on his
outlay, as distinguished from a landlord who is in the receipt of
rent proper.

It is true that the adoption of the new rate would probably lead
to the abandonment of the complicated system which has grown
up in this old country. And why not ? say some. But surely
the fact that the system has grown up should give us pause. The
calmness with which the ruin of an established industrial system
is contemplated is comparable only to the confidence with which
the Protectionist would divert and reshape the course of his
country's trade to suit his own ideas.

It is possible, of course, to admit what has been above contended—that the proposed rate on site-values would largely fall
upon occupiers—and yet to approve of the new rate. But it
must be approved on the same kind of grounds as other taxes
which fall upon the consuming public. The site-value rate, as
compared with other forms of additional impost on the urban
public, may have the kind of advantage which one form of tax
on the beer-drinking public may have over another form. The
site-value rate has the kind of advantage which may be claimed

for a tax on wine in preference to one on beer on the ground (already indicated) that part of the burden *may* fall elsewhere than upon the consumer. If additional municipal taxation is required for the sake of salubrity or other paramount object, and if the site-value rate is the best form of additional levy on the urban public, let that rate by all means be adopted. But do not pretend that it will fall mainly upon affluent monopolists and idle landlords. Do not claim for it the authority of Mill.

(X)

MINIMUM SACRIFICE VERSUS EQUAL SACRIFICE

[THIS Paper, published in the *Quarterly Journal of Economics*, May 1910, under the title " The Subjective Element in the First Principles of Taxation," is a defence of minimum sacrifice as the criterion of taxation against objectors who had not realised its bearing on Progressive Taxation. Whereas in order to deduce progressive taxation from the principle of equal (or that of " proportional ") sacrifice, there is required in addition to the law of diminishing utility, some further datum which is not generally given; the principle of least sacrifice does not require us to assume that of which we are ignorant. This difference is illustrated by adducing a not very complicated formula for the relation between means and utility, which satisfies the only condition known to us, the law of diminishing utility. For all we know this might be the true law. If so, according to the principal of equal sacrifice (however interpreted) the taxation would be *regressive;* the rate of taxation increasing as the income decreases. No such paradox is attributable to the principle of minimum sacrifice.]

The following observations are designed as a supplement to the observations on the first principles of taxation which I have contributed to the ECONOMIC JOURNAL.[1] It is unnecessary to restate my theses, as they have been reproduced with a very flattering fulness in a work which commands universal attention, the second edition of Professor Seligman's *Progressive Taxation.* It will be sufficient here to recall that I divide the first principles of taxation—so far as they are subjective, and abstracting from the more objective *productional* conditions—into two classes, say A and B; characterised by the difference that the criterion of right taxation is for A an equation, for B a maximum condition. Each class is subdivided into two species. Thus A, denoting that *like*—or in a large sense of the term, *equal*—sacrifice should

[1] Vol. VII., " Pure Theory of Taxation "; Vol. X., " The Incidence of Urban Rates"; above, S and U.

234

be imposed on each taxpayer, is subdivided into equal in a narrow or *proper* sense, and equi-proportional sacrifice in a sense explained and preferred by Professor Seligman; say, respectively, A_1 and A_2. Likewise B, the general principle that the total net utility produced by taxation should be a maximum, is subdivided into what I have called the " primary problem," namely, " to determine the distribution of those taxes which are applied to common purposes, the benefits whereof cannot be allocated to any particular classes of citizens "—say B_1; and " the secondary problem, namely, to determine the distribution of taxation, not being limited to that amount of which the benefit is indiscriminate," [1] say B_2. Some additional reflections on these topics suggested by Professor Seligman's weighty criticism may be arranged under three heads.

I. First as to the main question whether formula A, in particular A_2, or formula B, is to be adopted as the first principle. Proof of this, in the ordinary sense of demonstration or deduction from axioms, on such a subject is not to be expected.[2]

It might be suggested in favour of A_2 that it is less *subjective*, less " sicklied o'er with the pale cast " of speculative thought, than the rival criteria of taxation. For conceivably, in order to apply A_2, we need not attempt to " compare the amount of feeling in one mind with that in another." [3] But in order to obtain a ratio between two " lots " of satisfaction—one of them, the total amount of satisfaction due to the possession of an income—there is required a precision of hedonic units which few utilitarians would venture to postulate. Practically, I think, in order to apply A_2—to show, for instance, that the richer class should contribute a larger sum of money (I do not say a larger *proportion* of income)—we must presuppose the sympathetic comparison of wants and feelings experienced by different persons. As thus : if it be possible, let the contribution of the rich man be the same as that of the poor man; then the ratio, which according to A_2 ought to be the same for all the contributions, is a fraction of which—by the law of diminishing utility—both the numerator is smaller, and the denominator is larger than what they are for the poor man. Therefore the ratio in the case of the rich man is too small, and must be increased by augmenting his contribution.

Thus the point which I have adduced in favour of A_2 is not

---

[1] See above, p. 152.

[2] Compare J. S. Mill, " To be incapable of proof by reasoning is common to all first principles." *Utilitarianism*, p. 52 and context.

[3] Jevons, *Theory of Political Economy*, p. 15 (2nd ed.).

of much practical importance; and I must leave the issue in the obscurity which envelops the first principles of conduct.

II. A subsidiary issue is presented by Professor Seligman's thesis that the authorities who have laid down " equal sacrifice " as the criterion have always meant A_2, not A_1. " When economists speak of equal sacrifice they mean relatively proportional sacrifice.[1] . . . ' Equal sacrifice ' is then merely a rough way of expressing the idea of ' proportional ' sacrifice." [2] " The demand for absolutely equal sacrifice in the formal mathematical sense [our A_1] has never, so far as I know, been advanced by any one." [3] Statements so confident, made by one who is so conversant with the history of financial doctrine, naturally carry great weight. They compel me to reconsider my *obiter dictum :* " It may well be doubted whether Mill entertained the notion of proportional sacrifice." [4] On reconsideration, I am disposed to omit the word " well."

It will be admitted, I trust, that I am a fair controversialist when I go on to adduce an additional piece of evidence in favour of my critic's thesis. I have been able to question one of the authorities who have professed the doctrine of equal sacrifice, a singularly clear writer and thinker on economic questions, and one who has carried economic principles [5] into public affairs, Lord—formerly known as Mr. Leonard—Courtney. Having observed that Mr. Courtney, in the answers which he submitted to the Royal Commission on Local Taxation, maintained " that taxation for common purposes should be levied from each member of a community according to the law of equal sacrifice, meaning thereby that each individual should be mulcted of such a sum as would, having relation to his means, involve the same sacrifice to the common want," I lately wrote to Lord Courtney asking which of the two formulæ (here distinguished as A_1 and A_2) his words were intended to designate. Lord Courtney replied with his usual lucidity—after explanations and definitions which I have not space here to transcribe—with reference to a certain graphical construction, " the law of equal sacrifice would be represented by the exaction of the same proportions of area, (the area representing the ' total satisfaction of the owner ') . . .

[1] *Progressive Taxation* (2nd ed.), p. 213.
[2] *Loc. cit.*, p. 214.
[3] *Loc. cit.*, p. 215.
[4] Above, **S**, p. 107, note.
[5] The scheme of graduated death duties, introduced by Sir William Harcourt's Budget of 1894, was rested by Mr. Courtney on the first principles of taxation (Parliamentary Debates, May 20, 1894).

Seligman and I are practically in agreement as to the measure of equal sacrifice."

I make Professor Seligman a present of this weighty testimony in his favour.   I am not like that commentator who, with reference to his own interpretation of a certain vexed passage in a classical work, said that he would not believe the author himself—Ne ipsi quidem Ciceroni crediderim—affirming that the passage meant something different.

I ought to confess that the present which I have made to Professor Seligman is not of much importance to myself, as the subsidiary issue (II) is one in which I am not much concerned. In fact the side which Professor Seligman takes in that issue is the one more favourable to my main theory, namely, that formula B supersedes, or at least subsumes, the formulæ of Class A (A_1, and A_2).   For *ceteris paribus* [1] the distribution of fiscal burden which A_2 prescribes tends to be more progressive than that of A_1.[2]   Accordingly, to show that classical authors have meant by the doctrine of " equal sacrifice " A_2 rather than A_1 lends additional plausibility to the synthesis which subsumes A under B.   If Mill interpreted equal sacrifice as Professor Seligman contends, it is all the more explicable that Mill should have enounced in the same breath both the principle of equal sacrifice and that of least sacrifice.[3]

III. Professor Seligman raises an issue in which I am more concerned when he concludes that " the minimum sacrifice theory is thus really not a whit more successful than the equal sacrifice theory, and possesses the additional disadvantage of being less applicable to the problems of actual life." [4]   " Neither in the version of Professor Edgeworth nor in that of Professor Carver does the doctrine of minimum sacrifice afford us any real help, or constitute any improvement on the doctrine of equal sacrifice."[5]

With reference to these passages and the context I have first to remark that the utilitarian position, as I have conceived it, does not reduce from B to B_1 so unreservedly as Professor Seligman interprets.   The greatest-happiness principle, that the total net utility procured by taxation should be a maximum, reduces to

---

[1] That is, supposing any form of the law of Diminishing Returns to be assigned.

[2] As noticed in the ECONOMIC JOURNAL, Vol. VII. p. 561; above, p. 110.

[3] "Whatever sacrifices it (a Government) requires from them (persons or classes) should be made to bear as nearly as possible with the same pressure upon all, which, it must be observed, is the mode by which least sacrifice is occasioned on the whole."   J. S. Mill, *Political Economy*, Book V. ch. ii. § 2, p. 1, referred to in the ECONOMIC JOURNAL, Vol. VII. p. 564; above, p. 115.

[4] *Progressive Taxation* (2nd ed.), p. 286 and context.

[5] *Loc. cit.*, p. 289.

the condition that the total disutility should be a minimum, not *simpliciter*, but *secundum quid*, with reference to the *primary* problem, namely, to determine the distribution of those taxes which are applied to common purposes.[1] The *secondary* problem, namely, to determine the distribution of taxation, not being limited to that amount of which the benefit is indiscriminate, is indeed immediately clouded over by doubts and reservations. It is cut into by productional and other interests; but I am not prepared to say that it is entirely cut away. Rather, I have maintained Mill's advanced, yet guarded, position. "That the State should use the instrument of taxation as a means of mitigating the inequality of wealth," is not to be demanded when by " a tax on industry and economy " a check to the growth of wealth is imposed. But the utilitarian will be as " desirous as anyone that means should be taken to diminish those inequalities " : such means as the limitation of inheritances and the taxation of unearned increments, so far as these means are free from the dangers above noted.[2]

But, secondly, even with respect to the narrowed utilitarian formula, I am surprised at Professor Seligman's suggestion that the principle of least sacrifice is not a whit more efficacious than the other forms of subjective canon.[3] I should have thought that one who deduced progressive taxation from premises which involve in part subjective considerations of sacrifice would have welcomed a statement of the subjective premises which leads more directly to the conclusion than the ordinary statement does. But the advantage which formula B_1 possesses over both forms of A in this respect was no doubt obscured by the comments of a critic whom Professor Seligman has followed, namely, Mr. Weston.[4]

Mr. Weston thinks it strange that a mathematical economist should " find satisfaction in a theory based upon a principle that

[1] See ECONOMIC JOURNAL, Vol. VII. p. 553, referred to above. I quote word for word from this page passages which Professor Seligman has done me the honour of quoting. But not to distract the reader's attention, I reserve quotation marks (in this paragraph) for quotations from Mill.

[2] The words within quotation marks are quoted from Mill, *Political Economy*, Book V. ch. ii. § 3. The rest of the passage is mostly quoted from the ECONOMIC JOURNAL, *loc. cit.*, p. 555; above, p. 106.

[3] " If we base our doctrine of the equities of taxation on the theory of faculty, both the production and the consumption sides of the theory seem to point to progressive taxation." Seligman, *loc. cit.*, p. 293 and context, from which it appears that the consumption element in faculty is equivalent to the sacrifice theory.

[4] *Justice and Taxation :* Columbia University Studies in History and Economics, Vol. XVII. (1903).

does not admit of an exact mathematical expression." [1] He bases this disparaging remark on my statement that " the reasoning from the principle of minimum sacrifice assumes no exact relations between utility and means." [2] But the meaning of that statement, as the context shows, is not that the principle of minimum sacrifice abandons the character of mathematical reasoning, but that it does not require all the data which are required by the rival principle of equal sacrifice. This is the first time that the parsimony of assumptions has been made a reproach to a mathematical argument. After Clerk Maxwell had shown that the observed laws of pressure and so forth were accounted for by the hypothesis that a gas consisted of an indefinite number of perfectly elastic minute spheres encountering each other in a molecular chaos, was it a sign of satisfaction in the absence of an exact mathematical relation, was it any imperfection, to show that much the same conclusion was deducible even without assuming the sphericity of the molecules ? Is it a confutation of the method of least squares, that it does not require us to postulate—what we are commonly ignorant of—the exact relation between the frequency of an error and its extent ? The method of least squares is content with some very simple and easily ascertained data as to the character of the observations dealt with ; [3] just as the principle of least sacrifice requires *only* the law of diminishing utility, not also some more exact datum as to the rate at which utility (*i.e.*, the increase of utility) diminishes with the increase of means.

This prerogative distinguishes the principle of " equimarginal " sacrifice from the other two principles, which indeed are concerned with sacrifice and involve margins in a certain sense, but do not employ the margin of utility to determine the minimum of sacrifice. [4] For example, suppose that the law of diminishing utility, the relation between total satisfaction, Z, and amount of income, y, is represented by the form $Z = H\sqrt{\dfrac{y}{b}}$, where H is a

[1] *Loc. cit.*, p. 206.

[2] ECONOMIC JOURNAL, pp. 566-7; above, p. 117.

[3] In particular the mean square of error (or deviation) pertaining to the class of observations with which we are dealing.

[4] Mr. Weston does not seem adequately to recognize the diversity under the appearance of similarity when he writes : " In fact Professor Edgeworth does not claim to do more than to bring out a little more definitely what was already implied in Mill, Sidgwick, Meyer, and others. At any rate as we have understood these authors the marginal sacrifice occasioned by the tax has meant an equimarginal sacrifice; one in which the tax imposes exactly equal sacrifice upon every tax-payer."

constant, for amounts of income greater than b, then according to
the principle of *equal* sacrifice the rate of taxation ought to be
regressive, varying in inverse proportion to the square root of y,
for small taxes. But according to the principle of *proportional*
sacrifice the rate ought to be constant, neither progressive nor
regressive. Again, suppose that the law of diminishing utility
is represented by the formula $Z = He^w$,[1] where $w = \left(\dfrac{y-a}{b}\right)^{\frac{1}{2}}$,
for amounts of income greater than a, and less than $a + 8b$; then
the rate of taxation ought to be *regressive* both for the principle
of *equal* and that of *proportional* sacrifice.[2] But no one is in a
position to affirm [3] that the assigned functions do not correspond
to the true law of utility. For they both fulfil the only condition
which may be taken for granted, namely, that utility should
increase with the increase of income at a decreasing rate.[4] The
principles of equal and proportional sacrifice give an uncertain
sound in cases like the above which may be multiplied indefinitely.
But the principle of least sacrifice in trumpet tones proclaims
that the rate of taxation ought to be progressive; except so far
as this distributional presumption is cut into by the productional
and other utilitarian conditions.

Not being certain that Mr. Weston has understood the distinctive characteristics of my formula, I am naturally not much
affected by his dissent; the rather that I am unable to understand
what is distinctive in the formula which he prefers. " The ideal,"
he thinks, " would seem to be the minimum of sacrifice to the
greatest number." This formula appears to be open to the sort
of criticism which I have elsewhere ventured to apply to the more
familiar phrase " greatest happiness of the greatest number ";

---

[1] Where e is the well-known constant (which forms the base of the Napierian
logarithms) namely 2.71828 . . .

[2] These conclusions may be deduced from the proposition that, if η (a function
of y) denotes the rate of taxation for any amount of income, y, and accordingly
ηy is the contribution of each tax-payer whose income is y, then for small taxes,
(1) according to the principle of equal sacrifice $\eta y \dfrac{dZ}{dy} = c_1$; (2) according to the
principle of proportional sacrifice $\eta y \dfrac{dZ}{dy} = c_2 Z$; c_1 and c_2 denoting appropriate
constants. The conclusions obtained for small taxes may be extended to taxes
of finite magnitude on the principle employed by Cournot (*Principes Mathématiques de la Théorie de la Richesse*, Section 32). [See note added at p. 242,
below.]

[3] Some *probability* that the law of utility is not on what may be called the
regressive side of Bernouilli's law may be discerned; above, S, p. 208.

[4] $\dfrac{dZ}{dy}$ positive, and $\dfrac{d^2Z}{dy^2}$ negative, for the values of y with which we are concerned.

which I contend is a loose synonym for " the greatest quantum
of happiness." " The more familiar statement has, indeed, some
advantages. That it is more familiar is no small advantage;
another is that it emphasises an essential condition of greatest
happiness, that the means of happiness should not be monopolised
by a few. The popular, as compared with the exact, formula
has only one disadvantage; that it is nonsense. To find the
maximum of one quantity A ' of,' or in relation to, the maximum
of another quantity B is a statement of a problem in the calculus
of variations which no amount of authority can render other
than inaccurate—not the authority of Mill, not even that of
Bentham." [1] Analogously, a phrase like that proposed by Mr.
Weston might be used to emphasise a condition of minimum
sacrifice : that the burden of taxation should not be *very* unequally
distributed. The phrase might also serve to recall the productional
considerations which I have thus worded, " The large relief from
the burden of taxation which *primâ facie* on distributional grounds
should be afforded to the less prosperous, is restricted by the
productional principle that those who have a share in calling the
tune should have a share in paying the piper." [2]

I do not deny that for popular use other expressions of the fiscal
first principle may be more effective than the utilitarian formula.
Among such variants the one which Professor Seligman prefers
is pre-eminent. It was a master-stroke of practical wisdom
to include the distributional, as well as the productional, criterion
of taxation under the category of " faculty," [3] which has the
appearance of being more definite than the *summum genus* utility.[4]
Let those who with M. Leroy-Beaulieu deny the collateral
authority of the subjective principle describe this diction as " en
quelque sort un jeu des mots." To one who believes in the double
nature of the fiscal *summum bonum* the happy ambiguity of the
proposed canon renders it all the more acceptable. It has a
Parliamentary sound. It is like the celebrated resolution of the
House of Commons declaring the throne vacant after the flight

[1] Above, **U**, p. 155, referring to **S**.

[2] Above, **U**, p. 159; there referring to municipalities, but with the omission
of a couple of words equally applicable to individuals.

[3] " The elements of faculty, then, are twofold, those connected with acquisition
or production, and those connected with outlay or consumption . . . the elements
of faculty which are connected with outlay or consumption bring us right back
again to the sacrifice theory. Faculty is the larger, sacrifice the smaller conception." *Progressive Taxation*, pp. 291–2.

[4] The summum genus under which I include the two modes of detriment :
diminution of the total production and aggravation of unequal distribution.
Above, **U**, p. 162.

of James II; in which, Macaulay says, " there was a phrase for every subdivision of the majority. The one beauty of the resolution was its inconsistency." [1]

It is pleasant to believe that, with respect to practical application, I am in complete accord with the eminent critic of my theory. The differences which remain are perhaps not more than verbal. We could both, I think, subscribe to Professor Nicholson's moderate doctrine, " that the ideal of equality of sacrifice, although vague and ill-defined, is one of the supports of certain kinds of exemption." [2] Professor Nicholson expresses entire agreement, in which I entirely concur, with Professor Seligman's reservations as to the equal sacrifice theory " regarded as the paramount consideration in the construction of any definite rate," rather than only one factor in the problem.[3] With regard to the proposal " to state the ideal as ' minimum ' sacrifice instead of equal," Professor Nicholson thinks " this statement seems the more logical on the pure utilitarian theory. On grounds of formal justice the equality of sacrifice may be preferred." [4]

(Note referring to p. 239.)

If $Z = He^w$, where $w = \left(\dfrac{y-a}{b}\right)^{\frac{1}{3}}$, $\dfrac{dZ}{dy} = Z\frac{1}{3}(y-a)^{-2/3}/b^{\frac{1}{3}}$; $> O$ if $y > a$; $\dfrac{d^2Z}{dy^2} = Z\{\frac{1}{9}(y-a)^{-4/3}/b^{2/3} - \frac{2}{9}(y-a)^{-5/3}/b^{\frac{1}{3}}\} < O$, if $y > a$, and $(y-a)^{1/3} < 2b^{1/3}$, or $y < a + 8b$.

To observe whether the rate η decreases (or otherwise) with the increase of the income y; consider first the case of *proportional* sacrifice, where $\eta y \dfrac{dZ}{dy} = C_2 Z$. The sign of $\dfrac{d\eta}{dy}$ is then the opposite to that of

$$\frac{d}{dy} y \frac{1}{Z} \frac{dZ}{dy} = \frac{d}{dy} y\frac{1}{3}(y-a)^{-\frac{2}{3}}/b^{\frac{1}{3}} = \frac{\frac{1}{3}(y-a)^{-5/3}}{b^{1/3}}\{(y-a) - \frac{2}{3}y\};$$ which is

positive if $y > 3a$. Accordingly $\dfrac{d\eta}{dy}$ is negative, the rate is *regressive*

for values of y between $3a$ and $a + 8b$. In the case of *equal* sacrifice regression sets in at an earlier value of y, before $y = 3a$. That equal sacrifice should thus be *more regressive* is consonant with the fact that it is in general *less progressive* than proportional sacrifice. (See above, p. 237.)

---

[1] *History of England*, ch. x. The whole of the brilliant context may be read with advantage by those who would put a finer point on fiscal apparatus than the nature of the material permits.

[2] *Principles of Political Economy*, Book III. § 5.

[3] *Loc. cit.*

[4] *Loc. cit.*, § 4, note.

GRADUATION OF TAXES

[REPRINTED from the ECONOMIC JOURNAL, 1919, where the fuller title describes the taxes which are to be graduated as taxes on income and capital. It is argued that the simple scheme proposed by Cassel is not appropriate to the very high taxation now prevalent. For the calculation of the tax from the taxable amount Multiplication and Division must now be supplemented by Involution or Logarithm. Not otherwise can there be realised the two conditions, the first productional and the second distributional, (i) that the taxpayer should not be deprived of motive to increase his income, (ii) that the rate of taxation should continually increase with the increase of the income. The use and purpose of " graduation " are more fully described in the following paper (Z) and the introduction thereto.]

METHOD OF GRADUATING TAXES ON INCOME AND CAPITAL

Among the formulæ known to me as having been suggested for the purpose of graduating taxation, a foremost place is due to the scheme proposed by Professor Cassel in the ECONOMIC JOURNAL.[1] Varying his notation, we may write

(i) $$T = r(X - E);$$

where T is the amount of the tax (in pounds sterling, or other monetary unit); r is a percentage or (decimal) fraction; $X - E$ is the taxable income; E is an abatement, not a fixed minimum, as Mill proposed, but varying with the income—not in an opposite sense as in many contemporary systems, but *increasing* with the increase of income.

(ii) $$E = \frac{XM}{X + M - e};$$

where e is the *minimum* of subsistence below which the tax does not descend, *e.g.*, £130 in the present British income-tax; M is the maximum abatement, a limit which is more and more nearly

[1] Vol. XI. (1901), p. 485 *et seq.*

approached (but never reached) as X increases. Substituting the value of E in the expression for T, we have

(iii) $$T = r\frac{X(X-e)}{X+M-e};$$

an expression which becomes zero, as it ought, when $X = e$.

Distinction may be claimed for this scheme on the following grounds :—

(1) It is elementary, " intelligible to the most untaught capacity," a great merit in a principle of currency according to Mill, and doubtless some merit in a principle of graduation.[1]

(2) It exhibits a mathematical elegance, which is also a fiscal excellence,[2] in that it is capable of representing a great variety of tax systems by means of a very few adjustable coefficients or " constants."

(3) Of its constants two, e and M, are determinable *a priori*, so to speak, from a knowledge of the people's wants and habits; the third, r, being adjustable according to the needs of the Treasury.

The *first* merit is conspicuous. The formula involves only the common arithmetical processes; the operation which is highest in a mathematical sense being *division*.

To illustrate the *second* feature I proceed to show how the formula is adaptable to actual tax systems. The first scale which I adduce is one relating to the continent of Europe before the war. The scale is constructed from the statistics of income-taxes in several European States as presented in a Blue-book dated 1913.[3]

TABLE I.—PRE-WAR CONTINENTAL INCOME TAX.

Income	£40–	80–	100–	150–	300–	500–	1,000
Tax per cent.			2·64	2·92	3·47	4·29	4·84 5·11
Income	£1,500–	2,000–	3,000–	5,000–	10,000	Maximum.	
Tax per cent.		5·53	5·84	6·29	6·66	6·98	7·2

Each rate in this table is obtained by taking a Mean—that mean which is called the Median—of the rates pertaining to an assigned amount of income in each of several States. For this purpose several Swiss Cantons have been lumped together so

---

[1] Mill, *Political Economy*, Book III. chap. xiii. § 2. The condition is less imperative in the case of taxation, inasmuch as the mathematical basis on which the contribution of the taxpayer is calculated need not be obtruded on his notice; it suffices that the authorities should promulgate an *arithmetical* schedule of the amounts payable on each amount of income or capital.

[2] As pointed out in *A Levy on Capital* (by the present writer, 1918), p. 85.

[3] [Cd. 7100.]

as to count as one State. Also three minor German States have been similarly treated. For example, in order to determine the figure which is to be put for the rate of taxation of an income of £100 (up to £150) I utilise the following data :—

Prussia.	Bavaria.	Other German States.	Denmark.	Norway.	Sweden.	Holland.	Switzerland.
3·19	2·65	3·20	3·80	2·39	2·27	2·27	4·82

The " Other German States " are Saxony, Wurtemberg, and Baden, with rates respectively 3·00, 3·20, and 4·25; whereof the *second* in the order of magnitude is taken as the Mean. Likewise, 4·82 is the Median (half-way between the third and fourth in the order of magnitude) of the rates for six Swiss Cantons. The Median of the eight figures thus obtained is 2·92 (half-way between 2·65 and 3·20). The exempted minimum for the majority of the States appears to be 40; and accordingly, I take that for the value of *e*. But as the tax for some States does not descend to 40, I have not formed a mean value for the rate between 40 and 80. At the other extremity the fixed proportion designated by *r* in the formula is evidently 7 per cent. (approximately).

As to M, I have not attempted to verify the *third* claim by determining this constant, as theoretically possible, from the conditions of Continental life. For the purpose of illustrating the adaptability of the formula, it suffices to determine M from the condition that for some assigned income the rate given by the formula (with the two given constants) should be the actual rate shown in the table. Consider, for instance, the income £1,000, the rate against which in the table is 5·11 per cent., the tax therefore being £51·1. We have then by equation (iii) :

$$51 \cdot 1 = 0 \cdot 07 \frac{1000 \times 960}{M + 960},$$

whence $M = 355$. If we had taken the rate for 2,000 as the datum, we should have the equation :

$$2000 \times 0 \cdot 0584 = 0 \cdot 07 \frac{2000 \times 1960}{M + 1960}$$

whence $M = 390$.

If we put for M the nearest round figure, 400, that will be found, with the other constants, to give fairly good results. For instance, for the income £1,500 the tax as calculated by the formula is £82·4; actually it is £82·9. For income £5,000 the tax calculated is £324; actually it is £333.

The formula fits well many other pre-war tax systems, characterised by the feature that as the income increases indefinitely, the rate approaches a fixed and small proportion.[1]

But when we turn to war income-taxes we find that the ultimate fixed proportion is no longer a small percentage. Thus the British Income-Tax as modified by the Budget of 1918, rises to above 50 per cent. From the new scale as given in full by Mr. W. M. J. Williams in the *Journal des Économistes* [2] I select some specimen data. The earlier figures relate to " wholly unearned income." For the later figures income-tax (at 6s. in the £) and sur-tax are combined.

TABLE II.—BRITISH INCOME-TAX, 1918.

Income in pounds.	Tax in pounds.	Shillings per pound.
200	12	1·2
1,000	187·5	3·9
10,000	4,187·5	8·4
20,000	9,437·5	9·5
40,000	19,937·5	10·0
100,000	51,437·5	10·3

Proceeding as before, let us put 50 per cent. as (approximately) the ultimate fixed proportion, while for e we have 130. From these data there follow inferences as to the abatement which are not consonant with the *third* of the merits above claimed for the Cassel formula. In accordance with equation (i) put $T = 0\cdot5(X - E)$. Then in order that the equation may be satisfied when $X = 10,000$, we have $4187\cdot5 = 0\cdot5(10,000 - E)$. Whence E, the abatement, is £1,625; rather a high figure for necessaries ! But it is not the highest figure implied. Employing equation (iii) we have :

$$4187\cdot5 = 0\cdot5\frac{10,000 \times 9870}{9870 + M},$$

whence $M = 1915$! [3]

If we are to abandon the *rationale* of Professor Cassel's formula, and to treat it as simply empirical, a further simplification may be advised. Let us no longer treat the tax as a *function* of the abatement. On that arrangement if the taxpayer is, in

---

[1] Seven per cent. in the example above given, eight per cent. in the example worked by Prof. Cassel (with a somewhat different notation) in the ECONOMIC JOURNAL for 1901, p. 491.

[2] June, 1918, p. 316.

[3] The practice of the English Law with respect to the "necessaries" of "infants" may be referred to as justifying some extravagance in the estimate of what is necessary for persons in a high station of life. See Anson, *Contracts*, *sub voce* "Infants."

Latin idiom, increased by a child, and obtains a corresponding increase of exempted income, an entirely new schedule has to be calculated.   There would be as many schedules as there are varieties of abatement.   But it is much simpler to treat the tax as a function of the surplus of the taxable income over and above the deducted abatement.   There is thus room for the greatest variety in the grounds for abatement : children, wife, insurance ; perhaps invalidity, perhaps change in the value of money, perhaps station in life.[1]

This change is easily effected by putting $e = 0$ in the above written formula (iii), and for X (the total income) x, the surplus above the untaxed abatement, which does not now figure in the formula.   The formula thus generalised may be written :

(iv)
$$T = x \frac{rx}{M + x}.$$

For instance, utilising data furnished by the British income-tax for 1918, let us determine M and r from the equations :

(1)
$$r \frac{39870^2}{M + 39870} = 20,000,$$

(2)
$$r \frac{870^2}{M + 870} = 187 \cdot 5,$$

from which I find $M = 1217$, $r = 0 \cdot 517$.   Applying the formula thus determined to an income of £100,000, that is, a surplus of taxable income of £99,870, I find for the tax £51,140—much the same as the actual tax, £51,437 10s.

Is there any reason to think that we should fare better with any other formula involving only *three* constants (two in addition to the abatement, which is not *explicit* in the formula as now modified) ?   We shall be better able to answer this question after considering two defects which may be attributed to the formula, whether in its original or its generalised shape.

First, the formula is not suited to represent very steep graduations ; the case when the rates of taxation increase very much more rapidly than the taxable incomes.   Let x_1 and x_2 be two taxable incomes, the latter being the greater ; and let ρ_1 and ρ_2 be the corresponding rates of taxation.   Then by hypothesis, since the tax is to be progressive, ρ_2 is greater than ρ_1 ; say, $\frac{\rho_2}{\rho_1} = q$, where q is an improper fraction.   Substituting for ρ_1 and ρ_2 their

---

[1] The Australian Commonwealth appears to be particularly select and generous in the specification of grounds for exemption.   See Commonwealth Report cited below.

values obtained from equation (iv) (and remembering that $\dfrac{T}{x} = \rho$),

we have $\dfrac{\rho_2}{\rho_1} = \dfrac{M + x_1}{M + x_2} \dfrac{x_2}{x_1}$. Whence it follows that q is less than $\dfrac{x_2}{x_1}$.
But this is a limitation upon the progression which may be un-
desirable. It may be required that, as in the present American
income-tax, while the tax on £1,000 is £16, the tax on £2,000
should be £71 [1]; and accordingly that, while

$$\frac{x_2}{x_1} = 2, \quad \frac{\rho_2}{\rho_1} = \frac{35 \cdot 5}{16} = 2 \cdot 2 \ldots$$

It may be pleaded that such steep graduation is abnormal. But
it is doubtful whether any norm or standard can be prescribed for
the income-tax as distinct from the *tax system* of a country. For
the income-tax is usually complementary to other parts of the
system, in particular to taxes on commodities and local taxation.
Where the taxes on commodities were very heavy—pressing most
heavily on the lower incomes—such a scale as that which has
been instanced might well be appropriate. A formula adopted to
general use ought to be better guarded against the objection which
has been exhibited.

But grant that this objection is not very serious, especially
with respect to taxes on capital. Admit that the formula under
consideration affords as good a fit as any other function involving
only three constants, to the taxes on income and capital which are
in actual use. Yet adaptation to existing forms is not the sole
test of the adaptability which we require. Our task is not
exactly that of the statistician who employs a favourite formula
to represent a concrete set of data—a given " histogram." Our
part is not so much that of the portrait-painter as of one who
draws ideal " subjects." Our formula should be adapted to
represent graduation, not only as it is, but as it ought to be. Now
the Swedish designer of fiscal forms falls short of ideal perfection
at one point. He may be contrasted with the sort of artist that
was to be found in Rome, capable of modelling hair and nails to
perfection, but unsuccessful in the composition of a whole.[2] Contrariwise, Professor Cassel's work as a whole is admirable. But
he fails to represent one extremity in its ideal perfection. He
copies it indeed perfectly as it actually occurs, compressed and
deformed like a Chinese lady's foot. Such, I submit, is the

---

[1] It is true that in the actual tax the £1,000 and the £2,000 include the
abatement, and so correspond to our X, not our x, but it might have been
otherwise.   [2] Horace, *Ars Poetica*, 32.

character of the graduations commonly in use which approach, but never pass, a certain finite rate. Can any good reason be given for thus exempting the higher incomes and capitals from progression ? Surely the exemption has not been adopted by officials as a deduction from the principle of " equal sacrifice " in accordance with the ingenious reasoning of Mr. Cohen Stuart.[1] " As soon as all personal wants are pretty well satisfied," he argues, " the possession of income has no longer any influence on consumption. It is a figure the increase of which by a certain percentage would give about the same pleasure to a man with 10 millions of francs per annum as to one with 100 or 500 millions." Or is the reason one of those given by other theorists with less lucidity ?[2] Could it be fear of alarming the millionaire, even when the final rate was so moderate as 7 per cent., as in the pre-war Continental taxes above cited ? Was it a not unfounded belief that the condition of continual progression could not be secured by elementary arithmetical operations ? Or simply poverty of mathematical resource ?

II. Whatever may have been the reasons in the past for this lenity to millionaires, it may be doubted whether it will continue to appear reasonable in the future. There will be a demand for a formula fulfilling the condition of an effectual continual progression. The following formula seems to satisfy those conditions :

$$(\text{v}) \qquad\qquad x - T = ax^{\beta},$$

where, as before, x is the excess of income or capital above a specified minimum ; T is the amount of the tax ; $x - T$, say, y, may be described as the "available surplus," that which remains to the taxpayer (over and above the exempted minimum) after he has paid the tax ; a and β are numerical constants, β being always fractional.

An example will form the simplest explanation of the scheme. The example is furnished by the American Federal Income-Tax of 1917.[3] I transcribe part of the schedule, commuting dollars into pounds sterling.

TABLE III.—AMERICAN FEDERAL INCOME-TAX.

Income......	£1,000	2,000	4,000	12,000	20,000	100,000
Tax.........	£16	71	236	1,356	13,236	38,536

From the information given I assume that £400 may be treated as an exempted minimum.

[1] Discussed by the present writer in the ECONOMIC JOURNAL, Vol. VII. : above, S, p. 110. [2] *Loc. cit.*, p. 109.

[3] As stated by the Guaranty Trust Company, New York.

To determine a and β we must utilise two of the data, say, the tax on £1,000 income and that on £12,000. We have thus two equations :

(1) $a(12,000 - 400)^\beta = (12,000 - 400) - 1,356(= 10,244).$
(2) $a(1,000 - 400)^\beta = (1,000 - 400) - 16(= 584).$

Whence (taking logarithms and eliminating a) I find for β, 0·967, and thence for a, 1·202, nearly. The construction will be found to fit fairly well at different points. For instance, for an income of £4,000 the calculated tax is £296, the actual tax is £236. For an income of £20,000 the calculated tax is about £3,000, the actual £3,236. Of course, if we had selected other points for an exact fit, we could have secured greater closeness of fit than now, in the neighbourhood of those points. But we cannot expect with only three constants at our disposal to obtain a good fit at all points.

There is one tract, however, for which it is not in general possible to secure a good fit, namely, the lower extremity. As the income diminishes, we come to a point at which the tax is zero; and if we descended below that point the tax would pass into a bounty ! This limit is given by equating the available income to the total (untaxed) income above the minimum, *i.e.*,

$$\text{(vi)} \qquad\qquad ax^\beta = x,$$

whence $x = a^{1/1-\beta}$. Thus in the example just now given, if Log $a = 0·079$, $\beta = 0·967$, we have for the limiting value the number of which the logarithm is 2·4 nearly, *i.e.*, about 251. Which, added to 400, the minimum exempted, gives 651 for the figure below which the construction is not applicable.

III. The new formula seems specially suited to serve as a sur-tax. It may thus complement the Cassel formula when that fails at the upper extremity. At a certain point the new tax may be as it were yoked on to one of the Cassel type. To avoid a *jolt*, it should be arranged that at the point of junction the sur-tax should be zero.

To illustrate the composition of the formulæ I recur to the statistics of the American income-tax, and proceed to arrange that when the income has reached £2,000, a sur-tax of the kind described should be superimposed on a Cassel tax. For the calculation of the Cassel tax I make the convenient assumption that the highest abatement for " necessaries " which the American millionaire can claim, the M of the formula, is £800. As before, I take £400 as the minimum abatement. Then by equation (iii) for any assigned income, X, we have $T = r\dfrac{X(X - 400)}{800 + X - 400}.$ This formula must give us the whole tax for an income of £2,000, since the sur-tax is to be zero at that point. Putting for X 2,000, and for T the given taxation on an income of that size, viz. 71 (£), I find $r = 0.05325$. Now let us take an income well above £2,000, e.g., £20,000, and determine the co-efficients of a sur-tax so that it may both (1) start at £2,000, and (2) at £20,000 may prescribe a tax which, superadded to the Cassel tax for that income, may be equal to the given tax, viz., £3,236. First, for the Cassel tax with the constants above stated I find 1023·25. The sur-tax therefore should contribute (3236 — 1023·25), or 2212·75. That is, the available income (on the supposition that the sur-tax only acted) should be (19600 — 2212·75) or 17387·25. We have thus the two equations :

$$(1) \quad a19600^\beta = 17387 \cdot 25.$$
$$(2) \quad a1600^\beta = 1600.$$

Whence I find for β 0·952, and for a 1·425. It will be found that this construction gives a fairly good fit at points not too distant from those at which the fit is by construction exact. Thus for an income of £4,000 the tax is by calculation £311, actually £236.

Satisfactory as this result appears, the formula from which it is deduced cannot be accepted as universally appropriate. For it violates the canon that, however large the income or capital may be, the tax should not be such as to deprive the taxpayer of the motive to work and save. To be sure, in the instance given the breakdown is far enough off. The taxable amount would have to rise to some millions of trillions sterling before reaching the point at which an increase of the total income would result in a diminution of the available income. And very generally, if, as commonly, I think, it could be arranged that the fixed ratio r of the Cassel part of the formula should be small, not exceeding, say, 0·1 (10 per cent.), it may be expected that the breakdown is at a safe distance.[1] But possibly, and especially in a case above noticed,[2] the data may prove recalcitrant.

IV. To be safe from the danger which has just been indicated, it might be better to yoke the new formula with that of Professor Cassel, not abreast, so to speak, but *tandem*. Let the Cassel tax act by itself up to an assigned figure, say, as before, £2,000; and thereafter let the new tax by itself rule. We have only to arrange that the new formula should give the same figure for the tax on that income as the Cassel formula, namely, the given figure 71; and also that it should satisfy the datum for any other income,

---

[1] Compare note 3 to p. 252, below.   [2] Above, p. 247.

say, as before, £20,000. We thus obtain two equations for the constants a and β, namely :

(1) $a(1600)^\beta = 1600 - 71.$

(2) $a19600^\beta = 19600 - 3236.$

From which I find $\beta = 0.946$; $a = 1.42$.

V. Another method of employing the new formula (introduced in Section II.) as a sur-tax is to take for the primary tax, not the Cassel formula, but one of the new type, that one which does not become a bounty.[1] This condition is secured by putting $a = 1$ in the expression for the available income; which thus becomes of the form x^b (b less than unity). At a suitable point there is to be either added to, or, better, perhaps, substituted for, this formula one of the more general type ax^β.[2]

The first arrangement is not perfectly safe. But the danger is not in practice, I think, to be much apprehended. Consider, for instance, the example given in the lecture above referred to (*Levy on Capital*). According to the formula there offered as representative of the present English income-tax, the "available" income, say y (*i.e.*, the amount in excess of the exempted minimum, say x, less by the tax), may be written :

$$y = x^{.974} + 1.22x^{.962} - x.$$

The expression for y continues to increase with the increase of x, up to a value of x which is above £10,000,000,000 ![3]

A geometrical representation of these constructions is offered on p. 253.

The abscissa measured along the horizontal OA from the origin O denotes income or capital. The ordinate Xy corresponding to any abscissa OX denotes the amount that the taxpayer has at his disposal after paying the tax—including an exempted minimum. The ordinate can never rise above OB, a right line, making an angle of 45° with OA. OE denotes the exempted minimum; an abatement varying for different persons, according to the number of children, etc. The abscissa ox measured from o as origin denotes the taxable income. The ordinate xy denotes

---

[1] More exactly, does not become a bounty until the taxable income is less than £1.

[2] The expression for y the ordinate which represents the available income becomes on the first plan $x^b - T$, where T is the sur-tax; $= x^b - (x - ax\beta) = x^b + ax\beta - x$. Accordingly $\frac{dy}{dx} = bx^{b-1} + \beta ax^{\beta-1} - 1$; an expression which may ultimately become negative; just as the compound formula of Section III.

[3] Analogously the example given below in Section VII., though manufactured to exemplify difficulties, has no terrors for the present method, which would continue to be applicable up to incomes over £100,000,000 !

the available surplus, being the taxable amount minus the tax.
The length intercepted between y and the line oB represents the
tax. A right line, oC, dividing all ordinates in the same proportion, represents a uniformly proportional tax above a certain
exempted minimum (Mill's ideal). The curve-line oy is intended
to represent a tax according to the formula of Professor Cassel.
It will be observed that the rate of taxation (whether relatively
to the total or the taxable surplus) continually increases. The
abatement, too, continually increases. For, by equation (1),
the abatement $E = (rX - T) \div r = (rx - T) \div r + e$. Now
rx is denoted by TR in the figure; and T by yT; and the curve
is such that yR (as well as Ty) continually increases.

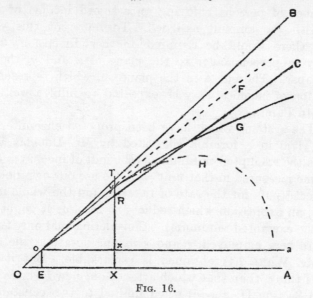

FIG. 16.

The Cassel tax is supposed to function independently up to
the point y in the curve corresponding to x on the abscissa. At
that point the new tax is substituted. Beyond that point the
dotted curve yF represents the continuation of the Cassel curve,
the rate continually approximating to r; the vertical distance
of the curve from the right line OC approximating to the limit
$r (M - e)$. The thick curve-line beyond y, yG, represents the
new tax, as employed by itself in Section IV. The tax is such
that y, the available surplus, continually increases; while, at
the same time, $T \div x$, the rate of taxation, also increases up to
the limit of 100 per cent. The *broken* curve, which also diverges
from y, represents the compound tax constituted by superim-
posing the new formula upon that of Professor Cassel after the

manner shown in Section III. The *hump* at H in the curve, representing the available surplus, is designed to illustrate the particular case in which the compound formula would be inappropriate.

The figure also serves to illustrate Section V. The thick curve to the right of the point y may still represent the new formula as substituted in Section IV. The line to the left of y is suited to represent the curve $y = x^b$ as well as the curve which designates the available surplus according to the (generalised) Cassel formula;

for both of which curves $\dfrac{dy}{dx} > 1, \dfrac{d^2y}{dx^2} < 1$.

So far, we have taken no account of the circumstance that the number of persons enjoying an assigned income or capital varies with the amount assigned. To represent this varying number, there would be required another dimension, a third axis—say z—perpendicular to the plane of x and y, the plane of the paper. The curve in the plane xz, which represents the distribution of incomes, may be expected to fulfil a well-known law due to Pareto.

VI. The systems which have been proposed encounter a formidable rival in a formula suggested by Mr. Douglas White.[1] He takes the exempted minimum as the unit of income. Then if the income measured in that unit $= X$ (to use our own notation), he in effect [2] puts for the rate of taxation (on the whole income) $r \operatorname{Log} X$, an expression which reduces to zero, as it ought, when $X = e$ (the exempted minimum). Considering that only two constants are here employed, r and e in our notation, the success which Mr. White has obtained is remarkable. But it is not greater, I think, than that which attends our new formula (introduced in Section II. above) when limited to two constants (*including* the abatement) by putting $a =$ unity, as in Section V. The formula thus presented has the advantage of not involving the exempted minimum. It is free also from defects which may be attributed to the White formula in common with a more general form to which we now proceed.

VII. Mr. White's formula may be generalised by employing a similar form, with a new constant, referring to the taxable income (above the exempted minimum); as thus,

$$\rho = r \operatorname{Log}\!\left(1 + \frac{x}{c}\right);$$

[1] ECONOMIC JOURNAL, Vol. XXI. (1911), p. 371 *et seq.*

[2] I must apologise to Mr. White and other authors for making rather free with their notations and conceptions for the purpose of the comparisons here instituted.

where x is now, as before, the taxable surplus and ρ is the rate of taxation on that surplus; c is a new constant. For example, to obtain a graduation on the lines of the American income-tax, let us operate on the data for incomes of £1000 and £50,000. We have then (putting for e, as before, 400) the two equations :

(1) $$r \operatorname{Log} \left(1 + \frac{49600}{c}\right) = \frac{13936}{49600}$$

(2) $$r \operatorname{Log} \left(1 + \frac{600}{c}\right) = \frac{16}{600}.$$

Easily eliminating r, we obtain an equation for c which is approximately satisfied by $c = 1,600$. The corresponding value of r is roughly 0·19. The formula thus obtained will be found to fit the given scale at different points fairly well.

But the construction will not work so well in all cases. It is open to the same objection as the Cassel formula that it is unsuited to represent very steep graduation. If $\frac{\rho_2}{\rho_1}$ is very large, larger than $\frac{x_2}{x_1}$, then it may not be possible to find a value of c which complies with the data. A more serious defect is the liability to excess of taxation at the upper extremity. To exhibit this, suppose it to be prescribed that the taxation of an income of £1000 should be what it is for the present British income-tax, namely, £187 10s. on £870 (the surplus above £130); but that for the smaller income of £200 the tax should be much less than what it is according to the British income-tax, say, instead of £12, only £2 or a trifle less (on £70). As above remarked,[1] we cannot be certain that a progression which looks anomalous may not be appropriate to a (complementary) income-tax. The constants which satisfy these conditions are (roughly) $r = 0·5$, $c = 512·4$. Accordingly, in the neighbourhood of the points utilised, the formula thus furnished complies with the conditions of a workable progressive tax. But consider a point at some distance from these tracts, above £50,000. For this size of income the formula gives a tax greater than the income ! But the extent of the failure is not fully shown by this result. At a much earlier stage, namely, just above £6,000, the formula ceases to be admissible because by increasing his income beyond this limit the taxpayer would incur *loss*. The *broken* curve yH in the figure may serve to represent this failure. On the suppositions just now made, H would correspond to a taxable surplus just above £6000. The point corresponding to £51,000 would be *below* the axis oa !

[1] Above, p. 248.

This fiasco may be avoided by dovetailing a curve of the Type II. on to an initial tract of Type VII., after the manner shown in Section IV.

VIII. There is a certain affinity between Mr. White's formula and another which has been proposed in the ECONOMIC JOURNAL by Mr. Steggall.[1] Mr. Steggall's scheme presents two distinctive features : (a) that between certain limits, e.g., between 100 and 1000 the tax on successive equal increments of income increases by an equal increment, e.g., on the first hundred (exempted), 0 ; on the second hundred, 2d. in the pound; on the third hundred, 4d.; and so on. The total paid for ten hundreds will thus be 0 + 2 + 4 + . . . + 18, an arithmetical progression of which the sum is 90, and accordingly the *rate* for 1,000 is 9d. in the pound. If this rate of progression were to continue, we should reach the rate of a pound in the pound too soon. Accordingly (b) it is arranged that the rise of 9d. in the rate per pound which occurred in the tract of income from £100 to £1000 should thereafter be spread over a larger tract from £1000 to £10,000. After £10,000 the next rise of 9d. is spread over the tract £10,000 to £100,000. And so on. It is this latter arrangement which has some affinity to Mr. White's construction.[2]

The other feature (b) of Mr. Steggall's plan is one that frequently appears in popular schemes of taxation. Numerous examples will be found in recent reports on the Income Tax.[3] A particularly good instance is furnished by the Wisconsin system. There the tax on successive increments of 1000 dollars each rises from the first thousand to the fifth by $\frac{1}{4}$ per cent, for each 1000 dollars up to the fifth thousand inclusive; and the result of these rates on successive increments is shown as the " true rate on whole amount " (of taxable income);[4] that is, the rate in the usual sense which has been here all along adopted. There is no essential difference between the " Tariff System," [5] as it is called in the Report, in which each successive increment is subject to a rate increasing in arithmetical progression and the simpler plan

---

[1] Vol. XXV. (1915), p. 136, *et seq.*

[2] Observing that the logarithm of the taxable income, x, increases by equal increments as the tax increases by increments of 9d., let us suppose these increments to become indefinitely small; and we obtain the simple relation $X = 10^{bR}$; where R is the rate of taxation ($= T/X$); b is a constant : whence $R = \frac{1}{b} \log X$, which corresponds to Mr. White's formula, *mutatis mutandis.*

[3] See 1906, 365; and 1913 [Cd. 7100], *passim.*

[4] *Loc. cit.* (1913), p. 178. The rise of the rate by steps of half per cent. from the fifth to the thirteenth thousand is similarly treated.

[5] *Loc. cit.*, p. 6.

in which the rate reckoned on the whole taxable quantity increases in an arithmetical progression.[1]

To obtain a continuous curve corresponding to the series of steps presented by such arithmetical progression, let us suppose that in any tract in which there is a uniform progression of the sort the steps become smaller and smaller.[2] In the limit the curve representing the rate of taxation will be a parabola. The common parabola emerges as an *eighth* form, as a candidate for the representation of the *rate* of taxation; and accordingly for the tax and the available surplus, a parabola of the third degree. The construction is only applicable to short tracts; otherwise, the continued increase of the tax would be fatal.

IX. The parabola of higher degrees naturally follows here. The formula is recommended by its common use in many branches of physics. It is not, however, applicable to all branches. It is not adapted, for instance, to represent the extremities of groups of observations. For much the same reason it seems unsuited to represent taxation of the higher incomes and capitals. It has, however, the distinction of being, as far as I know, the highest in the mathematical sense of all formulæ actually adopted in the financial regulations of a great country. In the income-tax adopted by the Commonwealth of Australia,[3] for the tract of income between £2,000 and £6,500, the expression for the tax (in pounds sterling) is :—

$$5333\cdot3 - 5x + \frac{12\cdot583x^2}{10^3} - \frac{1\cdot06}{10^6}x^3 + \frac{0\cdot03}{10^9}x^4;$$

where x is the taxable income over and above the abatement which is deducted from the total income. For incomes between £546 and £2000 there is another parabola, one of the third degree. Below £546 the formula is more simply arithmetical. There is an abatement decreasing with the amount of income. If we regard each boundary of a discontinuous tract as impairing

---

[1] Some relations of the two systems are well exhibited in the *Mathematical Gazette* for May 1916, referring to the Australian Commonwealth income-tax.

[2] Let us suppose that the tract of finite extent a is divided into an indefinitely large number of steps, each measuring Δx. Now at each of these small steps let there be added to the rate of taxation the very small quantity $b\Delta x^2$ (b a finite constant). Then the sum of the arithmetical progression which represents increase of the rate in the tract under consideration is $\frac{1}{2}\frac{a}{\Delta x}\left(\frac{a}{\Delta x}-1\right)\times b\Delta x^2$; i.e. $\frac{1}{2}ba^2$.

Thus the increase of the rate of income is given by a *parabola*, of which a measured from the beginning of the finite tract may be taken as the abscissa.

[3] See Official Year-book of the Commonwealth of Australia for 1901–15; No. 9, 1916, pp. 725–26.

simplicity and mathematical elegance in the same degree as an additional constant, we must pronounce the Australian tax somewhat deficient in that quality; taking into account the number of arbitrary boundaries, as well as of constants proper. In spite of, or rather in consequence of, its mathematical elaboration, the Australian formula has hardly any advantage in respect of continuity over the formless British income-tax.

X. If it is thought desirable to employ more constants than enter into the formulæ of Sections III. and IV.—that is, four excluding the exempted minimum—it is easy to take on an additional tax of the new type after the manner shown in those Sections.

To resume and conclude. Several formulæ old and new have been compared in respect of their use for the purpose of graduating taxes. In this comparison regard has been had to certain general conditions which should be fulfilled so far as practicable and consistent with each other. The conditions taken account of are chiefly (1) that the *functions* employed should be continuous; (2) that they should be familiar; (3) that the amount of taxation should never be so great as to make it the interest of the taxpayer not to increase his income or capital; (4) that the rate of taxation, as the income or capital increases indefinitely, should converge not to a proper fraction (a percentage less than 100), but to unity (100 per cent.); (5) that the abatement which is to be free from taxation on various grounds (children, insurance, etc.) should not enter as a constant into the formula for graduation. To which it is perhaps to be added (6) that some of the constants should be, like the abatement, determinable from considerations of expediency other than their effect upon the result of the calculation, the amount of contribution prescribed by the formula. Comparing proposed schemes, it is not possible to arrange them in an order of merit abstractly, without knowing firstly the end in view—in particular at what points of taxable income (or capital) it is expedient to lighten or tighten taxation—and secondly, the means available—in particular how many constants may be employed. If the graduation required is not very steep, several formulæ may be appropriate which would otherwise become impracticable. If the number of available constants is given, certain hypothetical preferences may be expressed.

If (exclusive of, or in addition to, the exempted minimum) only *one* constant is allowed, the form recommended is

$$T = x - x^b,$$

where T is the tax, x is the taxable income or capital, b is a proper fraction. If there are (besides the abatement, as before) *two* constants, we have a choice between these two expressions :

$$(1)\ T = \frac{rx^2}{M + x} \qquad\qquad (2)\ T = xr \operatorname{Log}\left(1 + \frac{x}{c}\right).^1$$

Sometimes, if the graduation is not very steep, the latter is preferable; but it may be much worse. If it is advisable to have as many as, and not more than, *three* constants (besides the abatement) there is recommended a combination of two prescriptions,[2] namely, (1) $T_1 = x - x^b$, (2) $T_2 = x - ax^\beta$.

If *four* constants are to be utilised, there may be advised a combination of the two taxes :

$$(1)\ T_1 = \frac{rx^2}{M + x} \qquad\qquad (2)\ T_2 = x - ax^\beta.$$

By taking on an additional T, or more than one, any number of constants, odd or even, may analogously be employed.

[1] Ordinary logarithms.

[2] T_1 is to be taken by itself up to a certain point—such a point, for instance, as that at which the super-tax begins in the British system. After that point either T_1 and T_2 are to be compounded, or, perhaps preferably, T_2 is to be employed by itself.

(Z)

FORMULÆ FOR GRADUATING TAXATION

[THE following article appeared in the ECONOMIC JOURNAL, 1920, under the title " Mathematical Formulæ and the Royal Commission on the Income-tax." The formulæ which it is the purpose of the article to recommend, though described as " Mathematical," involve no higher mathematics than the operations mentioned in the preceding article (Y). There is here emphasised a caution which was alluded to in that article : that formulæ are only means to ends which must be prescribed by other than mathematical considerations (Y, p. 258). Where and how much to lighten or tighten the pressure of taxation must be, as Professor Pigou teaches (below, p. 262), " arrived at by general reasoning." There is no connection between graduation undertaken for the purposes herein described and the schemes of the graduation-crank who assumes that a distribution of fiscal burdens must be equitable because it conforms to a neat and pretty formula.

It may be well perhaps to quote some evidence bearing on this point given by the present writer before the late Royal Commission on the Income-tax [Cmd. 288, 4]. Sir Josiah Stamp having asked with reference to curves representing different principles of graduation : " Is there anything which tells us which is really the more just curve ? " (Q. 11,815), the answer was : " No, I am rather doubtful about the point at which you should lighten or tighten the tax. Certainly, from mere knowledge of curves, you cannot get any such ethical proposition as that. It must be from people who have knowledge of the facts, and make mathematics their servant to carry out their ideal. How they would get it, I am sure I don't know. . . ." But " some formulæ would assist common-sense." . . . (11,816). " It may assist you to have only one or perhaps two screws to turn ; you can let out here and tighten there with more facility than you otherwise could ; but as to showing exactly where you should tighten or not, that is beyond my science."]

The grounds on which the Commission reject the use of graduation formulæ are to be examined here. Their objections are summarised in the form of quotations from two expert witnesses (Report, 132).

I. The first passage, from the evidence of Dr. Stamp, is directed against the use of a formula purporting to express the ideal relation between amount of income and amount of tax. In the context Dr. Stamp shows that it would be very difficult to obtain " a single comprehensive tax return for a year," as the practical application of such a graduation form would require (9583).[1] Moreover, whereas different formulæ are proposed, " it is impossible to say which of the various curves truly represent that principle of equality of sacrifice they purport to embody " (9609). " That function is necessarily unknown," as Professor Pigou puts it (4274). Again, as Professor Pigou suggests, it is not enough to secure equal sacrifice; " minimum aggregate sacrifice " must be taken into account (4256). Where the data are so vague the deduction must be " in the air " (Pigou, 4271, 2).

Yet the premises, however inadequate to the deduction of a definite formula, may suffice for a certain negative conclusion. The ground which will not serve as the foundation of the elaborate edifice designed may yet be solid enough to support a battering-ram capable of being directed against simpler edifices in the neighbourhood. First (a), so far as equal sacrifice is supplanted by minimum aggregate sacrifice, whatever presumption in favour of progressive taxation is afforded by the principle of equal sacrifice becomes strengthened. " The case for (progressive) graduation is stronger " (Pigou, 4258). Now (β) some presumption in favour of progressive taxation is afforded by the principle of equal sacrifice. " The function," according to which the satisfaction attending income—and the sacrifice attending taxation—varies, is, indeed, " necessarily unknown " (4274). But something about that function is known, or at least strongly presumed, namely, that satisfaction as dependent on income increases at a rate which diminishes more rapidly than does the rate of increase pertaining to the simple function proposed by Bernoulli as apt to represent the relation of means to satisfaction.[2] At least it may be safely assumed that the function has not the opposite

[1] The bracketed figures refer to the paragraphs in the Evidence.
[2] In short it is presumed that the function is of the hyper-Bernoullian kind described above, S, p. 108; where evidence in favour of the presumption is submitted. More recently Professor Pigou in *Wealth and Welfare* lends his authority to the presumption; and it is now commonly, though not universally, accepted.

character, that which would justify regressive taxation.[1] Thus, if either of the propositions a and β—and, *a fortiori*, if both—hold good, it follows that the common arrangement according to which the rate of taxation (the ratio of the tax to the total, or to the taxable, income) rises to a certain maximum, and thereafter remains constant [2] (however large the income), is contrary to the (distributional) first principles of taxation. The graduation proposed by the Commission is open to this criticism, in so far as the rate of taxation, though not perfectly stationary, increases very gently for incomes above £20,000. It is not significant for the purpose of this negative conclusion that super-tax and the income-tax proper are based on returns for different years. The additions by which the " effective rate " for the " total " of income-tax and super-tax is computed by the Commissioners in the tables of the second Appendix to the Report are accurate enough to justify this criticism.[3] Of course, the unprogressive character of the scheme may admit of justification on *productional* grounds. (*Cp*. 4012, 4119, 4356, 11787, *et passim.*)

II. The above use of the materials which some enthusiasts have attempted to use for the purpose of constructing an ideally just graduation is quite consistent with the view that such a construction is impossible. Having exposed that impossibility, Professor Pigou, in the course of his searching questions, goes on to educe " the real purpose of the thing " (4271). " When you have got certain points on your scale arrived at by general reasoning,[4] then a mathematical formula can give you a means of interpolating." The " interpolation " contemplated (by the present writer at least) is of the kind which, given a set of figures (forming, say, the " argument," or first column of a table), deduces a corresponding set of figures (to form the entries in the table) by means of a *formula*, or definite function. It is thus that actuaries deduce the mortality at different ages by means of the Gompertz or Gompertz-Makeham Law. The Pearsonian curves which play a great part in modern statistics are of this type.

To interpolation of this kind it may be objected that, in the words of the second passage adduced by the Commission, " it would try the temper of all taxpayers " (Report 132). Or, as

[1] Above, S, p. 108.

[2] *Cp.* above, p. 249.

[3] Nor need the objection that the income-tax does not form the *whole* of taxation (*cp.* above, p. 248) give us pause, with reference to so rough an estimate; especially when it is observed that indirect taxation (and part at least of local taxation) is proportional to expended income.

[4] *Cp.* Stamp, " the common sense and instinctive judgment of the people (Report, *loc. cit.*); Hopkins, " a matter of common judgment " (213).

Mr. Hopkins, the witness cited, says elsewhere, " a mathematical formula would try the intelligence of a large proportion of the general public." " The time of the tax officials would thus be occupied . . . in striving to appease distracted taxpayers by explaining the complications of the system " (4017). But why, it may be asked, should the general public want to have the complications explained ? They are concerned only with the amount that each has to pay. A statement in the form of a table of the amounts calculated by the formula is sufficient (cp. 4337, 11,827). Cannot the general public read the dial of a town clock without going behind to inspect the works ? Must not even the more intelligent be content with a general knowledge of the principle on which time is measured, without going into the niceties of " escapements," " gridiron pendulums," and the like ? May not the general public be satisfied that the dictates of " general reasoning," " common-sense and instinctive judgment," [1] are fulfilled by the scale of graduation, without comprehending the particular method of interpolation ? This is one of the questions on which the logic of a student is of little weight against the judgment of official experts; so long, at least, as that judgment is confined to particular concrete cases—for instance, the testimony of Mr. Hopkins that mathematical formulæ have " no practical application to the income-tax as it stands in this country at the present day " (4079).

A similar remark applies to the objection described by the Commission as " most serious and almost insuperable," namely, " the necessity of determining the exact total income of the taxpayer " (Report 133).[2] But that this objection is not universally applicable may be shown by an argumentum ad hominem or ad vigintiviros, the Commissioners, whose own scheme is nearly as open to this objection as one founded on a mathematical formula. To show this let us compare their scheme with formulæ of graduation proposed in the ECONOMIC JOURNAL.[3] We may employ the tests which they prescribe, namely, " (a) practicability, especially so far as the conditions under which total income may be calculated are concerned; (b) equity, that is to say, the necessity for increasing the rate of tax steadily as the total income

---

[1] Above p. 262, note 4.

[2] Cp. Hopkins (4017). " If the present simple methods of graduation were discarded in favour of some mathematical formula under which the rate of tax varied with, say, each pound of income, it would be necessary to know the exact amount of the total income before an assessment upon any part of the income could be accurately made."

[3] Above, p. 249 et seq.

increases . . . ; (c) simplicity in explanation and ease in comprehension " (Report, 135). The comparison is most conveniently made in the simple case of the taxpayer being a " single " person, and the income all " investment." The taxation proposed by the Commission is twofold, income-tax (proper) and super-tax.

The first tax is arrived at thus. Deduct £135 from the total income, and on the remainder, the " taxable income," impose a tax of 3s. in the pound, up to the limit of £360 total income, that is, on £225 taxable income. On the portion of taxable income above that limit impose a tax of 6s. in the pound. This scheme may challenge comparison with one proposed in the ECONOMIC JOURNAL, according to which the rate of taxation is given by the formula

$$r\frac{x}{x+L};$$

where x is the taxable income, the remainder over and above an exempted minimum; r and L[1] are constants to be adjusted to conditions such as those stated by Professor Pigou in a passage above cited.

With reference to the first tract of income from £135 to £360, it may be admitted that, at least in this country at the present day, the Commission's scheme passes the first test better than its rival. If the taxpayer is charged at the uniform rate throughout that tract, he is under less temptation to transfer his income by misrepresentation to a figure at which the rate is lower; and there will be less need of revising local assessments (Report, 133). But this advantage ends at the limit £360. Thereafter the " effective rate of taxation " on the total income, or on the taxable income—an equally appropriate conception—varies continuously for the Commission's scheme, just as well as according to the formula. If l is the limit at which the tax ceases to be simply proportional, and r is the standard rate (Report, 149), the

---

[1] This constant L, called M in article Y, is not to be identified with the constant, also called M, there employed in Prof. Cassel's scheme to represent the maximum abatement. L might be regarded as the excess of the maximum abatement above the minimum of subsistence, say £135. But that conception is not sufficiently general. Thus the formula might well be adapted to present a set of rates corresponding to the scale (income-tax *plus* super-tax) proposed by the Commission between incomes of £2000 and £20,000. If we determine L (and r) so that the taxes at those points should be the same as given by the formulæ and by the Commission (for single persons and income all investment), L proves to be above £1500, the total abatement above £1600 ! In the words of the Commission, a " difficulty would be experienced in convincing people with small incomes " that taxpayers with large incomes might properly receive an abatement so much larger than that allowed to small incomes (Report, 138). *See* above, p. 246.

rate of taxation on the taxable income is $r\dfrac{x - \frac{1}{2}l}{x}$; where, as before,

x is the taxable income.[1] This rate varies continuously with x just as much as that above given by the formula. Whatever practical expedients are employed to meet the difficulty in the one case are surely equally admissible in the other. On the first count, then, (a) the two candidates are equal. Considering next the third test (c), simplicity, can it be maintained that there is much difference in this respect between the two expressions for the effective rate

on the taxable income, viz. $r\dfrac{x - \frac{1}{2}l}{x}$ and $r\dfrac{x}{x + L}$? Lastly, (b) as

to equity and steady increase, let us compare the graduation determined by the formula with that prescribed by the Commission (for incomes above £360). Whereas there are two constants at our disposal, r and L, let us determine them so that the formula may coincide with the Commission's scheme at two points considered as the " certain points on your scale arrived at by general reasoning " (Pigou) or " instinctive judgment " (Stamp).[2] The limit £360 (£225 above the exempted minimum (£135)) may properly be taken as one of those points.[3] Let us take £2000 for the other point.[4] We have then two simple equations to determine r and L.[5] The resulting values are $r = 0{\cdot}32058$ (6s. 6d. in the pound); $L = 255{\cdot}869$.[6] Using these values for the constants, let us determine the tax according to the formula at several points, and compare the figures with those of the Commission.

TABLE I.—*Comparing Taxes according to* A *the Scheme of the Commission, and* B *the Formula.*

Income in pounds	360	500	700	1000	1500	2000
Tax A	33·75	75·75	135·75	275·75	375·75	525·75
Tax B	33·75	68·79	124·75	214·00	367·30	525·75

There seems to be no significant difference between the two

[1] The tax is $\frac{1}{2}rl + r(x - l) = r(x - \frac{1}{2}l)$. Accordingly the *rate* of taxation is $\dfrac{r(x - \frac{1}{2}l)}{x}$.   [2] Above, p. 262.

[3] Especially if it be conceded that the formula is not to apply below that limit, the effective rate for the tract below (and at the limit) being the same as what it is in the Commission's scheme, viz. 3s. per pound on the taxable income.

[4] Of course, if preferred, we might take for the other datum the " standard " ratio $r = \cdot3$; with the result of greater consilience for the higher incomes, less for the lower ones.

[5]   (1) $r\dfrac{225^2}{L + 225} = 33{\cdot}75$ (2) $r\dfrac{1865^2}{L + 1865} = 525{\cdot}75$

The figures on the right of the equations are obtained from the directions given in Part I. of the Report; supplemented by Table I. in Appendix II.

[6] Of course in practice round numbers would be employed.

sets of figures.   A similar indifference is shown by a comparison
of the effective rates of taxation.

TABLE II.—*Comparison of Effective Rates according to* A *the
Commission Scheme,* B *the Formula.*

Income in pounds . .	360	500	700	1000	1500	2000
A	1/10½	3/0½	3/10½	4/6	5/0	5/3
B	1/10½	2/9	3/7	4/3½	4/11	5/3

The effective rates of taxation on the *taxable income* present a
similar comparison.   In point of equity and gradual increase
there is nothing to choose between the two schemes.

The above comparison illustrates a property of some importance belonging to the sort of " interpolation " with which we are
here concerned.   If the constants are determined so that the
formula shall fit exactly at a few points, it will generally be found
to fit approximately in the neighbourhood of, and even to a considerable distance from, these points.   The property was brought
prominently under the notice of the Statistical Society on the
occasion when Dr. Brownlee read a paper advocating a new
formula for the graduation of a Mortality Table.[1]

Now let us go on to the second tax with which the Commission deals, the super-tax.   And let no difficulty be created by the
circumstance that the two taxes are not based on returns for the
same year.   The task of interpolation is not hampered by that
circumstance; test (*a*) is passed triumphantly.   For all that we
have to do is to find a simple formula which will adequately represent the scheme proposed by the Commission (Report, 152).
Here is the scheme :

TABLE III.—*Showing Rates of Super-tax proposed by the
Commission.*

Income in thou-sands . . .	2	2·5	3	4	5	6	7	8	9	10	20
Rates in succes-sive zone . .		1/6	2	2/6	3	3/6	4	4/6	5	5	5

This scheme is like the " Scene of Man " according to Pope—
" A mighty maze, but not without a plan."   Over a portion of
the tract dealt with, from three to nine thousand, a certain law
is discernible.   With reference to that portion we may say, in

[1] *Journal*, Vol. LXXXII. (1919).   Dr. Major Greenwood, giving his own and
Mr. Yule's experience, said " they could fit the same data to this (the same)
degree of accuracy by formulæ from two contradictory theories, the mathematical
expressions of which were totally distinct one from another " (*loc. cit.* p. 67).
Similar testimony was borne by another speaker (p. 75), with the reservation
that the functions employed should be of a kind suited to the subject matter.

the words of a Commissioner, " the regularity of the curve ought to be sufficient almost to satisfy the soul of a mathematician " (4128). The satisfaction would be greater if, instead of making five steps each of length corresponding to £1000 and of height 6*d*., there was a *continuous* rise in the rate; represented by a simple equation.[1] The total tax (above the point where regularity set in) would then be represented by a simple parabola instead of a discontinuous series of right lines.

But we are not concerned now with this partial regularity; our task is, rather, to represent the whole scheme by a simple formula. To carry in mind and comprehend the Commission's scheme, a number of features must be attended to; there are a great many " things to remember," in the phrase of one of the expert witnesses.[2] There is first the starting-point, £2000; but this need not be counted against the scheme, as any rival scheme must also have a starting-point. Then there are the length £500 and the height 1*s*. 6*d*. of the first step, two " things to remember "; likewise the length of the second step £500 and the height 6*d*., two more things. Then we enter on a tract characterised by steps of equal length £1000, and equal height 6*d*. There are thus only two things to remember about that tract up to the point at which it stops, £9000, which makes another thing. The length and breadth of the next step (up to £10,000) count for two more things; and the step to £20,000 means two more.[3] Altogether, in order to comprehend the scheme, *eleven* details must be carried in mind. A tyro at golf complained that he could only make a good stroke when he kept in mind, and simultaneously attended to, a dozen rules (as to the position and movement of his clubs and limbs) which he had been taught by the professional. Now suppose, as some experts teach, that all the points which the golfer should observe are summed up in this one commandment, " Keep your eye on the ball; " would not this be favourable to " simplicity in explanation and ease in comprehension " (test *c*) ? That is the sort of advantage which an interpolating formula offers to the practice of finance. There can be found an expression for the super-tax at any point of the scale from £2000 to £20,000 which involves only *two* constants. Nor are they involved in a complicated fashion. Indeed, the expression is

---

[1] E.g., $y = rx$; x being the income above £3000, and y the rate on that excess. The total tax would be given by the *integral* of y, viz. $\frac{1}{2} rx^2$. Contrast the expression for the total tax according to the Commission's scheme given below. Note to p. 268.

[2] Mr. Hopkins, deprecating the use of a table giving the tax payable on each of several incomes.   [3] *Cp.* below, p. 268.

simpler than the expression for the super-tax at a point in that part of the Commission scale which alone admits of a general expression, the tract beginning at £3000 and ending at £9000.[1] The rule to be proposed is nearly as simple as that which applies to the *first* tract of the Commission's *income*-tax; which is the simplest possible, simple proportion. According to that rule, if x is the taxable income, and t is the tax to be paid thereon, $t = rx$, where r is a proper fraction. It comes to the same to say that, if y is the disposable income, that which remains over after the tax t has been paid, $y = bx$, where $b = 1 - r$ (also a proper fraction). That is the formula for unprogressive taxation. For progressive taxation, let us put a formula which seems next to that in simplicity, namely :

$$\text{Log } y = b \text{ Log } x.$$

Mr. Hopkins, who so ably voices official objection to mathematical complications, would, it may be hoped, not object to the use of logarithms as calculated to try the temper and intelligence of the general public. For Mr. Hopkins himself employs logarithms for the purpose of exhibiting schemes of taxation. He writes : " The divisions of the line representing the amount of income in this and the following graphs are based not on the actual amount of the income, but on the logarithm of the amount of the income " (Royal Commission on Income-tax, Instalment II., p. 81 *et seq.*). Our graph would differ from his only in having *both* axes based on logarithms. Let the axis of x represent the logarithm of taxable income; and let the disposable income be measured on the axis of y. Then the simple equation, $y = bx$, represented by a line on a diagram, represents the (logarithm of the) disposable income corresponding to any assigned value of the (logarithm of the) taxable income. If another constant is required, there should be added to the expression for y another constant, say, A, or Log a.[2] With reference to the case under consideration, the ratio of any y to the corresponding x is taken to be about 0.9; and the

---

[1] If x is the amount in pounds of income above £3000 (and below £9000), and n is the number of *integer* thousands in x, the general expression for the super-tax on $3000 + x$ is according to the rules of the Commission :

$$87.5 + x\left(\frac{1}{10} + (n+1)\frac{1}{40}\right) - \frac{n(n+1)}{2}\frac{1}{40} 1000.$$

$$\left[500\frac{1.5}{20} + 500\frac{1}{10} + 1000\left(\frac{1}{10} + \frac{1}{40}\right) + 1000\left(\frac{1}{10} + \frac{t}{40}\right) + \ldots + 1000\left(\frac{1}{10} + \frac{n}{40}\right)\right.$$

$$+ (x - n1000)\left(\frac{1}{10} + (n+1)\frac{1}{40}\right) = 87.5$$

$$\left. + x\left(\frac{1}{10} + (n+1)\frac{1}{40}\right) - n(n+1)\frac{1}{40}1000 + \frac{n(n+1)}{2}\frac{1}{40}1000.\right]$$

[2] The equation Log y = Log a + b Log x is identical with the perhaps less familiar form given above, $y = a x^b$.

constant addendum 0·32; constants determined as follows. To fit the formula to the Commission's super-tax, assumed to be agreeable to the judgment of the wise, let us take as the points "arrived at by general reasoning," in Professor Pigou's phrase, £2000 and £10,000; for which the amounts of super-tax are respectively *nil* and £1462 (for single persons, with income all "investment"; Report, Appendix II., Table No. 4). We have thus two simple equations [1] whereby to determine the constants *a* and *b*. Solving these equations, we obtain : Log $a = 0·32419$, $b = 0·90179$. These constants are employed to find the disposable income and thence the tax payable for any amount of income between £2000 and £20,000. Some comparisons with the scheme of the Commission are presented.

TABLE IV.—*Comparing Super-tax* A *according to the Commission, and* B *according to the Formula.*

Income in pounds . .	2000	5000	7000	10,000	15,000	20,000
Super-tax A	0	362	737	1462	2712	3962
Super-tax B	0	443·4	853·6	1462	2697	4050 [2]

The comparison of these figures with those proposed by the Commission will show that test (*b*) is satisfied by the new curve.

No doubt, if we advance far beyond £20,000, the characteristic property of interpolation which has been noticed [3] will cease to operate; there arises discrepancy of the kind shown below :

TABLE V.—*Comparing the Effective Rates of Super-tax on Incomes above* £20,000 *according to* A *the Commission's Scheme, and* B *the Formula.*[4]

Income in pounds . .	20,000	50,000	100,000	500,000	1,000,000
Effective rate A . .	3/11½	4/10½	5/2½	5/5	5/5½
Effective rate B . .	4/0½	5/6	6/4½	8/4½	9/1½

---

[1] (1) Log $a + b$ Log $2000 =$ Log 2000; (2) Log $a + b$ Log $10,000 =$ Log $(10,000 - 1462)$.

[2] Of course other *pivots* might have been used for the purpose of obtaining a formula of the proposed type corresponding to the scheme of the Commission (presumed to be just); for instance, 2000 as before, and 7000 for which the super-tax, according to the Commission, is 737. Whence by parity of reasoning there is found $b = ·91101$ and Log $a = ·29376$. Which constants being inserted in the formula will give a scale similar in its general features to Table IV.

[3] Above.

[4] When an income-tax of so much (*e.g.*, 6*s.*) per pound is added to a super-tax framed as above, there will *ultimately* (for incomes above some millions sterling per ann. !) be reached a stage at which the tax-payer will have no motive to increase his income (*see* above, p. 251 *et seq.*). But, if necessary, this breakdown can be indefinitely deferred by putting for "Log x" in the formula "Log $(1 - \gamma)x$;" where γ is a proper fraction not exceeding the rate of the income-tax (*e.g.*, ·3).

If, then, the flattening of the rate for the upper incomes was deliberate on the part of the Commission, the new formula will cease to correspond to their judgment. But if there was a minority, as we may surmise,[1] in favour of a more severe progression, they might welcome a formula which embodies their ideal without any additional complication; whereas, to effect a similar graduation (above £20,000) on the lines of the Commission, some dozen additional " things to remember " might be required. Or, if the requirements of a just progression were thought not to be quite satisfied by the formula, it would be easy to introduce one or more additional functions of the same type, tightening or lightening the tax at different points according to the judgment of experts and the sense of the community.[2] The Chancellor of the Exchequer, employing a formula which of all appropriate to progressive taxation seems one of the simplest,[3] may hope with some confidence to construct a scale of taxation not very different from the ideal scale, could it be discovered. He would be in the fortunate position of the statistician when, having to combine observations dispersed according to some unknown law, he selects, out of the innumerable possible methods of averaging, a familiar one—the arithmetic mean; or when, in the construction of an index-number, he employs some handy system of weights, the true system not being ascertainable. The statistician may be certain that the methods practised will not yield the best result conceivable; but he may also presume that the result of the ideally best method is likely not to differ widely from that of his fairly good method. Something of the confidence which the theory of probabilities imparts to statistics the characteristic property of interpolation [4] may impart to fiscal practice.

Altogether, the Commission seem not to have done justice to the use of mathematical formulæ for the purpose of interpolation. They justly reject formulæ purporting to express an ideal scale of taxation. But they do not recognise that some approach to the ideal is possible by way of interpolation.

[1] Asked if he agreed to graduation leading to " practical extinction beyond a certain point," Dr. Stamp replied, " I hesitate to say extinction, but I think severe progression " (9791).   [2] Cp. above, p. 262.

[3] As the classical utility-function $\log x/c$ (where x is the total income and c the minimum of subsistence), perhaps the simplest function which fulfils the condition of continual increase at a decreasing rate, leads to the (unprogressive) rate of taxation $r = \text{constant}$; so the next simplest function that increases less rapidly, viz. $\log \log x/c$, leads to the (progressive) rate $r = \text{const.} \times \log \dfrac{x}{c}$.

[4] Above, p. 266.

SECTION VI
MATHEMATICAL ECONOMICS

SECTION VI

MATHEMATICAL ECONOMICS

(a)

ON THE APPLICATION OF MATHEMATICS TO POLITICAL ECONOMY

[THIS is the Presidential Address delivered to Section F of the British Association in 1889. Mathematics are described as a useful, though not an indispensable adjunct to economic studies; a finish to the training of an economist comparable with a knowledge of the Classics as part of a general education. Mathematical conceptions are found to be specially appropriate to the cases, frequent in economics, where there are several mutually dependent variable quantities; and where it is required to determine the maximum value of a quantity dependent on several variables.

If the subjects which would now be described as "quasi-rent" and "external economies" are inadequately treated in this Address, it should be remembered that the Address was delivered before the publication of the *Principles of Economics*.]

At the meeting of the British Association which was held at Cambridge about a quarter of a century ago, Jevons submitted to this section a "general mathematical theory of political economy," which, as he himself records, was "received without a word of interest or belief." I propose to consider the justice of the unfavourable verdict which our predecessors appear to have passed on the mathematical method introduced by Jevons.

There is some difficulty in discussing so abstruse a subject in this place. It is as if one should discourse on the advantages of classical education on an occasion on which it might seem pedantic to cite the learned languages. I shall evade this difficulty by addressing to students some appended notes,[1] which, like the boy of the proverb, are to be seen, not heard.

The cardinal article of Jevons's theory is that the value in

[1] The appended notes are referred to by letters of the alphabet, thus : (a).

exchange of a commodity measures, or corresponds to, the utility of the least useful portion of that commodity. What a person pays per month or year for a sack or ton of coal is not what he would be willing to give for the same rather than be without fuel altogether. Rather the price is proportioned to the advantage which the consumer expects from the portion which he could best dispense with—to the " final utility," in Jevons's happy phrase.

I shall not be expected here to dwell on a subject which has been elucidated in treatises of world-wide reputation, such as those of Professors Marshall, Sidgwick, Walker, and I would add Professor Nicholson's article on Value in the *Encyclopædia Britannica*. Those writers seem to present what I may call the economical kernel of Jevons's theory divested of the mathematical shell in which it was originally enclosed; whereas my object is to consider the use of that shell: whether it is to be regarded as a protection or an encumbrance.

I may begin by removing an objection which the mere statement of the question raises. The idea of reducing human actions to mathematical rule may present itself to common sense as absurd. One is reminded of Swift's " Laputa," where the beef was cut into rhomboids and the pudding into a cycloid, and the tailor constructed a very ill-fitting suit by means of rule and compasses. It should be understood, however, that the new method of economical reasoning does not claim more precision than what has long been conceded to another department of science applied to human affairs, namely, Statistics. It is now a commonplace that actions such as suicide and marriage, springing from the most capricious motives, and in respect of which the conduct of individuals most defies prediction, may yet, when taken in the aggregate, be regarded as constant and uniform. The advantage of what has been called the law of large numbers may equally be enjoyed by a theory which deals with markets and combinations.

But, indeed, even the limited degree of arithmetical precision which is proper to statistical generalisations need not be claimed by our mathematical method rightly understood. It is concerned with quantity, indeed, but not necessarily with number. It is not so much a political arithmetic as a sort of economic algebra, in which the problem is not to find x and y in terms of given quantities, but rather to discover loose quantitative relations of the form: x is greater or less than y; and increases or decreases with the increase of z.

Such is the character of what may be called perhaps the leading proposition in this calculus, namely, the mathematical theory of Supply and Demand.   The use of a curve introduced by Cournot to represent the amount of a commodity offered, or demanded, at any particular price, supplemented by Jevons's theory of final utility (a), does not indeed determine what price will rule in any market.   But it assists us in conjecturing the direction and general character of the effect which changes in the condition or requirements of the parties will produce.   For example, in the case of international trade the various effects of a tax or other impediment, which most students find it so difficult to trace in Mill's laborious chapters, are visible almost at a glance by the aid of the mathematical instrument (b).   It takes Professor Sidgwick a good many words to convey by way of a particular instance that it is possible for a nation by a judiciously regulated tariff to benefit itself at the expense of the foreigner.   The truth in its generality is more clearly contemplated by the aid of diagrams such as those employed by the eminent mathematical economists Messrs. Auspitz and Lieben (c).

There seems to be a natural affinity between the phenomena of supply and demand and some of the fundamental conceptions of mathematics, such as the relation between function and variable,[1] between the ordinate of a curve and the corresponding abscissa,[2] and the first principles of the differential calculus, especially in its application to the determination of *maxima* and *minima*.   The principle of Equilibrium is almost as dominant in what Jevons called the mechanics of industry as in natural philosophy itself (d).   In so many instances does mathematical science supply to political economy what Whewell would have called " appropriate and clear " conceptions.   Their use might, perhaps, be illustrated by comparing—however fancifully, and *si parva licet componere magnis*—the advance in economics which Jevons initiated or continued to the advance in mathematics which the higher method invented by Sir William Rowan Hamilton appears to have effected.   Algebra and geometry are to ordinary language in political economy somewhat as quaternions are to ordinary algebraic geometry in mathematical physics; if we

---

[1] The treating as constant what is variable, e.g., *supply, margin, wages-fund*, is the source of most of the fallacies in political economy.

[2] For instance, the two meanings of increased demand—which Mr. Sidgwick has contrasted as the *rise* and the extension of demand—are most easily and with least liability to logomachy distinguished as the variation of an ordinate (1) due to the displacement of the curve, the abscissa not varying, or (2) corresponding to an increment of the abscissa, the curve being undisturbed.

accept the view of the latter relation which has been given by a very competent judge, Clerk-Maxwell. " I am convinced," he says, " that the introduction of the ideas as distinguished from the operations and methods of quaternions will be of great use in the study of all parts of our subject, and especially . . . where we have to deal with a number of physical quantities, the relations of which to each other can be expressed far more simply by a few expressions of Hamilton's than by the ordinary equations." [1] This is the spirit in which the economist should employ mathematics—" the ideas as distinguished from the operations and methods."

In considering the above given, and indeed any concrete, instances, it is hardly possible to keep to what may be called the simplest type of supply and demand, the ideal market in which we contemplate only two groups of competitors and only two articles of exchange : say, gold for corn, or any other *quid pro quo*. In general, and especially when considering what rates of exchange tend to rule in an average of transactions, it is proper to take into account that the dealings in one market will affect those in another. If the entrepreneur has less to pay for machinery, *ceteris paribus*, he will be able to offer more on the labour market. Thus we obtain the idea of a system of markets mutually dependent. In a general view of this correlation it is not necessary to distinguish whether the state of one part is connected as cause or effect with the other parts of the system. As Professor Marshall says : [2] " Just as the motion of every body in the solar system affects and is affected by the motion of every other, so it is with the elements of the problem of political economy " (e).

This conception of mutually dependent positions is one in which minds disciplined in mathematical physics seem peculiarly apt to acquiesce. In other quarters there may be observed a restless anxiety to determine which of the variables in a system of markets is to be regarded as determining or regulating the others. In one of the principal economic journals there has lately been a pretty stiff controversy on the question which of the parties in the distribution of the national produce may be regarded as " residual claimants upon the product of industry "; [3] whether it

[1] Clerk-Maxwell, *Electricity and Magnetism*, Art. 10. He says in the context, " As the methods of Descartes are still the most familiar to students of science, and as they are really the most useful for purposes of calculation, we shall express all our results in the Cartesian form." Compare Professor Marshall's dictum with respect to the use of the vulgar tongue in economic reasonings, cited below, p. 287.

[2] In a remarkable review of Jevons's Theory in the *Academy* of 1st April, 1872.   [3] *Quarterly Journal of Economics*, 1887, p. 287; 1888, p. 9.

is the working class which occupies this preferential position, or if the " real keystone of the arch " is interest. Such questions certainly admit of a meaning, and possibly of an answer. But they will probably appear of secondary importance to those who accept, as the first approximation to a correct view of the subject, the principle of mutual dependence—what may be called the Copernican theory of distribution, in which one variable is not more determined by another than the other is by that one (*f*).

Among the factors of this economic equilibrium I have not as yet explicitly included cost of production. Rather, the system of markets which so far I have had in view is that which would arise if all the articles of exchange were periodically rained down like manna upon the several proprietors, and each individual sought to maximise his advantage according to the law of final utility. But now we must observe that self-interest does not operate only in this fashion. We must take account of efforts and sacrifices.

Here again the language of symbol and diagram is better suited than the popular terminology to express the general idea that all things are in flux, and that the fluxions are inter-dependent. In Professor Marshall's words, " as a rule, the cost of production of a thing is not fixed; the amount produced and its normal value are to be regarded as determined simultaneously under the action of economic laws. It, then, is incorrect to say, as Ricardo did, that cost of production alone determines values; but it is no less incorrect to make utility alone, as others have done, the basis of value." [1] Among those who may have gone astray in the latter sense, who, in their recoil from Scylla, are at least sailing dangerously near Charybdis, may be placed the important Austrian school, who have rediscovered and restated the theory of final utility without the aid of mathematical expression. To amplify a figure suggested by one them,[2] let us figure the hard conditions of industrial life by the austerity of a schoolmaster who, in order to cultivate patience and fortitude in his scholars, should distribute among them certain rewards—it might be toys and sweets—in return for certain amounts of fatigue and pain endured. Thus the cost of procuring a marble might be writing

---

[1] *Economics of Industry*, p. 148.

[2] *Cp*. Professor Böhm-Bawerk : " Es kann ein Erzieher einem Knaben, um ihn gegen Weheleidigkeit abzuhärten, für die tapfere, freiwillige Erduldung von Schmerzen ein sehnlich begehrtes Spielzung in Aussicht stellen. So untergeordnet das Vorkommen solcher Fälle auch sein mag, so wichtig ist es für die Theorie festzustellen, dass Arbeit und Arbeitsplage doch nicht der einzige Umstand ist, auf den sich . . die Wertschätzung gründen kann." *Konrad's Jahrbuch* 1866, p. 43.

out twenty lines, the cost of a top standing half an hour in the stocks. Supposing exchange to be set up among the members of the youthful population, free competition being assumed, there would theoretically arise an equilibrium of trade in which the value of each article would correspond to its final utility. That is, if a top exchanged for ten marbles, it might be expected that each boy would prize the last top about as highly as the last decade of marbles which he thought fit to purchase. So far final utility might be regarded as the regulating principle.

But it is equally true that the final *dis*-utilities of the exchanged articles will be equal. If a top is worth ten marbles, we are entitled to expect such an adjustment of trade that each and every boy would as soon stand in the stocks half an hour as write out two hundred lines—the cost of ten marbles at twenty lines per marble.

To be sure final utility may be conceived as operating by itself without reference to cost of production, as we tacitly assumed in our first paragraphs. Whereas the converse conception of a traffic in discommodities [1] has less place in real life.

But it is not worth while weighing the two principles against each other, *in vacuo*, so to speak, and abstracting the real circumstances by which each is differently modified. As these are introduced the balance will oscillate now in favour of one side, now of the other; perhaps leaving it ultimately uncertain whether cost of production or final utility is the more helpful in the explanation of economic phenomena.

For instance, in our allegory let us introduce the supposition that there is only one variety of cost—say the common labour of writing out verses. If now the authorities fix twenty lines as the cost of a marble, and two hundred as the cost of a top, it is predictable that a top will be worth ten marbles. It is equally true, indeed, now as before, that the final utility of a top will be equal to the final utility of ten marbles. But the latter proposition, though equally true, is not equally useful. For it does not afford

---

[1] Suppose our allegorical schoolmaster should discontinue the system of rewards, and prefer to cultivate diligence by requiring each boy from time to time to bring up a certain number of lines, written out—whether by himself or another would not be scrutinised—or to be responsible for the cleaning of a window, after the manner of Mr. Squeers's practical method and so on. In the traffic of discommodities which would be set up on this supposition the (negative) value of each article of exchange would be measured solely by its disutility. However, it must be admitted, I think, that this latter hypothesis is rather more absurd than the former abstraction—with reference to ordinary life at least; for, as it happens, the traffic in impositions more nearly resembles what is said to occur in schools.

the simple and exact method of prediction which is obtained by the Ricardian view upon the supposition made. But then the supposition that there is only one variety of sacrifice is not always appropriate. And even if it were appropriate, it might not be helpful when we introduce the condition that the cost of procuring each article is not fixed definitely, but varies increasingly or decreasingly with the amount procured. Thus the cost of the first marble given out might be twenty lines; of the next marble. twenty-one lines; with an equally varying scale for tops. Upon this supposition the two propositions that value corresponds to final utility and also final disutility might be equally true, but equally useless for the purpose of prediction.

Again, it may be that a man is freer to vary the extent of his expenditure than the duration of his work (g). The final disutility experienced by the secretary of the British Association during its meetings must be fearful. For it is not open to him to terminate at pleasure his day's work, as if he were employed by the piece. He would not, however, have accepted the office unless the advantages, less by all the trouble, were at least as great as in any other position open to him. Now this equation of the net advantages in different occupations is—co-ordinately and (in a mathematical sense) *simultaneously* with the equation of final utility for different kinds of expenditure—a condition of normal economic equilibrium (h). Yet again, the free play of this tendency is impeded by the existence of " non-competing groups."

I cannot be expected here to enumerate all the conditions of economic equilibrium. For a complete exposition of the complexities, at which I have thought it necessary to glance, I must refer to the second book of Professor Sidgwick's *Political Economy*. It will be evident to his readers [1] that what may be called the

---

[1] There occurs to me only one point at which the use of mathematical illustrations more complicated than those which I have referred to in my first two headings would conduce to the apprehension of Mr. Sidgwick's theorems. I allude to his repeated statement that, not only in international trade, as Mill pointed out, but also in trade in general, there may be several rates of exchange at which the supply just takes off the demand. This statement, taken without reservation, goes the length of destroying the prestige which is now attached to competition. Professor Marshall in an important passage recommends arbitrators and combinations to imitate the method of a celebrated engineer, who, in order to make a breakwater, first ascertained the slope at which a bank of stones would naturally be arranged under the action of the waves, and then let down stones so as to form such a slope (*Economics of Industry*, p. 215). Now, if gravitation acted sometimes vertically and sometimes at an angle of 45°, if the forces of competition tended to two distinct positions of equilibrium, the construction of the economic breakwater would become arbitrary. It is important, therefore, to show the limits of Professor Sidgwick's theory.

general economic problem of several trading bodies distributing and exchanging *inter se* under the influence of self-interest, and in a regime of competition, is much more hopelessly difficult than the as yet imperfectly solved dynamical problem of several material bodies acting on each other *in vacuo*. When Gossen, the predecessor of Jevons as exponent of the law of final utility, compares that principle to the law of gravitation, and the character of our science to that of astronomy, he betrays a parental partiality. A truer, though still too flattering, comparison would be afforded by some very immature and imperfect specimens of physics, say the theory of fluid motion applied to the problems of house ventilation.

There is a certain resemblance between the uniformity of pressure to which the jostling particles of a gas tend, and the unity of price which is apt to result from the play of competition. As the architect is guided by studying the laws according to which air flows, so it will help the builder of economic theory to have mastered the principle of movement towards equilibrium. But even in the material constructions practice is apt to lag far behind theory, as every reader in the British Museum knows. Much less are we able to predict what currents will flow between the different compartments of the industrial system. We know so imperfectly the coefficient of fluid friction, and the other conditions of the general problem : what compartments may be regarded as completely isolated and hermetically sealed, which partitions are porous and permeable.

Indeed there has been noticed one mode of competition, which it does not seem easy or helpful to represent by physical analogies —the transference from one occupation to another, the equation of net advantages or total utilities in different employments ; industrial as distinguished by Cairnes from commercial competition. The latter operation appears to me to admit much better of mathematical expression than the former, which is not so well represented by the equilibrium of a physical system.[1] Accordingly the equation of net advantages has been judiciously omitted by Jevons in his formulation of the cost of production. And the Helvetian Jevons, as we may call Professor Walras,

[1] Commercial competition might be likened to a system of lakes flowing into each other; industrial competition to a system of vessels so communicating by means of valves, that when the level in one exceeded that of another to a certain extent, then *per saltum* a considerable portion of the contents of that one (a finite difference as compared with the differentials of the open system) is discharged into the other.

appears to have altogether made abstraction of the cost of production considered as importing sacrifice and effort.*

Professor Walras, illustrating the operation of a simple market, supposes each dealer, before going to market, to write down his scale of requirements—how much he would be willing to buy or sell at each price.   From these data it would be easy to calculate beforehand the rate of exchange which would prevail in the market formed by those individuals.   But, when we advance from the simplest type of market to the complexities introduced by division of labour, it is seen to be no longer a straightforward problem in algebra or geometry, given the natures of all the parties, to find the terms to which they will come.   Here, even if we imagine ourselves in possession of numerical data for the motives acting on each individual, we could hardly conceive it possible to deduce *a priori* the position of equilibrium towards which a system so complicated tends.

Accordingly it may be doubted whether the direct use of mathematical formulæ extends into the region of concrete phenomena much below the height of abstraction to which Jevons has confined himself.   However, the formulation of more complicated problems has still a negative use, as teaching the Socratic lesson that no exact science is attainable.   As Dupuit, one of the greatest of Jevons's mathematical predecessors, points out, " Quand on ne peut savoir une chose, c'est déjà beaucoup que de savoir qu'on ne sait rien." [1]   If, he says, the early theorists, instead of formulating the balance of trade, had confined themselves to declaring the question above their powers, they would probably have done a greater service than the successors who refuted them.   So Cournot, referring to his own mathematical treatment of economics.   " Aussi nos modestes prétensions étaientelles non d'accroître de beaucoup la domaine de la science proprement dite, mais plutôt de montrer (ce qui a bien aussi son utilité) tout ce que nous manque pour donner la solution vraiment scientifique de questions que la polémique quotidienne tranche hardiment." [2]   Similarly Jevons says,[3] " one advantage of the theory of economics, carefully studied, will be to make us very careful in our conclusions when the matter is not of the simplest possible nature."

In the vineyard of science to perform the part of a pruninghook is an honourable function; and a very necessary one in this

* For a defence of this statement see below, p. 310.
[1] *Annales des Ponts et Chaussées,* 1844, p. 372.
[2] *Revue Sommaire.*
[3] *Theory of Political Economy,* p. 157, second edit.

age of luxuriant speculation, when novel theories teem in so many new economic journals. I give in the appended notes an example of this corrective process applied to a theory of great worth and authority, and concerning the most vital interests, such as the relations of employer and employed, and the socialistic attack on capital (*i*). In directing this weapon of criticism against Professor Walker, I act upon the Miltonic rule for selecting an adversary :

> "Best with the best, more glory will be won,
> Or less be lost."

In the preceding remarks I have had in view, as presumably most favourable to computation, the case of bargains in which there is competition on both sides. It is now to be added that the mathematical method is nearly as applicable to a regime of monopoly. Here Cournot, rather than Jevons, is our guide. Cournot's masterly analysis of the dealings between a monopolist seller and a number of buyers competing against each other has been copied out of mathematics into the vulgar tongue by many well known writers, and need not here be repeated (*k*).

It is in this department perhaps that we can best answer Cairnes's challenge to Jevons to produce any proposition discovered by the mathematical method which is not discoverable by ordinary reasoning. Not, indeed, that the economist is bound to answer that challenge; any more than, in order to prove the advantages of international trade, he is concerned to deny that claret may be produced in Scotland.

The following proposition is a particular case of a more general theorem given by Cournot. Let there be a railway and a line of steamers, each forming part of a certain through journey, and separately useless : the fares will be lower when both means of transport belong to a single company than where there is less monopoly, the two services being in the hands of two companies, each seeking its own gain independently of the other.*

The *rationale* of this somewhat paradoxical proposition is not easily discerned without the aid of symbols. Cournot, in a popular [1] redaction of the theories which he first conceived in a mathematical form, suggests, as a generally intelligible explanation, that it is better to be at the mercy of a single master than of several petty tyrants. But this seems to be a commonplace of the sort which, in the absence of rigid reasoning, has so often deceived the amateur economist. Might it not be applied to the case of monopoly in general?

* For a more exact statement, see **E**.   [1] *Revue Sommaire.*

It would be hard to say how much this remarkable proposition may add to the arguments in favour of the Government monopolising railways. Nor would I undertake to estimate the practical significance of Cournot's numerous mathematical theorems on the taxation of monopolists. We might perhaps compare the function of the sovereign science with respect to the theory of monopolies to the duty of Government as to their management—to exercise a general supervision without attempting to control details.

We have in the last few paragraphs been supposing monopoly on one side of the market, on the other side a public competing with each other. Let us now consider the bargain between two monopolists, whether individuals, or rather corporate trading bodies, combinations in the most general sense of the term. The mathematical analysis of this case brings very clearly into view the important property, which is not very prominent in writings of the pre-Jevonian era, that the bargain between two self-interested co-contractors is not determinate in the same sense as in a regime of perfect competition.

No doubt, if we take a very simple case—such as that imagined by De Quincey, of a bargain between the owner of a musical box and a colonist already on his way to a distant region where no luxuries can be purchased—it is easy to see that the bargain may settle down at any point between certain limits. But where both the amount of commodity to be sold and money to be paid are variable, as in the momentous case of the bargain between a combination of employers on the one hand and employees on the other, it is a less familiar truth that the terms of the contract are in general to some extent indeterminate. For instance, the bargain may be either all in the interest of the one party, say long hours and small pay, or on the other hand high wages with much leisure.

The significance of this proposition has been missed by many of those who have treated the subject without the aid of the appropriate apparatus. Some fail to see that there is any peculiarity in the bargain between isolated units. Another discerns the indeterminateness of the bargain only in the special case in which the article exchanged is a large indivisible object, like a house. Another limits the difficulty to the case of a single negotiation as distinguished from a contract which, as in the actual labour market, may be modified from time to time. Another tells us that in such a bargain the most anxious party gains least.

All these phrases seem to obscure the cardinal distinction that perfect competition tends to a determinate settlement, whereas in a regime of combination a principle of adjustment is still to seek. What is that principle ?

At a former meeting of the British Association, on the occasion of a discussion on sliding scales, I stated the difficulty which there might be, in the absence of competition, in defining fair wages and reasonable terms, and I asked the eminent professor who introduced the subject in what direction one should look for a solution of this difficulty. His reply imported, as I understood, that no other general rule can be given but this : to obtain a full knowledge of, and bring a candid judgment to bear on, all the circumstances relevant to each case. To which I would add that one circumstance relevant to this whole class of cases is just the fact that there is in the abstract such a marked difference between combination and competition.

Possibly the dry light of abstract science may enable us to see a little further into this difficulty. Analysis strongly suggests that the right solution is what may be called the utilitarian arrangement, that which is productive of the greatest sum-total of advantage for all concerned. The utilitarian determination is clearly discerned to be by no means necessarily coincident with the settlement towards which competition tends. For instance, the " vrai prix," in Condillac's sense, as determined by the play of supply and demand in the labour market, might be such that the entrepreneur class should take the lion's share, leaving the labourer a bare and painful subsistence ; but there is no ground to believe that this is the best possible arrangement. From an abstract point of view it is by no means evident that a free labour market is the only way to equity, that any interference with it must involve injustice." [1] Nor need it appear " a great fundamental principle—as inevitable in its action as gravitation—that a fair day's wages for a fair day's labour is determined by the proportion which the supply in the market bears to the demand." [2] It may be true indeed, in a practical sense, that perfect competition is " not less harmonious and beneficent in its operation than gravity ; " [3] but theoretically it is tenable that there is an adjustment of contracts more beneficent than that which the mechanical play of competition tends to establish (l).

To introduce these philosophical conceptions of utilitarianism will doubtless seem irrelevant to those who are immersed in the details of business. But the practical man should be reminded

Danson, *Wealth of Households.*   [2] Rupert Kettle on " Arbitration."
[3] Walker, *Political Economy.*

that in other spheres of action, politics and morals, the principle of utility, however badly received at first, has exercised a great influence—though doubtless not so great as was expected by the theorists of Bentham's school, and needing to be largely tempered with common sense.

Such, I think, are the principal points at which mathematical reasoning is capable of being applied to political economy. [In estimating the use of this method, it is natural to take as our standard the helpfulness of mathematics in other departments of science.

As compared with mathematical physics, the mathematical theory of political economy shows many deficiencies. First, there is the want of numerical data, which has been already noticed. It is true that there is a faint hope of obtaining what Jevons too confidently expected, statistical data for the relations between demand and price. It is true also that in the higher mathematics conclusions which are quantitative without being numerical are more frequent than is usually supposed. Some political economy is as exact as some mathematical physics. The fields cultivated by Section A and Section F may overlap, but it must be admitted that the best part of our domain corresponds to what is the worst part of theirs. If you inquire as to the products of inferior soils, we must confess, if we do not wish to conceal the nakedness of the land, that over a large portion of our territory no crop is produced. We are employed only in rooting out the tares which an enemy has planted. Much of our reasoning is directed to the refutation of fallacies, and a great part of our science only raises us to the zero point of nescience from the negative position of error. " Sapientia prima stultitiâ caruisse." In this introductory portion of political economy we have seen that the mathematical method is likely to be serviceable.[1]

It is not to be supposed, however, that the work of our section is wholly destructive; that like the islanders of whom it is said that they earned a precarious livelihood by washing one another's clothes, so we are occupied only in mangling each other's theories. Like imprudent sectaries, by our mutual recriminations we have obscured the virtues common to our profession. What Jevons said of Cairnes, that his own opinions were much more valuable than his objections against other people's opinions, is true of Jevons himself and other controversial economists. Now, this possibility of mutual misunderstanding by persons who are both in the right is connected with a circumstance which it is not

[1] See above, p. 281.

irrelevant here to notice. It is that in our subject, unlike physics, it is not often clear what is the prime factor, what elements may be omitted in a first approximation. One writer on rent may emphasise distance from the centres of population as the main attribute, and introduce fertility of soil as a perturbation of the abstract result given by the first view. Another fixes attention on the powers of the soil, and allows for other elements, as for friction. So, in the theory of money, the state of credit, or the quantity of metal, have each been regarded as the prime variable.[1] It need not be pointed out how unfavourable to exact science is such a state of the subject matter. Imagine an astronomer hesitating whether in the determination of Jupiter's movements the sun or the planet Saturn played the most important part. That is the condition of many of our speculations.

It will not be expected that from such materials any very elaborate piece of reasoning can be constructed. Accordingly another point of contrast with mathematical physics is the brevity of our calculations. The whole difficulty is in the statement of our problems. The purely computative part of the work is inconsiderable. Scarcely has the powerful engine of symbolic language been applied, when the train of reasoning comes to a stop. The case is like that of the " swell " in *Punch*, who, about to enter a hansom, inquires solicitously of the driver whether he has got a good horse. " Yes, sir; very good 'oss." " Aw—then dwive to next door." However, our road, though short, is so slippery as to require every precaution.

It follows that in economics, unlike physics, the use of symbols may perhaps be dispensed with by native intelligence. It must be admitted that the correct theory of value has been rediscovered by Menger, and restated by his follower, Böhm-Bawerk, without the explicit use of mathematics. Without the law, they have done by nature the things contained under the law. Still, under a higher dispensation, they might have attained greater perfection. Nor can equal accuracy be ascribed to all the followers of Menger. Nor is the terseness which comes of mathematical study a characteristic of this Austrian school (m).

Another point of contrast between the mathematical science of the physicist and the economist is that the former appeals to a larger public. Mathematics is as it were the universal language of the physical sciences. It is for physicists what Latin used to

---

[1] Compare Cournot : " Ce que l'un néglige dans une première approximation comme un fait secondaire et accessoire, un autre le regardera comme le fait principal et dominant."—*Principes*, Book IV. chap. vii.

be for scholars; but it is unfortunately Greek to many economists. Hence the writer who wishes to be widely read—who does not say, with the French author, *J'imprime pour moi*—will do well not to multiply mathematical technicalities beyond the indispensable minimum, which we have seen reason to suppose is not very large. The parsimony of symbols, which is often an elegance in the physicist, is a necessity for the economist. Indeed, it is tenable that our mathematical constructions should be treated as a sort of scaffolding, to be removed when the edifice of science is completed. As Professor Marshall, one of the highest authorities on this subject, says: "When a man has cleared up his mind about a difficult economic question by mathematical reasoning, he generally finds it best to throw aside his mathematics and express what he has to say in language that is understanded of the people."[1] Upon this view mathematical discipline might be compared to grammar or to the study of classical literature, which it is profitable to have learnt thoroughly, while it is pedantic to obtrude one's learning.

From these considerations it may appear that our little branch of learning is of quite a rudimentary form. The solid structure and regular ramifications of the more developed mathematical sciences are wanting. A less unfavourable contrast would be presented if we compared our method, not with applied mathematics generally, but with that particular branch of it which comes nearest to ours in its proximity to human interests—the use of the Calculus of Probabilities in social statistics.

There is really only one theorem in the higher part of the calculus, but it is a very difficult one, the theory of errors, or deviations from an average. The direct applications of this theory to human affairs are not very considerable. Perhaps the most conspicuous example is afforded by an investigation to which, if I had undertaken to review the work done in our subjects during the past year, I ought to have directed particular attention—Mr. Galton's rigid proof of the fact and amount of *regression*, or reversion, in children compared with parents and other relationships.

But, beyond the isolated instances in which the theory of deviations is applied in social statistics with the same strictness and cogency as in physics, there is a wide zone of cases in which the abstract theory is of use as giving us some idea of the value to be attached to statistical results. Mr. Galton justly complains of the statisticians who "limit their inquiries to averages, and do

[1] *Academy*, June 11, 1881.

not revel in the more comprehensive views" of the deviations from averages. "Their souls seem as dull to the charm of variety as that of the native of one of our flat English counties, whose retrospect of Switzerland was that, if its mountains could be thrown into its lakes, two nuisances would be got rid of at once." But great caution is required in transferring the theory of errors to human affairs; and the Calculus of Probabilities may easily be made, in Mill's phrase, the "opprobrium of mathematics."

Now, in all these respects there is a considerable resemblance between the higher parts of the two branches of science which are cultivated in this section. It may be said that in pure economics there is only one fundamental theorem, but that is a very difficult one : the theory of bargain in a wide sense. The direct application of mathematical reasoning is, as we have seen, limited—more limited, I think, than the corresponding function of the higher statistics. But, on the other hand, the regulative effect, the educational influence, of studies like those of Cournot and Jevons are probably very extensive.

How extensive, it would be difficult to decide without defining the limits of a province within which our special subject is included—the use of abstract reasoning in political economy. Now, on this vexed question, and with reference to the heated controversy between the historical and the deductive schools, the mathematical economist as such is not committed to any side. It may be dangerous to take wide general views; it may be better to creep from one particular to another rather than ascend to speculative heights. Our only question here is whether, if that ascent is to be made, it is better to ascend by the steep but solid steps of mathematical reasoning, or to beguile the severity of the ascent by the zigzag windings of the flowery path of literature. It is tenable that the former course is safest, as not allowing us to forget at what a dangerous height of abstraction we proceed. As Professor Foxwell has well said,[1] with reference to the mathematical methods in the hands of Jevons and Professor Marshall, "It has made it impossible for the educated economist to mistake the limits of theory and practice, or to repeat the confusions which brought the study into discredit and almost arrested its growth."

I trust that I have succeeded in distinguishing the question what is the worth of abstract reasoning in political economy from the much more easily answered question whether, if it is

[1] In his important letter on "The Economic Movement in England " in the *Quarterly Journal of Economics* for October, 1888.

worth doing, it is worth doing well.[1] The mathematical economist is concerned to separate his method from that mathematical and metaphysical reasoning which Burke repudiates as inapplicable to human affairs; from the abstract method which he has in view when he says :—" The geometricians . . . bring from the dry bones of their diagrams . . . dispositions that make them worse than indifferent about those feelings and habitudes which are the supports of the moral world." [2] Burke is referring to the Jacobin philosophers; but our withers are unwrung, if similar words should be applied to some of the " sophisters and calculators " of a later generation. Just as a political party, if popularly suspected of complicity with crime, would do well to take every opportunity of clearing themselves from that imputation, so the mathematical economist is called on to disown emphatically all sympathy with the flagrant abuses to which the injudicious use of abstract reasoning is undoubtedly liable.

To continue the comparison which I was instituting between the mathematical theory of economics and the Calculus of Probabilities, they have one very unpleasant property in common—a liability to slips. As De Morgan says,[3] " everybody makes errors in probabilities at times, and big ones." He goes on to mention a mistake committed by both Laplace and Poisson, the ineptitude of which he can only parallel by the reasoning of a little girl whom he had called a " daughter of Eve " ; to which she retorted, " then you must be a daughter of Adam." It is not to be concealed that economic reasoning, even in its severest form, is sometimes equally inconsistent. I should have hesitated to assert that Cournot has made some serious mistakes in mathematics applied to political economy, but that the authority of the eminent mathematician Bertrand [4] may be cited in support of that assertion.

Again, the more abstract theories of value and of probabilities seem to resemble each other in their distance from the beaten curriculum. Each forms, as it were, a little isolated field on the rarely crossed frontier and almost inaccessible watershed between the moral and the physical sciences.

[1] *Cp.* Professor Foxwell, *loc. cit.* " What the new school protest against is first the unscientific and meagre way in which deduction was used. In their view, though it is worth while to study, and therefore worth while to study accurately, the workings of private interest under a system of competition, yet human nature is not all self-interest. . . ."   [2] *Letter to a Noble Lord.*
[3] Writing to Sir W. R. Hamilton (*Life of Hamilton*, by R. Graves, vol. iii.).
[4] *Journal des Savants*, 1883. I hope to show on some future occasion that M. Bertrand's censures of Cournot and Professor Walras are far too severe.

The same character of remoteness belongs perhaps to another province, which is also comparable with ours—the mathematical side of formal logic, the symbolic laws of thought which Boole formulated. There was a certain congruity between Jevons's interest in his logical machine and in what he called the " mechanics of industry." But I venture to regard the latter pursuit as much more liberal and useful than any species of syllogism-grinding.

If you accept these parallels, you will perhaps come to the conclusion that the mathematical theory of political economy is a study much more important than many of the curious refinements which have occupied the ingenuity of scientific men ; that as compared with a great part of logic and metaphysics it has an intimate relation to life and practice ; that, as a means of discovering truth and an educational discipline, it is on a level with the more theoretical part of statistics ; while it falls far short of mixed mathematics in general in respect of that sort of pre-established harmony between the subject matter and the reasoning which makes mathematical physics the most perfect type of applied science.

But we must remember—and the mention of the theory of probabilities may remind us—that any such judgment is liable to considerable error. We cannot hope to measure the utility of a study with precision, but rather to indicate the estimate on either side of which competent judges would diverge—a central point, which will be found, if I mistake not, equally removed from the position of Gossen, who compares the new science to astronomy, and the attitude of Dr. Ingram towards the researches which he regards as nothing more than " academic playthings, and which involve the very real evil of restoring the metaphysical entities previously discarded." [1]

One more general caution is suggested by another of the technical terms which we have employed. What we are concerned to discover is not so much whether mathematical reasoning is useful, but what is its " final utility " as compared with other means of research. It is likely that a certain amount of mathematical discipline—say as much as Mr. Wicksteed imparts in his excellent *Alphabet of Economic Science*—is a more valuable acquisition to a mind already stored with facts than the addition of a little more historical knowledge.

But, in reverting to the subject of final utility, I am reminded

[1] See the passage relating to Jevons in the article on Political Economy in the *Encyclopædia Britannica*, 9th edit.

that presidential addresses, like other things, are subject to this law; and that a discourse on method prolonged beyond the patience of the hearers is apt to become what Jevons called a *discommodity*.

NOTES

(a) SIMPLE EXCHANGE.—The simplest case of exchange is where there are two large groups of uncombined individuals dealing respectively in two commodities, *e.g.*, corn and money. To represent the play of demand and supply, let any abscissa, Ox in Fig. 1, represent a certain price, and let the quantity of commodity demanded at that price be xp. The locus of p may be called the demand-curve. Similarly, xq represents the quantity offered at any price, Ox; and the locus of q is called the

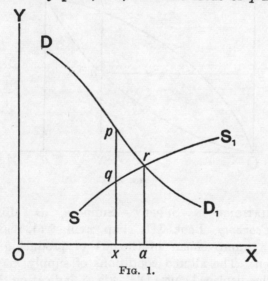

FIG. 1.

supply-curve. The price Oa, at which the demand is just equalled by the supply, is determined by the intersection of these curves. This is Cournot's construction. The converse construction, in which the abscissa stands for quantity of commodity, the ordinate for price, is employed by Mr. Wicksteed in his excellent *Alphabet of Economic Science*.

The diagrammatic representation which most closely corresponds to Jevons's formulæ is that which the present writer, after Professor Marshall, and Messrs. Auspitz and Lieben, independently, have adopted. In this construction the two co-ordinates respectively and symmetrically represent the quantities of the two commodities exchanged, the *quid* and the *pro quo*. For instance, Fig. 2 may represent the state of supply and demand in the international market between Germany and England. The curve OE denotes that in exchange for any amount of "linen," Oy, England is prepared to supply the quantity of "cloth" yp ($= Ox$); or, in other words, that in exchange for the quantity Ox of cloth England demands xp ($= Oy$) of linen. The curve OG is similarly related to Germany's supply and demand. The position of equilibrium is determined by the intersection of these curves.

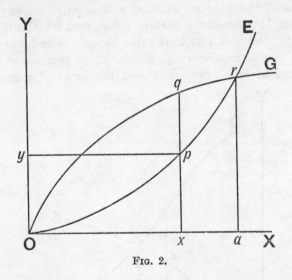

FIG. 2.

(*b*) VARIATIONS IN SUPPLY.—Suppose, as Mill supposes (*Political Economy*, Book III. chap. xviii. § 5), that there has occurred an improvement in the art of producing Germany's export, linen. The altered conditions of supply may be represented by the displaced curve OG′, Fig. 3, indicating that whereas before the improvement Germany in exchange for any quantity, Ox, of cloth offered only xq, she now offers xq'. The effect of the improvement on the rate of exchange will depend upon the form of the curve OE beyond the point r. If the intersection of the curve OE is at r_2, vertically above r, we have the case where, as Mill rather awkwardly says, the demand of England for linen increases "in the same proportion with the cheapness." The other cases in which the demand for linen—and accordingly the price, so to speak, of cloth in linen—are increased more or less than the cheapness, are represented by the points of intersection r_1, r_3.

Again the same construction may be used to facilitate the comprehension of the theory of international trade which Professor Sidgwick has recently proposed. Let the curves OE and OG′ represent the conditions of supply and demand, on the hypothesis that cost of transport is annihilated, that England and Germany are in juxtaposition. Now restore the abstracted sea, and the altered conditions of supply and demand *in a market on the English shore* will be represented by the change of OG′ to OG. According to the form of the curve OE the different effects on the rate of exchange are visible at a glance. (*Cp.* Sidgwick, *Political Economy*, Book II. chap. ii. § 3.)

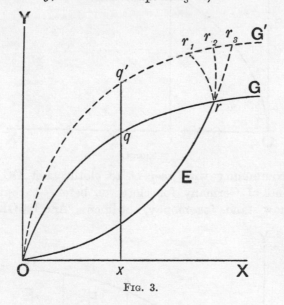

FIG. 3.

(*c*) GAIN OF TRADE.—To measure the variations in the advantage accruing from trade by the variations of price—or more generally rate of exchange—is a confusion which could hardly have occurred to the mathematical economist. The simplest method of illustrating the gain of trade is that proposed by Messrs. Auspitz and Lieben. In Fig. 4, let O*n* be the locus of a point *t*, such that a certain individual in exchange for the quantity O*x* of one commodity will just be willing to give the quantity *tx* of another commodity, will neither gain nor lose by that bargain. Then, if he obtain O*x* in return for only *rx*, he is a gainer by that bargain to the extent of *tr*. The curve thus defined is called the *utility-curve*.

By combining properly the utility-curves for all the individuals of a community, we obtain what may be called a collective utility-curve. There is a peculiar propriety in taking one axis, say the ordinate, to stand for money. Let ON then in Fig. 5 be the collective utility-curve, in this sense, for the

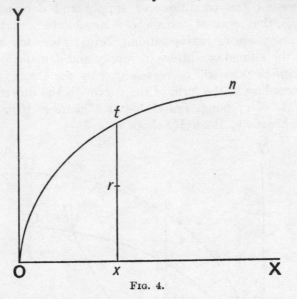

FIG. 4.

German community with respect to cloth. Let OG represent the demand of Germany for cloth, as before, except that the ordinate now stands for money, not linen. And let OE represent

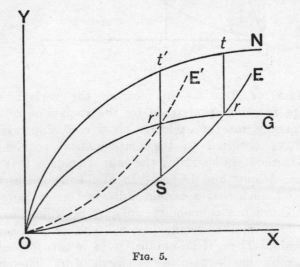

FIG. 5.

the supply of cloth in exchange for money on the part of England. Then the gain to Germany of the trade with England is represented by a vertical distance *tr*.

Now let Germany impose a tax on the import of cloth. The effect of the tax will be to displace the supply-curve OE in the manner indicated by the dotted curve OE'. Let r' be the new point of intersection between the demand—and (displaced) supply-curve. The advantage to Germany in the way of trade is now $t'r'$. To which is to be added the tax $r'S$—accruing to Germany. Since $t'S$ may very well be greater than tr, Germany may gain by the imposition of the tax.[1]

What difficulties the reader may feel about the proposition will disappear on reference to Messrs. Auspitz and Lieben's beautiful and original reasoning (*Theorie der Preise*, §§ 80–82). In the light of their constructions it will be at once seen what conditions of supply and demand are favourable to the endeavour of one nation to gain by taxing the imports from (or exports to) another. It will be noticed that the particular supposition entertained by Professor Sidgwick (Book III. chap. v. § 2)—that the quantity consumed of the taxed import is constant—is not essential.

It may be observed that the *utility-curve* is a particular case of the " *indifference-curve* " employed by the present writer (*Mathematical Physics*, p. 21). Also the lines tr and $t'S$ are particular cases of· the " preference-curve " (*ibid.*). If these more general conceptions are employed, the demonstration will not require that we should put the ordinate for money, regarded as a constant measure of utility. The interpretation assigned to the curves OG and OE in our second and third figures may still stand.

(*d*) ECONOMIC EQUILIBRIUM.—By analogy with well-known physical principles, economic equilibrium may be regarded as determined by the condition that the advantage of all parties concerned, the integrated utility of the whole economic system, should be a *maximum*. This *maximum* is in general subject, or in technical phrase *relative*, to certain conditions; in particular what Jevons called the " law of indifference," that in a market all portions of a commodity shall be exchanged at the same rate. But occasionally this condition is suspended : as often as we take what may be called a socialistic or utilitarian view as distinguished from that incommensurability of pleasures appertaining to different persons, which Jevons in a remarkable passage of his *Theory* (p. 15) has postulated. It will be found that this postulate

---

[1] The construction only applies accurately to trade on a scale so small that the opening of the trade does not alter the value of money in the country.

must be abandoned when we consider the gain of trade, as in our note (c), or the theory of combinations, as in note (l), and on other occasions.

In general, the first condition of a maximum, that the first term of variation should vanish, gives the Jevonian equations of exchange the demand curves of other writers.

The second condition of a maximum, that the second term of variation should be negative, finds its fulfilment in certain well known propositions which involve the conception of a decreasing rate of increase, viz. the law of diminishing returns, the law, or laws, of diminishing utility and increasing fatigue.

For some propositions it is proper to take account not only of the sign, but also the magnitude, of the second differential of utility. Thus when Professor Walker is contending that in case of " any increase of product resulting from the introduction of any new force into industry," the whole increment will fall to be added to the share of the working class; he argues, quite correctly upon his premises, that if the improvement does not " increase the amount of tools and supplies required in production "—since there is no greater demand for capital in the case supposed— " . . . there can be no increase in the rate or amount of interest " (*Quarterly Journal of Economics*, 1887, pp. 283 and 284). Analytically we should find that the variation in the rate of interest due to the disturbance of equilibrium, say $\Delta\iota$, was indefinitely small as compared with the variation in the rate of wages, say Δw, because the decrease in the rate at which the utility of capital increases is indefinitely great. The argument requires that this second differential should be immense at the position of equilibrium.

(e) COMPLEX EXCHANGE is the general case of simplex exchange above analysed. We have now several, instead of two, categories of dealers and commodities. In both cases equilibrium is determined upon the principle that each individual seeks to maximise his own advantage, subject to the conditions (1) that in a market there is only one price for any article, and (2) that all which is bought is sold, and all which is sold is bought. Let there be m dealers and n articles. And the first article being taken as the measure of value, let the prices of the remaining articles be p_2, p_3, . . . p_n. Let the quantities of commodities bought or sold by any individual, say No. r, be x_{r1}, x_{r2}, ... x_{rn}; each variable with its sign, *plus*, if bought, *minus*, if sold. Let the advantage of the individual, regarded as a function of his purchases and sales, be ψ_r $(x_{r1},\ x_{r2}\ .\ .\ .\ .\ x_{rn})$. There is sought the system of values assigned to the variables for which this function is a maximum, subject (a) to the condition which follows from the first assumption above made : $x_{r1} + p_2 x_{r2} +$ etc. $+ p_n x_{rn} = 0$. In order to determine the maximum of ψ_r subject to this condition, we obtain (β) by the Calculus of Variations ($n - 1$) equations of the form—

$$\left(\frac{d\psi_r}{dx_{r1}}\right) = \frac{1}{p_2}\left(\frac{d\psi_r}{dx_{r2}}\right) = \ldots = \frac{1}{p_n}\left(\frac{d\psi_r}{dx_{rn}}\right)$$

(with certain conditions as to the second term of variation). To which is to be added the equation (a). We have thus n equations relating to the rth individual. The same being true of each of the m individuals, we have in all $m\,n$ equations of the forms (a) and (β). We have also (γ), from the condition that everything which is bought is sold, and conversely, n equations of the following form : $x_{1s} + x_{2s} + $ etc. $ + x_{ms} = 0$.

But of the ($m + n$) equations of the forms (a) and (γ) only ($m + n - 1$) are independent. For adding the m equations of the form (a) we have :

$$\left.\begin{array}{l} (x_{11} + x_{21} + \ldots + x_{m1} \\ + p_2(x_{12} + x_{22} + \ldots + x_{m2} \\ + \quad - \quad - \quad - \quad \quad - \\ + p_n(x_{1n} + x_{2n} + \ldots + x_{mn} \end{array}\right\} = 0.$$

Now, if any ($n - 1$) of the equations of the form γ, say all but the first, are given, then in the last written equation the coefficients of $p_2 \ldots p_n$ vanish. Therefore the first equation of the form (γ), viz. $x_{11} + x_{21} + $ etc. $+ x_{m1}$, is also given. We have thus $mn + (n - 1)$ equations to determine $mn + (n - 1)$ quantities, viz. the x variables, which are mn in number, and the ($n - 1$) p's.

The great lesson to be learnt is this. The equations are *simultaneous*, and their solution *determinate*. That the factors of economic equilibrium are simultaneously determined is a conception which few of the literary school have received. The reader is referred for fuller statements to Professor Walras's *Économie Politique*, 2nd edit., and to Messrs. Auspitz and Lieben's Appendix IV.

(*f*) COMMERCIAL COMPETITION.—Abstracting that change of occupations which Cairnes ascribed to " Industrial " as distinguished from " Commercial," competition (comp. Sidgwick's *Political Economy*, Book II. chap. i.), let us suppose that the x's of the last note, which primarily denoted commodities ready for immediate consumption, include also agencies of production, (the use of) land, labour, and capital. We may conceive entrepreneurs buying these agencies from landlords, labourers, and capitalists, and selling finished products to the public. We have thus the appropriate idea of rent, wages, interest, and (normal) prices determined *simultaneously* (in the mathematical sense).

In a primary view of complex exchange it is proper with Jevons to regard each portion of commodity sold, each negative variable, say, $- x_{rs}$, as a deduction from an initial store, say ξ_{rs}. But when we consider production, we regard ξ as a function of the outlay of the entrepreneur. Supposing that the entrepreneur confines himself to the production of a single article, let the gross produce, in money, after replacing capital, be $f_r(c_r, \, l_r)$, where f_r is a function depending on the individual's skill, energy, opportunities, etc., c_r is the amount of capital borrowed by him, and l_r the number of acres of a certain quality which he rents. The net produce is obtained by deducting from this quantity the payments $c_r \iota + l_r \rho$, where ι is the rate of interest and ρ is the rent per acre. Thus the advantage which the entrepreneur seeks to maximise is of the form

$$\psi_r(x_{r1}, \; x_{r2} \ldots \; [f_r(c_r, l_r) - c_r \iota - l_r \rho] - x_{rr} p_{rr}, \; \ldots);$$

whence $\dfrac{df_r}{dc_r} = \iota$ and $\dfrac{df_r}{dl_r} = \rho$. The first of these equations expresses

a well-known proposition regarding the final utility of capital. The second equation expresses a less familiar condition with respect to the number of acres which will be rented on an ideal supposition of the homogeneity and divisibility of land above the margin of cultivation.

What then, and where, is the Ricardian theory of rent? Its symbolic statement is $l_r \rho = f(c_r, l_r) - f(c_r, \, o) = f_r(c_r, \, l_r) - c_r \times \iota$; where $f(c_r, o)$ is the gross produce of c_r capital laid out by the individual numbered r, on land below the margin obtainable for nothing in as large quantities as desired. It will be found that these equations postulate that the quantity of land above the margin is small as compared with the number of applicants, and that $f(c_r, \, o)$ is identical with $c_r \times \iota$, which are the common Ricardian assumptions. The validity of these assumptions as a first approximation, the need of correction where greater accuracy is required (truths which some minds seem incapable of holding together), have been admirably pointed out by Mr. Sidgwick (*Political Economy*, Book II. chap. vii. § 2). The second approximations made by him may be usefully expressed in the symbols which have been proposed, or rather in those which the student may construct for himself. I do not put forward those which occur to me as the best—if, indeed, there is any absolutely best in the matter of expression. For some purposes it would have been proper to take account of the various qualities of land (as I have elsewhere done—*British Association Report*, 1886). For other purposes it would be well to put labour hired by the entrepreneur as an independent variable. When this or any other variable is omitted, we are to understand that there is implied the best possible arrangements with respect to the variables which are not expressed. The nature of this implication is shown in the following note.

(*g*) So far we have been taking for granted that the entrepreneur does his best, without reference to the motives acting upon him, the pleasures procurable by the sale of his product. Formally it would be proper to take account that the utility-function ψ_r involves the *effort*, say e_r, explicitly, as fatigue diminishes advantage, and implicitly, as exertion increases production. Corresponding to the new variable we have a new equation, the complete differential of ψ_r, with reference to e_r, say $\left(\dfrac{d\psi_r}{de_r}\right) + \left(\dfrac{d\psi_r}{df_r}\right)\dfrac{df}{de_r} = 0.$ It is a nice question how far effort should be regarded as an independent variable; how far the essential principle of piece-work prevails in modern industry.

(*h*) INDUSTRIAL COMPETITION.—The condition that net advantages should be equal in industries between which there is mobility may thus be contemplated. Let us put the advantage of an individual, say No. r, engaged in the occupation s as a function of his net income, the price of the articles on which his expenditure is made, and the disutility of effort. Say ϕ_{rs} (f_{rs} ($\pi_1, \pi_2, \ldots . e_{rs}$), $p_1, p_2 \ldots . - e_r$); where ϕ_{rs} is a utility-function, not necessarily the same for the same individual in different occupations, since his indulgences may vary with the nature of his employment; f_{rs} — a symbol not identical with the f of the last but one note—is the individual's net earnings in the business s, involving prices $\pi_1, \pi_2,$ etc., of all manner of agents of production, involving also as stated in note (*g*) the effort e_{rs}; p_1, p_2, etc., are prices of articles of consumption as a function of which the individual's advantage may be obtained by means of the equations (*a*) and (*β*) in note (*e*)— eliminating the quantities consumed. The last variable in the function ϕ_{rs}, the explicit e_{rs}, has a negative sign prefixed, to indicate that the direct effect of increased fatigue is diminished advantage.

The equation of Net Advantages imports that the advantage, ϕ_{rr}, of the occupation of which the individual chooses is not less than ϕ_{rs}, the advantage of any other occupation open to him. It is important to observe that for all occupations the complete differential with regard to e is zero ; in symbols $\left(\dfrac{d\phi}{d\mathfrak{f}}\right)\dfrac{d\mathfrak{f}}{de} + \left(\dfrac{d\phi}{de}\right) = 0.$ But this equation conveys no presumption that the final disutility in different occupations is the same that $\left(\dfrac{d\phi_{rs}}{de_{rs}}\right) = \left(\dfrac{d\phi_{rt}}{de_{rt}}\right).$ The equation of final disutility holds only where efforts and sacrifices are capable of being applied in " doses " to any number of occupations. The latter is the only case, I think, contemplated by Jevons in his analysis of Cost of Production (*Theory*, chap. v.). The inquiry, what is meant in general by saying that the cost of production of two articles is equal, must start from right conceptions about Final and Total Utility. But this is not the place to follow up the difficult investigation. I do not attempt here to discuss any matter fully, but only to illustrate the suitability of the subtle language of mathematics to economical discussions.

(*i*) PROFESSOR WALKER'S THEORY OF BUSINESS PROFITS.— Professor Walker's theory, as stated in the *Quarterly Journal of Economics* for April, 1887, involves the proposition that the remuneration of the lowest, the least gifted employers, is on a level with that of the labouring class. Concerned as we are here with methods rather than results, it is allowable to posit this premiss without expressing an opinion as to its accuracy. It is fortunate not to have to take side on an issue concerning which the highest authorities are divided, and statistical demonstration is hardly possible.

But, though the expositor of method is not called upon to dispute the truth of this proposition, he has something to say against the evidence which has been adduced in proof of it. He must enter a protest against the form of the following argument :—

" Let our hypothesis be clearly understood. We assume, first, that there is in a given community a number of employers, more or fewer, who alone are, by law or by custom, permitted to do the business of that community, . . . or else who are so exceptionally gifted and endowed by nature for performing this industrial function that no one not of that class would aspire thereto, or would be conceded any credit or patronage should he so aspire. Secondly, we assume that neither in point of ability nor opportunity has any one member of this class an advantage as against another . . . all being, we might say, the exact copies of the type taken, whether that should involve a very high or a comparatively low order of industrial power.

" Now, in the case assumed, what would be true of business profits, the remuneration of the employing class ? I answer that if the members of this class were few, they might conceivably effect a combination among themselves, and . . . fix a standard for their own remuneration. . . . If, however, the community were a large one, and if the business class . . . were numerous, such a combination . . . would be impracticable, . . . the members of the business class would begin to compete with each other. From the moment competition set in it would find no natural stopping place until it had reduced profits to that minimum which, for the purposes of the present discussion, we call *nil*.

" What, in the case supposed, would be the minimum of profits ? I answer : This would depend upon an element not yet introduced into our problem. The ultimate minimum would be the amount of profits necessary to keep alive a sufficient number of the employing class to transact the business of the community. Whether, however, competition would force profits down to this low point would depend on the ability or inability of the employing class to escape into the labouring class. We have supposed that labourers could not become employers; but it does not follow that employers might not become labourers and earn the wages of labourers. . . ."—(*Quarterly Journal of Economics*, 1887, p. 270 and context.)

This reasoning will puzzle those who have received the abstract theory of supply and demand as formulated by the mathematical school [above, notes (a) and (d)]. Because the dealers on one side of a market, as the employers in the labour market, compete against each other without combination, it does not follow that the advantage which they obtain from their bargains is *nil*. The *minimum* to which the play of competition tends is not necessarily small in the sense of a bare subsistence. It is a *minimum* only in the mathematical sense in which every position of equilibrium is a minimum (of potential energy in physics ; in psychics, may we say, of potential utility. See note (d)).

Representing the entrepreneur's demand for work by the curve OG (Fig. 5), where the abscissa measures work done, and the ordinate money payable out of the wages and profit fund, and putting OE for the offer of the workmen, we see that the point r may be distant to any extent from the utility-curve ON, which indicates the advantage of a transaction (see note (c)). As far as abstract theory, without specific data, carries us, the competing entrepreneurs may make very good bargains. They may be ever so prosperous; they may be, in Burke's fine phrase, " gambolling in an ocean of superfluity."

So far, on the hypothesis that neither in point of ability nor opportunity has any one member of this class an advantage as against another. The heterogeneity of faculty will, of course, introduce a graduation of gain. But in this flight of steps it is not necessary that the lowest should be on a level with the grade of common labour. The scale of profits may be a sort of Jacob's ladder, culminating in a paradise of luxury, and having its lowest rung suspended high above the plain of ordinary wages.

Let us suppose, however, that the writer has tacitly made some assumption as to the numbers of the " numerous " business class relatively to the " large " community (compare the parallel passages in his *Political Economy*, pars. 280, 236). Still what does the consideration of business profits as rent do more than the received principle of supply and demand ? If the workmen, believing that in the distribution regulated by competition too much has been assigned to brain and too little to muscle, determine to reduce profits by means of a combination, should they stay their hand because they are told that profits (above the lowest grade) are of the nature of rent ? The terms " rent " and " margin " may indeed suggest that the extra profits of the abler entrepreneurs exactly corresponds to their greater ability. It might seem that if, so to speak, we pushed down all the higher faculties to the level of the lowest grade of business power, the diminution of the total distributed, of the wages and profits fund, would exactly correspond to the subtraction from the earnings of the degraded entrepreneurs, while everything else remained constant. Conversely it might be argued that the increment of produce due to the existence of superior ability may justly be assigned as extra profit.

But how little appropriate is this precise conception will at once appear from the annexed diagram. Let OE in Fig. 6 represent the entrepreneur's demand, OW the workmen's offer of the labour, the abscissa representing work done, and the ordinate wages payable out of the wages and profits funds (abstraction being made of interest and rent for land). Let OE be formed by the composition of Oe_0, the collective demand curve for the lowest entrepreneurs, and one or more curves, such as Oe_1, appertaining to the entrepreneurs of higher ability. Now let us shrink these higher natures to the zero of business ability. The individual demand curve for each degraded entrepreneur will become identical with that from which Oe_0 was formed (by the combination of all the demand-curves for the lowest grade). The new demand-curve will therefore be of the form OE′ intersecting with OW as at the point r'. (Whether the disturbance will stop there will depend upon the nature of the communication between the departments of employer and workman; whether the mobility is one-sided, like that of fluid allowed by a valve to escape from one vessel to another, but not back again—see the end of the passage cited on our p. 301 from the *Quarterly Journal of Economics*—or whether the permeation is perfect.) If Oe_0 is small, if the part played in production by the marginal employers is insignificant, it is probable that the annihilation of

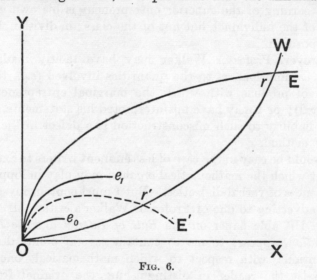

FIG. 6.

the higher grades will result in the destruction of the greater part not only of profits, but also of wages.

Accordingly it appears in general inexact to say that the "surplus which is left in the hands of the higher grades of employers . . . is of their own creation" (*Quarterly Journal of Economics*, April, 1887, pp. 274 and 275); if we define their own creation as the difference between the actual produce and that which would have existed if their superior faculties had not been exercised. In that sense (and what other sense is there?) the surplus of the higher grades is likely to be much *less* than their own creation (especially in the case where the marginal employers are relatively few). We seem to have proved too much. But may we not deduce the *quod est demonstrandum*, that actual profits are deserved, from the larger proposition that the entrepreneurs " own

creation " is by a certain amount greater than their profits ?
No ; for that larger proposition is blocked by the antinomy that
the workmen (or the higher grades of them) may by parity claim
the greater part of the produce as *their* " own creation "—what
would not have existed but for the exertion of their faculties.

In short, we know no more than we knew at first—viz. that
the distribuend is produced jointly by the owners of brain and
muscle, that the terms of the distribution are determined by
supply and demand, and that in this, as in every other market,
each more favoured nature enjoys a *rent*, or differential advantage [the nature of which is well illustrated by Messrs. Auspitz
and Lieben's construction indicated in our note (*c*)]. That the
surplus earning of the superior entrepreneur is his own creation
is true of the individual, but not of the class ; in division, but not
in composition.

However, Professor Walker may have tacitly made some
specific assumptions as to the quantities involved (*e.g.*, the proportion of produce with which the marginal entrepreneurs are
concerned) ; or I may have misinterpreted his statements. Even
so, the liability to such misconstruction is a defect in the purely
literary method.

It would be easy in the case of less eminent writers to exemplify
the part which the mathematical *organon* may play in lopping the
excrescences of verbal dialectics. But I must content myself with
briefly adverting to one of Professor Walker's critics, Mr. Sidney
Webb. His able paper on the *Rate of Interest and the Laws of
Distribution*, appears to me to contain several points deserving
of attention ; with respect to which mathematical conceptions
may assist the reader in distinguishing the original from the
familiar, and the true from the misleading.

(1) Mr. Webb restates the theory formulated by Jevons, that
capital is ideally distributed according to the law of " equal
returns to the last increments." (*Rate of Interest and Laws of
Distribution*, by S. Webb, pp. 10, 11, and 21 of paper reprinted
from *Quarterly Journal of Economics*, January, 1888.)

In symbols (see above, note (*f*), p. 562) let the net earning of
any individual be $f_r(c_r) - \iota c_r$; where f_r is a function differing for
different individuals according to their faculties and opportunities,
c_r is the amount of borrowed capital employed by the individual ;
ι is the rate of interest ; land and labour are not expressed. In
equilibrium

$$\frac{df_r(c_r)}{dc_r} = \iota = \frac{df_s(c_s)}{dc_s} = \frac{df_t(c_t)}{dc_t} = \ldots$$

(2) Again, Mr. Webb discerns that the " law of diminishing returns " is applicable to capital as well as to land (*ibid.*, pp. 9 and 20, etc.). This is probably a new truth to the literary economist, who will have some difficulty in reconciling it with the *law of increasing returns* received into the text-books. To the mathematician it is evident that, in order to maximise the net earnings $f(c) - \iota c$, not only must the first differential of this expression vanish, but also the second differential $\dfrac{d_2 f}{dc^2}$ must be negative, which is the *law of diminishing returns*. It is quite consistent with the supposition that for certain values of the variable, not admissible as a solution of the problem, $\dfrac{df}{dc}$ should be positive, agreeably to the *law of increasing returns*.

(3) Mr. Webb dwells much on " the special industrial advantages not due to superiority of site or skill " which are enjoyed by some individuals. The use of an expression for the product like our f_r may serve at least to keep in mind the existence of such specialities. It also brings into view a difficulty which has not been sufficiently noticed by those who use *rent* in its metaphorical or secondary sense.

Suppose the extra produce is a function involving several variables (or parameters) like land, ability, opportunity. Say $f_r = F(\lambda, a, \omega \ . \ . \ .)$, where F is a form common to the community, and λ, a, ω denote the quality of land, ability, and opportunity peculiar to the individual. If the extra produce is $F(\lambda \ a \ \omega) - F(o, o, o)$; is $F(\lambda, o, o) - F(o, o, o)$ the " economic rent " of land, $F(o \ a \ o) - F(o, o, o)$ the rent of ability, $F(o \ o \ \omega) - F(o, o, o)$ the extra produce due to opportunity ? (*Ibid.*, pp. 16 and 17.) If so, the three parts do not make up the whole !

(4) Anyway, to call the third extra produce *interest* is very unhappy. Its affinities are evidently with rent. (*Cp.* Sidgwick, *Political Economy*, Book II. chap. vii. § 4.)

(5) I should not have complained about the use of a term, but that it is connected with Mr. Webb's main contention against Professor Walker, to which I am unable to attach significance : that " this, not the ' rent of ability,' is the real keystone of the arch." (*Ibid.*, p. 17.) From the point of view here taken (above, p. 276) this search for the " keystone " among the factors of distribution is nearly as hopeless as the speculation of the ancients about the real *up* or *down*.*

* There is here omitted a note (designated " J " in the original) dealing with the phenomenon of " increasing returns," upon the supposition that the collective

(*k*) ONE-SIDED MONOPOLY.—In Fig. 7 let the curve DD′ represent the demand of the public for a monopolised article, the abscissa denoting price, the ordinate quantity. Then, as Cournot shows, if there are no expenses of production the rectangle O*yrx* should be a *maximum* (*Recherches*, art. 25); or rather the *greatest possible*. The solution is not likely to be indeterminate, except in the particular case where the demand-curve is an equilateral hyperbola. Indeterminateness is similarly exceptional when there are expenses of production (*cp.* Sidgwick, *Political Economy*, Book II. chap. ii. § 4).

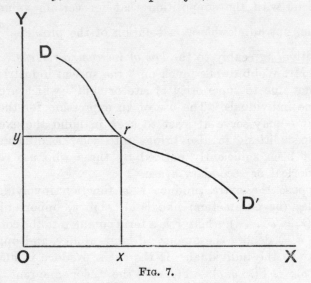

FIG. 7.

(*l*) TWO-SIDED MONOPOLY.—In Fig. 8 let O*p* and O*q* represent the curves of constant satisfaction, or indifference curves (above note (*c*); *Theorie des Preises*, Appendix II.; *Mathematical Psychics*, p. 21) drawn through O for two individuals or combinations respectively. Then the locus of bargains which it is not the interest of both parties to disturb is the *contract-curve, pq* (*Mathematical Psychics*, loc. cit.). At what point then on this curve will the transaction settle down? If we assume that the conditions of a market are retained, the required point is at *r* the intersection of the supply- and demand-curves which is on the contract-curve. That is the solution of Messrs. Auspitz and

---

supply-curve is formed by simple addition from curves of which each represents the offer of an individual at an assigned price, and at one and the same time. This treatment is now obsolete, not taking into account the possibility of " external economies " explained by Dr. Marshall subsequently to the publication of the present paper.

Lieben (*Theorie*, p. 381). It corresponds to the principle laid down by Professor Marshall for the action of arbitrators (referred to above in note to p. 279). But Professor Menger, who has a numerical scheme equivalent to a rudimentary contract-curve (*Grundsätze*, pp. 176–8), and Professor Böhm-Bawerk, referring to the " Spielraum " afforded by the indeterminateness of bargain, recommend to " split the difference." Instead of " equal," " *equitable* " division has been proposed by the present writer, namely, that adjustment which produces the maximum of utility to all concerned ; not subject to the conditions of a market, but irrespectively thereof (equations (β) and (γ), without equation (a)

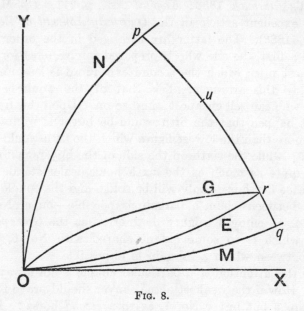

FIG. 8.

in note (*e*) above), the utilitarian arrangement, which also is represented by a point in the contract-curve, say *u* in Fig. 8. Such might seem to be the ideally most desirable arrangement ; but very likely the practically best, the πρακτὸν ἀγαθόν, is in the neighbourhood indicated by Professor Marshall and Messrs. Auspitz and Lieben.

(*m*) THE AUSTRIAN SCHOOL.—Professor Menger and his followers have expressed the leading propositions of the economic calculus—the law of diminishing utility, the law of demand and supply, and so forth—by means of numerical examples, supplemented with copious verbal explanation. Their success is such as to confirm the opinion that the mathematical method is neither quite indispensable nor wholly useless, *nec nihil nec omnia*, like most scientific appliances. Conceding that in the main they impart a saving knowledge of the true theory of value, it may still be maintained that they occasionally emphasise the accidents of a particular example as if they formed the essence of the general rule; that their explanations are excessively lengthy; and yet their meaning sometimes is obscure. For instance Professor Böhm-Bawerk may seem to attach undue importance to his conception of the *Grenzpaar*. He illustrates the play of demand and supply by supposing a market in which on the one hand there are a number of dealers each with a horse to sell, and on the other hand a number of would-be buyers (Konrad's *Jahrbuch*, 1886; *Kapital* . . ., p. 211. *Cp.* Mr. James Bonar's excellent article in the *Quarterly Journal of Economics*, October, 1888). The latter are arranged in the order of their strength : first, the one who is prepared to give most for a horse, the highest price which the second can afford is less, and so on. Parallel to this arrangement is that of the would-be sellers : first, he who can sell cheapest; and so on. Upon this hypothesis it might happen that the fifth would-be buyer is willing to give a little more than the lowest figure which the fifth would-be seller will take; while the sixth on the side of the buyers is not willing to give quite as much as the sixth horse-dealer stands out for. In this case five horses only will be sold; and the couple who are the last between whom a bargain is possible—buyer No. 5 and seller No. 5—enjoy a mighty distinction as the *Grenzpaar ;* an honour which is to some extent shared with No. 6, the first couple between whom a bargain is impossible.

Now this attention to a particular couple is not always appropriate. How if the weakest actual buyer should prove to be, not buyer No. 5 but buyer No. 1, as to a *second* horse ? Professor Böhm-Bawerk, indeed, has thought of this case, and called attention to it in a note to his later redaction (*Kapital* . . ., p. 218).* So far—although the whole simplicity of the scheme is destroyed when we permit second and third horses to the different buyers and sellers—the conception of a " limiting couple " may still be retained. It will be found, however, that this idea is not appropriate to the general case of a divisible commodity, which a single individual on one side of the market may buy from or sell to a large number on the other side. That general case is much more clearly represented by a diagram like Fig. 9, where the inner broken curves represent the dispositions of the individual dealer, the outer thick curves collective supply and

* But see note to **B**, Vol. I. p. 37 below.

demand (*cp.* Auspitz and Lieben, *Theorie des Preises*). No doubt Professor Böhm-Bawerk's conception is appropriate to a particular case, that in which the *Kleinste Marktübliche Mengeneinheit*, in the phrase of Messrs. Auspitz and Lieben (*ibid.*, p. 123), is considerable. But it is better with those eminent theorists to begin with the general or, at least, the simple case.

As an instance of the excessive circumlocution to which the purely literary method is liable, we may notice the doctrine of objective and subjective value, which occupies many pages in one of the works to which we have referred. Is there really much

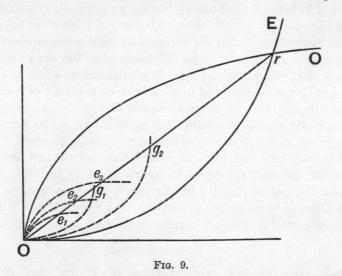

FIG. 9.

more in the distinction than what is visible on a glance at the appropriate diagram? The individual's subjective estimate of worth is expressed by his particular demand- or supply-curve Oe_1, Oe_2, Og_1, Og_2, etc., in Fig. 9. The proper combination of those individual curves gives the collective demand- and supply-curves, of which the intersection represents the " objective " value.

Moreover, verbal circumlocutions are so little adapted to express mathematical conceptions that we are sometimes left in uncertainty as to our author's meaning. When Professor Böhm-Bawerk remarks that there is something special in the labour market, in that the buyer will vary his arrangements according to the price of the article, the rate of interest (*Kapital* . . ., p. 407), does he specify the property which Messrs. Auspitz and Lieben have stated as general; that the utility function (our ψ, note (*e*) above) is discontinuous, being different for large and small values of the variable under consideration?

These deficiencies are more conspicuous in other writings of
the Austrian school.   A glance at Fig. 9, an intuition of the
corresponding algebraic formulæ, will show that the notion of
an *average* imported into the doctrine of value by Dr. Emil Sax
(*Staatswirthschaft*) is not quite appropriate. As an instance in
which great abridgment would be effected by mathematical
expression, we might notice the last three chapters of Dr. Zucker-
kandl's *Theorie des Preises*. Again the difficulty of conveying
technical propositions without the proper phraseology may be
illustrated by Professor Wieser's *Der natürliche Werth*, when he
speaks of value and final utility having place in a communistic or
socialistic state (page 26 note and *passim*). May his meaning
thus be formulated ? In an economical regime distribution and
exchange are regulated by the condition that the final utility of
all concerned should be zero, the total utility a maximum, *subject
to the law that there should be only one rate of exchange in a market*.
In a communistic or utilitarian regime the limitation which the
last italicised clause expresses is removed. In terms employed
in our note (*e*) the economical adjustment is determined by the
equation (*a*), (*β*), and (*γ*); the utilitarian adjustment is determined by (*β*) and (*γ*) only—in short, there is the distinction
between the points *r* and *u* in our Fig. 8 referring to note (*e*).

In offering these trenchant criticisms I regret that my limits
impose a curtness which is hardly consistent with courtesy.

(Note referring to p. 281.)

[A passage in this paper relating to Walras was severely
criticised by Professor Bortkevitch in the *Revue d'Économie Politique*,
January–February, 1890. He rightly connected the passage with,
and interpreted it by, a review of Walras's *Éléments d'Économie
Politique Pure* (deuxième édition) which I had contributed to *Nature*
(September, 1889). I replied to Professor Bortkevitch's criticisms in
the *Revue d'Économie Politique*, January 1891. Looking back at
these controversial writings—the Address here reprinted and the
contemporary review in *Nature*, Professor Bortkevitch's criticism, and
my rejoinder—I desire to withdraw any passage which suggests that
Walras was at a disadvantage, as compared with Jevons, in that he
did not analyse the final disutility of labour so fully and exactly as
Jevons did. Professor Bortkevitch (*loc. cit.*) and Professor Pareto
(*Giornale degli Economisti Cambi Forestieri*, 1894) are right about
that. It was not necessary for Walras's purpose that he should do in
that matter exactly as Jevons had done. There is not the connection,
which I incidentally suggested but now disown, between Walras's
difference from Jevons in this respect and his agreement with Jevons

in another respect which constituted the gravamen of my criticism. But I do not retract the remarks which apply equally to Jevons and Walras : namely, that while they elaborated " final "—or, as we now say, " marginal "—conditions, they left untouched the all-important condition that the *total* utility—the " net advantages," in the phrase introduced by Marshall—in different occupations should be equal (above, p. 280). It was not made a matter of reproach that this condition had not been treated mathematically. Rather, it was pointed out that it would have been very difficult to do so. In my rejoinder of 1891 I illustrate the difficulty by reference to a problem in Todhunter's *Calculus of Variations*, which has for *quæsitum* not simply a *maximum* (or *minimum*), but the *greatest* (or *least*) *possible* value ; to determine the course of a ship between two given points, so that the voyage may be accomplished in the shortest possible time. A stroke of the pen gives us the *marginal* condition, from which it follows that the course must be rectilinear. But a series of tentatives may be required to determine what combination of right lines affords the quickest passage. (On the difference between a *maximum* and the *greatest possible* value as the *quæsitum* compare ECONOMIC JOURNAL, 1922, p. 435, and references there given.)

It is not a matter of reproach to mathematical economists to have stopped short of these complexities. But economic theory, as distinguished from mathematical expression, does require the recognition of the important principle designated by Cairnes as " Industrial Competition " and its opposite, " Non-competing Groups." Now Walras's peculiar doctrine of an entrepreneur who makes neither gain nor loss cuts him off from this essential principle. Nothing must everywhere be equal to nothing ; and it is difficult to see how the equality—or it may be inequality—of profits in different occupations can be reconciled with this favourite tenet of the Lausanne School. Of course it may be tolerated as an extreme abstraction ; a simplification permissible to a path-breaker (*cp.* Pareto, *loc. cit.*). But it seems to deserve pardon rather than praise.

In two of the writings mentioned, the review in *Nature* and the article in the *Revue d'Économie Politique*, criticism is directed against another part of Walras's *Éléments :* namely, his description of the process by which the price in a market is evolved. He describes *a* way rather than *the* way by which economic equilibrium is reached. For we have no general *dynamical* theory determining the path of the economic system from any point assigned at random to a position of equilibrium. We know only the statical properties of the position ; as Jevons's analogy of the lever implies (*Theory*, p. 110 *et seq.*). Walras's laboured description of prices set up or " cried " in the market is calculated to divert attention from a sort of higgling which may be regarded as more fundamental than his conception, the process of *recontract* as described in these pages and in an earlier essay (see β). It is believed to be a more elementary manifestation of the propensity to truck than even the effort to buy in the cheapest and sell in the dearest market. The proposition that there is only one price in a perfect market may be regarded as *deducible* from the more axiomatic principle of recontract (*Mathematical Psychics*, p. 40 and context).]

(β)

ON THE DETERMINATENESS OF ECONOMIC EQUILIBRIUM

[THIS is a translation of an article which appeared under a slightly different title in the *Giornale degli Economisti*, 1891. The inquiry takes its start from a passage in the then recently published second edition of Marshall's *Principles*, where he adduces from the present writer's essay on *Mathematical Psychics* a construction there largely employed in the investigation of economic equilibrium, the *contract-curve*. Apart from this connection the discourse is not closely related to the text. For Marshall in the passage cited has in view a market in a special sense distinguished from normal, whereas the process which I analyse has much in common with the determination of normal equilibrium. Besides, as argued by Mr. Berry in the same volume (XL.) of the *Giornale*, the term "determinate" is used by Marshall in a somewhat different sense from that which I have adopted.

Apropos, it may be remarked that there is a certain indeterminateness about the use of the term "determinate" by economists. Thus Pareto has demurred to the description (above, **E**) of the transactions between two monopolists as indeterminate. There being more equations than unknowns, the problem, he thinks, cannot properly be described as "mathematically indeterminate."

I dispute no man's definition of terms; concerned, rather, with the truth of propositions. The proposition which I seek to establish here relates to a typical market consisting of two groups of individuals, say A's and B's : the A's offering the commodity a in exchange for β supplied by B's. Each A makes agreements with B's independently of and not in concert with other A's; and the B's likewise act independently. The term "market" applied to this transaction is not to be understood in a sense opposed to "normal" or "natural." Rather there is conceived to be a certain normality about the proceedings. They need not be supposed to take up a long period; rather the contrary, since the disposition and circumstances of the parties are assumed to remain throughout constant. But it is supposed

313

that agreements are renewed or varied many times. A " final
settlement " is not reached until the market has hit upon a set
of agreements which cannot be varied with advantage to all the
re-contracting parties. The re-contract most favourable to the
disturbance of a temporary equilibrium is one in which an A deals
with a great many B's. If that power is not used, *e.g.*, if each
A confines himself to dealing with one B, it is quite possible (as
will appear below) that re-contract thus hampered would not
disturb the equilibrium. Thus the condition that perfect finality
should be reached may be stated as follows, in the case, say, of
equal numbers on both sides of the market, m A's and m B's;
it must be impossible for any number of A's, say $m-n$, dealing
(each for himself) with any number of B's to enter into a new set
of agreements with advantage to all the re-contracting parties.
Since in general the less restriction there is on the number of B's
who re-contract the greater is the possibility of a new equilibrium,
the condition is adequately expressed by the proviso that it
should not be possible for $(m-n)$ A's to re-contract with *all*
the B's. This " all " has proved a stumbling-block to a critic
who writes in the same *Giornale* for June, 1891. But I think
it might have been difficult to recall the explanation above given
by any other concise phrase. I trust that I shall not suffer like
the plaintiff in the old state of the English Law who lost his case
because in describing an article which had been stolen from him
he spoke of a " ham " where he should have used the words
" part of a ham." At any rate before condemnation is passed,
reference should be made to the writer's essay on *Mathematical
Psychics ;* on which the article in the *Giornale* is largely based.
In the reproduction of the article here presented I have omitted
several long passages which purported to be restatements of
theories more accurately enunciated in that essay.

I illustrate the theory of determinate equilibrium by two
examples in which first appearances are deceptive. There is first
the case in which the marginal utility of both articles for at least
one of the parties varies with the terms of an agreement. This
circumstance may seem at first sight unfavourable to determinateness. It may be to some kinds of determinateness, but not to
that which has been above defined. Rather, it is the general
rule that both articles should vary in respect of final utility for
both parties. If we have to do not with the general problem,
but with the particular case in which the marginal utility of
one commodity remains constant—as in the instance cited below
from Auspitz and Lieben—the equilibrium does not on that

account, I think, become more determinate than in the general case, theoretically at least, and apart from " friction."

If this view is correct, indeterminateness is not to be attributed to the labour market, because the marginal utility of money varies with the price of labour that may be set up. But a certain indeterminateness is to be attributed to that market for a quite different reason, namely, the circumstance that a man cannot, or at least does not, simultaneously serve two masters. This point is disputed by the aforesaid critic in the *Giornale* (June, 1891). But, as appears from the passages cited below from the *Giornale*, he seems not to have taken account of an essential condition in our problem, viz., that the competing work-people should not act in concert.]

The theory of Exchange is founded on the principle of Barter, which has been discussed by Marshall with remarkable originality and accuracy. He has avoided the common error of attributing to two persons who are bargaining with each other a fixed rate of exchange governing the whole transaction. A uniform rate of exchange, he remarks, is applicable only to the case of a perfect market. By way of example he puts the case of A having a basket of apples and B a basket of nuts; A desiring nuts and B apples. Referring to this example, I would express the process of barter mathematically in the following manner.

Let the abscissa x denote the number of apples given by A and received by B; the ordinate y, the number of nuts given by B and received by A. Thus every point in the plane (x, y) represents a barter of so many apples for so many nuts. Let u be the utility, or satisfaction, of A so far as it depends on the one hand on the number of nuts that he gains, and on the other hand the number of apples that he retains, that is the number initially in the basket less by the number that he has parted with. Let v be the similarly defined advantage of B.[1] Bartering will continue as long as it is possible for both parties to gain thereby. Let Δx be the *quid* given by A and Δy the *pro quo* received by him at any stage of the transaction. The process of exchange

---

[1] It may assist the formation of correct conceptions to put $u \equiv \phi_1(a - x) + \psi_1(y)$, where a is the original stock of apples; with a corresponding expression for v. But we are not limited to this simple form. We are at liberty to use for it an expression of the form $\chi(a-x, y)$.

can only continue as long as the gain (of satisfaction) by A and likewise B's gain is positive; in symbols,

$$\frac{du}{dx}\Delta x + \frac{du}{dy}\Delta y > 0. \quad \frac{dv}{dx}\Delta x + \frac{dv}{dy}\Delta y > 0.$$

Now this condition will cease to be fulfilled when the total quantities exchanged, x and y, are such as to satisfy the equation

$$\frac{du}{dx}\frac{dv}{dy} = \frac{dv}{dx}\frac{du}{dy}.$$

The locus thus represented I have called the *contract-curve*.

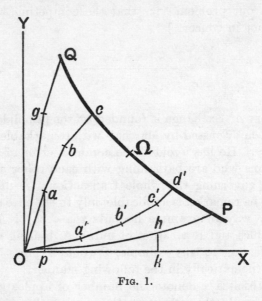

Fig. 1.

In Fig. 1 any point, for instance a, denotes the exchange of, or contract for the exchange of, the number of nuts represented by the ordinate ap against the number of apples expressed by the abscissa Op. The series of short lines Oa, ab, bc, corresponds to successive barters (at different rates of exchange) of a few nuts for a few apples. The broken line $Oa'b'c'd'$ indicates a possible set of exchanges more favourable to B.

Alike at c and at d' the bartering comes to a stop, those points being situated on the contract-curve PQ. Of this curve the only part with which we are concerned is that which is intercepted by the *curves of constant satisfaction*, or *curves of indifference*, for A and B respectively which pass through O; viz., OhP and OgQ. The *curve of indifference* which passes through a given point is the locus of all the contracts that procure to the contractor the same satisfaction as the contract designated by the given point. For instance, the contract designated by the point h, that is Ok apples given for hk nuts, or, again, the contract designated by P, procures for the contractor A the same satisfaction as the contract (or absence thereof) designated by O. It is indifferent to A whether he makes either of the first two deals, or none at all. Similarly, it is indifferent to B whether the dealing is represented by the point O, or g, or Q.

At what point on the tract of contract-curve between P and Q the process of bartering will come to a stop cannot be predicted. The position of equilibrium may be described as indeterminate. The essential condition of this indeterminateness is the absence of competition.

The essential condition is not to be sought in an incident of the case before us, namely, that the marginal utility of both the commodities varies in the course of the dealing. The phenomenon of indeterminateness may very well exist without that incident. Whether or not the marginal utility of one commodity, say y, is regarded as varying with the additions or subtractions incidental to exchange, there will always remain—in the case of barter between two individuals—an indeterminate tract on the contract-curve, every point of which is a position of equilibrium. True, the curve will sometimes degenerate into a right line parallel to one of the axes.[1] An example is furnished by Messrs. Auspitz and Lieben in that part of their important book in which they discuss the contract between a monopolist entrepreneur and a union of operatives. Assuming that the marginal utility of money may be treated as constant, they justly observe that " the determination of price seems to be between wide limits arbitrary."

Thus the imperfections of the labour market do not depend on the circumstance that the marginal utility of money varies for the work-people according to their bargain with the employers, according as their wages afford only bare necessities or superabundant luxuries. The imperfections of that market are rather

---

[1] In symbols if the final utility of y is constant for both dealers, we may put for u the satisfaction of the contractor A the expression $\phi_1(a-x) + \alpha y$, and for v (pertaining to B) $\phi_2(x) + \beta y$; where α and β are constants. Accordingly we obtain for the contract-curve $\dfrac{\phi_1{}'(a-x)}{\alpha} = \dfrac{\phi_2{}'(x)}{\beta}$; or x = constant; representing a line parallel to the axis of y. This line fulfils the characteristic condition of the contract-curve that at any point of the locus the inclination of the tangent to a curve of indifference passing through that point should be the same for both parties.

to be sought in certain peculiarities which Marshall has pointed out, as noticed at the conclusion of this paper.

Apropos of impediments to the play of competition in the labour market there may be observed from the point of view here adopted two incidents which are more curious than important.

Suppose that every A can contract with only one B, and likewise every B with only one A. Then it is no longer possible that $(m-n)$ A's—each acting independently—should form a set of new contracts with all—or any number of—the B's (and likewise impossible for $(m-n)$ B's to re-contract); which variation of contracts—when it can be effected with advantage to all the re-contracting parties—is here regarded as the essential attribute of competition. Accordingly, the equilibrium would be in the case supposed as indeterminate for a set of couples, as we have seen that it is in the case of a single couple. There may possibly exist types of domestic service which fulfil the supposed condition. But practical importance is not claimed for this *curiosum*.

There is another unobserved peculiarity of the labour-market which is the more curious in that it constitutes a positive advantage to the work-people in their dealings with entrepreneurs. Suppose that the system of contracts is initially at any point on the contract-curve (Fig. 1) d' on the right of the position hereinafter defined Ω; that is to the advantage of the B's who supply the article y. It may be shown that the advantage which the B's thus possess is lost through the action of $(m-n)$ of their number who carry off, so to speak, the whole (or a large part) of the A group.* Suppose now that the A's are work-people, the B's entrepreneurs. The terms first proposed may be very much to the advantage of the entrepreneurs. But they will lose that advantage through competition against each other. Assuming that an entrepreneur can employ several men, it will be to his advantage to offer to some of his rivals' workmen better terms than they were receiving, and so carry them off. And this process will theoretically continue until the system of agreements reaches the position of stable equilibrium symbolised by the point Ω, the point at which the demand curves (not shown in the figure) intersect on the contract-curve. Analogously it might be supposed that if the terms are at first too favourable for the work-people, if, for instance, the point c (left of Ω) represented an initial system of contracts, the work-people would lose that advantage, by mutual competition. But such competition would imply, according to our analysis, that a workman

* See note at end of article.

takes on several entrepreneurs; that a man *can* serve two masters simultaneously. In the case of painters, no doubt, and many home-workers plurality of employers is common. Still, the general rule is that no man can serve two masters, and so far as this is true the work-people have an advantage over the entrepreneurs in that they cannot equally beat down the price of their services by mutual competition.

I do not, however, regard these nice points as more than *curiosa*, of little practical importance in comparison with the conditions of the labour-market on which Marshall has dwelt; in particular, the tendency of any accidental disadvantage under which the work-people may be suffering to become perpetuated through the lowering of their vitality and efficiency, and the fact that employers are few in comparison with the number of work-people. In this field Marshall has thoroughly reaped the harvest, leaving nothing to those who come after him but to glean some logical niceties.

(Note referring to p. 318.)

[The argument that if a rate of exchange unduly favourable to the work-people is set up they will not beat the price down by their mutual competition is disputed by an able critic in the June number (1891) of the *Giornale*, on grounds of which the following quotation (*loc. cit.* p. 553) contains the gist. " Though it is true that ' no man can serve two masters,' yet it is quite possible for a number of work-people to increase the number of entrepreneurs whom they serve. If, on average, 100 work-people serve one employer, 500 may at pleasure renew their contract with six or with four. The first proceeding tends, according to Professor Edgeworth's reasoning, to favour the entrepreneurs, the second the work-people."

To which I reply in the October number of the *Giornale* (1891) suggesting that the critic has not taken account of the condition that the work-people should not act in concert.

" Say five entrepreneurs employ each on average 100 men. Four of these entrepreneurs are disposed to employ a larger number of workmen, and they offer higher wages, each finding that he can thus make a bargain more advantageous for himself and for his employees. What can be simpler? But now consider the opposite case. How can 400 work-people originally employed by four entrepreneurs find occupation with five entrepreneurs by way of an initiative on the part of the work-people, each acting independently, and not in concert with others. This case is not analogous to the first; because it is not in the power of any operative to purchase, so to speak, a fraction of an entrepreneur, other than, or in addition to, that which he already enjoys in virtue of his present engagement."]

VARIORUM THEORIES ON CONSUMERS' SURPLUS, RENT, DUOPOLY, ENTREPRENEURS' REMUNERATION

[IN this Paper published under the title " Appreciations of Mathematical Theories," ECONOMIC JOURNAL (pp. 221–231 and pp. 524–531), 1907, some points raised by (then) recent writers on mathematical economics are discussed. Attention is called to Professor Pigou's views on utility or " satisfaction " as an object of economic theory, and its relation to utilitarian ethics. There is raised the question how far it is possible and desirable to contemplate simultaneously—as it were in one and the same picture—a series of (short-period) laws of demand (or supply) which change with time and circumstance (*cp.* Review of Cunynghame). The properties and proper designation of Consumers' Surplus are also considered.

Professor Flux suggests a variant of the construction commonly employed to represent the return of agricultural produce to successive " doses " of outlay. He proposes to represent the *total* return by an ordinate corresponding to an abscissa representing outlay. This representation would have the advantage of fixing attention on what we know in general about the relation of the product to the outlay, namely, its increase at a decreasing (or sometimes increasing) rate with the increase of outlay. The concavity (or convexity) of the curve traced by the extremity of the ordinate representing total production exhibits the character of diminishing (or increasing) returns without bringing into view so conspicuously as in the alternative scheme the assumption involved in the shape of the diagram about a coefficient not known to us, the rate at which the rate of decrease (or increase) varies, the third differential of product with respect to outlay.

In connection with the discussion on outlay and return, reference is made to the old theory that improvements in the art of cultivation are apt to be attended with a fall in rent.

Professor Loria's principal contribution to the Symposium consists of an objection to our description of the indecisive fight between monopolists (**E**); on the ground that in concrete fact they would cease fighting and make a compact. In this connection the reader should bear in mind that the monopolists to whom the theory relates are not necessarily purveyors of the *same* article. The articles which they respectively control may be not identical, but only partial substitutes for each other. They may be not substitutes for, but *complements* of, each other. The difference in the kind of indeterminateness, according as the articles are rival or complementary, is illustrated in the ECONOMIC JOURNAL, September 1922 (Review of Amoroso).

The theory propounded by American theorists, that the remuneration of the entrepreneur is exactly equatable to the loss which his removal from industry would occasion, is examined in the light of Professor Chapman's constructions; and it is found that the proposition is neither quite true nor very useful.]

Some theories which have recently been published in the ECONOMIC JOURNAL are the object of the following reflections :—

I. Beginning with Mr. Pigou's article in the ECONOMIC JOURNAL for 1903,[1] I remark that he has justly described the relations between the economic measure of utility and the philosophic doctrine of utilitarianism. The measure of utility proposed by Dupuit is applicable in its first intention and obvious interpretation to a great number of transactions.[2] But the cautions with which the second author of the method has qualified its statement [3] are often required. His followers are not committed to Mill's doctrine, " that to think of an object as desirable (unless for the sake of its consequences), and to think of it as pleasant, are one and the same thing; and that to desire anything except in proportion as the idea of it is pleasant is a physical and metaphysical impossibility." [4] Like Browning, as elsewhere portrayed by Mr. Pigou, the philosophical economist may think of himself as " able, if he so chooses, to resist his own pleasure-seeking desires " . . . " not an inert mass chained, as Bentham believed, to the irresistible power of imagined pain and pleasure." [5] It is not inconsistent with the use of the money-measure to indulge in a disinterested pursuit of the happiness of others, or even aim at some good distinct from the joy of

---

[1] " Some Remarks on Utility," ECONOMIC JOURNAL, Vol. XIII. p. 58.
[2] *Loc. cit.*, p. 68, last par.
[3] Marshall, *Principles of Economics*, Bk. I. ch. iii. § 5, note.
[4] *Utilitarianism*, p. 58.
[5] *Browning as a Religious Teacher*, p. 103.

sentient beings.   Nor can the technical apparatus for the measurement of economic utility be employed for " the summation of
total happiness." [1]

Agreeing with the general tenor of Mr. Pigou's remarks on
these sublime topics, I still think that the economic measure of
utility may have some tendency to establish the end proposed
by utilitarianism, and considerable efficacy in supplying means
thereto.   Economics cannot indeed prove that to procure the
greatest possible sum of satisfaction for all is the criterion of
what is right for each.   But the authority of an accredited
science is lent to show that this object is not absurd [2] as some
metaphysicians have suggested :   T. H. Green, for example,
when he says that " the aggregate of possible enjoyments " of
which modern utilitarians tell us " simply represents the vain
attempt to get a definite by the addition of indefinites.   It has
no more meaning than ' the greatest quantity of time,' would
have." [3]   A scruple worthy of the Eleatic school is solved by
walking in the way of the modern economist.   To some it is not
simply the addition of pleasures, but the addition of pleasures
belonging to different persons, which forms a stumbling-block.*
The familiar and successful application of the conception collective total utility, *Gemeinnutzen*,[4] is calculated, I think, to
dispel this prejudice.   Moreover, the technical apparatus may
conceivably be employed as a means towards ascertaining the
greatest possible sum of satisfaction in a utilitarian sense, in
two large departments of economics which border on ethics and
politics.   A utilitarian end, the least possible sacrifice on the
part of all concerned, may be accepted as the criterion of taxation.[5]   Against the principle of arbitration between combinations
there has been suggested the maximum total utility, not so much
that of society as a whole, as that of the parties to the agreement.[6]

However we define the " satisfactions " which are measured
by the method under consideration, the question may arise :
With what unit are they measured ?   Professor Irving Fisher's
unit, " the desire of an arbitrarily chosen individual A for a
small increment of a given commodity under given circum

---

[1] Pigou, ECONOMIO JOURNAL, *loc. cit.*, p. 68.

[2] *Cp. ibid.*, 1895, p. 587.

[3] Introduction to the moral part of Hume's Treatise, § 7.   [*Cp.* Sidgwick
Lectures on Ethics of T. H. Green.]

* To Jevons even, *Theory of Political Economy*, p. 14.

[4] Auspitz and Lieben, *Theorie des Preises*, p. 23 *et passim*.

[5] *Pure Theory of Taxation*, above, S.

[6] Index, s.v. *Arbitration*.

stances," is preferred by Mr. Pigou to a " just perceivable increment of pleasure." * Perhaps it is better to say, with Professor A. Voigt,[1] that no unit is required : quantities like utility
are to be measured only by *ordinal* numbers. In confirmation
of this conception Professor Voigt refers to the view, now prevalent
among mathematicians,[2] " which sees in ordinal number rather
than in cardinal the primary conception of number." †

In a first view of the measure under consideration utility
may be considered as related to money in the way of a continuous function. Thus if travel is the commodity enjoyed,
and a lowering of fares (which may be supposed to be reckoned
on the " zone " system) enables the consumer to procure more
of this article, he may simply take new tours, in addition to
those which he would take even at the higher fare. He may,
however, be induced by the change of fares to rearrange his
whole scheme of travel. The difficulties connected with such
change of function appear to be minimised by the plan which
Auspitz and Lieben have adopted for representing total utility.

A more serious disturbance of the relations between Demand
and Total Utility arises when the amount that any one person
demands is affected by the amount which other persons demand.[4]

* This unit was proposed in my essay on *Mathematical Psychics*. I have
suggested that its use has some affinity to physical measurement.—*Mind*, 1922,
p. 274.

[1] " Zahl und Mass in der Oekonomie," *Zeitschrift für die Gesamte Staatswissen-
schaft*, 1893, No. 3; referred to in the ECONOMIC JOURNAL, Vol. III., p. 202.

[2] *Cp.* Professor Love in the article on " Functions of Real Variables " in the
Encyclopædia Britannica, Ed. X. Vol. 28.—" The capacity of numbers to answer
questions of how many and how much—in other words, to express the results of
operations of counting and measuring—may be regarded as a secondary property
derived from the more fundamental one of expressing order. Natural
numbers form a series with a definite order, and the expression ' greater than '
and ' less than ' mean ' more advanced ' and ' less advanced ' in this order."

† *Cp.* Poincaré's pronouncement on the measurement of utility; cited below
(θ), p. 472, and published by Walras in the brochure *Économique et Mécanique*,
Lausanne, 1909.

[3] *Theorie des Preises*, pp. 9, 78, 87, 141, *et passim*.

[4] The conception may be illustrated by the common supposition that at social
gatherings which are cheered by alcoholic beverages the consumption of liquor per
head is likely to be greater the more numerous the company. An opportunity of
testing this belief is afforded by the varying size of the dinners at a certain Oxford
College whose members are thought to be susceptible to the influences of good
fellowship. The dinners on the Sundays during that part of the Terms which is
described as " full " seem well suited for the purpose of verification, the number
varying considerably—from seven to forty-two in the course of the period which
I have observed—while the character of the entertainment is not otherwise
materially altered. The amount of wine (of different kinds) drunk on each
occasion, and the cost thereof, have been recorded. I have utilised the records
for four years, 1903–1906 inclusive, employing the following assumptions. I
take the cost of the wine consumed as the measure of the quantity; and I take the

Mr. Pigou, improving on Mr. Henry Cunynghame's speculations

variations in the quantity consumed per head as an index of variation in effective demand.   The demand is, indeed, not measured as usual : for the total cost of the wine drunk on each occasion is divided equally among all who have taken part in the potation.   Accordingly the final utility of the last dose which an individual consumes is not, as in ordinary cases, balanced by the cost of that dose ; the set-off is only an nth part of that cost, where n is the number of the company.   I assume, however, that this peculiarity does not appreciably stimulate the consumption of wine at a College dinner, and that the amount of wine drunk at these social gatherings may be taken as an index of effective demand, just as well as if each individual, as happens at Club dinners, paid for what he individually consumed. I may add that if the circumstance which I neglect were really of account, the conclusion to which I am coming would be *a fortiori*.   To test whether the size of the party has any influence upon the depth of the potations, I first find the average size of a party, and then I find the average cost per head, on the one hand, for parties that are below the average size, and on the other hand for parties that are above the average size ; for each year, and for the whole period.   The results are exhibited in the subjoined table.   For example, in the year 1906 the records of 25 Sunday dinners were examined.   The average attendance was 21 (the smallest attendance being 10, the largest 42).   The average cost per head of the wine drunk at all the 25 dinners in 1906 was a sum which comes to 95·4 per cent. of the average cost per head of the wine drunk at all the 102 parties in the four years 1903–6.   The average cost of the wine drunk at those dinners numbering 12 (or more exactly construed, 12½), at which the number of diners was below the average for the year, was 97 per cent. of the aforesaid general average for the whole period. The average cost for the parties at which the numbers were above the average of the year was 93·8 per cent. (of the general average for the whole period).   I have thought it sufficient to give the costs as percentages.   The statement of the actual figures is forbidden by a scruple such as that which deterred Gibbon from disclosing the amount of his income ; lest he should excite the envy of some and the contempt of others.

	Number of parties.	Average size of party.	Cost per head per cent. of average cost for period 1903–6.		
			Small parties.	Parties of all sizes.	Large parties.
1903	25	18·4	99·8	*103·4*	106·2
1904	26	17·8	97·6	*99·8*	101·7
1905	26	19·2	104·5	*101·4*	98·3
1906	21	21·0	97·0	*95·4*	93·8
1903–6	98	19·1	100·5	*100*	99·4

It appears from an inspection of this table that no constant or considerable excess of consumption is shown by the larger as compared with the smaller parties. When it is added that the " probable error " incident to the difference between the average consumption of large parties and that of small parties in any one year is about 3 per cent. (per cent. of the general average cost as before), it will be apparent that in this example the influence of the amount demanded by all on the average demand of each is inappreciable.

on this subject,[1] points out that a " consideration of the distribution of the commodity, as well as of the mere quantity of it," should be taken into account.[2] His elaborate formulæ far transcend the resources of statistics ; but they subserve the useful purpose which Dupuit, referring to the impossibility of determining even the simpler law by statistical observation, has thus indicated : " quand on ne peut pas savoir les choses c'est déjà beaucoup que de savoir qu'on ne sait rien." [3]

The theory improved by Mr. Pigou has useful analogies with the extended theory of supply. The latter, indeed, does not, I think, equally require the consideration of distribution. But both theories profit by the method of representing the element of time which Mr. Pigou has exhibited in a subsequent article.[4] As I understand his construction, " the ordinary demand curve," at a time which is represented by a point on the axis of X, is in a plane passing through that point, parallel to the plane of YZ; Y denoting the scale of consumption, and Z the price. The diagrams, which are presented at successive epochs, do not occur like the slides which an exhibitor inserts in a regular sequence into his lantern. What diagram at the time $x + \Delta x$ will succeed the diagram presented at the time x will not depend simply on the time. To continue the metaphor, according as a certain index [the intersection of the supply- and demand-curves] is directed to one point or another in the diagram pertaining to the time x, the diagram at the time $x + \Delta x$ will take on different shapes.[5] The curve which expresses the movement of the scale of production in time is like the path of a particle in a Galtonian error-machine, a path determined partly by a prearranged constitution of things, partly by accidents affecting each step. The pre-arrangement forms the portion of truth in Mr. Cunynghame's doctrine that " a group of successive curves is the expression of a state of facts existing at one time, and is not a group of successive time phenomena."

[1] ECONOMIC JOURNAL, Vol. II. p. 37.

[2] The new conceptions of collective in relation to individual demand are analogous to the departure in the theory of probabilities according to which the elements or components which generate the law of error are no longer regarded as perfectly independent (see *Journal of the Statistical Society*, 1906, Vol. LXIX.). When each element is correlated with the sum of all, we have a simple case like that conceived by Mr. Cunynghame (*cp.* review reprinted Vol. III. p. 138); the case in which each element is correlated with some only of the other elements resembles Mr. Pigou's more exact conception.

[3] *Annales des Pontes et Chaussées*, 1844.

[4] *Monopoly and Consumers' Surplus*, ECONOMIC JOURNAL, Vol. XIV. p. 388.

[5] I have stated my meaning more fully in a criticism of Mr. Cunynghame's doctrines in the ECONOMIC JOURNAL, Vol. XIV. p. 63 *et seq.*

Referring to Mr. Pigou's article on "Monopoly and Consumers' Surplus," I select, among many points worthy of notice, his account of the pressure whereby the monopolist is able to exploit the "consumers' surplus" of his consumers. It may be suggested that the position of the monopolist is strengthened when the total amount which he controls is, or is supposed to be, limited.[1] The consumers of mineral water controlled by a monopolist, as in Cournot's illustration, are likely to agree to his terms more quickly when it is known that he has only a fixed quantity of the commodity per day at his disposal.

I cannot dismiss this article without commending Mr. Pigou for having followed the highest authority on the subject in substituting "consumers' surplus" for "consumers' rent." I submit that it is better to limit the term "rent" to the income derived from things the supply of which is limited, and cannot quickly be increased,[2] or some neighbouring definition, rather than to extend the term, as suggested by Professor Clark,[3] to all kinds of differential gains. Rent, as defined above, is a species of surplus which differs from other kinds of surplus in important respects.[4] These nice distinctions may be contemplated more clearly if different words are used for the species, rent, and that which is predicated thereof, the genus surplus.

II. An easy transition leads to Professor Flux's article in the ECONOMIC JOURNAL for 1905, of which a leading feature is the use of a line to represent the surplus constituting economic rent. Professor Flux's construction may be regarded as a variant of that which is employed by Messrs. Auspitz and Lieben.[5] The use of the ordinate rather than an area seems to have, on the side of supply, the same sort of advantage which we have already attributed to it on the side of demand;[6] it smooths over discontinuities of function.[7] A similar construction is suitable to represent producers' surplus considered as depending on several

---

[1] The description given by Mr. and Mrs. Webb of the bargain between the individual workman and the capitalist employer is very instructive : *Industrial Democracy*, Part III. ch. ii. p. 654, ed. 1902.

[2] See Marshall, *Principles*, Bk. II. ch. iv. § 7.

[3] See his article in the *Quarterly Journal of Economics*, 1891, and his book, *Distribution*. The claims of the wider definition are ably stated by Dr. J. Schumpeter in his paper on *Das Rentenprinzep* in the *Jahrbuch für Gesetzgebung*, 1907.

[4] As shown by Professor Marshall's *Principles*, pp. 479, 626 *et passim*.

[5] So far, at least, as Professor Flux uses the ordinates to represent *money* Reference should also be made to J. D. Everett's *Geometrical Illustrations of the Theory of Rent* read before the British Association, and published in the *Journal of the Statistical Society*, 1899.

[6] Above, p. 323.

[7] *Cp.* Flux, *loc. cit.*, p. 282, referring to his Fig. IV.

variables. Thus if the outlay of borrowed capital is measured on the axis of X, the amount of land rented on the axis of Y, the surplus accruing to a particular farmer, or to farmers collectively, may be represented as the intercept between a certain plane corresponding to Professor Flux's line O E, and a certain surface corresponding to his curve O P.[1] Of course, this is a very abstract conception, neglecting, *e.g.*, sales at particular times and in particular markets on terms which would not pay if adopted generally, and other incidents of a somewhat monopolistic character.[2]

But I must keep to the subject " improvements and rentability." Among the " controversies of a past age " to which Professor Flux recalls attention is the thesis that the " sudden and general introduction of agricultural improvements " would tend to lower rent.[3] I gather that Malthus took the opposite side from Ricardo and the Mills on this question, since he held that the tendency of rents to decrease might be " counterbalanced by extraordinary improvements in the modes of cultivation."[4] I do not understand that Professor Flux takes either side in this controversy. His construction may indeed be employed to show that neither the Ricardian thesis nor its contradictory is universally true. The mathematical weapon to which Professor Flux has imparted new refinement may be directed against the Ricardians with at least as much effect as Mr. Cannan has turned against them their own primitive instrument of arithmetical illustration.[5]

But I submit that the Ricardian thesis is not refuted by the proof that it is not universally true. For, interpreted generously, the theory purports to be only *probable*. The probability with which we have here to do is not merely the sort of credibility short of certitude which characterises empirical knowledge generally, but rather a species of presumption not founded on specific experience, which is peculiar to the Calculus of Probabilities. Such is the postulate that when an event must occur in one of two ways, and is not known to occur more frequently in one way than another,[6] then the event may be considered

---

[1] Cp. *Quarterly Journal of Economics*, 1904, Vol. XVIII. p. 165.

[2] *Cp.* ECONOMIC JOURNAL, Vol. VII. p. 238.

[3] J. S. Mill, *Political Economy*, Bk. IV. ch. iii. § 4.

[4] Quoted by Professor Flux, *loc. cit.*, p. 277.

[5] *Theories of Production and Distribution*, p. 322 *et seq.*

[6] While, if there was a difference of frequency, it would have come to our knowledge—I am disposed to add, in accordance with the view which I have expressed respecting " The Philosophy of Chance."—*Mind*, 1884.

as equally likely to occur in one way as in the other. With this may be connected the postulate that—in the absence of specific knowledge to the contrary—the coefficients with which we have to deal have not extreme values; in particular that the differential coefficients are not infinite; and accordingly the functions not discontinuous; and so forth. These probabilities might be conveniently called " *a priori*," from their use in the Calculus. I have elsewhere [1] dwelt on this kind of probability as required in the human sciences, and content myself now with an additional example. Investigating the incidence of our import duties Mr. Pigou properly begins an argument thus : " Presuming, as in the absence of knowledge is reasonable, that the elasticity of production is the same at home and abroad." [2] So Mr. Bickerdike, in a paper to which we are coming, properly presumes that the coefficients of elasticity with which he has to do have not extreme values. [3]

Now let us apply this principle to the problem in hand, one datum of which, it should be remembered, is that the total quantity of corn [4] consumed before and after the improvement is the same. We suppose with Mill " population stationary, and a sudden improvement made in the arts of production "; [5] and we also follow Mill in treating it as a matter of general knowledge that of an article, " such as the habitual food of the people of England, wheaten meal," " there is probably as much consumed, at the present cost price as there would be with the present population at a price considerably lower." With these presuppositions, and—to begin with—treating the amount of land used as constant, let us look first at the construction which Professor Marshall has made familiar, in which the degrees of the abscissa represent successive doses of outlay and the ordinates the corresponding increments of " corn." [6] The total area of produce being constant, the consequence of an improvement is to shorten the abscissa representing the amount of capital which

---

[1] Explicitly and in general in the article in *Mind*, which has been referred to, and in *Metretike* a pamphlet published in 1887 by the now defunct Temple Company; summarily, and with reference to Economics, in *Giornale degli Economisti*, 1897, Vol. XV. p. 318; and in ECONOMIC JOURNAL, *passim*. See Index, s.v. *A priori probabilities*. [See also *Mind*, 1922, p. 261.]

[2] *Protective and Preferential Import Duties*, p. 29.

[3] ECONOMIC JOURNAL, Vol. XVI. p. 532. *Cp.* Vol. XVII. p. 100 *et seq.*

[4] J. S. Mill, *Political Economy*, Bk. IV. ch. iii. § 4, par. 1. *Ibid.*, par. 5, " if no greater produce is required."

[5] *Ibid.*, Bk. III. ch. iii. § 2, par. 2 ; Bk. III. ch. ii. § 4, par. 2.

[6] Used in the general sense defined by Professor Marshall, *Principles o Economics*, Bk. V. ch. viii. § 3, par. 1, with reference to the classical theory of rent.

is laid out on the given land; and to lengthen the ordinates representing the returns to doses of capital—if not for every dose, every value of the abscissa, at least in general, and on the whole so that an equal area may stand on that smaller value of the abscissa which represents the capital outlay after the improvement. We must give up the pretension to formulate the variation in the law connecting the ordinate with the abscissa. We must neither affirm that the improvements always add an equal absolute amount to the produce of each of the successive doses of capital, nor yet that they always add an equal percentage.[1] But we may argue, I think, that there is no reason for expecting the average slope of the new curve to be either larger or smaller than that of the old curve; that as to its general trend the new curve will *probably* resemble the old one. It follows that corn rents will probably go down; and money rents very probably.

The argument is easily translated into the form proper to Professor Flux's construction. The argument is, I think, not affected by taking into account the circumstance that the amount of land rented by an entrepreneur-farmer is theoretically in general variable.[2]

III. I go on to the year 1906, which was fruitful in mathematical contributions. There is first the article [3] in which Professor Loria has honoured me by his criticism. Referring to an article of mine in the *Giornale degli Economisti* of 1897,[4] some of which is embodied in the ECONOMICAL JOURNAL of the same year,[5] Professor Loria, as I understand, does not traverse the abstract reasoning which I have applied to the case of dual monopoly. Rather he appeals to what may be called scientific common sense when he intimates that the case is not worth treating, since it could not long exist : " the two monopolists, instead of carrying on an unprofitable war . . . will settle the value between them." Now if each of the monopolists were producing the same article, this consummation might, perhaps, with propriety be assumed as the general rule. As Mill says, in a passage which is surely remarkable when the date at which it is written is taken into consideration, which is, perhaps, even

[1] *Cp.* Cannan, *loc. cit.*

[2] The relation between rent and the productivity of the marginal dose of land is elegantly exhibited by Mr. J. D. Everett in the paper which has been referred to, *Journal of the Statistical Society*, 1899, p. 707.

[3] Marshall and Edgeworth on Value. ECONOMIC JOURNAL, Vol. XVI. p. 365.

[4] *Giornale degli Economisti*, II. pp. 23–24 (misprinted " ECONOMIC JOURNAL," in the reference given in a note to Professor Loria's article).

[5] Vol. VII. pp. 237–8.

truer now than it was then, " Where competitors are so few they always end by agreeing not to compete." [1] But the two monopolists whom I am considering are not always producers of the same commodity. That case might be of no practical importance, and yet its analysis might be useful, for the sake of the analogous concrete cases in which the two monopolists control *correlated* articles, either " complementary " or " rival." These two cases are hardly comprised under Professor Loria's description of my theory : " it is assumed that the production of a given commodity is monopolised by two producers only." [2] I gave as instances of complementary articles owned by different monopolists the ground and the water-power required by millers.[3] The following comment on this case was given in the article of the same date in the ECONOMIC JOURNAL :—

" The theorem may have some bearing on a system which is regarded by some as the ideal of the economic future, that each industry should be consolidated into a trust or combination. Such a system would be characterised by instability, by fluctuations of prices such as now occur in railway wars, but more prolonged; for in so far as the combatants, like the two landlords in the example given, are not direct competitors, the combat seems less likely to be terminated by either the ruin of one party or the amalgamation of the two." [4]

I admitted that when the two monopolists supply rival commodities amalgamation is more apt to occur.

" But," I added, and still submit, " even in this case the proposition that value is between certain limits—over a certain range of prices—indeterminate, may well be of theoretical importance." [5]

The problem raised in Cournot's Chapter VII., as well as the problem of his Chapter IX.,[6] may repay attention. If he was not right in his solution of either problem, he may have been right in thinking them both worth solving.[7]

As to the remainder of Professor Loria's article directed against Professor Marshall's theory of value it would be presumption on my part to speak on behalf of one so capable of

[1] *Political Economy*, Bk. I. ch. ix. § 3, par. 3.

[2] ECONOMIC JOURNAL, Vol. XVI. p. 366.

[3] *Giornale, loc. cit.*, p. 20 *et seq.*

[4] ECONOMIC JOURNAL, Vol. VII., above, S, p. 99.

[5] *Loc. cit.*

[6] It is discussed in the *Giornale degli Economisti*, 1897. Above, E.

[7] Some considerations supporting this judgment will be found in the article on " Paradoxes of Competition," by Mr. Henry L. Moore, in the *Quarterly Journal for Economics*, Feb. 1906.

defending himself as Professor Marshall. I am concerned to notice only one point in the position which Professor Loria attacks. It appears, from the context of the passage in the *Principles of Economics* [1] to which Professor Loria adverts, that Professor Marshall is there dealing with market value in the sense in which it is contrasted with normal value. He adduces [2] a mathematical construction adapted to his purpose; which I notice here only because I am about to adapt a similar construction to a somewhat different purpose, contemplating not market value but normal value. I shall not suppose two sets of dealers to meet and settle their bargains at one go-off, so to speak. On the contrary, I shall suppose them to meet again and again under like initial conditions continually renewed, and to resume bargains until a system of contracts, not likely to be varied by recontract, has been set up. A conception of this sort [3] is required for the full discussion of the topic to which I proceed, Professor Chapman's remarks on the " Remuneration of Employers." [4]

IV. Continuing my examination of mathematical theories contributed to the ECONOMIC JOURNAL, I come to Professor S. J. Chapman's article on the " Remuneration of Employers." [5] Professor Chapman takes up a question which has been agitated in recent economic literature,[6] whether the remuneration of an employer is to be regarded as just equal to his final productivity in the same sense as the remuneration of the workman, or more generally the payment for a unit of any agent of production. He brushes away [7] the more extreme statements of this analogy which would oblige us to suppose the entrepreneur's work capable of being bought by the piece, like an ordinary commodity. As I understand, Professor Chapman rightly addresses himself to this issue : whether, if an additional employer is taken on, the total product of a society tends to be increased by an amount that is just equal to the normal remuneration of an employer. It is thus that the thesis has been conceived by one of its ablest supporters,

[1] *Principles*, Bk. V. ch. ii. Note on Barter.

[2] In his Mathematical Appendix.

[3] I have endeavoured in the article on " The Theory of Distribution " in the *Quarterly Journal of Economics*, 1904, Vol. XVIII. p. 187 *et seq.*, to win conceptions appropriate to normal exchange value. [Vol. I., **B.**]

[4] ECONOMIC JOURNAL, Vol. XVI. p. 523.

[5] See *ibid.*, December, 1906.

[6] For a *résumé* of authorities and arguments see the article on " The Theory of Distribution," Vol. I., **B.**

[7] Chapman, *loc. cit.*, p. 528.

Professor T. N. Carver. " The law of marginal productivity,"
he says,[1] " can be applied to the earnings of business management
as well as to the wages of other labour. The amount which any
individual business man can get by means of his superior management (not through his superior bargaining capacity [2]) depends
upon the amount which he can add to the product of the community over and above the amount which it would produce
without his help."

Assuming that there exists only one industry, and making
other simplifications which are legitimate with reference to the
extremely abstract proposition under consideration, Professor
Chapman supposes z employers, each managing a firm in which
there are x employés, the total number of employés in each of
the firms being constant, say c. The wage of an employé in any
firm is the addition to the product of the firm which is made by
taking on an additional employé; multiplying that final productivity by x, the number of employés in any firm, we obtain the
total wages paid in any firm; subtracting the total wages from
the product of the firm, we have (making a legitimate abstraction
of other agents of production) the profits of an employer. Professor Chapman investigates the question, whether if the number
of employers be increased from z to $z + 1$, the addition thus made
to the total produce of all the firms will be just equal to the
profits of an employer. He finds the new and remarkable result
that this equation holds good, so long as we abstract the effect
on the organisation of industry which may be produced by the
introduction of an entrepreneur. It is a nice question how far,
through what range of instances, it may be legitimate to neglect
this effect. Professor Chapman is no doubt right in treating
the effect as not negligible in general. Distinguishing the cases
in which an increase of entrepreneurs " raises or lowers the curve
of marginal value of labour to employers," [3] he finds that the

[1] *The Distribution of Wealth*, p. 263. *Cp.* p. 262 :—" That is the amount
which the community is able to produce with his [the business man's] help over
and above what it could produce without his help, and this is the only sense in
which any factor can be said to be productive."

[2] The parenthesis is explained by the remarks at p. 261.

[3] He uses the hard-worked terms " increasing and diminishing " returns to
distinguish these cases. The use of these terms is apt to breed confusion, because,
as I have elsewhere pointed out (see Index, s.v. *Increasing Returns*), there are
two essentially different meanings, according as that which diminishes (or
increases) is (1) the rate at which product increases with the increase of means,
or (2) the product divided by the means, the share of a unit factor of production in the product. A further sub-division is formed by the distinction between
(*a*) the cases in which there is only one species of means, and (*b*) the general case
of several kinds of factors. The definition of 1*b* is not obtained by mere

statement in question exceeds or falls short of the truth, according as one or other of these cases prevails.

The proposition, then, is not in general true. It might still, however, be useful if it were true in a typical case. It might then, in our ignorance whether it exceeds or falls short of the truth, be treated as the most *probable* general statement; upon the principle of *a priori*—or unverified—probability [1] which was adduced in a preceding section.

This sort of usefulness proves to be less than it appears to be at first sight, when, pushing the investigation up to first principles, we consider the labour market as a species of the general theory of exchange. The mathematical method of presenting this theory may, it is hoped, become more popular now that M. De Foville has recognised it by employing curves of Demand and Supply to explain the " mechanism of prices." [2] M. De Foville would certainly not have diverged from the literary method in which he excels, unless, in his authoritative judgment, the advantages of the technical expression had justified the departure from classical usage.

The Corn-market, M. De Foville's illustration, is not the only type of market to which curves of Supply and Demand are appropriate. They apply also to transactions in factors of production, such as the labour-market; and not only to " market value " in the sense of the term which refers to short periods, but also to " natural " or normal value, provided that the periods considered are not so long but that the dispositions, and " disponibilities " in M. De Foville's phrase, may be supposed constant. [3] We are to conceive two groups of dealers encountering each other, not once only, but from time to time, and ascertaining by repeated tentatives a rate of exchange at which a steady flow of trade is maintained. [4] With respect to this kind of exchange we may say of the mathematical representation, in M. De Foville's words,

---

composition from the simple case of 1*a*; the character of a *maximum* which distinguishes diminishing returns now involves an additional condition. Likewise 2*b* differs from 2*a* in requiring a principle of distribution among the different factors.

Professor Chapman's use of the terms may be referred to the heading 2*b*.

[1] The use of the term *a priori* is unhappy so far as it is employed to mean, not only, as here intended, probabilities established by general presumption, without specific experience, but also " antecedent " probabilities which enter into the investigation of causes (*cp.* Mill, *Logic*, Book III. ch. xviii.) Probabilities which are *a priori* in the second of these senses are often, but not always, *a priori* in the first sense. [See Index, s.v. *A priori probabilities*.]

[2] In his last book, *La Monnaie*, p. 150.

[3] A conception favoured by the stability of averages.

[4] See Index, s.v. *Normal Equilibrium*.

" This image, purely symbolical though it is, is good to keep in mind, because it tells us clearly and roundly (*nettement*) that in a free market there is nothing arbitrary in the formation of the prices." That under stable conditions things tend to a definite level, is not the only lesson to be derived from the mathematical method. It is also employed to answer questions of this sort : If the conditions are disturbed in an assigned manner, in what direction will the level be altered ? One example of such problems is afforded by the imposition of a tax; another example, by the addition of a new dealer on one side of the market—in the case before us a new entrepreneur put on the labour-market.

To start from first principles, let us suppose the market to consist of a set of dealers X_1, X_2, etc., on one side, and another set Y_1, Y_2, etc., on the other side; each X supplying commodity x in return for commodity y, and likewise each Y supplying commodity y in return for x. The attainment of a determinate level at which exchange is maintained is explicable by two principles : (a) contract, and (b) competition.[1]

(a) In virtue of the first principle, if any X deals exclusively with only one Y, they will agree to vary the terms on which they deal up to a limit at which further variation would cease to be advantageous to one or other of the parties.[2] Even if one X is not restricted to dealing with only one Y, a similar statement still remains true with respect to the *final increments* disposed of by each X and Y.

(b) Now let competition be introduced. Then, as M. De Foville has it, " we won't see (*on ne verra guère*) transactions concluded simultaneously on different bases. Why should Peter give up for twenty francs what Paul has just sold for twenty-five ? " If each X is restricted to dealing with only one Y, and, conversely, the number of X's and Y's being equal, then the position of one X will be as good as that of another X, and likewise the positions of the Y's will tend to equality. Yet the positions are not determinate.[3]

Now let us render competition perfect by removing this

---

[1] Cp. *Mathematical Psychics*, by the present writer.

[2] A point on the *contract-curve* relating to the two parties considered (*loc. cit.*).

[3] If, for the sake of illustration, we suppose all the X's to be of one type in respect of their dispositions or disponibilities, and likewise all the Y's to be of one type (not the same as that of the X's), then the system, which, under the supposition of the preceding paragraph, consisted of a set of points on the contract-curve between an X and a Y, is now reduced to a single point on the contract-curve. But that point is not determined without the condition of perfect competition, which is about to be introduced in the text.

restriction. Then the conditions of equilibrium will no longer be satisfied by an indefinite number of arrangements. For in general it will be possible for a dealer of one type or the other, e.g., an X, say Xr, to offer his commodity x in small parcels to several Y's on such terms that not only each of these Y's disposes of a parcel of his y to greater advantage than before, but also the position of Xr, as defined by the total quantity of x which he gives, and the total quantity of y which he receives in exchange, is bettered.[1] This sort of disturbance will continue until an arrangement is reached in which every portion of x is exchanged for a portion of y at one and the same rate; a rate such that every X gets as much y as he is willing to purchase, and not more than he is willing to purchase, at that rate; and every Y is similarly satisfied.

This " symbolical image " is no doubt an artificially simplified representation of the actual processes by which a uniform rate of exchange comes to be determined. It is thus that, in a first view of the molecular theory of gases, the physicist is allowed to imagine a system of equal perfectly elastic spheres. If we are to compare our theory with the hypotheses of Mathematical Physics, we must admit that in the economic molecular theory there is wanting the cogency which is conferred by a nice adaptation of premises to conclusions. But it is worth considering whether our premises, human motives evidenced by consciousness and sympathy, do not possess the character of a *vera causa* in a higher degree than the foundations of some received hypotheses as to the constitution of matter.

The conditions which determine the equilibrium of the market are indicated by the curves OP and OQ in the accompanying figure. These are Demand and Supply curves, but not of the kind proposed by Cournot and accredited by M. De Foville. They are, rather, of the kind proposed by Professor Marshall in an unpublished pamphlet referred to in his *Principles* and in Professor Pantaleoni's *Principii*.* In this, as in the more familiar system, one of the above elements represents the amount of a commodity supplied. But the other co-ordinate does not now represent a rate of exchange, but the amount supplied of another commodity. The explanation is most easily enunciated in the simple case in which one of the commodities, say y, is money.[2] Then any point

---

[1] The proof primarily applicable to the simple case may be extended to the general case.

* The substance of the papers referred to has been published by Marshall in his *Money Credit and Commerce*, 1923.

[2] According to the construction of Messrs. Auspitz and Lieben.

P, on the curve OPA indicates that Op, where p is the foot of the perpendicular let fall from P on OX, is the amount of x supplied by the X's at a price which is equal to Pp divided by OP ; a price which is assigned by the angle POX.[1] The amount of x *demanded* by the Y's at the same price is in Or, where Or is the foot of the perpendicular let fall from R on OX. Rr may be described as the amount of money supplied by the Y's at the given price; and Pp as the amount of money demanded by the X's at that price. The intersection of the curves indicates the terms at which Supply equals Demand.

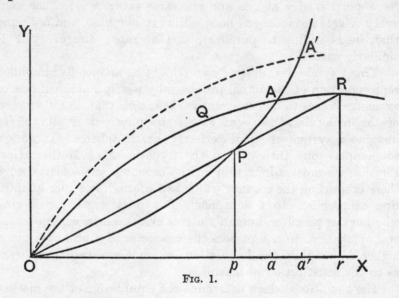

Fig. 1.

Now let us introduce the character of *Distribution* ; let us suppose that the x offered by one party is work, and the y offered by the other party is wages paid out of product.[2] The most general conception would include the case in which not only each employer employs several employés, but each employé is free to work for several employers. But with reference to modern industry, it seems proper to suppose that while each master employs several men, no man can serve two, or more, masters. The limitation does not impair the essential characteristics of a market, provided that the number of the employers continues to be large. But the limitation is not entirely inoperative. For, as I have elsewhere argued,[3] it is apt to obstruct the process by which

---

[1] Equal to the *tangent* of POX.
[2] *Theory of Distribution* (*loc. cit.*), p. 161.
[3] *Giornale degli Economisti*, 1891. (Above, β.)

workmen competing against each other lower wages.[1] The incident seems to be of little practical importance, and to have no direct bearing on the question now at issue. But it may serve to render more conceivable the view which will presently be suggested : that between the position of the employé and the employer there may be an asymmetry to the disadvantage of the class usually supposed to be the most favoured—the employers.

Let us now disturb the equilibrium which we have contemplated, by introducing an additional employer. And at first let us abstract that effect on the organisation which Professor Chapman has particularly considered. The abstract proposition which is found by his reasoning when that effect is neglected is now to be reconsidered. That reasoning appears to presuppose that not only the total number of workmen, but also the total quantity of work done, is constant. But in general this is not to be supposed. The raised offer on one side of the market is apt to be attended with an increased offer on the other side. In our figure, let OA' denote the curve pertaining to the employers, varied by the introduction of an additional employer. Then A' is the new position of equilibrium. Oa' where a' is the foot of a perpendicular (not shown in the figure) let fall from A' on OX is the new quantity of work supplied; greater than the old quantity Oa. To be sure, the curve pertaining to the employés might be shaped so that Oa' would be less than Oa. But there is some reason to think that the shape represented in the figure is the more probable and typical. At any rate there is no presumption that Oa' is equal to Oa.*

The same result may be shown by way of symbols.** The product of each firm is now to be regarded as a function, not only of x the number of employés in the firm, but also of e the average amount of work which they put forth, an average which may be supposed the same for each firm. With e should be included, theoretically, another variable E, the work of the entrepreneur.

[1] Consider the analysis above given (p. 334). But observe that the number of X's is there supposed to be equal to that of the Y's. When each Y employs several X's, the competition of these X's against each other, the quasi-monopolistic position of the Y with whom they deal, no doubt neutralises the incident noticed in the text.

* Still less is there any presumption, if P was the total product before the disturbance and AP is the increment due to the taking on of an additional entrepreneur, that (as the disputed theory requires) $\Delta P = \dfrac{P + \Delta P - A'a}{n + 1}$, or approximately $\dfrac{P - Aa}{n}$, where n is the original number of entrepreneurs.

** I have abridged the argument, which is somewhat confused as originally stated.

The work put forth by each employé is subject to the condition that the final disutility to him of the work is equal to the final utility to him of the remuneration.   Whence it follows—account being taken of the maximum condition on the part of the entrepreneur to which production is subject—that the total output of a firm is determined as a function of x, the number of employés in the firm, and w, the rate of remuneration per unit of e.   Now the product of x and z is by hypothesis constant. Whence it is deducible that the total product involves z, not only explicitly, but also implicitly in that x and w are functions of z. Accordingly, when the number of employers is varied from z to $z + 1$, the quantities which we have to compare receive variations depending on differential coefficients about which we have not in general sufficient knowledge to sustain the theorem in question.   If it is still the most probable statement, yet it is less probable than appeared; less useful as a typical mean of possible cases.

It may be added that even if the theorem were accurately true, it would not have the importance attached to it by some writers; among whom, however, Professor Chapman is not to be included.   This may be shown by considering a case in which Professor Chapman's abstract reasoning holds good without qualification.   Let the entrepreneurs be cottiers, renting a homogeneous tract of land limited in extent.   If an additional entrepreneur is introduced, the addition to the total product is found by parity of reasoning to be exactly [1] equal to the remuneration of an entrepreneur.*   But what of that?   Where is the consolation to the cottiers whose complaint is that their share of the product is so small, that " this principle of remuneration is in itself an injustice." [2]

So it is no *eirenicon* between employers and employed to affirm that, according to the definition of Professor J. B. Clark, " every workman gets the product of his work."   He is not thereby deterred from desiring more than what is his product according to that definition.   " You may call it what you please provided you hand it over," the Socialists would say, as Mr. Cannan happily observes.[3]

On the whole I see no reason to modify the opinion that the theorem in question is neither quite true nor very important.

---

[1] That is, to within quantities which are negligible.

* See note at the end of this article.

[2] Mill, *Political Economy*, Book II. ch. i. § 4.

[3] *Quarterly Journal of Economics*, " The Division of Income," May, 1905

If it could have been saved, it would have been by the more abstract part of Professor Chapman's brilliant reasoning.

(Note referring to p. 338.)

[Let $f(l)$ be the amount of produce which the cottier will produce (per unit of time) if he rents l units of land. This expression may be considered as derived from data connecting the amount of produce with several variable data, the amount of energy (measured objectively) put forth by the worker—which will depend partly on the rent which he has to pay—and any number of " gratuitous factors," arrangements which it is in the power of the worker to vary (*cp.* **I**, Vol. I. p. 298). Or is it simpler to suppose that there is determined by the Calculus of Variations the *form* which most advantageously connects the produce with the extent of land, the amount of work done on it and the rent per acre? Say we thus obtain for the worker's net advantage $U = F(l, e) - \rho l - \phi(e)$; where ρ is the rent per unit of land, $\phi(e)$ is the money-measure of the disutility attending the exertion e, F is the money-value of the produce (the price of which may be supposed constant). Differentiating U with respect to e and eliminating e with the aid of the equation $\left(\dfrac{dU}{de}\right) = O$ from U, we obtain for U an expression of the form $U = f(l) - \rho l$. We may suppose a population homogeneous in respect of circumstances and disposition so that the above formula applies adequately to each member.

A perfect land-market being assumed—cottier-entrepreneurs in competition with each other dealing with competitive landlords— the rate of rent ρ will be so related to l, the holding of each cultivator, that for each (at any assigned rate) U shall be a maximum; that $f'(l) = \rho$. Suppose that the total extent of land available is limited ($= L$, say) and all of the same quality. Then if there be n cultivators, the portion cultivated by each will be L/n; the value of the crop raised by each, $f(L/n)$; the rent (per unit of land), $f'(L/n)$; the gain of the cultivator, his producers' surplus, $f(L/n) - (L/n)f(L/n)$. The total value produced will be $nf(L/n)$. Now let one entrepreneur be abstracted. The value of the total produce becomes then

$$(n-1)f(L/n-1) = nf(L/n) - \left\{ f(L/n) - \left(\frac{L}{n}\right)f'\left(\frac{L}{n}\right) \right\};$$ fractions of the order $1/N$ being neglected. Thus the amount lost to the community by the abstraction of an entrepreneur is just equal to his remuneration.]

MR. BICKERDIKE'S THEORY OF INCIPIENT TAXES AND CUSTOMS DUTIES

[THE continuation of " Appreciations " in the ECONOMIC JOURNAL for 1908 deals with some interesting conceptions and propositions due to Mr. C. F. Bickerdike.

Any country has the power of securing to itself some net advantage by the imposition of an import tax. For if the tax be moderate, " incipient " in Mr. Bickerdike's happy phrase, the gain accruing from the proceeds of the tax will be greater than the loss incurred by the disturbance of industry. This is deducible from the general principle that in the neighbourhood of a maximum a small change in the conditions—in the values of the independent variables, on which the quantity to be maximised depends—is attended with a *very small* change in the quantity that was prior to the change at a maximum. This argument is to be distinguished from that which Cournot often employs (*Recherches Art, et passim*); the assumption that relations of greater or less which are true of differential increments in the neighbourhood of a maximum will continue to be true of finite differences. The extension practised by Cournot—when he reasons, for instance, that a monopolist will raise his price in consequence of a tax and *ceteris paribus* will raise it more the heavier the tax—is not threatened by any counter argument, as Mr. Bickerdike's paradox is by the ordinary anti-Protectionist arguments. In this respect his paradox is comparable with ours respecting the possibility of both producers and consumers being benefited by differential prices (**D**, Vol. I.). On probable suppositions as to the law of Demand, it has been found that a similar paradox would be verified for rates of taxation as high as 12½ per cent. (Below, ζ, p. 418.) Experimenting in a similar spirit on probable cases, Mr. Bickerdike has found that his paradox holds good for taxes of about the same order.

Having introduced his theorem by a construction proper to domestic trade, Mr. Bickerdike goes on to the subject of international trade. He employs the useful conception of a currency special to each country.   (It might with advantage be conceived as based on the Labour standard of monetary value (see Index)). There is thus realised what is desiderated by Mangoldt and others, an objective measure of the " virtual exchange " (Pigou, *loc. cit.*) between two nations.

The demand-and-supply curves proper to international trade are at first treated as if they were " primary " or short period contrasted with secondary curves, " supply curves proper," which express the result of external economies (see Index, s.v. *Primary*). But it may be argued that what is true of primary curves is *probably* true of secondaries, especially when the latter retain the shape that is usual with the corresponding primary curves relating to short periods.

My presentation of an argument which shows that it is generally possible to tax the foreigner, concludes with a warning against the practical application of the theory. The practices, based on the new argument, would be peculiarly liable to retaliation ; and would be at least as liable as other theoretically admissible arguments in favour of Protection to exaggeration and abuse.]

Continuing my retrospective survey of mathematical papers contributed to the ECONOMIC JOURNAL,[1] I come to Mr. Bickerdike's article on the " Theory of Incipient Taxes," published December, 1906. The article should be read with Mr. Bickerdike's review of Professor Pigou's *Protective and Preferential Import Duties*, with Professor Pigou's remarks on that review, and Mr. Bickerdike's rejoinder.[2]

Mr. Bickerdike has accomplished a wonderful feat. He has said something new about Protection. The novelty is perhaps not conspicuous in the first of the two propositions which constitute his thesis : " That in pure theory advantage is always possible in normal circumstances from either import or export taxation when the taxes are small enough." [3] This may seem at first sight to be a repetition of the doctrine which Mill and Sidgwick and Professor Nicholson have made familiar : that under certain circumstances a country may benefit itself at the

[1] See ECONOMIC JOURNAL, Vol. XVII. p. 221 and p. 524.

[2] *Ibid.*, pp. 98, 289, 583.

[3] The words which follow in the original, " except in one peculiar and unlikely case," are here omitted ; for it will be argued in the sequel that this peculiar case is not merely unlikely but impossible.

expense of the foreigner by a customs duty.· But it will be found that Mr. Bickerdike adds to our knowledge of the circumstances. He predicates advantageousness of a new class, " incipient "— or small finite—taxes. There is novelty also in his second proposition : " In the case of incipient import taxes, the tendency to advantage is greater the more elastic the demand of the taxing country for the articles taxed." That demand, it is explained in the context, is more elastic when there is an untaxed home supply, that is, when the tax is protective. This is a division very different from Mill's which expresses a generally received view : " Duties on importation may be divided into two classes, those which have the effect of encouraging some particular branch of domestic industry, and those which have not. The former are purely mischievous both to the country imposing them and to those with whom it trades." [1] . . . " A protecting duty can never be a cause of gain, but always and necessarily of loss, to the country imposing it." [2]

Observing this contrast, the reader will perhaps modify his first impression, and, not denying that Mr. Bickerdike's doctrine is new, will begin to question whether it is true. But the appearance of extreme paradox will, I think, disappear upon further consideration. The opposition between Mill's received doctrine and Mr. Bickerdike's new thesis is not diametrical, as Mill was not adverting to the particular species of customs duties which Mr. Bickerdike characterises as " incipient." Mr. Bickerdike's second proposition, read with his first, is in keeping with the most recent results of the mathematical method applied to international trade. Thus Professor Pigou, in his *Protective and Preferential Import Duties*—published contemporaneously with Mr. Bickerdike's article—argues that in a certain case, which I might describe as that of an " incipient " tax,[3] in Mr. Bickerdike's phrase, " the direct burden [incident to raising an assigned amount of revenue] under a protective can be proved smaller than that under a customs *plus* excise duty." He finds that " there is no general *a priori* presumption either for or against the imposition of protective duties as a means to raising revenue." " This conclusion," he observes, " is of course very different from the sweeping condemnation with which popular Free Trade

---

[1] *Political Economy*, Book V. ch. iv. § 6, paragraph fifth from the end. Remote consequences such as the development of industries are not here in question.

[2] *Loc. cit.*, antepenultimate paragraph.

[3] Professor Pigou's words, *loc. cit.* p. 31, are : " Where all second powers can be neglected, including the loss of the consumers' surplus on that part of the consumption which the tax destroys."

theory envelops all proposals in any way tainted with Protection."[1]
I submit that free traders of the classical school have " the root
of the matter," as Ricardo would say. In the balance of advantage they weigh the items of first magnitude. They " take care
of the pounds." The pence which they neglect may as often
occur on one side of the account as the other. But the balance
would seldom be turned by taking account of the pence. Thus,
on the one hand, it is little discredit to practical free trade that
it neglects mathematical refinements; on the other hand, it
is no presumption against Mr. Bickerdike's thesis that it appears
unacceptable to free traders of the purely classical school.

As if addressing first those who are least disposed to accept
his propositions, Mr. Dickerdike begins with an " attempt . . . to
show, by general reasoning, that they are not opposed to common
sense." [2] When he has gone as far as it is possible to go by
the highway of purely verbal reasoning, he strikes into a tract
which is more arduous indeed, yet not unfamiliar, a mathematical
method employed by Dr. Marshall in the *Principles of Economics*.
When with the aid of this method our guide has come within
sight of his conclusion, he makes for it by a direct path of his
own construction. Let us follow him as he proceeds by these
convenient stages.

I. *Pace* Aristotle,[3] a mathematician's appeal to common sense
and ordinary probabilities is not inadmissible when he deals with
applied mathematics and the application is to human affairs.
Mr. Bickerdike's use of popular arguments would perhaps have
been more persuasive if he could have found an illustration less
quaint than the group of milkmen who are supposed to " agree
that every time one of them sold milk he should make a contribution to a collective fund, in token of the fact that by putting
his milk on the market he is doing something to lower the price
of milk to the disadvantage of his fellows." [4] But it is difficult
to illustrate by domestic transactions the peculiarities of international trade. It has, indeed, in common with internal trade
between non-competing groups, the essential attribute, exchange
without mobility. But the *proprium* regional separation is
attended with peculiarities that are hard to parallel. How
else can we conceive as practicable that monopolistic power
which a State exercises by its control of the transit over a boundary
in space ? Where else shall we observe the phenomenon of a

---

[1] *Loc. cit.* p. 32.　　　　[2] ECONOMIC JOURNAL, Vol. XVI., *loc. cit.*
[3] *Ethics*, Book I. ch. iii.
[4] ECONOMIC JOURNAL, Vol. XVI. p. 530.

level of prices in the transaction between members of a group raised or lowered by regulation of the transactions between members of the group and outsiders, some of the articles of which the price is thus affected being " non-exportable ? " [1]

Whatever illustration is adopted, we must not expect to find any easy substitute for mathematical reasoning. It is very difficult, as Mr. Bickerdike observes, to give a convincing proof of his propositions by purely verbal reasoning. I have endeavoured, without success, to lighten the difficulty by following the usual method of illustrating problems in international trade, namely, constructing simple cases of such trade. It is worth while describing these tentatives in order to exhibit more clearly the points at which the new theory purports to be an advance on the classical doctrine. In order to minimise the difficulties connected with the use of money, I adopt Professor Nicholson's helpful conception, that of two countries whose mutual dealings are considered, one is large relatively to the other, so large that the level of general prices within that country is not disturbed by changes in the terms of international trade. If the theory in question—which has no connection with the relative size of the trading countries—cannot be proved by ordinary reasoning in this case, neither can it be so proved in general. Let the large country be " England " and the small one " Guernsey," these proper names being used, like Mill's " England " and " Germany," in a conventional sense abstracted from the actual facts of commercial geography. Let us begin by considering an extreme case, that in which one country has such a rigid sort of demand for the commodities imported from the other country, that, in Mill's phrase, " a certain quantity is all that is wanted at any price; and that when that quantity is obtained, no fall in the exchange value would induce other consumers to come forward, or those who are already supplied, to take more." [2] The conception implies, in virtue of the continuity attributable to laws of demand, that a small rise in the exchange value will not induce the consumer to take much less. We may refer the case to the third of Mill's " three possible varieties in the influence of cheapness or demand." [3] Or let us rearrange his three varieties

---

[1] As to the magnitude of this class the following opinion is expressed by Professor Taussig in his article on " Wages and Prices in relation to International Trade," *Quarterly Journal of Economics*, August 1906). " The quantity of such commodities is very great, and in all countries probably much exceeds that of commodities having a world range of price."

[2] *Political Economy*, Book III. ch. xviii. § 2, second paragraph from the end.

[3] *Ibid.*, § 5.

so as to form two classes, namely, E (elastic), " the demand increased more than the cheapness," and I (inelastic), " less than the cheapness "; the intermediate variety " as much as the cheapness " being treated as a mere limit. Then one of our countries possesses the attribute I in an extreme degree. Let the other country belong to Class E.[1]

First let the home country, that is, the country imposing the tax, enjoy the property E. For example, let England have a rigid demand of the sort defined for the early vegetables imported from Guernsey, but not so Guernsey for the metals, hardware, and other miscellaneous articles which she imports from England; what would be the effect of an export duty imposed by Guernsey? England would continue to take the same amount of early vegetables at a money value augmented by the tax; and the balance of indebtedness could only be restored by her sending to Guernsey a larger quantity of her own products (the price of which by hypothesis remains constant).

Now let Guernsey impose an import—instead of an export—duty. The duty will tend to check the amount of imports, and therefore their money value (Guernsey belonging to Class E). But England must pay for her imports of early vegetables, of which she will continue to take the same amount even if she has to pay more for them. The balance will be settled by England sending a greater quantity of hardware, etc., in return for the same quantity of early vegetables. But since the greater quantity of hardware, etc., has a greater money value (prices of English products being constant), the same quantity of early vegetables must have a greater money value; the price of early vegetables must be higher. But the producers of early vegetables being supposed, in abstract theory, to be in industrial competition with the producers of all other articles in Guernsey, the prices of all other articles, and in particular of labour, in Guernsey must rise. In the new equilibrium the national income of Guernsey, both real and nominal, will be greater than before;[2] the Treasury will obtain a net gain.

Similarly it may be shown that if England belong to Class E, Guernsey to the extreme form of I, England, by imposing either

---

[1] The case in which both countries belong to Class I is not adapted to popular illustration, as it presents difficulties which can hardly be removed without the use of mathematics.

[2] It may be supposed that Guernsey has no other foreign customers b t England, as Mill at first supposes with respect to Germany, and that the tax s a general one on all imports from England.

an import or an export tax, may draw to herself, as Mill would say, the whole tax.

Now let us reverse the supposition, and, the other data being the same, suppose that the tax is imposed by the country which belongs to Class I. For example, let England, having a rigid demand for the early vegetables of Guernsey, impose an import tax thereon. The whole of the tax would be paid by the English consumer. The result is virtually the same if an export duty is imposed by England, England still requiring the same amount of early vegetables. In exchange for that amount of vegetables Guernsey is willing to take the same amount of hardware, etc., as before. But the prices of exported hardware, etc., will rise by the full amount of the tax (the prices of these English products being constant in England). In the new state of equilibrium the level of general prices in Guernsey will be higher than before. But Guernsey will derive no advantage from this circumstance, since the prices of the articles in her international market have risen in a corresponding degree.[1] The English consumers pay more money for the same amount of vegetables as before. The English Treasury gains as much as the consumer loses. England, as a whole, neither gains nor loses, abstraction being made of the *friction* incidental to manipulation of tariffs.

It might be expected that the proposition thus easily proved for a species of Class I could be extended to the class generally. But, as we recede from the limiting case of rigid demand, there becomes sensible an item which baffles the estimate of advantage to the taxing country, namely, the privation of those who are deterred from consuming the taxed commodity in consequence of the rise in its price.

Nor is the matter any clearer in the case which Mr. Bickerdike seems to regard as typical,[2] where both the countries belong to Class E, each having an extensible demand for the products of the other. It is evident certainly that the reduction of consumption consequent upon taxation involves privation to the consumer. It may be argued that a country which by a customs duty limits its supply to the foreigner obtains thereby some advantage. But is it visible to the eye of ordinary reason, unaided by mathematical instruments, that for taxes not exceeding a certain magnitude this gain exceeds that loss ? Of course, the duty may be so high that, in Mill's words, " the trade and

---

[1] On the supposition made in the last note.

[2] ECONOMIC JOURNAL, Vol. XVI., *loc. cit.*, p. 532. [Compare Marshall *Money Credit and Commerce*, Book III., chap. vi., s. 5.]

its advantage would cease entirely." The disadvantage certainly preponderates for very heavy taxes; but where is the proof that as we pass from heavy to light and ultimately nominal duties, the gain to the Treasury by the foreigners' contribution exceeds the loss in the way of privation to the consumer? Common sense and ordinary economics can discern nothing about a small tax except that it is small. " The only thing that can be said for it is that it is a very little tax," [1] as Lowe said about the registration duty on corn, when proposing its abolition. Something more could be

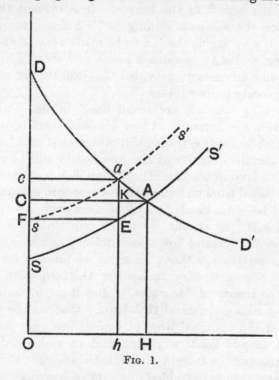

Fig. 1.

said for it on Mr. Bickerdike's theory. But we have hardly begun the proof of that theory while we confine ourselves to verbal reasoning. We have not even got so far as the candidate at an examination in Euclid who pleaded that, if he had not proved the propositions set by the examiner, at least he had made them seem probable.

II. Mr. Bickerdike advances much further by the use of a construction which he borrows from Dr. Marshall. As this construction was originally employed to illustrate the " pure theory of domestic values," [2] so the case of international values

---

[1] Hansard, April 1869, Vol. 195, p. 388.

[2] Pantaleoni, *Pure Economics* (translated by T. B. Bruce), p. 190.

to which it may seem most appropriate is that which resembles domestic trade, in not requiring a change of price-level to be taken into account. Suppose, for instance, that the " England " of the preceding section puts a small duty on the imports from " Guernsey," neither party urgently requiring to trade with the other. Let us begin with a supposition of this sort.

(A) It will be sufficient here to reproduce Dr. Marshall's diagram, and to refer the reader to Mr. Bickerdike's use of it in the Economic Journal : [1] " Imagine that the tax is going to be spent for the benefit of the buyers. It is evident that they gain or lose on the whole, according as $CFEK$ is greater or less than AKa. If we imagine the tax to be made very small, $CFEK$ becomes a line, and AKa becomes a point, and there is, therefore, necessarily some advantage, provided that the supply curve SS' is not an absolutely horizontal line."

This reasoning will not commend itself to those who have learnt too well the formulæ of the classical text-books. The common or Cobdenite free trader will object that in consequence of the tax a certain quantity of the commodity will be produced under more unfavourable conditions than before, industry will have been diverted from its " natural " course into less productive channels. If he condescends to look at a diagram, he will fasten attention on h H, the amount by which importation is reduced, and triumphantly demand how the deficiency can be made good by the home producer without resorting to inferior methods of production. Nor is it easy to answer this objection without recourse to the theory of " margins." But it ought to be intelligible to those who understand that theory that, as the marginal workman and the marginal dose of capital are only just worth applying, so an additional workman and an additional dose of capital, in excess of the margin of profitableness, are only just not worth applying. Now the added quantity of home production, a quantity of the same order as the amount by which importation is diminished, may be considered as obtained from marginal doses of productive force; corresponding to an amount of profit which is small comparatively, compared with the tribute levied from the foreigner.

To the mathematician, of course, the principle that quantities of the second order may be neglected in comparison with those of the first order presents no novelty. But he is apt hastily to conclude that the whole theory, being *de minimis*, may for

[1] Vol. XVI. p. 533.

practical purposes be neglected. It may be well, therefore, to exhibit the character of the reasoning at some length.

Mr. Bickerdike's theory involves an important principle in that branch of mathematics which is most applicable to human affairs, the Calculus of Probabilities grafted on the Calculus of Variations. The principle may be enunciated with sufficient accuracy as follows :—When a variable magnitude is in the neighbourhood of a maximum, the increment of that variable corresponding to a small finite increment of a variable on which it depends is likely to be particularly small.[1] A familiar example is afforded by the length of the day as dependent on the time of the year.   In Whitaker's Almanack you find that, day after day for eight days in the neighbourhood of the summer solstice there is no change in the length of the day measured by the interval between the time of the sun's rising and that of his setting; while in other months there is a difference of two or three minutes from day to day.   More precise astronomical examples of the principle may be found in the Nautical Almanack.* Here the following homely illustration may suffice.   Let there be a flight of steps shaped like an arch—as an iron bridge is sometimes constructed.   If the steps are all of the same length, the height becomes smaller as the summit is approached.   Say the radius of the (circular) arch is thirty feet, and the (horizontal) length of each step is a foot; then the (vertical) height of the step nearest the summit will be about a fifth of an inch; at a lower point, where the slope of the arch is 30°, the vertical height of a step will be more than half a foot; it is a whole foot where the slope of the arch is 45°.

The principle may well be of importance in utilitarian philosophy in cases where the very best is the enemy of the very good.   The economic application of the principle takes the following form : A *small* change of an economic variable quantity at the margin[2] commonly causes a *very small* change in the

---

[1] More exactly : if y is a variable depending on x, both variables being positive, and when $x = x_0$, y has a maximum value, viz. y_0 ; then commonly and probably, a finite positive quantity a can be found, such that for any quantity a not greater than a.

$$y_0 - y_{\Delta x} < y_a - \Delta x - y_a ;$$

where Δx is a small finite difference ($< a$); the ratio of the first member of this inequality to the second becoming smaller the smaller Δx and the greater a is; and this proposition may be extended *mutatis mutandis* to the cases of negative increments and of negative variables, to the case of several variables, to minimum values, and other cognate cases.

* Some instances are given in the ECONOMIC JOURNAL, 1922, p. 439.

As to the sense in which the term is here employed, see the article " Margin " in Palgrave's *Dictionary of Political Economy*.

corresponding surplus. As we are concerned here both with Consumers' and Producers' surplus, we may take an example from a species of the latter class, the profits of a monopolist. The numerical instances given by Cournot [1] at the end of his chapter on monopoly will serve our purpose; for, as he framed them, *aliud agens*, they may be regarded as random specimens with respect to the present object. It is allowable also to substitute in his examples a tax for an increase in the cost of production.

In his first example the price of the article before the tax is 20 fcs., and the profits of the monopolist are the fortieth part of a sum designated by the symbol a; say, profits $= 25,000$ fcs., putting $a = 1,000,000$. According to the assigned relation between price and quantity demanded,[2] when a tax of 2 fcs. per unit of commodity is imposed, the price rises by a slightly greater amount, the new price being nearly 22·1 fcs.[3] The loss of profits due to this rise of price—irrespectively of the tax, not taking into account that the loss is incurred to avoid a greater loss through the tax—is nearly 124 fcs.[4] The same change of price at a distance from the point would produce a greater change in profits. A price of 30 fcs., for instance, would afford a profit of 23,077 fcs.; but a rise of 2·1 fcs. in the price will reduce the profits by some 636 fcs., greater than the loss of profits due to the rise of prices from 20 to 22·1, viz. 124 fcs. That loss is small compared with the proceeds of the tax, viz. 2,251 fcs.[5] The disparity would be greater if the tax and the consequent change in price were less. For instance, let the tax be 0·2 fcs. The additions to the price will then be nearly 0·201. The loss of surplus due to this rise of price is 1·3 fcs.; while the yield of the tax is 247·5 fcs. Similar verifications may be obtained from Cournot's next example.[6]

A case of two variables is presented by an instance of monopoly which I have given elsewhere with a different object in view.[7] The price of a first-class ticket for passengers on an imagined

---

[1] *Principes Mathématiques de la Théorie des Richesses*, Art. 34.

[2] $F(p) = \dfrac{a}{b^2 + p^2}$ where p is the price, $F(p)$ the amount demanded at the price; $b = 20$.

[3] More exactly $2 + 20 \times 1{\cdot}004987$. See the English translation, where an arithmetical mistake made by Cournot is corrected.

[4] $1,000,000 \ [0{\cdot}025 - 22{\cdot}1/(400 + 22{\cdot}1^2)]$.

[5] $1,000,000 \times 2{\cdot}/(400 + 22{\cdot}1^2)$.

[6] It will be found convenient to assign the new *price*, and thence find the tax requisite to produce the rise of price.

[7] See **F**, Vol. I. p. 132.

railway being £4 10s., for a third-class ticket £2 6s. 4½d. (nearly), a tax of 16s. 10½d. per ticket is put on first-class tickets. The consequent loss of profits to the company through the diversion of travellers from the first to the third class is £200. The yield of the tax is £16,009 12s., some eighty times greater than the loss of receipts. The disparity between the yield of the tax and the loss of receipts is much greater when the tax is smaller. When the tax is (a little more than) 2d. per first-class ticket, the loss of receipts is 1s. 8½d. The yield of the tax is £171 7s. 7d.; nearly two thousand greater than the loss of receipts.

What these illustrations illustrate is the probable smallness of that loss of surplus which is attributable to change of margins consequent on the tax, comparatively with the yield of the tax. But what we have to prove is that the loss of surplus is small comparatively with a part of the yield, namely, that part which is levied on the foreigner. For this conclusion there is required an additional premiss : that the proportion contributed by the foreigner is sensible, considerable as compared with the ratio of the lost surplus to the proceeds of the tax. Thus in the case represented by Fig. 1 $CFEK$ is large relatively to AKa when CF is small.

It follows as a corollary that the privation consequent on the imposition of Customs duties tends to be smaller with respect to the proceeds of taxation the greater (a) the number of objects over which the taxation is spread, (b) the portion of it contributed by the foreigner.[1]

(B) So far the level of prices has been supposed undisturbed.[2] We go on to the general case, in which the change in the value of money within the home country cannot be neglected. Let us begin with a simple instance already adduced. England, having an urgent—perfectly inelastic—demand for goods imported from Guernsey, while Guernsey has not an urgent demand for English goods, Guernsey imposes a duty on imports from England.

In Fig. 1 the supply curve SS' now becomes a horizontal line, since by hypothesis the price of the English product is constant, the English producer being prepared to supply any amount (that Guernsey can want) at that price. When a tax of so much per cent., or, what comes to the same in this case, a specific tax, is imposed by Guernsey, the level of prices in Guernsey, as above shown, rises by the assigned percentage. A new demand-curve

---

[1] Proposition (a) was stated by me (with reference to taxation in general in an article on the " Pure Theory of Taxation," ECONOMIC JOURNAL, 1897 (above, S, p. 118).   [2] See above, p. 348.

is formed by adding that percentage to each ordinate of the old demand-curve. This new demand curve, say dd' (not shown in the figure), may meet ss', the supply-curve (now a line), raised to the extent of the tax, in a point which indicates that there is no loss of consumers' surplus, as if the consumers in Guernsey now take as great a quantity of hardware, etc., as before, and pay for it the same price in vegetables—if the expression is allowed—that they would have been willing to pay before, while their willingness to exchange vegetables for hardware, depending on the real relations between the supply of and the demand for things, is not affected by a change in the pecuniary measuring rod. There is then a net gain for the Guernsey Treasury.[1]

If the demand of England for early vegetables is not perfectly elastic, we have no longer the datum that the level of prices in Guernsey will rise to the full extent of the tax. Still, it is easy to see that the theory holds in the neighbourhood of the limiting case which has been considered. Advancing from that limit, we may get far on the way to a general proof. We may get further by ascribing to the home country a currency peculiar to itself. But this is to take a leaf from that stricter demonstration for which this method is but a makeshift.[2]

III. All that precedes may be regarded as merely preliminary to the beautiful mathematical construction on which Mr. Bickerdike mainly rests his theory. In building up this edifice of science he employs certain unessential simplifications, which may be regarded as a sort of scaffolding. I shall first describe, then contemplate in use, then remove, three pieces of this subsidiary apparatus.

First (a) it is supposed that the demand-curve and the supply-curves employed are of the simple kind which Dr. Marshall has defined as curves of constant elasticity.[3] Perhaps the relevance of the concept " elasticity " to the present investigation may be made clearer to readers of the classical school by observing that the distinction between elasticity of demand greater or less than unity [4] corresponds to the distinction between Mill's first

---

[1] Some modification of these statements is required if it is conceived that the Treasury employs its new purchasing power in obtaining from England hardware, etc., to be distributed in Guernsey.

[2] *Cp.* Bickerdike, Economic Journal, 1906, p. 531.

[3] Bickerdike, *ibid.*, 1897, p. 101; Marshall, *Principles of Economics*, Mathematical Note iii.

[4] See J. S. Mill, *Political Economy*, Book III., ch. xviii. § 5; and above, p. 345. If the "linen" which the home country imports is denoted by a_1, the cloth which he exports by a_2, it may be shown that the home country belongs to Class E or I

and third varieties of demand—the E and I of our first section. This distinction persists, though the levels of price, according to the usual conception of international trade, may alter.

(b) A second simplification is effected by imagining each country to use a money peculiar to itself. This money, as I understand, may be conceived as of the kind which Ricardo usually presupposes, the kind of which he says, " I shall suppose it to be invariable." [1] We might imagine the national money in Mr. Bickerdike's system to be an inconvertible (or at least unexportable) `currency, regulated, as some theorists have proposed, so that its value should remain constant. Constancy of value might be secured by one of the methods of measuring the value of money which I have elsewhere described, preferably the one called Ricardo's Method, or the Labour Standard.[2]

(c) It is further postulated that supply and demand on the part of the community are related in the simplest possible manner to the supply and demand on the part of the individuals which make up the community; the collective demand (at any assigned price) being the sum of the demands of the individuals (at that price); and likewise the community's supply (at a price) being the sum of the amounts supplied by the individuals (at that

---

according as $\dfrac{da_2}{da_1}$ $\left(\text{or}\,\dfrac{da_1}{da_2}\right)$ is positive or negative; where a_1 and a_2 are connected by a Supply-and-Demand curve of the kind proposed by Marshall for the " pure theory of foreign trade " (see Pantaleoni, *Principii di Economia Pura*, or the English translation thereof, for an authorised version of Marshall's doctrine). The equation to this curve may be written $a_1 f_1(a_1) = a_2 F_2(a_2)$; if with Mr. Bickerdike we put $y = f_1(x)$ for the equation of the home country's demand for imports, and $y = F_2(a_2)$ for her supply of exports, y denoting price in a money which (as postulated in our text) is peculiar to the country. Accordingly

$$\frac{da_2}{da_1} = \frac{f_1(a_1) + a_1 f_1{}'(a_1)}{F_2(a_2) + a_2 F{}'_2(a_2)}$$

(by the usual rule for the differentiation of an implicit function)

$$= \frac{f_1(a_1)(1 - 1/e_d)}{F_2(a_2)(1 - 1/e_s)}$$

in the (slightly varied) notation of Mr. Bickerdike, who after Marshall (*Principles of Economics*, Mathematical Note iii), puts for e_d, the measure or coefficient of elasticity of demand, the *negative* of the (negative) increment of commodity corresponding to a (positive) increment of price, and (without, I think, Marshall's authority) extends this notation to elasticity of supply. Thus $(- e_s)$, e_s being the *negative* of the increment of supply corresponding to an increment of price, is positive, the third of the postulates in the text being granted. Also $f_1(a_1)$ and $F_2(a_2)$, denoting prices, are essentially positive. Therefore $\dfrac{da_2}{da_1}$ is positive or negative according as $1/e_d$ is less or greater than unity. Therefore the home country belongs to Class E or I according as e_d is greater or less than unity.

[1] *Principles*, ch. i. § 6.
[2] Vol. I., A.

price). I propose to define this class of curve as *primary*; [1] taking between *primary* and *secondary* the distinction drawn by Mr. Cunynghame between the simpler and the more complicated curves which he has described in a well-known article.[2] I assume that primary demand-curves are always inclined negatively, and primary supply-curves positively, to the abscissa.

With the aid of these three postulates, by a chaste use of mathematical reasoning, Mr. Bickerdike establishes his two propositions.* Obtaining an expression for the rate at which advantage increases with the increase of a small tax, he infers the first proposition from the *sign* of that expression, and the second proposition from its magnitude.[3] "The formula shows only the tendency of a very small tax," as he observes. But we may extend the reasoning from a very small, to a small tax—from an infinitesimal, to a small finite change in the independent variable—by a procedure which Cournot has largely employed in investigating the effects of taxation.[4] Begin with a very small tax levied by the home Government from buyers of foreign commodities. If every buyer has to contribute to his Government so much on each purchase, his effective demand will be altered much as the demand of a customer for goods sold at a shop might be altered, if, instead of having the goods delivered gratis at his house as heretofore, he had to pay for their carriage. In short, the demand-curve of the home country—the curve which represents the amount of foreign commodity which the home country will take at each price (in the money of that country)—has been disturbed and subjected to a slight variation. There results a new system with a new position of equilibrium. Operating on the new system, let us *de novo* impose a new small tax. And so on. The inferences which were primarily true only of a single

---

[1] See Index, *Secondary Supply-curves.*

[2] See ECONOMIC JOURNAL, Vol. II. p. 35, and for my interpretation of Mr. Cunynghame's distinctions, Vol. III. p. 138, *et seq.* As I understand, the two kinds of relation between price (y) and quantity of commodity supplied (x) may be symbolised by one form $y = \psi(x, \mathrm{x})$; where x is treated as constant when the curve is primary, is identified with x when the curve is secondary; the dependence of ψ upon x corresponding to the " external economies " varying with the scale of production, or more generally to the influence which the action of all has on the " dispositions and disponibilities " (in M. de Foville's apt phrase) of each. Demand-curves may be similarly divided. For example, $y = x + 1 - \frac{1}{2}\mathrm{x}$ represents primary supply-curves inclined positively at an angle of 45°, a secondary supply-curve inclined negatively to the abscissa at an angle of about 26° 34'. Likewise $y + x = 2 - \mathrm{x})$ represents primary demand-curves inclined negatively at an angle of 45°, a secondary demand curve inclined negatively to the abscissa at an angle of about 62° 26'.   * Above, p. 342.

[3] ECONOMIC JOURNAL, Vol. XVII. p. 100.

[4] *Principes Mathématiques*, Art. 32.

step, may now be extended to a whole flight of stairs. We may suppose the stairs to be in a vertical plane; the horizontal length of each step depends on the increment to the tax, and the increment of height corresponding to an increment of length represents an increment of advantage. The steepness of the stairs will in general diminish as we advance, until a point of maximum elevation is reached.[1] In accordance with the theory we perceive (1) that the stairs will be in general of finite length (measured horizontally from the starting-point to the position of maximum elevation); (2) that if the construction be altered by an increase of the elasticity of the home demand, *ceteris paribus*, the first step of the new stairs will be higher than the first step of the old stairs,[2] the second step of the new higher than the second step of the old, and so on; the comparison, in favour of the new system, being facilitated by the interesting circumstance pointed out by Mr. Bickerdike, that there are, so to speak, the same number of steps in each of the flights of stairs, that the *position* of the maximum elevation remains constant.

The safety of these steps is secured by the condition that the equilibrium of the trade with which we are concerned is stable. The case of failure excepted by Mr. Bickerdike as " peculiar and unlikely " [3] is rendered practically impossible by that condition. For it secures that the denominator of the expression for the rate at which advantage (to the home country) increases with the increase of the duty, is always positive.[4] (The numerator of the expression is positive by the third postulate.)

[1] Compare the illustration given at p. 349, above.

[2] The curve of supply and that of demand on the part of the foreigners and the curve of supply for the home country are not disturbed; and accordingly their coefficients of elasticity remain constant. The curve of demand for the home country is indeed disturbed; but it appears from Mr. Bickerdike's equation (ECONOMIC JOURNAL, 1907, p. 100) that at the point defined by the new amount of imports, say a'_1, the elasticity of the disturbed curve is the same as the elasticity of the old curve at the point defined by the co-ordinate a'_1. But the elasticity of the old curve at that point is the same as at all other points, viz, the constant e_4. Thus the whole expression for $\frac{du}{dr}$ given by Mr. Bickerdike remains constant.

[3] Referred to above, p. 341.

[4] In order that the equilibrium of trade should be stable there must be fulfilled by the Marshall curves, at their point of intersection, a certain condition (Pantaleoni, *Pure Economics*, p. 207); which may be thus stated. If the abscissa represent exports from the home country (a_2) the ordinate imports into the same country (a_1), then the tangent of the angle which is made with the abscissa by a tangent to that country's Supply-and-Demand at the point of intersection, say the *slope* of the curve at that point, must be greater *in absolute magnitude* than the slope of the foreign country's Demand-and-Supply curve at the same point; whenever the two slopes are either both positive or both negative. Now for the home country the slope is—

The theory may be extended, as Mr. Bickerdike intimates, to duties upon exports; which form what may be called the " external case " of the theory. I follow Mr. Bickerdike in leaving this case to be worked out by the reader. Nor do I enter into the varieties which are presented by the partial taxation of particular imports or exports. For the purpose of this Appreciation it is allowable to lump together the imports, and likewise the exports, under one head, like Mill's " cloth " and " linen." [1]

Some parts of the theory may be enunciated with reference to the premiss by which each is principally supported.

(a) Mr. Bickerdike's first assumption affords an easy method of forming a judgment as to the magnitude of a tax which may be consistent with advantage to the taxing country. After the experiments which we have performed above with laws of demand taken at random, we shall not be surprised at Mr. Bickerdike's result :—" Rather strong assumptions have to be made as to the elasticity of foreign supply and demand if the rate of the tax affording maximum advantage is to come below 10 per cent." [2]

(b) Mr. Bickerdike's second device—a national money of constant value—is no less serviceable. It is free from the dangers to which the use of money in the theory of international trade is liable; while it is not open to the objections which Cournot

---

$$\frac{F_2(a_2)(1 - 1/e_s)}{f_1(a_1)(1 - 1/e_d)}$$

as follows from note 4 to p. 352. And the slope for the foreign country is

$$\frac{f_2(a_2)(1 - 1/\eta_\delta)}{F_1(a_1)(1 - 1/\eta_\sigma)},$$

by parity of reasoning, in Mr. Bickerdike's notation.

We have, therefore, if the slopes are either both positive or both negative,

$$\frac{F_2(a_2)(1 - 1/e_s)}{f_1(a_1)(1 - 1/e_d)} \bigg/ \frac{f_2(a_2)(1 - 1/\eta_\delta)}{F_1(a_1)(1 - 1/\eta_\sigma)} > 1.$$

Now by Mr. Bickerdike's equation (1) (loc. cit.) we have (his " r " being initially = 1)

$$\frac{F_2(a_2)}{f_1(a_1)} = \frac{f_2(a_2)}{F_1(a_1)},$$

therefore $(1 - 1/e_s)(1 - 1/\eta_\sigma) - (1 - 1/e_d)(1 - 1/\eta_\delta)$ the denominator of the expression for $\frac{du}{dr}$ is positive.

For the case in which the two Supply-and-Demand curves are not both positively or both negatively inclined to the axis, this reasoning is no longer available. But it is no longer required. For the case can only occur when one of the coefficients of elasticity, e_d or η_δ, is greater than unity and the other less. And in that case the second term of the denominator to which a negative sign is prefixed is negative. Accordingly the denominator is the sum of two parts, both of which are positive.

[1] Cp. Bickerdike, ECONOMIC JOURNAL, Vol. XVII. pp. 100, 101.

[2] Ibid., p. 101.

and others have brought against the classical conception of barter without the use of money. It avoids also a certain danger attending the conception of barter which, in the light of Mr. Bickerdike's theory, has become visible. When demand and supply are expressed in terms of the commodities exchanged (abstraction being made of money), there is a difficulty in representing a money tax on imports in the case of inelastic demand.[1] I must confess to have fallen into the trap which is here, and to have made statements about a tax on imports which are only true of a tax in kind, not in money.[2]

The use of a peculiar money allows us, with more security than in the preliminary stage,[3] to employ the curves proper to domestic trade for the purpose of exhibiting the loss of surplus advantage consequent upon a customs duty. We have only to imagine that in Fig. 1 DD' now represents the demand-curve for imports from abroad in terms of the *national* money; while SS' represents the supply of such imports by the foreigner at prices reckoned in the same money, that of the home country. When the duty is of the kind supposed, the national currency is appreciated with respect to the international money; and accordingly the foreign supply is raised, the curve SS' being thrust

---

[1] The difficulty may be cleared up as follows. When an import duty of *p* per cent. *ad valorem* is imposed by the home country the Supply-and-Demand curve becomes transformed to Mr. Bickerdike's equation (1) $ra_1f_1(a_1) = a_2F_2(a_2)$, where $r = 100/(100 + p)$. To exhibit the position of the new curve in relation to the old one let us suppose OE in Fig. 2 (a reproduction of Mr. Bickerdike's first figure) to be the undisturbed Supply-and-Demand curve for the home country; and let us consider with reference to any assigned value of the ordinate a_1, any point on the perpendicular passing through O, what is the abscissa, the new value of a_2 as compared with what the abscissa would have been if the curve OE had not been disturbed by the import duty. Let a_2 be the old abscissa, $a_2 + \Delta a_2$ the new abscissa (corresponding to the assigned value of a_1). Then to determine Δa_2, we have, putting $(1 - \tau)$ for (the proper fraction) r,

$$(1 - \tau)a_1f_1(a_1) = (a_2 + \Delta a_2)F_2(a_2 + \Delta a_2); (1 - \tau)a_1f_1(a_1) = a_2F_2(a_2) + \Delta a_2(F_2 a_2)$$
$$+ a_2F'_2(a_2)); - \tau a_1f_1(a_1) = \Delta a_2 F_2(a_2)(1 - 1/e_s)$$

Now e_s is positive (by the third postulate). So is τ. Accordingly Δa_2 is negative; the new curve is swung to the left of the old one, the change in OE being, as Mr. Bickerdike has pointed out, of the kind represented in Fig. 3 of my article on International Values, ECONOMIC JOURNAL, Vol. VI. p. 430. The foreigners' Demand-and-Supply curve remaining unchanged, we may reason with Mr. Bickerdike (ECONOMIC JOURNAL, Vol. XVI. p. 532) that the new position of equilibrium, say Q, is one of increased advantage to the home country.

[2] See Bickerdike, ECONOMIC JOURNAL, Vol. XVI. p. 532, referring to my Vol. IV. p. 432. I had recognised that a distinction which I had drawn between export and import taxes was not applicable to ordinary taxes in money, only to certain customs duties in kind—not a very important exception, I admit. (See Index, s.v. *Imports*.)

[3] See above, p. 348.

down. In the limiting case above supposed, where SS' was

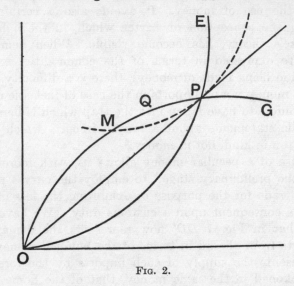

Fig. 2.

originally a right line, it will be lowered in such wise that the whole tax will accrue to the Treasury, without any loss of Con-

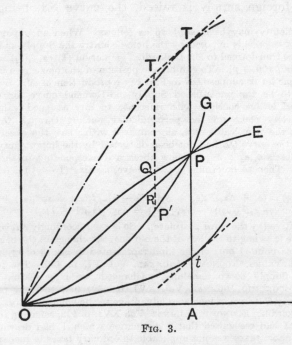

Fig. 3.

sumers' Surplus. In general the preliminary argument becomes *a fortiori* through the change of price-level.

(c) The third postulate allows us to evaluate the advantage obtained by the home country. For this purpose I shall employ another construction, that of Auspitz and Lieben, which, as already suggested, may offer some advantages. It will be remembered that they employ even in domestic trade a construction like that which Dr. Marshall invented for foreign trade But in their construction the ordinate represents, not an amount of commodity, but an amount of money given in exchange for a commodity, which may at first be supposed to be altogether produced at home. Thus, in Fig. 3, AP represents the quantity of money offered for OA, a quantity of commodity, at the price represented by the (tangent of) the angle POA, OPE being the demand-curve. Likewise the dispositions of sellers are represented by the supply-curve OPG. If through the point O is drawn the (collective) indifference-curve (to use my own terminology), OT pertaining to the buyers, the vertical distance between the demand-curve and the indifference-curve measures the Consumers' Surplus, the collective total utility incident to purchasing at a certain price. Thus for the price (tan) POA, PT is that total utility. Likewise the vertical distance between the supply-curve and the corresponding indifference-curve represents the gain of the sellers, e.g., Pt. The total advantage to the community (Consumers' + Producers' Surplus) is Tt. The last proposition remains true even if we suppose that the indifference-curve pertaining to buyers does not pass through O, but through a point at a vertical distance from O,[1] with a like supposition as to the curve pertaining to sellers.

When a tax is imposed on the commodity the effect is to diminish Consumers' Surplus from TP to $T'Q$, that is (since TT', the tangent at the point T, is parallel to the line OP) by an amount QR, which is less than the yield of the tax QP', and than the foreigner's contributions to the yield $P'R$.[2]

So far with respect to a domestic commodity. We have next to suppose the curve OPE to represent the Demand-curve of the home country for imports from abroad; OPG the foreigners' supply of those commodities (at prices reckoned in national money). We are now not concerned with the surplus advantage accruing to the foreign sellers. In estimating the advantage which the home country obtains from the trade, we must take

---

[1] As sometimes supposed by Auspitz and Lieben; whose terminology I do not follow literally.

[2] In this reasoning it is taken for granted that the vertical distance between T' and the curve OT may be neglected in comparison with QR and RP'; in virtue of the general principle enounced in the last section, above, p. 354.

into account not only the gain of the consumers, but also the loss of the home producers. It will be found that this collective utility is represented by a new curve OT, which has the same relation to the new OPE as the old OT had to the old, namely, that if a straight line in any direction through O meets the demand-curve at a point P, and a perpendicular through P cuts the indifference-curve O in T, the tangent to that curve at T is parallel to the line OP. Auspitz and Lieben establish this extension of their construction through the appropriate conception of a certain amount of commodity distributed gratis among the consumers and producers of the home country in accordance with the laws of final utility—a conception pertinent to scientific Socialism.[1]

So far as to imports abstracted from their concomitant exports. To represent the interest of the home country in the amount of exports, let OG now represent the home-country's supply of exports. By a parity of reasoning we may show that Pt now represents the net gain in the way of exportation.

The two together are equivalent to the sum-total which Mr. Bickerdike defines as the net advantage of trade.[2]

Having now shown the use of the scaffolding, I shall proceed to remove it bit by bit.

(a) First it may be remarked that the assumption of constant elasticity is not essential to Mr. Bickerdike's conclusions. The *initial* rate at which advantage is increasing with a small tax has

---

[1] We may also reason thus. Let y be the ordinate of the curve (not shown in the figure) which represents the *total* demand of the home country for the commodity whether home-made or imported. This curve lies *outside* OPE (which now represents the demand of the country for *imports* of the commodity); a vector drawn through O, making an angle θ ($< 90°$) with the abscissa, meets the total demand-curve in a point, say Π (not shown in the figure), such that the distance of Π from O along the vector is greater than the distance of P, the point where the vector meets the demand-curve for imports. For $O\Pi = OP + O\pi$, where π is the point at which the vector meets the home country's supply-curve of the commodity (not shown in the figure, OPG is now the *foreigner's* supply-curve). Let (x, y) be the co-ordinates of Π, (x_1, y_1) of P, (x_2, y_2) of π. Then (for every value of θ) $\Delta x_1 \tan \theta = \Delta x \tan \theta - \Delta x_2 \tan \theta$. Now $\Delta x \tan \theta$ is the pecuniary measure of the marginal utility to the consumers in the home country of an increment of the commodity; $\Delta x_2 \tan \theta$ is the loss to the home producers consequent upon the decrement of production Δx_2. Accordingly, $\Delta x_1 \tan \theta$ represents the net gain to the home country of an increment of importation Δx_1. But $\tan \theta = \dfrac{y_1}{x_1}$, where y_1 is that function of x_1 which forms the equation of the curve OPE. The curve OT obtained by integrating $\dfrac{y_1}{x_1}\Delta x_1$ now measures by its vertical distance from a point on OPE the net utility resulting from a certain amount of importation in the same way as it before measured the consumers' surplus for a certain amount of home production.

[2] The expression for u, ECONOMIC JOURNAL, Vol. XVII. p. 100.

the same expression, whether the elasticities be considered as constant or not. The argument by way of steps holds good provided that, as before, in the two compared flights of steps (corresponding to different degrees in the elasticity of demand on the part of the home country for the imported goods), each step of the one is higher than the corresponding step of the other.[1] Even the expression for " the maximum advantage rate " in terms (only) of the elasticities of foreign demand and supply still subsists.[2] But when these elasticities are not constant, the formula cannot be used for purposes of verification as before. The formula in its generality may be employed to show that the home Government, by means of a customs duty, may exercise a power of monopoly, and screw up the terms of international trade to the very point which the home country, acting as a Combination, would fix.

(b) When we abandon the supposition of a money peculiar to each country, we must base the theory of foreign trade on a more abstract conception, such as the " unit of productive power,"

[1] A condition which does not now admit of so neat a symbolic statement as before.

[2] To determine the rate of the tax which affords the greatest advantage to the home country, we have the condition that the disturbed Supply-and-Demand curve for the home country should intersect the (undisturbed) curve for the foreign country, viz. OG (Fig. 2) in a point Q which represents a state of trade of maximum advantage to the home country. In order that this condition should be fulfilled the tangent to OG at Q ought to coincide with the indifference curve pertaining to the home country which passes through Q. (See *Mathematical Psychics*, p. 116.) Now the differential equation to an indifference curve, relating to the home country, is

$$\frac{da_1}{da_2} = \frac{F_2(a_2)}{f_1(a_1)}.$$

The expression on the right denotes the slope, at the point (a_1, a_2), of an indifference curve passing through that point. Also the slope of the foreigners' Demand-and-Supply curve at the point (a_1, a_2) is

$$\frac{f_2(a_2)(1 - 1/\eta_\delta)}{F_1(a_1)(1 - 1/\eta_\sigma)}$$

Equating the two expressions for the slope and employing Mr. Bickerdike's equation (1) we have

$$r = \frac{1 - 1/\eta_\delta}{1 - 1/\eta_\sigma};$$

which is Mr. Bickerdike's result extended to the general case of variable elasticities.

Considering Fig. 2 to represent a market in the general sense of the term we see that if the dealers on the one side of the market for which the Supply-and-Demand curve is OE were to act as a Combination, the terms which they would force on their customers competing against each other are represented by the point Q in the curve OG; discrimination between customers being forbidden (*Mathematical Psychics*, *loc. cit.*, and p. 116). The point thus defined is coincident, I think, with the " maximum utility point " investigated by Prof. Pigou in the Appendix A to his *Methods of Industrial Peace*. The analogy between monopoly and the action of a tariff is exhibited by Auspitz and Lieben (*Theorie des Preises*).

which Professor Bastable has found it necessary to introduce,[1] or the " unit of work " which I have employed.[2] For, I think with the classical writers, it is not in general safe to ignore the change in the level of gold prices within the home country consequent upon a variation in the terms of international trade. How, except by means of a change in the price-level, can we explain the benefit which a country whose exports are in great demand in foreign countries can obtain by imposing a duty on commodities imported from those countries.[3] To determine, or at least define, the " unit " supposed to be constant while the level of gold prices is altered, we may have recourse to the principle of the Labour Standard already referred to as the regulator of the money imagined by Mr. Bickerdike. Of that money, as compared with this ideal standard, we may say what Adam Smith says of " a particular commodity " compared with " a quantity of labour " : " The one is a plain, palpable object ; the other an abstract notion, which, though it can be made sufficiently intelligible, is not altogether so natural and obvious."

(c) The last limitation to be removed is the postulate to which Professor Pigou has objected, that " a *supply-curve* can be treated as a *particular expenses curve*," [4] together with a corresponding assumption on the side of demand. " This is not legitimate in general," as Professor Pigou observes, " but it may be in special cases." I submit that this is one of the cases in which the assumption may be safely employed.

First, the postulate in question is " the least arbitrary assumption in the absence of special knowledge," a " neutral condition " [5]

[1] *International Trade*, ch. ii. p. 23 (ed. 4).

[2] " Theory of International Values," above, **R**, p. 53.

[3] The case of the " Guernsey " supposed above, p. 345. But in order that a change of price level should occur and have to be taken into account, it is not necessary that the home country should be very small (in relation to the foreign country); it is sufficient that it should not be large. Of course the amount of trade affected by the tax must be considerable in order to produce a sensible result on general prices in a measurable time.

[4] ECONOMIC JOURNAL, Vol. XVII. p. 290.

[5] If, as above (p. 354), the supply-curve is designated by the equation $y = \psi$ (x, x), the conditions are co-operative or anti-co-operative, according as $\left(\dfrac{d\psi}{dx}\right)$ is negative or positive. Like distinctions apply to the demand-curve $y = \phi(x, \mathrm{x})$.

It may be observed that $\left(\dfrac{d\psi}{dx}\right)$—the partial differential with respect to x only— is always positive, $\left(\dfrac{d\phi}{dx}\right)$ always negative ; $\dfrac{d\psi}{dx}$—the complete differential when $x \equiv \mathrm{x}$—and likewise $\dfrac{d\phi}{dx}$, may be either negative or positive, but $\dfrac{d\phi}{dx}$ cannot (in stable equilibrium) be positive while $\dfrac{d\psi}{dx}$ is negative.

between two conditions of which neither is known to prevail. These outlying conditions are described, with special reference to supply, as " Co-operative " and " Anti-co-operative," conditions correlated to, but not coincident with, Increasing and Decreasing returns as usually understood.   I accept this presumption, based, as I understand, on the principle of what I have called *a priori*, or unverified Probability.[1]   The presumption is confirmed by an appeal to authority evidencing that the assumption has worked well.   Mr. Bickerdike claims the authority of Professor Pigou [2] on the ground of his admission respecting Consumers' Surplus, to which I have already adverted.   I may add that in his mathematical reasoning about Arbitration,[3] Professor Pigou explicitly abstracts complications of the kind here called " secondary." A similar abstraction has been unconsciously practised with good effect by other authorities.   Many a humble votary of pure science has been edified by the truth as it is in Jevons, without having so much as heard whether there be a superadded complication.

Altogether there seems to be a considerable probability that the third postulate may be taken for granted; and accordingly that the theory holds good.

Such being the proof of the theory, what is its application ? May we not answer in the words employed by Hume with reference to his theory of Interest ?   " Besides that the speculation is curious, it may frequently be of use in the conduct of public affairs.   At least, it must be owned that nothing can be of more use than to improve by practice the method of reasoning on these subjects, which of all others are the most important, though they are commonly treated in the loosest and most careless manner." It is the latter sort of advantage—light rather than fruit—which I principally expect from Mr. Bickerdike's speculations.   He has improved by practice a method of reasoning which may be brought to bear on other questions of more direct practical importance.

The direct " use in the conduct of public affairs," to which the theory is applicable, is " making foreign countries contribute something to its [the home country's] revenue," in Mill's phrase, and more generally to its Real Income, in excess of the gain which it would enjoy under a free trade.   The feasibility of such projects is considered by Dr. Marshall in his judicial observations

---

[1] See Index.
[2] ECONOMIC JOURNAL, Vol. XVII. p. 585.
[3] *Methods of Industrial Peace.*

respecting an Export Duty on Coal.[1] His careful statement of the *pros* and *contras*, alike in the case of export and import duties, dispenses me from the necessity of treating the subject generally. I need dwell only on those considerations which are special to Mr. Bickerdike's particular scheme for taxing the foreigner.

Mr. Bickerdike's plan has the advantage of dispensing with a detailed inquiry into the conditions of demand and supply. It really looks as if it were sufficient for his purpose that the relevant elasticities of demand and supply should not be of an extreme character—extremely small for the home country or extremely great for the foreigner; that there should be nothing peculiar and exceptional in the conditions of the trade. A *datum* of this sort, the ascertainment of which cannot be considered chimerical, seems, in the light of Mr. Bickerdike's theory and experiments, to justify the imposition of small customs duties, say from $2\frac{1}{2}$ to 5 per cent., on a great number of articles. The objection that industry is thereby directed into less advantageous channels is not admissible; for by the theory the disadvantage in the way of production is overbalanced by the gain accruing to the Treasury. Abstracting the practical difficulties to which we are coming, on the platform of pure theory the Free Trader must abandon his hectoring tone with respect to the defence of a Protectionist tax on the ground that it is a little one.[2]

It may be added that Protection, in losing its evil, would not lose its attractiveness. It could not be objected to this, as to many ingenious schemes hatched by students, that it could never be started. It would be only too easy to start this scheme.

These considerable advantages are counterbalanced by weighty objections. At best, and even in the abstract, the theory is but probable. In the computation of the chances in its favour there is largely involved what I have called *a priori*, or unverified, probability. But it is yet to be seen how far such probabilities— though countenanced by their use in the treatment of physical observations—are available in the conduct of human affairs. It may be suggested that the evidence is good enough to afford a regulative idea for the adjustment of indispensable taxation, but not good enough to justify the imposition of taxes for the express purpose of putting the foreigner under contribution. The distinction might be illustrated by a comparison with the principle

---

[1] In a letter to *The Times* published April 22, 1901; reprinted in the ECONOMIC JOURNAL, Vol. XI. p. 265.

[2] The tone of Robert Lowe, for instance, in the speech referred to above, . 347.

of equal (or least) sacrifice, which is generally considered good enough to regulate the distribution of indispensable taxation, while only Socialists propose increasing taxation expressly for the purpose of carrying out that utilitarian principle. Upon this view Mr. Bickerdike's theory might have that limited application which Professor Bastable allows to the presumption in favour of small taxes in general which I have based on the theory of small quantities.[1] There are in practice much more important considerations; still, the presumption is worth mentioning.

Of course, the general presumption may be overridden by positive evidence that, with reference to any proposed customs duty, the contribution of the foreigner is likely to be smaller than the theory requires. There is some ground for believing that the conditions of British trade are particularly unfavourable for levying a contribution on foreigners.

Among practical considerations particularly relevant to the scheme before us is the danger of retaliation. The novelty in the scheme, that it may be practised by a country which has no special advantages, nothing like a " monopoly " as producer or consumer, no doubt increases the home country's power of hitting the foreigner. But it equally increases the power of the foreigner to hit back. Practised on the grounds peculiar to this theory, the scheme of taxing the foreigner is peculiarly open to Mill's objection : " it would be a means which it would seldom be advisable to adopt, being so easily counteracted by a precisely similar proceeding on the other side." [2] The mathematical method shows rather more clearly than appears in Mill's discussion, that, short of the case in which " the trade and its advantage would cease entirely," [3] bilateral taxation would damage both parties.

Again, the system of many small taxes minimises, indeed, the loss incident to changes in the course of industry; but it does not minimise the amount of trade-hampering constraint that taxation, high or low, involves. On the contrary, that sort of *friction* in proportion to the proceeds of taxation is likely to be greater the more numerous the taxes.

Thus the direct use of the theory is likely to be small. But it is to be feared that its abuse will be considerable. It affords to unscrupulous advocates of vulgar Protection a peculiarly specious

---

[1] *Public Finance*, ed. 3, p. 353 referring to ECONOMIC JOURNAL, Vol. VII. p. 568, above, S.

[2] J. S. Mill, *Political Economy*, Book V. ch. iv. § 6, ante-penultimate paragraph. *Loc. cit.*, penultimate paragraph.

pretext for·introducing the thin edge of the fiscal wedge. Mr. Bickerdike may be compared to a scientist who, by a new analysis, has discovered that strychnine may be administered in small doses with prospect of advantage in one or two more cases than was previously known; the result of this discovery may be to render the drug more easily procurable by those whose intention, or at least whose practice, is not medicinal. It was thus that the " drama of poison " perpetrated in the reign of Louis XIV. was initiated by one whose baleful receipt was obtained from Glaser, a chemist of eminence, the discoverer of a new substance.[1] Let us admire the skill of the analyst, but label the subject of his investigation POISON.

[1] Funck-Brentano, *Le Drame des Poisons*.

APPLICATION OF THE DIFFERENTIAL CALCULUS
TO ECONOMICS

[THIS fragment, published in *Scientia*, 1909, under a slightly different title, deals with the mechanics of wealth in the narrow sense which excludes what Jevons calls a " common denominator of feeling." The principle of " recontract " (above, β) is employed in a variant proof of the theorem that the position of stable equilibrium is at the intersection of the demand-curves pertaining to the respective sides of a market. The abstract theory of Supply-and-Demand is applied to international trade; and to the analogous case of transactions between the parties to Distribution. But it is pointed out that this analogy may prove misleading if there is not taken into account a certain characteristic of domestic trade which Professor Pigou has described as the elasticity of the Demand for Common Labour (cp. *Economics of Welfare*, Book V. ch. iii. s. 8). The conceptions of Producers' Surplus and of the margin of production are illustrated by critical references to well-known writers.]

Description and Division.

The extension to Social Science of principles approved in Mathematical Physics is a theme worthy of *Scientia*. For this journal, as announced at its inception, is " born of the desire to co-ordinate the work carried on in different fields of knowledge." Alone in a world of specialists it seems to realise that part of Plato's scheme of education which consisted in bringing the sciences together and contemplating them in their mutual relations.

There is indeed a certain resemblance between the ancient philosophy and the modern study of Mathematical Psychics in so far as both attain large general views rather than particulars adapted to art and practice. But we are not committed to the contempt of fact which seems to characterise the Platonic precept that " in astronomy, as in geometry, we should employy problems, and let the heavens alone, if we would approach the subject in the right way." [1] The Newtonian astronomy is rather the model of our Science; but we can only follow it at a great distance owing to the multiplicity of variables in Social Science and the want of a unit for measuring advantage in a subjective sense. Often we must be content with knowing that knowledge is unattainable without more data than we possess—the Socratic lesson of modesty which was taught by Cournot and Jevons.[2]

This description is applicable generally to the subject designated by the main portion of my title—" the use of the Differential Calculus "—and more particularly to that part of the subject which is demarcated by the limiting clause—" to determine conditions of maximum advantage." The subject thus limited is, if we understand " Economics " in its largest sense, almost coincident with—only slightly narrower than—the field which is covered by the well-known dictum of Malthus : " Many of the questions, both in morals and politics, seem to be of the nature of the problems *de maximis et minimis* in fluxions." Such is the little territory, on the borderland between Physics and Psychology, which I attempt here to survey.

One main division has already come into view, that which separates Economics in a narrow or " proper " sense from the wider Science of Political or rather Social Economy, of which the object is not simply wealth, but welfare, so far as dependent on wealth. We might define Economics proper—the subject of our Section I—by the limitation that in Jevons's words " the motive in one mind is weighed only against other motives in the same mind, never against the motives in other minds." [3] Whereas in Social Economy—the subject of Section II*—what Jevons calls " a common denominator of feeling " must be postulated.

According to the postulate, the relation between the individuals of a Society may be described by the familiar metaphor of

[1] *Republic*, vii. 529, Jowett's translation; a precept which Macaulay contrasts unfavourably with Bacon's method.

[2] The use of Mathematics to make clear the nature and extent of the assumptions implied in dealing with economic problems has been noticed by Professor J. S. Nicholson in a recent lecture (*Transactions of the Faculty of Actuaries*, No. 35, Vol. I. Part IV.).

[3] *Theory of Political Economy*, edition 3, p. 14. *Cp.* Pareto, *Manuel d'Économie Politique*, chap. iii. § 11.

* The design of a sequel dealing with a subject wider than economics proper, was not destined to be executed. The definition of the wider subject may be illustrated by the writer's article in the ECONOMIC JOURNAL for December 1923.

solidarity. But the physical analogy of Economics proper does not lie so ready to hand. The particles of an economic system neither cohere as a solid, nor collide with the independence of a gas. Their liquid movements are comparable to a dance in which youths and maidens move in unison; harmoniously, but subject to a change of partners.

To learn the steps of this peculiar dance consider first the movement of a single couple. One of the pair, say X, gives to the other, say Y, a quantity x of the commodity x in return for the amount y of the commodity y given by Y to X. The terms of such an arrangement may be represented by a point (x, y) on the plane of the paper. The variation of the terms of contract is represented by the movement of the point in the plane. The parties cannot move separately. They are in the same boat. They both have hold of the rudder, but the directions in which they respectively prefer to move are not the same. The magnetic pole towards which X would steer lies to the south-east, supposing that the axis of y points to north. The centre of attraction for Y lies to the north-west. Motion is possible only as long as both parties are winning towards their respective goals.[1]

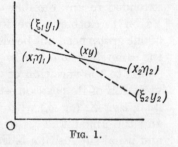

Fig. 1.

Next let there be two individuals on each side, say X_1 and X_2 dealing with Y_1 and Y_2. (The motives or dispositions of X_1 may at first be supposed identical with those of X_2; the psychic forces acting on Y_1 and Y_2 being also identical.) X_1 is free to move in any direction to any distance, provided that either Y_1 or Y_2 accompany, or at least move parallel to him; and the like is true of X_2 with regard to the Ys, and of each of the Ys with regard to the Xs. The conditions are expressed by Fig. 1, in which the point (x_1, η_1) represents the amount of commodity x which the individual X_1 gives and the amount of commodity y which he receives (partly, it may be, from Y_1, partly from Y_2). The point (ξ_1, y_1) denotes the amount of commodity y which Y_1 gives and the amount of commodity x which he receives (in general, partly from X_1, and partly from X_2). The points (x_2, η_2), (ξ_2, y_2) are similarly interpreted. The two points (x_1, η_1) and (x_2, η_2), may be considered as moving along a rod which passes

[1] See the construction in the writer's *Mathematical Psychics*, Part II. p. 20 *et seq.*, and *cp.* Pareto, *Manuel d'Économie Politique*, ch. iii. § 58 *et passim*.

through a point (x, y); subject to the condition that those two points are equi-distant from the point (x, y). The points (ξ_1, y_1) and (ξ_2, y_2) are similarly related to the point (x, y); which may thus be described as the centre of gravity of the system. The system moves towards a position of equilibrium—a position of maximum energy, as it may be considered—under the influence of forces acting on the constituent particles; subject to the constraints which have been indicated. Among those conditions is one very unusual in Physics, very difficult to represent mechanically, that no part of the system does work against another. For instance, the point (x_1, η_1) cannot suffer a change by the subtraction of Δx_1 from x_1, the addition of $\Delta \eta_1$ to η_1, if such a step in the direction defined by the ratio $\Delta \eta_1 : \Delta x_1$ is one in which the individual is averse to move. The conception may be extended to any number of Xs on one side, and any number of Ys on the other. The forces actuating the different members of one group need not be identical; they need to act, not in exactly the same *direction*, but in what may be called the same *sense*.

As to the variation of the forces acting on a particle with the variation of its position—the change in the motives of an individual, *e.g.*, X_r (or Y_r) with the amount of x (or y) that he retains, and the amount of y (or x) that he has obtained—the natural and usual supposition is that the forces are a function only of the position defined by those amounts, viz. x_r and y_r. This state of things is here designated by the term "independent dealing," the symbol (A). But we shall also have to entertain the supposition, not very usual in Physics, that the forces acting on any particle at the point (x, y) depend not only on the co-ordinates which define that position, but also on the position of the system— upon the co-ordinates of its centre of gravity, as we may say, when the number of particles on each side is equal. The supposition will be more fully explained in the sequel, under the head of "interdependent dealing," labelled (B).

I do not attempt here to cultivate the fields which have been indicated; but as I pass in the course of a rapid survey, I may sometimes root up a weed which has proved noxious, or drop a seed which may germinate.

I. ECONOMICS PROPER

(A) *Independent Dealing.*

Simple Exchange.—This heading is meant to designate the simplest form of *market*, the conception of which has been attained in the introductory description of two groups of Xs and Ys, dealing respectively in two commodities x and y. This is the economic molecule; itself, as we have seen, a compound of curiously interrelated atoms. In the fragmentary system of only two particles, their identical position (which may be equally in our notation denoted by the symbols (x, η), (ξ, y), (x, y)) would be varied under the influence of forces tending to maximum advantage up to a limit investigated by Jevons, in his *Theory of Exchange*, and now commonly known as the *Contract-Curve*.[1] When there are one, two or more dealers on each side of the market, a like condition of contract must still be fulfilled. Thus in the case above put of two dealers on each side, either of the Xs, say X_1, will continue to deal with one of the Ys, say Y_1, up to a point beyond which it is impossible to advance a single step with benefit to both parties. The like is true of X_1 with respect to Y_2, and of X_2 with respect to either of the Ys.

Moreover, in addition to this purely *contractual* condition, the circumstance of *competition* introduced by the duality of the dealers on each side imports a new condition. There cannot be equilibrium unless the slope of the final step taken by any X in conjunction with (parallel to) any Y is the same as the slope of the final step taken by (that or) any other X with any other (or that) Y. For if it be possible let Fig. 1 correspond to a state of equilibrium in which X_1 gives to Y_2 a final increment of x, say $(\Delta x_1)_2$, in return for the final increment of y $(\Delta y_2)_1$; while X_2 gives to Y_1 the final increment $(\Delta x_r)_1$ and receives the final increment $(\Delta y_1)_2$; this arrangement cannot stand if the slope designated by the respective pairs of corresponding increments are different. For in that case it would in general be to the advantage of one of the Xs and one of the Ys to desert their respective partners and take one step at least, and probably several, with each other.

Yet another condition is imposed by competition when we advance to the typical case of indefinitely numerous dealers on each side of the market—a crowd of competitors all of the same order in respect of the possible magnitude of their transactions.[2] Suppose that, in accordance with the conditions of equilibrium which have been already established, all the economic

---

[1] See the writer's *Mathematical Psychics*, p. 21 *et seq.*

[2] Or more generally of such relative magnitude that the power of any one competitor to influence the market is very small. This condition may be illustrated by its analogy with the condition which must in general be fulfilled by the relative magnitudes of independent statistical quantities, in order that their aggregate may fluctuate in accordance with the normal law of error.

particles are disposed at points such that no *indefinitely small* change of the system is possible; the final step which any one X can be induced to make in conjunction with one Y having the same slope for all, corresponding to a rate of exchange for small quantities $\Delta\eta : \Delta x$. Now by the assumption introduced in this paragraph, it is open to any individual on either side of the market, say X_r (or, *mutatis mutandis*, Y_r), to supply himself by exchanging small quantities with a great number of dealers. In other words, his whole course from zero to the point (x_r, η_r) may be made up of steps taken in conjunction with different Ys, each small step in the direction of the common slope $\Delta\eta : \Delta x$. If now X_r by multiplying steps of this kind can reach a point, say (x'_r, η'_r), which represents greater advantage to him than the point at which he was just now supposed to be at (x_r, η_r), he will tend to proceed to that point. He cannot do so, it may seem, because there will not be increments of y forthcoming on the terms offered to proceed to the new point; since they are as advantageously employed by their owners in dealing with other Xs. But it will be worth the while of X_r to offer rather better terms (with respect to short terminal steps) to a number of Ys than those which are represented by the given slope; since if it is advantageous for X_r to move from (x'_r, η_r) to $x'_r, \eta'_r)$, it will in general [1] be advantageous for him to move to some point in the neighbourhood of (x'_r, η'_r). Thus the system cannot be in equilibrium unless any individual dealer X_r (and similarly each Y) whose dealing consists of η_r received in return for x_r given, obtains as much y as he is willing to take at the rate of exchange defined by the ratio $\eta_r : x_r$. In other words, the point (x_r, η_r) is on the *demand-curve* of the individual X_r, and accordingly the point of equilibrium for the system is on the collective demand curve which represents the total demand (on the part of the Xs) for y at each compared rate of exchange between x and y. Likewise the point of equilibrium is on the collective demand-curve which represents the total demand on the part of the Ys for x; or, in other words, the curve representing the supply of y. Therefore the point of equilibrium is at an intersection of the collective Supply and Demand Curves.[2]

It may be asked, what is the good of thus deducing an obvious matter of fact, that there is one price in a market? I reply,

---

[1] In the absence of *singularities*, the usual continuity in the functions with which we are concerned may postulate.

[2] For a variant deduction of the familiar generalisation, see *Mathematical Physics*, p. 34 *et seq.*

may we not hope for the sort of advantages which explanation of empirical laws affords in Physics—always enlarged breadth of view, often increased power ?   We should hope humbly, indeed, mindful of the imperfections of the human, as compared with the physical, sciences.

The hope may derive some encouragement from the instance which comes nearest to our case, being the explanation of a law which applies to human affairs, in part at least, though its principal applications are physical.   I refer to the Law of Error, the so-called Gaussian law, which in the present connection at least might more properly be called Laplace's law; [1] the law prevalent in Statistics, which is explained by the action of numerous independent agencies supposed to underlie statistical phenomena.

It may be observed, parenthetically, that there is a resemblance not only between the subject-matter of the two laws explained—so far as both relate to human affairs—but also in the causes which form the explanation, the action of great numbers being a necessary part of each cause.   But the relation of the economic to the statistical theory is rather a resemblance than an analogy. There is not one law, but two laws; the law of competition, and the law of averages.   They are to be condemned who say or imply that the steadiness of normal value is altogether explained by the principle of Statistical Stability. [2]

To return to our explanation of a market; it may be held that this shows badly compared with the explanation of the Law of Error and other more familiar derivations of observed uniformities.   For there is no other probable explanation available in many of those cases; whereas here there is a very simple alternative explanation, namely, that exchange with different parties at the same rate is dictated by the simplicity of the

---

[1] For a summary of the present writer's views on this law see the paper on " The Application of the Calculus of Probalities to Statistics " in the *Bulletin of the International Institute of Statistics* for 1909.

[2] Suppose a market, with ten Xs on one side, ten Ys on the other; if, as above supposed, their natures or dispositions were constant from one (market-) day to another, the price determined by the play of competition would presumably be much the same from day to day, the range of indeterminateness being very small.   Suppose next that the demand-and-supply schedule for each individual oscillates from time to time; the steadiness of the rate of exchange (though not its determinateness) would be impaired.   But suppose further that the numbers on each side are raised from ten to a hundred.   Then steadiness may be restored by the principle of averages.   But alone it is not sufficient to secure steadiness, since it does not secure determinateness; for instance, in the case of two combinations, their average motives might be constant, but their bargains might vary from time to time.

arrangement—by an unconscious pressure of general convenience of the kind usually supposed to have brought about the adoption of money. No doubt this cause will explain something, but not, I think, everything. It will explain why a monopolist, apart from law and ethics, would probably not want to make separate terms with every individual, as strict theory might suggest. But it will not explain why in a monopolistic regime there may be several prices for (practically) the same article, but only one in a perfect market. To have analysed the conditions of a perfect market will be of assistance when we come to deal with monopolies and imperfect markets.

Composite Exchange.—A separate heading is scarcely required for the generalisation of the preceding theory. By supposing that the Xs offering x deal not only with Ys offering y, but also with Zs offering z, Ws offering w, and that dealers in each of these groups deal with two or more of the remaining groups. As Mill says, after analysing a certain case of simple exchange : " trade among any number of countries and in any number of commodities must take place on the same essential principles as trade between two countries and in two commodities." [1]

Economic Mobility.—The groups of Xs, Ys, etc., which supply different articles, may be imagined occupying different islands, between which there is a great gulf fixed, so that they which would go from one to the other island cannot. It is not possible for an X to assume the part of a Y, or vice versa. There is on this supposition no equation between the labour required in order to supply a certain quantity of x and the labour required to supply the quantity of y which is exchanged for that quantity of x. The quantities of labour, it should be remarked, must in the present section in strictness be conceived as measurable by an objective standard—so many foot-pounds, for example. But it is not easy, nor I think, usual, to treat Economics proper with such abstract rigour, as entirely to keep out of sight the cognate proposition—strictly belonging to our Section II *—that in the absence of mobility there will be no comparison between the trouble and benefit (in a subjective sense) resulting on an average to the parties on the different sides of the channel. On one side may be fruits growing wild, or quails rained from heaven, obtainable with a minimum of labour—with (practically) no labour at all if we suppose the amount of the commodity obtainable (per diem) to be limited. The denizens of this favoured

---

[1] *Political Economy*, Book III. chap. xviii. § 3; referring to International Trade. * See added note on p. 368, above.

island may be luxuriating in superfluity, while their customers have to toil hard in order to obtain the necessities of a miserable existence.

Though exchange without mobility may appear the simpler conception, it is not that which the classical writers have primarily entertained. To illustrate their conception of value dependent on and proportionate to quantity of labour, we may conceive regions which are at times islands, at times connected by dry land. The market is held, say at the time of high tide, and goes on much as we have already supposed. But it is no longer possible that any X should permanently fare worse than if he were to be transformed into a Y; since it is now open to him to transfer himself, at low tide, from one island to another. The passage between two islands may be more or less free; sometimes, perhaps, only available at *neap* tides, so that a long period is required for a change in " market value " to lead to a change in " normal " value.

International Trade.—Exchange being the genus, and the absence of mobility the differentia of international trade, there is deducible from these essential attributes a characteristic property which may be enunciated as follows. The price [1] of the commodities imported in (relation to) the commodities exported is less than what it would be if, *ceteris paribus*, the trade were closed. For suppose that a nation of Xs being dealers of the sort above defined,[2] export x to and import y from a nation of Ys; if the price of y in x would be unaffected by the cessation (and reopening) of the foreign trade, there would be no motive for the continuance of the trade. This characteristic property includes as a particular case the classical principle of Comparative Cost. The property is more general as it applies to cases of value depending only on rarity, not (also) on effort and sacrifice. For example, before trade was opened between Japan and the Occident in the early 'fifties, the rate of exchange between gold and silver in Japan was about $1:6$; while in the outer world it was about $1:15\frac{1}{2}$. There was accordingly fulfilled the condition that gold should be exported from Japan to the Occident, silver exported from the Occident into Japan. The condition would have existed on the supposition that the value of the precious metal had nothing

[1] I follow M. Walras in thus employing price in the more general sense of rate-of-exchange.

[2] Otherwise if there were one or two predominant it might be in their interest and in their power to open the trade for the sake of obtaining the advantage of increasing returns by turning on to *one* commodity the productive forces which had hitherto been employed on *two*.

to do with cost of production, but depended entirely on rarity, or the total amount in existence (as possibly in the later Roman Empire). The re-statement proposed is not only more general, but less equivocal than the doctrine of Comparative Cost as stated by the earlier writers. For the Comparative Costs must be interpreted in the words of Professor Bastable [1] as "those which would exist at the margin on the hypothesis that each country is isolated; in the general case (not explicitly considered by the earlier writers) of cost varying according to quantity produced."

Distribution.—So far we have ignored the heterogeneity of the factors which co-operate in production. Our Xs and Ys might have been small independent artisans or peasant proprietors. We have now to take into account the stratification of modern industry—that the class of workmen is, as it were, on a different level from the class of landlords, and from the various strata which compose the capitalist employing class. We have to conceive, in the metaphor of Jevons, a horizontal as well as a vertical cleavage. If the vertical cleavage before represented by the isolation of islands is now represented by the separation between the wings and towers of a mansion, the horizontal cleavage may be represented by the separation between the flats which form the different stories of the mansion. In domestic or internal trade there is assumed to be more or less perfect mobility between the compartments on the same story; but not mobility between the stories, one of which may be imagined to contain the working classes, the other the capitalist employing class.[2]

In economics it is often difficult to hold fast general resemblances without ignoring—or appearing to ignore—specific differences. In the present matter, while apprehending that the transactions between the operative and the employing classes are the genus international trade, we must not forget that the exports and imports in this trade are of a very peculiar character. The peculiarity might be partially illustrated by the trade which

[1] ECONOMIC JOURNAL, Vol. XI. p. 228, last par., and p. 229, first par.; referring to the present writer's analysis at Vol. X. p. 391. *Cp.* Vol. XI. p. 589.

[2] The propriety of conceiving the transactions between employers and employed as a sort of international trade was discerned by J. S. Mill (*Political Economy*, Book III. chap. ii. last par.). Professor Pigou seems to sanction the view here presented when referring to the presentation of it in the ECONOMIC JOURNAL; he says: "Is it not the better view that the great divisions of the industrial world, land, capital, brain-power, trained hand labour, muscular labour, are now competing in the sense that against those who would pass from one to another there is a great gulf fixed" (*Edinburgh Review*, Vol. CCIII. p. 23, January 1906—an article of which Professor Pigou has acknowledged himself the author in his book on *Import Duties*).

used to flourish between England and the Southern States of America; these States exported to England raw cotton, receiving in return cotton manufactures. If the offer of raw cotton with the demand for cotton manufactures were to be increased on one side of the international market by a change such as the growth of population in the Southern States, other things being the same, the offer of manufactures on the other side of the market on the part of a large and flourishing England would be 'likely to keep pace with the offer of raw material, in such wise as not to alter the terms of international exchange to the disadvantage of the average Southerner. But, indeed, the illustration hardly does justice to the expansiveness of the trade which we are now considering. Let us rather suppose the export to consist of that rawest and most extensively demanded material, mechanical power. Let us imagine, for the sake of illustration, Niagara harnessed in the service of man to belong wholly to the United States, not in part to Canada; and that by improved means of transmitting force the means of production may be conveyed from Niagara to any department of Canadian industry. If the supply of power from Niagara to Canada were to be increased by some dislocation, for instance, some impediment to its supply elsewhere, then it might be expected that—in the long run, and abstracting temporary disturbance—the offer on the part of Americans owning Niagara would be met by the demand for additional power on the part of the entrepreneurs in a large and flourishing Canada.

This peculiarity of the quasi-international trade must be borne in mind when it is argued that the transition from a regime of Protection to Free Trade may place a portion of the working-classes in the position of a " nation " for whose exports there has ceased to be a demand. In thus arguing in the course of an exchange of views with Professor Bastable in the ECONOMIC JOURNAL, I ought to have emphasised the peculiarity which has just been illustrated. It is true that I guarded against mis-apprehension by comparing the increase in freedom of trade to an improvement in machinery, and quoting Mill to the effect that an improvement in machinery may be " very injurious to the labourers " on a supposition " purely ideal." [1] But I may have quoted, without sufficient reservation, Ricardo's conclusion that (in a certain supposed case) " population will become redundant and the situation of the labouring classes will be that of distress

[1] ECONOMIC JOURNAL, Vol. XI. p. 583. Cp. *ibid.*, Vol. X. p. 392, where the issue is described as " so minute a point in so hypothetical a case."

and poverty." Ricardo has " been supposing " (as he explains
in the context) [1] " that improved machinery is *suddenly* discovered." Moreover, the probability of such a case was really
different for Ricardo from what it is for us after a century's
experience of improvements in machinery. Similarly, the proposition that the improvement in the mechanism of importation
which is effected by the liberation of trade, though it may divert
the direction, will (in the long run) not impair but increase the
efficiency of the productive forces in the country, rests partly,
I think, on specific experience of what improvements in arts of
production have done for the benefit of the working classes.
To distinguish empirical evidence of this kind from the still
more diffused and universal experience on which the first principles
of exchange (communicated in preceding paragraphs) are founded
is, I think, philosophically just ; and may be practically important
in certain peculiar pathological cases.

Function of the Entrepreneur.—The central figure in the
productive system is the entrepreneur. Buying the factors of
production, the use of land, labour, machinery, and working
them up into half-manufactured or finished products, which
he sells to other entrepreneurs or consumers, at a price covering
his expenses and remunerating his work and waiting. The
symmetry of the entrepreneur with respect to the factors of production was first, I think, clearly enunciated by M. Leon Walras.
Justly, or with very slight exaggeration, on the occasion of M.
Walras's anniversary in June 1909, the leading economists and
statisticians of Italy have declared : " The model that he was
first to furnish for the comprehension of economic phenomena,
the theory of economic equilibrium, constitutes the greatest
advance which our science has received, since the impulse (*l'avvia-
mento*) given to it by Ricardo." [2] All the more deserving of
examination must be any tenet in the doctrine of such a teacher
that challenges attention as paradoxical. In this spirit I have
before now noticed the peculiar proposition that the entrepreneur
normally makes neither gain nor loss. At first sight the dictum
might pass as a *façon de parler*, as Companies make their liabilities
and assets exactly balance by including among the liabilities
of the Company the property of its members. But the latest
utterance of the Lausanne school makes it indisputably clear
that the proposition is to be interpreted literally. Professor
Pareto recognises as fully as one could desire that the entrepreneur

---

[1] Ricardo, MacCulloch's edition, pp. 237 and 241.
[2] *Giornale degli Economisti*, June 1909.

is constantly pursuing his maximum advantage. But, we read, "cette fin elle-même peut se modifier par l'effet des moyens dont on veut se servir pour l'attendre." [1] The " curve of pursuit " along which the entrepreneur thus moves lands him in a position of null remuneration, through the action of competitors in the pursuit. " De cette façon les entreprises concurrentes, aboutissent là ou elles ne se proposaient nullement d'aller. Chacune d'elles ne recherchait que son propre avantage et ne souciait des consommateurs que dans la mesure où elle pouvait les exploiter, et au contraire par suite de toutes les adaptations et réadaptations successives enforcées par la concurrence toute cette activité des entreprises tourne au profit des consommateurs." [2]

Admitting that a process of the sort described may occur in certain phases of competition to which we are coming,[3] I do not recognise the description as typical of the entrepreneur's function in general, in a condition of stable equilibrium, or steady flow. In the pursuit of his maximum advantage he is rather to be compared to the lover on the Grecian vase, celebrated by Keats, who, though winning near the goal, does not advance—but does not therefore recede. Professor Pareto puts the case of an entrepreneur renting land from a landlord and producing wheat.[4] " If the entrepreneur has a monopoly he will procure for himself the maximum of advantage or profit (*bénéfice*)." [5] Agreed; assuming, what is indeed not explicably affirmed, that there is a plurality of competing landlords. " If there is competition between the entrepreneurs," the proprietor " will take all the *bénéfice* of the production and the entrepreneur nothing." Again agreed; assuming, what is now affirmed, that there is a single landlord and a plurality of competing entrepreneurs. But neither of these assumptions is appropriate to the normal case of Production and Distribution. We ought to assume a plurality both of landlords and entrepreneurs, like the Xs and Ys in the above paragraphs. In this typical case I cannot see that " lorsqu'il y a concurrence entre les entreprises celles-ci doivent se tenir sur les transformations complètes; elles n'ont donc ni profit ni perte." There is probably more than I have been able to apprehend in Professor Pareto's doctrine concerning the " complete transformation " of the factors of production by the entrepreneur [6] in a regime of competition. But I cannot see how it is inconsistent with the theory that the wheat produced flows partly into the hands of the entrepreneur, partly into the

---

[1] *Manuel d'Économie Politique*, ch. v. § 11.   [2] *Loc. cit.*, § 74.
[3] Subdivision B.   [4] *Loc. cit.*, § 62.   [5] § 64.
[6] *Loc. cit.*, chap. iii. §§ 75, 150 *et passim*.

barns of the landlord, in a proportion determined by the play of demand and supply; with no presumption that, in general, the proportion is extremely unequal, and tends to be unity to zero (or the reverse).

The conception of a set of cultivator entrepreneurs dealing with a set of landlords has been employed by me in criticising another paradoxical doctrine about the function of the entrepreneur, propounded by other eminent writers, on another continent. These writers do not regard the remuneration of the entrepreneur as null, but as precisely equivalent to the loss which would be occasioned to the community by the subtraction of an entrepreneur. The proposed equation would, as it happens, be verified by the particular case above instanced; but not, I have maintained, in the general case when instead of, or in addition to, landlords we have the owners of other factors of production, in particular hired labour.[1]

It will be understood that it is only the exact mathematical analogy between the marginal productivity of the entrepreneur and that of an operative in a large establishment which I dispute; I do not deny, I all along imply, that there is a general resemblance between the motives and winnings of the employer and employed, sufficient to justify Dr. Marshall's doctrine, that there is a supply price for business power.[2]

Nor do I dispute that part of Professor Pareto's exposition, which is in accordance with Dr. Marshall's doctrine, that the net advantages of a business are balanced against the incident efforts and sacrifices, in prospect rather than in the result at the stages of " quasi-rent." [3] Professor Pareto may be quite right in his surmise [4] that the actual remuneration of employers on an average is very small. It is the deduction of that tendency to zero from the theory of Competition that I cannot follow. Let me take another illustration. Suppose a set of competing landlords as before, each owning a portion of the land, which may be supposed limited in quantity and all of the same quality. But instead of competing cultivators, suppose now citizens competing for sites of bungalows and gardens in which to take holiday. We have once more a typical case of simple exchange between

---

[1] Above, p. 339 and context.

[2] *Principles of Economics* under the head of " Business Management."

[3] *Ibid.*, Book VI. chap. viii. (4th edition).

[4] *Manuel*, chap. v. t. 69, referring to certain Belgian Statistics. See the Hungarian statistics compiled by Korösi, to which reference is made in the ECONOMIC JOURNAL, Vol. XII. p. 251, and compare Marshall, *loc. cit.* Book VI. chap. viii. § 8, which may be considered the *locus classicus* on the subject.

Xs and Ys, a marginal price affording a maximum of advantage in the sense above explained.[1] That character of a market would be maintained even though it were true, in accordance with the shrewd remark of Sidgwick, that human beings have a tendency to over-value leisure as a source of happiness.[2] I am aware that Professor Pareto would not admit the parallel suggested between Consumers' and Producers' surplus.[3] But with reference to the purpose in hand I fail to see the difference. However, I am quite prepared to find that there is no material disagreement between us, that we are looking at different sides of the same shield—I at the gold side, he at a side which is devoid of all precious metal.

Marginal Productivity.—I go on to consider some objections which, though not so serious, on a question of pure theory, as the dissent of a great mathematical economist, yet deserve and may reward attention. I refer to the difficulty about the function of *Margins* in Economics which is felt by some who have not specially attended to maximum problems. No one has expressed these difficulties more strikingly than Mr. J. A. Hobson. The following extract is typical of his objections to Dr. Marshall's doctrine of the " Marginal Shepherd."

In order to measure the productivity of the last dose of labour let us remove it. The diminution of the total product may be 8 per cent. This 8 per cent. according to Marshall's method we ascribe to the last dose of labour. If now, restoring this dose of labour, we withdrew the last dose of capital, the reduction of product might be 10 per cent. This 10 per cent. is regarded as the product of the last dose of capital. Similarly the withdrawal of the last dose of land might seem to reduce the product by 10 per cent. What would be the effect of a simultaneous withdrawal of the last dose of each factor ? According to Marshall's method clearly 28 per cent. But is this correct ? " [4]

Quite correct, I have elsewhere replied,[5] adding, with reference to objections continued in the same vein as the passage above quoted : Imagine " an analogous application of the differential calculus in physics. . . . An objector substituting x wherever a mathematician had used dx or Δx."

To which Mr. Hobson retorts : " Professor Edgeworth appears to think that the Differential Calculus will assist him to find the

---

[1] Above, p. 368 *et seq.*   [2] *Political Economy*, Book III. chap. vii.

[3] According to Professor Pareto the producer is obliged to remain on the " line of indifference " corresponding to " complete Transformation " and null remuneration. " Il y a là une différence essentielle avec les phénomènes qui se réfèrent avec gouts "—*Manuel d'Économie Politique*, chap. iii. § 79, and context).

[4] Hobson, *The Economics of Distribution*, p. 146.

[5] *Quarterly Journal of Economics*, Febuary 1904, p. 167.

productivity of the Marginal Shepherd· by starting from the productivity of an infinitesimal margin of him." [1]

To which I rejoin that the introduction of Δx in conjunction with dx in the passage above quoted was not without significance. There was understood the presumption which must be borne in mind wherever, as in the present papers, we deal with applications of the Differential Calculus to Economics—that propositions true of *differentials* may often be extended to *small finite differences* [2] with sufficient accuracy for practical purposes. Such is

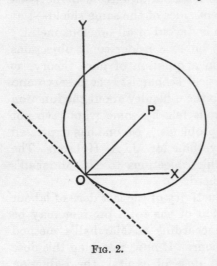

FIG. 2.

the proposition now in question, that the effect of taking (or rejecting) in succession two or more small doses of different factors of production is sensibly the same as taking (or rejecting) both the doses together. Mr. Hobson has presented a contrary result by selecting for his illustration too large doses, not typical of the fine adjustments practised by the organisers of modern industry. A similar objection may be taken to an illustration which he has given in his latest treatment of the subject,[3] where the tenth dose, the difference between a " ten group " and a " nine group " of shepherds adds twenty sheep, while the eleventh dose adds only five sheep. There is a discontinuity between the returns to successive doses which is hardly typical of an establishment in which many operatives are employed.

Let me take my own illustration. Let there be two factors of production x and y (*e.g.*, common labour and a certain kind of machinery); and let the amounts of each factor which a certain entrepreneur employs be respectively x and y. Let these amounts be measured from the point O along the abscissa and the ordinate respectively of Fig 2. Let the net return—the difference between the gross receipts and the total outlay [4]—be represented by z,

---

[1] *Journal of Political Economy*, 1904. Vol. XII. p. 460.

[2] In virtue of that continuity of functions which is commonly experienced. Compare ECONOMIC JOURNAL, Vol. XVIII. 1908, p. 399; and below, p. 389.

[3] *The Industrial System*, p. 110.

[4] We might represent the *gross* receipts by adding to z as above defined $kx + ky$, the perpendicular distance from the point (y, x) to the corresponding point in a plane above the paper, whose section with the plane of the paper is

the perpendicular distance measured downwards from any point (x, y) in the plane of the paper to the corresponding point on the (concave) surface of a spherical—or rather hemispherical—bowl underneath, the rim of which is the circle shown in the figure (being a " great circle " of the sphere of which the bowl forms a hemisphere). Thus initially when x and y are each zero, z is zero. As x and y are increased z will increase up to the maximum which occurs at the point P; for which if R is the radius of the sphere and of the (great) circle shown in the figure, $x = \frac{1}{\sqrt{2}}R$, $y = \frac{1}{\sqrt{2}}R$. Now let us consider the effect of removing—first successively, then simultaneously—small doses of each factor, say one per cent. of each, or, as more convenient to calculate, while less favourable to our thesis, $\sqrt{2}$ per cent. of each that is $0{\cdot}01R$. Whereas R measured the maximum net profit, the diminution of profit caused by reducing the abscissa from $\frac{1}{\sqrt{2}}R$ to $\frac{1}{\sqrt{2}}R - 0{\cdot}01R$, the ordinate remaining unchanged, is found to be

$$R - \sqrt{R^2 - 0001R^2} = R(1 - \sqrt{0{\cdot}9999}).$$

Likewise the diminution of the ordinate by $\sqrt{2}$ per cent. thereof is $R (1 - \sqrt{0{\cdot}9999})$. The sum of these two effects, viz. $2R (1 - \sqrt{0{\cdot}9999})$ is to be compared with the effect of taking the two doses together, viz. $R (1 - \sqrt{0{\cdot}9998})$. It appears that while the former subtrahend is $0{\cdot}0001000014..R$, the latter is $0{\cdot}000100005..R$—not a very important difference, per cent. of net profits (or gross receipts). The difference will still be insignificant even when we take away doses so large as $0{\cdot}1R$, that is, above fourteen per cent. of each factor. The sum of the effects of (removing) the two doses separately is now $0{\cdot}010025..R$; the effect of the two doses together is $0{\cdot}01005..R$.

Of course if we go on increasing the size of the doses, we shall reach a case in which the difference under consideration is significant. Thus if all industry were organised on a scale in which no entrepreneur could take on more than one or two

---

the tangent to the circle at O, its equation being $z = kx + ky$. Of course in general the coefficients of x and y would not be equal, the line in which the plane thus designated cuts the plane of the paper would not make a half right angle with each of the axes. The coefficient k may be interpreted as the price of the corresponding factor, " accumulated," as explained by Dr. Marshall, so as to be comparable with prospective receipts.

employees, the remuneration of the last employee taken on would very imperfectly measure—might afford only a very superior limit to—the remuneration of an employee. In fact that remuneration would be indeterminate (in the mathematical sense) within certain limits;[1] unless indeed under the appearance of selling work by the day there really lurked a traffic in hours of work,[2] and so the requisite comminution of doses reappeared. Except, of course, also the cases in which the remuneration of the hired operatives is equated by competition to the remuneration of small independent artisans, of settlers on free land, and so forth. In short, I do not deny that there *might* be an industrial system such as Mr. Hobson seems to suppose in which the marginal productivity of an operative does not (with any accuracy) measure wages. But I opine that such a system is not typical of modern industry in the concrete. And I affirm, what Mr. Hobson in the passage above quoted seems to deny, that the following theorem is true in the abstract. If the labour market consisted only of a number of employers on one side, and a much greater number of employees all of the same efficiency on the other side, with no limitations on the size of establishments, wages would be approximately measured by the marginal productivity of an operative.[3] This simple corollary to the doctrine of maximum advantage does not seem to be touched by Mr. Hobson's dialectic, of which I subjoin some more specimens.[4]

" Margins are derivative, not determinative."

" This [the author's doctrine] does not imply that the marginal factors exercise any special determinant influence as causes of the price."

" It is far more accurate to say that the price per unit causes the margin to be where it is than to attribute any causative power to the margin, as margin, in relation to the price per unit."

Does this dialectic add anything to the warning which Dr. Marshall in connection with his doctrine of the Marginal Shepherd had clearly pronounced? " It must, however, be remembered that the price which at first was worth while for the farmer to pay for this labour merely gauged the outcome of multitudinous causes which between them govern the wages of shepherds; as the movements of a safety-valve may gauge the outcome of the multitudinous causes that govern the pressure in a boiler."[5]

[1] Index, s.v. *Determinate Equilibrium*.

[2] *Loc. cit.*, p. 189.

[3] The law of diminishing returns, proper to the case here designated A, being postulated.   [4] *The Industrial System*, p. 102.

[5] *Principles*, Book VI. chap. i. § S. (3rd ed., 1895), and context.

I submit that difficulty and logomachy might be avoided by contemplation of a physical analogue, the principle of maximum energy. Suppose in the construction pertaining to Fig. 2 that a weight sliding down towards the lowest point of the bowl from the rim does so many foot-pounds work. The point at which the maximum energy will have been put forth, the position of the minimum potential energy, or equilibrium, is (corresponds to) P. Is it necessary to inquire whether the last step of the path which stops at P is " derivative " or " determinative " ?

Incipient Taxes.—An interesting example of the transition from differential to small finite differences—where what is strictly true *de minimis* is predicated also *de parvis*—occurs in the remarkable paper of which I have here borrowed the title.[1] The author, Mr. C. F. Bickerdike, argues that theoretically in normal circumstances it is always possible for a country to obtain a net advantage by the imposition of small import or export duties without supposing (as usual when such admissions are made by economists) that the country has a kind of monopoly as seller or buyer. The argument is based on the proposition that the loss of *consumers' surplus* occasioned by the disturbance of industry is of a negligible order as compared with the gain to the Treasury.

This proposition is a particular case of a wide principle which may thus be worded : " A small change of an economic variable quantity at the margin commonly causes a *very small* change in the corresponding surplus." The principle is not confined to Economics, being based on the general theory of maxima. Good examples are afforded by astronomical quantities of which the variation is recorded in the Nautical Almanack. For instance, the distance of the sun at noon (along a great circle) from the celestial equator varies more rapidly when the distance is near its maximum, about the times of solstice, than at other times. Thus the variation in the sun's declination[2] per hour at the time of the summer solstice (at noon of the day on which the solstice occurs) is 0·36 second. The variation at the time of the spring equinox per hour is 59·25 seconds. The change is more than 160 times greater at the equinox than what it is at the solstice. If we consider a degree (or small finite difference) of time larger than an hour, say a day, there will still exist the same kind of

---

[1] " Incipient Taxes," by C. F. Bickerdike, ECONOMIC JOURNAL, Vol. XVI. p. 529; *cp.* Vol. XVII. p. 98.

[2] The *apparent* declination; Nautical Almanack, 1909. The variation per hour, at noon of the day on which the hourly variation is a minimum, is larger or smaller according as the actual moment of solstice is further from or nearer to noon.

contrast, but less in quantity—as theory leads to expect. The change in declination per day at the spring equinox is very much greater than what it is at the summer solstice.* Like propositions are true of the winter solstice, and all similar cases. The principle may be extended from variations of *quantities* to variations of *form* (the special object of the Calculus of Variations).

This principle seems to be of wide application in Political Economy, more especially in the larger sense of the term to which we are coming in our second section.** It has been employed as an argument in favour of the diffusion of taxation over a great number of commodities.[1] It may be employed to justify small interferences with the natural course of industry for the sake of large ulterior advantages. A small readjustment of the entrepreneur's plan of production and " margins of profitableness," recommended for some considerable non-economic advantage, becomes additionally advisable by the theorem that the economic loss is likely to be not merely small, but *very* small.[2] No doubt it is a dangerous doctrine to enunciate ; very liable to be abused by Protectionists and other unscrupulous controversialists, who if you give them a *differential* will take an *integral*.

* See Index, s.v. *Maximum*.
** See introduction to this article above, p. 367.
[1] Above (δ), p. 351, referring to S. The argument is no doubt overborne by practical considerations on the other side.
[2] See on the principle of incipient taxes. Above, δ.

(ζ)

APPLICATIONS OF PROBABILITIES TO ECONOMICS

[THE Probability of which the application to Economics forms the subject of this article (published in the ECONOMIC JOURNAL, June 1910) is largely of the sort which has been called *a priori*, or " unverified." The controversy with Professor Seligman concerning the incidence of taxation in a regime of monopoly—prolonged by his return to the subject in the third edition of his *Shifting and Incidence*—illustrates the use and need of such Probabilities.

They are employed in the second part of the article to show the advantages of Discrimination, or differentiation of prices, in a regime of Monopoly, and even in one of pure Competition. In this argument I have perhaps practised unnecessary moderation in dwelling somewhat exclusively on the case where the disturbance of price caused by discrimination is inconsiderable. True, in the case where differential prices are compared with the single price of pure competition there is no ground for expecting that the advantageous divergence of prices will be considerable. But in the case of discrimination introduced under a regime of monopoly there is room for considerable differentiations advantageous to both parties. Also the proposition, placed third below (p. 407), that the monopolist may be induced for a small consideration to adopt a system of prices through which the customers, as well as himself, may be materially benefited by the introduction of discrimination in the place of a unique monopoly price—this useful proposition may well hold good of considerable discrimination, in virtue of a property of a maximum to which attention has been often called in these pages (see Index, *sub voce* " maximum "). Indeed the verifications of the theory which have been offered are by no means confined to indefinitely small discriminations. The examples observed are such that in each the price of one of the articles is raised by $12\frac{1}{2}$ per cent.]

Probability, in that general sense in which it has been called the guide of life, is of wider application to Political Economy than dogmatic theorists imagine. Of this extensive field one corner only is here explored, namely, that species of Probability which is amenable to mathematical theory. The Calculus of Probabilities and the principles of Economics may seem, indeed, quite distinct branches of knowledge. Yet I submit that they have a root in common. The theory of Probabilities lends to Economics, as to other sciences, certain premises which are evidenced, neither by pure intuition, nor by formal induction, but by general impressions, and what may be called mathematical common sense. Of this character is " the assumption that any probability-constant about which we know nothing in particular is as likely to have one value as another "—an assumption made by Laplace and endorsed by Pearson.[1] This so-called *a priori* probability is employed in the theory of measurement, not only with respect to probability-constants, but also for the determination of other kinds of constants. The coefficients which characterise curves and surfaces and analytical *functions* corresponding to these geometrical forms are presumed, in the absence of evidence to the contrary, not to have extreme values, not to be enormously great or indefinitely small. For where the possible values range over a certain tract with some approach to equality of distribution, it may be presumed that they do not often occur at the limits of that tract. The curves with which we have to deal in practice do not abound in *singularities*. The increment of a function corresponding to an increment of the independent variable is not commonly immense. There usually holds good, or is tenable as a working hypothesis, the fundamental principle that of interdependent variable quantities an increment of one is attended with a (simply) *proportional* increment of the other; throughout a tract of sensible extent.[2]

" Commonly " and " usually " may seem strange terms to occur in a mathematical proposition. But I submit that the conception is required by mathematicians. Thus Hamilton, in explaining the definition of " differentials " (with reference to his

---

[1] Pearson, *Grammar of Science*, second edition, p. 146.

[2] Beyond a certain tract—a certain amount of change in one of the quantities, considered as the independent variable—it may be expected that the *proportion* itself changes, yet not *per saltum*; it being assumed, when nothing is known to the contrary, that $\frac{d^2y}{dx^2}$, as well as $\frac{dy}{dx}$, is not immense. In short, the Taylorian expansion in ascending powers is presumed to hold good for two or three terms at least. Much use will be made of this presumption in the sequel of this paper.

own original calculus) has to employ the phrase " in all ordinary cases." [1] The following is a typical extract from Laplace.[2] It relates to the problem of *correcting* an " element " [quantity under measurement] already approximately determined, by means of numerous observations each of which represents, or purports to be equal to, a known *function* of the element.

" If we substitute in that function instead of the element its [known] approximate value *plus* the correction [called] z; then develop the function in ascending powers of z,[3] and neglect the square of z [and higher powers thereof], the function will assume the form $h + pz$ [where h and p are constants]."

Now, of course, it may happen that the coefficient p (and accordingly the coefficient of z^2 in the expansion) is enormously great, and so the proposed simplification will not be available. Laplace, however, in the above cited and many other passages, tacitly assumes that this will not happen.

The sort of continuity which must be postulated for practical purposes is not of exactly the ideal continuity about the definition of which mathematicians dispute. A broken line, or succession of dots, may often be treated as if continuous. In Probabilities curves of " error," or " facility," are to be conceived, I hold, as series of discrete points. In Physics the received molecular theory seems to require a similar conception. Thus Clerk-Maxwell, with reference to Atoms :—

" The principle of continuity, which is the basis of the method of fluxions and the whole of modern mathematics, may be applied to the analysis of problems connected with material bodies by assuming them, for the purpose of this analysis, to be homogeneous. . . . Thus if a railway contractor has to make a tunnel through a hill of gravel, and if one cubic yard of gravel is so like another cubic yard that for the purposes of the contract they may be taken as equivalent, then in estimating the work required to remove the gravel from the tunnel he may, without fear of error, make his calculations as if the gravel was a continuous substance. But if a worm has to make his way through the gravel, it makes the greatest difference to him whether he tries to push right against a piece of gravel, or direct his course through one of the intervals between the pieces; to him, therefore, the gravel is by no means a homogeneous and continuous substance." [4]

[1] *Quaternions*, Joly's edition, Vol. I. p. 432.
[2] *Théorie Analytique des Probabilités*, Liv. II. ch. iv. § 20.
[3] So I freely translate " en réduisant en série par rapport à z."
[4] Article on " Atoms," *Encyclopædia Britannica*, ed. 9, Vol. III. p. 38.

I cannot pretend to give an adequate exposition of the philosophy which underlies the science of Mathematical Physics. But if there is a part of that mysterious substructure which at all corresponds to the description above given, then it cannot be considered as paradoxical that a less exact science should rest in part upon similarly inexact axioms.

I submit, therefore, that in Economics we must sometimes be content with premises not better evidenced than those which have been above attributed to Physics. For example, Professor Pigou, reasoning about the incidence of a differential duty on foreign wheat, very properly begins : " Presuming, as in the absence of knowledge is reasonable, that the elasticity of production is the same at home and abroad." [1] If anyone specially conversant with the trade in wheat is able to correct this presumption, that does not prove Professor Pigou wrong in making it, or adhering to it until more exact information is forthcoming. In this world it is often necessary to act though we know only in part. Thus M. Colson, for the important purpose of estimating the utility of a " public work," prescribes that, adopting a mean value [en moyenne], in the absence of more exact data, we may evaluate the benefit per unit of new traffic,[2] by a formula which amounts to this, as I understand. Whereas we know nothing of a certain curve, bounding an area which is to be measured, except that the curve joins two given points and that it slopes continually downwards.[3] Under these circumstances we may, for the purpose of the measurement, put for the curve the right line joining the given points.[4] Of course this kind of a priori presumption is liable to be superseded by specific evidence as to the shape of the curve; for instance, if there were sometimes ground for supposing it to be convex, as was, in fact, suggested by M. Colson's distinguished predecessor, Dupuit.[5] There is required, I think, in a case of this sort, in order to override the

---

[1] Cp. ECONOMIC JOURNAL, Vol. XIX. p. 105.

[2] Cours d'Économie Politique, Liv. VI. p. 203.

[3] By which condition an indefinitely large divergence of the curve from the line is excluded.

[4] In Professor Marshall's construction—more familiar to English readers than M. Colson's (see the review of the Cours d'Économie Politique (Liv. I.), III. p. 169)—the sought measure is the mixtilinear figure bounded by the horizontal line representing the increase of traffic, the vertical line representing the decrease of price and the demand-curve; the area PRA in Professor Marshall's Fig. 10, Principles of Economics, Book III., ch. vi. § 3, ed. 4, corresponding to an increase of output from OM to OH; an area like BB''b''$_2$ in the diagram representing M. Colson's conception in the review just now mentioned.

[5] Annales des Ponts et Chaussées, 1844, Vol. II. p. 367.

a priori probability, either very definite specific evidence, or the consensus of high authorities.

Another application of *a priori* Probabilities to economic curves is made by M. Colson with reference to the probability of neutral equilibrium between demand and supply; the supposition that the equation of demand and supply " might be equally satisfied by every numerical rate which could be supposed," in the phrase of J. S. Mill. Mill has entertained this conception in that central part of his chapter on International Value which has seemed to many the least satisfactory part of the chapter and of the whole work.[1] Of this sort of neutral equilibrium M. Colson says [2] :—

" A coincidence such that two functions should preserve the same value, for all values of the variable extending over an interval not indefinitely small presents a degree of improbability which is equivalent to a mathematical impossibility."

Another example of *a priori* probability is the presumption, in the absence of evidence to the contrary, that demand (and supply) curves will not be of an extreme and limiting form—not very rigid or very inelastic. Unfortified by a general presumption of this sort, we are apt too easily to let pass arguments which take for granted that the demand for some article under consideration, for instance, house-accommodation, is perfectly inelastic.[3]

The issue whether an economic curve slopes rapidly or gently is distinct from the question at what degree of minuteness the continuity of the curve breaks down; what is the *minimum divisible* of currency, the *minimum vendible* of commodity. Thus the question whether there would be a great increase in the consumption of alcoholic liquors, if the heavy taxes now imposed on them were removed, is not much affected by the circumstance that the retail price of a pot of beer can only decrease (say) by a halfpenny at a time. That comparatively trifling circumstance may often be abstracted by the theoretical economist. He cannot always be adjusting his speculative instruments to the two scales of magnitude distinguished in Maxwell's parable of the gravel

---

[1] It is criticised by Professor Marshall in his unpublished papers on Foreign Trade (the papers referred to in the Preface to his *Principles*), by Professor Bastable in his *International Trade*, p. 11, ed. 3, and by the present writer in the ECONOMIC JOURNAL, Vol. IV. (1894), p. 611. Above, **R**, pp. 1, 23.

[2] *Cours d'Économie Politique*, Liv. I., with reference to the supply of and demand for work : not referring particularly to Mill.

[3] See on this point ECONOMIC JOURNAL, Vol. X. pp. 187–9 (above, **U**, p. 168). *Cp.* above, **S**, p. 71.

hill.   He may permissibly devote himself to the difficult calculations proper to the contractor, while he leaves to his critics the easy task of making allowances for the idiosyncrasies of the worm.

Referring for further observations on *a priori* Probability to former publications,[1] I now go on to consider some examples.

I.—THEORY OF TAXATION

For the purpose of securing attention to the obscure subject of this study, it happens, fortunately, that the subject bears upon Professor Seligman's deservedly popular treatise on *Shifting and Incidence of Taxation*.   Many of the criticisms with which Professor Seligman has honoured my observations on the theory of taxation in a regime of monopoly turn upon the question whether the assumptions above described are legitimate.

The suggested difficulties about my use of the term " in general," as applicable to the case of continuity, and of " friction " in the contrary case,[2] may, I hope, be removed—or at least reduced to questions of terminology—by the explanation above given.   Continuity of the rough sort which characterises curves in Physics and Probabilities may be properly, or at least intelligibly, described as " general " in Economics, affording as it does a first approximation beyond which it is frequently unnecessary to proceed.

Professor Seligman still continues (in his third edition) to ask :

" Is it fair to assume that a small change of price is ' more general ' than a great one ?   And would Professor Edgeworth's elaborate formulæ all hold good if the change of price were substantial ? " [3]

To which I reply, as I have already replied (to the second edition) :—

" Certainly, the formulæ hold good for substantial changes of price as long as the conditions of a maximum continue to be fulfilled, that is, presumably for some finite distance. . . . Because the mathematical investigation advances by tentative steps it is not precluded from going in the direction of the rise of price as far as any other method [can go safely]." [4]

Cournot's method of short steps is the only (tolerably) safe one ; Professor Seligman's giant steps over the space of a quarter

---

[1] See Index, s.v. *A priori Probabilities.*
[2] *Shifting and Incidence*, third edition, p. 345.
[3] *Ibid.*, third edition, p. 345; second edition, p. 276.
[4] ECONOMIC JOURNAL, Vol. IX. (1899), pp. 308, 309; F, p. 163.

of a dollar in his favourite illustration [1] may terminate in a precipice. It is true that not even Cournot's method is perfectly safe. Pure Mathematics—exclusive of applied Probabilities—can only guarantee the safety of a single step; or not even that in case of a *singularity* occurring at the point (of the demand curve) with which we are concerned. In order to obtain a practical conclusion the Calculus of Probabilities must be grafted on the Differential Calculus,[2] as I have elsewhere explained.

Had Professor Seligman entertained the, I think, received assumptions as to the curves employed in applied Mathematics, he would have prevented some misunderstanding of his doctrine as to the relation of elasticity to taxation in a regime of monopoly. Professor Seligman had said (in his first edition) :—
" The greater the elasticity of demand the more favourable—other things being equal—will be the position of the consumer." [3] This proposition I very naturally understood to imply that if in the long run of general practice we could distinguish those cases in which the elasticity of the demand-curve was particularly great, we should find that the liability of the consumer to suffer by taxation (in a regime of monopoly) was particularly small. I not only disputed this thesis, but the method of proving it, which seemed to me to consist in the observation of examples not taken at random, but selected as having an attribute favourable to the thesis.[4] It was Voltaire, I think, who said that you could kill a flock of sheep with incantations—if accompanied by arsenic. Now it seemed to me that Professor Seligman, while professing to observe the effects of " incantations," had taken care that " arsenic " should be present in each instance. But on considering his amplified statement (in the third edition) I am led to believe that I was mistaken; that he meant " arsenic " all the time—though he said " incantation." I surmise that, instead of the false thesis above cited, there was intended the true thesis which is obtained by substituting in that statement for " elasticity of demand," *increment* of that elasticity. Or rather we ought to put as that quantity of which the thesis affirms that the greater the said quantity the more favourable will be the position of the consumer, the following, or some equivalent coefficient; the increment, with the increase of price, of the decrement-of-demand-corresponding-to-increment-of-price.[5] For there now comes into

---

[1] Cited below, p. 395.

[2] ECONOMIC JOURNAL, Vol. XVIII. (1908), p. 399. Above, p. 351.

[3] *Shifting and Incidence*, ed. 1, p. 191; quoted by me in the ECONOMIC JOURNAL, Vol. IX. p. 303; amplified by the author in his third edition, p. 345.

[4] ECONOMIC JOURNAL (*loc. cit.*), p. 304.

[5] The phrase made up of words connected by hyphens is used to denote the

view a distinction which might be safely ignored so long as we were concerned only with a single point on the demand-curve (a point which might, however, be treated as representative of the neighbouring tract, in virtue of the principle just now explained). The distinction which now arises is between elasticity in the *proper* sense of the term as defined by Professor Marshall,[1] and elasticity in a popular sense, presumably the coefficient above defined; or more simply, the slope of the demand-curve. The complications connected with the use of *elasticity proper* were evaded in my former paper,[2] as they will be in the present paper, by the device of (in effect) taking as the unit of commodity and price respectively the values which render the monopolist's revenue a maximum. For the slope and the elasticity of the curve then coincide. But when we pass from the attribute itself to the *increment* thereof, a choice between the two meanings must be made. There can be little doubt, I think, but that our author would choose the popular sense. An intelligible and true meaning can thus be assigned to his statements :

" Demand is said to be more elastic when each successive increase of price leads to a greater falling off in demand." [3]

" After the point of maximum monopoly revenue has been reached, the more elastic the demand the smaller will be the proportion of the tax that he [the monopolist] is apt to shift to the consumer." [4]

---

positive quantity $[-F'(p)]$, if with Cournot we put $F(p)$ to denote the amount demanded at the price p. We might, of course, equally well—*pace* Professor Seligman—designate this coefficient as the increment-of-demand-corresponding-to-decrement-of-price. The increment of this coefficient with the increment of price is the greater the smaller that $F''(p)$ is; since by an increment of price, Δp, $[-F'(p)]$ becomes $[-F'(p) - \Delta p F''(p)]$. But the smaller that $F''(p)$ is the less (other things, and in particular $F'(p)$, being the same) is the increase of price due to a small increase of cost of production or taxation, say τ per unit of commodity. For by Cournot's theory (*Principes Mathématiques*, ch. v. § 31) that increase is $\tau \dfrac{F'(p)}{2F'(p) + pF''(p)}$, which may be written $\tau \dfrac{[-F'(p)]}{2[-F'(p)] - pF''(p)} t$, where the denominator is necessarily positive. The smaller that $F''(p)$ is, the greater is the denominator of the above fraction; and, therefore, the smaller the fraction itself, the less the rise of price in consequence of the tax; in accordance with the thesis enunciated in the text. (It may be well to warn the reader that " smaller," as here applied to $F''(p)$, means that this quantity is less, *account being taken of its sign*. When, as frequently, $F''(p)$ is negative, its value is less the greater its *absolute quantity* is—as a man is poorer the greater his debt is.)

[1] *Principles of Economics*, Book III. ch. iv. Compare Palgrave's Dictionary : article on " Elasticity " (by the present writer).

[2] See ECONOMIC JOURNAL, Vol. IX. p. 291 (F, I. p. 157), and below, p. 428, note. In the sequel we shall have to do with cases in which the elasticity proper is (at assigned points) the same for demand-curves with different slopes.

[3] *Shifting and Incidence*, third edition, p. 346.

[4] *Loc. cit.*, p. 345; more explicit than the corresponding passages in the second edition (p. 277).

It will be apparent that it is impossible even to enunciate the writer's thesis without the use of the methods which he contemns. The above interpretation is put forward with diffidence as it is perfectly consistent with the sort of continuousness which I have all along postulated for demand-curves. Professor Seligman seems to call for a " Deus ex machinâ " where no " dignus vindice nodus " occurs, if my interpretation of his thesis is correct. But the absence from his view of the matter of those conceptions and presumptions which are the subject of this paper is, I fear, fatal to our mutual understanding.[1]

I take to myself blame for the misunderstanding that has occurred, so far as it may have been aggravated by my neglecting to point out the distinction between increment of slope and increment of elasticity proper. But we are not now concerned with ordinary negligence. Such human error is to the defect which we are now considering as ordinary mistakes in spelling are to those which are perpetrated by a type-writing machine. The latter exhibit a want of that minimum of orthography which is common to articulate men. A similar absence of conceptions and presumptions present to the general mind seems to be evinced by our author's persistent use of a certain demand-schedule, with wide intervals between the entries. I once more reproduce in a variant form this scheme of data.[2]

PROFESSOR SELIGMAN'S DATA.

Price in $	4	5	$5\frac{1}{4}$	$5\frac{1}{2}$	$5\frac{3}{4}$	6
Amount demanded	1200	1000	900	825	750	700
Gross receipts ...	4800	5000	4725	4537·5	4312·5	4200
Net receipts A ...	2400	3000	2925	2887·5	2812·5	2800
Net receipts B ...	2100	2750	2700	2681·25	2625	2625

Net receipts A are based on a cost of two dollars per unit of product, without tax.

Net receipts B are based on the same cost, together with a tax of a quarter of a dollar per unit of product.

---

[1] The following quotation, with the comment thereon, may illustrate our mutual inaccessibility. "My assumption," says Professor Seligman, " is that of a demand which becomes more or less elastic after the point of maximum monopoly revenue has been reached. Professor Edgeworth's assumption is that of a demand which is more or less elastic from the outset, before, as well as after this point." (Shifting and Incidence, p. 347. Note, par. 1.) Upon which I remark : (1) I can accept the assumption which Professor Seligman takes to himself if, as is possible to interpret, it involves no more than the usual presumptions that the slope of a curve and the increment to the slope $\left(\text{say } \frac{dx}{dp}, \text{ and } \frac{d^2x}{dp^2}, \text{ where}\right.$ p is the price and x the quantity demanded at the price) both vary gradually. And (2) I cannot accept the assumption attributed to myself if, as is natural to interpret, it involves something more than those usual presumptions.

[2] See Shifting and Incidence, third edition, pp. 343, 344; second edition, pp. 275, 276; and cp. ECONOMIC JOURNAL, Vol. IX. pp. 307, 308.

Now if it is merely meant that the transaction is of such a kind that differences of price less than a quarter of a dollar cannot be taken into account, *cadit quæstio*. I have fully admitted that reasoning based on ordinary degrees of continuity does not apply to this particular case.[1] If my critic meant no more than this, he would hardly have repeated (in his new edition) his schedules and arguments. It is incredible, too, that he should regard an exception of this kind as a refutation of Cournot's theory of taxation in a regime of monopoly. One might as well pretend to have damaged the Ricardian theory of taxation in a regime of competition by adducing the well-known little fact that, in the words of a distinguished Chancellor of the Exchequer,[2] a very small additional duty " can hardly fall on the individual consumer of a glass of spirits or a pot of beer." Besides, if this had been our author's meaning, why keep to such wide intervals of price as a quarter of a dollar ?

Upon whatever principle constructed, this schedule may be likened to a net with meshes so wide as to lose half the catch. To remedy this defect we might fill up the vacant spaces with a finer reticulation. This will be effected if we put a continuous curve through six points representing the specified amounts of commodity corresponding to the several prices ; an appropriate form being assigned to the curve, and the constants being then calculated from the data. Or, as it is rather a troublesome matter to construct such a curve, it must suffice to construct a continuous curve complying with the parts of the data which are essential to the argument.

Here is a particularly simple curve of the sort :—

$$x = 900 + 200 \sqrt{5\tfrac{1}{4} - y} ;$$

where x denotes the quantity of commodity demanded at any price y. Here, in accordance with the data, $x = 1000$ when $y = 5$; and $x = 900$ when $y = 5\tfrac{1}{4}$. Also xy is, as it ought to be, a *maximum* when $y = 5$; as is proved by general reasoning,[3] and may be verified by actually trying values of y in the neighbourhood of 5, *e.g.*, 4·9 and 5·1.

Now let us suppose, with Professor Seligman,[4] that the cost of production—the tax imposed by the nature of things—is \$2 per unit of commodity. The quantity to be maximised by the

---

[1] *Loc. cit.*, p. 307.　　　　[2] Vernon Harcourt, Budget Speech, 1894.

[3] When $y = 5, \frac{d}{dy}xy = 0$, while $\frac{d^2}{dy^2}xy < 0$.

[4] *Loc. cit.*, p. 343.

monopolist is then $x(y - 2)$. And we cannot suppose with Professor Seligman that the price continues to be $5;[1] unless, indeed, it is postulated—a postulate surely not of general validity and one to which Professor Seligman has not called special attention—that the monopolist cannot charge a price intermediate between a dollar and a quarter of a dollar. If the formula which we have assigned for the demand-curve were perfectly exact, the phenomenon perfectly continuous, the price would now theoretically be 5·1439 (nearly); that being the value of y which renders the above expression a maximum.[2] The actual price will be an approximation to this ideal limit. If the price can be graduated to a cent, the monopolist will charge, in addition to the original 5 dollars, 14 or 15 cents; whichever of the two makes the net proceeds greater.[3] If, in addition to nature's tax of 2 dollars per piece (for cost of production), there is imposed an ordinary tax of a quarter-dollar per piece, the principle is just the same. We have now to find y so that $x(y - 2\frac{1}{4})$ should be a maximum. The value of y which fulfils this condition is found to be 5·1583. . . .[4] Accordingly, the monopolist will charge an additional 15 or 16 cents, whichever makes the net proceeds greater (no doubt here the latter).

If half-dimes are the lowest admissible denomination, he will charge either 5 dollars and 3 half-dimes, or 5 dollars and 4 half-dimes; if dimes are the lowest denomination, either 5 dollars and 1 dime or 5 dollars and 2 dimes; if quarter-dollars are the lowest admissible denomination, the monopolist will charge either

---

[1] *Loc. cit.* "He will always prefer the price $5." Compare the "net receipts A" in our Table, embodying Professor Seligman's data.

[2] We have now to determine y the equation :

$$\frac{d}{dy}(y - 2)(900 + 200 \sqrt{5\frac{1}{4} - y}) = 0.$$

Whence :

$$900 + 200 \sqrt{5\frac{1}{4} - y} - \frac{100}{\sqrt{5\frac{1}{4} - y}}(y - 2) = 0.$$

Reducing, we obtain a quadratic equation of which the only available root (the other root being negative) is 5·14389 . . .

[3] The integer preferred is not necessarily the one nearest to the theoretical price.

[4] This value is found from a quadratic equation by reasoning of a parity with that employed in the preceding note. It may be well to remind the reader that the reasoning and conclusion are similar in the case of an (*ad valorem*) tax on gross receipts, as distinguished from a (*specific*) tax on gross product. Suppose that an *ad valorem* tax of 5 per cent. is imposed on the gross receipts. The amount which the monopolist will now seek to maximise is $\frac{19}{20}xy - 2x = \frac{19}{20}x(y - 2\frac{2}{19})$; an expression of the same form as that which it was proposed to maximise in the case of a specific tax.

5 dollars, or 5 dollars and 1 quarter-dollar—in each case adopting that alternative which makes the net proceeds a maximum. The last case might be designated by the proposition for which Professor Seligman contends, namely, that " the monopolist will continue to find his greatest profit in continuing to charge the original price "; if we could suppose that an able controversialist in a considered rejoinder would reaffirm as decisive in his own favour a proposition understood by himself and intended to be interpreted in exactly that qualified sense in which it had been explicitly affirmed by the other party to the controversy.[1]

The simple curve which has been adduced is sufficient for the purpose of showing the various results of a tax—all comprehended under one simple law—according as different degrees of continuity prevail. But the illustration is suitable only for taxes of a limited magnitude, as the curve stops short at the price $5\frac{1}{4}$. Here is a more appropriate, though less easily manageable, representation of the proposed law of demand :—

$$x = 842 \cdot 265 + 246 \cdot 227 \ (5 \cdot 26289 - y)^{\frac{1}{2}}$$

Here, as before, when $y = 5$, $x = 1000$ (approximately); when $y = 5\frac{1}{4}$, $x = 900$; and xy is a maximum when $y = 5$.[2] Moreover, now when y is greater than $5\frac{1}{4}$ (as well as less than 5), a series of values of x are presented not very different from and corresponding in their general trend to Professor Seligman's data, and equally favourable to his thesis. Thus when the price, $y = 4$, I find [3] that the amount demanded, x, is now $= 1108 \cdot 4$ (instead of 1200); and when $y = 6$, $x = 619 \cdot 8$ (instead of 700). Now let us introduce the cost of production, $2 per unit piece; and as before we can prove by general reasoning and verify by actual trial that a price intermediate between 5 and $5\frac{1}{4}$—namely, about $5 \cdot 13$—affords the maximum monopoly revenue. Additions to the tax may be exemplified as before, but now on a larger scale.

But, indeed, it is not necessary for the purpose of rendering our author's data typical to adapt thereto an analytical expression, a curve defined by an equation. It suffices to draw with a

---

[1] See ECONOMIC JOURNAL, Vol. IX. p. 307, where, quoting the proposition again quoted here, I add, " He will " [continue to " charge the original price "] " if he can only alter the price *per saltum* by leaps of $\frac{1}{4}$ dollar. . . . If the monopolist can adopt an intermediate price between $5 and $5\frac{1}{4}$, I submit that he will tend theoretically to do so. . . ." This proposition is entirely in accord with the explanation which has been given by Professor Jannacone (referred to by Professor Seligman) in his " Questione Controverse," first published in the *Riforma Sociale*, xii. (1902).

[2] When $y = 5$, $\dfrac{dy}{dx} = 0$, $\dfrac{d^2y}{dx^2} < 0$.

[3] With the aid of logarithms.

free hand a continuous curve passing through points which
represent the data as to price and corresponding demand. Or
let us take the series of points each of which have for abscissa
(measured on the axis OX) the amount of commodity put by the
monopolist on the market, and for ordinate that amount multiplied by the price at which that amount is demanded. We may
then have a curve in its general shape resembling that in the
accompanying diagram; which is copied from an illustration
which I employed in a former paper.[1] The revenue which the
monopolist seeks to maximise was there compared to the height
which a prisoner confined in a narrow vaulted cell seeks to
maximise, namely, the vertical distance from the crown of his
head to the sole of his foot. That position of greatest comfort is
defined by the point P, while the floor OX is horizontal (in the

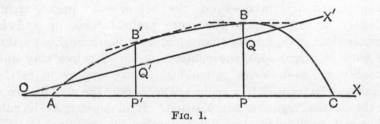

Fig. 1.

absence of taxation, including cost of production). But when
(corresponding to the introduction of a tax) the floor is tilted up
into the position OX', then the position of greatest comfort
recedes from P to P' (the amount put on the market diminishes).

I proceed now to enlarge the cell of the prisoner in order to
illustrate a theorem to which Professor Seligman has not, I
think, done justice. While he expends labour in proving what
comes to nothing but the obvious and admitted fact that when
the law of demand is sensibly discontinuous there may occur a
suspension *pro tanto* of the general rule that taxation is attended
with an increase of price, he passes by slightingly, and fails to
see the significance of the theorem that, even though the law of
demand be perfectly continuous, taxation in a regime of monopoly
may not only not injure, but actually benefit the monopolist's
customers—in the case of articles which are to some extent
substitutes for each other, such as first-class and third-class
accommodation on a railway journey. Reverting to the parable
of the prisoner in the cell, we have now to regard the area bounded
by the curve $AB'BC$ in the diagram as the section no longer of a

[1] ECONOMIC JOURNAL, Vol. VIII. (1898), p. 236.

narrow cell, but of a vaulted curve which extends far into a third dimension perpendicular to the plane of the paper. Let the reader hold the page before him with its plane perpendicular to that of the table; and let him measure, in a direction from him, along a new axis Y, perpendicular to the plane of the page and parallel to that of the table,[1] a length y representing the amount of a second commodity, say third-class accommodation. Let the amounts of the two commodities (first-class and third-class accommodation) be initially x_0 ($= OP$) and y_0; and after the imposition of a tax x_1 ($= OP'$) and y_1. Then x_1 is less than x_0. But what about y_1? For all we know the output of the second quantity also may be diminished in consequence of the tax on the first commodity. But this is the less probable alternative; as I have argued from an inspection of the symbols employed.[2] In the case of this the less probable alternative, the phenomenon now in question, the fall of both prices, cannot possibly occur.[3] But in the more probable case of y_1 being greater than y_0 (y_2 greater than y_1, and so on, throughout a tract of sensible magnitude), the concurrent fall of prices may quite possibly occur—however ridiculous it may appear to careless thinkers who transfer to a regime of monopoly the maxims proper to the classical regime of competition. It all depends on the value of certain coefficients which determine the change in prices. The values of these constants which are favourable to the double event are not, I think, a priori, extremely improbable. The conditions which they must fulfil * are not excessively exacting. Here is an example which does not strike one as specially unlikely. The number of first-class passengers (per day, week, or other unit of time) being x, and the number of third-class passengers being y, the fares in pounds sterling, p_1 and p_2 respectively, are connected by the equations : [4]

---

[1] A line parallel to the vertical PB in the diagram may be taken for the axis of Z, on which is measured the amount of the monopolist's net revenue corresponding to assigned outputs, x and y, of the two commodities.

[2] "Teoria pura del Monopolio," *Giornale degli Economisti*, 1897. (**E**, I. p. 135.)

[3] If not self-evident, this proposition may be deduced from the formulæ (*mutatis mutandis*) in the Note at the end of this paper.

* The conditions are investigated in the Note at the end of this section; in the ECONOMIC JOURNAL (Vol. XX.), not reprinted here. For a popular statement of the *rationale* of the phenomenon see ECONOMIC JOURNAL, Vol. VII. (1897), p. 231 (**S**, p. 94), and Vol. IX. (1899), p. 288 (**F**, I. p. 145).

[4] The reader is advised to substitute for $\dfrac{x}{100,000}$ the new variable x,

and for $\dfrac{y}{200,000}$ the new variable y.

$$p_1 = \text{Ll}\left[\frac{17}{5}\left(\frac{x}{100,000}\right) - 2\left(\frac{x}{100,000}\right)^2 - \frac{2}{5}\left(\frac{y}{200,000}\right)\right]$$

$$p_2 = \text{L}\tfrac{1}{2}\left[\frac{73}{30} - \frac{22}{15}\frac{y}{200,000} + \frac{13}{30}\left(\frac{y}{200,000}\right)^2 - \frac{2}{5}\left(\frac{x}{100,000}\right)\right]$$

The form of these equations is the simplest consistent with (1) the hypothesis that the demand for one commodity is diminished by the possession and consumption of a certain amount of the other commodity, and (2) the presumption that a demand curve is not a right line.[1] As the *form of the functions* presented is ordinary so the *values of the coefficients* do not appear *outré*. And yet a tax on first-class tickets will cause *both* fares to drop.

To show this let us begin with the simple supposition that cost of production (the working expenses assignable to the varying numbers of passengers) may be left out of account. Then the revenue which the company, acting as a monopolist, seeks to render a maximum, is $xp_1 + yp_2$. If p and p_2 are connected with x and y in the manner supposed, this expression will be a maximum, when $x = 100,000$ $y = 200,000$; that is, when $p_1 = £1$, $p_2 = \frac{1}{2}$ £1 $(= 10s.)$; as is proved by general reasoning,[2] and may be verified by actual trial of values x and y in the neighbourhood of 100,000 and 200,000 respectively (corresponding to values of p_1 and p_2 in the neighbourhood of £1 and 10s. respectively).

Now let a tax of 1s. 3 mites per ticket be imposed on first-class passengers. It will then pay the monopolist company to lower first-class fares by about $3\frac{7}{8}$d. and third-class fares by about $3\frac{3}{4}$d.* For at these new prices the numbers of passengers will be

[1] Unless there occurred the term involving x *squared*, the demand curve for x, which represents the amount of x varying with the price thereof while the amount of y is kept constant, and the corresponding demand curve for y, would degrade to a right line.

[2] Substituting x for $\dfrac{x}{100,000}$ and y for $\dfrac{y}{200,000}$, and putting $V = 100,000\,xp_1 +$ 200,000 y p_2 we have for the conditions that V should be a maximum, the two (simultaneous) equations :

$$\frac{34}{5}x - 6x^2 - \frac{4}{5}y\left(= \frac{dV}{dx}\right) = 0$$

$$\frac{73}{30} - \frac{44}{15}y + \frac{13}{10}y^2 - \frac{4}{5}x\left(= \frac{dV}{dy}\right) = 0$$

(together with three inequations—relating to the second term of variation). The two equations (and the three inequations) are satisfied by the system of values x = 1, y = 1. Whence $x = 100,000$, $y = 200,000$, $p_1 = 1$, $p_2 = \frac{1}{2}$.

* In the example as now stated there has been substituted for the tax originally considered, viz. 2s. per first-class ticket, the smaller figure given above, or more exactly £0·05166. The difficulties attending the use of a strong case for the purpose of illustration are thus lessened. These difficulties were pointed out in a note appended to the original article when it was too late to alter the text. They are summarised below (p. 427).

about 97,880 first-class and just 214,000 third-class. It follows that the gross receipts will be diminished by a matter of £64.* But on the net receipts there will be a gain; for though £64 has been lost, there has been saved about £109, the tax which the monopolist would have had to pay on the 2,120 first-class passengers who have dropped out. There is thus a net saving of about £175.

It is no serious objection that the transaction instanced, passenger fares, is of a kind which does not admit (like some wholesale transactions) of making prices in fractions less than the lowest coin in currency; that a mite ($\frac{1}{8}d.$), and even a farthing, can hardly figure in passenger fares. In such a case, as above fully explained, the monopolist will fix that integer number of the lowest available units (say half-pence)—in the neighbourhood of what we called the " theoretical price "—which affords the maximum revenue. The degree of fineness to which the currency is graduated is a matter of quite secondary interest in relation to a theorem of the kind which we are now considering.

So far we have made abstraction of cost of production. But it may easily be shown that to take it into account is not fatal to the possibility of both prices falling in consequence of a tax. Consider any case of the kind hitherto considered—where there is no cost of production—in which the conditions are favourable to the occurrence of the double event. In such a case it may be presumed, by *a priori* Probability, that as the tax is increased from zero up to some finite amount, say t, the monopolist will continue to subtract more and more from both prices. Now suppose that a part, say half of t, is not an ordinary tax, but that loss of gross receipts which the niggardliness of nature imposes, namely, cost of production. The consequence of imposing a tax (in the ordinary sense) of $\frac{1}{2} t$ per unit (in addition to nature's tax of $\frac{1}{2} t$) will be, under the circumstances, to lower both prices.[1]

* Suppose that y is changed in consequence of the tax from 1 to 1·07 (y from 200,000 to 214,000). Then in order that $\frac{dV}{dy}$ should vanish we must have $x = ·978796$ ($x = 97,880$ nearly). In order that $\frac{d}{dx} (V - x\tau)$ should vanish, $\tau = ·05166$. From the new values of x and y we find for the new prices $p_1 = £·983824$; $2p_2 = £·9686$; each lower than the original figure, namely £1. For the gross profits, $xp_1 + yp_2$, we have now $97879·6 \times £·98382 + 107,000 \times £·9686 = £199,936$. There is thus a loss on the gross profits of some £64. But there is saved on the tax (100,000 — 97,880) £·05166 above £109.

[1] *Cp.* ECONOMIC JOURNAL, Vol. IX. (1899), p. 292 last par. and p. 293. (**F**, p. 154.)

The improbability of the event in question is, I grant, very considerable; but it is not enormous, does not amount to practical impossibility. The improbability is not even very considerable, I think, if the paradoxical characteristic, benefit to consumers (in consequence of a tax), is defined so as to include, besides the case of both prices falling, the case in which, though one price rises, the " consumers' surplus " is not as usual impaired, but, on the contrary, increased.[1] To secure this result only one condition [2]—not as before, two—must be fulfilled. If Δp_1 and Δp_2 are the increments of the respective prices consequent on an increment of taxation, it is now postulated—not that both Δp_1 and Δp_2 should be negative—but only that $x'\Delta p_1 + y'\Delta p_2$ (where x' and y' are the respective outputs—prior to the tax) should be negative.

The theory in this more general form may seem open to the sarcasm which Professor Seligman directs against the primary form of the theory : that it " will surely be a grateful boon to the perplexed and weary secretaries of the treasury and ministers of finance throughout the world." [3] The suggested discrepancy between common sense and mathematical inference may seem really to be made out when it is inferred that benefit to the consumers as a whole is not a very improbable consequence of a tax. But the appearance of absurdity is obtained by looking only at one aspect of the theory. We have so far confined ourselves to the case in which the output of the untaxed commodity is increased in consequence of the tax. But, if the alternative—quite possible, though a priori less probable—case occurs, then the consumer will be damnified in consequence of the tax to an extent beyond what might be supposed. Professor Seligman might with almost equal plausibility have suggested as the outcome of the theory that—whereas it is natural to suppose that the displacement of first-class passengers by the tax will swell the numbers of the second-class—the theory implies that the accommodation of both kinds will be restricted with, of

[1] Professor Seligman's words (employed in another connection) " the more favourable . . . will be the situation of the consumer " (Shifting and Incidence, second edition, p. 191, quoted in the ECONOMIC JOURNAL, Vol. IX. p. 303) seem well adapted to describe the increase of Consumers' Surplus ; and I had supposed that the words might bear this meaning. But I now find (Shifting and Incidence, third edition, p. 348) that Professor Seligman repudiates this interpretation; and I apologise for having supposed that he might have entertained an appropriate conception.

[2] In the symbols before employed the condition requires that $\dfrac{d^2 V}{dx\,dy}$ should be negative, and Δy positive; the fulfilment of this requirement being necessary but not sufficient.   [3] Shifting and Incidence, third edition, p. 214.

course, considerable rise of prices. The " boon " to weary
financiers might now be represented as the lesson that it is
inexpedient to tax the more expensive species of a commodity,
as the consumption of the less expensive species also will thereby
be seriously restricted.

But in truth the boon which the theory confers is not a
definite rule, but the warning to distrust rules transposed from
the regime of competition to that of monopoly.[1]

I hope to adduce, under head II, an example of *a priori*
Probability more directly applicable to practice.*

II.—Discrimination of Prices

This second exemplification of applied Probabilities is, like the
first, furnished by the theory of Monopoly. The feature of that
theory with which we are now concerned is the power of the
monopolist to discriminate between different species of commodities and customers, not preserving that unity of price which
characterises a perfectly competitive market. The subject may
fittingly be introduced by a quotation from the earliest, and still,
I think, the highest authority on the theory of discrimination,
Dupuit. In his epoch-making paper on the measurement of
utility Dupuit puts the following case :—

" Waterworks are constructed for the use of a town situated on
a hill which had before great difficulty in procuring water. The
value of water had been so high that an annual subscription of
50 francs was required to pay for a daily supply of a hectolitre
[22 gallons] . . . . But now that pumps have been set up, that
amount of water costs only 30 francs. As a consequence, the consumer will now employ water for less pressing, less essential wants.
. . . Again, owing to the improvement of the pumps, or by the mere
fact of increased consumption, the price is reduced to 20 francs.
Our man will now want to have four hectolitres, so as to be able

---

[1] Even the terms proper to the regime of competition are to be transplanted
with caution; and I agree with Professor Jannacone (" Questione Controverse,"
Riforma Sociale, Vol. XII.) as to the infelicity of the term *Shifting* applied to
taxation under the regime of monopoly.

* There is here omitted, not as erroneous, but as elaborated out of proportion
to its importance, a note on the probability of a tax on one of two articles which
are partially substitutes for each other producing a fall in the prices of both
articles, in a regime of monopoly. It suffices to state the conclusion that the
phenomenon appears to be quite possible, though far from probable. The note
also pointed out that the reasoning must be applied with caution when the tax
considered is very heavy.

to clean his house every day. Supply him with water at 10 francs per hectolitre, and he will demand ten hectolitres, so as to be able to water his garden. At 5 francs he will demand twenty hectolitres, to maintain a sheet of ornamental water; at 1 franc he will want a hundred hectolitres, to have a fountain constantly playing." [1]

With reference to this illustration, it may be asked : supposing that water for use within the house and water for external use, in the garden or pond, form two categories between which it is possible for a monopolist to discriminate ; is it to be supposed that when the price is lowered from 20 francs to 10 francs, and accordingly water begins to be employed for external uses, the whole of the additional six hectolitres are employed on external uses or part on (additional) internal uses ? The question is not explicitly raised by Dupuit; being indeed not relevant to his context. But I am concerned to postulate for the cases of discrimination with which I deal that a lowered price *is* attended with an increased demand for both of the uses. The species of discrimination which I have in view may be made more conspicuous by noticing its absence from another illustration given by Dupuit :—

" A footbridge is constructed between two populous quarters of a large town at a cost of 150,000 francs. At the rate of 5 centimes per passenger the proceeds prove to be only 5,000 francs [per annum]. The concern is accordingly a failure ; the entrepreneur who had borrowed the greater part of the 150,000 francs, being unable to pay the interest on this sum, is soon ruined. The bridge is sold to an intelligent man who studies the demand for the use of the bridge, with the object of increasing his own profits. Thus he observes that his bridge connects a quarter of the town in which there are manufacturing works with the quarter in which the workmen live ; and that they have, morning and evening, to make a long detour in order to reach their destination. The use of the bridge would greatly shorten the distance which they have to traverse ; but a workman could not afford to pay out of his wages as much as ten centimes a day. . . . [Under the circumstances] the proprietor might insert in his tariff a clause to this effect : ' For passengers wearing a cap, blouse, or jacket [2] the toll is reduced to 1 centime.' [He will thus, suppose, gain an additional 3,000 francs from 300,000 new passengers—per working year of 300 days ; but he may lose a part of his original profits, 5,000 francs, as] " a certain number of passengers at 5 centimes will, by reason of their attire, benefit by the reduction which was not intended for them."

[1] *Annales des Ponts et Chaussées*, 1844, Vol. II. p. 337.
[2] *En casquette, en blouse ou en veste.*

[However] " by new artifices he may succeed in reducing the loss. Thus he may stipulate that the reduction of the toll shall be given only at the hours at which the workshops open and close, or only to workmen showing a certificate [1] of employment." [2]

In this and other passages Dupuit suggests a type of discrimination which may thus be formulated. Considering the demand for the undiscriminated commodity (*e.g.*, passage of the bridge without respect of persons) as made up of the demands for different species between which discrimination is possible; it is (*a*) conceived that the demand for one species is independent of, uncorrelated with, the demand for another species—Dives will not offer less because the toll is lowered for certificated workmen; (β) it is admissible, if indeed it is not essential, that the demand for each species is practically limited (*e. g.* the amount of water employed in internal uses will not be materially increased, however low the water-rate falls). A similar conception is entertained by M. Colson, who walks in the way of Dupuit.[3] I recognise that the conception is of great importance for the purposes of both theory and art. But I emphasise it here only to make clear that it is not the case with which I am about to deal. I am indifferent about the attribute (*a*), and I am not indifferent about (β); I postulate that when price is lowered the amount of each species— as well as of the genus—increases. For example, if there are two species (such as water for internal, and water for external use) whereof the amounts x_1, x_2 are demanded at the prices y_1, y_2, I suppose that (for any assigned value of y_2) x_1 continually increases as y_1 diminishes.[4] The case is quite sufficiently important to reward attention to its properties. In dealing with it, I shall for convenience of enunciation confine my statements mostly to the variety in which only two species are discriminated; but the propositions thus enunicated are readily adapted to any finite number of species.

Concerning the kind of discrimination thus defined, I propose to prove the three following theses :—

1. *Very probably a system of prices can be assigned, such that both the monopolist and his customers may gain by discrimination.* The gain to consumers may possibly be so great that they are better off than they would have been, other things being equal, under a regime of competition.

[1] *Livret.*   [2] *Loc. cit.*, 1849, p. 220.

[3] See, for some account of M. Colson's conception, the review of his *Cours*, III., 170; and compare below, p. 421.

[4] Thus in the example designated C at p. 417 below, each of the components (as well as the compound) demands tails off towards infinity as the price sinks to zero.

2. *Probably the prices which the monopolist will fix in order
to render his profit a maximum are such that the customers will
lose through discrimination;* except when the amount demanded
of one species before the discrimination is much less than the
amount then demanded of the other.

3. *Probably, if the disturbance of prices caused by discrimination is not considerable, the portion of the monopolist's maximum
which is due to the infliction of loss on the customers is inconsiderable.* For a small consideration the (perfectly self-interested)
monopolist may be induced to adopt a system of prices such that
the customers will not lose through discrimination; for a small
addition to that consideration he may be induced to adopt a system
of prices such that they will be materially the gainers.

The general presumptions above described as *à priori* are available to show that the first proposition is probable. The gain of
the monopolist by discrimination depending on the addition to
or subtraction from each price, may be likened to the height, say
z, of a surface shaped like a hill, varying with co-ordinates
x and y, such as the longitude and latitude of any position on the
hill. Now, in general one can reach a higher position on a hill
when free to move in any direction than when one is restricted
to motion along a certain path. In the case before us a limitation
of this sort exists prior to discrimination; the monopolist being
constrained to charge only one price for the whole class of
commodity, or in other words equal prices for the two species.
When this limitation is removed, the monopolist will tend to start
off in a direction which has been called the *line of preference*;[1]
perpendicular to another line on the plane of *xy* called the *line
of indifference*. Likewise the consumer will have his lines of
preference and indifference. But from our general knowledge of
the relations between buyer and seller, we may presume that the
lines pertaining to one party are not coincident with the lines
pertaining to the other party. Accordingly the direction in which
both parties can move together (from the original position), both
being gainers by discrimination, is probably represented by an
angle of sensible magnitude; the probability of mutual gain is
measured by the ratio of that angle to four right angles.

The probability thus discerned will appear greater if we
formulate what is known about the relation of the monopolist
to his customers. On Fig 1 let the addition to, or subtraction
from the price of one species be measured from *O* on the axis *OX*,
OX', and likewise the alteration of the other price on the axis of *Y*.

---

[1] *Mathematical Psychics*, p. 22, and context.

Prior to discrimination, the monopolist was constrained to move
along a right line, representing the condition that the two prices
must be the same, the line TT' making equal angles with the
axes. When the monopolist becomes free to move, otherwise
than in this line, his line of preference is evidently not in the same
quadrant as this line; not in the direction implying that both the
variations of price are positive—between OX and OY—nor yet in
a direction implying that both variations are negative—between

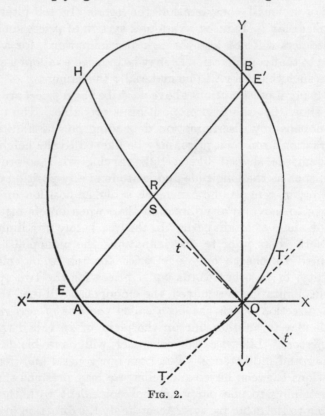

Fig. 2.

OX' and OY'. For if either of these directions represented the
monopolist's preference, he would not, prior to the discrimination,
have stopped at O. Not his line of preference, but his line of
indifference slopes in the same general direction as the original
path. In the figure the line TT' does duty both for the path of
constraint and the line of indifference; but these loci are not
in general coincident. But the line of preference pertaining to
the customers is evidently in the direction between OX' and
OY' since the variation most advantageous to the purchasers is
the fall of both prices. Accordingly, their line of indifference will

slope in the general direction represented by the line tt' in the figure. The interests of the two parties are concurrent for variations of price which are represented by a step in any direction between OT and Ot.

To obtain an idea of the distance to which they may travel concurrently, we may employ a more elaborate construction; which is also required for the proof of the second and third theses. Let us begin by assigning a particular form to the demand-curves of the customer; and first of all the simplest of all forms, the right line. Let x_1 be the amount of one species of commodity, x_2 that of the other demanded at any price, y; and let $2x = x_1 + x_2$ be the amount of the generic commodity (*e.g.*, water for any purpose) demanded at the price of y. Then by hypothesis x is connected with y by a (linear) relation of the form $x = A - By$; where A and B are numerical coefficients. The monopolist's profit, supposing at first that cost of production may be left out of account, $= xy = Ay - By^2$. This will be a maximum when $y = \frac{1}{2}A \div B$ [1] and accordingly $x = \frac{1}{2}A$. If we call this maximum value of x, a, and the corresponding value of y, b, we have $A = 2a$, $B = a \div b$; and accordingly the equation of the (average, generic) demand-curve may be written in the form

$$\frac{x}{a} = 2 - \frac{y}{b}.$$

This line is represented by BA in Fig. 3; on the supposition that $a = b$ (as may always be effected by properly taking the units of commodity and price).

Let us at first suppose (in accordance with the main portion of thesis 2) that x_1 and x_2 are equal at the price which is fixed by the monopolist prior to discrimination. Let us also for the present suppose that there is no correlation [2] between the demands for the two species of commodity. Then the two specific demand-curves (as they may be called, although they are straight lines) will intersect at the point P, which represents the price and *half* of the quantity demanded before the discrimination. The two curves will diverge at that point as represented by the dotted lines in Fig. 3, in such wise that any horizontal line intercepts between the *average* demand-line (AB) and either of the specific demand-lines (*e.g.* A_1B_1) a length equal to that which it intercepts between the former line (AB) and the other specific demand-line

---

[1] I use the old-fashioned sign of division $\div$ in the text, but in the more technical notes the now generally adopted sloping line, as thus, A/B.

[2] *Cp.* above, p. 406.

A_2B_2. For instance, on the horizontal line through ω, the intercepts aa_1 and aa_2 are equal. Likewise $AA_1 = AA_2$.

This property may conveniently be represented by the following construction :—

$$\text{Let } x = a(1 + \xi); \ y = b(1 + \eta).$$

Then if ξ and η are measured from P along the rectangular axes, the relation of ξ to η is represented by the line AB (provided that $a = b = 1$). In other words, $\xi = -\eta$.

Likewise, if $x_1 = a(1 + \xi_1)$, $y_1 = b(1 + \eta_1)$,
$$x_2 = a(1 + \xi_2), \ y_2 = b(1 + \eta_2).$$

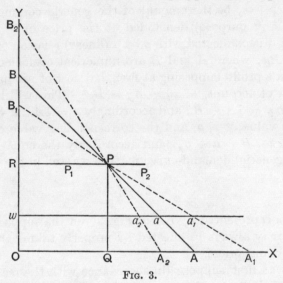

FIG. 3.

$\xi_1 = -q_1\eta_1$, $\xi_2 = -q_2\eta_2$, where q_1 and q_2 must be so selected that $q_1 + q_2 = 2$; say $q_1 = 1 + \beta$, $q_2 = 1 - \beta$, where β is a proper fraction.[1]

The apprehension of the general theorem may be facilitated by assigning a particular numerical value to β. Let us assign a value which is neither very great nor very small, namely $(0\cdot2)$.

$$\text{Thus } \xi_1 = -1\cdot2\eta_1; \ \xi_2 = -0\cdot8\eta_2.$$

Now the gain of the monopolist through discrimination, say R, being the difference between his profit after the discrimination and what it was before

$$= x_1y_1 + x_2y_2 - 2ab.$$
$$= ab(\eta_1 + \xi_1 + \eta_1\xi_1) + ab(\eta_2 + \xi_2 + \eta_2\xi_2).$$

[1] As follows from the condition that the line representing a demand-curve must be inclined negatively to the axis of x.

Substituting for ξ_1 and ξ_2 their respective values in terms of η_1, η_2 we have (if $a = b = 1$)

$$R = (- 0 \cdot 2\eta_1 - 1 \cdot 2\eta_1{}^2 + 0 \cdot 2\eta_2 - 0 \cdot 8\eta_2{}^2).$$

Thus the relation between (changes in) prices, which afford the same profit, the locus of constant revenue, is given by equating the expression within the brackets to a constant. This locus is an ellipse, which when $R = o$ passes through the origin from which ξ and η may be measured (on rectangular axes). In Fig. 1 O represents this origin, and the curve $OAHB$ is supposed to fulfil the condition

$$1 \cdot 2\eta_1{}^2 + 0 \cdot 8\eta_2{}^2 + 0 \cdot 2\eta_1 - 0 \cdot 2\eta_2 = O.$$

Likewise the locus of constant Consumers' Surplus is found from first principles to be an ellipse with equation

$$\tfrac{1}{2}1 \cdot 2\eta_1{}^2 + \tfrac{1}{2}0 \cdot 8\eta_2{}^2 - \eta_1 - \eta_2 = constant.$$

In the figure the curve OSH represents the case in which the said constant is zero, the locus of null gain to the consumers through discrimination.

When the constant in the last written equation is positive, the curve of Consumers' Surplus lies below and to the left of OSH. Consider in particular the curve of this family passing through T, on the supposition that the point T represents the (lower, identical) prices which would prevail, other things being equal, if the regime were one of competition not monopoly. It seems quite possible that this curve (not shown in the figure) should *cut* the locus of null monopoly profit, the ellipse $OAHB$.* There will then be intercepted between these two curves an area any point in which represents a pair of prices which fulfil the secondary part of our first thesis.

The range of variations in price, from O the position before discrimination, that are advantageous both to the monopolist and his customers is represented by the space intercepted between the curves OSH and OAH. The point H may be described as the limit of the range and the index of its extent, if it is understood not to mean that the direct path from O to H can be travelled concurrently, with mutual advantage, by both parties. So the Pillars of Hercules are described by a geographical writer as the limit up to which the navigation of the early Mediterranean peoples extended; though a people situate like the ancient inhabitants of Marseilles could not sail in a straight line to that limit, but must hug a curvilinear shore (that of Spain) comparable with our curve OSH.

* *Cp.* **D**, I. p. 101 *seq.*

The index thus defined is found [1] to be the point of which the abscissa (η_1) is $- 0{\cdot}1855..$, and the ordinate (η_2), $+ 0{\cdot}2268..$; corresponding to prices relatively $18{\cdot}55$ per cent, lower and $22{\cdot}68$ per cent. higher than the prices prior to the discrimination. There is thus a considerable range of variation; considerably greater, as will presently appear, than that which corresponds to the monopolist's maximum profit. Thus the first thesis is verified.

Going on to the second thesis, we have first to determine the prices which render the monopolist's profit a maximum. They prove to be $\eta_1 = - \frac{1}{12}$, $\eta_2 = + \frac{1}{8}$.[2] We have now to observe how the Consumers' Surplus is affected by the adoption of these prices. Substituting the values of η_1 and η_2 in S, the expression for the consumers' gain by the discrimination, we find the gain to be *negative*, namely—$\frac{1}{32}$. The *sign* of this quantity is all that is required to fulfil the second thesis; but it is interesting to notice that the *amount* of loss is greater [3] than the amount of the monopolist's gain, viz., $\frac{1}{48}$ (that is, a gain of about 2 per cent. upon his profits before the discrimination).

To verify the third thesis, we have to compare the maximum monopoly revenue, R', as above determined, the *absolute* maximum as it may be called, with that *relative* maximum, which is the greatest possible gain to the monopolist consistent with the condition that there should be no loss to the consumer. The required positions may be explored by means of the theorem [4] that the maximum monopoly revenue *relative* to, or limited by, the condition that the Consumers' Surplus should have any assigned value is realised by a system of prices such that the elasticity [5] is the same for each of the demand-curves. In the simple case before us, the locus of equal elasticity is a right line inclined to the axis x at an angle of which the tangent is $\frac{9}{2}$,[6] and passing through the point R, the line ERE' in Fig. 2. Thus we have only to determine the intersection of this line with the curve of null gain to the consumers. Let θ_1 and θ_2 be the respective differences between the known co-ordinates of R, η'_1, η'_2, and the sought co-ordinates of the point of inter-

[1] The calculation is facilitated by the incident that the intersection of the two curves is also the intersection of either of them with the line $\eta_1(1 + \frac{1}{2}\beta) + \eta_2(1 - \frac{1}{2}\beta) = 0$.

[2] Differentiating R with respect both to η_1 and η_2, and observing that the second term of variation is negative.

[3] In absolute quantity.

[4] See Note at the end.

[5] The elasticity *proper*, referred to on a preceding page (above, p. 393).

[6] In general $\dfrac{1 + \beta}{1 - \beta} \Big/ \dfrac{1 + \frac{1}{2}\beta}{1 - \frac{1}{2}\beta}$.

section S, say η''_1 and η''_2. Substituting in the expression for S, the Consumers' surplus, for η_1, $-\frac{1}{12}+\theta_1$ and for η_2, $+\frac{1}{8}+\theta_2$, and then putting $\theta_2 = \frac{27}{22}\theta_1$, we obtain .for θ_1 a quadratic equation of which I find the root to be $-\cdot014067$. The corresponding value for θ_2 is $-0\cdot01726$. Whence we obtain for η''_1, $-0\cdot09740$ and for η''_2, $+0\cdot10774$. Substituting these values for η_1 and η_2 in the general expression for R, I find for the new value of R, R'', as we may call it, $0\cdot02035$. This is to be compared with R', the absolute maximum, namely $\frac{1}{48}$, or $0\cdot02083$. The difference between R' and R'' is very small, namely, $0\cdot00048$; about $2\cdot3$ per cent. of R'. That is the proportion of the monopolist's maximum profit which is dependent on the Consumers' loss—a very small proportion in accordance with our third thesis.

When, other things being the same, we suppose the extent of discrimination as measured by the constant β to be increased, it will be observed that the first and the second theses continue to hold good. But the subordination predicated by the third thesis becomes less and less; though it retains some significance for values of β much greater than that which we have considered— say up to $\frac{1}{2}$. To illustrate the failure of the third thesis (while the first and second are eminently fulfilled) put $\beta = 1$. Proceeding as before, I find for R' now $0\cdot8$, for $R' - R''$, $0\cdot1205$; the latter more than 15 per cent. of the former.*

The case which has been considered in which the demand-curves with which we are concerned are straight lines may be regarded as a *Lemma*, which forms a convenient introduction to the far more typical case in which the curves are of the second degree, to wit, parabolas. One obvious difference between the typo and the Lemma is the incident that whereas before in the expression for R and S there occurred only *squares* (and first powers) of the variables (η_1 and η_2), there now occur *cubes* of those quantities. But this difference is not from the present point of view the essential one; since the η's are supposed to be so small, or at least so far from great, that their *third* powers may be, I will not say " neglected," but *subordinated*, in comparison with the second powers. It is a more essential circumstance that the co-efficient of the second powers in the expression for R now takes on different values, depending on a certain coefficient which is of great significance in the theory of monopoly.[1]

* But see Introduction to this article.

[1] The coefficient ω, as to which see the final Note, p. 427. If the equation to the typical parabola is $\xi = -\eta - \lambda\eta^2$, the coefficient of η^2 in R, viz. $-(1+\lambda)$, $= -\frac{1}{2}\omega$.

Still facilitating the acceptance of general truth by a particular example, let us suppose that the demand-curve for $2x$ ($= x_1 + x_2$) prior to discrimination is a parabola of the kind sometimes called horizontal; so that x is of the form $A - By^2$ (A and B both positive). If as before we express the coefficients in terms of the values of x and y, for which xy is a maximum, we have

$$\frac{x}{a} = \frac{3}{2} - \frac{1}{2}\left(\frac{y}{b}\right)^2.$$

Whence, if as before $x = a(1 + \xi)$, $y = b(1 + \eta)$,

$$\xi = - (\eta + \tfrac{1}{2}\eta^2)$$

$$\xi_1 = - 1\cdot2(\eta_1 + \tfrac{1}{2}\eta_1{}^2); \quad \xi_2 = - 0\cdot8(\eta_2 + \tfrac{1}{2}\eta_2{}^2).$$

Proceeding as before, we shall now find

$$R = - 0\cdot2\eta_1 - 1\cdot8\eta_1{}^2 - 0\cdot6\eta_1{}^3, + 0\cdot2\eta_2 - 1\cdot2\eta^2{}_2 - 0\cdot4\eta^3{}_2$$

$$S = - \eta_1 + 0\cdot6\eta_1{}^2 + 0\cdot2\eta_1{}^3, - \eta_2 + 0\cdot4\eta_2{}^2 + 0\cdot13\eta^3{}_2.$$

The intersection of these curves forms the limit to the range of prices advantageous to both parties. If we leave out of account the terms in R and S which involve *third* powers of the η's, we may proceed as before to find the co-ordinates H_1 and H_2 of the intersection. They are respectively $0\cdot127$ and $0\cdot145$;[1] of the same order as the true values obtained by taking into account the third powers of the variables, namely $0\cdot1258$ and $0\cdot1438$ respectively.

The values of H_1 and H_2 prove to be in this instance, as in the Lemma, considerably greater, roughly speaking, about double those of η'_1 and η'_2, the co-ordinates which represent the prices affording maximum profit to the monopolist. For these I find :

By the summary method,

$$\eta'_1 = - 0\cdot05, \; \eta'_2 = + 0\cdot083;$$

Taking account of the subordinate cubic terms,

$$\eta'_1 = - 0\cdot05719, \; \eta'_2 = 0\cdot08012.$$

Whether calculated by the true or the approximate method, the values of R', the monopolist's maximum gain by discrimination, and S', the consequent loss to the customers, prove to be much the same; and accordingly the relation between them not materially different. As thus :—

	R'.	$- S'$	$S' \div R'$
Approximate	0·01388	0·02315	1·667
Accurate ...	0·01378	0·02222	1·612

[1] The calculation of the co-ordinates is facilitated by the circumstance that the point of intersection between the curves lies on the straight line $8\eta_1 + 7\eta_2 = O$. It happens (in this particular example) that this convenient proposition holds good for the true curves, including the cubic terms, as well as of the curves truncated by the omission of those terms.

The approximate calculation may evidently be trusted as a verification of the second thesis.

Going on to the third thesis, I find approximately after the manner of the Lemma, for the prices which make the monopolist's profit a maximum subject to the conditions that the customer is not a loser (or gainer),

$$\eta_1'' = \eta_1' - 0 \cdot 010044, \quad \eta''_2 = \eta'_2 - \tfrac{21}{16} = 0 \cdot 010044$$

where η'_1 and η'_2 have the approximate values above found, namely, $0 \cdot 0\dot{5}$ and $0 \cdot 08\dot{3}$ respectively. Whence it is deducible that the gain which the monopolist must forgo in order not to occasion loss to his customers is about $0 \cdot 0004$, about 3 per cent. of the absolute maximum (above stated).* To compare the true result with this approximate one would require a very laborious calculation. The following partial test must suffice. Assign to the ordinate η_2 a value less than that which affords the (true) maximum profit by an amount which the approximate investigation suggests; for example, put $\eta''_2 = 0 \cdot 07$, less than $\eta'_2 \,(= 0 \cdot 08012)$ by about $0 \cdot 01$. Now find that abscissa of the curve $S = O$ (roughly as to the general shape of that portion with which we are concerned illustrated by the curve OSH in Fig. 2), for which the ordinate is $0 \cdot 07$. That abscissa is found to be $- 0 \cdot 06548$. Accordingly, $+ 0 \cdot 07$ and $- 0 \cdot 06548$ represent prices for which the consumers' loss is null. But the gain which the monopolist forgoes by the adoption of those prices, say η''_1, η''_2 instead of η'_1, η'_2, is found (by substituting those values in the expression for R) to be a small percentage of R', namely, about 2 per cent.[1] But that percentage, small as it is, exceeds the true percentage which would be obtained by using the true η''_1 and η''_2 instead of the assumed or " trial " values.

The peculiar interest of this example is that it is typical of an immense variety of demand-curves, or *functions* representing x, the amount demanded in terms of y, the price.[2] Very generally,

---

* Three per cent. of the addition to his profit due to discrimination; but less than $\tfrac{1}{2}$ per mille of his total profits.

[1] About $\tfrac{1}{4}$ per mille of the monopolist's total profit.

[2] The essence of the general reasoning may be indicated as follows. In the notation above employed we have for R', the gain of the monopolist through discrimination

$$(1 + \xi_1)(1 + \eta_1) - 1, + (1 + \xi_2)(1 + \eta_2) - 1;$$
$$= - \beta\eta_1 - (1 + \beta)\tfrac{1}{2}\omega\eta_1^2 .., + \beta\eta_2 - (1 - \beta)\tfrac{1}{2}\omega\eta_2^2 ..;$$

the *dots* indicating omission of terms involving higher powers, and ω denoting the coefficient which in general terms, with reference to a monopolised article of which the quantity sold is x, the price y, the gain of the monopolist being $V = \tfrac{1}{x}\dfrac{d^2V}{dy^2}$. (See final note, below, p. 426, and remember that the quantity sold

in virtue of presumptions above enunciated,[1] such a function may be expanded in ascending powers of y of the type

$$A + By + My^2 + Ny^3 \cdots \qquad ,$$

with a coefficient M of such an order of magnitude in comparison with subsequent coefficients that, y being a small fraction, the first three terms of the expansion afford an approximation to the value of the function that is adequate for purposes like the present one. If a thesis like ours, not demanding numerical precision, is true of this approximation to the function, it is probably also roughly true of the function itself.

Of course, it must be presumed that the functions with which we are concerned are of an ordinary character—not discontinuous or otherwise abnormal. For example, suppose one of our demand-curves to have the following extraordinary form. Ascending from Q (at zero price) the locus is a vertical line, say as far as P—it is the perpendicular from P on the axis OX—in Fig. 3. From P the locus is a horizontal line, the perpendicular from P on the axis OY. In this peculiar case our first thesis would be fulfilled; all the better, as

---

before discrimination is here taken as unity.) Whence for the prices affording maximum profit we have

$$\eta_1' = -\frac{\beta}{(1+\beta)\omega} \cdot \cdot \, , \quad \eta_2' = \frac{\beta}{(1-\beta)\omega} \cdot \cdot \cdot$$

Also the gain of the customers by discrimination

$$= -\eta_1 - \int_0^{\eta_1}\xi_1 d\eta_1, \; -\eta_2 - \int_0^{\eta_2}\xi_2 d\eta_2$$

$$= -\eta_1 + \tfrac{1}{2}(1+\beta)\eta_1^2 \cdots , \; -\eta_2 + \tfrac{1}{2}(1-\beta)\eta_2^2 \cdots$$

Substituting in this expression for S the above-written values for $\eta'_1 \, \eta'_2$, we obtain for S'_1 the gain of the customers through the discrimination

$$-\frac{2\beta^2}{\omega(1-\beta^2)}\left\{1-\frac{1}{2}\frac{1}{\omega}\right\}$$

Which will be negative in accordance with the second thesis, unless ω is small, $< \tfrac{1}{2}$.

To prove the third thesis consider R and S as functions of θ_1, θ_2, where $\theta_1 = \eta_1 - \eta'_1, \theta_2 = \eta_2 - \eta'_2$. Then the position of relative maximum as above defined must lie on the locus of common tangents to curves of the respective families $R = const.$, $S = const.$; that is

$$\frac{dR}{d\theta_1}\Big/ \frac{dR}{d\theta_2} = \frac{dS}{d\theta_1}\Big/ \frac{dS}{d\theta_2}.$$

Whence we obtain (R not involving the first powers of the θ's) $\theta_2 = q\theta_1 \cdots$, where q is a coefficient of the order unity. Substitute this value of θ_2 for θ_1 in the equation to zero of S, which is of the form

$$S' - A\theta_1 - B\theta_2 \cdots,$$

where S' is of the order β^2, A and B are of the order unity; we find the required value of θ_1 and therefore θ_2 to be of the order of β^2. But R is of the form $R' - (1+\beta)\omega\theta_1^2 - (1-\beta)\omega\theta_2^2 \cdots$ Therefore $R' - R''$ (the difference between the absolute and the relative maximum profit) is of the order β raised to the *fourth* power.   [1] Above, p. 389.

there is avoided all *dead loss*—*perte sèche* in M. Colson's phrase—that is loss to the consumers, which is not gain to the monopolist. Also our second thesis would be eminently fulfilled; for it would be in the power of the monopolist now to charge prices (b_1 and b_2) by which not only one group of customers, but both groups, would have a bad bargain : Consumers' Surplus being theoretically zero or practically only just above it. But our third thesis in this peculiar case would fail altogether. Peculiar as it may seem, this example is not essentially different from one which is at least suggested by very high authority—the Dupuit-Colson type referred to on a previous page,[1] if the attributes there designated a and β are supposed predicable in their strictest form. We are presented with the conception of the area within the demand-curve resolvable into a series of separate columns—as it were so many sacks standing upright, each of which the monopolist can deplete down to any point which it pleases him to fix.[2]

To return to probable matter, if the discrimination is not so complete as to suspend the ordinary properties of demand-curves the theory above propounded may be considered as evident *a priori* in our sense of the term. Accordingly it does not stand in need of specific verification. Nevertheless, as even in mathematics seeing is believing, as the temperament of Didymus is prevalent among those whom I wish to persuade, I have thought it worth while to verify my theory by showing that it holds good for several different laws of demand. For this purpose I select four functions which are in very common use throughout applied mathematics.[3]

[1] Above, p. 404.

[2] As I interpret, there is supposed to be reached a stage of analysis at which the ordinary properties of a demand-curve break down; much as the soap-bubble breaks when the tenuity of the film approaches the dimensions of the constituent molecules. The distinguished economists who entertain this conception are aware of the impossibility of perfectly realising it in practice (*cp.* Dupuit, *Annales des Ponts et Chaussées*, 1842, Vol. I. p. 222; Colson, *Cours d'Économie Politique*, Vol. VI. p. 38. *Cp.* p. 227, par. 2).

[3] The following table exhibits the functions which are employed in two forms;

	x.	ξ.	$\tfrac{1}{2}\omega$.
A	$\tfrac{1}{4}(3-y)^2$	$-\eta + \tfrac{1}{4}\eta^2$	$\tfrac{3}{4}$
B	$\sqrt{3-2y}$	$\sqrt{1-2\eta}-1$	$\tfrac{3}{2}$
C	$-\log y/e$	$-\log(1+\eta)$	$\tfrac{1}{2}$
D	e^{1-y}	$e^{-\eta}-1$	$\tfrac{1}{2}$

the first referred to the zero of commodity and the zero of price as origin, and

There is first (A) the one most used and most useful of all, to evaluate which requires only the operations of arithmetic up to and including *Involution*; in short, the parabola—the common parabola, if no higher power than the second occurs. An example of this law has already been given. But it may be well to consider a second example of a variety less favourable to our third thesis. Next (B) we shall place a function which requires *Evolution* so far as the extraction of the *square root*. Next comes (C) a function which is of wide application in physics, and even in economics has been frequently employed,[1] the *logarithm*. Then follows (D) the nearly related function, which is sometimes called the *anti-logarithm*.[2] I have experimented on these functions in the following uniform manner. I take a curve of the kind under consideration to represent the *average* law of demand, the *half* of the amount demanded at any assigned price, of both species of the commodity. To represent the demands separated by discrimination, I suppose this curve to be thus disturbed, or strained. To half the quantity of x demanded at any price, y, there is added the quantity $\beta (x - a)$ to constitute x_1, the demand for one species at that price; and from the quantity of x there is subtracted the quantity $\beta (x - a)$ to constitute x_2; where, as before, β is a (not large) proper fraction, a is the amount of commodity sold and b the price which affords maximum profit to the monopolist prior to discrimination. (The enunciation applies primarily to the tract of curve for which x is larger than a; for the tract below that point we may read $a - x$ for $x - a$, and interchange the words " addition " and " subtraction.") The fraction β is in each case determined so as to render the increase of the price that is raised equal to $12\frac{1}{2}$ per cent. of the original price.[3] I now determine an

---

abbreviated by putting x for x/a, where x is any amount of commodity and a is that amount of which the sale affords maximum profit to the monopolist, and likewise putting y for y/b (*cp.* above, p. 209, par. 2). For the secondary form of the functions the point of which the co-ordinates are x $= 1$ y $= 1$ is taken as the origin and the co-ordinates are respectively

$$\xi \equiv x - 1 (\equiv (x - a)/a)$$
$$\eta \equiv y - 1 (\equiv (y - b)/b).$$

There is added in a third column a coefficient corresponding to M in the immediate context (to ω in the final Note), a coefficient which must be positive and is presumably not a very small fraction.

[1] To represent the law of diminishing returns and the law of diminishing utility.

[2] The inverse of the Napierian logarithm (of the ordinary logarithm divided by the constant $0.434. . .$)

[3] It might have been somewhat more elegant, but it would have been considerably more troublesome, to *assign* the coefficient β (as in the treatment of the Lemma) and thence *compute both* the changes of price.

index of the range of prices that are mutually advantageous—those Pillars of Hercules, up to which, as explained with reference to our Lemma, the two parties can travel concurrently.   Only it is not always convenient to find the actual position of the Straits; it suffices to find a point, as it were, on the African shore, as in example A, or even as in the other examples, a rock at some distance from that shore, on the Mediterranean side of the Straits.   The limits so understood are given in the first column of the subjoined table.   I then determine the prices which make the monopolist's profit a maximum, the (money-measure of) loss to the customers by the adoption of those prices, and compare the amount of that loss to the amount of the monopolist's profit when maximised.   The percentage given by that comparison forms the entry in the second column.   Further, I find a pair of prices which, while not causing any loss to the customers, yet require the monopolist to forgo only a small proportion of the addition (through discrimination) to his (possible maximum) profit; and accordingly a *very* small proportion of his total possible profit.   The amount thus forgone, as a percentage of the total profit obtained by discrimination, forms the entry in the third column.

Though I have expended much labour on these calculations, yet, as they are long and delicate, I can hardly hope to have entirely avoided mistakes.   Especially the decimals in the Table here following and the final and penultimate places of the decimal in the Table of Materials given in the Notes, are open to suspicion.   But I am sure that the computation is quite accurate enough to verify propositions in Probabilities.

TABLE [1] SHOWING VERIFICATIONS OF THE THREE THESES :—

| Law of Demand. | 1 | | 2 | 3 |
	−	+		
A	18·5	22·3	201	2·5
B	18	22	98	2·5
C	18	22	200·5	1·15
D	20	24	309	1·7

(1) Changes of price advantageous to both parties; per cent. of the price before discrimination.

[1] The subjoined table presents the materials from which the table in the text is constructed, namely—

(2) Loss to the customers by discrimination when the monopolist's gain thereby is a maximum; per cent. of the monopolist's maximum profit.

(3) Percentage of maximum profit resigned by the monopolist to avoid loss to the customers by discrimination.*

Is this multiplication of tests like using several triangles of different shapes in order to prove one of Euclid's propositions relating to triangles in general? Or, rather, have we made a contribution towards ascertaining by induction, less roughly than is given by *a priori* evidence, a limit up to which for purposes like ours fractions may be treated as *small?* [1]

β, the coefficient of discrimination;

$(- H_1, + H_2)$ changes of price advantageous to both parties;

$(- \eta'_1, \eta'_2)$ prices rendering the monopolist's gain by discrimination a maximum;

R', the monopolist's gain by discrimination when a maximum;

$- S'$, the loss to the customers by discrimination when the monopolist's profit is a maximum;

$(- \eta''_1, \eta''_2)$, prices in the neighbourhood of $(- \eta'_1, \eta'_2)$ at which the customers are neither gainers nor losers;

R'', the monopolist's gain by discrimination when the prices are $(- \eta''_1, \eta''_2)$.

The prices are relative to the prices before discrimination; the gains (and losses) are relative to the monopolist's profit before discrimination.

Designation of function.	β.	$- H_1$.	H_2.	$- \eta'_1$.	η_2.	$- S'$.	R'.	$- \eta''_1$.	η''_2.	R''.
A	0·149502	0·1856	0·2228	0·08324	0·125	0·03109	0·01547	0·0952	0·105	0·01508
B	0·30217	0·18	0·22	0·08356	0·125	0·03139	0·03213	0·095	0·105	0·03134
C	0·0953199	0·18	0·22	0·090918	0·125	0·0227	0·01132	0·099	0·11	0·01119
D	0·099383	0·2	0·24	0·08316	0·125	0·03117	0·01007	0·1032	0·115	0·0099

The table in the text is thus formed out of the materials.

Column 1 shows H_1 and H_2 each multiplied by 100.

Column 2 shows $- S'/R'$, multiplied by 100.

Column 3 shows $(R' - R'')/R'$, multiplied by 100.

* There should be added a fourth column presenting the more interesting set of percentages which compare the profit resigned by the monopolist (to avoid loss to the customers, viz. $R' - R''$) with the total profit which he might have obtained; viz. $1 + R'$ (*Cp.* Introduction to this article, above, p. 387). These percentages are for A, B, C, D, respectively, 0·04, 0·08, 0·02, 0·01.

[1] Compare Mr. Bickerdike's observation with reference to his theory of " incipient taxes " (ECONOMIC JOURNAL, 1907, p. 101), " Rather strong assumptions have to be made as to the elasticity of foreign demand and supply if the rate of the tax affording maximum advantage is to come below ten per cent."

As I understand (*cp.* ECONOMIC JOURNAL, XVIII. p. 399 *et seq.*), the quantity with which the writer is concerned, the net gain to the home country, consequent upon a small customs-duty, takes the form $Lx - Mx^2 \cdots$; where L is proportionate to the amount of commodity taxed, x is the rate of taxation per unit of commodity; M is such a coefficient as the M described in our text. Or as L must be considered

Having secured this central position, we can now easily extend the territory subject to our laws; removing limitations by which it has hitherto been circumscribed.

So far we have supposed that prior to discrimination the two categories of consumers were equally important to the monopolist, the amount demanded by each at the single price being the same. Now let us recall this assumption; and, beginning with the Lemma, suppose that at the price b ($= PQ$ in Fig. 3) the amount demanded by one group of consumers is $a(1 + a)$, while the amount of the other species demanded is $a(1 - a)$. The first demand corresponds to RP_2 in the figure if a is positive, the second to RP_1 ($P_1P = PP_2 = aa = a$, if $a = 1$). If the specific demand curves consisted respectively of the lines joining B to P_1 and P_2 (and produced) there would be no discrimination; the two new prices would be identical with the old price, b. But we are to suppose that the dotted lines—not now passing both through P, but one through P_1, another through P_2—are so inclined as to cause a dissilience of prices when the constraining condition that there should be only one price for the whole class is removed. Is it now probable that the consumers as a whole will suffer by the monopolist's using his power of discrimination so as to make his profits a maximum?

Common-sense will perhaps prejudge this question; pointing to instances in which a railway manager may afford a special rate to exceptional classes of travellers (excursionists and so forth). If the general scale of rates is not disturbed by the favour granted to the occasional passengers, if the one species is advantaged and the other is not affected, there must result advantage to the class as a whole.

Doubtless, I reply, in the extreme case of inequality where the demand of the class favoured by discrimination was so small prior to the discrimination as not sensibly to affect the rates fixed for other classes; for instance, the demand of the workmen for the use of the foot-bridge in the second of the illustrations above cited from Dupuit.[1] But we are not now considering extreme cases, but cases in which a—the measure of inequality—is a proper fraction and primarily at least a small one. For instance in the first of Dupuit's illustrations, suppose (what was, perhaps,

---

as varying with $x =$ say $L' - Nx \cdots$, we may write the quantity under consideration $L' - M'x^2(M' = M + N)$. The value for which this expression is a *maximum* (approximately $\frac{1}{2}L'/M'$) is probably much smaller than the limit up to which the expression is positive.

[1] *Cp.* above, p. 405.

not his meaning) that of the ten hectolitres of water which are demanded when the (single, undiscriminated) price is 10 francs per hectolitre per annum, six are required for *internal* use and four for *external* use; [1] and that both demands expand when price falls. In such a case are the consumers as a whole likely to suffer by discrimination? The answer given by mathematics to a question in the theory of Monopoly is often not that which is expected by common-sense.

As before, let us put ξ_1, ξ_2 for the proportional or relative changes in demand respectively consequent on the relative changes of price η_1 and η_2. Then we may write

$$\xi_1 = -a - (1 - a + \beta)\eta_1,$$
$$\xi_2 = +a - (1 + a - \beta)\eta_1;$$

simpliciter in the case of the Lemma, or with the addition of terms involving second powers of the η's to fit the more general type. Forming the general expressions for the Monopoly Revenue and the Consumers' Surplus we find that, as long as a and β remain small fractions, the triple thesis is fulfilled nearly as well as when we dealt with β only. Now, likewise, as either of the coefficients becomes large, the second thesis, that the monopolist tends to fix a set of prices prejudicial to the customers, ceases to be qualified by the third thesis, that his interest in their detriment is small.[2] The second hypothesis retains some probability even when the coefficients are considerable; in the absence of knowledge that the forms of the functions with which we have to deal —the higher powers of the variables which now come into play— are unfavourable to the thesis. We are, of course, here, as throughout, contemplating the money-measure of Consumers' Surplus; not taking into account that the consumers on a small scale may be the poor and needy.

If it is given that a is very large (nearly unity) then the exception [3] enounced in connection with Thesis 2 occurs. But if nothing is given about the coefficients, then we may still affirm the thesis in a certain *a priori* sense.[4] No doubt this kind of probability is not so useful as that which obtains when it is given that conditions favourable to the theses, such as the smallness of both a and β, are realised in the particular case with which we have to deal.

[1] Above, p. 405.　　[2] See observations on the Lemma above, p. 413, par. 3.

[3] This exception deserved to be specified on account of its importance in practice; the attribute by which it is defined—the ratio between the amounts demanded before discrimination—being commonly capable of identification. Theoretically, other exceptions have a right to be enounced; for instance, the case when β is (known to be) large, or γ (below, note 1), or ω small (final Note).

[4] Index, s.v. *A priori Probabilities*.

These considerations are readily extended to the general case.[1]

A further extension of our laws is effected by removing the condition that the commodities in which the monopolist deals should be, like the mineral waters in Cournot's classical illustration, unaffected by cost of production. First, let us make the simplest supposition, that there is a uniform cost of production for all articles of the class considered without regard to the species into which it may be discriminated, or to the total amount produced. This simple case may be represented by measuring in Fig. 2 the net price on which the monopolist's profits are calculated, no longer from the abscissa, but from a horizontal line at a distance from the abscissa, say $O\omega$, which represents the cost of production per unit.[2] The position of maximum profit (prior to discrimination) will now be given by bisecting ωa and ωB, instead of OA and OB. The units of the system being the same as before, the price and amount will not now be each unity. Or if we take the new price and the new amount as the units (in which lengths on the axes are respectively measured), the demand-curve referred to the new position of maximum as origin is no longer $\xi = -\eta$, but $\xi = -q\eta$, where q is a coefficient greater than unity.[3] The essential character of the reasoning is not altered by the modification of the data. Nor is that character altered when, instead of $k_1 x_1 + k_2 x_2$, representing the total cost of producing the quantities of the specific commodities x_1 and x_2, at the respective rates per unit k_1 and k_2, we have to add a term such as $\pm l_1 x_1^2 \pm l_2 x_2^2$;[4] where the positive sign corresponds to the *law of diminishing returns*, the negative sign to the *law of increasing returns*; nor when we add a term such as $- l_{12} xy$,[5] corresponding to *joint cost*.[6]

The reader will observe what a subsidiary rôle is here assigned

---

[1] In general there may be any number of coefficients of discrimination in addition to the α and β which have been introduced. Prior to discrimination let

$$\xi = x/(a - 1) = -\eta + \lambda\eta^2 + \mu\eta^3 + \nu\eta^4 \cdots$$

After discrimination

$$\xi_1 = \pm a - (1 \pm \beta)\eta_1 + (1 \pm \gamma)\lambda\eta_1^2 + (1 \pm \delta)\mu\eta_1^3 \cdots;$$
$$\xi_2 = \mp a - (1 \mp \beta)\eta_2 + (1 \mp \gamma)\lambda\eta_2^2 + (1 \mp \delta)\mu\eta_2^3 \cdots.$$

[2] M. Colson employs largely an equivalent construction.

[3] If k is the cost per unit in the new notation according to which the value of x and the value of y which afford a maximum under the new circumstances are now taken as units; then q may be deduced from the condition that $(1 + \xi)(1 + \eta) - k(1 + \xi)$, $= (1 - k) + \eta - q\eta - q\eta^2 + kq\eta$, should be a maximum when $\xi = 0$, $\eta = 0$. Whence it is deducible that $q = 1/(1 - k)$.

[4] The " l's," as well as the " k's," being positive.

[5] l_{12} being positive. The proposition is, of course, equally true when this coefficient is negative; that is, in the less frequently specified case of rival production (see Index, s.v. *Correlation*).

[6] Nor when higher powers of the variables occur; with the usual assumptions as to the magnitude of their coefficients.

to *joint cost;* which some distinguished writers on Railway Economics seem to emphasise as the principal cause of discrimination. Joint cost is no doubt favourable to discrimination; but there is a more essential condition, unity of management, monopoly.[1]

A further extension is effected by removing the condition that the specific demands should be uncorrelated. The character of the reasoning is not essentially altered by this alteration in the data. The principal difference in the result may thus be expressed. Whereas previously the amount of profits which the monopolist must forgo in order that the customers should not lose or should even gain by discrimination was (approximately) a quantity of the form $A\theta_1^2 + B\theta_2^2$, where A and B are coefficients of the order unity (roughly speaking), θ_1 and θ_2 are of the order β^2 (β being a small, or rather not large, fraction); now there is added to this expression a new term of the same order as the others, $C\theta_1\theta_2$.

I need not point out in detail that most of the propositions above predicated of the Lemma and the simple type are true of the generalised conditions. Enough has been said to show that these propositions hold good through a wide range of circumstances, with as much truth as can be expected of a theory which belongs at once to Mathematical Economics and to the Calculus of Probabilities. Indeed, I am disposed to claim for the theory a greater degree of practical importance than can generally be ascribed to those branches of study.

Mathematical economics serve generally to present comprehensive views as to the interdependence of variable quantities, rather than to solve particular problems; as Professor Pareto has recently pointed out in this Journal.[2] But I submit that there is an exception to this general limitation; that mathematics play a more direct part in the theory of monopoly. What if an exception should be formed by the application of the preceding theorems to one of the doctrines propounded by Professor Pareto himself— not certainly a particular problem, yet a general view which

[1] It may be objected that discrimination arises without monopoly in the case of large establishments; for instance, when an hotel keeper discriminates between wines of different species, though his profits are subject to competition with other hotel keepers. But I submit that he can practise discrimination just because he enjoys a certain degree of monopoly. If the wines were sold separately by open competition, if there was on the spot a sherry-market and a port-market, the prices paid by the customers would each of them—instead of as now on an average, summed up in the hotel-bill—conform to the cost of production. (See Index, s.v. *Quasi-monopoly.*)

[2] In his appreciative tribute to the memory of Walras, March, 1910.

purports to be of direct practical significance ?   I refer to his argument directed against Socialism, that at best it would not essentially alter the distribution and production of wealth.   " Economic
goods will be distributed according to the rules which we have
discovered in studying a regime of competition. . . ."   " Prices
reappear," or " will at most change their name." [1]   But we have
seen that a regulated discrimination of prices, such as might conceivably be practised by a Socialist Directory, but is not possible in
a regime of competition, tends to increase the sum-total of utility.
A conception still less familiar to popular Socialism is suggested by
what may be called the *external case* of our theory, that which
is presented when " monopolist " is interpreted to mean sole
buyer. The suggestion is that to discriminate between labourers
on grounds other than efficiency—not always to pay the same
wages for the same amount of work done—might diminish the
" dead loss " of Producers' Surplus which the contrary policy
involves.

But if this advantage is either of a negligible order in relation
to the stupendous consequences of a Socialist revolution, or is
over-balanced by the liability to enormous abuses; may we not
hope for a less precarious application to a more familiar kind of
monopoly, the control of railways and generally public works ? [2]
That hope is justified by experience.   For the mathematical principles on which our reasoning is mainly based are actually applied
under the skilful direction of M. Colson to the railway policy of
France.   Such is the proposition that a small reduction of price, so
small as to cause a very small sacrifice of profit to the monopolist,
is likely to be attended with considerable relief to the customers.
Our third thesis but superadds to this received proposition the
following one :—In the case of discrimination (in certain not
unusual circumstances) the relief to the customers afforded by
a small sacrifice of the monopolist's profits is likely to be so
considerable that they may be gainers, or at least not losers, by
the introduction of discrimination.[*]

It is true that these propositions are but probable; liable to
failure in particular cases.   But we are not altogether dependent
on the more precarious kind of *a priori* probability, that which
is exemplified by the predication of our second thesis [3] in the
absence of data as to the extent and elasticity of demand.   Such

---

[1] *Cours d'Économie Politique*, p. 1014 and context.
[2] In the sense of the term in which it is employed by M. Colson.
[*] See D, and Introduction thereto.
[3] Above, p. 407.

data would often be available sufficiently to show what case we had to deal with. The sun of full knowledge may illuminate part of our course. There may be enough of that daylight to enable us at least to select the proper path; which may then be pursued in safety by the starlight of Probabilities.

NOTE.—*On certain coefficients.* The first differential coefficient of a monopolist's profit with respect to price has an interesting relation to the elasticity of his customers' demand. The former coefficient may be written, in our notation, when there is no cost of production,

$$x + y\frac{dx}{dy} = x\left(1 + \frac{y}{x}\frac{dx}{dy}\right) = x(1 - e);$$

where e is the elasticity as defined by Professor Marshall (*Principles of Economics*). When cost of production is constant, c per unit, the expression becomes

$$x(1 - \epsilon), \text{ if } \epsilon = -\frac{y'}{x}\frac{dx}{dy'}, y' = y - c.$$

This proposition may be employed to prove the theorem above enounced (p. 412), that when a monopolist discriminates between different species of custom, subject to the conditions that the subtraction from (or addition to) the benefit of his customers as a whole should be nil, or have any other assigned value, the elasticity of demand is the same for the different species which are discriminated (cost of production being null or constant). For consider the Consumers' Surplus, say W, as the difference between the money-measure of the utility resulting from the consumption of the commodities, and the purchase-money thereof, we have, in the case of two species of commodity,

$$W = \int_0^{x_1} y_1 dx_1 + \int_0^{x_2} y_2 dx_2 - x_1 y_1 - x_2 y_2 = +\int_\infty^{y_1} x_1 dy_1 + \int_\infty^{y_2} x_2 dy_2.$$

Likewise the profit of the monopolist, say V, is, in the absence of cost of production, $x_1 y_1 + x_2 y_2$. Now the quantity which the monopolist aims at maximising is $V + \lambda W$; where λ is the indeterminate co-efficient proper to problems of relative maximum. We have accordingly

$$\frac{d}{dy_1}(V + \lambda W) = 0; \frac{d}{dy_2}(V + \lambda W) = 0;$$

Whence $\lambda = \frac{dV}{dy_1}\bigg/\frac{dW}{dy_1}$. Now $\frac{dV}{dy_1} = x_1(1 - e_1)$, and $\frac{dW}{dy_1} = x_1$. Therefore $\lambda = (1 - e_1)$. By parity of reasoning $\lambda = (1 - e_2)$. Whence $e_1 = 1 - \lambda = e_2$. As above, e is replaced by ϵ when the cost of production per unit is a constant, but the proposition loses its simplicity when the cost (per unit) involves the variables. It may be remarked that the property of equal elasticities is also characteristic of another kind of discrimination which may seem particularly suitable for a State Monopoly to practise, namely, that regulation of prices which has for its object the maximum benefit to the purchasers as a whole, consistent with the retention by the monopolist of a fixed profit—a fixed amount, or a fixed percentage of the output, that is, of the cost of production, supposing cost to be constant.

The affinity between elasticity and the increment of monopoly profits extends to the second order of differentials. Putting $V = xy$ we have $\frac{1}{x}\frac{dV}{dy}$ (or is it more elegant to write $\frac{y}{V}\frac{dV}{dy}$?) $= 1 - e$ (for any value of the variable). Accordingly, $\frac{1}{x}\frac{d^2V}{dy^2} = -\frac{de}{dy}$, at the point of maximum, since then $\frac{dV}{dy} = 0$. This coefficient, or rather its negative, namely $\frac{de}{dy}$, which has been called ω (above, p. 415), plays an important rôle in the theory of monopoly. It is closely related to, though not identical with, the coefficient designated ω in the note to the first section of this article in the ECONOMIC JOURNAL, Vol. XX. p. 301 (not reprinted here), ω there denoting $\frac{1}{y}\frac{d^2V}{dx^2}$. (*Mutatis mutandis* when cost of production enters.) The coefficient ω is necessarily positive and presumably not (often) very small. The smaller it is, the sooner, as we continue to increase the degree of discrimination, the extent to which prices are varied, is the limit reached at which our third thesis breaks down. Thus in the second of the two parabolas above instanced, a smaller value of η'_2 (β and $-\eta'_1$) will cause the third term of the expansion to become comparable with the second in the case of the second parabola, for which $\omega = \frac{3}{2}$, than in the case of the first parabola, for which $\omega = 3$.

[There is here omitted a paragraph referring to the theorem that a tax on one of two monopolised articles for which the demand is correlated may result in the *fall* of *both* prices. Some difficulties which the reasoning may present when the tax instanced is very heavy, restated in that paragraph, may here be summarised as follows. When the changes in the variables (prices and quantities) consequent on the tax are large, then there is no longer available the convenient generalisation of Cournot's formula for the change of price and quantity due to a tax on a monopolised article; the simultaneous equations of the first degree adduced in a former article (E). The neglect of the *third* powers of the increments which that method involves becomes inaccurate. The reasoning, too, may break down if the functions intended to represent the relation of price and quantity demanded are such and so simple that for the new values of the variables the functions no longer retain the character proper to the problem. This limitation is illustrated by the incident that the functions above employed to represent the relation of the price to the quantities x and y (above, p. 401) becomes inadmissible when x the number of first-class passengers is smaller than 85,000, while y the number of second-class passengers remains 200,000. For then $\dfrac{dp_1}{dx}$ is no longer, as it ought to be, *negative*.]

One more coefficient calls for one more remark : elasticity, in the popular sense, that is, $F'(p)$ in Cournot's notation, $\dfrac{dx}{dy}$ in ours. The sort of reader who is content with this usage may be apt to think that the distinction (*ante*, p. 290) which we have emphasised between elasticity and the increment thereof is a refinement of no great practical importance, that what is true of the increment is true enough of the quantity supposed to increase. It may be well, therefore, to point out that between the increment (first differential coefficient) of a variable and the variable itself, there may be all the difference that there is between the velocity at which a body is moving and the distance through which it has moved. Contrast the following propositions :— (1) The higher the speed of a motor-car the greater is the danger of accidents ; (2) the longer the distance (from any fixed point) that a motor-car has travelled (at whatever rate), the greater is the danger of accidents. The former presumption could doubtless be verified by the statistics of accidents. Governments are well advised in making regulations based on this presumption. But what should we think of an expert who advised Government to discourage motorists from travelling beyond a certain distance from, say, New York, in order to prevent accidents ? That advice would be of a piece with the theory which predicates of elasticity what is true of the increment of elasticity. No doubt it may be a proof of great natural ability to approach and half discern the truth in such a matter without the aid of the appropriate mathematical conceptions.

ON SOME THEORIES DUE TO PROFESSOR PIGOU

[THIS examination of some new theories due to Professor Pigou appeared in the ECONOMIC JOURNAL (June 1913) as a Contribution to the Theory of Railway Rates; in virtue of a connection which is explained in the opening sentences. The introductory contrast between Professor Pigou's terminology and that which is commonly employed in the present Collection brings into view the peculiarity that in our treatment of Value and Production there is contemplated more explicitly than is now usual the entrepreneur aiming at his maximum advantage, exercising something of the freedom of a monopolist; " external economies " not figuring conspicuously. (They are not ignored, because not presented in one comprehensive picture. Rather, they are, so to speak, shown on a " film," a moving series of pictures each of a differently constituted market, the conditions of supply— perhaps also of demand—changing with the time. See Index, sub voce *External Economies*.) Professor Pigou's conception of the Supply-curve, of which the ordinate includes payment for rent, is exhibited in relation to his new construction of the " curve of marginal supply prices." It should be observed that in reproducing this construction (June 1913) the writer had not the advantage of having seen Professor Allyn Young's criticism of the construction, nor the modifications introduced by Professor Pigou in deference to that criticism. However modified, the new curve, with the corresponding " curve of marginal demand prices," serves to sanction reasoned departures from the rule of *laissez-faire*, to extend Marshall's " limitations of the abstract doctrine of maximum satisfaction."

In subsequent paragraphs there is offered a defence of Professor Pigou's theory of Joint Cost as applied to Railway Policy (see Index, sub voce *Joint Production*).]

Graphical Representation of Cost.—The relations between cost of production and quantity produced present such a variety of aspects as almost to defy the subtlety of speech, even when rendered precise by mathematical conceptions. Similar shapes designated by the same name, a supply-curve, are often employed in a misleading manner with reference to quite different circumstances. For instance, it may make all the difference whether we are considering (a) long periods, or (α) short ones; (b) the presence, or (β) the absence, of what Dr. Marshall calls "external economies"; (c) collective cost, or (γ) that which pertains to a single individual (or constituent group); (d) the regime of competition, or (δ) that of monopoly; (e) the remuneration of the entrepreneur as included in the cost of production, or (ε) as a residue distinguished from the entrepreneur's expenditure. There is a less mistakable division between (z) the use of one of the co-ordinates to represent *price*, the construction which Dr. Marshall has made familiar, and (ζ) the use of one co-ordinate to represent the total amount of money demanded in exchange for the amount of product represented by the other co-ordinate.[1] There is a certain correlation between (corresponding members of) several of these dichotomies; and it is therefore the less surprising that throughout Professor Pigou should have adopted the positive and I the negative attribute. The supply-curves which he employs are mostly of the type *abcdez*; while mine are primarily of the type *αβγδεζ*. It is not to be expected, therefore, that there should be a close similarity between our representations. But I am concerned to show that there is no essential discrepancy.

For the purpose of instituting a comparison I construct in Fig. 1 a supply-curve of the type above distinguished as z; and I transfer here as Fig. 2 a curve of the type ζ which I have employed.[2]

For the present purpose it is not necessary to consider the simplest and most elementary transactions to which such curves may pertain : such transactions as international trade between two imaginary islands, or the bargain between ideal hunters of two different types—say white employers and black employees— as to the distribution of their joint quarry.[3] The curves of type ε proper to such conceptions are not considered here. Let us rather suppose SS_1 as representing, agreeably to common usage, the

---

[1] The ζ system is used by Mr. Flux in the ECONOMIC JOURNAL, Vol. XV., and commented on by the present writer, XVII (γ). It is not quite identical with, being less general than, Dr. Marshall's curves of International Trade referred to in the ECONOMIC JOURNAL, Vol. III., pp. 69 and 359.

[2] See III., Fig. 1.

[3] Compare *Quarterly Journal of Economics* on the "Theory of Distribution," 1904 (**B**, I., p. 14).

amount x of, say, agricultural produce offered by a set of farmers

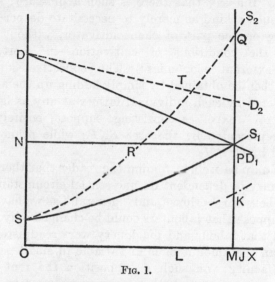

Fig. 1.

In Fig. 1 SS_2 is a parabola of which the equation is
$$Y = \tfrac{1}{4}(x + a)^2$$
whence
$$yx = \int_0^x Y dx = \tfrac{1}{4}(a^2 x + a x^2 + \tfrac{1}{3}x^3); \quad y = \tfrac{1}{4}(a^2 + ax + \tfrac{1}{3}x^2).$$

The unit in which x is measured is a ($=$ one inch). Accordingly, $MQ = 2 \cdot 25$ inches; $MP = 1\tfrac{1}{16}$ inch. The demand-curve DD_1 passes through D at the vertical distance of 2 inches from O, and intersects the supply-curve at P. DD_1 is a right line of which the slope relatively to the vertical is $2/1\tfrac{1}{2}$. Accordingly the slope of the curve of marginal supply prices DD_2 is *twice* that slope. DD_2 intersects SS_2 at T; nearer the origin than P as might be expected, the law of diminishing returns acting.

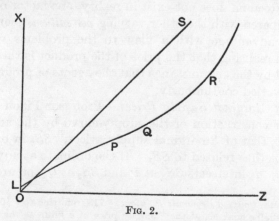

Fig. 2.

using implements, employing workmen, and paying rent. If the increase of produce did not involve any sensible (additional) pressure on the soil this supply-curve would be, suppose, a horizontal line. But say that there is such a pressure; and let it first be of such a kind as merely to necessitate deeper ploughing and digging on the part of each cultivator, without otherwise modifying the conditions of cultivation—in short, without *negative* " external economies." The collective supply-curve SS_1 would then be obtained by simply adding up the amounts of product offered by each individual farmer at any assigned price. The " general " expenses consisting, suppose, entirely of rent, would be represented by the area SNP; while prime costs are represented by $OSPM$.

Here it may be well to remind the reader that there is something arbitrary or dependent on unessential circumstances in the distinction between " prime " and " general " as we have used the terms. Suppose that labourers could be changed only after long notice, and that labour and machinery were readjusted less frequently than the amount of land variable in small parcels with imaginary facility; on such a supposition the rent might be regarded as prime cost, the other expenses as general. The same ordinate MP might now represent the price of that increment of land which corresponds to an increment of produce. More generally it is proper to regard the price PM as made up of two (in general, more) portions, MK and KP, corresponding respectively to the values (at the prevailing prices of the factors of production) of that increment of capital and that increment of land which the entrepreneur would take on if free to distribute an assigned increment of resources between the two uses.[1] Even where this freedom does not exist in reality, one factor of production as compared with the other varying *per saltum*, there is some theoretical advantage with a view to the problems which are before us in realising that the price of the product is theoretically not affected by the circumstance that the agents of production are or are not varied continuously.

Curve of Marginal Supply Prices.—Professor Pigou improves the familiar construction of the supply-curve by the addition of a new curve, that of " marginal supply prices," SS_2 in our Fig. 1. This curve is thus related to SS_1. If the ordinate at any point of the abscissa, M, intersects SS_1 at P and SS_2 at Q, the area $OMQS$

[1] See Pareto, *Cours d'Économie Politique*, § 718 (referring to § 100—1); and compare Marshall's analysis of the " supply price of a knife as the sum of the supply prices of its blade and handle."—*Principles of Economics*, Book V. ch vi. § 1; and his note on marginal product (with reference to J. A. Hobson's theories, *op. cit.*, p. 393, ed. 6).

is equal to the area $OMPN$.[1] But the area $OMPN$ represents the total expenses incident to the production of the quantity OM; inclusive of rent (the area PSN) and of entrepreneur's remuneration, which by our convention is included in the area $OSPM$. Accordingly, the line MQ—or, more exactly, the little rectangle of which that line is the height and a (small) unit of produce is the base—represents the addition to the total cost incident to the production of an additional unit.

But, it will be asked, Is not this the very definition of "marginal cost"? And have we not just seen that—however we manipulate the distinction between prime and general cost—the marginal cost incident to an increment of produce is OP? How then can that incremental cost be OQ? The answer is that both statements are true. The same predicate "marginal increment of cost" is truly coupled both with MP and with MQ; if in the one proposition it is understood *simpliciter*, in the other proposition as the logicians say, *secundum quid*. For MP is the increment of cost consequent on an increment of production, the cost of production of the units of commodity other than this increment being supposed constant. That is, MP is the marginal cost from the point of view of the entrepreneur producing a small part of the aggregate output in a regime of competition. But MQ is the increment of cost consequent on an increment of production, the price of the produced commodity not being supposed constant.[2] Rather, account being taken of the circumstance that the price is such that if a sale could be effected at that price the expenses of production would just be covered, that covering price changes (in the case supposed, increases) with the amount produced. Accordingly, MQ might be described as the marginal increment of cost from the point of view of a monopolist.

In this connection mention may be made of another piece of mechanism due to Professor Pigou: the curve of "marginal demand prices."[3] The relation of this curve to the ordinary demand-curve may be shown as follows : Let DD_1 be the demand-

---

[1] In symbols, if y is the ordinate of SS_1, Y that of SS_2,

$$\int_0^x Y dx = xy.$$

[2] Let $x \ (= OM)$ be the produce, $p \ (= MP)$ the supply-price, or cost of production per unit, $xp \ (= OMPN = OMQS)$ the total cost. Then $MP = \left(\dfrac{d}{dx}\right)xp$

(p being treated as constant) $= p$; $\ MQ = \dfrac{d}{dx}xp$ (the complete differential)

$= p + x\dfrac{dp}{dx}.$

[3] See ECONOMIC JOURNAL, Vol. X., " Producers' and Consumers' Surplus."

curve in our figure intersecting the supply-curve at P; DD_2 the curve of marginal demand prices. If the ordinate, not drawn on the figure, at any point on the abscissa, J, intersects DD_1 at D, and DD_2 at D_2, the area OJD_1D is equal to the area of the rectangle of which the base is OJ and the height OD_2.[1] But the area OJD_1D represents the total utility, or, in Professor Pareto's less equivocal phrase, " ophelimity " accruing to the customers from the quantity of commodity OJ (on the supposition of their obtaining it *gratis*). The corresponding money value is that which would be realised by a monopolist who practised discrimination of the kind defined by Professor Pigou as " ideal "—a conception which he has happily illustrated by the suggestion of a method whereby a monopolist of this particularly grasping type might conceivably touch the total value in question.[2] Accordingly, a monopolist of this type would push production up to, but not beyond, the point at which the increment to the said total value is just equal to the increment of total cost, that is, the point at which the curves DD_2 and SS_2 intersect, the point T in the figure, or the point L on the abscissa corresponding thereto. A nobler use of the two new curves will presently appear.

The moderately mathematical reader will have no difficulty in translating these constructions into the form which I have employed, above labelled ζ. The curve S_1 in Fig. 1 might be supposed to correspond to the curve PQR in Fig. 2, if we do not attend to the initial convex part of the latter curve, rather suppose it to start from O and be convex to (OZ) throughout. The abscissa OZ in Fig. 2 corresponding to OX in Fig. 1, the *ordinate* in Fig. 2 (*e. g.* a perpendicular let fall from R on OZ—not drawn in the figure) would correspond to the area $OMPS$ in Fig. 1. What line then in Fig. 2 corresponds to the area $OMQS$ in Fig. 1? It might be the ordinate of a certain curve derived from $OPQR$ in Fig. 2 which I have indicated as pertaining to the regime of competition,[3] the collective supply-curve (*Gesammt-*

---

[1] In symbols (corresponding to those used above with reference to supply) let y' be the ordinate of DD_1 Y that of DD_2. Then

$$\int_0^x y'dx = Y'x.$$

In the figure, DD_1 is intended to be a straight line inclined to the axis of Y at an angle with tangent 1. Accordingly DD_2 is inclined to the vertical at an angle with *twice* that tangent.

[2] Economic Journal, Vol. XIV. p. 391; *Wealth and Welfare*, p. 203. See also, with reference to this kind of monopoly, Economic Journal, Vol. XX. p. 453 (above, p. 417).

[3] Defined by me, Economic Journal, Vol. XXI., E, and more fully by Auspitz and Lieben in their *Theorie des Preises*, p. 13.

angebotscurve) of Auspitz and Lieben.[1] Or rather, as we are not here explicitly representing the profits of the entrepreneur as varying with the amount of product, it is proper to take our curve *PQR* as the cost-curve (*Gesammtkostencurve*) with the interpretation (not that of Auspitz and Lieben) that the intersection of any right line drawn through the origin with that curve designates the amount offered at the price represented by the inclination of the line.[2] With this interpretation the *vertical distance* defined by Auspitz and Lieben [2] as the measure of Collective Utility (*Gemeinnutzen*) corresponds to the *area DTS* in our Fig. 1.

I have given another construction in which the factors of production—in the case before us " capital " (= labour + implements × waiting) and land—appear as co-ordinates.[3] Say the amount of the former factor is measured along the bottom of the page from the left corner, while the other factor is measured from the same point along the left side of the page. The cost κ of any two quantities of the factors (at prices supposed to be given) is measured downwards on an ordinate perpendicular to the plane of the paper. The corresponding amount of produce multiplied by its price (which the monopolist is free to vary), say ζ less by the cost κ, gives z, the quantity which it is the object of the monopolist to maximise. The construction is such that z is measured upwards from the plane of the paper. In seeking this maximum the monopolist entrepreneur will describe a path on the plane of xy; which will be a broken sort of path in case one of the factors, such as land, comparatively with the other is varied *per saltum*. This construction is applicable to a regime of competition with a little modification. We may suppose different entrepreneurs to move by different paths in seeking each the maximum of the z pertaining to him. The height of the average z may be regarded as small or null; rather in deference to fact than as required by theory.[4] Each entrepreneur ever strives to make his z as great as possible. So each golfer in every match strives to make the difference between his score and " bogey," augmented

---

[1] The construction ζ thus interpreted will, I think, correspond to that which Mr. Flux has employed in his paper on " Improvements and Rentability " (ECONOMIC JOURNAL, Vol. XV.); it being observed that he takes cost for the abscissa and product for the ordinate, as in our Fig. 1 B in C, p. 65.

[2] *Op. cit.*, p. 370.

[3] See ECONOMIC JOURNAL, Vol. XI. p. 365.

[4] On the theoretical point, see Index, s.v. *Entrepreneur*. As to the facts, almost all that is known, I believe, is well presented by Ashley in the ECONOMIC JOURNAL, Vol. XX. p. 350.

by his handicap, as small as possible; though on an average, in well regulated golf links, probably the difference between the score and (bogey+handicap) is zero, or rather—having regard to very bad players—on the wrong side of zero.

So far we have supposed the curve of marginal supply prices to be ascending. Now let us consider a descending curve of the sort such as SB in Fig. 3 (see p. 437). If we retain the supposition that the collective supply-curve is formed by simple addition from the dispositions of the individual entrepreneurs, the supply-curve SS' derived from SB (according to the rule above given) will be insignificant in a regime of competition. For it represents only that amount of production which at any assigned price affords to entrepreneurs a *minimum* of profit—a position of unstable equilibrium. But in a regime of monopoly it might well happen in the case represented that production might be stable at any point between O and O'.[1]

In order that the descending supply-curve may be significant in a regime of competition it must receive a different interpretation. The height MP now denotes as before the price at which the quantity OM is evoked[2] in a state of industry adapted to that scale of production. But what corresponds to the curve SS_1 of Fig. 1 in our first example, considered as representing the sum of the amounts offered by each entrepreneur at any (one) assigned price, is a quite different curve from SS_1 of Fig. 3, an ascending curve, the "short-period" supply-curve. It is here represented by a right line—in the neighbourhood at least of any point P on the supply-curve, for it may be supposed lower down to twist and cut the axis OY near O. The construction is explained in my review of Mr. Cunynghame's *Geometrical Political Economy* in the ECONOMIC JOURNAL for 1905 (pp. 66–68). For the sake of convenience I virtually made the assumption which Professor Pigou has made on perhaps other grounds, that " the price at which anybody supplies a given quantity of commodity is made up by the addition of two parts, one depending on the quantity that the person himself supplies, and the other upon the quantity that the whole market collectively supplies."[3] The ascending part of the supply-curve SS_1 is similarly to be interpreted, and not as the curve SS_1 in Fig. 1.

[1] As noticed (with reference to the curve there employed), **C**, p. 73. ECONOMIC JOURNAL, Vol. XXI. p. 361.

[2] Defined more exactly by Professor Pigou, ECONOMIC JOURNAL, Vol. X. p. 358.

[3] Pigou, ECONOMIC JOURNAL, Vol. XIII. p. 21; the reference to " demand " there made being omitted to suit my context.

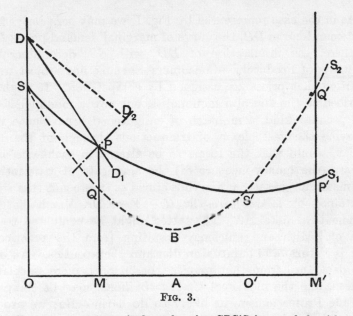

FIG. 3.

In Fig. 3 the curve of marginal supply prices $SBS'S_2$ is a parabola with vertical axis and apse at B. If $AB - b$ OA $= 2a$, $OS - 2a^2 + b$; the equation of the curve referred to O as origin is

$$Y = b + \tfrac{1}{2}(x - 2a)^2.$$

From this the expression for y the ordinate of the supply-curve is obtained by putting

$$yx = \int_0^x Y dx = bx + \tfrac{1}{6}x^3 - ax^2 + 2a^2x.$$

Whence $y = b + 2a^2 - ax + \tfrac{1}{6}x^2$. There is a minimum of y at the point of intersection S' between the two curves. This property is general; since

$$Y = \frac{d}{dx}xy = y + x\frac{dy}{dx};$$

and accordingly when $Y = y$, $\frac{dy}{dx} = 0$. In order to construct a simple system of short period supply-curves, formed by right lines with a positive slope of 45° (*Cp.* ECONOMIC JOURNAL, Vol. XV. p. 68), put

$$y \equiv x + \psi(x);$$

where $\psi(x) = b + 2a^2 - ax + \tfrac{1}{6}x^2 - x$. Then for the equation to any line of the family, we have

$$y = x + \psi(x'),$$

where x' is the abscissa of any point on the curve $SS'S_1$. For instance, when $x' = a(= OM)$, $\psi(x') = b + 1\tfrac{1}{6}a^2 - a$; and accordingly the equation of the corresponding line is

$$y - (b + 1\tfrac{1}{6}a^2) = x - a;$$

the equation of a line passing through P, the *broken* line in Fig. 3. In the figure the unit a is taken as three-quarters of an inch', and b is taken to be half an inch. Accordingly, OS ($ = M'Q'$) $= 2$ inches. The demand-curve is a right DD_1 starting from the point D which is at the height 2·5 above the origin. This demand-curve intersects the supply-curve at P of which the height is $1\tfrac{3}{8}$ inches. The slope of DD_1 with reference to the vertical is $\tfrac{2}{3}$. Accordingly that of DD_2 is $\tfrac{1}{3}$. The intersection of DD_2 with SS_2 (not shown in the figure) is at a greater horizontal distance than P from the origin; as might be expected, the law of increasing returns acting.

As in the case represented by Fig. 1, we may here derive from the demand-curve DD_1 the curve of marginal demand prices DD_2. As there, the intersection of DD_2 with SS_2 determines the maximum of Producers'+Consumers' Surplus, not subject to the condition that prices are assigned by competition. It might be described as the aim of a monopolist, but now a monopolist of a very peculiar kind, a monarch of enlightened benevolence who, surveying the vast plexus of transactions throughout the community, would wish the terms to be altered in such wise as to increase (the money-measure of) the aggregate of satisfactions. This maximum of satisfaction thus aimed at transcends that which is attained by *laissez-faire*, the $H - V$ of Dr. Marshall's deep mathematical note xiv. The latter might be compared to the state of health and efficiency resulting from the practice of what is natural and habitual in diet and therapeutics. An *arbitrary* departure from that practice, based on a mere association of ideas, like the mediæval *similia similibus*, may be compared to crude Protectionism, as likely to do harm. But we are not thereby forbidden to depart from what is called natural, in a direction pointed out by science. One of the directions in which it may prove possible to improve on *laissez-faire* is afforded by Professor Pigou's doctrine supplementing that of Dr. Marshall with respect to the "limitations of the abstract doctrine of maximum satisfaction." [1] The new and less abstract maximum, $H' - V'$, as we may call it, transcends the state of unrestricted competition of which it is sometimes said by mathematical hedonists, and implied by practical free traders, that "this regime realises the maximum of satisfaction and the minimum of sacrifice for each of the co-exchangists." [2] To advance some way in the direction of $H' - V'$ may be better than to have attained $H - V$; [3] just as you are higher when half-way up Mont Blanc than on the top of Snowdon.

Increasing Returns.—I cannot claim to have anticipated this sublime use of the new curves.[4] It is relevant here as bearing on

---

[1] *Principles of Economics*, Book V. ch. xiii. p. 467 *et seq.*; referred to by Professor Pigou in the ECONOMIC JOURNAL, Vol. XI. p. 366.

[2] I quote from *Histoire des Doctrines Économiques* (p. 636, ed. 2) of Gide and Rist, who are transcribing faithfully enough the doctrines of the mathematical economists. [3] Compare Pigou, *Wealth and Welfare*, p. 106.

[4] The system of co-ordinates here called ζ (above, p. 430) may be adapted as I have indicated (Index, s.v. *Increasing Returns*) to the system of long-period supply curve with intersecting short-period curves, proper to increasing returns in a competitive regime. The area DTS in Fig. 1 would then correspond to a line in a modified form of Fig. 2, the greatest vertical distance between two curves which are modifications of Auspitz and Lieben's Collective Cost and

a question which I have particularly considered, the signification of the term " increasing returns."   In view of much tedious discussion in recent literature I sought to fix the meaning of that evasive term.   I distinguished as " primary " and " secondary " two definitions respectively importing that an added dose of productive power increases (1) the marginal, or (2) the average produce.   Among other considerations in favour of the primary definition, I remarked : " When we contemplate the working of a competitive regime as bearing on the interest of the community, from the point of view of the philosophic statesman, then we welcome the phenomenon of Increasing Return (or deprecate its contrary) as tending to (or from) some quantity which it is proposed to maximise. But the criterion of such a maximum is analogous to our *primary* conception." [1]   Now the point of view of this philosophic statesman is exactly that of the benevolent monarch whom we have just imagined—except that the view of the latter is assisted by the new implement which has just been described.   Accordingly, I claim Professor Pigou's authority for my *primary* definition.   To be sure, the denotation is generally the same for the two connotations; but not always, as we may see in Fig. 3, where the tract (of produce) AO' presents diminishing returns according to the first definition, but increasing according to the second.   My interpretation is confirmed by Professor Pigou's use of terms in the important passage, too long to quote in full, in *Wealth and Welfare*,[2] which resumes " the general analysis of distribution developed by Dr. Marshall."   The " *law of diminishing* returns to individual factors of production," it is there said, " states that the increment of product due to the increase by a unit of any factor of production in any industrial field will in general be smaller, other things remaining the same, the greater is the supply of that factor already employed there."   If I mistake not, a typical instance of this doctrine is afforded by our introductory lemma; when the land being considered as constant the " capital " laid out thereon is increased.   As shown by the rise of the curve SS_1 (considered as a short-period supply-curve) in Fig. 1, the increment of product due to the increase by

---

Collective Utility Curves; the distance measuring the total utility called by them *Gemeinnutzen* (*op. cit.*, p. 370).   But neither they, I think, nor I proposed to employ this conception for the purpose of contemplating the ideally best distribution of resources; for instance, that as between two classes of industries of the types pertaining to our Fig. 1 and Fig. 3 (Diminishing and Increasing Returns) it would be theoretically advantageous to diminish the output determined by *laissez-faire* in the former case and to increase it in the latter.

[1] ECONOMIC JOURNAL, Vol. XI. p. 359. C, p. 72.

[2] Part II. ch. ii. § 3.

a unit of " capital " will be smaller (in the neighbourhood at least of the point of equilibrium) the greater the supply of that factor already employed.   Assuredly, the law of diminishing returns which such a factor fulfils is diminishing returns in the primary sense.   Professor Pigou evidently treats that as *the* sense of the term when he does not even notice that in the same circumstances *increasing* returns in the *secondary* sense *must* prevail—initially. Yet the term " increasing returns " is largely employed in such a case by the leading American writers on railway and general economics.   One whom I shall often quote as not only the latest but also one of the greatest of them, thus expresses himself : " The law originates primarily in the fixed conditions attaching to the heavy capital investment—the fact, namely, that fixed charges up to a given point of saturation tend to remain constant absolutely : but become proportionately less as the volume of business expands.   From this fact, therefore, rather than because of any marked economies of large-scale production, may it be affirmed that railroads offer a notable example of the law of increasing returns." [1]   It is in virtue of this fact that " a railroad theoretically presents a clear example of an industry subject to the law of increasing returns." [2]

Joint Cost.—In the case of another important term, Joint Supply (and its synonyms), I am disposed to accept Professor Pigou's usage for the primary definition, while admitting as secondary the definitions sanctioned by the authority of railway experts.   In the first section of this study I have given a general definition covering the cases included by the American writers; but I place in a special category the cases excluded by Professor Pigou; for instance, " where the Joint Cost depends upon a quantity such as total weight or volume which is the sum of two or more items each pertaining to one of the joint products." [3] My typical example, clover and honey, fulfils, I think, Professor Pigou's definition that " two products are supplied jointly when a unit of investment expended upon increasing the normal output of one *necessarily* increases that of the other also." [4]   This is not evident at first sight; for, of course, apiculture without clover seed would not result in an output of clover.   Professor Taussig makes a very natural criticism when referring to Professor Pigou's example of joint cost, back loading, he remarks : " Now

[1] W. Z. Ripley, *Rail-roads* (1913), p. 99.

[2] *Op cit.*, p. 71 *et seq.*   *Cp.* **C,** p. 84.

[3] ECONOMIC JOURNAL, Vol. XI. p. 560.   **C,** p. 88.   See Index, s.v. *Joint Cost.*

[4] *Wealth and Welfare*, p. 215.

in back loading, as in other cases where 'discriminating' rates
are made, it cannot be said that a railroad '*necessarily*' (I follow
Professor Pigou's example in italicising the word) puts on the
market a supply of one kind of service when it supplies another
kind.   There are always some separable expenses : for example,
in the case of back loading there are the terminal expenses and
the extra cost of hauling a loaded train over that of an empty
one." [1]   Ninety-nine out of a hundred critics would probably
endorse this criticism.   And they would be justified in so far as
ninety-nine out of a hundred writers might be supposed to use
the phrase " increasing the normal output " as meaning no more
than " increasing the output."   But it is not to be supposed that
the disciple and successor of Dr. Marshall employs the term
" normal " as a merely decorative epithet.   Professor Pigou has,
I think, all along very properly used " output " as the output of
something that is demanded, and has implied that the demand
is not of an exceptional, perfectly inelastic, character.   It follows
that the output necessarily tends to be, and we may therefore say
normally is, increased by the diminution of its marginal cost.
Now a diminution in the marginal cost of producing a commodity
such as the transportation of a back load is caused when new trains
are put on—not merely to meet a temporary emergency, but as a
permanent arrangement—to meet an increased *direct* traffic.
But the marginal cost of an article transported by a returning
" empty " is not similarly increased by another item in the back
load.   These statements are not affected by the existence of
" terminal expenses " and the like.

It were to be wished, perhaps, that Professor Pigou had
expressed himself in terms less liable to misconstruction.   But, in
fact, it would not be easy to give a more unequivocal definition
without making it either very long or very technical.   For an
explicit description which, I think, nearly covers the instances
contemplated by Professor Pigou I again quote Professor
Ripley :—

" Railroad expenditures, as Taussig clearly pointed out a
number of years ago, afford a prime illustration of the production
of several commodities by a single great plant simultaneously at
joint and indistinguishable cost.   The classical economists
illustrated this law by the joint production of wool and mutton
and of gas and coke.   In both of these instances neither commodity
could conceivably be produced alone. . . . The law of joint cost
with reference to the production of transportation is somewhat

[1] *Quarterly Journal of Economics*, Vol. XXVII. (1913), p. 380.

different. Compare, for instance, the carriage by a railroad of thousands of passengers and different commodities in every direction, under varying conditions, singly or wholesale, slowly or by express, over a given set of rails every day; with the operation of a great refinery, producing simultaneously kerosene, gasolene, lubricating oils, and greases, as well as various odd chemicals. Both are examples of production at joint cost, but with various important contrasts. In the refinery all the costs are joint. All the processes are interlocked. Every increase in the output of kerosene produces *pari passu* an increase of the other commodities. On the railroad not all, but only a part of the costs are joint, in such manner as has been shown. For, from the joint portion of its plant—roadway rails and locomotives—the railroad may produce transportation of different sorts quite independently. It may choose to especially cultivate its passenger traffic or cotton or coal business." [1]

The " important contrasts " so clearly exhibited by Professor Ripley would not be materially affected if the increase of other commodities *pari passu* with kerosene required some special or separable expense; just as the output of copperas as a joint product with wire, which Professor Pigou by implication instances as a genuine case of joint supply,[2] requires some special cost for the erection of necessary sheds.

A short but technical definition may be based on the form of the (mathematical) *function* which expresses the relation between assigned quantities of several commodities, x, y, u, v, w, etc., and z, the cost of producing the whole set. Materials for the construction of such a definition may be found on a former page.[3] There may be some doubt as to where the line should be drawn which separates the primary from the secondary definition of Joint Cost. But there can be no doubt that it should be drawn well above the case in which the total cost z is related to the quantities of the products simply as a *function* of their *sum :* that is, in the manner below indicated by a quotation from Professor Pigou. I apply the term " sum " to the addition of adjusted units (like those below supposed for pease and beans), ordinary (*e.g.*, avoirdupois) units each multiplied by a proper coefficient corresponding to special costs.[4] The ground of the distinction lies

---

[1] *Op, cit.*, p. 67.

[2] *Wealth and Welfare*, p. 299, *note* 1.

[3] **C**, p. 88 *et seq.*

[4] The bearing of Joint Cost proper on the power of predicting competitive price may be illustrated by supposing that normal equilibrium, after having been reached, is disturbed by a change in demand for each of two commodities; and

herein, I think, that in the case of joint cost proper we cannot, and in other case we can (theoretically), *predict* the relative charges for the different commodities without regard to the relative demand for the commodities.

"*Cost of Service*" *Principle.*—But the question what is the proper or primary definition of the term Joint Cost is itself of secondary interest. Professor Pigou will perhaps allow the Americans to have their terminology if they will concede to him his propositions. The main issue, of far deeper importance than the definition of a word, is whether Professor Pigou is right in concluding that, in the regulation of railways, discrimination or the "value of service" principle should, after an initial—probably brief—stage, give place to the "cost of service" principle.[1]

First appearances, it must be admitted, are against Professor Pigou. Using terms in a strange sense, and accusing distinguished economists of common fallacies, he propounds a thesis contradicting the doctrine of the highest authorities on railway economics. What though in power of mathematical reasoning he wields a bow which few can bend ! Does he not aim with it at the clouds ? An airship, indeed, would seem to be just the object which he has in view. For his refined reasonings would be admittedly sound if all transportation was effected by flying-machines. For then presumably each flying-machine might be worked to the full for one kind of traffic only. The case would in this respect resemble that of those railways for which discrimination is not claimed, where "each has in the main its own expenses

---

observing the effect according as Joint Cost proper is absent or present. Let the cost, z, $= F(T)$, where (1) $T = ax + by + cu + \ldots$, and x, y, $u \ldots$ are assigned quantities of the commodities designated X, Y, $U \ldots$. Then the respective prices, in competitive equilibrium, of the commodities X, Y, U are $F'(T)a$, $F'(T)b$, $F'(T)c \ldots$. Now let a change in the demand for X and Y occur. Then in general there will be a change in volume affecting cost. "Cost is unknown until volume is ascertained," as Professor Ripley well says (*loc. cit.*). But in the case before us the effect on price may well be small, if there are many commodities; the new set of prices being $F'(T + \Delta t)a$, $F'(T + \Delta t)b \ldots$. At any rate the *relative* prices, the ratios in which the total charge is distributed among the different commodities, are unchanged. (Compare Marshall, *Principles of Economics*, Mathematical Note xvii., par. 1.) Next (2) let $T = ax + 2hxy + by + cu + \ldots$. Now when x and y are "interlocked," to borrow a phrase from Professor Ripley, the prices are no longer as independent of the quantities as before. The new price of X is now $F'(T + \Delta T)[(a + 2h(y + \Delta y)]$ and the new price of Y is $F'(T + \Delta T)[a + 2h(x + \Delta x)]$. It is evident that the prediction of the prices from the costs is not such a simple affair as before. Once more (3) let $T = ax^2 + by^2 + \ldots$, or more generally $T = \phi(x) + \psi(y) + \chi(u)$. The disturbed price of each commodity will now involve, in a more disturbing manner than in case (1), the quantity of that commodity. But it will not do so in the same way as in (2). It is a nice question whether this case should be described as Joint Cost proper.

[1] *Wealth and Welfare*, p. 234, and context.

of operation as well as its own road-bed and other plant." [1]   But, as it is, " the freight service of a railway comprises the carriage of all kinds of goods simultaneously from the most valuable high-priced commodities, such as silk and satins, down to lumber, coal, cement, and even sand." [2]

Such are the first appearances.   But on reflection, in the light of the principles which have been above recalled, it will be discerned that if the flying-machines are perfectly competitive, no essential difference is introduced by their having mixed loads; supposing, with Professor Pigou, that " a unit of investment is responsible either for x units of one kind and y units of the other, or for $(x + h)$ units of the first kind and no units of the second, or for no units of the first kind and $(y + k)$ units of the second." [3] Thus, in our introductory Lemma,[4] suppose that the produce in wheat is destined for different kinds of cakes and bread.   The price of a unit of wheat for different destinations would still be the same.   And if the same ground is equally suitable for pease and beans—joint effects in the way of rotation of crops being abstracted—then if the prime costs (in the sense explained) of (properly assigned) units of pease and beans are the same, the same will be the selling price for pease and beans (of units so assigned).   The orthodox economist stating this familiar doctrine would not be put off by the affirmation that a great part of the cost was indeterminate, being joint for all the products in large part; that it is impossible to *allocate* the amount proper to each product.   This objection might be made to Professor Wieser's doctrine of " imputation "; [5] or to the pretension, censured by Mill, of assigning, in a philosophical sense, the amount due to each of two concurrent causes—like the blades of a pair of scissors.   But *this* indeterminateness is quite consistent with the determination of value in exchange—proportioned to marginal cost—in a regime of perfect competition.   But the prices so determined, according to the received theory, afford a maximum of advantage to producers and consumers.   A similar maximum of advantage must be ascribed to the charges for mixed loads which would be adopted by airships conceived as sufficiently

[1] Taussig, *Quarterly Journal of Economics*, Vol. XXVII. p. 379; and *cp.* p. 380.

[2] Ripley, *op. cit.*, p. 169.

[3] *Wealth and Welfare*, p. 218.

[4] Above, p. 431 *et seq.*

[5] Referred to by Marshall, *Principles of Economics*, p. 393 (6th edition), and unfavourably reviewed by the present writer in the ECONOMIC JOURNAL, Vol. IV. p. 281 (III, p. 50 *et seq*).

numerous to realise perfect competition.   Railways, indeed, cannot be conceived so numerous as to bring about that scale of charges through the play of competition; but it is to be believed that maximum advantage would be attained if there could be imposed by authority in this case that proportion of charge to marginal cost which is known in other cases to have that desirable result.

I must confess to have countenanced an erroneous view in this matter.   Concerned mainly with monopoly, I incidentally mis-stated a law of competition.   I argued that in general a single undiscriminated price might be replaced by two (or more) dis-criminated prices with advantage both to the (monopolist) producer and the customer.   For any value of monopolistic revenue or any value of customers' benefit assigned at random the maximum of advantage to the other party will be realised not by a unique price, but by discrimination.   But I omitted to notice that the case in which the initial unique price (or the assigned amount of advantage to one party) is that which occurs in a regime of perfect competition is a particular limiting case of which the statement generally probable is known not to be true.   The general reasoning breaks down when we suppose the initial (unique) price of two commodities to be equal to the (equal) marginal cost of each.[1]   In this case if any neighbouring system of discriminating prices be assumed, it will be the interest of one or both parties to return to the unique price.

I subscribe, then, to Professor Pigou's thesis; but with two considerable reservations, pointed out by Professor Pigou himself.

---

[1] It was shown in a previous paper (ζ, p. 412) that if b is the undis-criminated monopoly price of two articles (or species of the same article), and $b(1 + \eta_1)b$ $(1 + \eta_2)$ are any two discriminating prices in the neighbour-hood of b; then the curve representing that the Customers' Surplus (considered as a function of η_1 and η_2) is constant (the same as what it was when η_1 and η_2 each $= 0$) and the (likewise interpreted) curve of Constant Producers' Surplus *intersect*, in such wise that it is in general possible to adopt a system of discriminating prices which will be better both for the producer and the customer than the undiscriminated price b.   It is supposed (in the absence of joint cost) that the cost of production is the sum of two costs each a function of (the amount of) one of the products (*loc. cit.*, p. 423); or more generally a function of the sum (or of a linear function) of the quantities produced (above, p. 443, note).   The pro-position remains true *in general* when by b we understand not only the monopoly price, but any unique price for the two articles.   But in the *particular* case when the marginal cost of producing the amounts saleable at the unique price b is just equal to b the proposition breaks down; the curves do not intersect, but *touch* at the point ($\eta_1 = 0$ $\eta_2 = 0$), in such wise that it is not possible to move off from that point in a direction advantageous to both parties.   It should be observed that the existence of a *maximum* at this point is not inconsistent with the possi-bility that some other point represents *greater* advantage both to producer and customers, as suggested in the text (p. 438).   [But- see **Prefatory** note to **D**, Vol. I. p. 100.]

Firstly, if a railway cannot be made to pay with rates and fares assigned on the principle of cost of service, it is better that it should practise discrimination than that it should not exist.   More generally, let it be supposed possible to operate the railways of a country so that the marginal cost of each ton-mile is the same. Then the maximum of the type $H - V$ is attained.   But it may be better to pursue the type $H' - V'$ by employing discrimination so as to increase the output of transport for which the demand is very extensible, and where the advantages of increasing returns are thereby secured.   It might be one of the exceptions to the general rule that there should be equality of " marginal net products " in order to secure maximum satisfaction.[1]   No doubt the conditions are *a priori* improbable.[2]   But there is specific evidence of high authority for their existence; so far as we may thus interpret the dicta of the experts, such as " Much of this business is made possible only by special rates adapted to the case in hand.   A higher rate . . . would kill the business."   " To compel each of these classes of goods [silk and satin, . . . cement, and even sand] to bear its proportionate share of the cost of carriage would at once preclude the possibility of transporting low-priced goods at all." [3]   The testimony of high authorities would, no doubt, carry even greater weight if it should be repeated with a full recognition of the *a priori* improbability to which Professor Pigou has called attention.

Secondly, let it be granted that the cost of service principle, the system of charges which would be realised by perfect competition, is ideally the best.   Yet with regard to a system so complex, how can we ascertain in the absence of competition what charges would be fixed by competition ?   The attempts to do so for railway rates have often proved ludicrous.   They remind one of the pretension sometimes made by politicians to tell us what some dead chief—Mr. Gladstone or Lord Beaconsfield—would have thought about a measure which was never before them.   The defunct authority ought at most to be invoked only to sanction a general line of policy, not to furnish details such as, say, the items of a tariff.   As Professor Pigou says : " It is plain that anything in the nature of exact imitation of simple competition is almost impossible to attain." . . . " A considerable gap between the ideal and the actual is likely to remain." [4]

[1] Cp. *Wealth and Welfare*, p. 107.   [2] *Op. cit.*, p. 211 *et seq.*

[3] Ripley, *Railroads*, pp. 152, 168 *et passim*.   The *dynamic* use of discrimination claimed by Professor Ripley would, I think, be admitted by Professor Pigou as pertaining to an initial state (*op. cit.*, p. 234).

[4] *Op. cit.*, p. 265 *et seq.*

The impracticability of the cost of service principle seems to be largely the ground on which it is dethroned by leading economists from the sovereignty which it might otherwise claim. Professor Ripley begins : " There can be no question that for an indispensable public service like transportation, conducted under monopolistic conditions, the ideal system of charges would be to ascertain the cost of each service rendered and to allow a reasonable margin of profit over and above this amount." [1] But he goes on, in view of the difficulty of ascertaining those charges, to attribute a position of collateral supremacy to the principle of value of service : " Two general theories governing the rates chargeable by railways are entertained, known respectively as cost of service and value of service. . . . Neither of these views [pertaining to the two theories] is entirely sound by itself. Both have large elements of truth in them. Each qualifies the other." [2] " Our final conclusion then must be this : That both principles are of equal importance, and that both must be continually invoked as a check upon each other." [3]

These dicta no doubt embody the highest practical wisdom. And it is perhaps vain to desiderate that the limits of these practical principles should be defined more closely by reference to the more general conditions of welfare, the " equality of marginal net products," or the still more ideal principle that the money measure of economic satisfactions should be as great as possible.

Theory of Limited Monopoly.—Nor do I attempt here to formulate the relation between the cost of service principle and the mixed modes of monopoly which I have elsewhere discussed. Suffice it to submit that in the present state of scientific opinion about the subject those discussions seem not otiose. In this part of the work I have obtained support from the adjacency of Professor Pigou's constructions at two points. First, he lends countenance to the use of a right line for the demand-curve as a device for exploring the probabilities of more concrete cases; though he himself seems to use the construction chiefly for the sake of convenience. [4] I am fortified in the assumption that the right line may be provisionally taken as the type of the demand-curve pertaining to the customers of a railway company. [5] I am

---

[1] *Op. cit.*, p. 168.   [2] *Op. cit.*, pp. 166, 167.   [3] *Op. cit.*, p. 184.

[4] Once at least to show that as there is nothing knowable in this simple case, " our ignorance would not be lightened " by abandoning the assumption of linearity (p. 107).

[5] But the claim which I have made in favour of the right line that it is intermediate between the convexity predicated by Dupuit and the concavity predicated by Professor Pigou (ECONOMIC JOURNAL, Vol. XXIII. p. 65) must be retracted. It was based on a misinterpretation of Professor Pigou's doctrine concerning the

therefore confirmed in the deduction that discrimination accompanied with a moderate control is likely to be better, both for the customers and the monopolist, than monopoly forbidden to discriminate.[1]

In this and other theories I have largely employed a sort of Probability which has been described in this journal as *a priori*,[2] and elsewhere perhaps more unequivocally as " unverified." This species of probable inference bears to the more solid parts of statistics and economics a relation something like that which Adam Smith has pointed out between literary and mathematical compositions. The authors of the latter kind, he says, " may have the most perfect assurance both of the truth and importance of their discoveries "; and accordingly they are, much more than the others, " indifferent about the reception which they may meet from the public." [3] Now the unverified or non-statistical part of Probabilities, though it is but common sense reduced to formula, yet is not so commonly recognised, not so obviously objective, but that those who employ it should desiderate the approbation of good authorities." This sort of confirmation is largely afforded by Professor Pigou, who employs this sort of inference repeatedly and with respect to the most momentous interests.[4]

The problem in my second section, which comes nearest to one of those which Professor Pigou has handled, is that which relates to the effects of discrimination in a regime of monopoly.[5] Supposing with him that the law of demand is linear, and that the law of constant return holds, I find with him that the monopolist will produce the same quantity after discrimination as before.[6] But I have not attended particularly to the alteration

---

third differential of utility (*Industrial Peace*, p. 70). I forgot that the theorem related not to a particular commodity, such as railway service, but to money income, being in fact an improved version of what I had myself (ECONOMIC JOURNAL, Vol. VII. p. 559) described as " the circumstance that as the income is increased by equal increments the differences between the successive increments of utility become less." My misapplication of the doctrine was facilitated by a misprint in Professor Pigou's statement of it.

[1] (, p. 412 *et seq.*

[2] See Index, s.v. *Probability.*

[3] *Theory of Moral Sentiments*, Part III. ch. ii.

[4] See Index, s.v. *Pigou.*

[5] *Wealth and Welfare*, p. 210.

[6] From the equations indicated at p. 446 *et seq.* in the ECONOMIC JOURNAL, Vol. XX., it appears that if ξ'_1 and ξ'_2 are the proportional deviations of the output in consequence of discrimination from what it was before discrimination

$$\xi'_1 + \xi'_2 = - (1 + \beta)\eta'_1 - (1 - \beta)\eta'_2 = 0,$$
$$\text{where} \quad \eta' = - \tfrac{1}{2}\beta/(1 + \beta), \quad \eta'_2 = + \tfrac{1}{2}\beta/(1 - \beta)$$

of the output; which, as pointed out by Professor Pigou, has not the significance in a regime of monopoly which it has in one of competition.[1] He uses it here only as a stepping-stone towards a *quæsitum* which I have sought more directly.

The only other remark which seems called for in connection with the problems in my second section is that they are not open to the criticism which has lately been directed against Professor Pigou as one " trained in the mathematical school," and accordingly applying a well-rounded theory of monopoly which does not take account of the *incompleteness* characterising monopoly in the concrete.[2] My conception of a monopolist seeking a maximum of gain, *subject to limitations* imposed by the threat of competition, by public spirit (or State control), admits, I 'think, of *degrees* much clearer than the expressions commonly employed in a similar connection, such as " equal sacrifice," or " not charging what the traffic will not bear." [3] Not that I mean to endorse the criticism as applicable to Professor Pigou. A sense of continuity is not likely to be wanting in the follower of him whose motto is *Natura non facit saltum.*

[1] *Loc. cit.,* § 17.
[2] *Quarterly Journal of Economics,* Vol. XXVII. (1913), p. 384.
[3] See **G**, pp. 186, 189, *et passim.*

(θ)

ON SOME THEORIES DUE TO PARETO, ZAWADSKI, W. E. JOHNSON AND OTHERS

[THESE " Recent Contributions to Mathematical Economics "
(as they were entitled when published in the ECONOMIC JOURNAL,
March and June 1915) are divided, not very sharply, according to a
distinction suggested by some of the writers reviewed, into two
parts dealing respectively with the general theory of economic equilibrium and "tentative applications of mathematical economics outside the general theory of equilibrium." To the first class belong
Mr. W. E. Johnson's original representation of supply and demand
free from a certain particularity which confines the usual representations; also the analogy which is drawn between Producers'
and Consumers' surplus; and the treatment of utility or satisfaction as an object of economic science with the countenance of the
great mathematician Poincaré. But we can hardly describe as
belonging to the general theory of economic equilibrium a *curiosum*
which is pointed out by Zawadski after Pareto and independently
by Mr. W. E. Johnson : namely, that where the demand for commodities is correlated (in the way of rivalry) a rise in the price
of one of the articles (due to a tax, for instance) may cause an
increase in the consumption of that article. The proposition
should rather be referred to the chapter of tentatives, if it can be
supposed to have a bearing on practice. More important examples
of applied—or applicable—mathematical economics are afforded
by Professor Pigou's theory that production tends to be a
maximum when the marginal productivity is equal in every
branch; his proof that the elasticity of the demand for common
labour is in general highly elastic—a tenet favourable to Free
Trade; his doctrine of Joint Cost, showing that the " Cost of
Service " principle—the rule proper to simple Competition—is
appropriate in cases which had previously been supposed subject
to the rule of " What the traffic will bear."]

RECENT CONTRIBUTIONS TO MATHEMATICAL ECONOMICS

Théorie Mathématique de l'Echange. ANTONIO OSORIO. Ave une introduction de Vilfredo Pareto. Traduit par Jos D'Almada. (Paris : Giard. 1913.)

Principes d'Economie Pure. La Théorie de l'Échange sous le régime de la libre concurrence. E. ANTONELLI. (Paris : Rivière. 1914.)

Les Mathématiques appliquées à l'Économie Politique. W. E. ZAWADSKI. (Paris : Rivière. 1914.)

The Vagaries of Recent Political Economy. Professor J. S. NICHOLSON. (*Quarterly Review*, October, 1913.)

The Pure Theory of Utility Curves. W. E. JOHNSON. (*Economic Journal*, December, 1913.)

Contributo alla Teoria dell' Offerta a costi congiunti. MARCO FANNO. (Rome : *Athenæum* Supplement to *Giornale degli Economisti*, October, 1914.)

The purport of these pages is to report the progress in mathematical economics which may have been made since last a contribution to the subject was noticed in the ECONOMIC JOURNAL, namely, June 1913. We do not define the limits of the subject strictly. "To clear up the relations of fundamental economic conceptions"—in the words applied by one of our authors to the work of Cournot and his successors—is no doubt the principal achievement, but we are not prepared to say that it is the only hopeful employment, of mathematical economics. We do not, with M. Antonelli, restrict the subject to what he and other of our authors describe as the general theory of economic equilibrium. We rather follow M. Zawadski, who indeed makes that general theory his main object, yet adds a chapter on "tentative applications of mathematical economics outside the general theory of equilibrium." So we in our *first* and main section will confine ourselves to the commonly recognised territory, the domain proper, of our science; but in a supplementary *second* section we shall examine the zone of influence extending beyond that territory.

SECTION I.

The subject of this section may be broken up—anatomically so to speak and for the purpose of demonstration, though not in life and fact—into three parts. *Firstly*, we shall consider the pure theory of exchange, making abstraction of the concrete fact that most things exchanged have been produced. *Secondly*, we shall introduce the circumstance of production and observe what progress has been made in what has been called the Mechanics of Industry. Corresponding to the rôle of Energy in the theory of Mechanics is the predominance of utility or satisfaction in mathematical economics. The conception is indeed immanent in all our reasonings; but it may be artificially isolated for special consideration in a *third* sub-section.

(1) *Theory of Exchange.*—This part of the subject has received special attention from three of our authors. Their predilection and success may be traced to the influence of the economist who first stated the theory of exchange in all its generality, Léon Walras. M. Antonelli's work, indeed, may be regarded as an abridgment of Walras's *Éléments d'économie pure ;* a task which the illustrious author himself had commenced. This work of a disciple is valuable as a clear and simple exposition of the founder's doctrine. M. Osorio's treatise is based not only on the work of Walras, but also on that of his distinguished successor, Professor Pareto. The treatise is, we may be sure, a most valuable addition to the economic literature of Portugal. The translation into French has to encounter the formidable rivalry of the original writers. To what extent the free adaptations of their theories are to be considered improvements will depend partly on the concurrence of the reader with M. Osorio in attributing " extreme concision " to " Walras's and Pareto's deductions." M. Zawadski also is deeply imbued with the doctrines of those original writers. But he is not bound to adopt the words of any master. He views the school of Lausanne in just relation to other schools, of which he had taken a comprehensive survey.

In his statement of the problem M. Zawadski makes an assumption about the data which we regárd as important. For the purpose of the abstract theory—which "affords an approximate image of the real phenomenon "—we should think of " dealers who often meet having each at his disposal [*porteurs de*] about the same quantity of goods " (p. 200). Again, " the economic tendencies imaged by the abstract theory are the more decided (*plus prononcées*) the more the phenomena are regular, continually repeated under analogous conditions " (p. 201). And again, with special reference to *production :* " Only transactions frequently repeated under analogous circumstances can present a certain character of regularity, so it is only to these that our theory is in general applicable " (p. 215).[1]

M. Zawadski is also happy in his view of the function of money, or, in Walras's more general terminology, *numéraire*, in a theoretical market. He starts with the assumption that one out of *m* commodities plays the part of money, and so in a perfect market there are (*m* − 1) prices; but he does not regard this proposition as axiomatic, rather as deducible (by way of "arbitrage") from a greater number, conceivably *m(m* − 1), rates-of-exchange between different commodities (p. 134, p. 124). We may add that even the existence of a uniform rate-of-exchange between any two commodities is perhaps not so much axiomatic as deducible from the process of competition in a perfect market (X. 85).[2]

However this may be, we incur no serious loss of generality in postulating that one out of the *m* commodities acts the part of *numéraire*. If there are *n* individuals each buying or selling any number of the *m* commodities, it is beautifully shown that to determine the state of equilibrium there are given as many equations as there are unknown quantities, namely, the (*m* − 1) prices and the amounts of each commodity (including the money) acquired positively or negatively, so to speak, by each of the *n* individuals—*mn* (in addition to the said *m* − 1) quantities—on the ideal supposition of each individual dealing in all the commodities. Here, as throughout his work, M. Zawadski appears to us to present the cream of Walras's and Pareto's thoughts.

He justly claims for Walras priority with respect to the general theory of exchange. But he appears to us to do less than justice to the *doyen* of English economists when he suggests that the interdependence of economic quantities is not recognised in the *Principles of Economics* (Zawadski, p. 307). Surely Dr. Marshall has adequately presented this great truth in passages relating to "joint demand" and "composite demand," to "joint supply" and "composite supply"; for instance, in Note XXI. of his Mathematical Appendix. There Dr. Marshall affirms that cardinal principle which is the main outcome of Walras's teaching :

---

[1] A cognate conception has thus been expressed (see **B**, I., p. 40) in relation to the labour-market : " On the first day a set of hirings is made which proves not to be in accordance with the dispositions of the parties. These contracts terminating with the day, the parties encounter each other the following day, with dispositions the same as on the first day—like combatants *armis animisque refecti*— in all respects as they were at the beginning of the first encounter, except that they have obtained by experience the knowledge that the system of bargains entered into on the first occasion does not fit the real dispositions of the parties."

[2] The references of this form relate to the list of writings given below at p. 477.

"However complex the problem may become, we can see that it is theoretically determinate, because the number of unknowns is exactly equal to the number of equations which we attain." In the text to which that note refers and in many other passages [1] Dr. Marshall reaffirms the interdependence in question. He is quite aware that a demand-curve representing the connection between two economic quantities—in particular price and the amount demanded—may become less serviceable than usual—may, for instance, ascend with a rise of price—when the commodity demanded is related in a certain peculiar and exceptional way to some other commodity.[2] But he is also aware that " there are very few practical problems in which the corrections to be made under this head would be of any practical importance." He does not think it necessary to repeat continually that " the neglected elements would generally belong to the second order of quantities." In short, he appears to have assigned to the doctrine just the amount of space which is due to it in a treatise not primarily concerned with mathematical abstractions.

The sin of omission is with more plausibility imputed to professedly mathematical writers. In M. Zawadski's otherwise too flattering notice of some articles dealing with Monopoly which have appeared in this Journal there is made—by implication and cross-reference—an objection apparently identical with that to which we have alluded. The " superiority of Pareto's solution " (p. 203) over Cournot's is affirmed on grounds apparently common to Cournot's *Recherches* and the Articles in question. With respect to Cournot's equation for the determination of price in a regime of monopoly [3] it is objected : " It is not this equation by itself which determines the price of the commodity by itself, but it is this equation simultaneously with all the others pertaining to the system which determines all the prices and all the quantities exchanged " (p. 303). " The demand [' débit '] for a commodity is a function not simply of its price, but also of the quantities bought and the prices of the other products. These latter cannot be considered constant, theoretically at least, when the corresponding magnitudes relative to the first commodity are varied " (p. 58, note ; compare p. 60, note). The dilemma stated with respect to the use of plane curves appears, therefore, to be applicable here. Either " the other economic quantities

---

[1] See, in particular, *Principles of Economics*, 6th edition, pp. 100, 105, 130, 132.

[2] See below, pp. 460, 479.

[3] $\dfrac{d[p_y f(p_y)]}{dp_y} = 0$, in M. Zawadski's notation.

exercise no influence on the quantities offered or demanded [of the quantity under consideration] "; or " the other quantities are constant " (p. 299). We are not concerned to defend Cournot— " Deorum injuriæ Diis curæ "; but we demur to the description as applicable to the articles in the ECONOMIC JOURNAL. In the first of them (IV. 56, 234) the transactions contemplated are thus typified : " Suppose three islands, A, B, C, engaged in this sort of international trade. A imports from B goods for the manufacture of which B has to import materials from C." The consumers in A, forming a monopoly, dictate the price of the goods which, regard being had to the quantity of imports forthcoming at each price, affords the greatest advantage to the monopolist purchaser. It is not assumed that the other economic magnitudes, such as the price and quantity of the materials imported from C, have no influence on the price of the product exported from B, nor that they remain constant.[1] On the contrary, attention is directed to the influence of the other quantities. In short, the dilemma is escaped by the process which M. Zawadski describes as the " third eventuality " (loc. cit., note); the relation between the price and the offer is determined by the elimination of the " other quantities." The example is no doubt a particular case. The monopolist is a buyer ; and the total quantity of the factors of production is for a purpose in hand supposed constant. Complications of demand and supply are expressly abstracted; " correlation of supply or demand not being now supposed " (V. 234). That complication is, however, mentioned in the immediate context ; and elsewhere in the series of papers referred to has been frequently, in the view of some inordinately, recognised. Altogether the example of the principle on which monopoly price is determined may be taken as fairly representative.

We do not expect that our author will press his objections to the " third eventuality "—the elimination of the economic quantities other than the one which is immediately under the control of the economist—when it is explained that the process is virtually equivalent to " Pareto's Solution " (Zawadski, p. 202, last par.; p. 220, last par.); abridged, it may be, for the purposes of practice or exposition. We do not suppose that there is any substantial difference between our author's position and our own. We quite agree with him in holding that when complicated

---

[1] See (VI.) referred to in the ECONOMIC JOURNAL (V.). The monopolist purchaser there considered (p. 19) " will go on varying p_1 " [the price of the article purchased corresponding to M. Zawadski's p_x] directly, and indirectly p_2 [the price of the factor of production, one of M. Zawadski's " other economic quantities "] by means of an equation which might be used for eliminating p_2.

eliminations of " other economic quantities " are necessary, " the process would leave us in the most complete ignorance of even the elementary properties [such as, we presume, the *descending* character of the demand curve] of the resulting functions " (*loc. cit.*, p. 300). We notice with complete approval his tacit postulate that something more than theoretical determinateness, " certain additional properties of the functions," as he elsewhere says (p. 165), may reasonably be looked for. In this connection he has some very wise observations, which we have not space to transcribe, on the possibilities and limits of mathematical economics (*loc. cit.* and p. 187). We gather that it is not the only, though a principal, use of this study to show that there exists a determinate solution of the problems, the equations being neither more nor less in number than the unknowns. Even with reference to the " general theory of equilibrium," even in the limited and recognised sphere to which our first section is restricted, some additional propositions may be expected, some laws of contract (I. 146) which might be available in practice if we only had corresponding minor premises. Such hypothetical applications are presented by M. Zawadski in his section on the *laws of individual demand and offer* (pp. 180–187), and by Mr. Johnson in his article on *Utility-curves*. We shall endeavour to present some salient features of these theories, without attempting to make an abstract of writings which hardly admit of compression—one of them being adequately, and the other exceedingly concise. Comments and corollaries, more than copies, will be offered.

We may begin by recalling the construction which Dr. Marshall employed many years ago to illustrate the theory of international trade.[1] Let the amount of goods imported by a country (such as the " cloth " of Mill's example) be X, and let the equivalent amount of exports (such as " linen ") be Y. A point (X, Y) represents an international exchange; the inclination (to one of the axes) of the line joining the point to the origin represents the rate of exchange between exports and imports. The Demand-and-Supply Curve pertaining to a country is the locus of points at which trade may be in equilibrium. Subsequent writers have applied the construction to exchange in general; and in particular to the case now under consideration, exchange without reference to production. It has been shown that the

---

[1] In the papers put under contribution by Pantaleoni in his *Principii di Economica Pura*. They may be seen, as we are informed by the learned M. Zawadski, in the Goldsmiths' Library at the University of London. The construction is reproduced and discussed in the ECONOMIC JOURNAL (IX. (b). *Cp.* VIII. 70). See below, p. 477.

Demand-and-Supply Curve may be regarded as the locus of points at which a straight line passing through the origin touches an *indifference-curve ;* that curve being the locus of points representing bargains between which there is nothing to choose. To fix the ideas we might suppose the indifference-curves to consist of concentric circles with centre C in Fig. 1. The person to whom the construction relates—conceivably a typical individual—desires always (or at least for all the cases which our construction is apt to represent, say the space bounded by the axes through O and, on the right, by a perpendicular through C) to pass from any point at which he may be placed to another on an indifference-curve nearer the centre. But he has no interest in the change

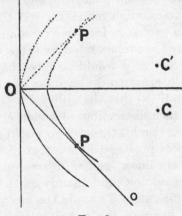

FIG. 1.

of terms represented by movement from one point to another on the same indifference-curve. The curves thus defined are also and will here usually be called " utility-curves."

Now let X be an addition to an initial quantity x_0, and likewise Y be subtracted from y_0; x_0 and y_0 being the co-ordinates of O relatively to an origin below and left of O, say the left corner at the bottom of the page. Let x (measured from that origin) $= x_0 + X$; $y = y_0 - Y$. Then in order to represent in terms of x and y the series of bargains which have been above described, it is proper to substitute for any point at a distance Y above the horizontal through O a point at the same distance *below* that horizontal (the horizontal distance from O, viz. X, remaining unchanged). Thus the utility-curves in the transferred construction will consist of concentric circles about a centre C' (which is *above* the horizontal through O).

The convexity (towards the axes of x and y) of the utility-curves which are thus presented is not accidental; it is an important essential property. It follows from the axiomatic, or at least commonly experienced, circumstance that an individual possessing x_o of one commodity and y_o of another will in general find it his interest to give some of one commodity in exchange for some of the other; and that if there is fixed rate of exchange between the commodities there will be a point x, y at which it will just cease to be to his interest to exchange at this rate. Accordingly at that point, as shown in the figure, the utility-curve must be convex to the line $O\ o$ representing the rate of exchange —the " price-line " in Mr. Johnson's phrase—and accordingly, as the line descends from left to right, convex to the axes of x and y, say, as before, the bottom and the left edge of the page. In the figure the transaction represented is the giving of some of commodity (y) in exchange for some of commodity (x).[1] But if the initial amounts are represented by some point on the same price-line *below O*, say o, p would still be that point at which the individual would cease to do business at the assigned rate.

The analytic condition that the utility-curve should be convex brings into view a nice distinction, of which Mr. Johnson makes much use. In discussing his theories we would gladly imitate the parsimony of symbols practised by another of our authors. We should like to draw the line at *partial differential coefficients*.[2] But unfortunately the reasoning turns mainly on the conceptions connoted by those coefficients. To avoid the use of the appropriate symbols would be open to the criticism which Todhunter has passed on that section of Laplace's introduction to his Theory of Probabilities in which, for the benefit of the general reader, the operations of the higher mathematics are expressed in ordinary language. Todhunter describes the section as " a complete waste of space." " It would not be intelligible to a reader unless he were able to master the mathematical theory delivered in its appropriate symbolical language, and in that case the section would be entirely superfluous."[3] We can only practise temperance, not abstinence, in the matter of symbols.

Let $f(x, y)\ (\equiv u) = $ constant be the equation to a utility curve. The slope of the tangent at any point x, y on the curve is

---

[1] The *genus*, as distinguished from *a quantity* of a commodity, is expressed by the use of brackets.

[2] More exactly partial *finite differences*—differences not always very small, absolutely or relatively to the variable (e.g., x) to which the difference (Δx) relates (XI. 565).

[3] *History of Probabilities*, p. 497.

$-\left(\dfrac{df}{dx}\right) \Big/ \left(\dfrac{df}{dy}\right)^1$; where the bracketed differential coefficients are *partial*. The condition that the curve should be convex (to the axes) at the point (x, y) is that the (complete) differential coefficient of this expression for the slope, which we may call t, should be positive. This condition may be written $a\theta_1 + b\theta_2 < o$,[2] where a and b are positive quantities, θ_1 and θ_2 are made up of partial differential coefficients derived from the utility-function, u. In order that the inequation should be satisfied, one or other of two alternatives must hold good; we must have either (a) both θ_1 and θ_2 negative, or (β) one of them only negative, while the other is positive (the limiting case in which one of them is zero being neglected). The first alternative (a) is properly described by Mr. Johnson as the "standard case"; the second (β), the exceptional alternative, is shown by him to have some important properties.

His theory relates principally to the case of three variables, two commodities and money. But we may introduce the subject without considering more than two variables. Let x be the quantity of a certain kind of commodity that is purchased at the price ξ. Let z be the purchase-money taken from an initial store of money μ; so that after the purchase our man has $\mu - z$, say Z, money to expend in other ways. Now if the utility of commodities other than (x) is entirely independent of the quantity of (x) consumed, we may consider the total utility realised, say u, as the sum of two terms, say $f(x) + F(Z)$. This total is to be maximised *subject to the conditions that* $z + Z = \mu$ (a constant). In other words, there is to be maximised $u - m[x\xi + Z - \mu]$; where m is the undetermined coefficient proper to problems of *relative* maximum, the expression within the square brackets being equated to zero. We have, then, to determine the three quantities x, Z, and m, the three equations

$$(1)\ \frac{df}{dx} = m\xi;\quad (2)\ \frac{dF}{dZ} = m;\quad (3)\ x\xi + Z = \mu.$$

---

[1] Brackets outside partial differential coefficients will be sometimes omitted where no doubt can arise. A sloping line is used to denote *division*.

[2] $\theta_1 \equiv \left(\dfrac{du}{dy}\right)\left(\dfrac{d^2u}{dx^2}\right) - \left(\dfrac{du}{dx}\right)\left(\dfrac{d^2u}{dxdy}\right)$; $\theta_2 \equiv \left(\dfrac{du}{dx}\right)\left(\dfrac{d^2u}{dy^2}\right) - \left(\dfrac{du}{dy}\right)\left(\dfrac{d^2u}{dxdy}\right)$;

$a \equiv 1 \Big/ \left(\dfrac{du}{dy}\right)^2$; $b \equiv \left(\dfrac{du}{dx}\right) \Big/ \left(\dfrac{du}{dy}\right)^3$. From the essential properties of a utility function it is evident that a and b are both positive.

It may be noted that in Zawadski's (Pareto's) notation (p. 171), $\phi_y\phi_{xx} - \phi_x\phi_{xy} \equiv \theta_1$; $\phi_x\phi_{yy} - \phi_y\phi_{yx} \equiv \theta_2$. Mr. Johnson's $\dfrac{dV}{dx}$, $\dfrac{dW}{dz}$ differ only by positive factors respectively from our θ_1 and θ_2.

Accordingly, if the data are changed, in particular if the price ξ is raised, we are in a position to determine how the variables x and Z will be affected thereby. If we consider only a small change of ξ we may obtain (differentiating each of the equations by ξ) three equations for the three differential coefficients $\dfrac{dx}{d\xi}, \dfrac{dZ}{d\xi}$ and $\dfrac{dm}{d\xi}$, whence it is deducible that with the increase of ξ x must decrease, z may increase or decrease.

This familiar proposition is introduced here only as a stepping-stone to the less simple case in which the expenditure *on x* and *of Z* are not independent of each other, some of the commodities on which Z is to be expended being correlated [1] to, and in particular competitive with x. On this supposition it will be proper to put for u, $f(x, Z)$ [2]; and to then proceed as in the simple lemma. We have now three equations for the aforesaid three differential coefficients with respect to ξ. [3]

Eliminating two of the variables, we obtain for $\dfrac{dx}{d\xi}$, the *increase* of x corresponding to an increase of its price, an expression of the form $-a + b\theta_2$; where a and b are positive quantities (not the same as those lately employed) and θ_2 is the quantity above defined (Z now being substituted for the commodity y), which is generally negative, but occasionally positive. In the latter case the quantity purchased, x, *may increase* with the rise of price. In that case it is evident from equation (3) that Z must decrease.

This reasoning may easily be turned so as to treat explicitly of two commodities; supposing that the whole available income [4] is to be expended on two [5] commodities. We have only to suppose that Z now represents the amount of a second commodity of which

---

[1] The term " correlated " being used for the genus comprising complementary and competitive. See Index, s.v. *Correlation.*

[2] " f " as here used to denote a function involving *money* as one of its variables is not quite on a par with the " f " in the context, which denotes a function of commodities used—a utility function. The former kind of function is to be conceived as obtainable from the latter kind (by proper eliminations).

[3] (1) $\left(\dfrac{d^2f}{dx^2}\right)\dfrac{dx}{d\xi} + \dfrac{d^2f}{dxdZ}\dfrac{dZ}{d\xi} - \xi\dfrac{dm}{d\xi} = m;$

(2) $\dfrac{d^2f}{dxdZ}\dfrac{dx}{d\xi} + \dfrac{d^2f}{dZ^2}\dfrac{dZ}{d\xi} - \dfrac{dm}{d\xi} = x;$

(3) $\xi\dfrac{dx}{d\xi} + \dfrac{dZ}{d\xi} \qquad\qquad = -x.$

[4] As here used, μ denotes the whole available income (not a part arbitrarily earmarked to expenditure on two commodities); otherwise the change in the marginal utility of money as measured by $\dfrac{du}{d\mu}$ would not be significant.

[5] More concretely two kinds of commodities.

the price is *unity* (as may be supposed without serious loss of generality).

The reasoning may be extended to three variables if we put $u = F(x, y) + f(Z)$ where x and y are the amounts of two commodities which are purchased for the sum of money z at the prices ξ and η, and $Z + z =$ constant, the maximum of u being thus relative to the condition $x\xi + y\eta + Z =$ constant. We leave it to the reader to deduce conclusions similar and additional to those which we have enounced with respect to two dimensions. For the general analysis, which we have adapted to some sim plified cases, the reader is referred to Professor Pareto's *Manuel*, or to M. Zawadski's abridged, but lucid, exposition (p 180 *et seq.*).

Some interesting results *in pari materiâ* are obtained by Mr. Johnson with the aid of analytic geometry. To introduce his theories let us extend to three dimensions the construction in two dimensions above described. Let us now suppose a system of utility-*surfaces ;* such as concentric spheres with centre in the positive quadrant bounded by the planes xy, xz, yz. The construction is suited to represent two commodities of kinds (x) and (y) purchased in quantities x and y for the sum of money z; it being understood that z is a variable conditioned by equations like those written in the last paragraph. If the prices of (x) and (y), ξ and η respectively, are given, the amounts demanded and offered, the value of the variables x, y, z are determined. The system of values x, y, z is represented by the point at which one of the utility-spheres is touched by the *price-plane*, as we may say. This is a plane parallel to one passing through the origin of x and y and through two lines in the planes (xz), (yz) respectively corresponding to the given prices, the lines of which the equations are $z = x\xi$, $z = y\eta$. As in the case of two dimensions the system of quantities x, y, and ξ (quantity of commodity purchased, purchase money and price) becomes determinate when any *one* of them is given, or more generally any one equation connecting them; so in the case of three dimensions the system of quantities x, y, z, ξ, η becomes determinate when any *two* of them, or any two equations connecting them, are given. As in the case of two dimensions when not one variable or equation is given, we can construct a curve, the demand-and-supply curve, connecting one of the variables with another or with a function of the two others (x with y, or with y/x—the rate of exchange $\equiv$ say $\tan \theta$); [1] so in the case of three dimensions when one and only one variable, or equation

---

[1] Or, using polar co-ordinates, we may connect θ with ρ ($\equiv \sqrt{x^2 + y^2}$).

connecting the variables, is given we can construct a curve in three dimensions representing the course of the three quantities x, y, z as one of the other quantities, in particular one of the prices, is varied. The projection of that curve on the plane (xy) exhibits the change in the magnitudes of x and y consequent upon a change of one of the data.

Mr. Johnson has employed that plane curve to contemplate the variation of x and y in two or three instances which lend themselves particularly well to analytical geometry. Thus, suppose the one equation given to be this : that the ratio between the prices, ξ and η, is constant. For example, we may suppose a general rise or fall of prices not materially altering the relation between the prices of the different commodities; while incomes remain constant. To determine how a certain individual (or a particular class of individuals) will respond to such a change, we may write as the equation of the demand-and-supply curve in the plane of (x, y) in our notation, $t = $ constant.[1] Accordingly, for the slope of this curve we have $- \left(\dfrac{dt}{dx}\right) \Big/ \left(\dfrac{dt}{dy}\right)$. Therefore in general (a) the slope is positive, the values of x and y both decrease when the prices rise (both increase when the prices fall). But in the exceptional case (β) when one of the θs is positive more of one commodity and less of another will be demanded.

The construction may also be applied to the following problem. Suppose that the amount of money at the disposal of the individual, the total which we have called μ, is increased (or diminished), the utility-function remaining in other respects unaltered. What will be the effect on the quantities purchased, x and y; the prices ξ and η now both remaining constant ? As before, it may be shown that in general both purchases will be augmented; but in the exceptional case when one of the θs, e.g., θ_1 (in our notation), is positive, the case of " x urgent " in Mr. Johnson's terminology, much more of x but less of y will be purchased.

" What is the value of such a conclusion ? " asks M. Zawadski (p. 186), with reference to his own demonstration that a fall of price may be attended with a diminution in the amount purchased. " Does the case really occur, otherwise, than by way of exception ? " We can only answer, with Dr. Marshall,[2] " Such cases are rare; when they are met with each must be treated on its own merits." A good preparation for that requisite treatment

---

[1] Above, p. 459.

[2] *Principles of Economics*, Book III. ch. vi. § 4, p. 132, 6th edition.

appears to be afforded by the exercises in abstract reasoning provided by Professor Pareto and Mr. Johnson. We shall return to the subject under our third head. Under the present head we shall only add some observations on certain leading economic conceptions which Mr. Johnson has employed successfully.

In the construction for the representation of exchange between two commodities the plan of measuring the amount of one given in exchange *downwards* [1] (negatively) has certain advantages. It enables the indifference- or utility-curves from which the demand-curves are derivable to be expressed more simply; utility being treated as a function of the quantities consumed. The utility-curve does not now vary with variations in the conditions of the market, such as the amounts of each commodity in the hands of the dealer at the opening of the market. There is avoided a certain unreal heterogeneity imparted to the indifference-curves when the amount given is measured positively. When thus represented, the curves necessarily appear to belong to two distinct types, whereas conceivably the law of utility might be identical for buyers and sellers. In order that exchange should take place it is only necessary that the distribution at the opening of the market should be different. Thus in Fig. 1, if the point O represented the position of half the market, say $\frac{1}{2}n$ dealers, and the point o the position of the other $\frac{1}{2}n$ dealers, all having identical *laws* of utility, there would be an exchange characterised by the point P, supposing that $OP = Po$. If the initial distribution were different there would still be (in general) exchange; though it might happen that some who had been buyers under the first conditions would become sellers under the second.[2]

This praise is not to be understood as disparagement of the older constructions for the representation of exchange between the two kinds of commodity. No doubt the last-mentioned advantage on the side of the newer representation is considerable, at least when we leave international trade proper, to which Dr. Marshall's curves were originally adapted, and apply them to exchange in general. The advantage, however, may be partly secured by supposing two groups between which there is a certain mobility so that the numbers on each side of the market may vary according to circumstances.[3] The intersection of the two demand-and-supply curves pertaining respectively to buyers and sellers is particularly well calculated to bring out the principal outcome of mathematical

[1] Above, p. 457.

[2] The construction proposed by Mr. Wicksteed in the ECONOMIC JOURNAL fo September, 1913, seems designed to secure this sort of advantage.

[3] *Cp.* X. 88.

theory, the determinateness of economic equilibrium. The constructions mentioned in the last paragraph are not so well suited for this purpose. The case there put, in which half the market would be massed at one point, is quite imaginary. Usually the initial positions of the dealers would correspond to points scattered over the plane. The geometrical representation of this system would have little advantage over algebraic analysis—such as that which is given by M. Zawadski, after Walras and Professor Pareto—when reduced so as to apply to two commodities.

Mr. Johnson does not claim superiority for his construction as a representation of exchange between *two* commodities. It is the case of *three* articles, one of them being money, which he has specially illuminated. His work appears to us to be in respect of mathematical technique a unique contribution to the subject. In a remarkable degree geometrical elegance is coincident with economic importance.

Mr. Johnson has thrown additional light on the peculiar case which we have called β ; [1] a case to which Professor Pareto had already called attention.[2] Mr. Johnson proposes to define " competitive " as distinguished from " complementary " commodities by the characteristic of class β ; from which it follows that " in the former case changes along the demand-curves [of the kind described above] involve an opposite variation in x and z [our y], in the latter the two increase or decrease together " (Johnson, p. 496). This subtle distinction is now to be compared with the simpler definition which was proposed some years ago (V., 21), and appears to be accepted by M. Zawadski (p. 173). According to this definition, two commodities of the kinds (x) and (y) are, for the quantities x and y, complementary or competitive according as the partial differential coefficient [3] which represents the increase in the marginal utility of one commodity consequent on the gratuitous acquisition of an increment (or small unit) of the other commodity is positive or negative; in symbols, according as $\dfrac{d^2u}{dxdy} >$ or $< o$. It will be observed that the class *complementary* as thus defined is entirely included within the larger class which Mr. Johnson denotes by that term. For when $\dfrac{d^2u}{dxdy}$ is positive both θ_1 and θ_2 are negative.

[1] Above, p. 459.

[2] *Manuel*, p. 573. *Cp.* Zawadski, p. 170.

[3] See note 2 to p. 458. It often depends on the magnitude of the differences (Δx, Δy) under consideration whether a case is to be classed as Joint Production or not (XIII. 565).

Mr. Johnson's class *competitive* also includes a part of our class *competitive*; the greater part, indeed, since β is admitted to be an exceptional phenomenon. Which of these two definitions is preferable?

In favour of the older definition it may be urged that a distinction so fundamental should not be made to depend upon the incidents of a comparatively advanced regime, such as the distribution of money among different purchases, or even the more elementary distribution of doses of labour among different kinds of production. The distinction should be more *intrinsic*; one which Robinson Crusoe might have drawn between articles found by him on the derelict ship. Among such, for example, were barrels of powder, "fowling-pieces," and pistols. The first two commodities were complementary in our sense, since by the acquisition of the one the other became more useful. But the relation between guns and pistols was different; for the more of one article that was acquired, the less the other would be a desideratum. Might not these relations be usefully predicated, although the Johnsonian criterion would not be available? Or, again, consider the rice and barley to the cultivation of which Robinson Crusoe directed his primitive agricultural labours. Might he not decide whether one food went well with the other or the reverse, without waiting to observe whether, in case he obtained command over a greater quantity of labour (say through the accession of Friday), he would require (for his own consumption) more of both commodities, or much more of one and less of another?

On the other hand, as most of us live under a monetary regime, a definition relating thereto may well be useful. Propositions relating to money form a large part of economic theory. But of that part a large proportion does not admit of the distinction on which Mr. Johnson dwells. For the possibility, or at least the significance, of class β presupposes variability in the marginal utility of money.[1] But very generally, with reference to internal trade at least, the marginal utility of money may be treated as constant.[2] It is, therefore, not surprising that many of the deductions which have been made respecting commodities correlated in the way of demand presuppose constancy in the value of money (VI. 21) and employ only the older definition (V., *cp.*

[1] If m is constant, it is clear that when μ (the outlay in money) is increased (prices being constant) all that will happen is that more both of x and of y will be purchased.

[2] *Cp.* Marshall, *cited* above, p. 39, note. M. Zawadski, indeed, complains that constancy in the marginal value of money is too freely postulated by economists.

note 2, p. 468, below).   In international trade, indeed, the value
of money is normally variable.   Probably with respect to some
difficult problems in international values, the new conceptions,
if not the new terminology, may be particularly appropriate.

We shall have more to say about this matter under the head
of Production.   We may also postpone some further points
relating to the exchange of consumable commodities until we have
considered Production—a subject closely connected in Mr.
Johnson's treatment with Consumption.

Theory of Production.—The formulæ which have been obtained
in relation to consumption may be transferred almost unaltered
to production.   As the consumer seeks to lay out any assigned
sum of money so as to obtain a maximum of satisfaction, so the
producer seeks to incur a minimum of cost in producing any
assigned quantity of product.   The mathematical expression of
the conditions is almost identical; at least with reference to a
single product, in the absence of joint production.   Whether is it
easier to say that

$$f(x, y) - m[x\xi + y\eta - \mu]$$

shall be a maximum, where μ is an assigned outlay of money and
the other symbols have the same signification as before; or to say

$$(x\xi + y\eta) - \frac{1}{m'}[f(x, y) - v] \text{ [1]}$$

shall be a minimum; where now x and y are quantities of factors-
of-production—*two* doing duty as representative of any number—
ξ and η are their prices, v is the quantity of a product connected
by a " production-function " (in Mr. Johnson's phrase) with x
and y, $1/m'$, like m, is the constant proper to a relative maximum
(or minimum).[2]

The theorems which have been proved for utility-functions

[1] The form of the function f is, in general, to be determined by the Calculus of
Variations.   Or, what comes to much the same, we may consider v as depending not
only on the factors of production, x, y, etc., but also on certain adjustments
defined by quantities which may be called " gratuitous constants " (XIII. 357);
for instance, the *time* or *place* at which some operation is to be performed—within
limits not affecting the total cost—might well be constants of the character.   Say
$v = \phi(x, y; p, q)$ to each of the gratuitous constants $p, q, \ldots$ there corresponds an
equation $\frac{dv}{dp} = 0$; by means of which equations the said constants may be
eliminated.   [The " gratuitous constants " in the production-function are cognate
to the coefficients or "parameters," u, v, w, which Dr. Zotoff introduces and
eliminates in his interesting development of Mr. Johnson's theory (ECONOMIC
JOURNAL, Vol. XXXIII. (1923), p. 115.]

[2] More exactly the quantity to be maximised is subjective, the utility obtained
by the entrepreneur from profits less by the disutility attending production
(cp. II., note h).

may be transferred by analogy to production-functions. In particular the mathematical distinction between *complementary* and *competitive* goods should be the same, whether the goods are, in the terminology of the Austrian School, of the first or of a higher order. Here, then, we have a new argument against the suggested innovation in the definition of these terms. For, with reference to production, it is equally tenable that the terms should designate a difference which is *intrinsic*. We need not now go to Robinson Crusoe's island for an illustration. Whenever an industry is *integrated*, in the sense that the factors of production and the product are manufactured by the same firm, it may be important to distinguish between the cases in which the increase of one factor increases the efficiency of another factor, or the reverse. But that distinction is expressed by the sign of the partial differential coefficient $\dfrac{d^2v}{dx\,dy}$ rather than by the signs of expressions corresponding to the quantities which we have called θ_1 and θ_2.

The constant $m'\left(\dfrac{1}{\kappa}\text{ in Mr. Johnson's notation}\right)$ is well described by him as the marginal efficiency of money. In fact, the increment of the product effected by applying a (small) unit of money to increase any factor (e.g., x) is measured by the price of the factor multiplied by m'; since $\left(\dfrac{dv}{dx}\right) = m'\xi$. For any assigned quantity of product v there are, when the prices ξ, $\eta \cdots$ are given, determinate values of x, $y \ldots$, and accordingly a determinate value of μ, the total expenditure, $= x\xi + y\eta \cdots$. We have thus $\mu = \chi(v)$ where v is the product corresponding to Mr. Johnson's " p " (p. 507); and χ is a function corresponding to the " cost-curve " defined elsewhere [XIII. 362, and context]. For the price of the commodity we may put the reciprocal of the marginal efficiency of money $1/m'$; abstracting not only the circumstance that there is an interval of time between the outlay on the factors and the completion of the production, but also the distinction between prime and general expenses and other circumstances of high importance on any but the most abstract view of the subject. On this hypothesis the exchange value of the outlay (μ) in terms of the commodity produced (v) would be $\mu\dfrac{dv}{d\mu}$. The excess of the product over the cost thus measured would be $v - \mu\dfrac{dv}{d\mu}$.

In applied mathematics (as Mr. Johnson reminds us, p. 503)

we are often concerned not so much with the simple differential coefficient, the relation of two increments, say $dv : d\mu$, as with the ratio between the *relative* changes $dv/v : d\mu/\mu$; in short, with the elasticity $\dfrac{\mu}{v} \dfrac{d\mu}{dv}$. The last written elasticity has a very important property. According as this elasticity, say ϵ, is greater or less than unity, the ratio v/μ increases or diminishes as μ increases. But the increase or decrease of that ratio forms the criterion of *increasing returns* [1] in a common and very important sense of the term. If ϵ is less than unity industry cannot be in a state of equilibrium, in a regime of competition.[2]

It is pointed out by Mr. Johnson that, as production is increased with the increase of outlay, the " marginal efficiency " of money changes, but does not necessarily increase or diminish (p. 510). In this connection he investigates the condition that the production-function should be such as to afford a true minimum (of cost). He shows that as production—and therewith outlay—is increased the locus (in space of many dimensions generally) of the system of simultaneous values $x, y \ldots$ (in our notation) is " analogous to a line for cutting across the equipotential surfaces " $v = f(x, y \ldots)$ (p. 509). That family of surfaces are shown to be in all directions *convex* to the axes of (our) $x, y. \ldots$ This last statement may seem inconsistent with the illustration of progressively increasing production which was given in the former paper, to which reference has been made. There the cost attending the use of the factors was represented by a *plane* (XIII. 365). It must be remembered, however, that the analysis there offered—much less rigid than Mr. Johnson's—refers specially to *monopoly*. In a regime of monopoly equilibrium may very well be reached, though the production-function has not the normal convexity. It should be added that the analysis in the context referred to is specially directed to the explanation of a particular incident, *increasing returns*. Mr. Johnson's more general theory is adapted to wider applications.

The analogy between consumption and production, between maximising utility and minimising cost, is calculated to elucidate

---

[1] See XIII. 354 *et seq.* (Below, p. 477.)

[2] See XIII. p. 358; and *cp.* Johnson, p. 507. The difference between our statements and Mr. Johnson's as to the elasticity ϵ is explained by the fact that we, in accordance with the very abstract suppositions which may be ascribed to the Continental writers, suppose an entrepreneur producing such a relatively small part of the aggregate output as not to affect (through the action of increasing or diminishing returns) the price of the product. Mr. Johnson's formulæ are doubtless appropriate to the practically more important case of *long-period supply-curves* (*cp.* XIV. 6, par. 1, and note 1; VIII. 66, and context).

one or other of the phenomena, whichever is the less clear and familiar. It is usually the more subjective of two compared phenomena which gains in clearness by the comparison. Yet the poets, those masters of allegory, occasionally illustrate things of sense by things of soul. A skylark is " like an unbodied joy." The way of Phæacian ships was " like a thought." So those to whom the working of their own minds are more familiar than the ways of business men may be helped by the proposed analogy to understand the nature of entrepreneurs' profits. They may be encouraged to question the paradox propounded by the school of Lausanne and repeated by M. Zawadski that " the entrepreneur *quâ* [en tant qu'] entrepreneur makes neither gain nor loss." Those who would uphold this tenet are, in virtue of the said analogy, placed under the heavy burden of having to prove that the consumer *quâ* consumer obtains no pleasure. The consumer's surplus of utility, of the form $F(x, y) - m\mu$, is by common consent not equatable to zero. Why should we equate to zero the producer's surplus of product (the total product *minus* the equivalent in product of the amount of money laid out), viz. $f(x, y) - m'\mu$? [1] We know no more about the function F than about the function f.[2] Competition, it may be said, presses upon profits. But so it does upon utility ; the net advantages in different occupations being reduced to a level by industrial competition (in Cairnes' phrase). That level may be low; the remuneration of the average occupied person, measured in the pleasure that money can command, may in fact be small. But that it is normally *zero* neither common sense nor economic theory compels us to believe.

So far abstracting (among other concrete circumstances) the *general expenses* of a business; which it is interesting to note that Walras left out of account. If they are taken into account, the argument becomes *a fortiori*. For why should not a

---

[1] That is, upon the very abstract suppositions above specified (p. 468, note). With respect to most of the circumstances abstracted it may be observed that their great importance was first pointed out by Dr. Marshall. The type of industry formed by their abstraction is identical with the conception entertained in a paper to which M. Zawadski alludes (p. 205. *Cp.* Osorio, p. 28), a paper (II) written before the appearance of the *Principles of Economics*. The deficiency there noticed (p. 688, and *note* h) in the then prevailing mathematical systems in relation to *Industrial* (as distinguished by Cairns from *Commercial*) competition has since then been remedied by Marshall's " *Long-period* " Supply-curve and Pigou's *Curve of marginal supply prices*.

[2] It was perhaps the exigency of the theory in question which led a distinguished economist to maintain that the product was a *homogeneous function* of the factors of production (VII. 182), and has led other theorists to make by implication statements about the function which are only less preposterous because less distinct.

substantial remuneration for the entrepreneur be included in the general expenses of the business ? In fact, that is probably the meaning of the more moderate disciples, if not the leaders,[1] of the School of Lausanne. If the paradox is only a figure of speech, ' solvuntur risu tabulæ." The entrepreneur is transformed, like the father of the Bourgeois Gentilhomme, who, it was discovered, had after all not been a shopkeeper. 'Tis true he was a very good-natured and obliging man, and as he was a connoisseur in drapery be used to get together goods of that sort and make presents of them to his friends—" pour de l'argent."

M. Zawadski writes (p. 211) : " L'entrepreneur réel apporte dans son entreprise des facultés et connaissances qui le distinguent des autres, son travail, son crédit, ses relations, etc. ; l'entrepreneur idéal n'apporte rien de tout cela : il est absolument égal à tous les points de vue à ses collègues ou, plus exactement, pour tout ce qui le distingue, il n'est pas entrepreneur, mais fournisseur de services ; il n'est que la personification de son entreprise." We do not suppose that there is any material difference between the meaning of these statements properly interpreted and our view of the matter. We regard the formulæ which are piously repeated by M. Zawadski as we do Mill's dictum that " demand for commodities is not demand for labour," [2] or any other of the paradoxical dogmas consecrated by the usage of the older English economists who, as Mr. and Mrs. Webb have remarked,[3] had " almost a genius for publishing what they did not mean to say." We, too, conceive an ideal entrepreneur who makes nothing by way of monopoly, or rent-of-ability, or " konjunctur " —though our formula is well adapted to take account of those concrete circumstances when they are present. " We may suppose that the entrepreneur's remuneration is totally unmixed with rent, so that it is open to any worker to transform himself into an entrepreneur, the difference of remuneration [between the profits of an entrepreneur and the wages of common labour] compensating for the efforts and sacrifices attending the transformation." [4]

[1] Walras by not admitting general expenses has cut himself off from this explanation; and, as remarked on a former occasion (X. 92), the theory in question appears to be for Pareto more than a *façon de parler.*

[2] Of this dictum Dr. Marshall has said " it expresses his meaning badly " (*Principles of Economics*, note on the doctrine of wages, 4th edition), and Sidgwick has said " This proposition which has occasioned a good deal of polemical discussion is, I believe, perfectly true when properly explained. . . . I think, however, it is all in form unsatisfactory. . . . I think most reflective readers of Mill find it puzzling after all the pains that he has taken to make it clear " (Sidgwick, *Political Economy*, Book I. chap. v., note).

[3] *Industrial Democracy*, Part III. chap. i.

[4] XI. 570. Other passages referring to the question are, VI. 82, VIII. 530, IX. 92.

There is thus a "supply-price," in Dr. Marshall's terminology, for the services of an entrepreneur, just as there is a supply-price of a workman's service; differing only in that the former is paid out of a surplus, the latter is commonly a marginal outlay. It is not quite clear to us how M. Zawadski would deal with the surplus which must arise [1] upon the supposition, which he at least entertains as sometimes appropriate, that the price of the product is equal to its marginal cost,[2] in the absence of general expenses (p. 212).

In this connection we should mention the coefficients of production formulated by Walras and adopted by his successors. Certainly it seems a natural conception, and agreeable to the habits of the business man, to split up the price or the cost-of-production of a (unit of) product into a number of elements each formed by the price of a factor multiplied on the amount of that factor which goes to a unit of product. Thus, in our notation, if in the state of equilibrium μ is the total expenditure, x, y, etc., are the amounts of the factors employed, n is the number of units produced, $\frac{\mu}{n} = \frac{x}{n}\xi + \frac{y}{n}\eta + \cdots$. But when the coefficients $\frac{x}{n}$, $\frac{y}{n}$ are to seek, in case of what is called "variability of the coefficients-of-production," it seems to us more natural to determine the quantities x, y, etc., with the aid of the production function $f(x, y \ldots)$, in terms of the product v, as above explained; without bringing in the coefficients of production. However, the same heights of contemplation may be scaled on different sides. In the selection of the route habit properly counts for much.

The conception which we recommend has the advantage of being readily applicable to the case of two or more products, Joint Production; with which may be coupled what has been called Rival or Disjunctive Production (XIII. 558). As before, we have to minimise the cost, $x\xi + y\eta + \cdots (\equiv \mu)$; subject now to the condition that two (or more) products, say v and w, are produced; that is, the *propositum* which is to be minimised is

$$\mu - \frac{1}{m_1}[f_1(x, y \ldots) - v] - \frac{1}{m_2}[f_2(x, y \ldots) - w]$$

where f_1 denotes the quantity of v and f_2 that of w which results from the application of the (amounts of the) factors x, $y \ldots$ in the best available manner;[3] $1/m_1$ and $1/m_2$ are relativity-constants

---

[1] In the absence of unwarrantable and unworkable assumptions as to the form of the production-function (above, p. 466, note).

[2] Walras's conception as to which, see III.   [3] *Cp.* XIII. 357.

of the kind already employed.[1] Thus the prices of the factors, namely, ξ, η... being given, we have the cost in terms of the amounts of the products, say $\mu = \phi(v, w)$.

Analogous to the distinction between complementary and competitive *factors-of-production*, a distinction between *products* is now presented. Products are complementary or competitive (joint [2] or rival) according as the increase of one product alleviates or aggravates the expense of increasing the other product : in symbols, according as

$$\frac{d^2\phi(v, w)}{dvdw} < \text{or} > 0.$$

It can hardly be doubted that the above is the true distinction appropriate to difficult problems relating to railways or, more generally, " public works " (XIII. 217). Analogy and the economy of language make against Mr. Johnson's usage of the terms with respect to joint demand and its opposite.

(3) *Utility.*—Now let us turn back from the " production-function " to the analogous expression for utility, and see what new light is thrown on the more subjective conception. With reference to the difficulty of measuring satisfaction, M. Antonelli aptly quotes a letter written by the eminent mathematician Poincaré to Walras : [3]

" Can satisfaction be measured ? I may say that one satisfaction is greater than another, because I prefer one to the other; but I cannot say that one is two or three times greater than another. . . . Satisfaction then is a magnitude, but not a measurable magnitude. Now is a magnitude that is not measurable therefore not amenable to mathematical theory ['par cela seul exclué de toute spéculation mathématique'] ? By no means. Temperature, for instance (at any rate before the term ' absolute temperature ' had acquired a signification with the rise of Thermodynamics), was a non-measurable magnitude. It was arbitrarily defined and measured by the expansion of mercury. It might

[1] It may be well to remind the reader that the " best available " use of the factors does not depend on the selling-prices of v and w. *Any* two values of v and w having been *assigned* the minimising of the *propositum* affords equations enough to determine the corresponding values of x, y..., together with m_1 and m_2 (the equation to zero of each of the expressions within the square brackets being, of course, taken into the account). Of course, in order to *determine* the quantities v and w the selling-prices of those articles have to be taken into account.

[2] The subject will be treated at length in the next section, with reference to the views of Professor J. S. Nicholson and Professor M. Fanno.

[3] At the end of Walras's study entitled " Économie et Mécanique "; quoted by Antonelli at his p. 66.

quite as legitimately have been defined by the expansion of any other substance and measured by any function of that expansion, *provided that it was a continually increasing function.* Likewise, in the present case, you may define satisfaction by an arbitrary function, provided that the function continually increases along with the satisfaction which it represents." . . .

Poincaré's ruling is in accordance with the view now generally prevalent among mathematicians, that the capacity of numbers to express the results of counting and measuring "may be regarded as a secondary property derived from the more fundamental one of expressing order. Natural numbers form a series with a definite order, and the expressions ' greater than ' and ' less than ' mean ' more advanced ' and ' less advanced ' in this order." These are the words of another eminent mathematician, Professor Love.[1]

Professor Pareto is therefore in very good company when, scrupling to designate utility as a function (say u) of quantities of commodities (say x, y..), he contemplates a family of successive *indifference-curves* (or generally surfaces in space of many dimensions) in the plane x, y (or corresponding hyper-surface); such that the advance from any one indifference-locus to the next in succession affords an *index*, rather than a measure, of the advance in satisfaction, or as Professor Pareto prefers to say, *ophelimity.* According to M. Osorio (p. 312), not only should the combinations which are preferred have a higher index; but also if in passing from Combination I. to Combination II. one experiences a greater difference in pleasure than in passing from Combination II. to Combination III., the difference between the Indices I. and II. ought to be greater than that between the Indices II. and III.[2] The form of doctrine adopted by Professor Pareto would imply a substantial difference from received theories if the negation that u is a *function* of x, y (in our notation) in the ordinary sense of the terms involved the corollary that the system of values x, y.. does not normally correspond to the same amount of utility ; that amount varying with the *path* by which we have attained the point x, y.. (starting from any initial point).[3] But it would be difficult to reconcile this possibility with

[1] See the articles of Professor A. E. Love and Professor A. Voigt referred to (IX. *a* 222).

[2] If it is objected that this statement implies the *measurability* of satisfaction, it may be replied that there are those to whom this implication does not appear a *reductio ad absurdum* (I. 60).

[3] *Cp.* Zawadski, p. 150, note (referring to Pareto, *Manuel*, pp. 547–557), p. 176, p. 209, note.

that character of repetition under similar circumstances which we have attributed to the phenomena under consideration; we do not understand that Professor Pareto would press his suggestion; and M. Zawadski, with his usual good sense, seems not to attach to it much practical significance.[1]

The matter is well put by Mr. Johnson with reference to two commodities [x and y] : " There are no lines in the figure which measure the utility itself. The several utility-curves are arranged in a scale of increasing value as we pass to the right and above [in the plane of x, y]; and thus the ' distance ' (measured arbitrarily) from one curve to another ' indicates ' without measuring the increase in utility. But this impossibility of measurement does not affect any economic problem " (p. 490).

Walras appears to be fully justified in the use of terms such as maximum satisfaction by the authorisation which he received from Poincaré. We have not caught the distinction on the ground of which M. Antonelli classes Walras with Cournot as dealing with objective phenomena, rather than with the " mathematico-psychological " school initiated by Gossen and developed by Pareto [2] (Antonelli, p. 17).

Identity of expression in a matter so speculative is not to be expected. But there appears to be a substantial agreement among experts that things go on as if the satisfaction obtained by an individual from an assigned set of goods was a quantity dependent on the quantities of the goods. To proceed as if there was such a dependent variable appears to be legitimate. (See Antonelli, p. 68, referring to Walras's brochure, *Économique et Mécanique*; and p. 111, " nous pourrons le supposer "; and *cp*. Zawadski, p. 154.)

If utility, say u, is a function of goods purchased for use, it follows that, prices of the goods being assigned, u is a function of μ, an amount of money which is to be expended on the purchase of those goods.[3] The differential coefficient of u with respect to μ is the marginal utility of money, which we have called m $\left(\text{Mr. Johnson's } \dfrac{1}{\kappa}\right)$. The relation between a *relative* (indefinitely small) change in the amount of money and the corresponding *relative* change in utility, that is $\dfrac{du/u}{d\mu/\mu}$ or $\dfrac{\mu}{u}\dfrac{du}{d\mu}$ is defined by

---

[1] *Loc. cit.*

" ce cas semble avoir assez peu d'importance . . ."

" des cas de ce genre ne jouent pas un grand rôle en pratique."

[2] The appreciative reviewer of M. Antonelli's work in the *Journal of the Statistical Society* for July, 1914, appears sensible of the obscurity which we notice.

[3] The function which is the inverse of (the analogue of) Mr. Johnson's χ (p. 507).

Mr. Johnson (p. 504) as the elasticity of u in terms of money. This coefficient plays a part in economic theory analogous to that which we have assigned to the *elasticity of money*.[1] As long as the elasticity of utility is greater than unity the ratio u/μ increases with the increase of money. Thus if the " net advantages " of an occupation (including profits) increase with the increase of investment in that line, there will be a crowding into that occupation up to a point at which u/μ, having ceased to increase, becomes equal for all occupations between which there exists " Industrial Competition " (as defined by Cairnes). The ratio u/μ, which each individual tries to maximise, is not to be confounded with the marginal utility of money. The *reciprocals* of these quantities are likewise to be distinguished; Mr. Johnson's κ, the reciprocal of our m, is not to be equated to π, which he calls the price (of a unit) of utility.

The postulate here adopted that utility or welfare " can be brought under the category of greater and less " [2] rests primarily on the testimony of consciousness, the psychological observation that there are degrees of felt satisfaction. This personal experience is then extended by sympathy to the evaluation of other people's pleasures. Jevons's suggestion that the theory of utility is limited to the motions of a single mind, that "no common denominator of feeling seems to be possible " appears to us untenable. The contrary is postulated throughout large tracts of economic science; for instance, the theory of taxation and that of industrial conciliation. Even a more fundamental part of political economy, the theory of value and distribution, involving the equation of net advantages in different occupations, suggests at least, if it does not require the comparison between, the welfare of different persons.[3] This kind of comparison no doubt presupposes some homogeneity between the persons compared, such that presumably exists between " a thousand persons living in Sheffield and another thousand in Leeds, each with about £100 a year." [4] So when we use a change in the level of prices as an index of a variation in welfare, the indications obtained are then most useful when the persons affected by the alteration of prices are of one and the same type, for instance workpeople having similar family budgets.[5]

In the example last given the rough estimation of welfare

[1] Above, p. 468.   [2] Pigou, *Wealth and Welfare*, Part I. chap. i. sect. 1.
[3] See VII. 22.

[4] Part of a passage which is quoted more fully in the ECONOMIC JOURNAL (III. p. 66), from Marshall's *Principles of Economics* (3rd edition).

[5] The British Association Committee for measuring the value of money recommend construction of different index numbers for different classes.

is commonly improved by a semi-objective measure, a stable average (of percentage variations in price).

But a rough estimate would still be possible, even though the *sporadic* character proper to a good average were wanting, if, for instance, price-variations under treatment consist of two large groups, one clustering about a percentage above 100, the other about a percentage below 100. Something of the sort occurs when the price of a large item in the family budget, of house-accommodation for instance, rises while the remainder as a whole falls. A rough estimate of the change in the value of money may still be possible.[1]

This conception is sufficiently definite to enter into significant propositions. Thus it is recorded of a local dearth that, the price of bread rising very high, the price of meat and other articles fell off owing to the fact that the purchasers of those articles had to expend so much of their money on bread. In this instance, presumably, the less necessary articles followed the law of " short periods " (" market value "); the dealers sold their goods below cost price.[2] Otherwise we might suppose the prices of articles other than bread (including that of meat) to be kept constant. Under these conditions, as shown above,[3] it is conceivable that more bread might be purchased. But this occurrence is attended with a rise in the marginal utility of money.[4] In other more important cases the direction of the change in the marginal utility of money cannot be similarly predicted. In the normal conditions above designated case *a*, when a rise of price in one article—while the prices of other articles remain constant—is attended with a fall in the demand for the article which has become more expensive, the marginal utility of money may or may not rise. Again, suppose the income available for the purchase of different kinds of goods to be increased (as in the case adduced above, p. 402), the marginal utility of money will normally fall, but in exceptional cases may rise. In this and other respects the marginal utility of money in the way of consumption is analogous to its " marginal efficiency " in the way of production.

---

[1] Compare Bowley, *National Progress in Wealth and Trade*, pp. 26–7.

[2] In some previous enunciations of cognate theories (IV. and V.) a supply curve of the sort pertaining to reciprocal demand or international trade is implied (by reference to Auspitz and Lieben's constructions) so that the result of assigned changes in the price—or quantity—of one article x is given in terms of the change in the *price* of the article y as in this particular passage of the present article; not in terms of the change in *demand* for y as elsewhere in the present article.

[3] Above, p. 460.   [4] *Cp.* Marshall, *loc. cit.*

∴ Publications relating to mathematical economics, by the writer of the present article, referred to in the course of the article :—

I.—*Mathematical Psychics* (1881).

II.—*On the Application of Mathematics to Political Economy* (Report of the British Association for the Advancement of Science, 1889).

III.—" La théorie mathématique de l'offre et de la demande " (*Revue d'Économie Politique*, 1891).

IV.—" The Pure Theory of Taxation " (ECONOMIC JOURNAL, 1897).

V.—" Teoria Pura del Monopolio " (*Giornale degli Economisti*, 1897).

VI.—(*a*) Review of Bastable's *Theory of International Trade*, second edition. (*b*) Review of the same, third edition. (*c*) " Disputed Points in the Theory of International Trade " (ECONOMIC JOURNAL : (*a*) 1897, p. 397 ; (*b*) 1900, p. 389 ; (*c*) 1901, p. 582).

VII.—" Theory of Distribution " (*Quarterly Journal of Economics*, 1904).

VIII.—Review of Cunynghame's " Geometrical Political Economy " (ECONOMIC JOURNAL, 1905, p. 62).

IX.—" Appreciations of Mathematical Theories " (ECONOMIC JOURNAL : (*a*) 1907, (*b*) 1908).

X.—" On the Use of the Differential Calculus in Economics " (*Scientia*, Vol. VII., 1910).

XI.—Article on " Probability " in the *Encyclopædia Britannica* (eleventh edition).

XII.—" Applications of Probabilities to Economics " (ECONOMIC JOURNAL, 1910).

XIII.—" Contributions to the Theory of Railway Rates," Parts I. and II. (ECONOMIC JOURNAL, 1911).

XIV.—(*a*) Review of Pigou's " Wealth and Welfare " (ECONOMIC JOURNAL, March, 1913). (*b*) " Contributions to the Theory of Railway Rates : Digression on Professor Pigou's Theories " (ECONOMIC JOURNAL, June, 1913).

SECTION II

The theories which we have been contemplating would be
demarcated by some writers from the more tentative problems
to which we now proceed. Thus M. Antonelli, appreciating the
work of Walras, sharply distinguishes his pure theory of economic
equilibrium from his application of mathematical reasoning to
bimetallism. We are more impressed by the similarity than by
the difference between the more and the less general propositions
which admit of mathematical treatment. Alike they are " sicklied
o'er with the pale cast " of abstract thought " and lose the name
of action." This similarity is indeed likely to be forgotten when,
instead of x and y, some concrete matter is the subject of our
theorising. When Walras prescribes for Indian currency he
forgets the limitations of mathematical theory. It is not surprising that the English Government do not set much store on his
bimetallic scheme, as Professor Pareto observes in the vigorous
preface which he contributes to M. Osorio's volume. We heartily
agree with Professor Pareto when, in this connection, he says :
" Anyone who expects [" *veut* "] to derive the solution of a practical problem simply and solely [" *exclusivement* "] from the
theories of pure economics, or even those of applied economics, is
generally wrong " [" *est généralement dans le faux* "] (*loc. cit.*,
p. xvii). But while agreeing that both the pure mathematical
theory and that which has the semblance of being applied are
nearly equally false in a certain sense, if taken too literally, we
also think that they may be nearly equally useful as showing
probability or tendency. As M. Zawadski says of the pure
theory, which predicates maximum " ophelimity " of free competition : " It does not follow that [because it cannot be applied
directly] it is altogether without bearing on practice [" *soit privée
de toute portée pratique* "] (p. 289). As a champion of Free Trade
Professor Pareto has assuredly derived support from the principle
of maximum satisfaction, as it is called in English ; though he
is aware that the unqualified assertion of *laisser faire* is folly
(Zawadski, p. 288, note). We submit that a similar use may
be made of less general propositions. There is attained a presumption analogous to that scientific common sense, that almost
unconscious record of experience, which underlies many of the
theorems of Probabilities.[1] The designation " *a priori* " or
" unverified " which has been applied to such presumptions is

[1] See, on p. 477, *ante*, XIV. 225 ; XIII. 205 ; XII. 287, 459, 463, and earlier
writings there cited.

not intended to cut from under them the ground of experience, but rather to mark the absence of that third stage in the " Concrete Deductive Method " which Mill called " Verification." [1] The presumptions which we postulate are analogous to the " antecedent probability " which Mill (after Laplace) employs in the calculation of chances—" it would be impossible to estimate that probability with anything like numerical precision," yet " we may be able to form a conjecture " adequate to sustain " a practical conclusion." [2]   Such presumptions are of the kind which " would naturally be assumed " in Dr. Marshall's words " to start with, . . . and until cause to the contrary were shown." [3]

Of this kind is the presumption that the imposition of a tax will diminish the demand for a commodity.   It is almost sufficient to say that the negative would be violently contrary to common sense [4]; calculated to excite the derision which was bestowed by an economist of the highest sagacity upon the cognate paradox that a tax upon a (monopolised) article might prove beneficial to the consumer. [5]   Common sense in the example before us is further justified in the case of a *small* tax by a presumption resting on a higher, more expert, sort of common sense, that the marginal utility of money may be treated as constant.   When the tax is so large as to render this presumption hazardous, we must fall back on the first presumption, strengthened by a consideration of the conditions on which the rise or fall of price depends.   It will be seen from the formula which expresses those conditions (above, p. 460) that the consumption of the taxed article will be diminished when its correlation in the way of demand with untaxed articles is small.   Now this is a datum, like Mill's " antecedent probabilities," about which we may be able, in his words, to " form a conjecture " sufficiently accurate for " a practical conclusion."   Some other conclusions of less practical importance may be gathered from the study of the formula.

It is difficult to formulate the presumptions of common sense

[1] *Logic*, Book III. ch. xi. ;   Book VI. ch. ix.

[2] *Logic*, Book III. ch. xviii. § 6.

[3] *Principles of Economics*, Book III. ch. vi. § 3, p. 30; referring to the assumption that " a shilling's worth of gratification to one Englishman must be taken as an equivalent with a shilling's worth to another."   The passage including the note should be studied in its bearing on the treatment of utility as a quantity (*ante*, p. 58 *et seq.*).

[4] Thus Professor Carver expresses a generally and almost universally valid belief when in his scholarly paper on " The Shifting of Taxes " (*Yale Review*, November, 1896), he says : " It is scarcely conceivable that a tax can increase the demand for the thing taxed."   Yet we have seen that this hardly conceivable, is not impossible.

[5] XII. 296 *et seq.*;   and earlier writings there cited.

so unequivocally as not to admit of being misrepresented and misapplied by captious critics and stupid practitioners. There must ever be understood a saving clause like that which Aristotle appended to his definition of moral virtue, " ὡς ἀν ὁ φρονιμός." The nature of the presumptions postulated may best be exhibited by examples. We shall take these from Professor Pigou's *Wealth and Welfare*, a work which abounds in " tentatives " (as they would be described by M. Zawadski), going beyond the received applications of mathematical method.

The same work has been utilised by the writer of the article in the *Quarterly Review*, which we have cited, to point a different moral. But the difference is perhaps not so great as it appears. The reviewer, indeed, maintains that " between this pure science and the application of practice there seems to be a deep gulf fixed." Whereas, we attempt to bridge that gulf. But we are careful to put up a conspicuous notice to the effect that " this bridge is not adapted to carry heavy traffic." Our " antecedent probabilities " will generally require to be strengthened by concrete materials in order to lead to practical conclusions. It is not clear that the polemic in the *Quarterly Review* is intended to demolish the inchoate construction which we describe. The attack is rather directed against the form of exposition adopted by a particular writer. The questions involved pertain mostly to literary criticism. How far is it advisable to employ a technical terminology ? What is the happy mean between abruptness and diffuseness of style ? There is room for some diversity of judgment on such questions. But we do not venture to oppose our judgment to that of one who is a master of the arts of exposition. We are not, however, precluded from citing in illustration of a particular point passages which have been criticised on grounds not relevant to that particular point.

Our first example consists of the leading principle which Professor Pigou thus enunciates in the form of two propositions. " The first is that the dividend necessarily stands at the maximum attainable amount when the marginal net product of resources is equal in all uses ; the second, that self-interest, if not interfered with, tends to make these marginal net products equal." [1] Professor Pigou may be open to criticism for having alluded to Adam Smith's corresponding theory as " highly optimistic," without mentioning the serious qualifications of the general theory which were introduced by Adam Smith (*Quarterly Review*, p. 420). We do not venture to dispute about Adam Smith's meaning with the

[1] Pigou, *Wealth and Welfare*, Part II. ch. iii. § 1.

editor of the *Wealth of Nations*. We are ready to admit that *Wealth and Welfare* might be improved by fuller references; and we may add, by a more complete index. But we are not here concerned with the form of the treatise. What interests us is the substantial identity between the leading principles enunciated by Professor Pigou, and those which propounded by Adam Smith have revolutionised the world of industry and commerce. What the *Quarterly Reviewer* disparagingly describes as " Professor Pigou's translation of the plain language of Adam Smith into the language of marginal net products " appears to us an improved restatement of fundamental doctrines—a revised version which, though not comparable in respect of style with the authorised version, has the advantage in respect of accuracy. The mathematical statement brings more clearly into view the essential characteristic of a maximum. What the critic suggests (*loc. cit.*, par. 2), and what others more loudly proclaim, that the mathematical statement of a general proposition involves a neglect of practical limitations, is not, we submit, true of Professor Pigou.[1] In the immediate context of the leading principle which we have cited he introduces exceptions, and throughout makes it clear that he treats the general propositions of political economy as " truths only in the rough," as Mill says. Many of the exceptions which he points out are of that *recherché* species which the mathematical method is peculiarly adapted to discover, thereby " making clear how far we are from being able to solve with full knowledge of the case a multitude of questions which are boldly decided every day." These words of Cournot are quoted with approbation by the writer in the *Quarterly Review*, in an earlier writing,[2] where he shows how the mathematical economist, " by making clear the nature and extent of the assumptions implied in dealing with

---

[1] If it be objected that in the above cited enunciation of leading principles Professor Pigou uses the word " necessary " and in several other passages an italicised " *must*," it may be replied that Adam Smith, who admittedly recognises practical limitations, is yet very fond of the word " necessary." For instance, in connection with the principle now under consideration :

" The study of his own advantage naturally, or rather necessarily, leads him to prefer that employment which is most advantageous to the Society " (Book V. ch. ii. par. 4).

" Every individual who employs his capital in the support of domestic industry necessarily endeavours so to direct that industry that its produce may be of the greatest possible value " (*loc. cit.*, par. 7).

" The industry of the country therefore is thus turned away from a more to a less advantageous employment, and the exchangeable value of its actual produce instead of being increased, according to the valuation of the law-giver, must necessarily be diminished by every such regulation " (par. 12).

[2] Transactions of the Faculty of Actuaries, Vol. IV. Part I. *The Use of Mathematical and Legal Ideas in Economic Problems.* By J. Shield Nicholson.

economic problems . . . invites the statesman to proceed with caution."

It often happens, as we have had occasion to notice, that a mathematical writer who enounces some *recherché* exception is in consequence supposed to be denying the general rule.[1] It is hard that he should be also suspected of affirming the general rule unreservedly as if it did not admit of exceptions. It was said of some narrow-minded specialist that he was a man who could see a fly upon a barn door without being able to see the door or the barn. A double degree of blindness seems to be attributed to the mathematical economist; now represented as incapable of seeing the barn, and now the fly. The truth appears to be that the relation between the large and the small, the general and the particular,[2] is better conceived by one who has been trained in mathematics, including probabilities, than by one whose soul this science has not taught to stray beyond generalisations of the Ricardian type. However this may be, it is certain that whoever employs general propositions in economics, whether expressed mathematically or not, is exposed to the suspicion of neglecting facts; especially on his first appearance, and before he may have acquired a reputation for caution and good sense. Adam Smith himself is no exception to this rule. Adam Smith stands accused of " Smithianismus." Nor is it only to pedants of the German historical school that Adam Smith has appeared too abstract, but also to practical English genius. It was Burke who said,[3] " You, Dr. Smith, from your professor's chair, may send forth theories upon freedom of commerce as if you were lecturing on pure mathematics; but legislators must proceed by slow degrees." Fox was not so much impressed as the *Quarterly Reviewer* is by the limitations with which the generalisations of Adam Smith are guarded. For, as reported by Lord Colchester, " in talking of books upon political economy he said (as I have often heard him say in debate) that he had but little faith in Adam Smith, or any of them, their reasons were so plausible but so inconclusive." [4]

Imputations of this sort have, no doubt, sometimes been

---

[1] *Cp.* F., p. 144.

[2] The relation is well expressed in the following passage, one of a large class of similar conclusions : " All that we have proved is that situations are *possible* in which a diminution in the falsity of judgment or a diminution in the costs of movement will make marginal net products more unequal. When, however, we are contemplating, from a general point of view, the consequences of these diminutions it is not the *possible* but the probable effect which concerns us " (*Wealth and Welfare*, Part II. ch. iv. § 10).

[3] As related by (the second) Lord Lansdowne, *Hansard*, 1820, Vol. I. p. 550.

[4] *Diary of Lord Colchester*, Vol. II. p. 7.

deserved, not, indeed, by Adam Smith, but by some of his followers, for instance, Miss Martineau. But our withers are unwrung. We have been careful to explain with Professor Pareto that the solution of practical problems is not to be expected from economic theory pure and simple. We do, indeed, claim that general propositions of the kind which Adam Smith qualifies with the adverb " necessarily," may afford general directions which are useful " to start with," and in the absence of knowledge to the contrary. We should not expect the first principle now under consideration, whether as stated by Adam Smith or in Professor Pigou's version, to be of much avail in an emergency, say for the direction of a committee providing employment for the wives of absent soldiers. But with reference to some wider question *in eodem genere*, to one taking a general view of women's work, the principle may well be significant. Suppose it to be ascertained that, as Mr. Sidney Webb finds probable, " women's work is usually less highly paid than work of equivalent difficulty and productivity done by men." [1] *Pro tanto*, the productive resources of the community would not be distributed so that marginal net products should be equal. Against such a distribution there is the presumption that in the words of Mrs. Sidney Webb,[2] " it is by the fullest possible use of all the productive faculties of the whole population that we shall obtain the largest yield of services and commodities." This presumption is of great importance. It is of the kind which—tempered with common sense and regard to fact—has worked mighty revolutions in industry. Yet the presumption is not by itself decisive. Before giving play to the Smith-Pigou principle, we require, having regard to the concrete circumstances, marriage and domestic life, to be secured against the danger of that process of degradation through subsidised competition which is described by Mrs. Webb as " industrial parasitism." [3]

As a second example of an economic tendency let us take Professor Pigou's proposition that the elasticity of the aggregate demand for labour is much greater than unity.[4] There is room for difference of opinion as to the form in which this presumption

---

[1] ECONOMIC JOURNAL, Vol. I. p. 635 *et seq*. Compare Mrs. Fawcett, ECONOMIC JOURNAL, Vol. II. p. 174; arguing that women are crowded into classes of industry less remunerative than those open to men.

[2] *The New Statesman*, July 25, 1914; one of a series of valuable articles on " Personal Rights and the Woman Movement."

[3] Cp. *loc. cit.*, Aug. 1.

[4] *Wealth and Welfare*, Part II. ch. ii. § 11 *et passim*. The proposition is criticised in the *Quarterly Review, loc. cit.* p. 417, and defended by Professor Pigou in the next number of that Review (Jan. 1914).

should be stated. So experts differ about the statement even of geometrical axioms. But we submit that some such general proposition, resting on the sort of evidence to which we all along appeal, underlies the received arguments in favour of labour-saving machinery and free trade. How else can the free trader reply to specious objections like those employed by Byles in his *Sophisms of Free Trade*.[1] The objections urged in former numbers of the ECONOMIC JOURNAL against some of the arguments in favour of free trade employed by Professor Bastable in his *International Trade* are similarly to be answered by presumptions as to the way in which productive forces probably act. It was objected that the transaction between the employing and employed class in a country is of the same genus as international trade, that a removal of barriers to the trade between nations may well—and not infrequently does—prove permanently injurious to a particular nation; and therefore that the removal of restrictions on importation into a particular country may well prove permanently detrimental to the employed class as a whole. The answer is to be sought in common sense, and probabilities founded on general experience. An answer in this sense has been given by the objector himself.[2]

[1] *E.g.*, " Suppose stockings to the value of £500,000 a year are made in Leicester and exchanged annually for gloves to the amount of £500,000 a year made in Dover. . . . Suppose now the Leicester people instead of exchanging their stockings for gloves from Dover exchange them for gloves . . . say from Calais. Dover loses what Calais gets. . . ." *Sophisms of Free Trade*, Edition 1904, p. 26.

[2] " In economics it is often difficult to hold fast general resemblances without ignoring—or appearing to ignore—specific differences. In the present matter, while apprehending that the transactions between the operative and the employing classes are of the genus international trade, we must not forget that the exports and imports of this trade are of a very peculiar character. The peculiarity might be partially illustrated by the trade which used to flourish between England and the Southern States of America; these States exported to England raw cotton, receiving in return cotton manufactures. If the offer of raw cotton with the demand for cotton manufactures were to be increased on one side of the international market by a change such as the growth of population in the Southern States, other things being the same, the offer of manufactures on the other side of the market on the part of a large and flourishing England would be likely to keep pace with the offer of raw material, in such wise as not to alter the terms of international exchange to the disadvantage of the average Southerner. But indeed, the illustration hardly does justice to the expansiveness of the trade which we are now considering. Let us rather suppose the export to consist of that rawest and most extensively demanded material, mechanical power. Let us imagine, for the sake of illustration, Niagara harnessed in the service of man to belong wholly to the United States, not in part to Canada; and that by improved means of transmitting force the means of production may be conveyed from Niagara to any department of Canadian industry. If the supply of power from Niagara to Canada were to be increased by some dislocation, for instance some

Another example of an advance in applied mathematical economics is presented by Professor Pigou's theory of joint production in railway rates. That theory has been severely criticised in the *Quarterly Review*. And it may be admitted that the criticism has weight so far as it is directed against the form of the exposition. That the gist of the theory should have been completely missed by a very discerning critic certainly argues some defect in the exposition. Perhaps it was injudicious on the part of Professor Pigou to use expressions which might suggest that his difference with the railway experts related only to definitions—" an accident of language." [1] Whereas the real issue relates not to the definition of terms, but to a distinction between things. There is a great difference between a condition of industry in which the cost of producing x of one commodity (say gas) is the same as that of producing x of that commodity plus y of some other commodity (say coke), and a condition in which the cost of producing x and y, say transportation of coal and transportation of copper, does, indeed, depend upon a single variable, but not now x or y, but z the *sum* of the two [2] (the number of tons of copper transported *plus* the number of tons of coal). The difference might be illustrated by the contrast between two methods which have been proposed for linking gold and silver so as to form a double standard of value. According to one method, which was called by its distinguished inventor " true bimetallism," [3] and has subsequently become known as " symmetallism," a sum of say £3 17s. $10\frac{1}{2}d.$ in standard money would procure a fixed fraction, say half, of an ounce of gold *plus* a fixed weight of silver, say $\frac{1}{2} \times 15\frac{1}{2}$ ounces (or, more generally, $\frac{1}{2} \times r$, r being a legalised ratio). According to the plan commonly known as bimetallism, the sum of £3 17s. $10\frac{1}{2}d.$ would procure *any* (proper) fraction of an ounce of gold, say $\frac{1}{t}$th of an ounce, *plus* a weight of silver equal to $15\frac{1}{2} \left(1 - \frac{1}{t}\right)$—or, more generally, $r\left(1 - \frac{1}{t}\right)$. Suppose

---

permanent impediment to its supply elsewhere, then it might be expected that—in the long run, and abstracting temporary disturbance—the offer on the part of Americans owning Niagara would be met by the demand for additional power on the part of the entrepreneurs in a large and flourishing Canada." *Scientia*, 1909, p. 90. (Above, ϵ.)

[1] *Wealth and Welfare*, Part II. chap. xiii. §`3. *Cp.* § 4, where in denying a proposition about a certain kind of industry it is argued : " This is not Joint Supply."

[2] More exactly a *linear function* of the two quantities, say $ax + by$, where a and b are constants.

[3] Evidence of Professor Marshall before the Precious Metals Commission, 1887.

hasty thinkers to have confused the properties of these two very different systems. It would probably not be the best method of combating the confusion to ascribe it to an accident of language, a wrong definition of the term " bimetallism." Such a method of attack might seem to be met by the defence : " it would be strange if . . . experts, practical and theoretical, have fallen into a gross error by not understanding the words they use " (*Quarterly Review*, p. 421). Upon which we remark that the railway experts no doubt attached a clear conception to the words they used ; but it was not an appropriate conception.[1] The subtlety of their thought was not equal to the subtlety of the distinctions existing in the nature of things.

For an examination of these delicate, but vital, distinctions the reader is referred to former articles in the ECONOMIC JOURNAL.[2] They are summarily re-stated here,[3] in the new light which has been thrown on the subject by recent publications. It is proper to begin with the simple case defined by Mill, " when the same outlay would have to be incurred for either of the two [products] if the other is not wanted or used at all." Professor Fanno expresses this datum by treating the ratio between the quantities of the two products as a constant, viz. K. He represents the real unity underlying the apparent duality of the products by an appropriate unit. Thus equipped he successfully attacks the main problems which the case presents ; investigating the effects of a change in the demand of one or other of the commodities, of a tax or a bounty, now under the regime of competition, now under that of monopoly. The interest of these investigations extends beyond the simple case to which they primarily relate. The light which is applied at this particularly accessible point illuminates the comparatively inaccessible regions in the neighbourhood. This extension of illumination is effected by Professor Fanno through the introduction of a change in the value of the constant " K." This statement of the general problem has an advantage in respect of simplicity over that which has been given in a former number of the ECONOMIC JOURNAL.[4] The relation between the two presentations might be illustrated by the contrast between the modern and the older method of representing the relation between demand and price. This relation is

---

[1] Compare Whewell, *Inductive Sciences*, as to the part which clear and appropriate conceptions have played in scientific discovery.

[2] See XIII. p. 556, *et seq.* See Index, s.v. *Joint Production*.

[3] Before striking at what is here said the dissentient reader is requested to attend to what has been there said.

[4] IV. 54.

now commonly expressed by a curve or symbols. But the Ricardians preferred to say that " although the demand should be doubled, trebled, or quadrupled," [1] the price will ultimately fall to that " natural " price which is fixed by the cost of production. But the cost of production might vary; and in the case of agriculture at least it might vary in consequence of a change in the amount demanded.

As we leave the hard and fast limit formed by the classical instance of gas and coke we come to cases like wool and mutton, beef and hides, which are joint products in " a more partial sense," as Mill says; [2] a sense which has been made clearer by mathematical writers, in particular Dr. Marshall [3] and Mr. Flux. [4] " If we suppose the degrees of complementariness to be gradually diminished we shall pass through the zero point of absolute independence to a relation which may be distinguished as *rival* production; when the increased production of one commodity renders the increase of the other more difficult." [5] At the limit of this class, at the extreme which is opposite to the limit of Joint Production proper formed by Mill's instance, gas and coke, is placed the case now under consideration, where the cost of production depends on the simple sum of two (or more) quantities of product $(x + y)$, or, more generally, the *weighted* sum $(ax + by)$, where a and b are numerical constants, the dependence not being of the simplest sort, the cost not simply proportional to the said sum, but some *function* thereof, as may be expected where there are *general* expenses. The conception of this case as an extreme limit of rival production is countenanced by Mr. Johnson's parallel enunciation with respect to joint *demand*. He thus describes the " extreme cases " in which " the curves of utility degenerate into a series of parallel straight lines. " Here we may call x and z strictly or absolutely *competitive ; i.e.,* any

---

[1] Ricardo, *Political Economy*, ch. xxx.

[2] *Political Economy*, III. ch. xvi. § 1.

[3] *Principles of Economics, sub voce* Joint Supply.

[4] *Economic Principles.*

[5] Quoted from the discussion of the subject in an early paper (V. 54, referring to VI.), in which context, it may be as well to caution the possible reader, there are some bad misprints, noticed among the errata in the decennial index.   In a later paper (XIII. 558) it is proposed to use the term " disjunctive " as opposite to " Joint " (production). The class seems not to have been named by other writers, and perhaps with reason, since without further limitations it is too wide to be of service.   It will apply to almost all economic production if in accordance with the first of the passages referred to it is exemplified wherever " a limited amount of time, strength or resources may be spent on either of two sorts of otherwise unconnected production." It might be better to limit the class to cases where there is a more active technical incompatibility between two kinds of production.

given amount of x gives the same utility as a proportional amount of z " (*loc. cit.*, p. 495). Substitute " y " for " z," " cost " for " utility," and for " curves of utility " " curves of equal cost," and you have a statement corresponding to ours.

Such, then, is the case to which it is proposed to attribute properties proper to Mill's case of gas and coke, identifying two limiting cases which are at the opposite extremes of opposed categories.[1] It is as if you were to attribute the same properties to the extreme cases of Diminishing Returns and its opposite; identifying the case in which no amount of additional outlay will produce any additional return and a virgin soil or nascent industry in which Increasing Returns operate with the greatest activity. Against this inaccuracy of language and thought Professor Fanno lends the weight of his authority. In a passage too long to be quoted here in full he thus characterises the "broad" sense of joint cost which has been opposed to Professor Pigou's narrow [*ristretto*] sense. " This excessive [*soverchia*] extension of the concept joint cost does not seem to us correct or scientifically rigorous. For every group of phenomena formed by any classification ought to comprise phenomena which resemble each other [*che sieno fra loro omogenei*] not merely superficially [*formalmente*] but in material respects [*sostanzialmente*]. Now this is far from being the case with the group denoted by ' Joint Supply ' in the broad sense of the term. In the two cases [the broad and the limited sense] the character of the correlation between the prices is different; their behaviour [*comportamento*] and laws are different. We therefore reject the broad conception of joint cost as too vague and indeterminate." Professor Fanno writes with a knowledge of the vigorous but courteously conducted controversy —" *una vivace ma obiettiva polemica* "—between Professor Pigou and Professor Taussig in the *Quarterly Journal of Economics* (1913).

We are not so much concerned to prove that Professor Pigou's definition is the best, as to exhibit the importance of the new propositions which justify the definition. They relate chiefly to the characteristics of joint cost in the " broad " sense, what we have described as the limiting case of " competitive production." These properties are quite different from those which are com-

[1] Under the circumstances carefully defined by Professor Pigou, p. 218 (latter part). Compare ECONOMIC JOURNAL, Vol. XXI. p. 565; with reference to *certain magnitudes* of the increment Δx it might be impossible to increase the production of x by Δx without diminishing the cost of increasing y (the characteristic of Joint Production proper), *even though* the total cost was of the form $F(ax + by)$.

monly ascribed to joint cost of production. Of the latter, J. S. Mill writes : " Since cost of production here fails us, we must revert to a law of value anterior to cost of production, and more fundamental, the law of demand and supply." [1] So Professor Nicholson, referring to the case of joint products : " In this case the law of value is that the normal price of the two together is determined by the aggregate cost of production; and that the relative prices of the joint products, or the distribution of the aggregate between them, depends upon the demand and supply." [2] Well, the relative prices of the products, in the limiting case in question, do *not* depend upon the demand and supply in the sense which is evidently intended, the sense in which value depending on demand and supply only is opposed by J. S. Mill and the older writers to value depending on cost of production. It is *not* necessary now to " revert to a law anterior to cost of production." [3] It is as true now as in the normal case of value said to " depend on cost of production," that "although the demand should be doubled, trebled, or quadrupled," [4] prices tend to be the same if costs of production remain the same. Now, as in the normal case, " it is the cost of production which must ultimately regulate the price of commodities." [5] Only the regulating cost of production is not now, as usually to be understood, the total cost, but the prime cost, the cost of adding a unit of either product, other things being the same. Thus, suppose that the total cost of transporting x tons of coal *plus* y tons of copper depends only on $x + y$.[6] It follows from first principles that the increment in the total cost due to the increase (*ceteris paribus*) of x by any small weight τ is equal to τ multiplied by the rate at which the total cost increases with the increase of x. But that rate is the same as the rate at which the total cost increases with the increase of $x + y$, or of y only (x remaining constant).[7] Accordingly, the prime cost of transporting (a small unit of) coal will be the same as that of transporting copper. Therefore, according to the rule just now given, the price of transporting a ton of coal tends to be the same as the price of transporting a ton of copper, the general expenses being distributed equally between the two commodities. Again, supposing that the cost of transporting silver

---

[1] *Political Economy*, III. xvi. 1.

[2] *Principles of Political Economy*, Vol. II. p. 52. Cp. *Quarterly Review*, *loc. cit.*, p. 421.

[3] Any more than it is always, even in the general case of value said by Mill to depend on cost of production proper.   [4] Ricardo as quoted above, p. 198.

[5] Ricardo, *loc. cit.*   [6] *Cp.* XIII. p. 560.

[7] If the total cost of producing $x + y$ is $F(x + y)$ the rate at which this increases with the increase of either x or y is $F'(x + y)$.

and gold depends only on the weight (concrete circumstances, such as differences of risk and insurance, being abstracted); then in a regime of bimetallism (in the ordinary sense of that term) the prime cost of transporting a thousand pounds sterling in silver would be $15\frac{1}{2}$ times the prime cost of transporting a thousand pounds sterling in gold (supposing the bimetallic ratio to be $15\frac{1}{2} : 1$); and, accordingly, the price of transporting a thousand pounds sterling in silver would tend to be $15\frac{1}{2}$ times the price of transporting that sum in gold.

It may be objected that this proposition is not confirmed by observation; the predicated exact correspondence between prime cost and price is not observable throughout the real world of industry. It may be replied that the requisite condition of perfectly competitive production is often not perfectly fulfilled; and, further, that even when the condition is at least approximately fulfilled, the resulting tendency is obstructed by an element of monopoly. We may have to rely largely on general reasoning, of a piece with that which is generally accepted in proof of a correspondence between value and cost of production in ordinary cases. In the present case, indeed, the importance of the tendency consists in its not being fulfilled in practice. There is afforded a rule for the regulation of industries in which the fulfilment of the tendency is obstructed by monopolistic friction. This regulative idea may well be of far-reaching importance. A check is thus given to the spread of the heresy, as it would have seemed to the older economists, that there is no presumption against charging different prices for like services : electric power may properly be sold at different prices according to the use for which it is destined, a doctor may fairly vary his fees according to the means of the patient, and so on.[1]

It must be remembered that the tendency which has been stated rests on the sort of probability which is here all along understood. The rule holds good, *primâ facie* and provisionally, until cause to the contrary be shown. One cause that is to be looked for is a condition of supply and demand such that without discrimination contrary to the rule production cannot be made to pay. With reference to industries generally, " in an industry selected at random," as Professor Pigou has it,[2] it appears improbable, for reasons given by him, that this sort of exception should occur.

It is a question of great practical interest whether the excep-

---

[1] *Cp.* Acworth, *Railway Economics*, ch. ix.
[2] *Wealth and Welfare*, Part II. ch. xii., especially §§ 15, 16, 17.

tion is likely to occur in the class of industries for the regulation of which a rule is much required, " public works," in M. Colson's phrase, and, in particular, railways. Railway experts in general bear witness in favour of a discrimination inconsistent with the rule. But their testimony is obscured by the confusion attending the double signification of " joint cost " The answers of experts are then most authoritative when they are addressed to questions framed by correct theory. Pending further discussion, we are disposed to agree with Professor Pigou that, while discrimination or the " value of service principle " is required at a certain early stage of a country's development, the " cost of service principle " should be the rule for more developed countries.[1] Thus considerable weight is added to the reasons in favour of " the cost of service principle," which is now being enforced by the Interstate Commerce Commission.

At the same time, the weight on the other side of the balance is lightened. For the Competition to which advocates of discrimination appeal—Professor Hugo Meyer notably [2]—is found to be of the nature of *Duopoly*, a species of competition which has not in its favour the same presumptions as that which Professor Pigou calls " simple competition." [3]

Many other examples of mathematical reasoning based upon Probabilities and bearing upon practice are to be found in Professor Pigou's work. We do not conceal that there is something tentative in these applications. Nor do we put forward our explanation of their philosophical basis as final. Rather, in the words of the philosopher who first divined the deep connection between Probabilities in a technical sense and Induction in general,[4] we " shall think it sufficient if the present hints excite the curiosity of philosophers and make them sensible how defective all common theories are in treating of such curious and sublime subjects."

[1] *Wealth and Welfare, loc. cit.*, § 10. Compare as to objections and qualification, XIV.

[2] *Governmental Regulation of Railway Rates, passim,* and especially with reference to the system of " blanketing," which the Interstate Commerce Commission has since limited.

[3] *Wealth and Welfare,* Part II. ch. viii. and ch. vii. §§ 12–14; ch. xvi. §§ 2–3.

[4] Hume, " Of Probability," sec. vi. of *An Enquiry Concerning Human Understanding (Essays).*

END OF VOL. II.